FINANCIAL ACCOUNTING STANDARDS

Explanation and Analysis

FINANCIAL ACCOUNTING STANDARDS
Explanation and Analysis

Jon A. Booker, PhD, CPA
Associate Professor of Accounting
The University of Tulsa

Bill D. Jarnagin, PhD, CPA
Associate Professor of Accounting
The University of Tulsa

COMMERCE CLEARING HOUSE, INC.
PUBLISHERS of TOPICAL LAW REPORTS
4025 W. PETERSON AVE., CHICAGO, ILLINOIS 60646

Library of Congress
Catalog Number: 80-52956

Printed in the United States of America

To Diane, Brenda and Samantha

Table of Contents

Preface

The second edition of *Financial Accounting Standards* represents a significant improvement in both quantity and quality of material presented. The coverage of the book has been expanded to include all FASB Interpretations, FASB Technical Bulletins, and future considerations from the FASB as evidenced by Exposure Drafts and Proposed Interpretations circulating at the date of printing. This expanded coverage was designed to provide the reader with the most integrative material available in the area of accounting pronouncements. Of course, the coverage of the basic Statements of the Financial Accounting Standards Board has been made as current as possible. The first edition ended with coverage of SFAS No. 23, and the second edition extends the coverage through SFAS No. 34. The flowcharts have been improved visually and technically.

As with the first edition, the book groups pronouncements into subject matter Topics that, in turn, are arranged to follow major balance sheet headings as closely as possible. This organization allows the reader to find all current pronouncements that deal with a given subject in one section of the book. The Exposure Drafts and Proposed Interpretation of Statements are explained on the Contents page that begins each Topic. This material has not been included in the main body of the text because it is subject to substantial change and may never be published in the form of a Statement or Interpretation.

Three levels of explanation and analysis are offered for the Opinions and Statements. This "three-level" approach includes flowchart material, general discussion and detailed example material. First, a flowchart has been prepared to illustrate the general decision process and accounting procedures required by a pronouncement. Next, a general discussion of the major provisions of the Opinion or Statement is presented. This discussion is more detailed than the material presented in the flowchart, but does not attempt to incorporate computational aspects of the pronouncement. The third level of explanation and analysis consists of detailed example material that shows the reader specific computational and accounting requirements of the pronouncement. The example material is designed to progress from simple to complex considerations. Specific implementation problems are discussed in this section of the analysis. Where appropriate, disclosures from actual annual reports of selected companies complete the analysis of each Opinion or Statement.

Accounting practitioners should view this book as a working guide for solutions to many complex accounting problems. We have been pleased with the response of practitioners to the presentation of the material. Once again, we encourage a careful reading of the original pronouncement, before reading the material relating to a specific Opinion or Statement. The original pronouncements of the APB and FASB are viewed as an integral part of this book and should always be consulted as the final authority on accounting and disclosure matters.

CPA Examination candidates should benefit from this volume because approximately 60 percent of the questions on the Theory part of the Uniform CPA Examination, and a large percentage of the financial accounting questions on the Accounting Practice parts, are directly related to the professional pronouncements. Candidates are encouraged to pay particular attention to the computational notes and journal entries associated with the detailed example material.

We still find that, in the classroom, many accounting students become confused by the concise and technical presentation found in the original pronouncements, and many of the Interpretations do little to overcome this dilemma. Information contained in this text has proven to be invaluable when used as an interpretive instrument for students in the classroom. The use of this text will minimize classroom time devoted to explanations of technical provisions of the pronouncements and will free the instructor to spend more time dealing with the many conceptual issues in accounting. The book may be used as the main text or as a supplement in an undergraduate theory or pronouncements course. Graduate MBA students will benefit from the technical presentation that is often omitted from their coursework. We have found the book to be of benefit in Advanced Financial Accounting and a powerful supplement to Intermediate Accounting (especially Intermediate II). We have prepared a problems book which contains CPA examination questions relating to the pronouncements. The problems book and accompanying solutions manual reinforce the material in the text.

We wish to thank the American Institute of Certified Public Accountants and the Financial Accounting Standards Board for permission to quote from their publications, and the editors of the *CPA Journal* for permission to reproduce certain flowchart material.

It is our hope that *Financial Accounting Standards—Explanation and Analysis* will provide you with new insights into, and a practical understanding of, the Opinions and Statements of our professional organization. We invite your comments and suggestions for improvements in subsequent editions.

Jon A. Booker

Bill D. Jarnagin

The University of Tulsa
600 South College
Tulsa, Oklahoma 74104
(918) 592-6000

Topic 1

Basic Financial Statements

Detail Contents

APB Opinions and SFAS Statements

FASB Interpretations

FASB Technical Bulletins

APB Opinion No. 19 (March 1971)
Reporting Changes in Financial Position

Prior to the issuance of APB Opinion No. 19, the statement of changes in financial position, then referred to as the "statement of sources and applications of funds," was viewed as "supplemental information" that could be included with the financial statements of a company or omitted altogether. One problem created by this position was the diversity of reporting practices by businesses: even within the same industry, some companies elected to prepare a "statement of sources and applications of funds," while others elected not to present the statement. Another major problem dealt with the definition of the term "funds." The Accounting Principles Board issued Opinion No. 19 in an effort to provide consistency in reporting and to provide a more precise definition of what was meant by "funds."

As indicated in the Flowchart, APB Opinion No. 19 requires the presentation of the statement of changes in financial position for all profit-oriented businesses (Block 1) that issue a balance sheet and income statement (Block 2). The statement of changes in financial position now is considered to be one of the basic financial statements; i.e., it has been placed on equal footing with the balance sheet and statement of income and retained earnings. The definition of "funds" was broadened by APB Opinion No. 19 so that even those companies that did not prepare a classified balance sheet were required to issue a statement of changes in financial position. If a company prepares a classified balance sheet, the statement of changes in financial position may be prepared on the cash, near cash or working capital basis. The Opinion allows a company to

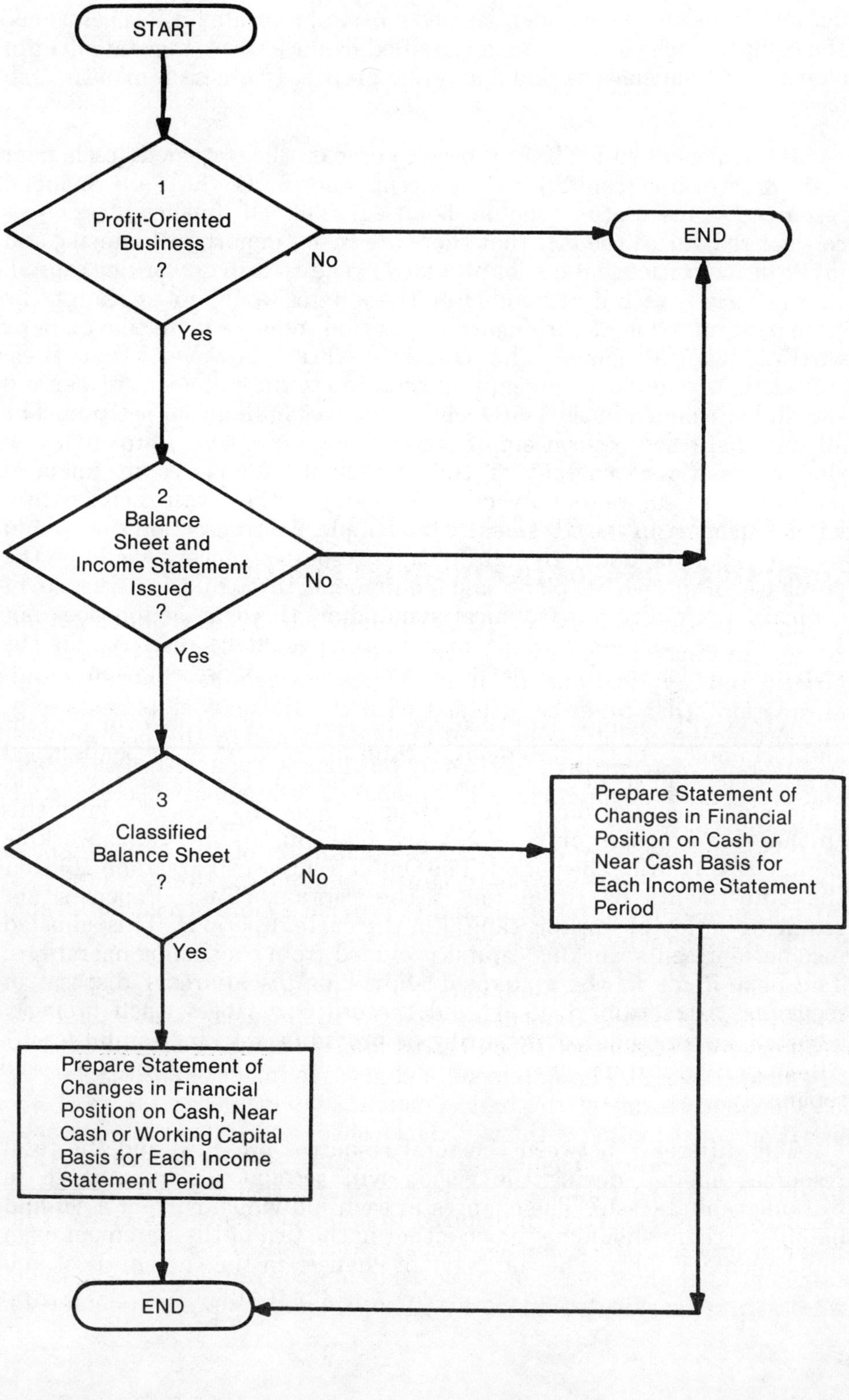
START
1
Profit-Oriented
Business
?
No
Yes
END
2
Balance
Sheet and
Income Statement
Issued
?
No
Yes
3
Classified
Balance Sheet
?
No
Yes
Prepare Statement of Changes in Financial Position on Cash or Near Cash Basis for Each Income Statement Period
Prepare Statement of Changes in Financial Position on Cash, Near Cash or Working Capital Basis for Each Income Statement Period
END

define "funds" in the manner deemed most appropriate for its operations. If a company does not prepare a classified balance sheet, the statement of changes in financial position should be prepared on a cash or near cash basis.

Regardless of which basis is used to prepare the statement (cash, near cash or working capital), the concept known as the "all financial resources" presentation should be used. The all financial resources concept recognizes the fact that there are many important financing and investing activities that do not provide or require cash or working capital. From a strictly technical standpoint, these items would not appear on the statement of changes in financial position prepared on the cash or working capital basis. The Opinion states, however, that these transactions provide meaningful information to the statement reader and should be included in the statement of changes in financial position. The all financial resources concept of presentation takes a very broad view of the informational content of the statement of changes in financial position and assumes that all activities of an investing or financing nature will be included in the statement. An example of a transaction that would require reporting under the all financial resources concept would be the purchase of property, plant and equipment through the issuance of common stock. From a technical standpoint, this transaction does not affect either cash or working capital, but would be disclosed in the statement under the all financial resources concept of presentation.

While APB Opinion No. 19 advocates flexibility in the form, content and terminology of the statement, certain information must be disclosed in accordance with the provisions of the Opinion. The statement should begin with income from continuing operations and should adjust this amount for expenses or revenues not requiring or providing working capital (cash) during the period. The Opinion suggests (Paragraph 10) that the adjustments be listed under the caption: "Add—Expenses not requiring outlay of working capital in the current period." This adjusted income represents working capital provided from continuing operations. The next items in the statement should be disclosure of disposal of segments, extraordinary items and accounting changes, each properly adjusted for amounts not requiring or providing working capital (cash). All major investing and financing activities should be disclosed separately.

The difference between the total resources provided and the total resources applied during the period will account for the change in working capital (cash). The changes in each individual current asset and liability account should be shown either in the text of the statement or in supplementary form. The summary of changes in the current asset and liability accounts provides the detailed information about the computation of the change in working capital. Of course, if the statement is prepared on the cash basis, the changes in current assets and liabilities should be shown as either sources or uses of cash.

A statement of changes in financial position must be presented for each income statement period. For example, if the company reported income for the last three periods, but presented only the current period balance sheet, then three statements of changes in financial position would be required. However, in this case, the detailed composition of current assets and liabilities would be disclosed only for the current period.

Paragraph 14 of the Opinion specifically identifies the following items as requiring individual disclosure in the statement:

1. Purchases of long-term assets—each separately identified;
2. Working capital or cash provided by the sale of long-term assets not in the normal course of business;
3. Conversion of equity securities into common stock;
4. Issuance and retirement of long-term debt;
5. Issuance or repurchase of common stock for cash or other consideration; and
6. Dividends, other than stock, distributed to shareholders.

While the actual statements shown at the end of this section illustrate formats that commonly are used to prepare the statement of changes in financial position, it sometimes is difficult to follow the presentation without some frame of reference. The statement format outlined below should give the reader a basis for examining statements contained in annual reports. The statement is designed to illustrate the format suggested in the Opinion when the working capital approach is used.

XYZ CORPORATION

Statement of Changes in Financial Position* for the Year Ended December 31, 197X

Financial Resources Generated:		
Net Income from continuing operations		$XX,XXX
Add—Expenses not requiring outlay of working capital in the current period		
Item 1	$X,XXX	
Item 2	XXX	X,XXX
Working capital generated by continuing operations		$XX,XXX
Working capital generated by discontinued operations		XXX
Working capital generated by extraordinary items		XXX
Working capital generated by an accounting change		XXX
Working capital generated by operations		$XX,XXX
Other sources of working capital		
Item 1		XXX
Item 2		X,XXX
Item 3		XXX
Total working capital generated		$XX,XXX
Financing and investing activities not generating working capital		
Item 1	$X,XXX	
Item 2	X,XXX	$ X,XXX
Total financing resources generated		$XX,XXX
Financial Resources Used:		
Uses of working capital		
Item 1		$ X,XXX
Item 2		XXX
Item 3		X,XXX
Total uses of working capital		$XX,XXX
Financing and investing activities not requiring the use of working capital		
Item 1	$ XXX	
Item 2	XXX	XXX
Total financial resources used		$XX,XXX
Increase (decrease) in working capital		$ XXX
Changes in Working Capital Accounts	**Increase (Decrease)**	
Current Assets:		
Account 1	$X,XXX	
Account 2	(XXX)	
Current Liabilities:		
Account 1	XXX	
Account 2	XXX	
Working Capital	$ XXX	

* APB Opinion No. 30 requires that discontinued segments and extraordinary items be shown as separate elements of income on the income statement. In addition, APB Opinion No. 20 requires a separate reporting of accounting changes. While these two Opinions do not specifically amend APB Opinion No. 19, it seems only logical to report these elements separately in the statement of changes in financial position.

International Harvester Company's Statement of Changes in Financial Position is shown for the years 1975 and 1974. Notice that the company reported a loss on the disposal of discontinued operations and showed the related adjustment to the loss. Working capital provided by operations is labeled "Financial Resources Provided from Continuing

Operations." Contrast the statement of International Harvester Company with that of Hudson Pulp & Paper Corp. Hudson Pulp & Paper has prepared its statement on a near cash basis, i.e., cash and short-term investments. Hudson Pulp & Paper also has included the change in the cash and short-term investments on the face of the statement. Notice that the current asset and liability accounts are included in the text of the statement under the funds provided or used headings.

Compare the Statement of Changes in Financial Position of Northrop Corporation, prepared for the years 1975 and 1974 on the cash basis, with that of Clark Equipment Company, prepared for the same years on the working capital basis. Notice that Northrop appropriately includes the elements of working capital within the statement itself. Since Clark is using the working capital format, the elements of working capital are presented in a tabulation at the bottom of the statement.

International Harvester Company (Oct)

Changes in Financial Position

	1975	1974
Financial resources provided		
	($000)	
Income from continuing operations	$ 115,920	$115,729
Items not affecting working capital:		
Depreciation and amortization	80,334	69,418
Undistributed earnings of nonconsolidated companies	(38,770)	(23,357)
Deferred income taxes	36,040	(423)
Other	628	(2,247)
Financial resources provided from continuing operations	194,152	159,120
Discontinued operation	(44,617)	2,200
Items not affecting working capital:		
Estimated loss on disposal of discontinued operation (less $5,250,000 estimated future costs)	65,708	—
Depreciation and amortization	6,668	6,097
Deferred income taxes	(34,140)	1,059
Financial resources provided by discontinued operation	(6,381)	9,356
Extraordinary income	—	6,124
Cumulative effect on prior years (to October 31, 1974) of change in accounting policy (before deferred income taxes of $7,392,000)	15,443	—
Total financial resources provided from operations	203,214	174,600
Additions to long-term debt	354,378	181,002
Other property disposals	8,457	20,183
Issuance of preferred stock	50,000	—
Total financial resources provided	616,049	375,785
Financial resources applied		
Capital expenditures	173,232	180,578
Cash dividends	49,649	44,447
Reduction of long-term debt	41,469	52,769
Increase in investments	39,638	23,933
Reclassification of working capital to estimated realizable value of assets, discontinued operation	41,576	—
Other	2,879	15,497
Total financial resources applied	348,443	317,224
Increase in working capital	267,606	58,561
Working capital		
At beginning of the year	947,277	888,716
At end of the year	$1,214,883	$947,277

Source: *Accounting Trends and Techniques,* Copyright © 1976 by the American Institute of Certified Public Accountants, Inc., pp. 328.

Hudson Pulp & Paper Corp. (Dec)

Statement of Changes in Financial Position

	1975	1974
Funds provided by:		
	($000)	
Net income	$ 9,039	$14,872
Charges/(credit) to income not affecting funds:		
Depreciation and depletion	7,601	6,501
Deferred Federal income taxes/(credit)	(353)	164
Total from operations	16,288	21,537
Issuance of long-term debt	10,000	—
Construction costs for water pollution treatment facility, reimbursed by trustee	—	91
Decrease in receivables	—	1,951
Decrease in inventories	71	—
Increase in accounts payable and accrued expenses	401	3,644
Increase in current portion of long-term debt	—	2,584
Increase in dividends payable	117	411
Book amount of properties sold	147	73
Other items—net	799	1,136
Total funds provided	27,826	31,431
Funds used for:		
Additions to plant assets and timber resources	33,911	12,114
Dividends	2,076	1,828
Capital stock acquired	772	708
Decrease in long-term debt	2,763	4,631
Decrease in current portion of long-term debt	1,867	—
Increase in receivables	1,895	—
Refundable estimated Federal income tax payments	2,325	—
Increase in inventories	—	5,655
Increase in other current assets	131	420
Decrease in Federal income taxes	4,167	401
Total funds used	49,910	25,760
(Decrease)/increase in cash and short-term investments	(22,083)	5,671
Cash and short-term investments at beginning of year	28,718	23,047
Cash and short-term investments at end of year	$ 6,635	$28,718

Source: *Accounting Trends & Techniques,* Copyright © 1976 by the American Institute of Certified Public Accountants, Inc., p. 339.

Northrop Corporation (Dec)

Statement of Changes in Consolidated Financial Position

	1975	1974
Factors increasing cash:	($000)	
Operations:		
Net income	$ 24,732	$18,136
Add non-cash items:		
Depreciation and amortization of property, plant and equipment	14,042	12,914
Increase in deferred income taxes and deferred credit	8,113	10,603
Cash provided from operations	47,487	41,653
Increase in progress payments received	36,124	49,024
Increase in income taxes currently payable	18,440	(425)
Increase in trade accounts payable, other current liabilities, accrued employees' compensation and minority interest	12,848	(5,259)
Additional long-term borrowings	8,865	8,381
Issuance of common stock	3,224	33
Carrying value of disposals of property, plant and equipment	2,851	3,162
Decrease in prepaid expenses	844	(202)
	130,683	96,367
Factors decreasing cash:		
Increase in inventories	48,981	70,043
Additions to property, plant and equipment	25,074	32,008
Decrease in advances on contracts	23,107	(49,912)
Increase in accounts receivable and unreimbursed costs and accrued profits	22,984	(19,692)
Dividends paid	6,515	5,373
Repayments of senior long-term debt	3,704	6,817
Increase in short-term investments	2,102	24,416
Repayments of notes payable	2,098	3,222
Increase in other assets	917	(592)
Purchase of common shares for treasury	318	4,200
Principal amount of subordinated debt purchased	312	3,233
Decrease in revolving credit borrowings	—	15,000
	136,112	94,116
Decrease in cash	5,429	(2,251)
Cash balance at beginning of year	14,534	12,283
Cash balance at end of year	$ 9,105	$14,534

Source: *Accounting Trends & Techniques,* Copyright © 1976 by the American Institute of Certified Public Accountants, Inc., p. 339.

Clark Equipment Company (Dec)

Statement of Changes in Financial Position

	1975	1974
Financial resources were provided by:	($000)	
Net income for the year	$ 46,618	$ 50,064
Add charges (deduct) credits to income not affecting working capital in the year:		
Net income of finance subsidiaries	(11,287)	(12,130)
Equity in unremitted earnings of minority-owned associated companies	(498)	(2,531)
Provision for depreciation of properties	23,502	18,652
Provision for deferred income taxes	(1,546)	7,660
Working capital provided by operations	56,789	61,715
Addition to long-term borrowings	26,432	133,458
Decrease in investments in and advances to finance subsidiaries and minority-owned companies	—	16,738
Sales of properties	2,754	3,677
Increase in accrued items, etc.	1,027	1,253
Other items	480	300
Increase in common stock:		
Proceeds from sale of stock under option plans	—	406
Upon conversion of debentures	—	146
	87,482	217,693
Financial resources were used for:		
Cash dividends	21,757	21,753
Additions to properties	60,820	72,428
Increase (decrease) in investments in rental equipment	1,614	(2,693)
Investments in and advances to finance subsidiaries and minority-owned companies	12,056	—
Long-term borrowings paid, converted to common stock, or becoming current liability	86,046	35,387
Decrease in rental equipment installment obligations	13,399	1,318
	195,692	128,193
Increase (decrease) in working capital	(108,210)	89,500
Accounted for by:		
Increase (decrease) in current assets:		
Cash	(8,672)	12,274
Accounts and notes receivable	(82,964)	57,716
Inventories	(54,697)	90,546
Prepaid expenses	(3,009)	4,695
	(149,324)	165,231
Less—Increase (decrease) in current liabilities:		
Notes payable	(23,243)	41,736
Accounts payable	(14,525)	24,116
Accrued payrolls	(5,463)	4,009
Accrued social security and general taxes	(4,075)	6,106
Installment obligations owed to finance subsidiaries	(10,107)	2,601
Taxes on income	15,915	(14,274)
Current installments on long-term debt	384	11,437
	(41,114)	75,731
Increase (decrease) in working capital, as above	(108,210)	89,500
Working capital at beginning of year	366,876	277,376
Working capital at end of year	$258,666	$366,876

Source: *Accounting Trends & Techniques,* Copyright © 1976 by the American Institute of Certified Public Accountants, Inc., p. 342.

APB Opinion No. 20 (July 1971) Accounting Changes

and

SFAS No. 32 (September 1979) Specialized Accounting and Reporting Principles and Practices in AICPA Statements of Position and Guides on Accounting and Auditing Matters

Flowchart and General Discussion

APB Opinion No. 20 deals with the broad areas of reporting and disclosing accounting changes and accounting errors. The major accounting changes identified in the Opinion are (1) changes in accounting principles, (2) changes in accounting estimates and (3) changes in reporting entities. While reporting of errors in previously issued financial statements is not an accounting change, it also is included in the Opinion.

Flowchart 1 depicts the general accounting principles and reporting requirements promulgated by the Opinion. The major decision points have been numbered for reference in the discussion that follows. Each of the sections below will be divided into three parts: (1) general discussion of specific accounting change or error correction; (2) technical considerations in accounting for and reporting the change; and (3) required disclosures with specific examples. This organization will allow the reader to go directly to the problem area of interest.

Changes in Accounting Principles—General Discussion

A change in accounting principles (Block 3) is the "adoption of a generally accepted accounting principle different from the one used previously for reporting purposes" (APB Opinion No. 20, Paragraph 7). Examples would include changing methods of depreciation from, say, straight-line to sum-of-the-years' digits method, or a change in the method of pricing inventories from specific identification to first-in, first-out.[1] A change in accounting principle must be from one generally accepted principle to another generally accepted principle. A change from an accounting principle that is *not* generally accepted to one that is generally accepted is treated as an error, rather than as a change in accounting principle.

---

[1] In addition to these examples, FASB Interpretation No. 1 requires that changes in the computation of the cost elements included in inventory be treated as a change in accounting principle.

APB Opinion No. 20 identifies four types of accounting changes that require special treatment. These four are: (1) a change *from* Last-in, First-out (LIFO) inventory method *to* some other method (Block 5); (2) a change *to* or *from* percentage of completion method of accounting for long-term construction contracts (Block 6); (3) a change *to* or *from* the "full cost" method of accounting used in the extractive industry (Block 7); and (4) special cases where companies are involved in initial public offerings of securities (Block 8). These four changes are handled differently from other types of changes in accounting principles. Discussion of these special cases will be deferred until the end of the general discussion for changes in accounting principles.

A change in accounting principles is accounted for by reporting the "cumulative effect" of the change in the income statement. The cumulative effect of the change is reported on a "net of tax basis" and should appear after any extraordinary items, but before net income. The cumulative effect will be a special line item on the income statement.

The cumulative effect is the difference between the *beginning* retained earnings balance of the year in which the change is reported and the beginning retained earnings balance that *would have been reported* if the new principle had been applied retroactively. The cumulative effect is measured by assuming that the "new" principle was used in all previous periods, and by comparing the results obtained under this assumption with the actual results reported. An important point to remember is that the cumulative effect is the impact on *beginning* retained earnings of the period in which the change in accounting principles occurred.

The amount calculated and reported as the cumulative effect includes only those adjustments that have a direct impact on income. Adjustments that may be required because of an indirect link to income are not considered as part of the cumulative effect. For example, a company may pay certain key employees a bonus based upon reported income. A change in accounting principle may affect the income previously reported and therefore the amount of the bonus. The amount of the change in the bonus, which is indirectly linked to income, is not part of the cumulative effect.

In addition to reporting the cumulative effect in the income statement, the company also must disclose in the footnotes the nature of the change, the justification of the change, certain pro forma information and the effect of the change on current operations.

Nature of the Change

The nature of the change is a short description of the change in accounting principles. The description should include the effective date of

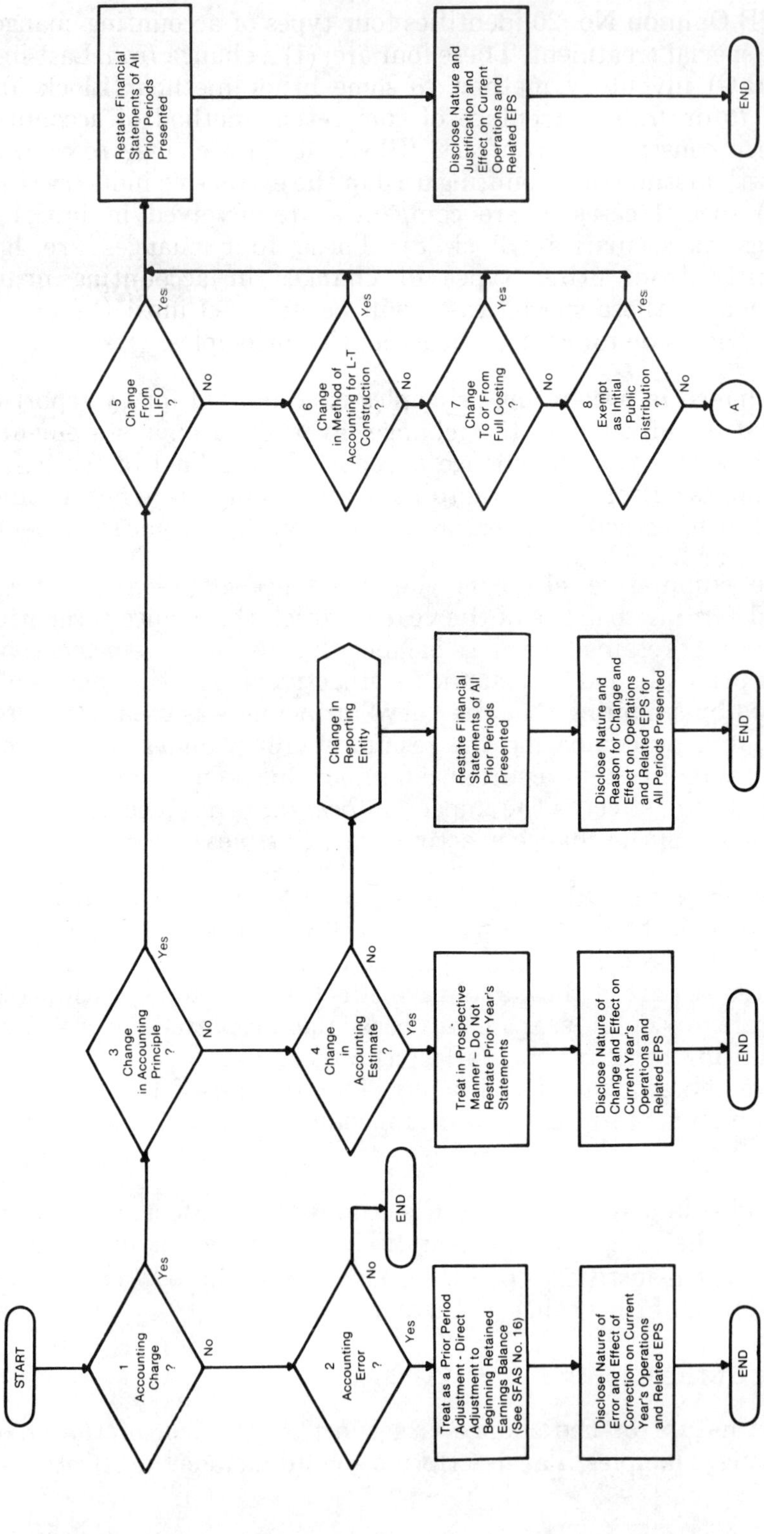
START
1 Accounting Charge ?
Yes
No
2 Accounting Error ?
Yes
No
END
Treat as a Prior Period Adjustment - Direct Adjustment to Beginning Retained Earnings Balance (See SFAS No. 16)
Disclose Nature of Error and Effect of Correction on Current Year's Operations and Related EPS
END
3 Change in Accounting Principle ?
Yes
No
4 Change in Accounting Estimate ?
Yes
No
Treat in Prospective Manner – Do Not Restate Prior Year's Statements
Disclose Nature of Change and Effect on Current Year's Operations and Related EPS
END
Change in Reporting Entity
Restate Financial Statements of All Prior Periods Presented
Disclose Nature and Reason for Change and Effect on Operations and Related EPS for All Periods Presented
END
5 Change From LIFO ?
Yes
No
6 Change in Method of Accounting for L-T Construction ?
Yes
No
7 Change To or From Full Costing ?
Yes
No
8 Exempt as Initial Public Distribution ?
Yes
No
A
Restate Financial Statements of All Prior Periods Presented
Disclose Nature and Justification and Effect on Current Operations and Related EPS
END

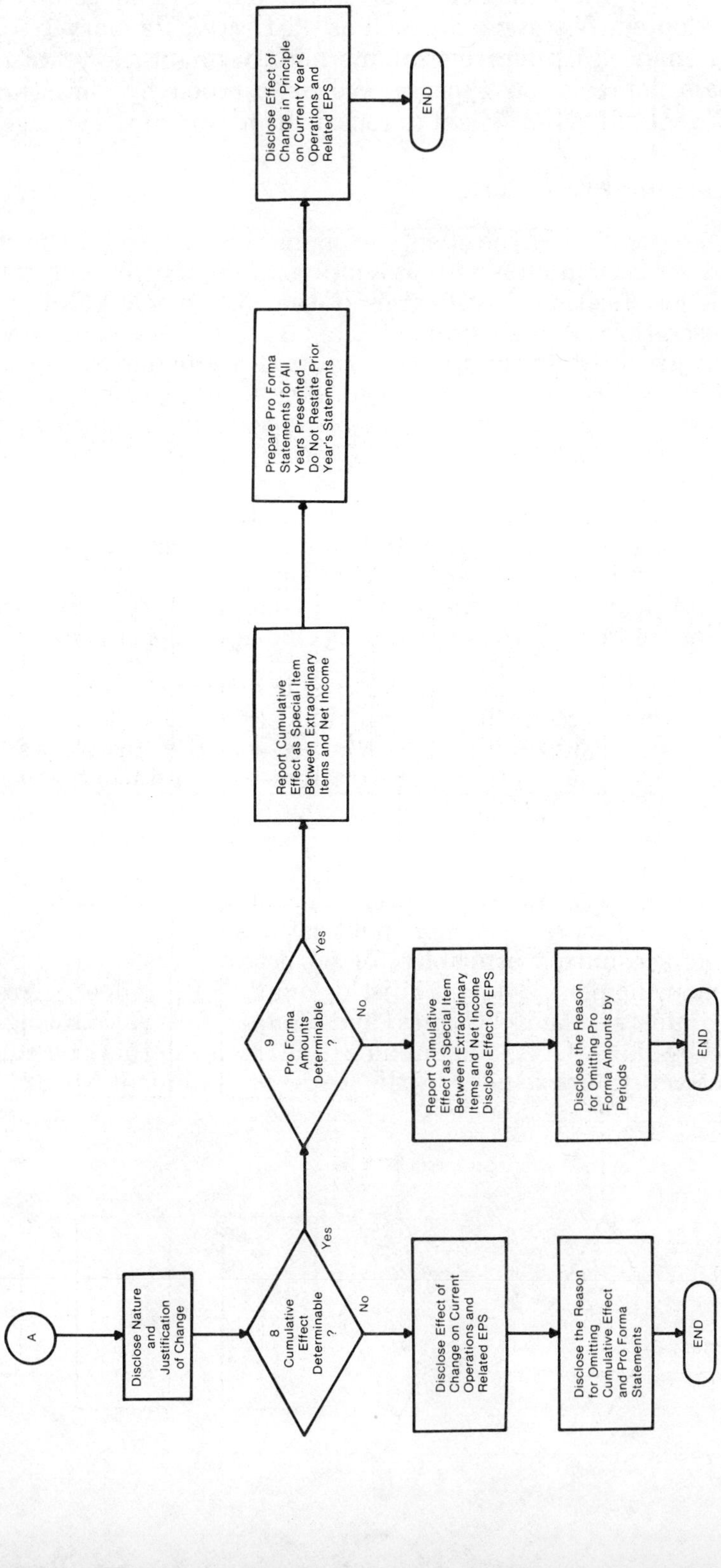
A
Disclose Nature and Justification of Change
8 Cumulative Effect Determinable ?
Yes
No
Disclose Effect of Change on Current Operations and Related EPS
Disclose the Reason for Omitting Cumulative Effect and Pro Forma Statements
END
9 Pro Forma Amounts Determinable ?
Yes
No
Report Cumulative Effect as Special Item Between Extraordinary Items and Net Income Disclose Effect on EPS
Disclose the Reason for Omitting Pro Forma Amounts by Periods
END
Report Cumulative Effect as Special Item Between Extraordinary Items and Net Income
Prepare Pro Forma Statements for All Years Presented – Do Not Restate Prior Year's Statements
Disclose Effect of Change in Principle on Current Year's Operations and Related EPS
END

the change, the method used prior to the date of change and the new method adopted. A statement, such as, "Effective January 1, 197X, the Company changed its depreciation method to sum-of-the-years' digits. In prior years depreciation expense was determined by the straight-line method," generally is sufficient to report the nature of the change.

Justification of the Change

The justification of the change explains the reasons for the change in principles. APB Opinion No. 20 provides little support for determining an acceptable justification. Justification of the change is left almost entirely to the discretion of management. The APB did state, however, that support or justification for a change exists if a pronouncement issued by the Board "creates a new accounting principle, . . . expresses a preference for an accounting principle, or . . . rejects a specific accounting principle" (APB Opinion No. 20, Paragraph 16). The Board issued Statement No. 32 in an effort to express an opinion on certain preferable methods of treating accounting changes in several specialized situations, i.e., in areas not specifically covered in the Opinion. Statement No. 32 is an amendment to Paragraph 16 of APB Opinion No. 20, and identifies several publications of the AICPA that may contain preferable justification for dealing with accounting changes in specific industries.

For several years, the AICPA has issued Statements of Position (SOPs), Industry Accounting Guides, Industry Audit Guides and Audit and Accounting Guides that have expressed the Institute's position regarding accounting and auditing matters in certain industries. FASB Interpretation No. 20, *Reporting Accounting Changes Under AICPA Statements of Position,* was the first pronouncement to indicate that accounting changes should be handled in accordance with the SOPs where such accounting treatment was specified. Statement No. 32 has indicated that SOPs and certain other publications of the AICPA contain "preferable accounting principles for purposes of justifying a change in accounting principle." Below is a listing of all SOPs, Industry Accounting Guides, Industry Audit Guides and Audit and Accounting Guides published by the AICPA, and an indication as to whether the publication has been accepted or excluded by the FASB in Statement No. 32:

Justification of the Change

Publications Accepted As Preferable Accounting Principles	Publications Not Accepted As Preferable Accounting Principles
SOP 74-6 Recognition of Profit on Sales of Receivable with Recourse	
SOP 74-8 Financial Accounting and Reporting by Colleges and Universities	
SOP 74-11 Financial Accounting and Reporting by Face-Amount Certificate Companies	
SOP 75-1 Revenue Recognition When Right of Return Exists	
SOP 75-2 Accounting Practices of Real Estate Investment Trusts	
	SOP 75-3 Accrual of Revenue & Expenditures by State & Local Governmental Units
	SOP 75-4 Presentation and Disclosure of Financial Forecasts
SOP 75-5 Accounting Practices in the Broadcasting Industry	
SOP 75-6 Questions Concerning Profit Recognition on Sales of Real Estate	
SOP 76-1 Accounting Practices in the Record and Music Industry	
SOP 76-2 Accounting for Origination Costs and Loan and Commitment Fees in the Mortgage Banking Industry	
SOP 76-3 Accounting Practices for Certain Employee Stock Ownership Plans	
SOP 77-1 Financial Accounting and Reporting by Investment Companies	
	SOP 77-2 Accounting for Interfund Transfers of State and Local Governmental Units
SOP 78-1 Accounting by Hospitals for Certain Marketable Equity Securities	
SOP 78-2 Accounting Practices of Real Estate Investment Trusts	
SOP 78-3 Accounting for Costs to Sell and Rent, and Initial Rental Operations of, Real Estate Projects	
SOP 78-4 Application of the Deposit, Installment, and Cost Recovery Methods in Accounting for Sales of Real Estate	
SOP 78-5 Accounting for Advance Refunding of Tax-Exempt Debt	
SOP 78-6 Accounting for Property and Liability Insurance Companies	
SOP 78-7 Financial Accounting and Reporting by Hospitals Operated by a Governmental Unit	
SOP 78-8 Accounting for Product Financing Arrangements	
SOP 78-9 Accounting for Investments in Real Estate Ventures	
SOP 78-10 Accounting Principles and Reporting Practices for Certain Nonprofit Organizations	
SOP 79-1 Accounting for Municipal Bond Funds	
SOP 79-2 Accounting for Cable Television	

SOP 79-3 Accounting for Investments of Stock Life Insurance Companies	
SOP 79-4 Accounting for Motion Picture Films	
INDUSTRY AUDIT GUIDES	*INDUSTRY AUDIT GUIDES*
Audits of Government Contractors	Audits of Service-Center-Produced-Records
	Audits of State and Local Governmental Units
Audits of Voluntary Health & Welfare Organizations	
Audits of Investment Companies	
Audits of Finance Companies	
Audits of Colleges and Universities	
Audits of Stock Life Insurance Companies	
Audits of Brokers and Dealers in Securities	
Hospital Audit Guide	
Audits of Employee Health & Welfare Benefit Funds	Medicare Audit Guide
Audits of Banks	
Audits of Personal Financial Statements	
Audits of Fire & Casualty Insurance Companies	
Audits of Construction Contractors	
INDUSTRY ACCOUNTING GUIDES	*INDUSTRY ACCOUNTING GUIDES*
Accounting for Franchise Fee Revenue	
Accounting for Retail Land Sales	
Profit Recognition on Sales of Real Estate	
Accounting for Motion Picture Films	
AUDIT AND ACCOUNTING GUIDE	*AUDIT AND ACCOUNTING GUIDE*
Savings and Loan Associations	

Through the issuance of FASB Interpretation No. 20 and Statement No. 32, the Board has attempted to give some guidance in the area of accounting for changes and providing suitable justification for such a change. Even with this expanded information, statements such as, "The change from FIFO to LIFO was made because management feels that LIFO more fairly reports current income by matching current costs with current revenues" typically were used to justify the change by many companies from FIFO to LIFO.

Pro Forma Information

"Pro forma" literally means "for the sake of form," but the phrase is used in accounting to indicate the presentation of information on a basis other than that actually reported. In this particular case, the financial information is to be presented "as if" the new principle always had been used. While the cumulative effect includes only direct adjustments to income, pro forma information will include both direct and indirect adjustments.

For a change in accounting principles, the pro forma information should include current income before extraordinary items, net income and the required EPS disclosure. The pro forma information should be prepared for all statement periods presented, under the assumption that the new principle was used in each of those periods.

Effect of the Change on Current Operations

The last disclosure to consider is the effect of the accounting change on current operations. The effect of the change on income before extraordinary items, net income and related earnings per share must be presented in the notes to the financial statements in the period of change. To illustrate the type of disclosure required, assume that a company changes its method of depreciation from straight-line to sum-of-the-years' digits in year 197X. A typical disclosure statement might read as follows: "The effect of the change in depreciation methods in 197X increased income before extraordinary items by $5,000 ($.25 per share)."

In addition to the reporting requirements for general type changes in accounting principles, discussed above, the Opinion outlined special considerations and special cases in reporting for changes in accounting principles.

Changes in Accounting Principles—Special Considerations

The discussion above assumed that a company could determine both the cumulative effect and the necessary pro forma information. There are cases where the cumulative effect cannot be determined (Block 9) and where the pro forma information cannot be developed (Block 10).

If the cumulative effect cannot be computed, the financial statements should contain a disclosure stating the effect of the change on current income before extraordinary items, net income and related earnings per share. If the cumulative effect cannot be determined, pro forma information is not required. However, the footnotes should contain a statement giving the reasons for omitting the cumulative effect and the pro forma information. One classic example of a change in accounting principles where the cumulative effect cannot be determined is a change in inventory costing methods from FIFO to LIFO.

If the cumulative effect can be determined, but the required pro forma information cannot be developed, the cumulative effect and the impact on earnings per share should be reported on the income statement, as discussed previously. It also is necessary to disclose the reasons for omitting the pro forma amounts.

In addition to these two problems, a company may face a problem when acquiring new assets. The company may choose to change an accounting principle, e.g., depreciation methods, for the newly acquired assets, but continue to use the same accounting principle for existing assets. In this case, reporting of the cumulative effect and the pro forma information would not be required. Disclosure of the nature of the change, its effect on current operations and related earnings per share is required, however.

Changes in Accounting Principles—Special Cases

Before concluding the general discussion on changes in accounting principles, it is necessary to discuss the four exceptions to the general accounting identified in Blocks 5 through 8 of Flowchart 1. As mentioned earlier, these changes will be handled in a different manner. The Board concluded that the special changes have such a significant impact on income in the year of change that special treatment is necessary. Accounting treatment of these four special changes requires a restatement of all financial statements presented, using the new accounting principle. This means that the accountants must reconstruct all previous statements presented, under the assumption that the new principle was in effect. Restatement of previously issued financial statements may cause some concern on the part of an investor because amounts shown on the restated financials will be different from amounts previously reported. In addition to the retroactive restatement of the financial statements, the nature of the change, justification for the change, the effect of the change on income before extraordinary items, net income and related earnings per share must be disclosed.

Changes in Accounting Principles—Technical Considerations

To illustrate the accounting and reporting for a change in an accounting principle, assume that a company purchased equipment in year 197A at a cost of $20,000. The equipment has a useful life of five years and a $5,000 residual value. The company used straight-line depreciation in years 197A and 197B, but changed to the sum-of-the-years' digits method during year 197C. Retained earnings of the company at the beginning of year 197C are $60,000.

This change in depreciation methods constitutes a change in accounting principle. The first step in the accounting process is to determine the cumulative effect of the change. To accomplish this, it is necessary to calculate depreciation for years 197A and 197B under both methods, and to compare the difference. Table I shows the computations necessary to determine the cumulative effect.

Table I

Calculation of Depreciation and Cumulative Effect

Calculation of Straight-line and Sum-of-the-years' Digits Depreciation

	Straight-line	Sum-of-the-years' Digits
197A	[a]$3,000	[b]$5,000
197B	3,000	[c]4,000
Accumulated depreciation before change	$6,000	$9,000
197C	$3,000	[d]$3,000

Calculation of the Cumulative Effect of the Accounting Change

Depreciation Using Sum-of-the-years' Digits	$9,000
Depreciation Using Straight-line	6,000
Cumulative Effect of the Accounting Change	$3,000

---

[a]

Cost	$20,000
Residual Value	(5,000)
Amount to Depreciate	$15,000
Asset Life	÷ 5
	$ 3,000

[b] 5/15 × ($20,000—$5,000) = $5,000
[c] 4/15 × ($20,000—$5,000) = $4,000
[d] 3/15 × ($20,000—$5,000) = $3,000

The cumulative effect is determined to be $3,000. An alternative method of computing the cumulative effect is to determine the effect of using the sum-of-the-years' digits method in years 197A and 197B on the retained earnings balance of $60,000 (the balance resulting from the use of the straight-line method). As shown in Table I, if the sum-of-the-years' digits method had been used in previous periods, $3,000 ($9,000 − $6,000) more depreciation expense would have been charged to income. Over the two-year period, income would have been $3,000 lower and, therefore, retained earnings would have been $3,000 lower. In effect, the retained earnings balance under the sum-of-the-years' digits method would have been $57,000. The cumulative effect would be determined as follows:

Retained Earnings Using Sum-of-the-years' Digits	$57,000
Retained Earnings Using Straight-line	60,000
Cumulative Effect of Change in Accounting Principle	$ 3,000

The journal entry necessary to record the cumulative effect in 197C is:

Cumulative effect of change in an accounting principle—Change from straight-line to sum-of-the-years' digits	$3,000	
Accumulated Depreciation		$3,000

The credit to accumulated depreciation brings the account balance up to $9,000, which is the balance under the sum-of-the-years' digits method of depreciation. The normal, adjusting entry for depreciation will be made in 197C using the sum-of-the-years' digits method regardless of when in 197C the decision to change methods was made. The entry to record depreciation for 197C is as follows:

Depreciation Expense (computed in Table 1, sum-of-the-years' digits column)	$3,000	
Accumulated Depreciation—Equipment		$3,000

Once the proper journal entries have been made, the next problem is to determine the appropriate pro forma disclosures. To illustrate the computation and presentation of the pro forma information, assume the same facts as presented above, except that a bonus of 10 percent of reported net income is paid at the end of each year to certain key employees. The following income statement information is provided for 197C and 197B (income tax considerations are ignored).

	197C	**197B**
Income before extraordinary items and cumulative effect of accounting changes (includes bonuses actually paid)	$25,000	$20,000
Extraordinary gain	5,000	—
Cumulative effect of a change in accounting principle	(3,000)	—
Net Income	$27,000	$20,000
Earnings per share (assuming 20,000 common shares outstanding in both 197C and 197B (see Topic 7 for a complete analysis of earnings per share computations)		
Earnings per common share		
Income before extraordinary items and cumulative effect of an accounting change	$1.25	$1.00
Extraordinary item	.25	—
Cumulative effect of a change in an accounting principle	(.15)	—
Net income	$1.35	$1.00

Based on this information and on the assumptions given above, the following computations are necessary to determine the proper pro forma amounts. Remember that the pro forma information is developed under the assumption that the sum-of-the-years' digits method was used in both 197C and 197B.

Income in 197B before adjustments	$20,000
Additional depreciation under sum-of-the-years' digits	[a](1,000)
Adjustment for bonus on lower income	[b]100
Pro forma income for 197B	$19,100

[a] Depreciation in 197B—Sum-of-the-years' digits	$ 4,000
Depreciation in 197B—Straight-line	3,000
Additional Depreciation	$ 1,000
[b] Bonus in 197B before additional depreciation ($20,000 × 10%)	$ 2,000
Bonus in 197B after additional depreciation ($19,000 × 10%)	1,900
Adjustment for Bonus	$ 100

The pro forma income before extraordinary items in 197B is $19,100. Notice that the pro forma income included an adjustment for depreciation and for the bonus, but did not include the cumulative effect of the change in accounting principle. The following pro forma presentation is appropriate for the example given:

	197C	197B
Pro forma information: Income		
Income before extraordinary items	$25,000	$19,100
Net income (including extraordinary gain or loss)	30,000	19,100
Pro forma information: Earnings per share		
Earnings before extraordinary items	$ 1.25	.96
Net earnings	1.50	.96

Pro forma presentation requires a restatement of income before extraordinary items and net income for all periods presented, as if the new method had been used all along. Since, in the year of change, 197C, the new method already is used, the only adjustment in 197C, for pro forma purposes, is to remove the impact on income of the cumulative effect. For all prior periods presented (year 197B in this case), adjustments are required for both the additional depreciation and the bonus.

The nature of the change and the effect on current operations are not illustrated in this example, since adequate discussion of the appropriate disclosures was presented above.

Changes in Accounting Principles—Disclosures

To illustrate an actual example of disclosure requirements under APB Opinion No. 20, the notes to the financial statements of IPCO Hospital Supply Corporation are shown in Exhibit I.

Exhibit I

IPCO Hospital Supply Corporation (Jun)

Statement of Consolidated Income	**1975**	**1974**
	($000 except per share amounts)	
Income before cumulative effect of accounting change	$ 1,736	$ 2,618
Cumulative effect on prior years (to June 30, 1974) for accountng change with respect to inceptive costs, net of income tax effect of $396,000 (Note 2)	(431)	—
Net Income	$ 1,305	$ 2,618
Earnings Per Common Share		
Income before cumulative effect of accounting change	$ .33	$ .50
Cumulative effect of accounting change	(.08)	—
Net Income	$ .25	$ .50
Pro forma amounts giving effect to retroactive application of writing off inceptive costs as incurred (Note 2)		
Net Income	$ 1,736	$ 2,517
Net Income Per Common Share	$ .33	$ .48
Average number of common shares outstanding and common stock equivalents	5,268,272	5,273,263

Note 2: Accounting Change—Effective July 1, 1974, the Company adopted the accounting policy of expensing as incurred all inceptive costs relating to the opening of new stores of its Optical division. In prior years such costs were deferred and amortized over a two-year period following the end of the first year of operation of newly opened stores. Management is of the opinion that this accounting change will result in financial reporting more consistent with that prevailing in industry today. The effect of the change on the results of operations for the year ended June 30, 1975, was to decrease net income by $683,000 ($.13 per share) of which $431,000 ($.08 per share) related to prior years' operations. The pro forma amounts shown on the Statement of Consolidated Income disclose the effect of retroactive application of the new accounting method as if the new method had been in effect in the prior year.

Source: *Accounting Trends and Techniques,* Copyright © 1976 by the American Institute of Certified Public Accountants, Inc., p. 35.

Changes in Accounting Estimates—General Discussion

Much of the accounting information presented in the financial statements is based on judgments of future events. These judgments involve estimates for items such as warranty costs to be incurred in the future, the amount of bad debts associated with accounts receivable and the useful life and residual value of depreciable assets. With the passage of time, new information may be obtained that requires a change in assessment about a previous estimate. If the original estimate was the best possible one based on available evidence at the time, and if new information is obtained that indicates the original estimate is not currently a proper assessment of the facts, a change in an accounting estimate (Block 4) has occurred. However, if an original estimate was *not* the best estimate based on then available facts, and if later information indicates that the original estimate was improper, an accounting error has occurred.

A change in an accounting estimate is handled differently than a change in an accounting principle. The change in accounting estimate is accounted for on a "prospective" basis, i.e., any adjustment is charged to the current or current and future periods. The financial statements of prior periods are not restated. In addition to any accounting adjustments, the company must disclose the nature of the change in estimate and its effect on income before extraordinary items, net income and related earnings per share.

Changes in Accounting Estimates—Technical Considerations

To illustrate the accounting for a change in estimate, assume a company purchased equipment on January 1, 197A, for $110,000. The equipment has a useful life of 10 years and an estimated residual value of $10,000. During year 197C, after two years of depreciation have been charged to income, new information is available that indicates that the useful life of the equipment should have been eight years, rather than the 10 years originally used. This change in the estimated useful life of the equipment qualifies as a change in an accounting estimate. The depreciation charged to income in 197C and future years will be affected by this change. No cumulative effect or pro forma information is required for a change in an accounting estimate.

In this example, the undepreciated asset balance will be depreciated over the remaining useful life of the equipment. The computations necessary to determine the appropriate charge for depreciation for 197C and subsequent periods, assuming straight-line depreciation is used, would be:

Original Cost of Equipment	$110,000
Estimated Residual Value	(10,000)
Amount to Be Depreciated	$100,000
Useful Life	÷ 10
Annual Depreciation Charge	$ 10,000
Original Amount to Be Depreciated	$100,000
Less: Depreciation for 197A and 197B ($10,000 × 2)	20,000
Undepreciated Balance at Beginning of 197C	$ 80,000
Revised Remaining Life (8 years - 2 years)	÷ 6
Current and Future Period Depreciation Charge	$ 13,333

The undepreciated equipment balance at the beginning of the year of change was $80,000, and there were six years remaining in the revised useful life of the asset; therefore, depreciation for years three to eight of the asset's life would be $13,333. The only entry in 197C would be the annual depreciation charge, determined by using the new estimated useful life. The entry would be as follows:

Depreciation Expense	13,333	
Accumulated Depreciation—Equipment		13,333

Changes in Accounting Estimates—Disclosures

Disclosure of the nature of the change and its effect on income before extraordinary items, net income and related earnings per share have been discussed previously and will not be repeated here. Exhibit II clearly shows the disclosure required for a change in an accounting estimate. The Exhibit is from the notes to the financial statements of APECO Corporation for 1975.

Exhibit II

APECO Corporation (Nov)

Notes to Consolidated Financial Statements

Note B: Changes in Accounting Estimates—In 1974 and prior years, the Company accrued for the possible payment of royalties to another corporation; these accruals totaled $1,291,000 at November 30, 1974. As a result of a court order issued in July, 1975, and an agreement signed in October, 1975, the Company was released from all liability for royalties under the subject patents, and the $1,291,000 accrual was therefore credited to income in 1975.

Additionally, during 1975, the Company changed the depreciable lives of certain assets and revised the basis of estimation with respect to certain accruals and income deferrals to more reasonably reflect the Company's actual experience. The effect of these changes in estimates was to increase operating income (before tax effect) by approximately $720,000.

In addition during 1975 the Company reversed, as income-tax credits, certain prior year provisions for accrued and deferred income taxes totaling $917,000.

The aggregate effect of the above items on the Consolidated Statement of Operations and Retained Earnings for 1975 was to reduce the loss before income-tax credit by $2,011,000 and increase net income by $2,928,000 (per share—$.28).

Source: *Accounting Trends and Techniques,* Copyright © 1976 by the American Institute of Certified Public Accountants, Inc., p. 31.

Changes in Reporting Entities—General Discussion

A company is faced with accounting for a change in reporting entity when the financial statements to be issued reflect a different group of enterprises than was shown in previous financial statements. A change in reporting entity may result from the preparation of consolidated statements rather than individual enterprise statements, or from a change in the composition of subsidiaries or companies making up the consolidated or combined group.

Proper accounting for a change in reporting entity requires a restatement of financial statements for all prior periods presented, using the new reporting entity. In addition to the retroactive restatement of the financial statements, the company must disclose the nature of the change, the reasons for the change, and the effect of the change on operations and related earnings per share for all reporting periods presented. A retroactive restatement is required so that the reader of the financial statements can have comparable information for all periods presented. While the accounting work involved in restating the financial statements may be very complex, the general example below is used to introduce the reader to the problem.

Changes in Reporting Entities—Technical Considerations

To illustrate the accounting for a change in reporting entity, assume that Parent Company, Inc. issued the following comparative financial statements for the years 197B and 197A. (The statements of changes in financial position and changes in retained earnings have been omitted from the example.)

Parent Company, Inc.
Income Statement
For the Years Ended December 31, 197B and 197A

	197B	**197A**
Sales	$500,000	$450,000
Cost of sales	365,000	340,000
	$135,000	$110,000
Operating expenses	50,000	45,000
Income taxes	40,000	31,000
Net income	$ 45,000	$ 34,000
Earnings per share (20,000 shares outstanding)	$ 2.25	$ 1.70

Parent Company, Inc.
Balance Sheet
December 31, 197B and 197A

	197B	**197A**
Assets		
Current assets:		
Cash	$ 20,000	$ 30,000
Accounts receivable	40,000	50,000
Inventories	30,000	40,000
Total current assets	$ 90,000	$120,000
Property, plant and equipment	$600,000	$550,000
Less: Accumulated depreciation	(75,000)	(55,000)
Property, plant and equipment net	$525,000	$495,000
Other assets	$ 30,000	$ 10,000
Total assets	$645,000	$625,000
Liabilities and Stockholders' Equity		
Current liabilities:		
Accounts payable	$ 10,000	$ 20,000
Other	15,000	12,000
Total current liabilities	$ 25,000	$ 32,000
Long-term debt	$300,000	$300,000
Total liabilities	$325,000	$332,000
Stockholders' equity:		
Common stock (20,000 shares outstanding in 197B and 197A)	$200,000	$200,000
Retained earnings	120,000	93,000
Total stockholders' equity	$320,000	$293,000
Total liabilities and stockholders' equity	$645,000	$625,000

Assume that, during 197C, Parent Company, Inc. acquired all of the stock of Subsidiary Manufacturing Company by issuing 10,000 of its common shares. The business combination qualifies as a pooling of interest. (See Topic 11 for a complete analysis of business combinations.) The Company plans to issue consolidated financial statements for 197C, and wants to also issue comparative statements for the years 197C and 197B. This transaction and the related plan of financial presentation represent a change in reporting entity. When the 197C comparative financial statements are prepared, the 197B statements must be restated to reflect the change.

To illustrate the restatement of the financials for 197B, assume the following information is available for Subsidiary Manufacturing Company for the year 197B on an individual company basis:

Subsidiary Manufacturing Company
Trial Balance
December 31, 197B

Cash	$ 10,000	
Accounts receivable	25,000	
Inventories	30,000	
Property, plant and equipment	400,000	
Accumulated depreciation		$100,000
Other assets	50,000	
Accounts payable		10,000
Other current liabilities		5,000
Long-term debt		200,000
Common stock		100,000
Retained earnings		100,000
Sales		300,000
Cost of sales	200,000	
Operating expenses	40,000	
Income taxes	28,000	
	$783,000	$815,000
Net income	32,000	
	$815,000	$815,000

There were no intercompany transactions or other complicating factors relating to the business combination. Each company's common stock has a par value of $10 per share, so Subsidiary Company exchanges its 10,000 shares for 10,000 shares of Parent Company stock. Under these limiting assumptions, the restatement would be a straightforward combination of amounts shown, and would result in the following restated 197B financial statements:

Parent Company, Inc. and Subsidiary
Consolidated Balance Sheet
December 31, 197B*

Assets	
Current assets:	
Cash	$ 30,000
Accounts receivable	65,000
Inventories	60,000
Total current assets	$ 155,000
Property, plant and equipment	$1,000,000
Less: Accumulated depreciation	(175,000)
Property, plant and equipment, net	$ 825,000
Other assets	$ 80,000
Total assets	$1,060,000
Liabilities and Stockholders' Equity	
Current liabilities:	
Accounts payable	$ 20,000
Other current liabilities	20,000
Total current liabilities	$ 40,000
Long-term debt	$ 500,000
Total liabilities	$ 540,000
Stockholders' equity:	
Common stock (30,000 shares outstanding)	$ 300,000
Retained earnings	220,000
Total stockholders' equity	$ 520,000
Total liabilities and stockholders' equity	$1,060,000

* As restated see footnotes to financial statements.

Parent Company, Inc. and Subsidiary
Consolidated Statement of Income
For the Year Ended December 31, 197B*

Sales	$800,000
Cost of sales	565,000
	$235,000
Operating expense	90,000
Income taxes	68,000
Net income	$ 77,000
Earnings per share (30,000 shares outstanding)	$ 2.57

* As restated see footnotes to financial statements.

The restated 197B financial statements would be shown with the 197C statements on a comparative basis.

Changes in Reporting Entities—Disclosures

The footnote disclosures would explain the nature and reason for the change and its effect on operations and related earnings per share for the years 197C and 197B. Exhibit III shows the footnote disclosures for Scovill Manufacturing Company as a result of a change in reporting entity for the years 1972 and 1973.

Exhibit III

Scovill Manufacturing Company (Dec)

Notes to Consolidated Financial Statements

Note B—As of January 1, 1973, the Company's Brazilian subsidiary was consolidated, since management is satisfied that economic conditions have reached sufficient stability to warrant consolidation. Previously this investment was carried at cost and income was recorded to the extent of dividends received. The effect of this change was to increase net earnings and net earnings per share as follows:

	Fiscal Year Ended Dec. 30, 1973	Fiscal Year Ended Dec. 31, 1972
Net earnings	$1,055,000	$509,000
Net earnings per share of Common Stock:		
Primary	.15	.08
Fully diluted	.11	.05

Also, in 1973, the Company acquired an additional 20% interest in an Australian subsidiary and commenced consolidation of the accounts of this subsidiary. Previously this subsidiary was carried at cost plus equity in undistributed earnings and, accordingly, net earnings and net earnings per share were not affected by this action.

The financial statements for the fiscal year ended December 31, 1972, have been restated for comparative purposes.

During 1973, the Company also purchased an interest in two small foreign and two small domestic businesses and sold a small domestic division. The results of operations of these businesses, and the gain on the disposition, are not significant in relation to the overall consolidated results.

Source: *Accounting Trends and Techniques,* Copyright © 1974 by the American Institute of Certified Public Accountants, Inc., p. 22.

Accounting Errors—General Discussion

Accounting errors (Block 2 of Flowchart 1) are the result of "mathematical mistakes, mistakes in the application of accounting principles, or oversight or misuse of facts that existed at the time the financial statements were prepared," according to APB Opinion No. 20, Paragraph 13. Naturally, if an error were made in a period *and* discovered before the financial statements were distributed, it should be corrected in that period. APB Opinion No. 20 deals with errors that were made in one period and not discovered until a subsequent period. Therefore, previously issued financial statements contain an error.

The correction of an accounting error should be reported as a direct adjustment to retained earnings as a prior period adjustment. If comparative financial statements are to be presented, all prior statements should be restated to correct for the error. In addition, the company must disclose the nature of the error and the effect of the error on current operations and related earnings per share for the year in which the error is found and corrected.

Accounting Errors—Technical Considerations

To illustrate the proper accounting and reporting for an accounting error, assume that equipment was purchased by a company in year 197A for $100,000 cash. The equipment has a useful life of 10 years with no residual value, and the company uses the straight-line method of depreciation. At the beginning of year 197C, it was discovered that the equipment had never been recorded or depreciated. This failure to record the asset and related depreciation constituted an accounting error. The company had understated the value of its depreciable assets and depreciation expense of 197A and 197B. The amount of the error will be treated as a prior period adjustment and is calculated below:

Cost of asset	$100,000
Estimated useful life	÷ 10
Annual depreciation expense	$ 10,000
Number of years omitted	× 2
Depreciation expense not recorded	$ 20,000

In addition to correcting for the depreciation not recorded, the company must also record the asset acquired. The entry to accomplish this in 197C is:

Prior Period Adjustment - Accounting Error	$20,000	
Equipment	100,000	
Accumulated Depreciation		$ 20,000
Cash		100,000

Assuming that the beginning retained earnings balance previously reported for 197C was $150,000, and that, during 197C, net income amounted to $50,000 and dividends were $20,000, the following correction to retained earnings is required:

Retained earnings previously reported	$150,000
Adjustment:	
Prior period adjustment for accounting error in recording depreciation	(20,000)
Adjusted beginning retained earnings	$130,000
Net income	50,000
Dividends	(20,000)
Retained earnings 12/31/197C	$160,000

If 197C and 197B comparative statements were presented, the correction for the failure to record the asset and depreciation would be shown through a retroactive restatement of 197B financial statements.

Accounting Errors—Disclosures

The disclosure requirements for an accounting error are shown in Exhibit IV. The example is for the W.R. Grace Company for the years 1974 and 1975, and relates to an error in accounting for a business combination.

Exhibit IV

W.R. Grace & Co. (Dec)

Consolidated Statement of Shareholders' Equity

In Thousands	Preferred Stocks	Common Stock	Paid in Capital	Retained Earnings	Total
	Years Ended December 31, 1974 and 1975				
Balance at January 1, 1974, as reported	$9,608	$29,979	$221,464	$514,618	$ 775,669
Adjustment for change in accounting for two business combinations	—	—	17,764	(23,699)	(5,935)
Adjustments for 1975 businesses combined in poolings of interests transactions	—	753	952	2,047	3,752
Balance at January 1, 1974, as restated	9,608	30,732	240,180	492,966	773,486
Net income for the year 1974	—	—	—	119,110	119,110
Business combinations	—	263	2	—	265
Exercise of stock options	—	1	35	—	36
Purchase of preferred stocks	(221)	—	1	—	(220)
Other	—	—	358	—	358
Dividends paid:					
Preferred	—	—	—	(700)	(700)
Common ($1.525 per share)	—	—	—	(45,390)	(45,390)
Balance at December 31, 1974	9,387	30,996	240,576	565,986	846,945
Net income for the year 1975	—	—	—	166,678	166,678
Common stock subscribed	—	4,000	100,000	—	104,000
Business combinations	—	262	8,593	—	8,855
Exercise of stock options	—	18	390	—	408
Purchase of preferred stocks	(146)	—	51	—	(95)
Other	—	—	(366)	—	(366)
Dividends paid:					
Preferred	—	—	—	(697)	(697)
Common ($1.625 per share)	—	—	—	(50,654)	(50,654)
Pooled company prior to combination with the company	—	—	—	(61)	(61)
Balance at December 31, 1975	$9,241	$35,276	$349,244	$681,252	$1,075,013

Notes to Financial Statements

Note 1 (in part): Changes in Accounting:

(a) Change in Accounting Treatment for Two Business Combinations

In May, 1975, the Company determined that the 1969 and 1971 acquisitions of two European consumer products businesses which had been accounted for as poolings of interests should have been treated as purchase transactions in accordance with generally accepted accounting principles in effect during those years. Accordingly, the 1974 financial statements have been restated to reflect a Swiss Franc obligation which at December 31, 1974 was equivalent to $40,447. During 1975, the obligation was partially retired through issuance of common stock which increased paid in capital by an amount equal to the excess of fair value over par value of such shares at time of issuance. In addition, goodwill, which amounted to $25,512 at January 1, 1974, has been recorded representing the excess consideration paid over net assets acquired. This change required a charge to 1974 net income of $8,611, principally for foreign exchange losses, thereby reducing earnings per common and common equivalent share by $.10, and earnings per common share assuming full dilution by $.11. In June, 1975, the Company paid cash to settle the remaining obligation.

Source: *Accounting Trends and Techniques,* Copyright © 1976 by the American Institute of Certified Public Accountants, Inc., pp. 281 and 282.

APB Opinion No. 22 (April 1972)
Disclosure of Accounting Policies

Flowchart and General Discussion

APB Opinion No. 22 establishes disclosure requirements for significant accounting policies used by a business enterprise in the preparation of basic financial statements. The increased demand by statement users for full disclosure of accounting information appears to have been the impetus for the guidelines established by the Opinion. Prior to the promulgation of APB Opinion No. 22, many companies were disclosing significant accounting policies, but the manner and extent of presentation varied widely. The Opinion provides for some uniformity and comparability of accounting information by providing guidelines for the content and format of disclosures relating to accounting policies.

The Flowchart outlines the basic decision process involved in determining if a particular accounting policy must be disclosed. Accounting policies of a business enterprise need be disclosed only if the financial statements to be issued are prepared in conformance with generally accepted accounting principles (GAAP—Block 1). The policies must be disclosed, even though *all* basic financial statements (income statement, balance sheet and statement of changes in financial position) are *not* prepared. As long as at least one basic statement is presented in conformance with GAAP, accounting policies must be disclosed.

Accounting policies are defined as "accounting principles followed by the reporting entity and the methods of applying those principles" (APB

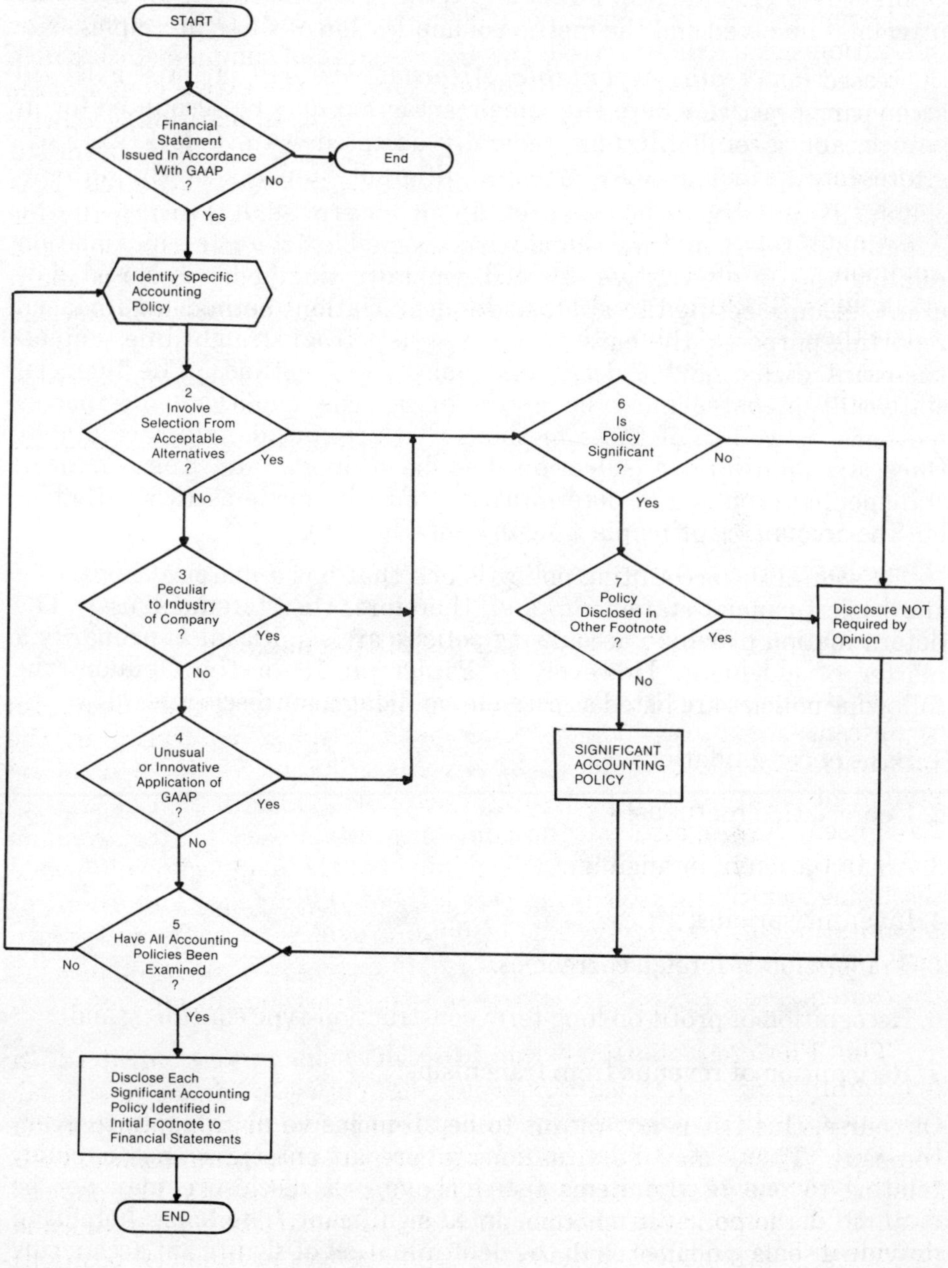
START
1 Financial Statement Issued In Accordance With GAAP ?
No
End
Yes
Identify Specific Accounting Policy
2 Involve Selection From Acceptable Alternatives ?
Yes
No
3 Peculiar to Industry of Company ?
Yes
No
4 Unusual or Innovative Application of GAAP ?
Yes
No
5 Have All Accounting Policies Been Examined ?
No
Yes
Disclose Each Significant Accounting Policy Identified in Initial Footnote to Financial Statements
END
6 Is Policy Significant ?
No
Yes
7 Policy Disclosed in Other Footnote ?
Yes
No
Disclosure NOT Required by Opinion
SIGNIFICANT ACCOUNTING POLICY

Opinion No. 22, Paragraph 12). The term "policies" refers to both the principles involved and the method of application of those principles.

Selection from Acceptable Alternatives.—Situations exist in accounting practice where the same transaction may be accounted for in any one of several different generally accepted ways (Block 2). Each alternative principle may have a different impact on the income statement and the balance sheet. If an enterprise is faced with the situation of selecting from alternative acceptable principles, information relating to the alternative selected generally should be disclosed. For example, in selecting the appropriate depreciation method for financial reporting purposes, the enterprise may select from straight-line, sum-of-the-years' digits, double declining balance, etc. methods. The financial statement preparer must be aware of all the applicable alternative methods, as well as of those methods that are considered unacceptable. Once an appropriate selection has been made and the financial statement(s) prepared, a determination must be made as to whether or not the accounting principle is significant (Block 6).

A significant accounting policy is one that has a material impact on the basic financial statements and, therefore, the statement user. The determination of which accounting policies are significant is primarily a matter of judgment. However, in Paragraph 13 of the Opinion, the following policies are listed as possible candidates for disclosure:

1. Basis of consolidation;

2. Depreciation methods;

3. Amortization of intangibles;

4. Inventory pricing;

5. Translation of foreign currencies;

6. Recognition of profit on long-term construction-type contracts; and

7. Recognition of revenue from franchising.

Of course, this list is not meant to be all-inclusive or to apply to every company. There may be situations where an enterprise has a policy relating to one of the items listed above, yet disclosure may not be required if the policy is not considered significant. The list is helpful in providing some guidance as to the determination of significant accounting policies.

The impact of the accounting policy on the user of the financial information is difficult to assess. However, if enterprise A has a material amount of inventory and uses LIFO inventory pricing, and enterprise B, in a similar situation, uses FIFO inventory pricing, the inventory costs and the cost of goods sold during the period would not be comparable. The lack of comparison is due to the difference in the accounting policy regarding inventory pricing. Each enterprise has selected a different acceptable accounting procedure for determining the cost of inventory. If each enterprise disclosed the accounting policy used, the informed reader would be able to assess more clearly the performance of each firm. In this case, disclosure of the accounting policy would provide some measure of uniformity and comparability between the two entities.

If a specific accounting policy results from the selection among acceptable alternatives and is determined to be a significant policy, it will require disclosure under the provisions of APB Opinion No. 22, if it is not disclosed elsewhere in the footnotes or financial statements (Block 7). The intent of the Opinion is to avoid duplication of information presented.

Policies Relating to Particular Industries

Some industries use specialized accounting principles and procedures in recording and reporting financial information (Block 3). A specialized accounting principle or procedure may be common to the enterprise's industry, but it differs from those normally followed by the majority of other industries. If the specialized accounting principle or procedure is significant (Block 6), and is not disclosed elsewhere in the footnotes or financial statements (Block 7), appropriate disclosure is required.

An example of a specialized industry accounting practice is identified in SFAS No. 12, "Accounting for Certain Marketable Securities" (see Topic 2 for a detailed analysis of SFAS No. 12). This pronouncement specifies that security dealers and brokers and investment companies have acceptable specialized accounting procedures for marketable securities. Marketable securities in these industries usually are shown on the balance sheet at *current market prices,* rather than at the lower of cost or market. Reporting the securities at lower of cost or market is the principle used by the majority of industries under the situation described in SFAS No. 12.

Another example of a specialized industry policy is where the operating cycle is considered to be longer than one year. This allows the inclusion in current assets of items that will not be converted into cash or consumed within one year. Most industries assume an operating cycle of one year and classify assets as current on this basis.

Even though enterprises in a particular industry use a given specialized accounting principle or procedure, it is necessary to disclose the policy, because the statement user may not be aware of the fact that the policy is peculiar to the industry. From a broad viewpoint, specialized accounting principles and procedures are, in effect, a selection from alternative acceptable accounting policies. An enterprise in an industry with specialized practices may elect not to follow those practices.

Unusual or Innovative Accounting Policy Application

The Opinion specifies that any generally accepted accounting principle that is applied in an unusual or innovative manner (Block 4) should be disclosed if the application is significant (Block 6) and is not disclosed elsewhere in the footnotes or financial statements (Block 7). By their very nature, unusual or innovative accounting policies are few in number. One example might be an unusual method of accounting for work-in-process inventory for a manufacturing firm. Accounting for work-in-process inventory can be a complex problem in cost accounting, especially when the manufacturing process is sophisticated. In an effort to simplify the accounting process, some manufacturing firms have adopted the policy of an instantaneous production process, i.e., inventories are either raw materials or finished goods, but there is never a work-in-process inventory. Under this system, goods that are "in process" are considered merely to be raw materials in a different form. Labor and overhead costs are accumulated in a clearing account, rather than applied to work-in-process inventory. The balance in the clearing accounts at any balance sheet date is considered current assets and is classified with inventories. When applied appropriately, this accounting policy is certainly unusual and innovative; and disclosure may be required if work-in-process inventory is considered to be material.

Format of Disclosures

The Opinion allows for some flexibility in the method of disclosure, but requires that any significant accounting policy be presented in such a manner as to be an integral part of the basic financial statements. It is recommended that disclosures be identified under the heading "Summary of Significant Accounting Policies" and be located as the first note to the financial statements, or preceding the first note.

Example Disclosures

The examples shown below are from the 1976 annual reports of Browning-Ferris Industries, Inc., Combined Communications Corporation and Franklin Mint Corporation. The three were selected to illustrate the routine disclosure of accounting policies, as well as specialized industry practices. Note the similarity of disclosures relating to inventories for Browning-Ferris Industries and Combined Communications, and the disclosures relating to property, plant and equipment for Combined Communications and Franklin Mint.

Careful reading of the notes indicates a specialized industry practice for all three companies. Review the Browning-Ferris note relating to "Landfill Sales," the Combined Communications notes relating to "Film Broadcast Rights" and "Outdoor Advertising Revenues," and the lengthy note of Franklin Mint relating to "Precious Metal Valuation and Related Product Costing." These all are excellent examples of specialized industry accounting policies.

Browning-Ferris Industries, Inc. (Sep)

Notes to Consolidated Financial Statements

Note 1: Summary of Significant Accounting Policies

Principles of Consolidation—The consolidated financial statements include the accounts of the Company and its subsidiaries. All significant intercompany accounts and transactions have been eliminated. The accounts of Canadian subsidiaries have not been translated into United States currency since the effect of translation would be insignificant. These notes include only amounts applicable to continuing operations, except where indicated otherwise.

Business Combinations—The financial statements include the accounts of businesses combined and stock issued in transactions accounted for on a pooling-of-interests basis for all periods presented. The accounts of purchased companies are included in the financial statements for all periods subsequent to the date of acquisition.

Inventories—Inventories, consisting principally of equipment parts, materials and supplies, valued under a method which approximates the lower of cost (first-in, first-out) or market, which entered into the determination of the cost of sales or operations, at the beginning and end of the two years ended September 30, 1976, were $7,962,000, $7,913,000 and $7,408,000.

Deferred Revenues—The Company's solid waste subsidiaries bill some of their customers for service from one to six months in advance. These revenues are deferred and taken into income in the period in which the related services are rendered.

Income Taxes—The Company uses the deferral method of accounting for the investment tax credit, under which the allowable credit is amortized over the useful lives of the assets acquired. Investment tax credits claimed were $1,825,000 in 1976 and $1,995,000 in 1975. Amortization of the accumulated credits increased net income $1,408,000 in 1976 and $1,180,000 in 1975.

Deferred income taxes are provided for timing differences resulting from inclusion of income and expense items in financial statements in years other than when recognized for income tax purposes. Timing differences result principally from the use of accelerated depreciation methods for income tax returns and the straight-line method in financial statements. The deferred income tax account is charged when the timing differences reverse. In 1976, timing differences resulted in a net decrease in the deferred tax account of $315,000. In 1975, deferred income tax expense was $2,110,000.

The Company and its domestic subsidiaries file consolidated Federal income tax returns.

Depreciation—Depreciation for financial reporting purposes is provided on the straight-line method based upon the estimated useful lives of the assets as follows: buildings, 10 to 40 years; equipment, 3 to 10 years; and furniture and fixtures, 5 to 10 years. Landfills are stated at cost which approximates estimated fair value, and landfill preparation costs are amortized over the useful life of the landfill.

Landfill Sales—The Company follows the policy of expensing, as incurred, both the cost of current landfill operations and the cost of landfill improvements made during the disposal process to increase the ultimate sales price of the completed landfill. Landfill sales activities were insignificant in 1976 and 1975.

Reclassification—Deferred investment tax credits and related accumulated amortization have been reclassified from property and equipment and accumulated depreciation to deferred income taxes. The amortization of the investment tax credit (amounting to $1,180,000 and $1,408,000 for the two years ended September 30, 1976), previously reflected as a reduction of depreciation expense, has been reclassified to income tax expense. These reclassifications did not affect net income.

Combined Communications Corporation (Dec)

Notes to Consolidated Financial Statements

Note A—Summary of Significant Accounting Policies

The Company's accounting policies reflect practices common to the industry and conform to generally accepted accounting principles. The more significant accounting policies are summarized below for the convenience of financial statement readers.

Principles of Consolidation—The Company's consolidated financial statements include the accounts of the Company and its subsidiaries, all of which are wholly-owned except Claude Neon Limited, a Canadian corporation, which is 99.8% owned. All significant intercompany investments, advances, transactions and profits have been eliminated.

Inventories—Inventories are valued at the lower of cost (first-in, first-out) or market.

Film Broadcast Rights—Rights to broadcast films are recorded as an asset when the films are available for telecasting; the current portion of unused rights represents the estimated costs of film to be expensed in the succeeding year. The amount charged to expense is based on varying rates as management deems appropriate to match related revenues with these expenses.

The liability for these rights, also recorded when the films are available for telecasting, is classified as current or noncurrent in accordance with the payment terms of the various agreements and is generally shorter than the useful life of the film.

Property, plant and equipment—Additions, improvements and expenditures for repairs and maintenance, and relocation of outdoor advertising structures, that significantly add to the productivity or extend the economic life of the assets are capitalized. Other expenditures for repairs and maintenance, and takedown costs of outdoor advertising structures, are charged to operations.

Depreciation and amortization, for financial statement purposes, is calculated principally on the straight-line method based on estimated average useful lives. When assets are retired, the assets and accumulated depreciation are removed from the respective accounts and any profit or loss on the disposition is credited or charged to income.

Intangibles—Intangibles, which include values assigned to broadcast licenses, network affiliations and goodwill (excess of purchase price over values ascribed to identifiable tangible net assets), are recorded at cost and generally considered by management to have continuing value over an indefinite period. Intangibles acquired subsequent to October 31, 1970 are being amortized on a straight-line basis over not more than forty years in accordance with Accounting Principles Board Opinion No. 17. Intangibles acquired prior to October 31, 1970 will be amortized only to the extent that a decline in value becomes evident or a definite term of existence is indicated.

Income taxes—The provision for income taxes includes deferred income taxes arising from timing differences between financial and tax reporting due principally to the use of accelerated methods of depreciation, the use of different depreciable lives, the recording of electric sign manufacturing profit, the recognition of certain gains and losses on dispositions of assets, the deferral of gains on involuntary conversions and the deferral of certain outdoor advertising revenues for tax purposes.

Investment tax credits are accounted for using the flow-through method.

Deferred charges—Deferred charges, including values assigned to purchased electric sign leases and certain other less significant costs, are deferred and charged to expense over a period management deems appropriate to match related revenues with these expenses.

Electric sign lease contracts—Electric signs manufactured by the Company are leased to customers generally on noncancellable three to eight year terms with renewal options. The sign sale price and related manufacturing costs are recorded at the time signs are installed and finance and maintenance income is recognized over the remaining lease term.

Translation of foreign currencies—For balance sheet purposes foreign currency assets and liabilities have been translated into U.S. dollars at market rates of exchange in effect at year-end, except for plant assets and certain other deferred items which are translated at exchange rates in effect at dates acquired. Income statement amounts, other than depreciation, are translated at annual average market rates of exchange. Gains and losses from currency adjustments which are not material in amount are included in costs and expenses on a current basis.

Outdoor advertising revenues—That portion of December billings pertaining to January space rental is recognized in December's operating income, which accounting practice is common to the industry. Proceeds from sign condemnations are taken into outdoor advertising revenue as follows: (1) when individual outdoor structures are condemned, the Company generally receives compensation as provided for by the Federal Highway Beautification Act and other federal and state laws. When the Company is permitted to retain the structure (which is common) for future use at a new location, the condemnation proceeds are credited to outdoor advertising revenue and the related takedown costs are expensed. If the Company is not permitted to retain the structure, the condemnation proceeds are credited to the reserve for depreciation of outdoor structures and takedown costs are expensed, (2) when the Company enters into a condemnation agreement for a group of signs the undepreciated cost of the structures given up is charged against the condemnation revenue received and the net is taken into outdoor advertising revenue.

Pension costs—Pension costs charged to current earnings include charges for current service costs, interest on the unfunded past service liability and amortization of unfunded past service liability over forty years as computed by independent actuaries. It is the Company's policy to fund pension costs as accrued.

Earnings per share—Earnings per share computations are based upon the weighted average number of shares of common stock and dilutive common stock equivalents (stock options, stock warrants and convertible Series A Preferred Stock) outstanding during the year and the adjustment of earnings, less applicable income taxes, for the amortization of original issue debt discount.

The number of shares used in the computation of primary earnings per share was 6,212,255 and 4,899,162 for the years ended December 31, 1976 and 1975, respectively. For fully diluted earnings per share the number of shares were 6,644,251 and 5,128,088 for the years ended December 31, 1976 and 1975, respectively.

Net revenue—Net revenue is advertising and other sales revenue after deducting advertising agency commissions and discounts.

Franklin Mint Corporation (Dec)

Summary of Significant Accounting Policies

Precious Metal Valuation and Related Product Costing—A major portion of the company's products are made from precious metals (silver and gold). Because these metals are subject to significant price fluctuations, the company hedges all its precious metal requirements by purchasing futures contracts to cover its fixed-price sales commitments. Sufficient contracts are assigned to each sales program to fulfill all orders, and the acquisition cost of the contracts establishes the cost of precious metal for the life of the program. The futures contracts are liquidated when bullion is purchased, and gains or losses resulting from the liquidation of the futures contracts adjust the bullion cost to the original program acquisition cost.

The market value of futures contracts purchased on the New York Commodity Exchange is fixed at the close of each business day. Any increase or decrease from the previous day's market value in the company's futures contracts is advanced to or paid by the company. These advances or payments are deferred until the contracts are liquidated.

For certain programs, the company's sales commitment period often exceeds the period for which precious metal futures contracts can be purchased on the commodities market. To extend the hedge position for the total program life, the company simultaneously sells expiring contracts and purchases new contracts. Gains or losses resulting from sale of these expiring contracts are deferred until the hedge is ultimately liquidated.

These deferrals are classified in the financial statements as either a current asset or current liability until bullion is purchased.

Accordingly, bullion and precious metal content of products in process are valued in inventory, and precious metal is charged to cost of products sold at time of shipment, at sales program acquisition cost.

Consolidation and Foreign Currency Translation—The consolidated financial statements include the accounts of the company and its domestic and foreign subsidiaries. Significant intercompany balances and transactions are eliminated in consolidation. Non-U.S. assets and liabilities are translated into U.S. dollars at year-end exchange rates, except that inventories, prepaid promotion costs and property, plant and equipment are translated at approximate rates prevailing when acquired. Income and expense items are translated at average rates of exchange prevailing during the year, except that inventories charged to costs of products sold, promotional and advertising costs and depreciation are translated at historical rates.

Forward exchange contracts are purchased to hedge, from time to time, against currency fluctuations affecting foreign operations of one or more foreign subsidiaries. Realized and unrealized gains and losses on these contracts are recorded in current income.

Sales Orders and Related Promotion Costs—The company's principal method of selling its products is through direct mail and newspaper or magazine advertisements. Advance payments from customers are received with the sales order on certain programs. Shipments are made either as single mailings or as a series over a number of months. Sales are not recorded, and income is not recognized, until shipment is made. Printing and mailing costs of direct mailing advertising and the cost of media advertisements, together with the cost of the collector albums or chests shipped to a customer at the beginning of a series, are deferred and charged against income over the shorter of the shipment period or fifty months. Costs incurred by company personnel in the development of sales programs, including salaries and wages, art work and other administrative expenses, are expensed in the period incurred.

Property, Plant and Equipment—Items capitalized as property, plant and equipment, including significant betterments to existing facilities, are carried at cost. Expenditures for maintenance and repairs are expensed when incurred.

Depreciation is computed by the straight-line method at rates adequate to recover the cost of the applicable assets over their estimated useful lives. Upon sale or retirement of property, plant and equipment, the cost and related accumulated depreciation are removed from the respective accounts, and the resulting gain or loss is included in income.

Income Taxes—The company provides for federal, foreign and state income taxes, at the statutory rates in effect on income before income taxes for financial reporting purposes. This includes certain income and expense items which are reported in different periods for financial and tax reporting purposes resulting in deferred taxes. For those foreign subsidiaries where dividends are expected to be declared, incremental U.S. income taxes, if any, have been provided on those earnings. No provision for U.S. income taxes has been made on the earnings of other foreign subsidiaries because it is the company's intention to reinvest such undistributed earnings. However, any additional U.S. income tax on dividends which might be declared in the future from reinvested earnings would be substantially reduced by foreign tax credits. Investment tax credits are accounted for as a reduction of the income tax provision in the year the related assets are placed in service.

Source: *Accounting Trends & Techniques,* Copyright © 1977 by the American Institute of Certified Public Accountants, Inc., pp. 28—30.

APB Opinion No. 30 (June 1973) Reporting the Results of Operations

Flowchart and General Discussion

APB Opinion No. 30 established accounting and reporting guidelines in three significant areas of income reporting. The three areas are (1) disposal of a business segment, (2) extraordinary items and (3) unusual *or* infrequent items. Prior to the issuance of APB Opinion No. 30, all three of these items generally were treated as extraordinary items for purposes of income reporting. The concept of an extraordinary item was much broader before the issuance of the Opinion than after issuance. Before APB Opinion No. 30 was issued, one would expect to find the reporting of income before extraordinary items, a line item reporting of extraordinary items, and then net income. This Opinion has increased the subdivision of income reporting. One now might expect to find the reporting of income from continuing operations (including unusual or infrequent expenses or revenues), loss from disposal of a business segment, extraordinary items, cumulative effect of accounting change, and, finally, net income. There has been a substantial increase in the line item reporting of items affecting income.

Because the number of subdivisions of income has increased, the definition of events that constitute extraordinary items has been significantly narrowed by the Opinion. Events that, in the past, were classified as extraordinary now are classified as segment disposals, extraordinary items and unusual or infrequent events. The Opinion has had the effect of providing the reader with more detailed information about the unusual transactions entered into by the enterprise.

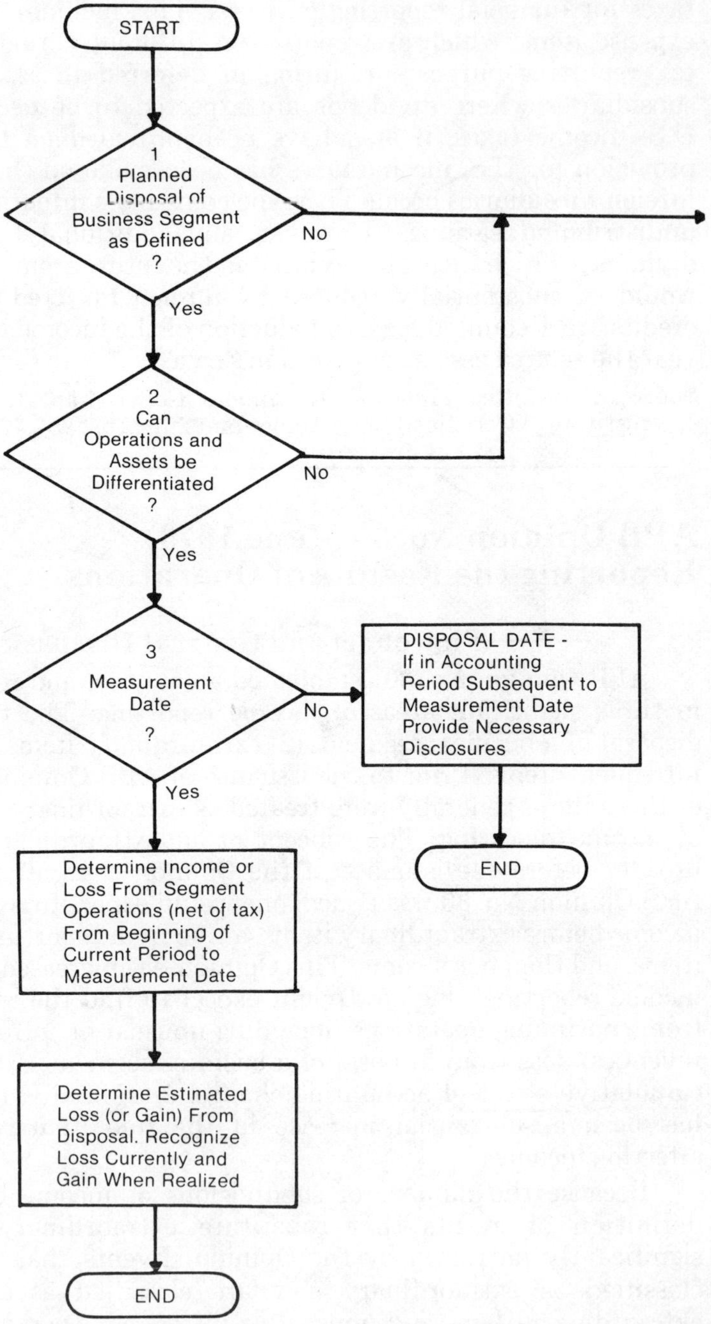
START
1
Planned
Disposal of
Business Segment
as Defined
?
No
Yes
2
Can
Operations and
Assets be
Differentiated
?
No
Yes
3
Measurement
Date
?
No
DISPOSAL DATE -
If in Accounting
Period Subsequent to
Measurement Date
Provide Necessary
Disclosures
END
Yes
Determine Income or
Loss From Segment
Operations (net of tax)
From Beginning of
Current Period to
Measurement Date
Determine Estimated
Loss (or Gain) From
Disposal. Recognize
Loss Currently and
Gain When Realized
END

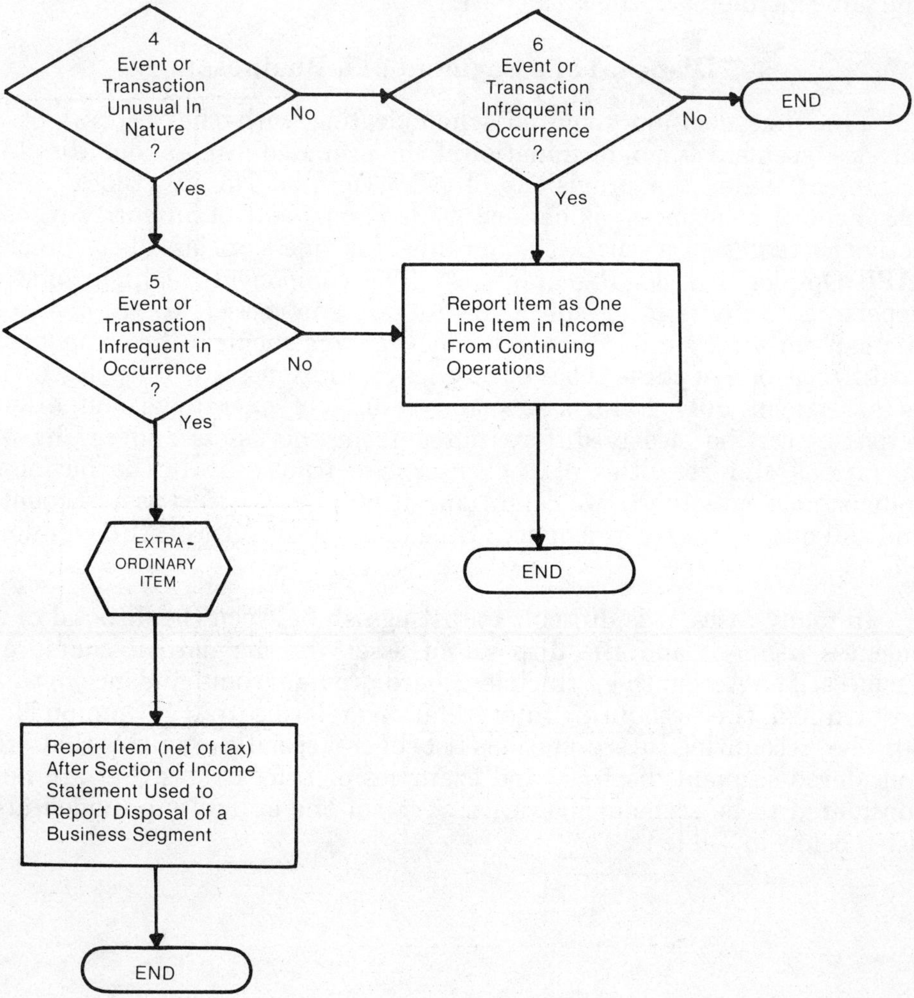
4
Event or
Transaction
Unusual In
Nature
?
No
6
Event or
Transaction
Infrequent in
Occurrence
?
No
END
Yes
Yes
5
Event or
Transaction
Infrequent in
Occurrence
?
No
Report Item as One
Line Item in Income
From Continuing
Operations
Yes
EXTRA-
ORDINARY
ITEM
END
Report Item (net of tax)
After Section of Income
Statement Used to
Report Disposal of a
Business Segment
END

The Flowchart of the Opinion indicates the major decisions required by the Opinion and the accounting procedures that follow from the decision process. The Flowchart is organized to deal with disposal of a business segment first, followed, in order, by extraordinary items and unusual or infrequent items. The discussion that follows is organized in the same manner as is the Flowchart.

Disposal of a Segment of a Business

The first decision required when dealing with the disposal of a business segment is a determination if the proposed disposal qualifies for treatment under the provisions of APB Opinion No. 30 (Block 1). A "segment of a business" is defined as "a component of an entity whose activities represent a separate major line of business or class of customer" (APB Opinion No. 30, Paragraph 13). The component might include a department, division or subsidiary of an enterprise, or an investee company or some similar type of business arrangement. If the component qualifies as one of these types of business operations, it will be classified as a segment only if its assets and results of operations and other activities can be clearly differentiated from the assets and results of operations and activities of the enterprise (Block 2). If the business component meets these two conditions, it will be classified as a segment, and will qualify for treatment according to the provisions of APB Opinion No. 30.

In many cases, it is difficult to distinguish between the disposal of a business segment and the disposal of assets in the normal course of business. The Accounting Principles Board provides some guidance in this area through the Accounting Interpretations relating to APB Opinion No. 30. The Accounting Interpretations list several specific examples that are considered segment disposals and examples of transactions that are not considered to be segment disposals. Some of the examples provided are listed below in Table I.

Table I

Accounting Interpretations of Disposal Classification[1]

Disposals Classified as Segment Dispositions	Disposals Not Classified as Segment Dispositions
1. A diversified company sold its only electronics division. Its assets and results of operations can be differentiated.	1. A mining company sold a foreign silver mining subsidiary which was the company's only activity in that particular foreign country. The sale is a sale of a part of a line.
2. A meat packing company sold its 25 percent interest in a professional football team. The investment was carried on the equity method. The company's only other interests are in the meat packing industry.	2. A diversified company sold a furniture manufacturing subsidiary. The company owns other subsidiaries that manufacture furniture. This represents a sale of a part of a line of a business.
3. A communications company sold all of its radio stations. The stations account for 30 percent of gross revenues. The company's only other interests are television stations and a publishing company. The radio station's assets and results of operations can be differentiated.	3. A company sold all its assets relating to woolen suit manufacturing. The sale was made in order to concentrate on suit manufacturing from synthetic products. The company has disposed of a product line.

[1] FASB, Financial Accounting Standards Original Pronouncements as of July 1, 1978, "Accounting Interpretations of APB Opinion No. 30," pg. 680-681.

Disposals that do not qualify as segment dispositions may be considered for treatment as extraordinary items. However, the disposal must meet the appropriate criteria before it properly can be classified as an extraordinary item.

Once a disposal has been properly classified as a segment disposition, there are *two* dates of accounting importance that control the timing of the recognition of any gain or loss. The first date, referred to as the "measurement date," is the first date that the management of an enterprise actually agrees to a plan of disposal (Block 3). The plan of disposal should be formalized and, according to APB Opinion No. 30, Paragraph 14, should include the following items:

(1) Identification of the major assets subject to disposition;

(2) Identification of the method of disposal;

(3) Statement of the time frame for completion of the disposition;

(4) Estimate of the results of operations of the segment from the measurement date to the date of actual disposition;

(5) Estimate of the proceeds or salvage value expected to be received upon disposition of the segment; and

(6) Identification, if the segment is to be sold, of the program to locate a buyer.

The second date of importance is referred to as the "disposal date." If the disposal is to be accomplished through abandonment, the disposal date is the date on which operations of the segment are discontinued. If the disposal is to be accomplished through a sale of the segment, the disposal date is the closing date of the sale.

The measurement date and the disposal date control the accounting for any gain or loss to be realized from the disposal of the segment. A disposal of a segment may be viewed as involving two types of potential gains or losses. The enterprise may experience income or loss from the segment prior to the disposal, and then may experience a gain or loss from the disposition of the assets of the segment. APB Opinion No. 30 requires that each of these parts be given separate accounting recognition. The total of the two represents, however, the reported gain or loss from the segment disposition. The enterprise that disposes of a segment must report income or loss from segment operations (net of tax) for the time period from the beginning of the accounting period containing the measurement date to the measurement date. The income or loss of the segment from the measurement date to the disposition date is considered to be part of the determination of the gain or loss from disposition.

A *loss* on the disposal of a segment must be *estimated* and recorded (net of tax) at the measurement date. The measurement date may occur in one fiscal year, and the disposal date may occur in the following fiscal year; but the estimated loss on disposal must be estimated at the measurement date. This estimated loss will be included in the operations of the enterprise in the accounting period containing the measurement date. The disposal could result in a gain to the enterprise. Gains are not accounted for at the measurement date, but are recognized only when realized. The realization of any gain normally would take place on the disposal date. The total loss from a segment disposition includes the expected income or loss from segment operations, from the measurement date to the disposal date, *and* the estimated loss on disposition of assets, determined at the measurement date.

If the segment is estimated to report income between the measurement date and the disposal date, the income included in the total loss may not exceed the estimated loss from disposition of the assets of the segment. The income estimated to be earned during this period may reduce the total loss to zero, but no further.

The loss on *actual* disposition must be adjusted for costs directly related to the disposition, and would include such items as additional pension expense resulting from the disposal and the costs of employee relocation.[1]

To illustrate the accounting treatment required for the disposal of a segment of a business, the assumptions listed in Exhibit I will be used.

Exhibit I

Segment Disposal—Example 1

1. Book-It, Inc., a highly diversified enterprise with a December 31 year end, is planning to dispose of a division in the lumber business. Book-It, Inc. has no other activities in the lumber industry. The assets and results of operations of the division can be clearly differentiated from the assets and results of operations of Book-It.

2. Book-It, Inc. approved a formal plan to dispose of the division on April 1, 197C.

3. The date of disposition is February 15, 197D. On this date, the expected selling price of the assets of the division is $1,000,000. The book value of the assets will be $3,000,000 on the disposal date. There are no disposal costs associated with the sale.

4. Net losses for the division amounted to $500,000 from January 1, 197C to April 1, 197C.

5. From April 1, 197C to February 15, 197D, the division is expected to incur losses of $200,000.

6. Income from continuing operations of Book-It, Inc., excluding the financial information presented in the preceding assumptions, is $4,000,000. Book-It had no extraordinary items, changes in accounting principles or unusual or infrequent items during the year.

7. The tax rate applicable to Book-It is 50 percent. This is also the rate applicable to items related to the disposal.

The transaction qualifies for treatment under the provisions of APB Opinion No. 30, because the business component is a division and its assets and results of operations can be differentiated from those of Book-

[1] FASB Interpretation No. 27 states that, if a sublease is part of a disposal of a segment of a business, the gain or loss on the sublease is treated as part of the overall gain or loss on the segment desposition.

It, Inc. The disposal also meets the examples given in the Accounting Interpretations of the Opinion, because this is the only division of Book-It operating in the lumber industry. The measurement date of the transaction is April 1, 197C, and the disposal date is February 15, 197D. This means that the measurement date and the disposal date fall in two different fiscal years.

The first step in the accounting process is to compute the estimated loss on disposal of the segment, net of any tax benefits of the loss. The determination of the loss is shown below:

Expected selling price of the division's assets	$1,000,000
Costs associated with the disposal	-0-
Net realizable value	$1,000,000
Book value of assets at date of disposal	3,000,000
Expected loss from disposition of assets	$2,000,000
Expected loss from operations of the division from April 1, 197C to February 15, 197D	200,000
Loss on disposal before tax benefits	$2,200,000
Income tax benefit ($2,200,000 × 50%)	1,100,000
Loss on disposal net of tax benefit	$1,100,000

Next, the operating loss from segment operations from January 1, 197C to April 1, 197C, and the related tax benefits must be computed.

Loss from January 1 to April 1, 197C	$500,000
Income tax benefit ($500,000 × 50%)	250,000
Loss from operations—January 1 to April 1, 197C, net of tax benefits	$250,000

Since Book-It, Inc. has no other income items requiring special reporting, the partial income statement for the year ended December 31, 197C would appear as follows:

Book-It, Inc.
Partial Income Statement
For the Year Ended December 31, 197C

Income from continuing operations		$4,000,000
Discontinued operations:		
Loss from operations of discontinued division (less applicable income tax benefits of $250,000)	$ 250,000	
Loss on disposal of discontinued division, including a provision of $200,000 for operating losses during phase-out period (less tax benefit relating to total loss on disposal of $1,100,000)	1,100,000	1,350,000
Net income		$2,650,000

This example assumed that the segment incurred losses from the beginning of the accounting period (197C) to the measurement date *and* from the measurement date to the disposal date. If the segment were to earn income during this period, a different presentation would be required. To illustrate this situation, the assumptions in Exhibit II will be used.

Exhibit II
Segment Disposal—Example 2

1. Jar, Inc., a highly diversified company with a December 31 year end, is planning to dispose of a division in the chicken business. Jar, Inc. has no other interests in the chicken business. The assets and results of operations of the chicken division can be clearly differentiated from the assets and results of operations of Jar, Inc.

2. Jar, Inc. approved a formal plan to dispose of the chicken division on November 1, 197B.

3. The date of disposition is April 1, 197C. On this date, the expected selling price of the assets of the chicken division is $1,500,000. The book value of the assets of the division will be $4,000,000 on the disposal date. Costs directly associated with the disposal are expected to be $25,000. In addition, Jar, Inc. expects to incur expenses of $10,000 to relocate several of its employees.

4. Net income reported by the division amounted to $560,000, for the period from January 1, 197B to November 1, 197B.

5. From November 1, 197B to April 1, 197C, the division is expected to report income from operations of $225,000.

6. Income from continuing operations of Jar, Inc. for the year ended December 31, 197B, excluding the financial information presented in the preceding assumptions, is $5,500,000. Jar, Inc. had no extraordinary items, changes in accounting principles or unusual or infrequent items during the year.

7. The tax rate applicable to Jar, Inc. is 50 percent, and this rate also applies to the items involved in the disposal.

This segment disposition is similar to the one described in Example 1, and qualifies for treatment under APB Opinion No. 30 for the same reasons. The measurement date is November 1, 197B, and the disposal date is April 1, 197C. Once again, the measurement date and the disposal date fall in different fiscal years.

The first step in the accounting process is to determine the loss on disposal of the segment. The computation of the loss is shown below:

Expected selling price of the division's assets	$1,500,000
Costs directly related to the disposal	(25,000)
Costs to relocate employees	(10,000)
Net realizable value	$1,465,000
Book value of division's assets	4,000,000
Expected loss on disposal of assets	$2,535,000
Expected income from operations of the division from November 1, 197B to April 1, 197C	225,000
Loss on disposal of segment	$2,310,000
Income tax benefits ($2,310,000 × 50%)	1,155,000
Loss on disposal net of tax benefits	$1,155,000

The income from operations of the division from January 1, 197B, to November 1, 197B, net of applicable taxes, would be computed as follows:

Income reported from January 1 to November 1, 197B	$560,000
Income taxes ($560,000 × 50%)	280,000
Income from division from January 1 to November 1, 197B, net of taxes	$280,000

Based upon this information, the partial income statement of Jar, Inc. for the year ended December 31, 197B, would be as follows:

Partial Income Statement
Jar, Inc.
For the Year Ended December 31, 197B

Income from continuing operations		$5,500,000
Discontinued operations:		
Income from operations of discontinued division (less applicable income taxes of $280,000)	$280,000	
Loss on disposal of discontinued division, including a provision of $225,000 for operating income during phase-out period (less tax benefit relating to the net loss on disposal of $1,155,000)	(1,155,000)	(875,000)
Net Income		$4,625,000

Appropriate footnote disclosures will be shown at the end of this section.

In addition to the financial presentation shown above, the enterprise is required to provide certain information in the footnotes to the financial statements. Paragraph 18 of the Opinion specifies the following disclosures:

1. Identification of the segment involved in the disposal.
2. The date of the disposal, if known.
3. Whether the disposal is to be accomplished through a sale or abandonment.
4. The assets and liabilities of the segment at the balance sheet date.

5. Proceeds from the disposition and income or loss from operations of the segment from the measurement date to the balance sheet date.

If the date of measurement occurs in one reporting period, and the date of disposal occurs in a subsequent reporting period, the enterprise must disclose the same information shown above in the subsequent period. In addition, the proceeds from the disposition and the income or loss from operations of the segment must be compared with the amounts reported in the preceding period.

Exhibit III shows a partial income statement and the related notes from the 1974 Annual Report of Hoffman Electronics Corporation. The information relates to the disposal of the Company's Metal Products Division. A careful reading of Note 4 will prove beneficial to an understanding of the reporting requirements specified in APB Opinion No. 30.

Exhibit III

Hoffman Electronics Corporation (Dec)

	1974	**1973**
Income From Continuing Operations	$ 720,190	$1,089,199
Discontinued Operations (Note 4):		
Loss from operations of discontinued business (less applicable income tax benefits of $446,400 in 1974 and $982,200 in 1973)	(483,549)	(826,399)
Loss on disposal of discontinued business (less applicable income tax benefits of $906,200)	(1,027,741)	—
	(1,511,290)	(826,399)
Net Income (loss)	$ (791,100)	$ 262,800

Note 4: Discontinued Operations—Effective August 16, 1974 the company made the decision to discontinue operations of its Metal Products Division. The results of operations of such business for periods prior to August 16, 1974, are included in the consolidated statements of income under the caption "Loss from operations of discontinued business." The following is a summary of the operations of this business for periods prior to August 16, 1974:

	1974	**1973**
Net sales	$5,811,667	$ 8,202,749
Costs and expenses	6,741,616	10,011,348
Income tax benefit	446,400	982,200
Net loss	$ 483,549	$ 826,399

"Loss on disposal of discontinued business," represents the estimated loss associated with the disposal of the assets of the business, together with a provision of $238,000 for estimated operating losses subsequent to August 16, 1974, including $220,000 to be incurred in 1975 during the phase-out period.

At December 31, 1974 assets associated with the Metal Products Division consisted primarily of trade receivables ($726,759) and machinery and equipment ($700,000). These assets are carried at estimated realizable value and are shown as "Assets of discontinued business" in the accompanying balance sheets.

The company's 1973 consolidated financial statements have been restated to conform with the current year's presentation.

Source: *Accounting Trends and Techniques,* Copyright © 1975 by the American Institute of Certified Public Accountants, Inc., p. 336.

Extraordinary Items

A second major area addressed by APB Opinion No. 30 is the proper accounting and reporting of extraordinary items. "Extraordinary items" are defined as "events and transactions that are distinguished by their unusual nature and by the infrequency of their occurrence" (APB Opinion No. 30, Paragraph 20). For a transaction to be classified as extraordinary it must be *both* unusual in nature (Block 4) *and* infrequent in occurrence (Block 5). The word "unusual" is defined in the Opinion (Paragraph 20) as follows:

> the underlying event or transaction should possess a high degree of abnormality and be of a type clearly unrelated to, or only incidentally related to, the ordinary and typical activities of the entity, taking into account the environment in which the entity operates.

As indicated by this definition, the determination of an extraordinary item depends, to a large extent, upon the nature of the operations of the enterprise. A given event or transaction may be considered extraordinary by one entity, but not extraordinary by a different entity. When considering the environment of the entity, proper attention must be given to the nature of the industry, the location of the entity, the extent of government regulation, etc.

The word "infrequent" is defined (APB Opinion No. 30, Paragraph 20) as meaning that "the underlying event or transaction should be of a type that would not reasonably be expected to recur in the foreseeable future, taking into account the environment in which the entity operates." Once again, the term "infrequent in occurrence" must be evaluated by reference to the entity's operating environment. Each entity must assess the probability of the event occurring in the future. If the event or transaction is likely to recur in the future, it probably will not be considered extraordinary.

One effect of the Opinion has been to significantly narrow the concept of an extraordinary item. However, three items are recognized as meeting the criteria for classification as an extraordinary item. These three items are (1) gains or losses resulting from major casualties, such as an earthquake, (2) an expropriation of assets or operations, and (3) a prohibition under a newly enacted law or regulation that meets both of the criteria for classification as an extraordinary item. The Opinion (Paragraph 23) also identifies the following items as generally not extraordinary:

(1) Losses from the reduction or removal of leased property, inventories, receivables, research and development costs, and intangible assets;

(2) Gains and losses resulting from foreign currency transactions or translations;

(3) Gains and losses resulting from the sale or abandonment of property;

(4) Gains and losses on segment disposition;

(5) Losses resulting from strikes; and

(6) Long-term contract adjustments.

Table II identifies items considered to be extraordinary, and other items not considered to be extraordinary, by the Accounting Interpretations of APB Opinion No. 30.

Table II

Accounting Interpretations of Extraordinary Items[1]

Events Classified as Extraordinary	Events Not Classified as Extraordinary
1. A large portion of a tobacco manufacturer's crops are destroyed by a hail storm. Severe damage from hail storms in the locality where the manufacturer grows tobacco is rare.	1. A citrus grower's Florida crop is damaged by frost. Frost damage is normally experienced every three or four years.
2. A steel fabricating company sells the only land it owns. The land was acquired ten years ago for future expansion, but shortly thereafter the company abandoned all plans for expansion and held the land for appreciation.	2. A company which operates a chain of warehouses sells the excess land surrounding one of its warehouses. When the company buys property to establish a new warehouse, it usually buys more land than it expects to use for the warehouse.
3. A company sells a block of common stock of a publicly traded company. The block of shares, which represents less than 10% of the publicly held company, is the only security investment the company has ever owned.	3. A large diversified company sells a block of shares from its portfolio of securities which it has acquired for investment purposes. This is the first sale from its portfolio of securities.
4. An earthquake destroys one of the oil refineries owned by a large multi-national oil company.	4. A textile manufacturer with only one plant moves to another location. It has not relocated a plant in twenty years and has no plans to do so in the foreseeable future.

[1] FASB, Financial Accounting Standards Original Pronouncements as of July 1, 1977, "Accounting Interpretations of APB Opinion No. 30," pg. 681-682.

Extraordinary items should be disclosed separately, net of taxes, just below the section of the income statement used to disclose the disposition of a segment of a business. A partial income statement and the related notes to the Financial Statements of Chicago Pneumatic Tool Company is shown in Exhibit IV. The information is from the 1976 Annual Report of the company, and demonstrates the proper accounting and disclosure relating to an extraordinary item.

Exhibit IV

Chicago Pneumatic Tool Company (Dec)

	1976	1975
Earnings before extraordinary item	$ 8,440,000	$18,765,000
Extraordinary item (net of applicable taxes)	2,800,000	—
Net earnings	$11,240,000	$18,765,000

1976 Financial Summary

Extraordinary Item represents the gain on the sale of a wholly-owned subsidiary, El-Jay, Inc. (net of applicable income taxes of $600,000), to Raytheon Company in September 1976 for $7.5 million in cash. El-Jay, Inc. was acquired in August 1975 for 254,545 shares of common stock and $143,000 in cash. The combination was accounted for on a "pooling of interests" basis.

Source: *Accounting Trends and Techniques,* Copyright © 1977 by the American Institute of Certified Public Accountants, Inc., p. 292.

Unusual or Infrequent Items

Certain transactions or events may be unusual in nature (Block 4) *or* infrequent in occurrence (Block 6), but not both. These items would fail to meet one of the two criteria necessary for classification as an extraordinary item. A transaction or event of this nature should be reported as a one-line item in the income from continuing operations. The nature and effect of the item should be disclosed in the footnotes to the financial statements. If there is more than one unusual or infrequent item, it would be appropriate to report similar items in the aggregate, providing that none of the items is individually material.

Exhibit V contains information from the 1976 Annual Report of Sterndent Corporation. The partial income statement and footnote relate to an unusual or infrequent item. In this case, the company has decided to withdraw from the domestic dental equipment manufacturing business. Notice that the item is reported in the aggregate in the income statement, and that detailed information about the aggregate amount is presented in the footnote.

Exhibit V

Sterndent Corporation (Dec)

	1976	1975
Operating income	$ 2,723,617	$8,863,728
Other income (expense):		
Interest expense—on short-term bank loans	(1,521,549)	(1,359,886)
Interest expense—other	(155,493)	(132,970)
Interest income	530,557	612,659
Other income (expense), net	(370,015)	(195,799)
	1,207,117	7,787,732
Unusual or non-recurring expenses (Note 9)	(9,115,000)	(1,209,000)
Income (loss) before provision (credit) for income taxes	$(7,907,883)	$6,578,732

Note 9: Unusual or Non-Recurring Expenses—Unusual or non-recurring expenses include the following:

	1976	1975
Estimated loss on withdrawal from the domestic dental equipment manufacturing business (a)	$6,431,000	
Estimated loss on abandonment of dental sundries distribution business in Brazil	2,084,000	
Loss on misappropriation of funds at the Company's dental subsidiary in Switzerland	600,000	
Expenses incurred to defend against an unfriendly tender offer for the Company's common shares		$ 502,000
Expenses related to flood damage at the Weber Consumable Products plant in Yonkers, New York		707,000
	$9,115,000	$1,209,000

a. In February, 1977, the Company decided to withdraw from the domestic dental equipment manufacturing business conducted by its Weber Dental Manufacturing Division ("Weber") in Canton, Ohio. Although the Company is actively seeking potential purchasers for this business, there is no assurance that a purchaser will be found, and the Company may have to liquidate the remaining assets of this division.

Source: *Accounting Trends and Techniques,* Copyright © 1977 by the American Institute of Certified Public Accountants, Inc., p. 235.

SFAS No. 16 (June 1977)
Prior Period Adjustments

Introduction

SFAS No. 16 establishes new accounting and reporting guidelines for the treatment of prior period adjustments for annual periods and accounting adjustments to be reported in preceding interim periods of the current annual accounting period. Prior to the issuance of this Statement, APB Opinion No. 9, "Reporting the Results of Operations," had established accounting principles for prior period adjustments. (Most of

APB Opinion No. 9 has been superseded by subsequent pronouncements. Do not confuse this Opinion with APB Opinion No. 30, "Reporting the Results of Operations," covered in this Topic.) Under the provisions of APB Opinion No. 9, if an event or transaction met four rather subjective criteria, it would be classified as a prior period adjustment. The adjustment was treated as a direct adjustment to the beginning balance in retained earnings, and therefore did not flow through the income statement. Based upon the four criteria established in the Opinion, the majority of prior period adjustments involved final settlement of income taxes and cases involving the company in litigation.

With the issuance of SFAS No. 16, the number of transactions or events that may be treated as prior period adjustments has been significantly narrowed. As a result, items that in the past were treated as prior period adjustments now are shown on the income statement, rather than as a direct adjustment to retained earnings.

The second major area covered by SFAS No. 16 deals with adjustments to preceding interim periods of the current accounting period. Basic interim reporting is covered by APB Opinion No. 28, "Interim Financial Reporting," and this Opinion is subject to the provisions of SFAS No. 16 (see Topic 12 for complete coverage of interim reporting). SFAS No. 16 has replaced APB Opinion No. 9 for the reporting of certain adjustments in the interim period.

Prior Period Adjustments

This Statement has significantly narrowed the type of items that may be considered prior period adjustments. Only two items are identified in the Statement. These two items (SFAS No. 16, Paragraph 11) are (1) accounting errors, and (2) adjustments that result from realization of income tax benefits of preacquisition operating loss carryforwards of purchased subsidiaries. Remember that several other pronouncements identify specific items that will be treated as prior period adjustments, but there are only two such items identified in SFAS No. 16. Most of the prior period adjustments identified in other pronouncements related to the transition period for adoption of the Opinion or Statement. Items that do not qualify as prior period adjustments will be treated as items of profit or loss and will flow through income in accordance with the provisions of APB Opinion No. 30. (See APB Opinion No. 30 in this Topic for a detailed analysis of the classification and reporting of gains and losses.) Prior period adjustments do not affect income, but are treated as direct adjustments to beginning retained earnings.

To illustrate the proper accounting and reporting for a prior period adjustment, classified as such by the provisions of SFAS No. 16, the assumptions listed in Exhibit I will be used.

Exhibit I
Prior Period Adjustments

1. Book-It, Inc. purchased a piece of equipment on January 1, 197A, for $100,000. The equipment has a useful life of 10 years, and there is assumed to be no residual value associated with the equipment.
2. On the purchase date, the accountant at Book-It charged the entire cost of the equipment to expense.
3. The Company uses straight-line depreciation for all owned assets.
4. Book-It, Inc. is preparing financial statements for the year ended December 31, 197C. Income reported for the year is $260,000. The Company paid dividends during the year of $100,000. The beginning balance in retained earnings is $85,000.

The event described in Exhibit I is an accounting error, and qualifies for treatment, under the provisions of SFAS No. 16, as a prior period adjustment. Assume that the error was discovered at the end of 197C. To simplify the solution to the example, income tax consequences of the error will be ignored. The entire cost of the equipment was charged to income in 197A, and the amounts properly charged to income should have been the depreciation for the years 197A through 197C. The depreciation for 197C will be charged to income of the period and will not enter into the determination of the amount of the prior period adjustment. The prior period adjustment is equal to the difference between the cost of the equipment, improperly charged to income, and the depreciation for years 197A and 197B. The computation of the amount of the prior period adjustment would be determined as follows:

Depreciation expense for 197A and 197B ($100,000/10 years = $10,000 × 2 years)	$ 20,000
Cost of equipment improperly charged to income	100,000
Prior Period Adjustment	$ 80,000

The correcting journal entry required by Book-It, Inc. at the end of 197C would be:

Equipment	100,000	
Depreciation Expense (for 197C)	10,000	
Accumulated Depreciation—Equipment		30,000
Prior Period Adjustment		80,000

As a result of this entry, the equipment is properly recorded as a part of property, plant and equipment; depreciation expense for 197C has been recognized, and the accumulated depreciation account has been properly established at $30,000 (depreciation for the years 197A through 197C). Since the error was discovered prior to the issuance of the financial statement, corrected income for 197C would be $250,000 ($260,000 as previously reported – $10,000 depreciation expense for 197C).

The proper presentation of Book-It's Statement of Retained Earnings for 197C would be as follows:

Book-It, Inc.
Statement of Retained Earnings
For the Year Ended December 31, 197C

Retained Earnings, January 1, 197C	$ 85,000
Adjustment:	
Prior period adjustment—error in recording equipment	80,000
Adjusted Retained Earnings, January 1, 197C	$165,000
Net Income for 197C	250,000
Dividends for 197C	(100,000)
Retained Earnings, December 31, 197C	$315,000

The prior period adjustment was treated as a direct charge to the beginning retained earnings balance, and did not flow through the income statement. The only income effect of the correction was to record the proper depreciation for 197C. The account "Prior Period Adjustment" will be closed directly to the retained earnings account.

The Statement of Consolidated Retained Earnings and related notes to the Financial Statements of Systron-Donner Corporation are shown in Exhibit II. The information comes from the 1975 Annual Report of the Company, and shows the proper accounting treatment and disclosure of an account error. The error relates to the recording of inventory that was sold.

Exhibit II

Systron-Donner Corporation (Jul)

Consolidated Statements of Earnings and Retained Earnings

	1975	1974
Net earnings	$ 1,422,072	$ 271,564
Reinvested earnings at beginning of year:		
As previously reported	12,333,057	11,869,993
Prior period adjustment	(191,500)	—
As restated	12,141,557	11,869,993
Reinvested earnings at end of year	$13,563,629	$12,141,557

Financial Review

Restatement of Prior Year's Financial Statements—Fiscal year 1974 has been restated to give effect to an error made in recording cost of goods sold in one unit of the Company. This restatement has resulted in a reduction of earnings from continuing operations for the year ended July 31, 1974 in the amount of $142,500, equal to $.09 per share; reduction of extraordinary income by $49,000, equal to $.02 per share, for related tax benefits from carryforward of operating losses; resulting in a total $191,500 reduction in net earnings, equal to $.11 per share.

Reclassifications have been made to 1974 financial statements to conform to the 1975 presentation.

Source: *Accounting Trends and Techniques,* Copyright © 1976 by the American Institute of Certified Public Accountants, Inc., p. 282.

Adjustments Required in Interim Periods

For an item to be classified as an adjustment to a preceding interim period of the current annual period, each of the following conditions (SFAS No. 16, Paragraph 13) must be met:

(1) The adjustment must be considered to be material;

(2) The adjustment must be directly related to the activities of preceding interim periods of the current annual period; and

(3) The amount of the adjustment could not be reasonably estimated in preceding interim periods, but can be estimated in the current interim period.

Examples of transactions or events that might meet these conditions would include cases involving litigation, public utility rate-making proceedings and final settlement of income tax matters.

When faced with a transaction or event meeting these three conditions, the company first must determine the amount of the adjustment applicable to the current interim period. This adjustment will be included in the income of the current interim period. Next, the amount of the adjustment associated with each preceding interim period of the current annual period must be determined. Income of each of these preceding interim periods should be restated to reflect the adjustments so determined. Finally, income of the first interim period of the current annual period should be restated to give effect to the amount of the adjustment relating to all prior annual periods.

To illustrate the proper accounting for adjustments to preceding interim periods, the assumptions listed in Exhibit III will be used.

Exhibit III
Adjustments to Preceding Interim Periods

1. Energy, Inc. is a public utility providing electric service to the towns of Ross and Prior and the surrounding area.

2. The state regulatory authority permits the company to increase its rates to customers as soon as an application for a rate increase is filed with the authority. The revenue collected as a result of the pending rate case is subject to refund, depending upon the findings of the authority.

3. In the middle of 197A, Energy, Inc. filed an application for a rate increase and immediately increased its rates to customers. Revenues collected, subject to refund, are as follows:

Collected during 197A	$110,000
Collected in First Quarter of 197B	58,000
Collected in Second Quarter of 197B	47,000
Collected in Third Quarter of 197B	52,000

4. In the third quarter of 197B, the regulatory authority rules that the rate increases were not justified, and the amounts collected must be refunded to the customers. The revenue earned as a result of the rate increase in considered to be material.

5. The company is in the process of preparing interim financial statements for the third quarter of 197B.

The facts presented in Exhibit III indicate that the events qualify for treatment as adjustments to preceding interim periods. The revenue collected is material, the amounts can be associated with preceding interim periods of the current annual period, and the amounts could not be reasonably estimated prior to the settlement of the rate-making proceedings.

An adjustment will be required to income of the third quarter of 197B, the second quarter of 197B and the first quarter of 197B. The adjustment in the first quarter of 197B must reflect amounts relating to the preceding annual period (197A). Table I shows the effect of the required adjustment on the income of the interim periods of 197B.

Table I

Adjustments to Prior Interim Periods

Adjustment	3rd Quarter	2nd Quarter	1st Quarter
	Interim Period—197B		
Overstatement of 197A revenues			$110,000
Overstatement in first quarter of 197B			58,000
Overstatement in second quarter of 197B		$47,000	
Overstatement in third quarter of 197B	$52,000		
Adjustment to income for each quarter of 197B	$52,000	$47,000	$168,000

Income for the first quarter of 197B must be restated by $168,000, the effect of the adjustment relating to the first quarter and the preceding annual period. The adjustments to income for the second and third quarters of 197B reflect the amounts specifically related to those periods.

In addition to the restatement of the income amounts, the following disclosures are required by the Statement (Paragraph 15):

1. The interim report prepared for the period containing the adjustment should disclose the impact of the adjustment on income from continuing operations, net income and related earnings per share amounts for each preceding interim period of the current annual period; and

2. The interim report prepared for the interim period containing the adjustment should disclose income from continuing operations, net income and related earnings per share amounts, restated as discussed in this section and as shown in the above example.

SFAS No. 33 (September 1979) Financial Reporting and Changing Prices

Introduction and Definition of Terms

Statement No. 33 is perhaps the most significant pronouncement issued by the Financial Accounting Standards Board to date. For the first time, major publicly held corporations are required to disclose information about the effects of inflation on the operations of the enterprise. Prior to the issuance of SFAS No. 33, the only source of detailed information concerning the impact of changing prices on certain selected financial statement accounts of large corporations was found in the Form 10-K filed annually with the Securities and Exchange Commission (SEC) by registered companies.

The SEC, by issuing Accounting Series Release No. 190, required the disclosure of "replacement cost" information as a *supplement* to the information contained in the basic historical cost financial statements. In general, the SEC required certain companies to determine the replacement cost of inventory and property, plant and equipment, and to restate the related cost of goods sold and depreciation expense for the period. The SEC viewed replacement cost as the cost of replacing existing assets with *new* assets that had a similar productive capacity. Under the SEC view, the enterprise would be required to take into consideration any technological changes that had occurred since the existing assets were first purchased.

Replacement cost information was not included in the annual report to shareholders. Interested readers of the financial statements were encouraged to request a copy of the most current Form 10-K to gain access to the replacement cost information. As a result of the nature of this reporting requirement, it has been difficult to assess the impact of replacement cost information on the decision-making process of the financial statement user. The basic historical cost financial statements contained in the Form 10-K were considered the primary financial statements and the replacement cost information was considered supplemental information. There was no *comprehensive* financial statement restatement required under the provisions of Accounting Series Release No. 190.

Like the SEC, the FASB has not required a change in the basic historical cost financial statements. Statement No. 33 requires that certain balance sheet and income statement accounts be restated to show the effects of inflation, and that such restated amounts be disclosed as *supplemental* information. Historical cost financial statements continue to be the basic yardstick for the accounting profession when reporting to shareholders.

The FASB approach to accounting for changing prices is quite different from the approach adopted by the SEC. As a result, it is essential that certain terms used in Statement No. 33, and in the discussion that follows, be defined. It is almost impossible to convey the precise meaning of each of the terms through a definition, but this will serve as a starting point to understanding the provisions of Statement No. 33.

Paragraph 22 of the Statement outlines the following terms:

Constant Dollar Accounting. A method of reporting financial statement elements in dollars, each of which has the same general purchasing power.

Current Cost Accounting. A method of measuring and reporting assets and expenses associated with the use or sale of assets, at their current cost or lower recoverable amount at the balance sheet date or at the date of use or sale.

Current Cost/Constant Dollar Accounting. A method of accounting based on measures of current cost, or lower recoverable amount, in terms of dollars each of which has the same general purchasing power.

Current Cost/Nominal Dollar Accounting. A method of accounting based on measures of current cost, or lower recoverable amount, without restatement into units each of which has the same general purchasing power.

Historical Cost/Constant Dollar Accounting. A method of accounting based on measures of historical prices in dollars each of which has the same general purchasing power.

Historical Cost/Nominal Dollar Accounting. The generally accepted method of accounting, used in the primary financial statements, based on measures of historical prices in dollars without restatement into units each of which has the same general purchasing power.

Upon first review of the terms, the reader may be confused as to the difference between them. Much of the terminology used in the definitions sounds the same. It may take some time to get used to this new terminology, but the authors hope that, after careful reading of the material that follows, the reader will develop an appreciation for the specialized terminology used in Statement No. 33.

If the terms listed above are viewed in their broadest aspect, there are two types of accounting for changing prices suggested. First, the terms deal with the problem of accounting for changes in the "general" prices of all goods and services. Second, the terms address the issue of accounting for "specific" price level changes relating to identified accounts. The treatment of "general" price level adjustments is referred to as "constant dollar accounting," and the treatment of "specific" price level adjustments is referred to as "current cost accounting." Statement No. 33 requires that the accountant report on *both* general and specific price level adjustments. Remember to associate "general" price level changes with **Constant Dollar Accounting,** and specific price level accounting with **Current Cost Accounting.**

The financial statements currently being prepared by accountants, i.e., historical cost statements, are referred to in the Statement as Historical Cost/Nominal Dollar financial statements. Historical cost refers to the measurement technique used by accountants, and nominal dollars refer to the measurement unit used. Primary financial statements use historical cost as the measurement technique and nominal dollars as the measurement unit. There are, of course, other measurement techniques and units that accountants may wish to consider in the preparation of future financial statements. One of the terms defined above was "Historical Cost/Constant Dollar Accounting." Remembering that constant dollars refer to dollars adjusted for changes in general price levels, this term implies that historical cost will be used as the measurement technique, and constant dollars will be used as the measurement unit. Put another way, accountants would continue to record transactions on the basis of historical cost, but, for financial statement presentation, these costs would be adjusted to constant dollars, i.e., dollars that have the same general purchasing power. Historical Cost/Constant Dollar Accounting would use the same measurement technique used today, but the measurement unit for financial presentation would be different. The constant dollar measurement unit could be expressed in terms of prior period dollars or in terms of current period dollars. In a period of rising prices, when constant dollars were expressed in terms of some base year, e.g., 1975, investments in assets would have to be deflated for the effects of rising prices. The use of constant dollars is an attempt to express account balances in different years in terms of the same amount of general purchasing power.

To accomplish the purpose of constant dollar accounting it is necessary to develop certain indexes that measure the change in the general purchasing power of the dollar. One such measure that most of us are familiar with is the *consumer price index.* This index represents an attempt to measure in constant dollars, the cost of typical goods and services purchased by consumers in general. Other price indexes have been developed to measure, in constant dollars, the cost to acquire specific goods and services. When accountants plan to use Historical Cost/Constant Dollar Accounting, they must decide upon the index to be used.

Current costs deal with the specific effects of changing prices on certain asset, equity, revenue and expense accounts. To be more specific, current cost is "equal to the current replacement cost of the asset owned, adjusted for the value of any operating advantages or disadvantages of the asset owned," according to Paragraph 99(f) of the Statement. The concept of current cost defined in the Statement "focuses on the cost of the service potential embodied in the asset owned by the enterprise." When dealing with Current Cost/Nominal Dollar Accounting, the accountant would use current cost as the measurement technique and nominal dollars as the measurement unit. For example, the cost of an asset would be expressed in terms of its replacement cost in nominal dollars. There would be no effort to express current costs in terms of general purchasing power units. This latter approach would be called Current Cost/Constant Dollar Accounting. Under this approach, asset costs would be measured in terms of current costs and reported in terms of constant dollars. This technique is an effort to measure the effects of both specific and general price level changes.

When determining current costs there is no need to use a price index. Each individual asset would have its own unique current cost. This is one of the major implementation problems encountered when attempting to convert historical cost information to current cost information. The determination of an asset's current cost can be an extremely difficult problem in practice; however, in theory the concept is easy to understand.

Another term identified in the Statement is the "lower recoverable amount" of an asset. Recoverable amount is defined in Paragraph 99(g) as the "net realizable value of an asset that is about to be sold or the net present value of expected cash flows (value in use) of an asset that is not about to be sold." The recoverable amount of an asset should always be equal to or greater than the "cost" of that asset. If this is not the case, the asset should be written-down to its net recoverable amount. In the case of reporting for changing prices, the accountant must compare the Historical Cost/Constant Dollar amount and the current cost value with the net recoverable amount of the asset to see which value is greater. As long as the cost (either historical cost/constant dollar or current) is equal to or less than the recoverable amount, no adjustment is required. In those cases where "cost" is greater than net recoverable amount of the asset, a write-down is in order.

A great deal of managerial judgment is required when attempting to calculate the proper current cost of an asset. If management does not intend to sell the asset under consideration, the computation of the recoverable amount requires that the expected cash inflows and outflows associated with the asset be identified. These cash flows must be discounted at an appropriate discount rate to determine the net present value in use of the asset. If management intends to sell the asset, the accountant must calculate the net realizable value of the asset. In some cases, the computation of net realizable value is not difficult; however, as in the case of work-in-process inventory, the computational problems can become quite complex.

Now that several of the terms identified in Statement No. 33 have been defined, attention can be turned to the general reporting requirements specified in the pronouncement.

Overview of the Disclosure Requirements

There are several different ways to view the disclosures required in SFAS No. 33. First, disclosures may be identified by the type of price level adjustment required, i.e., disclosures of current costs and constant dollar information. The disclosures could also be identified by the specific balance sheet or income statement account affected by the reporting for changing prices. The authors believe that the best approach to the discussion of the required disclosures is to combine both of the alternatives described above.

Disclosures may first be identified by the type of price level adjustment that is required and then by the specific accounts affected by the change. The first type of disclosures identified in the Statement relate to **Constant Dollar** information. These disclosures attempt to measure the effect of changes in the general purchasing power of the dollar. The specific disclosures identified in Paragraph 29 are:

(a) Information on income from continuing operations for the current fiscal year on a historical cost/constant dollar basis.

(b) The purchasing power gain or loss on net monetary items for the current fiscal year.

Merely listing these disclosures does not help the reader gain an understanding as to the true nature of the requirements specified in the pronouncement. To increase the level of understanding it is necessary to discuss the specific accounts affected by the items listed above.

As to requirement (a) above, the Statement permits the enterprise to provide for *comprehensive* restatement of the entire income statement, or to comply with certain *minimum* disclosures. At a minimum, the enterprise must restate (1) inventory, (2) property, plant and equipment, (3) cost of goods sold and (4) depreciation, depletion, and amortization expense on a historical cost/constant dollar basis. Notice that in the minimum required disclosures there are two balance sheet accounts and two income statement accounts. The reader will note that by changing the measurement unit for reporting inventories the cost of goods sold must be changed. Likewise, if property, plant and equipment are restated to a historical cost/constant dollar basis, the related depreciation, depletion and amortization will be affected. The changes in the income statement accounts are a direct result of restatement of the asset accounts.

If an enterprise elects to provide a comprehensive restatement of all balance sheet and income statement accounts on a historical cost/constant dollar basis, much more work will be required. SFAS No. 33 encourages experimentation by the enterprise and companies should not feel restricted to providing minimum disclosures. Certainly disclosures that went beyond the minimum but fell short of comprehensive restatement would be welcome by the FASB. Each business must decide just what type of disclosure it will elect.

Recall from previous discussion that when Historical Cost/Constant Dollar Accounting is used the accountant must decide upon the appropriate index to use for measuring constant dollars. Statement No. 33 specifies that the enterprise use the Consumer Price Index for All Urban Consumers. While one might debate the choice of the index, generally accepted accounting principles require the use of the Consumer Price Index. The Consumer Price Index for All Urban Consumers (CPI) is published in the *Monthly Labor Review* published by the Department of Labor. The Statement requires that the account restatement be made at "average-for-the-year" constant dollars, i.e., the average CPI should be used to restate the account balances.

The disclosure detailed in (b) above requires some explanation. The accountant is asked to compute the purchasing power gain or loss associated with the *net monetary assets* held at the end of the current fiscal year. Paragraph 47 of the Statement defines a monetary asset as "money or a claim to receive a sum of money the amount of which is fixed or determinable without reference to future prices of specific goods or services." Likewise, a monetary liability is defined as "an obligation to pay a sum of money the amount of which is fixed or determinable without reference to future prices of specific goods or services." Some examples of monetary assets would be cash, accounts receivable and investments in bonds. Examples of monetary liabilities would include accounts payable, dividends payable, bonds payable and other long-term debt. Appendix A to this Topic contains a schedule of monetary and nonmonetary assets and liabilities that is contained in Statement No. 33. The accountant must restate all monetary asset and liability accounts to constant dollar amounts using the average-for-the-year index. The gain or loss resulting from this restatement is not to be included in income from continuing operations but should be shown as a separate line-item after income from continuing operations, extraordinary items, disposals, etc.

The second set of disclosures are identified in Paragraph 30 of the Statement and include:

(a) Information on income from continuing operations for the current fiscal year on a current cost basis.

(b) The current cost amounts of inventory and property, plant, and equipment at the end of the current fiscal year.

(c) Increases or decreases for the current fiscal year in the current cost amounts of inventory and property, plant, and equipment, net of inflation.

Item (a) above means that income from continuing operations on a historical cost basis should be restated for the impact of depreciation, depletion and amortization and changes in cost of goods sold resulting from current cost information. Item (a) is really a result of reporting item (b) above. Once inventories and property, plant, and equipment have been restated to current costs, cost of goods sold and depreciation must be restated. The restatement of these accounts to a current cost basis is an attempt to measure the specific price level changes on the accounts identified. Determining current cost is a difficult task and involves many management decisions.

Item (c) above is an attempt to measure the change in current cost resulting from changing levels of inventory, property, plant, and equipment. Generally, the accountant will measure the current cost at the beginning of the fiscal year (or date of acquisition, if after the beginning of the year) and the current cost of the assets at the end of the fiscal year, and compute the net change. The amount of the net increase or decrease in the current cost of the assets identified should be reported *both* before and after eliminating the effects of general inflation. When considering the net change before the effects of general inflation, the enterprise would be dealing with just the current cost of the assets, i.e., the effects of specific price level changes. When considering the net change *after* the effects of general inflation, the enterprise would be adopting the current cost/constant dollar measurement approach. That is to say, the enterprise would attempt to measure the cost of the assets after giving effect to both *general* and *specific* price level changes. This certainly presents a challenge to the accountant to develop information that the profession is not familiar with. One of the most difficult practical problems will be to show the cost of an asset adjusted for both general and specific price level changes.

As in the case of reporting the effects of general price level changes, the enterprise has a choice of presenting a comprehensive restatement of the financial statements or providing the minimum information identified in the pronouncement. The discussion above relates to providing minimum disclosures.

The disclosures discussed to this point apply to the current fiscal period only. There is an additional disclosure requirement identified in Paragraph 35 of the Statement. These disclosures are for the five most recent fiscal years and include:

(a) Net Sales and Other Operating Revenues

(b) Historical Cost/Constant Dollar Information

(1) Income from continuing operations

(2) Income per common share from continuing operations

(3) Net assets at fiscal year-end

(c) Current Cost Information

(1) Income from continuing operations

(2) Income per common share from continuing operations

(3) Net assets at fiscal year-end

(4) Increases or decreases in the current cost amounts of inventory and property, plant, and equipment net of inflation

(d) Other Information

(1) Purchasing power gain or loss on net monetary items

(2) Cash dividends declared per common share

(3) Market price per common share at fiscal year-end

There are no new concepts introduced in disclosing the five year summary information; however, development of the information will require considerable costs to the enterprise. These should be viewed as start-up costs in the initial reporting year, and each subsequent year the cost will continue to decline. In the initial reporting year, the development of the five year summary of information may prove to be the most difficult task for the accounting department. Companies that have previously reported to the SEC on replacement cost information may find that the start-up costs will be slight. Other reporting entities may consider these costs to be excessive due to employee training and information gathering procedures.

The Board encourages experimentation with the disclosures identified above, and the authors concur with this notion. Companies should feel free to develop information about general and specific price level changes and report it in a manner deemed appropriate for its shareholders and other interested parties. The primary purpose of the Statement is to provide readers of the annual report with additional information for their decision-making processes. It may take several years for an individual enterprise to hit upon the right disclosures for their particular readership.

In addition to the conventional historical cost/nominal dollar information, the following *minimum* disclosures are required by SFAS No. 33:

	Historical Cost/ Constant Dollars	*Current Cost*
Restate Inventories	X	X
Restate Cost of Goods Sold	X	X
Restate Depreciation Expense	X	X
Restate Property, Plant and Equipment	X	X
Restate Depreciation, Depletion and Amortization	X	X
Purchasing Power Gain or Loss on Net Monetary Assets	X	
Increase or Decrease in Property, Plant, and Equipment Due to Specific Price Changes		X
Increase or Decrease in Property, Plant, and Equipment Due to General Price Level Changes	X	

The effects of the restatement of cost of goods sold and depreciation would impact the computation of income from continuing operations.

The discussion to this point has been concerned with the *general* provisions of SFAS No. 33. The introduction was intended to help the reader become familiar with the terminology and disclosure requirements of the Statement. It is now time to address the specific conceptual and technical problems created by the pronouncement.

Applicability of Statement No. 33

The first step in the accounting process outlined in the Statement is to determine if the reporting entity is subject to the provisions discussed in the previous section. Not all business entities are required to comply with the provisions of the Statement. Flowchart I is provided to detail the decision process required to determine if the entity under consideration is required to provide disclosures under SFAS No. 33.

FLOWCHART I

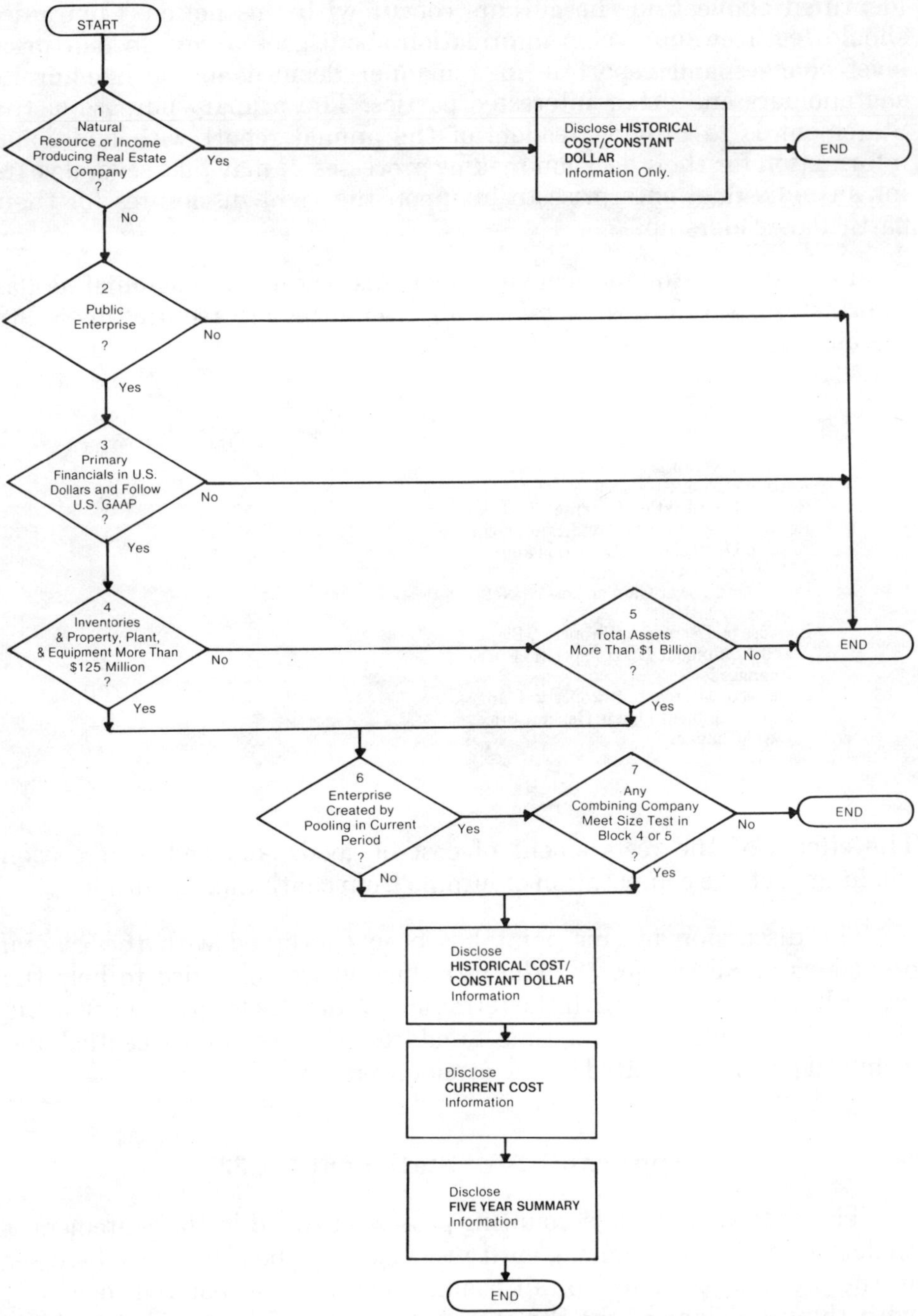
START
1
Natural
Resource or Income
Producing Real Estate
Company
?
Yes
Disclose HISTORICAL
COST/CONSTANT
DOLLAR
Information Only.
END
No
2
Public
Enterprise
?
No
Yes
3
Primary
Financials in U.S.
Dollars and Follow
U.S. GAAP
?
No
Yes
4
Inventories
& Property, Plant,
& Equipment More Than
$125 Million
?
No
5
Total Assets
More Than $1 Billion
?
No
END
Yes
Yes
6
Enterprise
Created by
Pooling in Current
Period
?
Yes
7
Any
Combining Company
Meet Size Test in
Block 4 or 5
?
No
END
No
Yes
Disclose
HISTORICAL COST/
CONSTANT DOLLAR
Information
Disclose
CURRENT COST
Information
Disclose
FIVE YEAR SUMMARY
Information
END

As shown in Block 1 of the Flowchart, companies in the natural resource and income producing real estate business do not have to comply with all the provisions of the Statement. These companies need only disclose the historical cost/constant dollar information described in the previous section. The Board plans to study the applicability of price level adjustments to several specialized industries including natural resource and income-producing real estate enterprises. The results of this study should be available in the near future.

To be subject to the provisions of SFAS No. 33 a business must be classified as a "public enterprise." A public enterprise is defined in Paragraph 22(h) as "a business enterprise (a) whose debt or equity securities are traded in a public market on a domestic stock exchange or in the domestic over-the-counter market or (b) that is required to file financial statements with the Securities and Exchange Commission."[1] This definition of a public enterprise may be considered a common sense definition. Accountants and others tend to think of companies whose securities are registered or traded on an exchange as being publicly held. Block 2 of the Flowchart indicates that public enterprises will be considered in further testing before one can determine if the provisions of SFAS No. 33 are applicable.

For a public enterprise to be considered further, its primary financial statements must be presented in United States dollars and prepared in accordance with United States generally accepted accounting principles (Block 3). Assuming that these conditions are met, there are two size tests that must be considered.

The enterprise must have inventories and gross property, plant, and equipment of more than $125,000,000, *or* have total assets of more than $1 billion to be subject to the provisions of SFAS No. 33. These size tests are similar but not identical to the size requirements imposed by the SEC in Accounting Series Release No. 190. Gross property, plant, and equipment includes land and other natural resources and capitalized leasehold interests, but not goodwill or other intangible assets. Gross property, plant, and equipment is shown *before* deductions for accumulated depreciation depletion, and amortization. Total assets are to be shown *after* deducting accumulated depreciation, depletion, and amortization. If the size test applies to a consolidated entity, relevant amounts should be taken from the consolidated financial statements. There is one final test to be conducted to determine if the enterprise should disclose the information required by the Statement.

---

[1] *FASB Technical Bulletin No. 79-8* (December 28, 1979) excludes closely held brokers or dealers in securities that file financial statements with the SEC from the provisions of SFAS No. 33. These entities are not considered to be "public enterprises" under the definition given in Statement No. 33.

If the enterprise under consideration was created by a pooling of interests in the current accounting period (Block 6), and any of the combining companies meet the size tests outlined in the preceding paragraph, the enterprise must comply with the provisions of SFAS No. 33. If, on the other hand, none of the combining companies meet the size tests, the entity would not be subject to the provisions.

When an enterprise meets all the conditions outlined in the Flowchart, it will be required to disclose the historical cost/constant dollar, current cost, and five-year summary information. Once it has been determined that the enterprise must comply with the disclosures, the next step is to identify the specific procedures required to meet the conditions specified.

The authors believe that the process of computing the historical cost/constant dollar, current cost, and five-year summary information is a very mechanical process. The computation phase of the accounting process would be greatly facilitated by the use of a computer. Manual preparation of the required schedules is extremely tedious. The challenge of SFAS No. 33 is to develop and accumulate all the information needed to begin the mechanical computation process.

The remainder of this discussion is divided into four parts, (1) an analysis of the provisions of SFAS No. 33 as they apply to property, plant, and equipment, (2) an analysis of the provisions relating to inventories, (3) computation of purchasing power gain or loss, and (4) a summary that brings all the information together to show the proper income reporting. The analysis of the Statement will begin with a detailed examination of property, plant, and equipment.

Technical Considerations—Property, Plant and Equipment

The authors have prepared Flowchart II to aid in the understanding of the specific provisions of SFAS No. 33 that apply to the reporting of property, plant, and equipment and related depreciation expense. The Flowchart blocks that run across the top of the page deal with the accumulation of information necessary for the computation phase of the work (Blocks 1, 6, 8, 12). The remaining blocks deal with the computation of price-level adjusted information and the proper disclosures required. The discussion that follows will refer back to the Flowchart so the reader will be able to see the logic of the computational process.

To illustrate the specific computational and accounting problems associated with the development and accumulation of necessary information required by the Statement, the assumptions listed in Exhibit I will be used.

Exhibit I

Property, Plant and Equipment—Example 1

1. Teal, Inc., a December 31 year-end company, has inventories and property, plant and equipment before considering accumulated depreciation, amortization and depletion of $130 million on December 31, 198D. Teal is a public enterprise that prepares its basic financial statements in accordance with generally accepted accounting principles. Teal has not been involved in a business combination for several years.

2. Teal's property, plant, and equipment is composed of the following elements (all amounts are shown in $000):

LAND

Acquisition Date	*Historical Cost*	*Current Cost 12/31/8C*	*Current Cost 12/31/8D*	*Net Recoverable Amounts 12/31/8D*
January, 198A	$ 50,000	$ 52,000	$ 80,000	$ 87,900
June, 198B	150,000	153,000	220,000	220,000
July, 198C	80,000	80,000	87,500	96,500
April, 198D	60,000	n/a	62,500	63,800
Total Land	$ 340,000	$285,000	$ 450,000	$ 468,200

EQUIPMENT

Acquisition Date	*Historical Cost*	*Current Cost 12/31/8C*	*Current Cost 12/31/8D*	*Net Recoverable Amounts 12/31/8D*
January, 198A	$ 100,000	$ 70,000	$ 68,000	$ 105,500
February, 198B	80,000	50,000	47,500	82,600
July, 198C	200,000	170,000	160,000	192,000
November, 198D	170,000	n/a	168,000	153,800
Total Equipment	$ 550,000	$290,000	$ 443,500	$ 533,900

BUILDINGS

Acquisition Date	*Historical Cost*	*Current Cost 12/31/8C*	*Current Cost 12/31/8D*	*Net Recoverable Amounts 12/31/8D*
January, 198A	$ 20,000	$ 21,000	$ 22,000	$ 30,000
January, 198B	30,000	35,000	36,500	39,800
July, 198C	50,000	52,000	53,000	55,300
September, 198D	60,000	n/a	60,500	60,700
Total Buildings	$ 160,000	$108,000	$ 172,000	$ 185,800
Total Property, Plant and Equipment	$1,050,000	$683,000	$1,065,500	$1,187,900

The equipment has a useful life of 10 years and the buildings have a useful life of 25 years. Depreciation is computed using the straight-line method with a full year's depreciation taken in the year of acquisition.

3. Information about the consumer price index on certain selected dates is shown below:

January, 198A	- 157.5	January, 198D	- 250.3	July, 198D	- 265.8
January, 198B	- 184.1	February, 198D	- 253.1	August, 198D	- 267.1
February, 198B	- 187.6	March, 198D	- 258.0	September, 198D	- 270.3
June, 198B	- 197.2	April, 198D	- 260.2	October, 198D	- 272.9
July, 198C	- 230.5	May, 198D	- 261.5	November, 198D	- 275.4
December, 198C	- 247.2	June, 198D	- 264.2	December, 198D	- 276.5

This consumer price information is the Consumer Price Index for All Urban Consumers for the hypothetical dates indicated.

After reviewing the information presented above, the reader should see that the first problem is to determine if the provisions of SFAS No. 33 apply to Teal, Inc. Teal is not in the natural resource or income producing real estate business (Block 1), and is a public enterprise as defined in the Statement (Block 2). Teal is a domestic corporation that prepares its financial statements in accordance with generally accepted accounting principles (Block 3). The enterprise meets the size tests because it has inventories and property, plant and equipment of $130 million at December 31, 198D (Block 5). Since Teal, Inc. has not been involved in any business combinations recently, it fails to meet the conditions in Block 6 of Flowchart I, and is, therefore, required to disclose certain information required in SFAS No. 33.

Knowing that the enterprise must comply with the provisions of the Statement, Teal must begin to accumulate certain information specified in Flowchart II. The information required in Blocks 1, 8, and 12 of the Flowchart is shown in Item 2 of Exhibit I. Information relating to Block 6 of the Flowchart is presented in Item 3 of Exhibit I. The information shown in Exhibit I is the data that must be accumulated by a company before the computational phase of the accounting process may begin. The information that is "given" in the Exhibit will be extremely difficult to develop in practice. The consumer price information will be the least difficult information to accumulate. Information relating to net recoverable amounts at the end of the year will be the most difficult information to develop under normal circumstances. Notice that Flowchart II has no specific "START" position. This means that the accountant may begin the data accumulation process at any of Blocks 1,6,8, or 12. Once a beginning point has been selected the accounting process will become somewhat structured as indicated by the remainder of the Flowchart. The authors believe that a logical place to begin is with the historical cost information because this type of data is most familiar to accountants. Therefore, the reader may wish to begin in the upper lefthand corner of the Flowchart, and proceed from left to right.

With this approach in mind, the first task is to develop information about the historical cost of property, plant and equipment at December 31, 198D. This information is shown in Exhibit I in the column headed "Historical Cost." Notice that Teal has Land, Equipment and Buildings in its property, plant and equipment category. Once the historical cost information has been developed, the next step is to compute the percentage depreciated for each asset at the end of the period (Block 2). The percentage relationship developed in this computation is needed to compute accumulated depreciation for the Historical Cost/Constant Dollar disclosure (remember that historical cost/constant dollar accounting refers to historical cost information converted into units that have the same *general* purchasing power). The percentage of property, plant and equipment depreciated at December 31, 198D is computed in Table 1.

Table 1

Computation of Percentage Depreciated at December 31, 198D—Historical Cost/Nominal Dollars

($000 omitted)

Acquisition Date (a)	*Historical Cost/ Nominal Dollars* (b)	*Useful Life* (c)	*Annual Depreciation* (d) = (b) / (c)	*Years Outstanding* (e)	*Accumulated Depreciation 12/31/8D* (f) = (d) × (e)	*Percentage Depreciated* (g) = (f) / (b)
			EQUIPMENT			
January, 198A	[1] $100,000	[1] 10	$10,000	[2] 4	$ 40,000	.40
February, 198B	80,000	10	8,000	3	24,000	.30
July, 198C	200,000	10	20,000	2	40,000	.20
November, 198D	170,000	10	17,000	1	17,000	.10
	$550,000				$121,000	
			BUILDINGS			
January, 198A	$ 20,000	[1] 25	$ 800	4	$ 3,200	.16
January, 198B	30,000	25	1,200	3	3,600	.12
July, 198C	50,000	25	2,000	2	4,000	.08
September, 198D	60,000	25	2,400	1	2,400	.04
	$160,000				$ 13,200	

[1] See Item 2 from Exhibit I.

[2] Recall that a full year's depreciation is taken in the year of acquisition, therefore, these time periods were computed by taking the difference in years between 198D and the year of acquisition.

Before it is possible to compute the necessary Historical Cost/Constant Dollar amounts, information relating to the consumer price index must be developed (Block 6). Teal, Inc. has planned to present the minimum required price level information for the fiscal year ended

FLOWCHART II
PROPERTY, PLANT AND EQUIPMENT AND RELATED DEPRECIATION

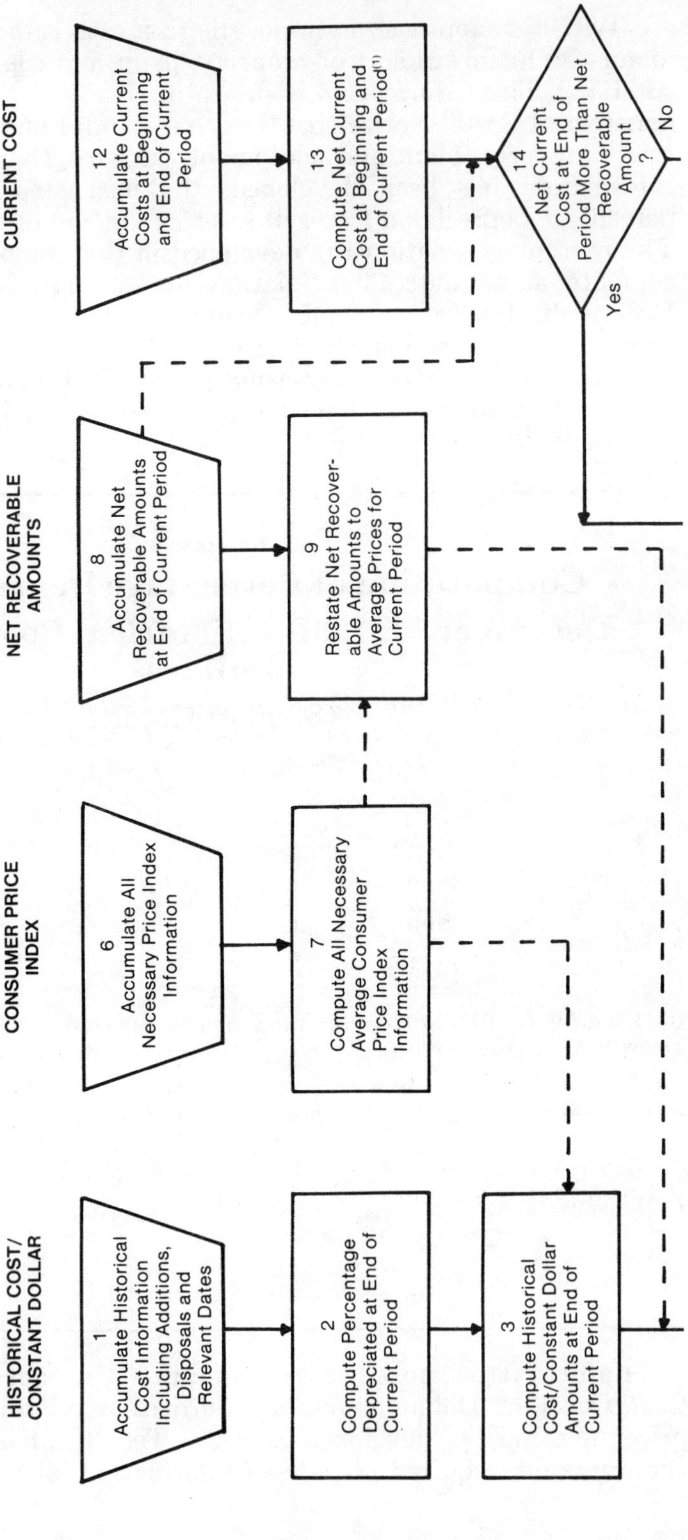

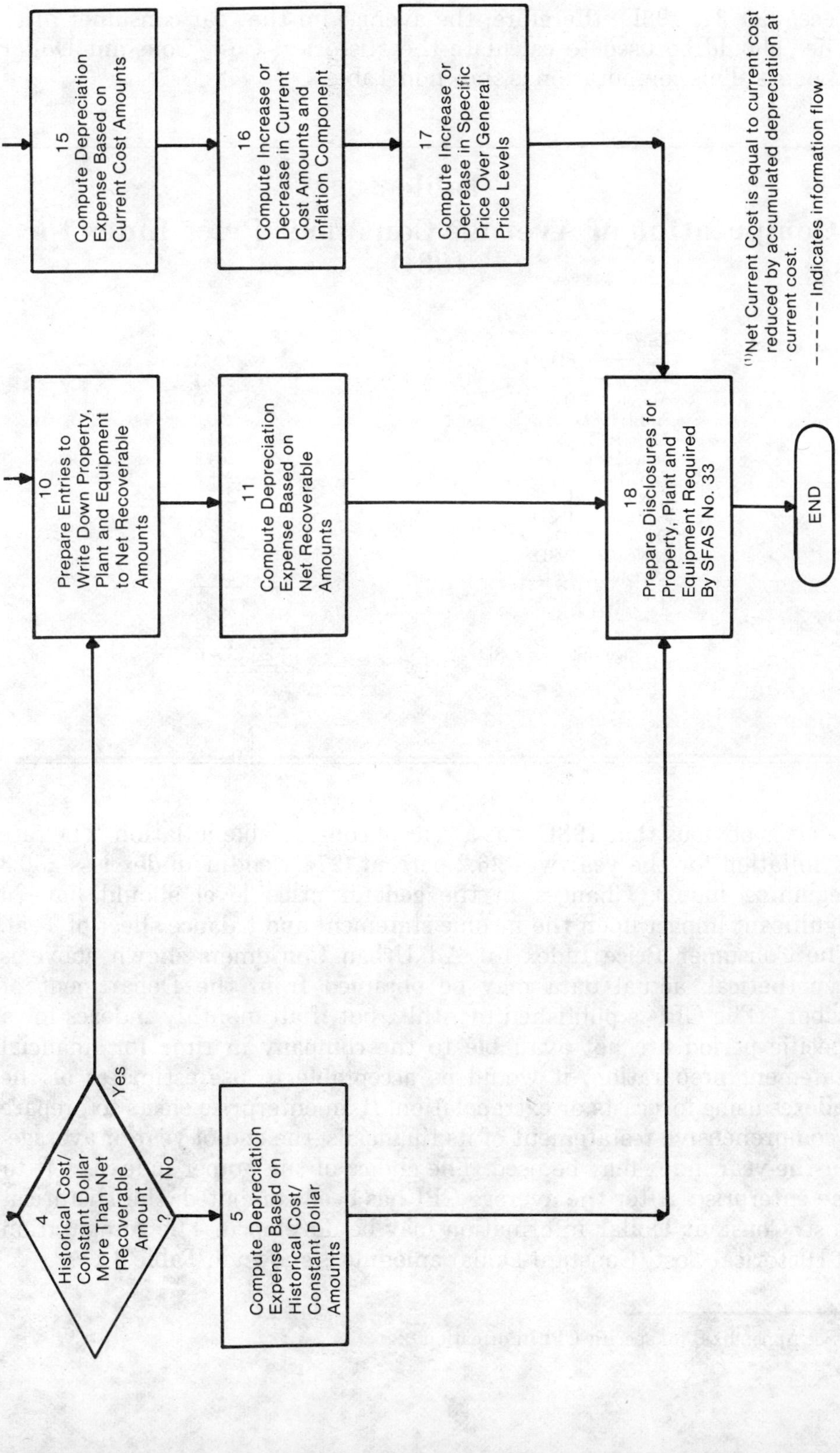
4
Historical Cost/
Constant Dollar
More Than Net
Recoverable
Amount
?
Yes
No
5
Compute Depreciation
Expense Based on
Historical Cost/
Constant Dollar
Amounts
10
Prepare Entries to
Write Down Property,
Plant and Equipment
to Net Recoverable
Amounts
11
Compute Depreciation
Expense Based on
Net Recoverable
Amounts
15
Compute Depreciation
Expense Based on
Current Cost Amounts
16
Compute Increase or
Decrease in Current
Cost Amounts and
Inflation Component
17
Compute Increase or
Decrease in Specific
Price Over General
Price Levels
18
Prepare Disclosures for
Property, Plant and
Equipment Required
By SFAS No. 33
END
(1)Net Current Cost is equal to current cost
reduced by accumulated depreciation at
current cost.
----- Indicates information flow

December 31, 198D, therefore, the average-for-the-year consumer price index should be used to calculate the Historical Cost/Constant Dollar amounts. This computation is shown in Table 2.

Table 2
Computation of Average Consumer Price Index for 198D

Date	*Index*
January, 198D	250.3
February, 198D	253.1
March, 198D	258.0
April, 198D	260.2
May, 198D	261.5
June, 198D	264.2
July, 198D	265.8
August, 198D	267.1
September, 198D	270.3
October, 198D	272.9
November, 198D	275.4
December, 198D	276.5
	3,175.3
	÷ 12
Average Index for 198D	264.6

It is obvious that 198D was a year of considerable inflation. The rate of inflation for the year was 26.2 percent (276.5 ending index less 250.3 beginning index). Changes in the general price level should have a significant impact upon the income statement and balance sheet of Teal. The Consumer Price Index for All Urban Consumers shown above is hypothetical; actual data may be obtained from the Department of Labor.[1] The CPI is published monthly, but if all monthly indexes for a specific period are not available to the company in time for financial statement preparation, it would be acceptable to use estimates of the indexes using forecasts or extrapolation. If an enterprise elects to prepare a comprehensive restatement of its financials, the end-of-year or average-for-the-year index may be used. The choice of the proper index is left to the enterprise. After the average CPI has been computed, the Historical Cost/Constant Dollar information may be developed. The computation of Historical Cost/Constant Dollar amounts is shown in Table 3.

[1] See Appendix B for specific CPI Information.

Table 3
Property, Plant and Equipment Expressed in Historical Cost/Constant Dollar Amounts—Average 198D Dollars ($000 omitted)

Acquisition Date (a)	*Historical Cost/ Nominal Dollars* (b)	*Conversion*[1] *Factor* (c)	*Historical Cost/ Constant Dollars* (d) = (b) × (c)[3]	*Percent Depreciated*[2] (e)	*Historical Cost/ Constant Dollar Accumulated Depreciation* (f) = (d) × (e)	*Net Historical Cost/Constant Dollar Amounts* (g) = (d) − (f)
			LAND			
January, 198A	$ 50,000	264.6/157.5	$ 84,000	n/a	-	$ 84,000
June, 198B	150,000	264.6/197.2	201,000	n/a	-	201,000
July, 198C	80,000	264.6/230.5	91,840	n/a	-	91,840
April, 198D	60,000	264.6/260.2	61,020	n/a	-	61,020
Total Land	$ 340,000		$ 437,860			$ 437,860
			EQUIPMENT			
January, 198A	$ 100,000	264.6/157.5	$ 168,000	.40	$ 67,200	$ 100,800
February, 198B	80,000	264.6/187.6	112,800	.30	33,840	78,960
July, 198C	200,000	264.6/230.5	229,600	.20	45,920	183,680
November, 198D	170,000	264.6/275.4	163,370	.10	16,337	147,033
Total Equipment	$ 550,000		$ 673,770		$163,297	$ 510,473
			BUILDINGS			
January, 198A	$ 20,000	264.6/157.5	$ 33,600	.16	$ 5,376	$ 28,224
January, 198B	30,000	264.6/184.1	43,110	.12	5,173	37,937
July, 198C	50,000	264.6/230.5	57,400	.08	4,592	52,808
September, 198D	60,000	264.6/270.3	58,740	.04	2,350	56,390
Total Buildings	$ 160,000		$ 192,850		$ 17,491	$ 175,359
Total Property, Plant, and Equipment	$1,050,000		$1,304,480		$180,788	$1,123,692

[1] The average for the year of 264.6 was taken from Table 2. The denominator of the conversion factor is the consumer price index on the date of acquisition of the asset involved, e.g., the first parcel of land was acquired in January 198A when the consumer price index was 157.5 (See Exhibit I, Item 3 for the detail consumer price index values).

[2] See Table 1, Column (g) for these amounts. Land is not depreciated.

[3] Values are rounded.

There are many important points that must be made about the information contained in Table 3. First, property, plant and equipment was divided into three categories; (1) land, (2) equipment, and (3) buildings. All equipment was assumed to have a useful life of ten years and all buildings were assumed to have a useful life of 25 years. In practice, there will be many different useful lives associated with equipment and buildings. This being the case, it will be necessary to subdivide major categories of depreciable assets to refine the computation process. One way to accomplish this is to group all the long-life assets together and all the short-life assets together. The only decision that must be made is what constitutes "long" and "short" lives. The entire matter of asset grouping is a management decision. Remember that the Statement encourages companies to experiment with the various disclosure requirements.

Another major point to consider is the fact that property, plant, and equipment were aged on the basis of acquisition dates, e.g., the first land purchase was aged from January 198A to December 31, 198D. For many large companies this type of aging process will place an extremely harsh clerical burden upon accountants. Schedules must be prepared in detail that may not be cost beneficial to the enterprise. The Board suggests that aging by year rather than acquisition date may be acceptable. In addition, it may be acceptable to group "older" assets into one aging group. For example, assets purchased between 1945 and 1960 may all be grouped together and aged based on the average index for the years specified. Yet another short-cut method may be to use First-In, First-Out as the basis of treating asset disposals. Some additional short-cut methods can be found in the FASB's publication, *Field Tests of Financial Reporting in Units of General Purchasing Power, 1977.* Statement No. 33 appears not to require absolute correctness in the application of its provisions, but allows experimentation and flexibility in the actual implementation of the Standard. Each enterprise is encouraged to devise its own short-cut methods as long as these methods fall within the guidelines of the pronouncement.

Notice that, in Table 3, Historical Cost/Nominal Dollar amounts were generally less than the Historical Cost/Constant Dollar amounts. This is due to the fact that inflation occurred at a rapid pace during 198D, and it would take more 198D dollars to purchase the same assets. A close look at the Table shows that in some cases the Historical Cost/Constant Dollar amounts were less than the Historical Cost/Nominal Dollar amounts. For example, look at the equipment purchased in November 198D and the building purchased in September 198D, in both cases the Historical Cost/Nominal Dollar amount was greater than the Historical Cost/Constant Dollar amount. This is because the average-for-the-year CPI was used as the conversion base and these assets were purchased at a time when the CPI was greater than the average-for-the-year amount. In such cases the Historical Cost/Nominal Dollar amounts will be deflated rather than inflated for the effects of changes in the general purchasing power of the dollar. Remember that the conversion process restates the assets in average-for-the-year *198D* dollars.

Once the Historical Cost/Nominal Dollar amounts have been converted to Historical Cost/Constant Dollar amounts, the accumulated depreciation associated with the constant dollar amounts must be calculated. This calculation is made by applying the percentage depreciated for the asset to the Historical Cost/Constant Dollar amounts. The net constant dollar amounts are just the Historical Cost/Constant Dollar values less the accumulated depreciation associated with the specific asset.

The next step in the accounting process is to compare the Historical Cost/Constant Dollar amounts with the net recoverable amounts to determine which value is larger. Before this comparison can be made the net recoverable amounts must be restated in terms of average 198D dollars. If the net recoverable amounts were not restated the comparison would be in terms of mixed dollars. The restatement is necessary so that the net recoverable amount will be comparable with the Historical Cost/Constant Dollar amount of the property, plant and equipment. Remember that property, plant, and equipment has already been restated in terms of average 198D dollars. For a company electing to disclose financial statements that have been comprehensively restated, end-of-year dollars or average-for-the-year dollars may be used. If assets have been restated in terms of end-of-year dollars then net recoverable amounts should be restated on the same basis.

If property, plant and equipment stated in Historical Cost/Constant Dollar amounts is *greater than* the related net recoverable amounts restated in terms of average 198D dollars, the Historical Cost/Constant Dollar amounts will be reduced by the difference, and this amount will be reported as a deduction in income from continuing operations. Remember from previous discussions that net recoverable amounts are the net realizable value of an asset that is about to be sold or the net present value of expected cash flows (value in use) of an asset that is not about to be sold. The computation of net recoverable amounts will be an extremely difficult problem in practice, and many subjective judgments will be required in the computation process.

For the assets listed in Exhibit I, the computation of the restated net recoverable amounts and the comparison with Historical Cost/Constant Dollar amounts is shown in Table 4.

Table 4
Restatement of Net Recoverable Amount and Comparison With Net Historical Cost/Constant Dollar Amounts ($000 omitted)

	Net Historical Cost/ Constant Dollars[1] (a)	*Net Recoverable*[2] *Amounts - 12/31/8D* (b)	*Conversion*[3] *Factor* (c)	*Restated 198D Net Recoverable Amounts* (d) = (b) × (c)	*Smaller of Net Historical Cost/ Constant Dollar or Restated Net Recoverable Amount* (e) × (a) − (d)
LAND					
	$ 84,000	$ 87,900	264.6/276.5	$ 84,117	$ 84,000
	201,000	220,000	264.6/276.5	210,532	201,000
	91,840	96,500	264.6/276.5	92,347	91,840
	61,020	63,800	264.6/276.5	61,054	61,020
Total	$437,860	$468,200		$448,050	$437,860
EQUIPMENT					
	$100,800	$105,500	264.6/276.5	$100,959	$100,800
	78,960	82,600	264.6/276.5	79,045	78,960
	183,680	192,000	264.6/276.5	183,737	183,680
	147,033	153,800	264.6/276.5	147,181	147,033
Total	$510,473	$533,900		$510,922	$510,473
BUILDINGS					
	$ 28,224	$ 30,000	264.6/276.5	$ 28,709	$ 28,224
	37,937	39,800	264.6/276.5	38,087	37,937
	52,808	55,300	264.6/276.5	52,920	52,808
	56,390	60,700	264.6/276.5	58,088	56,390
	$175,359	$185,800		$177,804	$175,359

[1] Net Historical Cost/Constant Dollar amounts are from Table 3, Column (g).

[2] Net Recoverable Amounts are from Exhibit I, Item 2, last column.

[3] The numerator in the conversion factor is the average-for-the-year CPI that has been previously computed. The denominator of the conversion factor is the CPI at the end of 198D because the net recoverable amounts are determined at the end of the current fiscal period.

By reference to Table 4 the reader can see that in all cases the net Historical Cost/Constant Dollar amounts were always less than the net recoverable amounts. This generally means that the net Historical Cost/Constant Dollar value of the various assets is less than the value in use or sale of that same asset. The enterprise would not incur a loss in selling the asset (if that is the intent of the company) or in use (if that is the intent of the company). In this case no write-down in value is required. As a result of this comparison (Flowchart II, Block 4), the net Historical Cost/Constant Dollar amounts shown in Table 4 will be used as the carrying value of the assets ($437,860 for land + $510,473 for equipment + $175,359 for buildings = $1,123,692 total carrying value).

The comparison of constant dollar amounts to net recoverable amounts was made on an acquisition-by-acquisition basis. However, it would have been just as acceptable to compare the total constant dollar amounts with the total net recoverable amounts by asset group. For example, the net Historical Cost/Constant Dollar amount of land could have been compared with the restated net recoverable amount for the land to see which is lower. The Board, in Paragraph 62 of the Statement, concludes that "decisions on the measurement of assets at their recoverable amounts need not be made by considering assets individually unless they are used independently of other assets." This would indicate that grouping of assets for comparison purposes is an acceptable practice. However, this statement does not rule out the comparison on an asset-by-asset basis when the assets are used independent of each other.

Because net Historical Cost/Constant Dollar amounts are less than the restated recoverable amounts, depreciation *expense* will be computed on the basis of the constant dollar amounts (Flowchart II, Block 5). It is necessary to compare constant dollar value with net recoverable amounts prior to the computation of depreciation expense because the expense is based on the lower of constant dollar or net recoverable amount. The comparison made in Table 4 to determine the smaller amount was based upon *net* Historical Cost/Constant Dollar amount, i.e., after reduction for accumulated depreciation. Depreciation expense is calculated on the gross amount of the asset carrying value, in this case, the gross Historical Cost/Constant Dollar amounts. The gross amounts for Historical Cost/Constant Dollar accounting are shown in Table 3, Column (d). It is these amounts that will be used to calculate depreciation expense in terms of constant dollar values. The computation of depreciation expense for 198D using these amounts is shown below:

Equipment (Historical Cost/Constant Dollars)	$673,770	
Straight-line Depreciation Rate	× 10%	
Depreciation Expense—Equipment		$67,377
Buildings (Historical Cost/Constant Dollars)	$192,850	
Straight-line Depreciation Rate	× 4%	
Depreciation Expense—Buildings		$ 7,714
Depreciation Expense for 198D on Historical Cost/Constant Dollar Basis		$75,091

Information about the Historical Cost/Constant Dollar depreciation expense will be disclosed. An example of the disclosure will be shown during the summary phase of the analysis of property, plant, and equipment.

The next major step in the accounting process involves the computation of certain current cost information. Remember that current costs deal with the effects of specific price level changes where constant dollar accounting addressed the question of general price level changes. Specifically, the accountant must compute the net current cost of the property, plant, and equipment as well as the accumulated depreciation on a current cost basis for both the current and immediately preceding fiscal year, i.e., in our case for 198C and 198D. Current cost information must be computed for both years in order to calculate the increases or decreases in the current cost of property, plant, and equipment for 198D. The current cost information for 198C is shown in Table 5.

Table 5

Computation of Net Current Cost and Accumulated Depreciation—Current Cost at December 31, 198C ($000 omitted)

Acquisition Date (a)	*Current Cost*[1] *12/31/8C (b)*	*Useful*[1] *Life (c)*	*Annual Depreciation (d) = (b)/(c)*	*Years Outstanding at 12/31/8C (e)*	*Accumulated Depreciation 12/31/8C (f) = (d) × (e)*	*Net Current Cost 12/31/8C (g) = (b) − (f)*
			LAND			
January, 198A	$ 52,000					$ 52,000
January, 198B	153,000					153,000
July, 198C	80,000					80,000
	$285,000					$285,000
			EQUIPMENT			
January, 198A	$ 70,000	10	$ 7,000	3	$21,000	$ 49,000
February, 198B	50,000	10	5,000	2	10,000	40,000
July, 198C	170,000	10	17,000	1	17,000	153,000
	$290,000				$48,000	$242,000
			BUILDINGS			
January, 198A	$ 21,000	25	$ 840	3	$ 2,520	$ 18,480
January, 198B	35,000	25	1,400	2	2,800	32,200
July, 198C	52,000	25	2,080	1	2,080	49,920
	$108,000				$ 7,400	$100,600
Total	$683,000				$55,400	$627,600

[1] Information about the acquisition dates and the current cost of the assets is found in Exhibit I, Item 2.

Current cost information for the fiscal year ended December 31, 198D is shown in Table 6. The computation of the values shown in Tables 5 and 6 are depicted in Flowchart II, Block 13. By examining the Flowchart, the reader can see that the next step in the accounting process is to compare the current cost information at the end of the current fiscal period with the net recoverable amounts at that date (Block 14). In our particular case, the current cost of the assets must be compared with the net recoverable amounts at December 31, 198D, to determine which value is lower. It is not necessary to restate the net recoverable amounts to average-for-the-year dollars because the current costs are computed at December 31, 198D, and are stated in year-end dollars. Net recoverable amounts are also stated in year-end dollars; therefore, the two amounts are comparable.

If the current costs are greater than the net recoverable amounts at the end of the period, it will be necessary to write-down the current costs to net recoverable amounts. The amount of the write-down will *not* be included in income from continuing operations, but will be included in the increases and decreases in current costs. The treatment is different than that required in the accounting for Historical Cost/Constant Dollar amounts. Recall that in that case, the write-down was included as a deduction from income from continuing operations.

The comparison of the current cost of the assets with the net recoverable amounts at December 31, 198D is shown in Table 7.

Table 6
Computation of Net Current Cost and Accumulated Depreciation— Current Cost at December 31, 198D
($000 omitted)

Acquisition Date (a)	Current Cost [1] 12/31/8D (b)	Useful [1] Life (c)	Annual Depreciation (d) = (b)/(c)	Years Outstanding at 12/31/8D (e)	Accumulated Depreciation 12/31/8D (f) = (d) × (e)	Net Current Cost 12/31/8D (g) = (b) − (f)
LAND						
January, 198A	$ 80,000					$ 80,000
June, 198B	220,000					220,000
July, 198C	87,500					87,500
April, 198D	62,500					62,500
	$ 450,000					$450,000
EQUIPMENT						
January, 198A	$ 68,000	10	$ 6,800	4	$ 27,200	$ 40,800
February, 198B	47,500	10	4,750	3	14,250	33,250
July, 198C	160,000	10	16,000	2	32,000	128,000
November, 198D	168,000	10	16,800	1	16,800	151,200
	$ 443,500				$ 90,250	$353,250
BUILDINGS						
January, 198A	$ 22,000	25	$ 880	4	$ 3,520	$ 18,480
January, 198B	36,500	25	1,460	3	4,380	32,120
July, 198C	53,000	25	2,120	2	4,240	48,760
September, 198D	60,500	25	2,420	1	2,420	58,080
	$ 172,000				$ 14,560	$157,440
Total	$1,065,500				$104,810	$960,690

[1] Information about the acquisition dates and the current cost of the assets is found in Exhibit I, Item 2.

Table 7
Comparison of Property; Plant and Equipment at Net Current Costs and Net Recoverable Amounts at December 31, 198D
($000 omitted)

Net Current Cost/ Nominal Dollars[1]	Net Recoverable Amounts—12/31/8D[2]	Smaller of Net Current Cost/Nominal Dollars or Net Recoverable Amounts
	LAND	
$ 80,000	$ 87,900	$ 80,000
220,000	220,000	220,000
87,500	96,500	87,500
62,500	63,800	62,500
$450,000	$ 468,200	$450,000
	EQUIPMENT	
$ 40,800	$ 105,500	$ 40,800
33,250	82,600	33,250
128,000	192,000	128,000
151,200	153,800	151,200
$353,250	$ 533,900	$353,250
	BUILDINGS	
$18,480	$ 30,000	$ 18,480
32,120	39,800	32,120
48,760	55,300	48,760
58,080	60,700	58,080
$157,440	$ 185,800	$157,440
$960,690	$1,187,900	$960,690

[1] This information is from Table 6, Column (g), which is the net current cost/nominal dollar amounts (current cost less accumulated depreciation).
[2] This information is from Exhibit I, Item 2, and is the net recoverable amounts *before* restatement.

A comparison of the net current cost of the property, plant, and equipment with the net recoverable amounts at December 31, 198D, shows that the net current costs are less than the net recoverable amounts, therefore, no write-down is required in this example. The net current cost of the property, plant, and equipment will be presented at $960,690, as shown in Table 7. Remember that the Board recommends a group-by-group comparison of costs for purposes of determining if a write-down is necessary. After the comparison has been made the next step is to compute depreciation expense based on the gross current cost of the assets

(Flowchart II, Block 15). If a write-down to net recoverable amounts had been required, depreciation expense would have been computed on the basis of net recoverable amounts (Blocks 10 and 11). The computation of depreciation expense on a current cost basis is shown in Table 8. Notice that depreciation expense is based upon the average current cost for the period, i.e., the current cost at the beginning of the current period plus the current cost at the end of the period divided by two.

Table 8
Current Cost Depreciation Expense—198D
($000 omitted)

Asset (a)	*Current Cost* [1] *12/31/8C* (b)	*Current Cost* [2] *12/31/8D* (c)	*Average Current Cost* (d) = (a + b)/2	*Depreciation Rate* (e)	*Current Cost Depreciation Expense* (f) = (d) × (e)
Equipment	$290,000	$443,500	$366,750	10%	$36,675
Buildings	108,000	172,000	140,000	4%	5,600
	$398,000	$615,500	$506,750		$42,275

[1] This information is from Table 5, Column (b), the gross current costs.
[2] This information is from Table 6, Column (b), the gross current costs.

The next Block on Flowchart II indicates that the increase or decrease in current cost amounts should be calculated (Block 16). Once depreciation expense has been computed, the increase or decrease in property, plant and equipment stated in terms of current costs may now be calculated. The increase or decrease is computed both before and after removing the effects of general price level changes from the account balances. The computation is designed to isolate the inflation component in the current cost information as well as show the effects of specific increases or decreases in the prices of assets owned. The computation of the increase in current costs of property, plant and equipment is shown in Table 9.

The difference between the Current Cost/Nominal Dollar amount and the Current Cost/Constant Dollar amount of $78,715 ($84,365 – $5,650) is the *inflation component* isolated from the current cost information. Table 9 represents some very complex computations from a conceptual standpoint. There are several major points that need to be discussed in relation to the Table.

First, it was necessary to restate the Current Cost/Nominal Dollar amounts to average-for-the-year constant dollars in order to isolate the inflation component included in the current cost information. If the assets acquired during the period were purchased uniformly during the

Table 9
Computation of the Increase in Property, Plant and Equipment Using Current Cost Amounts ($000 omitted)

	Current Cost/ Nominal Dollars	*Conversion Factor*	*Current Cost/ Constant Dollars*
Balance-January 1, 198D	[1] $627,600	264.6/247.2	[2] $671,776
Additions:			
Land-April, 198D	[3] 62,500	264.6/260.2	63,557
Equipment-November, 198D	[3] 168,000	264.6/275.4	161,412
Building-September, 198D	[3] 60,500	264.6/270.3	59,224
Depreciation Expense-198D	[4] (42,275)		(42,275)
Balance-December 31, 198D	[5] (960,690)	264.6/276.5	(919,344)
Increase in 198D	[6] $ 84,365		$ 5,650

[1] See Table 5, Column (g).
[2] $627,600 × 264.6/247.2 = $671,776.
[3] See Table 6, Column (b).
[4] See Table 8, Column (f).
[5] See Table 6, Column (g).
[6] Depreciation expense is added back to make all 198D values comparable.

period, no restatement would be called for because the assets would already be stated at average-for-the-year prices. In our example, each asset acquired was restated from its date of purchase. Whenever assets are purchased uniformly throughout the year, restatement may be avoided.

Depreciation expense for 198D need not be restated at average-for-the-year prices. If you recall, the depreciation expense for 198D was computed using an average of the beginning and ending balance in the asset accounts, this implies that depreciation expense was incurred uniformly during 198D, and no restatement is required.

The beginning and ending balances in the property, plant and equipment accounts were restated to average-for-the-year prices, so that the net change would be expressed in terms of dollars having the same purchasing power. The information in Table 9 can be used to complete the computation phase of the analysis by determining the increase in current costs due to changes in specific prices. The computation of this key amount is shown in Table 10.

Table 10
Computation of Excess of Increase in Specific Prices Over the General Price Level ($000 omitted)

Increase in specific Prices of Property, Plant and Equipment During 198D (See Table 9)	$84,365
Increase in the General Price Level (The Inflation Component Calculated from the Information in Table 9)	78,715
Excess of Increase in Specific Prices Over Increase in the General Price Level	$ 5,650

Using all the information developed to this point, it is possible to show the minimum supplementary information required by SFAS No. 33. The minimum disclosures are shown in Table 11.

Table 11
Minimum Required Supplementary Information for Property, Plant and Equipment ($000 omitted)

Net Property, Plant and Equipment at the Lower of net Current Cost/Nominal Dollars or Net Recoverable Amounts (Table 7)	$960,690
Historical Cost/Constant Dollar Depreciation Expense	75,091
Current Cost Depreciation Expense (Table 8)	42,275
Increase in Current Cost/Nominal Dollar Cost of Property, Plant, and Equipment (Increase in Specific Prices) (Table 10)	84,365
The Inflation Component (Difference Between Current Cost/Nominal Dollars and Current Cost/Constant Dollars) (Table 10)	78,715
Excess of Increases in Specific Prices Over Increases in the General Price Level (Table 10)	5,650

The illustration of the minimum required disclosures in SFAS No. 33 completes the analysis of the first example involving property, plant, and equipment. The first example omitted many of the complex problems associated with fixed assets. One major problem that was omitted was the impact of disposals of property, plant, and equipment on the calculations shown above. The second example is somewhat more complex than the first and will include the problem of asset disposals.

Since the computational phase of the accounting process is so mechanical in nature, the entire process will not be repeated in the second example. The second example will carry the reader through the computations involved in determining the Historical Cost/Constant Dollar amounts, after this the reader may refer back to the first example for the steps to follow in further computations. The only new aspect of the second example is the incorporation of asset disposals. Specific information about the second example is found in Exhibit II.

Exhibit II

Property, Plant and Equipment—Example 2

1. Sunglow Company, a December 31 year-end enterprise, began operations on January 1, 198A. At December 31, 198D, Sunglow has total assets after accumulated depreciation of $1.1 billion. The company is considered a public enterprise and prepares its basic financial statements in accordance with generally accepted accounting principles. The company has never been involved in a business combination.

2. Sunglow's property, plant and equipment at December 31, 198D is composed of the following ($000 omitted):

Acquisition Date	*Historical Cost*	*Disposals*	*Disposal Date*	*Date Disposal Acquired*
		LAND		
198A	$ 10,000	$ 2,000	198C	198A
198B	50,000	20,000	198D	198B
198C	-	-	-	-
198D	5,000	-	-	-
Total Land	$ 65,000	$22,000		
		EQUIPMENT		
198A	$ 80,000	$10,000	198B	198A
198B	60,000	15,000	198D	198B
198C	20,000	5,000	198D	198C
198D	90,000	5,000	198D	198D
Total Equipment	$250,000	$35,000		
		BUILDINGS		
198A	$ 50,000	$10,000	198C	198A
198B	-	-	-	-
198C	80,000	20,000	198D	198C
198D	20,000	-	-	-
Total Buildings	$150,000	$30,000		
Total Property, Plant, and Equipment	$465,000	$87,000		

The equipment has a useful life of 5 years, and the buildings have a useful life of 20 years. Depreciation is computed using the straight-line method, with a full year's depreciation taken in the year of acquisition and no depreciation in the year of disposal.

3. Relevant information about the consumer price index is shown below:

Average-for-the-Year 198A—185.6	December, 198C—247.2
Average-for-the-Year 198B—210.4	December, 198D—276.5
Average-for-the-Year 198C—235.2	
Average-for-the-Year 198D—264.6	

The first problem encountered by the accountant is to determine if the provisions of SFAS No. 33 apply to Sunglow. Sunglow is not in the natural resource or income producing real estate business and it is a public enterprise. The company prepares its basic financial statements in accordance with generally accepted accounting principles and meets the size test because its total assets exceed $1 billion. Sunglow has never been involved in a business combination, and as a result of meeting all of these tests, must comply with the provisions of Statement No. 33.

The next step is to accumulate all the pertinent information relating to the property, plant and equipment of Sunglow. Remember that this example will only be taken through the computation of the Historical Cost/Constant Dollar amounts. Knowing this, the information in Exhibit II will be used to begin the accounting process by computing the percentage depreciated for the assets owned by Sunglow.

The computation of the percentage depreciated is shown in Table 12, and the amounts are used to determine the accumulated depreciation on a Historical Cost/Constant Dollar basis. This is the same starting point used in the Example 1 material (See Flowchart II, Block 2).

Table 12

Computation of the Percentage of Property, Plant and Equipment Depreciated at December 31, 198D

Historical Cost/Nominal Dollars ($000 omitted)

Acquisition Date (a)	Historical Cost (b)	Cost Basis of Disposal (c)	Net Historical Cost of Asset (d)=(b) — (c)	Useful Life (e)	Annual Depreciation (f)=(d)/(e)	Years Out-standing[1] (g)	Accumulated Depreciation (h)=(f)×(g)	Percentage Depreciated (i)=(h)/(d)
				EQUIPMENT				
198A	$ 80,000	$10,000	$ 70,000	5	$14,000	4	$ 56,000	.80
198B	60,000	15,000	45,000	5	9,000	3	27,000	.60
198C	20,000	5,000	15,000	5	3,000	2	6,000	.40
198D	90,000	5,000	85,000	5	17,000	1	17,000	.20
	$250,000	$35,000	$215,000				$106,000	
				BUILDINGS				
198A	$ 50,000	$10,000	$ 40,000	20	$ 2,000	4	$ 8,000	.20
198B	-	-	-		-	-	-	
198C	80,000	20,000	60,000	20	3,000	2	6,000	.10
198D	20,000	-	20,000	20	1,000	1	1,000	.05
	$150,000	$30,000	$120,000				$ 15,000	

[1] The number of years outstanding is determined by taking the difference between the year of acquisition of the asset and December 31, 198D. Remember that a full year's depreciation is taken in the year of acquisition.

NOTE: Information in Columns a,b, and c are taken from Exhibit II, Item 2.

Once the depreciation percent has been computed, the Historical Cost/Constant Dollar information can be developed. The only difference between this example and the previous one is that the conversion to Historical Cost/Constant Dollars is made on the basis of the net historical cost of assets after giving consideration to the disposals. Table 13 shows the detailed computations necessary to restate the historical cost amounts and to determine the "net" Historical Cost/Constant Dollar values.

Table 13
Property, Plant and Equipment Expressed in Historical Cost/Constant Dollar Amounts
Average 198D Dollars
($000 omitted)

Acquisition Date (a)	Historical Cost (b)	Cost Basis of Disposal (c)	Net Historical Cost of Asset (d)=(b)—(c)	Conversion Factor[1] (e)	Historical Cost/ Constant Dollar (f)=(d)×(e)	Percent Depreciated (g)	Accumulated Depreciation Historical Cost/Constant Dollar (h)=(f)×(g)	Net Historical Cost/ Constant Dollar (i)=(f)—(h)
LAND								
198A	$ 10,000	$ 2,000	$ 8,000	264.6/185.6	$ 11,405	n/a	n/a	$ 11,405
198B	50,000	20,000	30,000	264.6/210.4	37,728	n/a	n/a	37,728
198C	-	-	-		-	-	-	-
198D	5,000	-	5,000	264.6/264.6	5,000	n/a	n/a	5,000
	$ 65,000	$22,000	$ 43,000		$ 54,133			$ 54,133
EQUIPMENT								
198A	$ 80,000	$10,000	$ 70,000	264.6/185.6	$ 99,795	.80	$ 79,836	$ 19,959
198B	60,000	15,000	45,000	264.6/210.4	56,592	.60	33,955	22,637
198C	20,000	5,000	15,000	264.6/235.2	16,875	.40	6,750	10,125
198D	90,000	5,000	85,000	264.6/264.6	85,000	.20	17,000	68,000
	$250,000	$35,000	$215,000		$258,262		$137,541	$120,721
BUILDINGS								
198A	$ 50,000	$10,000	$ 40,000	264.6/185.6	$ 57,026	.20	$ 11,405	$ 45,621
198B	-	-	-		-		-	-
198C	80,000	20,000	60,000	264.6/235.2	67,500	.10	6,750	60,750
198D	20,000	-	20,000	264.6/264.6	20,000	.05	1,000	19,000
	$150,000	$30,000	$120,000		$144,526		$ 19,155	$125,371
Total	$465,000	$87,000	$378,000		$456,921		$156,696	$300,225

[1] The conversion factor is determined by dividing the average-for-the-year 198D CPI by the average-for-the-year CPI for the year of asset acquisition.

NOTE: Information in Columns a, b, and c were taken from Exhibit II, Item 2. The percentage depreciated values were taken from Table 12, Column (i).

By reviewing Table 13, the reader can see that the consumer price information has already been computed. In practice these values will have to be computed, but the Example 1 material contained a section dealing with the computation of the average-for-the-year CPI. Notice that the calculation of the net Historical Cost/Constant Dollar amounts was very similar to the process followed in Example 1. To carry through the remainder of the example would be routine since many of the calculations would be identical to those shown in the Example 1 analysis. By this time the reader should be familiar enough with the basic technique used to be able to solve most problems associated with restating property, plant and equipment.

The information developed in this section dealing with property, plant and equipment will be used later in the discussion when we are concerned with financial statement presentation. Before we can reach this point, a discussion and analysis of the impact of SFAS No. 33 on inventories must be started.

Technical Considerations—Inventories and Cost of Goods Sold

Flowchart III has been prepared to help the reader follow the computational process required in SFAS No. 33. Reference to the Flowchart will be made as the discussion of the example material develops. In order to illustrate the specific computational and accounting problems associated with the accumulation of information required for the supplemental disclosures, two different examples will be presented. Information about the first example is found in Exhibit III.

Exhibit III

Inventories and Cost of Goods Sold—Example 1

1. Teal, Inc., the same company used in Example 1 of property, plant and equipment, will be used to illustrate the accounting for inventories and cost of goods sold. Recall from the previous example that Teal met all the conditions that require reporting under the provisions of SFAS No. 33.

2. The historical cost of inventories at December 31, 198C was $15 million, and the historical cost at December 31, 198D is $20 million. Teal uses a First-In, First-Out (FIFO) allocation method for pricing ending inventory.

3. Based upon past information and computations, inventory turnover for Teal is approximately six times per year. The company purchased 1,010,000 units of merchandise inventory during 198D for a total

FLOWCHART III
INVENTORIES AND RELATED COST OF GOODS SOLD

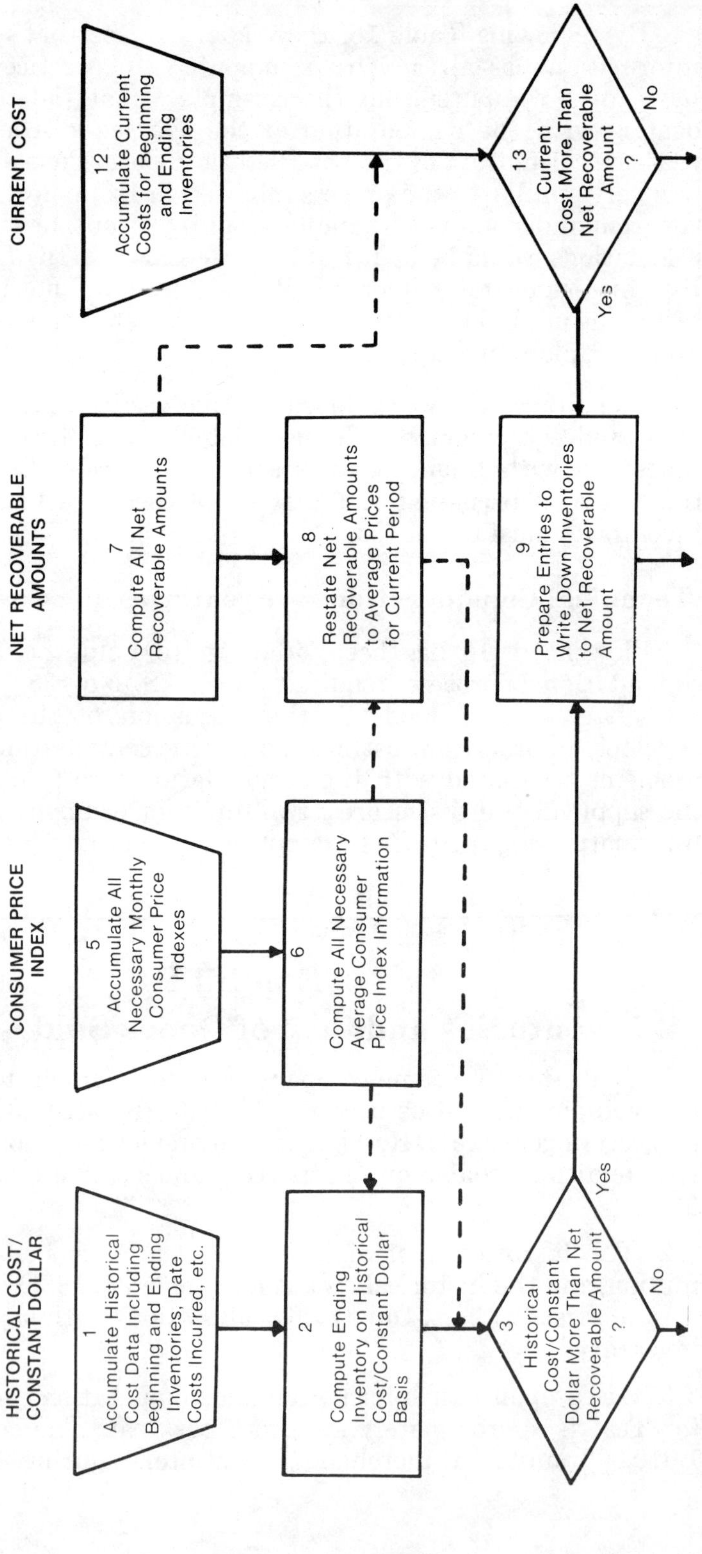

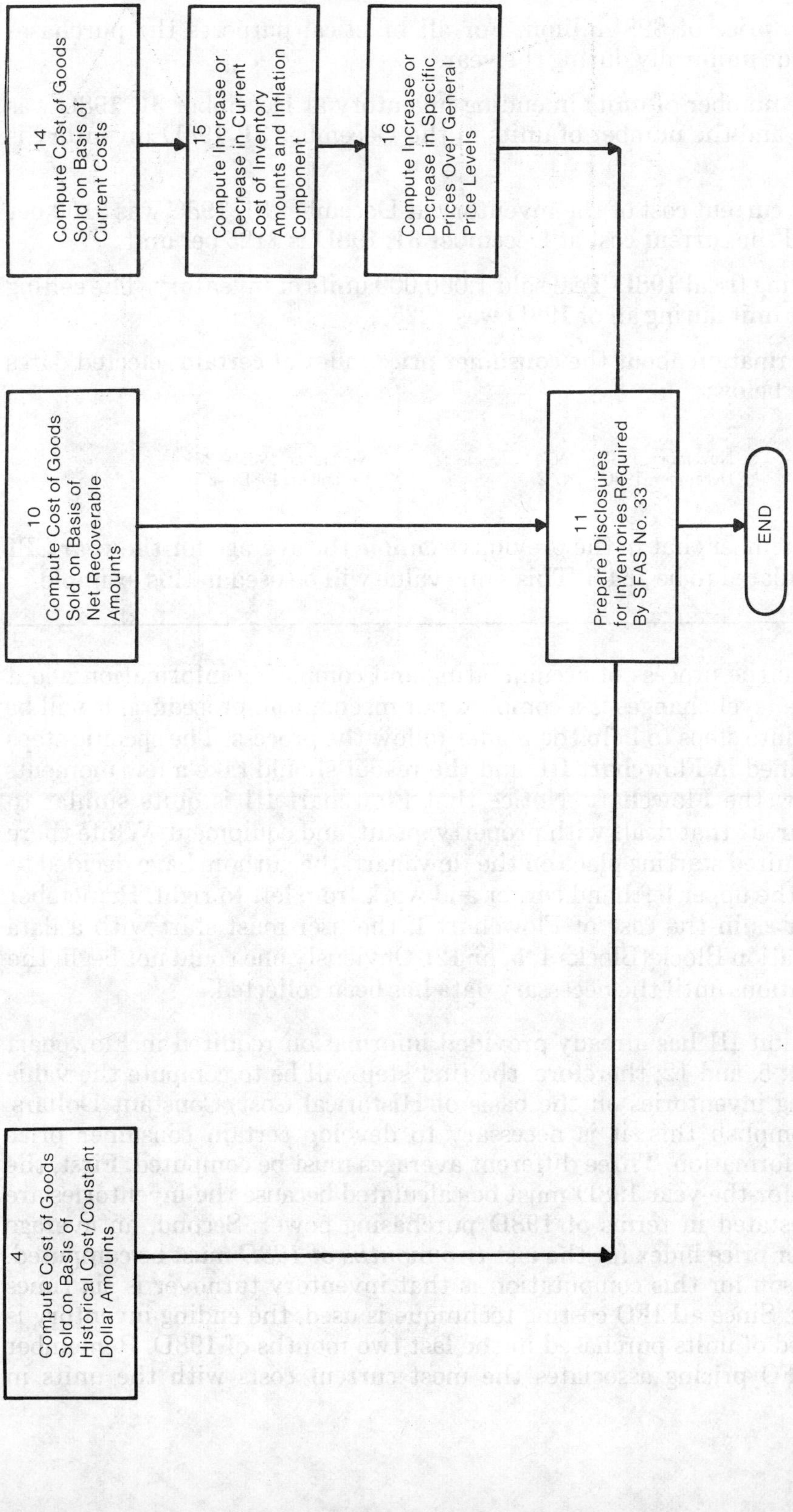
14
Compute Cost of Goods
Sold on Basis of
Current Costs
15
Compute Increase or
Decrease in Current
Cost of Inventory
Amounts and Inflation
Component
16
Compute Increase or
Decrease in Specific
Prices Over General
Price Levels
10
Compute Cost of Goods
Sold on Basis of
Net Recoverable
Amounts
11
Prepare Disclosures
for Inventories Required
By SFAS No. 33
END
4
Compute Cost of Goods
Sold on Basis of
Historical Cost/Constant
Dollar Amounts

purchase price of $98 million. For all practical purposes the purchases were made uniformly during the year.

4. The number of units in ending inventory at December 31, 198C was 150,000, and the number of units in the December 31, 198D inventory is 160,000.

5. The current cost of the inventory at December 31, 198C was $100 per unit, and the current cost at December 31, 198D is $125 per unit.

6. During fiscal 198D Teal sold 1,000,000 units of inventory. The selling price per unit during all of 198D was $225.

7. Information about the consumer price index at certain selected dates is shown below:

November, 198C—246.4	November, 198D—275.4
December, 198C—247.2	December, 198D—276.5

8. Remember that in the previous example the average-for-the-year CPI was calculated to be 264.6. This same value will be used in this example.

Since the process of accumulating and computing information about the price level changes is a complex, but mechanical, procedure, it will be divided into steps to help the reader follow the process. The specific steps are outlined in Flowchart III, and the reader should take a few moments to review the Flowchart. Notice that Flowchart III is quite similar to Flowchart II that dealt with property, plant and equipment. While there is no required starting place on the flowchart, the authors have decided to start in the upper lefthand corner and work from left to right. Remember that just as in the case of Flowchart I, the user must start with a data accumulation Block (Blocks 1, 5, or 12). Obviously one could not begin the computations until the necessary data has been collected.

Exhibit III has already provided information required in Flowchart Blocks 1, 5, and 12; therefore, the first step will be to compute the value of ending inventories on the basis of Historical Cost/Constant Dollars. To accomplish this, it is necessary to develop certain consumer price index information. Three different averages must be computed. First, the average-for-the-year 198D must be calculated because the inventories are to be restated in terms of 198D purchasing power. Second, an average consumer price index for the last *two months of 198D* must be computed. The reason for this computation is that inventory turnover is six times per year. Since a FIFO costing technique is used, the ending inventory is composed of units purchased in the last two months of 198D. Remember that FIFO pricing associates the most current costs with the units in ending inventory. Third, an average consumer price index for the last two months of 198C must be computed. The average index will be used to restate beginning inventory on a Historical Cost/Constant Dollar basis. The logic behind the use of the two-month index in 198C is the same logic that applied to the 198D index, i.e., the use of FIFO pricing and the inventory turnover.

The average-for-the-year consumer price index for 198D has previously been calculated to be 264.6. The average index for the last two months of 198C and 198D are computed in Table 14.

Table 14
Computation of Average Index for the Last Two Months of 198C and 198D

Month	*198C*	*198D*
November	246.4	275.4
December	247.2	276.5
Total	493.6	551.9
Divided By	2	2
Average 2-Month Index	246.8	275.95

Now that the necessary average consumer price indexes have been computed, ending inventories may be restated in terms of Historical Cost/Constant Dollars. The Historical Cost/Constant Dollar ending inventory in thousands of dollars is calculated below:

	Historical Cost/ Nominal Dollars (a)	*Conversion Factor* (b)	*Historical Cost/ Constant Dollars* (c) = (a) × (b)
Ending Inventory—198D	[1] $20,000	264.6/275.95	$19,177

[1] See Exhibit III, Item 2.

Notice that the conversion factor has a numerator of the average-for-the-year 198D consumer price index, and a denominator or the last two-month average index for 198D. Because Teal is facing a period of rising prices, the average index for the last two months is greater than the average-for-the-year index and the value of the ending inventory is actually deflated. This is because the restatement is in average for the year 198D dollars.

The next step in the accounting process is to make a comparison between the Historical Cost/Constant Dollar inventory and the net recoverable amount of the inventory. Before this can be done the net recoverable amount must be computed and restated in terms of average

198D dollars (the same base as the Historical Cost/Constant Dollar value.) The restated net recoverable amount may then be compared with the Historical Cost/Constant Dollar inventory value. The restatement of the net recoverable amount is shown in Table 15.

Table 15
Computation of Net Recoverable Amount and Comparison with Historical Cost/Constant Dollar Value of Ending Inventory
($000 except per unit amounts)

Selling Price per Unit of Inventory-December 31, 198D	[1] $225.00
Conversion Factor (264.6/276.5)	[2] X .957
Selling Price per Unit Expressed in Average 198D Dollars	$215.33
Units of Inventory at December 31, 198D	[3] X 160
Net Recoverable Amount	$34,453
Ending Inventory in Historical Cost/Constant Dollar Terms	[4] 19,177
Excess of Net Recoverable Amount Over Constant Dollar Amount	$15,276

[1] This information is from Exhibit III, Item 6.
[2] The conversion factor used is the average for 198D index divided by the index for December, 198D.
[3] Information about the 160,000 units in inventory is found in Exhibit III, Item 4.
[4] This amount was previously calculated.

As shown in Table 15, the Historical Cost/Constant Dollar value of ending inventory is not more than the net recoverable amount of the inventory; therefore, costs of goods sold will be computed on the basis of Historical Cost/Constant Dollar amounts. No write-down of the constant dollar value of inventory is required in this example.

The next step is to calculate the cost of goods sold using the Historical Cost/Constant Dollar amount for ending inventory. The computation will be made in Table 16, and a discussion of some of the important points that result from the computation will follow.

Table 16
Calculation of Cost of Goods Sold in Historical Cost/Constant Dollar Amounts for 198D
($000 omitted)

	Historical Cost/ Nominal Dollars [1]	*Conversion Factor*	*Historical Cost/ Constant Dollars*
Inventory, January 1, 198D	$15,000	264.6/246.8	$16,082
Purchases During 198D	98,000	—	98,000
Inventory, December 31, 198D	(20,000)	264.6/275.95	(19,177)
Cost of Goods Sold—198D	$93,000		$94,905

[1] See Exhibit III.

There are several important points that need to be covered in relation to the computations shown in Table 16. First, review the conversion factors used to restate nominal dollars to constant 198D dollars. The beginning inventory has a numerator in the conversion factor of the average-for-the-year 198D consumer price index, and a denominator of the last two-month index for 198C. Remember that the company uses the FIFO costing method and the goods in the January 1, 198D inventory were priced at the average index amount for the last two months of 198C (due to the inventory turnover). The conversion factor for the ending inventory has been discussed previously; refer back to Table 14 if additional help is needed. Purchases were incurred uniformly during 198D (see Exhibit III, Item 3) and are stated in average-for-the-year amounts. If purchases had not been incurred uniformly, some restatement would be in order. Notice that cost of goods sold on a Historical Cost/Constant Dollar basis is greater than the same amount on a nominal dollar basis. The real increase in the cost of goods sold is attributable to the beginning inventory. This is what one would expect to find in times of rising prices where the company uses the FIFO pricing method.

Now that the cost of goods sold has been computed on a Historical Cost/Constant Dollar basis, the next step in the process is to compare the current cost of the inventory with the net recoverable amounts to determine which value is larger (Block 13). The per unit current cost of $125 was given in Exhibit III, Item 5, and the net recoverable amount (selling price) of $225 per unit was also given in the Exhibit. Of course, in practice, this information must be developed by the accountant and will require considerable work. With the information given, the next step is to compare the two amounts to determine which is larger. The net recoverable amount should *not* be restated in terms of average dollars because both amounts involved in the comparison are stated at year-end prices. Since the $225 per unit net recoverable amount is in excess of the

$125 per unit current cost, no write-down is needed, and cost of goods sold will be computed on the basis of current costs.

Cost of goods sold on an average current cost basis is computed in Table 17.

Table 17
Average Current Cost of Goods Sold ($000 except for per unit amounts)

Current Cost Per Unit—January 1, 198D	$ 100
Current Cost Per Unit—December 31, 198D	125
Total	$ 225
Divided By	2
Average Current Cost Per Unit—198D	$ 112.50
Number of Units Sold During 198D	× 1,000
Average Current Cost of Goods Sold—198D	$112,500

After cost of goods sold has been computed on a current cost basis, the next step is to calculate the increase or decrease in current cost of inventory and isolate the inflation component in the current cost information (Block 15). The inflation component is the difference in the increase or decrease in Current Cost/Nominal Dollars and the Current Cost/Constant Dollar amounts. The inflation component must be isolated because it is needed to compute the excess of increases in specific prices over increases in general prices. The increase in the current costs of inventory and the identification of the inflation component are shown in Table 18.

Table 18
Computation of the Increase in Current Cost of Inventories and Isolation of the Inflation Component ($000 omitted)

	Current Cost/ Nominal Dollars (a)	*Conversion Factor* (b)	*Current Cost/ Constant Dollar* (c)=(a)×(b)	*Inflation Component* (d)=(a) − (c)
Inventory, January 1, 198D	[1] $15,000	264.6/247.2	$16,056	
Purchases—198D	[2] 98,000	-	98,000	
Average Current Cost of Goods Sold—198D	[3] (112,500)	-	(112,500)	
Inventory, December 31, 198D	[1] (20,000)	264.6/276.5	(19,139)	
Increase in Current Cost of Inventory—198D	$19,500		$17,583	$1,917

[1] This information is from Exhibit III, Item 2.
[2] This information is from Exhibit III, Item 3.
[3] See Table 17 for the computation of this amount.

The information developed in Table 18 is complex in nature and requires some explanation. The beginning inventory is restated using the average-for-the-year 198D index in the numerator and the index for December 198C in the denominator. Remember that purchases were incurred uniformly during the period and no restatement is needed. The average current cost of goods sold was computed in Table 17. The conversion factor used to convert the ending inventory is the average-for-the-year 198D index divided by the December, 198D index, this is because the current cost values were stated in end-of-year prices and needed to be restated to average for the year prices. The inflation component of $1,917,000 was isolated as the difference between the increase in current costs expressed in nominal and constant dollars. The inflation component will be used in the final step to separate the effects of general and specific price level changes.

This final step is to compute the increase in specific prices over the increases in the general price level. The computation is shown in Table 19.

Table 19
Computation of the Excess of Increases in Specific Prices Over the Increase in General Prices—198D ($000 omitted)

Increase in Specific Price of Inventory During 198D	[1] $19,500
Increase in General Price Level (Inflation Component)	1,917
Excess of Increase in Specific Price Over Increase in General Price	$17,583

[1] See Table 18 for all information in this Table.

This final computation completes the analysis of the inventory and cost of goods sold information for Teal, Inc. The minimum required supplemental disclosures specified in SFAS No. 33 for inventory and cost of goods sold is shown in Table 20. Remember that the total disclosures for Teal cannot be determined at this point, but must await further analysis.

Table 20

Minimum Required Supplemental Disclosures for Inventory and Cost of Goods Sold—198D

($000 omitted)

Cost of Goods Sold in Historical Cost/Constant Dollar Amounts (See Table 16)	$ 94,905
Current Cost of Goods Sold (Changes in Specific Prices) (See Table 17)	112,500
Current Cost of Inventory at December 31, 198D (See Table 18)	20,000
Increase in Current Cost/Nominal Dollar Cost of Inventory (See Table 18)	19,500
The Inflation Component (Difference between Current Cost/ Nominal Dollars and Current Cost/Constant Dollars) (See Table 18)	1,917
Excess of Increases in Specific Prices Over Increases in the General Price Level (See Table 19)	17,583

With the illustration of these disclosures, the analysis of the first example relating to inventories and cost of goods sold is complete. The example was designed to be relatively straightforward and involved the use of FIFO inventory pricing. When an enterprise uses a Last-In, First-Out (LIFO) inventory pricing technique, a problem arises as to how to handle the LIFO layers that may be added or reduced during the current period. The second example is somewhat more complex since it incorporates the use of Dollar Value LIFO.

Because most of the computations relating to price changes are mechanical in nature and have been sufficiently illustrated in Example 1, the second example will go through the computation of the Historical Cost/Constant Dollar ending inventory amounts. If the reader wishes to continue on with the example, reference should be made to the computations shown in Example 1.

Specific information about Example 2 material is found in Exhibit IV. Remember the only change has been in inventory pricing techniques.

Exhibit IV

Inventory and Cost of Goods Sold—Example 2

1. Dyer, Inc., a December 31 year-end company, began operations on January 1, 198A. Dyer has total assets after consideration of accumulated depreciation of $1.2 billion on December 31, 198D. Dyer is a public enterprise and prepares its basic financial statements in accordance with generally accepted accounting principles. The company has never been involved in a business combination.

2. Dyer uses a dollar value LIFO method of pricing its inventories. The historical cost of inventories at December 31, 198C and 198D are shown below:

	December 31, 198C (\$000 omitted)	*December 31, 198D (\$000 omitted)*
January 1, 198B Base Inventory	\$60,000	\$60,000
198B Layer	20,000	20,000
198C Layer	15,000	15,000
198D Layer	—	10,000
Ending Inventory	\$95,000	\$105,000

3. Inventory turnover, based upon previous information, is calculated to be four times per year. Purchases are made uniformly throughout the year. Dyer uses the earliest acquisition price to cost each LIFO layer.

4. Relevant consumer price index information is presented below:

January, 198A	- 157.5	January, 198C	- 221.5
February, 198A	- 158.6	February, 198C	- 223.8
March, 198A	- 159.4	March, 198C	- 224.2
January, 198B	- 184.1	January, 198D	- 250.3
February, 198B	- 187.6	February, 198D	- 253.1
March, 198B	- 188.1	March, 198D	- 258.0

Average-for-the-Year 198D—264.6

As in all other examples, the first problem is to determine if Dyer is subject to the provisions of SFAS No. 33. Dyer is not in the natural resource or income producing real estate business and is considered to be a public enterprise. The company prepares its basic financial statements in accordance with generally accepted accounting principles and meets the size test for total assets. Since the company meets all these requirements and has not been involved in a pooling-of-interests business combination, Dyer must comply with the provisions of SFAS No. 33.

The first step in the computation process is to calculate the Historical Cost/Constant Dollar amounts for inventory and cost of goods sold. To accomplish this, the accountant must first compute certain consumer price index information. In this example, the average-for-the-year 198D index of 264.6 will be used along with certain other price index data. Since inventory has a turnover of four times per year and LIFO layers are priced at the earliest acquisition price, each layer is assumed to be composed of dollar purchases in the first three months of each year (the first quarter). Remember that LIFO inventory pricing associates "old" prices with inventory and current prices with sales. Therefore, "old" for any particular year would be the first three months of that year. This requires the accountant to compute an average price index for the first quarter of each of the LIFO years, i.e., the base year plus each layer year. The average indexes for this period are computed in Table 21.

Table 21
Computation of Average Price Index Information

	LIFO Base 198A	*LIFO Layer 198B*	*LIFO Layer 198C*	*LIFO Layer 198D*
January	157.5	184.1	221.5	250.3
February	158.6	187.6	223.8	253.1
March	159.4	188.1	224.2	258.0
Total	475.5	559.8	669.5	761.4
Divided By	3	3	3	3
Average Price Index	158.5	186.6	223.2	253.8

If the inventory layers had been priced using the *last* price, the average index for the last quarter of each year would have been used. The consumer price index information developed in Table 21 will help restate the historical cost value for inventory to constant dollar amounts.

Once the appropriate consumer price index data has been developed, the ending inventory may be restated to Historical Cost/Constant Dollar amounts. This restatement is shown in Table 22.

Table 22
Restatement of Ending Inventory to Historical Cost/Constant Dollar Amounts
($000 omitted)

	Historical Cost/ Nominal Dollars (a)	*Conversion Factor (b)*	*Historical Cost/ Constant Dollars (c) = (a) × (b)*
January 1, 198B—Base	$ 60,000	264.6/158.5	$100,164
198B Layer	20,000	264.6/186.6	28,360
198C Layer	15,000	264.6/223.2	17,782
198D Beginning Inventory	$ 95,000		$146,306
198D Layer	10,000	264.6/253.8	10,426
198D Ending Inventory	$105,000		$156,732

The ending inventory priced at dollar value LIFO expressed in terms of average-for-the-year 198D dollars is $156,732.

Notice that the conversion factors used in Table 22 all have numerators that are the average for the year 198D consumer price index, and the denominator is the average price index computed in Table 21, i.e., the first quarter average price index for each year. This is because each LIFO layer is priced at the earliest price which is the first quarter average when consideration is given to the inventory turnover.

At this point, the Example 2 material can be discontinued because the remaining steps in the computation process would be the same as those described in connection with the Example 1 material. One important point about LIFO inventory needs to be made. The Statement, in Paragraph 60, Footnote 3, states that "cost of goods sold measured on a LIFO basis may provide an acceptable approximation of cost of goods sold, measured at current cost, provided that the effect of any decreases in inventory layers is excluded." When an enterprise uses the LIFO inventory pricing method, restatement to current cost may not always be required. This completes the discussion and analysis of the Example 2 material. The next major section deals with the determination of purchasing power gains or losses.

Technical Considerations—Purchasing Power Gains or Losses

Recall from previous discussion that Statement No. 33 requires the accountant to compute the purchasing power gain or loss resulting from net monetary items. A monetary asset was defined as money or a claim to receive a sum of money in a fixed amount, and a monetary liability was defined as an obligation to pay a sum of money the amount of which is fixed or determinable. In Appendix A to this Statement a list of assets and liabilities and their status as monetary or nonmonetary is provided. This is the same list provided in Statement No. 33 and the reader is encouraged to take a few minutes and look over the listing.

To illustrate the specific computational and accounting problems associated with the determination of the purchasing power gain or loss on net monetary assets, the information in Exhibit V will be used.

Exhibit V

Purchasing Power Gain or Loss on Net Monetary Assets ($000 omitted)

1. Teal, Inc., the company used in Exhibit I and III for the analysis of property, plant and equipment and inventories, will be used to illustrate the computation of purchasing power gains or losses. Remember that Teal met all the requirements for reporting under the provisions of SFAS No. 33.

2. Teal had the following monetary items at the end of 198C and 198D:

	December 31, 198D	*December 31, 198C*
Cash	$ 3,000	$ 4,500
Accounts receivable	10,000	9,500
Allowance for bad debts	(500)	(600)
Notes receivable	8,000	6,000
Cash surrender value of life insurance	6,000	5,500
Investment in bonds	15,000	16,000
Accounts payable	(15,000)	(16,000)
Notes payable	(30,000)	(26,000)
Bonds payable	(50,000)	(45,000)
Deferred income taxes	(8,000)	(7,500)
Net Monetary Liabilities	($61,500)	($53,600)

3. Relevant consumer price index data is presented below:

December, 198C—247.2

December, 198D—276.5

Average-for-the-Year 198D—264.6

The purchasing power gain or loss is defined in Paragraph 50 of the Statement as an amount "equal to the net gain or loss found by restating in constant dollars the opening and closing balances of, and transactions in, monetary assets and liabilities." To compute the purchasing power gain or loss, the beginning of the year net monetary items must be restated in terms of 198D dollars. The restated beginning balance, plus or minus the change in net monetary items, less the restated ending balance, will equal the purchasing power gain or loss.

The computation of the purchasing power gain or loss on net monetary items for Teal is shown in Table 23.

Table 23
Computation of Purchasing Power Gain or Loss ($000 omitted)

	Historical Cost/ Nominal Dollars (a)	*Conversion Factor* (b)	*Historical Cost/ Constant Dollars* (c) = (a) × (b)
Net Monetary Liabilities at December 31, 198C	$53,600	264.6/247.2	$57,373
Increase in Net Monetary Liabilities During 198D	7,900	-	7,900
			$65,273
Net Monetary Liabilities at December 31, 198D	$61,500	264.6/276.5	58,853
Purchasing Power Gain—198D			$ 6,420

The purchasing power gain computed above is $6,420,000. This seems logical because Teal is in a net monetary liability position in a period of rising prices. This type of situation would lead to a gain for the period. The $7,900,000 increase in net monetary liabilities during 198D is merely the difference between the beginning and ending net monetary liability position ($61,500,000 – $53,600,000). The conversion factors were taken from Exhibit V and use the average for the year 198D in the numerator and the consumer price index at December 31 of each year in the denominator. This factor converts the net monetary liabilities to the average for the year 198D dollars, i.e., constant dollars.

This completes the technical discussion and analysis of property, plant and equipment, inventories and cost of goods sold, and purchasing power gains or losses. Using all the information available about Teal, Inc., the necessary financial statement presentation can be developed. First the income statement of Teal, Inc. for the year ended December 31, 198D is presented and this is followed by the restated income statement as it would look when complying with the provisions of SFAS No. 33. Careful attention should be given to the restated financial statement, as it is as comprehensive as possible given the constraints of the previous discussion.

Teal, Inc.
Income Statement
For the Year Ended December 31, 198D
($000 omitted)

Sales		$225,000
Cost of Goods Sold	$93,000	
Depreciation Expense	61,400	
Selling, General and Administrative Expense	60,000	
Other Operating Expenses	5,000	
Total Operating Expenses		219,400
Income Before Taxes		$ 5,600
Income Taxes		2,800
Income From Continuing Operations		$ 2,800
Discontinued Operations:		
Income From Operations of Discontinued Division (Less Applicable Income Taxes of $200)	$ 200	
Loss on Disposal of Discontinued Division, Including a Provision of $50 for Operating Income During Phase-Out Period (Less Tax Benefit Relating to the Net Loss on Disposal of $300)	(300)	(100)
Extraordinary Item:		
Extraordinary Gain (Net of Income Taxes of $300)		300
Accounting Change:		
Cumulative Effect of a Change in Accounting Principle (Net of Income Taxes of $100)		100
Net Income		$ 3,100

Teal, Inc.
Income Statement Adjusted for Changing Prices
For the Year Ended December 31, 198D
($000 omitted)

	As Reported In The Primary Statements	*Adjusted For General Inflation*	*Adjusted For Changes In Specific Prices (Current Costs)*
Sales	$225,000	$225,000	$225,000
Cost of Goods Sold	$ 93,000	[1] $ 94,905	[2] $112,500
Depreciation Expense	61,400	[3] 75,091	[4] 42,275
Selling, General and Administrative Expense	60,000	60,000	60,000
Other Operating Expenses	5,000	5,000	5,000
Total Operating Expenses	$219,400	$234,996	$219,775
Income Before Taxes	5,600	(9,996)	5,225
Income Tax	2,800	2,800	2,800
Income from Continuing Operations	$ 2,800	$(12,796)	$ 2,425
Discontinued Operations:			
Income from Operations of Discontinued Division (Less Applicable Income Taxes of $200)	200	200	200
Loss on Disposal of Discontinued Division, Including a Provision of $50 for Operating Income During Phase-Out Period (Less Tax Benefit Relating to the Net Loss on Disposal of $300)	(300)	(300)	(300)
Extraordinary Item:			
Extraordinary Gain (Net of Income Taxes of $300)	300	300	300
Accounting Change:			
Cumulative Effect of a Change in Accounting Principle (Net of Income Taxes of $100)	100	100	100
Net Income	$ 3,100	$(12,496)	$ 2,725
Gain From Decline in Purchasing Power of Net Monetary Liabilities		[5] $ 6,420	[5] $ 6,420
Increase in Current Cost (Current Cost/Nominal Dollars) of Property, Plant and Equipment (Increases in Specific Prices See Footnote 1)			[6] $103,865
Effect of Increase in General Price Level			[7] 80,632
Excess of Increase in Specific Prices Over Increase in the General Price Level			$ 23,233

NOTE 1: At December 31, 198D, the current cost of property, plant, and equipment net of depreciation was $960,690, and the current cost of inventory was $20,000.

[1] See Table 20.
[2] See Table 20.
[3] See Table 11.
[4] See Table 11.
[5] See Table 23.
[6] $84,365 (Table 11) + $19,500 (Table 20) = $103,865.
[7] $78,715 (Table 11) + $1,917 (Table 20) = $80,632.

There are several important points that must be brought to the reader's attention about the information disclosed by Teal, Inc. First, take a close look at the amounts shown as depreciation expense under the three methods reported. Notice that depreciation expense adjusted for *general* price level changes is substantially larger than historical cost/nominal dollar depreciation expense. But also notice that depreciation expense on a current cost basis is lower than both historical cost/nominal dollar and historical cost/constant dollar amounts. This may be contrary to what you see in other examples, but the authors believe it is a very likely state to exist. Refer back to Exhibit I and look at the comparison of the historical cost and current cost of the equipment and buildings. Current cost is greater than historical cost in all cases, and this would be expected. Now look at Table 6 under the column "Net Current Cost" for equipment and buildings. The net amounts, i.e., amounts after considering depreciation, are significantly lower than the gross current cost amounts. This can be explained by the age of the equipment and buildings and the fact that technological changes and/or shifts in production methods and locations may cause equipment and buildings to show a reduced current cost amount. Remember there is a large second-hand market for equipment and real estate that reflects the current cost of an "old" piece of equipment.

Now look at the bottom line item presented in the income statement, i.e., "Excess of Increase in Specific Prices Over Increase in General Price Level." The general price level increase amounted to $80,632,000, while the specific price level changes amounted to $23,233,000. This latter amount is certainly material to the operations of Teal. The increase caused by changes in the specific prices is attributable to the fact that Teal held significant parcels of land during the period 198A through 198D. Refer back to Exhibit I and compare the historical cost of land with the current cost at December 31, 198D. There has been an increase of $110,000,000. Given the current market for land, this may not be unrealistic. Of course the remainder of the specific price increases were due to the equipment and buildings.

The final part of this analysis is an illustration of the current income statement and the five-year summary for a major automobile manufacturer. This example was taken from the FASB *Illustrations of Financial Reporting and Changing Prices* published in December 1979. The publication shows the disclosures that resulted from an experiment conducted by the Board. The authors suggest that interested readers obtain a copy of the illustrations.

SCHEDULE A

AUTOMOBILE MANUFACTURING COMPANY ILLUSTRATION
COMPARISON OF SELECTED DATA
ADJUSTED FOR EFFECTS OF CHANGING PRICES
($ In Millions except per share amounts)

Historical cost data adjusted for general inflation (constant dollars (a)) and changes in specific prices (current cost).

	1979	*1978*	*1977*	*1976*	*1975*
Sales—as reported	$31,670	$27,619	$23,696	$17,872	$15,774
in constant dollars	16,177	15,141	13,836	11,080	10,680
Net income—as reported	1,758	1,662	1,444	620	468
in constant dollars	727	804	736	101	48
in current cost	631				
Earnings per share—as reported	$ 6.00	$ 5.80	$ 5.00	$ 2.20	$ 1.60
in constant dollars	2.50 (b)	1.90	2.60	.40	.20
in current cost	2.20 (b)				
Common stock dividends per share—as reported	3.00	3.35	2.80	1.20	1.70
in constant dollars	1.50	1.90	1.60	.75	1.15
Profit margin—as reported	5.5 %	6 %	6 %	3.5 %	3 %
Net assets at year-end—as reported	8,785	7,880	7,190	6,540	6,265
in constant dollars	4,500				
in current cost	7,200				
Increase in specific prices of inventory and property over increase in general price level—net	1,372				
Unrealized gain from decline in purchasing power of net amounts owed	17				
Market price per common share at year-end	14	18	23	17	11
Average consumer price index	195.4	181.5	170.5	161.2	147.7

(a) Adjustment to constant dollar has been determined by applying the Consumer Price Index—Urban to the data with 1967 (CPI-100) as the base year as specified by Statement 33. Depreciation has been calculated on a straight-line basis for this calculation.

(b) These amounts will differ from those shown for constant dollar and current cost in Schedule B because a different base year has been used (1967 in Schedule A and 1979 in Schedule B) in order to illustrate the impact of changing prices in alternative forms.

SCHEDULE B

AUTOMOBILE MANUFACTURING COMPANY
ILLUSTRATION
SCHEDULE OF INCOME FROM CONTINUING OPERATIONS ADJUSTED FOR CHANGING PRICES
For the Year Ended December 31, 1979
(In Millions of Dollars)

	As Reported in the Financial Statements (Historical Cost)	Selected Data Adjusted for General Inflation (1979 Constant Dollar)	Adjusted for Changes in Specific Prices (Current Costs)
Sales	$31,670	$31,670	$31,670
Cost of goods sold	25,638	25,794	25,728
Depreciation and amortization expense	1,518	1,632	1,949
Other operating expense	1,034	1,034	1,034
Interest expense	178	178	178
Provision for income taxes	1,544 (a)	1,544 (a)	1,544 (a)
	29,912	30,182	30,433
Net income (loss) from continuing operations	$ 1,758	$ 1,488	$ 1,237
Earnings per share	$ 6.00	$ 5.10 (b)	$ 4.20 (b)
Unrealized gain from decline in purchasing power of net amounts owed		$ 33	$ 33
Increase in current costs of inventories and property over increase in the general price level—net (c)			$ 2,681

(a) In accordance with Statement 33, no adjustment has been made to the provision for income taxes. The effect is to increase the effective tax rate from the 46.8 reported in the financial statements to 50.9 and 55.5, respectively in the 1979 constant dollar and current cost calculations.
(b) These amounts will differ from those shown for constant dollar and current cost in Schedule A because a different base year has been used (1967 in Schedule A and 1979 in Schedule B) in order to illustrate the impact of changing prices in alternative forms.
(c) At December 31, 1979, current cost of inventory was $4,337 and current cost of property, plant and equipment, net of accumulated depreciation, was $8,685. The current cost of property owned and the related depreciation expense were calculated by applying selected wholesale price indexes to historical book values.

Appendix A

Listing of Monetary and Nonmonetary Items

Source: Statement of Financial Accounting Standards No. 33, Appendix D, September 1979.

ASSETS	*Monetary*	*Nonmonetary*
Cash on hand and demand bank deposits (U.S. dollars)	X	
Time deposits (U.S. dollars)	X	
Foreign currency on hand and claims to foreign currency†	X	
Securities:		
Common stocks (not accounted for on the equity method)		X
Common stocks represent residual interests in the underlying net assets and earnings of the issuer.		
Preferred stock (convertible or participating)		
Circumstances may indicate that such stock is either monetary or nonmonetary. See convertible bonds.	(see discussion)	
Preferred stock (nonconvertible, nonparticipating)		
Future cash receipts are likely to be substantially unaffected by changes in specific prices.	X	
Convertible bonds.		
If the market values the security primarily as a bond, it is monetary; if it values the security primarily as a stock, it is nonmonetary.	(see discussion)	
Bonds (other than convertibles)	X	
Accounts and notes receivable	X	
Allowance for doubtful accounts and notes receivable	X	
Variable rate mortgage loans	X	
The terms of such loans do not link them directly to the rate of inflation. Also, there are practical reasons for classifying all loans as monetary.		
Inventories used on contracts		
They are, in substance, rights to receive sums of money if the future cash receipts on the contracts will not vary due to future changes in specific prices. (Goods used on contracts to be priced at market upon delivery are nonmonetary.)	(see discussion)	
Inventories (other than inventories used on contracts)		X
Loans to employees	X	
Prepaid insurance, advertising, rent, and other prepayments.		
Claims to future services are nonmonetary. Prepayments that are deposits, advance payments or receivables are monetary because the prepayment does not obtain a given quantity of future services, but rather is a fixed money offset.	(see discussion)	
Long-term receivables	X	
Refundable deposits	X	

ASSETS	*Monetary*	*Nonmonetary*
Advances to unconsolidated subsidiaries	X	
Equity investment in unconsolidated subsidiaries or other investees*		X
Pension, sinking, and other funds under an enterprise's control The specific assets in the fund should be classified as monetary or nonmonetary. (See listings under securities above).	(see discussion)	
Property, plant and equipment		X
Accumulated depreciation of property, plant and equipment		X
Cash surrender value of life insurance	X	
Purchase commitments—portion paid on fixed price contracts An advance on a fixed price contract is the portion of the purchaser's claim to nonmonetary goods or services that is recognized in the accounts; it is not a right to receive money.		X
Advances to supplier—not on a fixed price contract A right to receive credit for a sum of money; not a claim to a specified quantity of goods or services.	X	
Deferred income tax charges† Offsets to prospective monetary liabilities.	X	
Patents, trademarks, licenses and formulas		X
Goodwill		X
Deferred life insurance policy acquisition costs† The portion of future cash receipts for premiums that is recognized in the accounts. Alternatively, viewed as an offset to the policy reserve.	X	
Deferred property and casualty insurance policy acquisition costs Related to unearned premiums.		X
Other intangible assets and deferred charges		X
LIABILITIES		
Accounts and notes payable	X	
Accrued expenses payable (wages, etc.)	X	
Accrued vacation pay Nonmonetary if it is paid at the wage rates as of the vacation dates and if those rates may vary.	(see discussion)	
Cash dividends payable	X	
Obligations payable in foreign currency	X	
Sales commitments—portion collected on fixed price contracts An advance received on a fixed price contract is the portion of the seller's obligation to deliver goods or services that is recognized in the accounts; it is not an obligation to pay money.		X
Advance from customers—not on a fixed price contract Equivalent of a loan from the customer; not an obligation to furnish a specified quantity of goods or services.	X	
Accrued losses on firm purchase commitments. In essence, these are accounts payable.	X	

LIABILITIES	*Monetary*	*Nonmonetary*
Deferred revenue Nonmonetary if an obligation to furnish goods or services is involved. Certain "deferred income" items of savings and loan associations are monetary.	(see discussion)	
Refundable deposits	X	
Bonds payable and other long-term debt	X	
Unamortized premium or discount and prepaid interest on bonds or notes payable Inseparable from the debt to which it relates—a monetary item.	X	
Convertible bonds payable Until converted these are obligations to pay sums of money.	X	
Accrued pension obligations Fixed amounts payable to a fund are monetary; all other amounts are nonmonetary.	(see discussion)	
Obligations under warranties These are nonmonetary because they oblige the enterprise to furnish goods or services or their future price.		X
Deferred income tax credits† Cash requirements will not vary materially due to changes in specific prices.	X	
Deferred investment tax credits Not to be settled by payment of cash; associated with nonmonetary assets.		X
Life insurance policy reserves Portions of policies face values that are now deemed liabilities	X	
Property and casualty insurance loss reserves	X	
Unearned property and casualty insurance premiums These are nonmonetary because they are principally obligations to furnish insurance coverage. The dollar amount of payments to be made under that coverage might vary materially due to changes in specific prices.		X
Deposit liabilities of financial institutions	X	

---

* If an investment is accounted for on the equity method, and if the investor is preparing comprehensive constant dollar financial statements, the financial statements of the investee theoretically should be restated in constant dollars and the equity method should then be applied. However, if restated financial statements cannot be obtained from the investee, the investor may be able to prepare such statements using nominal dollar information that is available, such as nominal dollar financial statements for a series of years. As a simpler alternative, an investor that prepares comprehensive constant dollar statements merely could restate the entries in the investment account as recorded in accordance with the equity method.

† Although classification of this item as nonmonetary may be technically preferable, the monetary classification provides a more practical solution for the purposes of constant dollar accounting.

Appendix B

Consumer Price Index—All Urban Consumers

For Additional Information Contact:

U.S. Department of Labor

Room 1539

Bureau of Labor Statistics

Washington, D.C. 20212

Consumer Price Index

(1967 = 100)

YEAR	JAN.	FEB.	MAR.	APR.	MAY	JUNE	JULY	AUG.	SEP.	OCT.	NOV.	DEC.	AVG.
1913	29.4	29.3	29.3	29.4	29.2	29.3	29.6	29.8	29.9	30.1	30.2	30.1	29.7
1914	30.1	29.8	29.7	29.4	29.6	29.8	30.1	30.5	30.6	30.4	30.5	30.4	30.1
1915	30.3	30.1	29.8	30.1	30.2	30.3	30.3	30.3	30.4	30.7	30.9	31.0	30.4
1916	31.3	31.3	31.6	31.9	32.0	32.4	32.4	32.8	33.4	33.8	34.4	34.6	32.7
1917	35.0	35.8	36.0	37.6	38.4	38.8	38.4	39.0	39.7	40.4	40.5	41.0	38.4
1918	41.8	42.2	42.0	42.5	43.3	44.1	45.2	46.0	47.1	47.9	48.7	49.4	45.1
1919	49.5	48.4	49.0	49.9	50.6	50.7	52.1	53.0	53.3	54.2	55.5	56.7	51.8
1920	57.8	58.5	59.1	60.8	61.8	62.7	62.3	60.7	60.0	59.7	59.3	58.0	60.0
1921	57.0	55.2	54.8	54.1	53.1	52.8	52.9	53.1	52.5	52.4	52.1	51.8	53.6
1922	50.7	50.6	50.0	50.0	50.0	50.1	50.2	49.7	49.8	50.1	50.3	50.5	50.2
1923	50.3	50.2	50.4	50.6	50.7	51.0	51.5	51.3	51.6	51.7	51.8	51.8	51.1
1924	51.7	51.5	51.2	51.0	51.0	51.0	51.1	51.0	51.2	51.4	51.6	51.7	51.2
1925	51.8	51.6	51.7	51.6	51.8	52.4	53.1	53.1	52.9	53.1	54.0	53.7	52.5
1926	53.7	53.5	53.2	53.7	53.4	53.0	52.5	52.2	52.5	52.7	52.9	52.9	53.0
1927	52.5	52.1	51.8	51.8	52.2	52.7	51.7	51.4	51.7	52.0	51.9	51.8	52.0
1928	51.7	51.2	51.2	51.3	51.6	51.2	51.2	51.3	51.7	51.6	51.5	51.3	51.3
1929	51.2	51.1	50.9	50.7	51.0	51.2	51.7	51.9	51.8	51.8	51.7	51.4	51.3
1930	51.2	51.0	50.7	51.0	50.7	50.4	49.7	49.4	49.7	49.4	49.0	48.3	50.0
1931	47.6	46.9	46.6	46.3	45.8	45.3	45.2	45.1	44.9	44.6	44.1	43.7	45.6
1932	42.8	42.2	42.0	41.7	41.1	40.8	40.8	40.3	40.1	39.8	39.6	39.2	40.9
1933	38.6	38.0	37.7	37.6	37.7	38.1	39.2	39.6	39.6	39.6	39.6	39.4	38.8
1934	39.6	39.9	39.9	39.8	39.9	40.0	40.0	40.1	40.7	40.4	40.3	40.2	40.1
1935	40.8	41.1	41.0	41.4	41.2	41.1	40.9	40.9	41.1	41.1	41.3	41.4	41.1
1936	41.4	41.2	41.0	41.0	41.0	41.4	41.6	41.9	42.0	41.9	41.9	41.9	41.5
1937	42.2	42.3	42.6	42.8	43.0	43.1	43.3	43.4	43.8	43.6	43.3	43.2	43.0
1938	42.6	42.2	42.2	42.4	42.2	42.2	42.3	42.2	42.2	42.0	41.9	42.0	42.2
1939	41.8	41.6	41.5	41.4	41.4	41.4	41.4	41.4	42.2	42.0	42.0	41.8	41.6
1940	41.7	42.0	41.9	41.9	42.0	42.1	42.0	41.9	42.0	42.0	42.0	42.2	42.0
1941	42.2	42.2	42.4	42.8	43.1	43.9	44.1	44.5	45.3	45.8	46.2	46.3	44.1
1942	46.9	47.3	47.9	48.2	48.7	48.8	49.0	49.3	49.4	49.9	50.2	50.6	48.8
1943	50.6	50.7	51.5	52.1	52.5	52.4	52.0	51.8	52.0	52.2	52.1	52.2	51.8
1944	52.1	52.0	52.0	52.3	52.5	52.6	52.9	53.1	53.1	53.1	53.1	53.3	52.7
1945	53.3	53.2	53.2	53.3	53.7	54.2	54.3	54.3	54.1	54.1	54.3	54.5	53.9
1946	54.5	54.3	54.7	55.0	55.3	55.9	59.2	60.5	61.2	62.4	63.9	64.4	58.5
1947	64.4	64.3	65.7	65.7	65.5	66.0	66.6	67.3	68.9	68.9	69.3	70.2	66.9
1948	71.0	70.4	70.2	71.2	71.7	72.2	73.1	73.4	73.4	73.1	72.6	72.1	72.1
1949	72.0	71.2	71.4	71.5	71.4	71.5	71.0	71.2	71.5	71.1	71.2	70.8	71.4
1950	70.5	70.3	70.6	70.7	71.0	71.4	72.1	72.7	73.2	73.6	73.9	74.9	72.1
1951	76.1	77.0	77.3	77.4	77.7	77.6	77.7	77.7	78.2	78.6	79.0	79.3	77.8
1952	79.3	78.8	78.8	79.1	79.2	79.4	80.0	80.1	80.0	80.1	80.1	80.0	79.5
1953	79.8	79.4	79.6	79.7	79.9	80.2	80.4	80.6	80.7	80.9	80.6	80.5	80.1
1954	80.7	80.6	80.5	80.3	80.6	80.7	80.7	80.6	80.4	80.2	80.3	80.1	80.5
1955	80.1	80.1	80.1	80.1	80.1	80.1	80.4	80.2	80.5	80.5	80.6	80.4	80.2
1956	80.3	80.3	80.4	80.5	80.9	81.4	82.0	81.9	82.0	82.5	82.5	82.7	81.4
1957	82.8	83.1	83.3	83.6	83.8	84.3	84.7	84.8	84.9	84.9	85.2	85.2	84.3
1958	85.7	85.8	86.4	86.6	86.6	86.7	86.8	86.7	86.7	86.7	86.8	86.7	86.6
1959	86.8	86.7	86.7	86.8	86.9	87.3	87.5	87.4	87.7	88.0	88.0	88.0	87.3
1960	87.9	88.0	88.0	88.5	88.5	88.7	88.7	88.7	88.8	89.2	89.3	89.3	88.7
1961	89.3	89.3	89.3	89.3	89.3	89.4	89.8	89.7	89.9	89.9	89.9	89.9	89.6
1962	89.9	90.1	90.3	90.5	90.5	90.5	90.7	90.7	91.2	91.1	91.1	91.0	90.6
1963	91.1	91.2	91.3	91.3	91.3	91.7	92.1	92.1	92.1	92.2	92.3	92.5	91.7
1964	92.6	92.5	92.6	92.7	92.7	92.9	93.1	93.0	93.2	93.3	93.5	93.6	92.9
1965	93.6	93.6	93.7	94.0	94.2	94.7	94.8	94.6	94.8	94.9	95.1	95.4	94.5
1966	95.4	96.0	96.3	96.7	96.8	97.1	97.4	97.9	98.1	98.5	98.5	98.6	97.2

(1967 = 100)

YEAR	JAN.	FEB.	MAR.	APR.	MAY	JUNE	JULY	AUG.	SEP.	OCT.	NOV.	DEC.	AVG.
1967	98.6	98.7	98.9	99.1	99.4	99.7	100.2	100.5	100.7	101.0	101.3	101.6	100.0
1968	102.0	102.3	102.8	103.1	103.4	104.0	104.5	104.8	105.1	105.7	106.1	106.4	104.2
1969	106.7	107.1	108.0	108.7	109.0	109.7	110.2	110.7	111.2	111.6	112.2	112.9	109.8
1970	113.3	113.9	114.5	115.2	115.7	116.3	116.7	116.9	117.5	118.1	118.5	119.1	116.3
1971	119.2	119.4	119.8	120.2	120.8	121.5	121.8	122.1	122.2	122.4	122.6	123.1	121.3
1972	123.2	123.8	124.0	124.3	124.7	125.0	125.5	125.7	126.2	126.6	126.9	127.3	125.3
1973	127.7	128.6	129.8	130.7	131.5	132.4	132.7	135.1	135.5	136.6	137.6	138.5	133.1
1974	139.7	141.5	143.1	143.9	145.5	146.9	148.0	149.9	151.7	153.0	154.3	155.4	147.7
1975	156.1	157.2	157.8	158.6	159.3	160.6	162.3	162.8	163.6	164.6	165.6	166.3	161.2
1976	166.7	167.1	167.5	168.2	169.2	170.1	171.1	171.9	172.6	173.3	173.8	174.3	170.5
1977	175.3	177.1	178.2	179.6	180.6	181.8	182.6	183.3	184.0	184.5	185.4	186.1	181.5
1978	187.2	188.4	189.8	191.5	193.3	195.3	196.7	197.8	199.3	200.9	202.0	202.9	195.4
1979	204.7	207.1	209.1	211.5	214.1	216.6	218.9	221.1	223.4	225.4	227.5	229.9	217.4

Topic 2

Investments

Detail Contents

APB Opinion No. 18 (March 1971)
The Equity Method of Accounting for Investments in Common Stock

Note: APB Opinion No. 18 does not apply to investments in common stock held by investment companies registered under the Investment Company Act of 1940 or by nonbusiness entities, such as estates, trusts and individuals.

Flowchart and General Discussion

Perhaps the most important decision the accountant must make to determine if APB Opinion No. 18 is applicable involves the computation of the percentage of ownership of the investor in the investee company's common stock. Exhibit I depicts the major points of Paragraph 17 of the Opinion. This paragraph will tell the reader if the other provisions of APB Opinion 18 are applicable.

As shown in Exhibit I, if the investor company owns 20 percent or more of the voting common stock of the investee company, the investment qualifies for equity method accounting. If the investor owns less than 20 percent interest, the equity treatment does not apply unless the investor can demonstrate the ability to exert "significant influence" over policies of the investee. (Significant influence may be indicated by membership on the board of directors, participation in policy making, intercompany transactions and others. See Paragraph 17 of the Opinion for a more complete discussion.)

The Flowchart of APB Opinion No. 18 also illustrates the percentage of ownership criteria, but goes on to show the general provisions of the Opinion that relate to accounting considerations. As shown in Blocks 1 and 2 of the Flowchart, if the investor company previously held an equity investment of less than 20 percent, but subsequently has increased its percentage ownership to more than 20 percent, a retroactive adjustment will be necessary before equity accounting treatment is begun. Naturally, if the percentage of ownership falls below 20 percent (and significant influence cannot be demonstrated), the investor would discontinue the equity accounting treatment (Blocks 5, 6 and 7).

When equity method accounting is found to be applicable, the investor company will recognize income from the investment as the income is earned by the investee. Likewise, losses from investee operations will be recognized, within certain limits, as such losses are incurred. Recognition of income or loss will be reflected as adjustments to the carrying value of the investment account. Recognized income will increase the carrying value, and losses will decrease the carrying value of the investment. One problem that is created by this treatment occurs when recognizable losses accumulate in an amount greater than the carrying value of the investment. This is likely to happen only in rare cases, and the proper accounting treatment is discussed below.

The amount of income or loss to be recognized by the investor company depends upon the percentage of ownership. The investor would multiply the percentage of ownership by the determined basis for income or loss recognition. As indicated in Note 2 to the Flowchart, this basis for income or loss recognition would be determined by starting with the investee's reported net income and subtracting any intercompany profits and cumulative preferred dividends. (These dividends would be deducted even if they had not been declared.) In the absence of intercompany transactions and cumulative preferred stock, the basis for income or loss recognition would be equal to reported income of the investee. The entry on the books of the investor company would be to increase its investment account and to credit an account entitled "Equity in Earnings of Investee Company." If the investee company reported ordinary income and extraordinary items, the investor would separate the two types of earnings, if the amounts were material to the investor.

The recognition of reported losses is somewhat more complex. Generally, the investor company can recognize its percentage share of reported losses so long as the total recognized losses do not exceed the carrying value of the investment. APB Opinion No. 18 allows the investor to reduce the investment value to zero, but special conditions must be met before further losses may be recognized. Once the investment has been written down to zero, the investor must discontinue the equity accounting treatment. After such a state is reached, the investor will not resume the

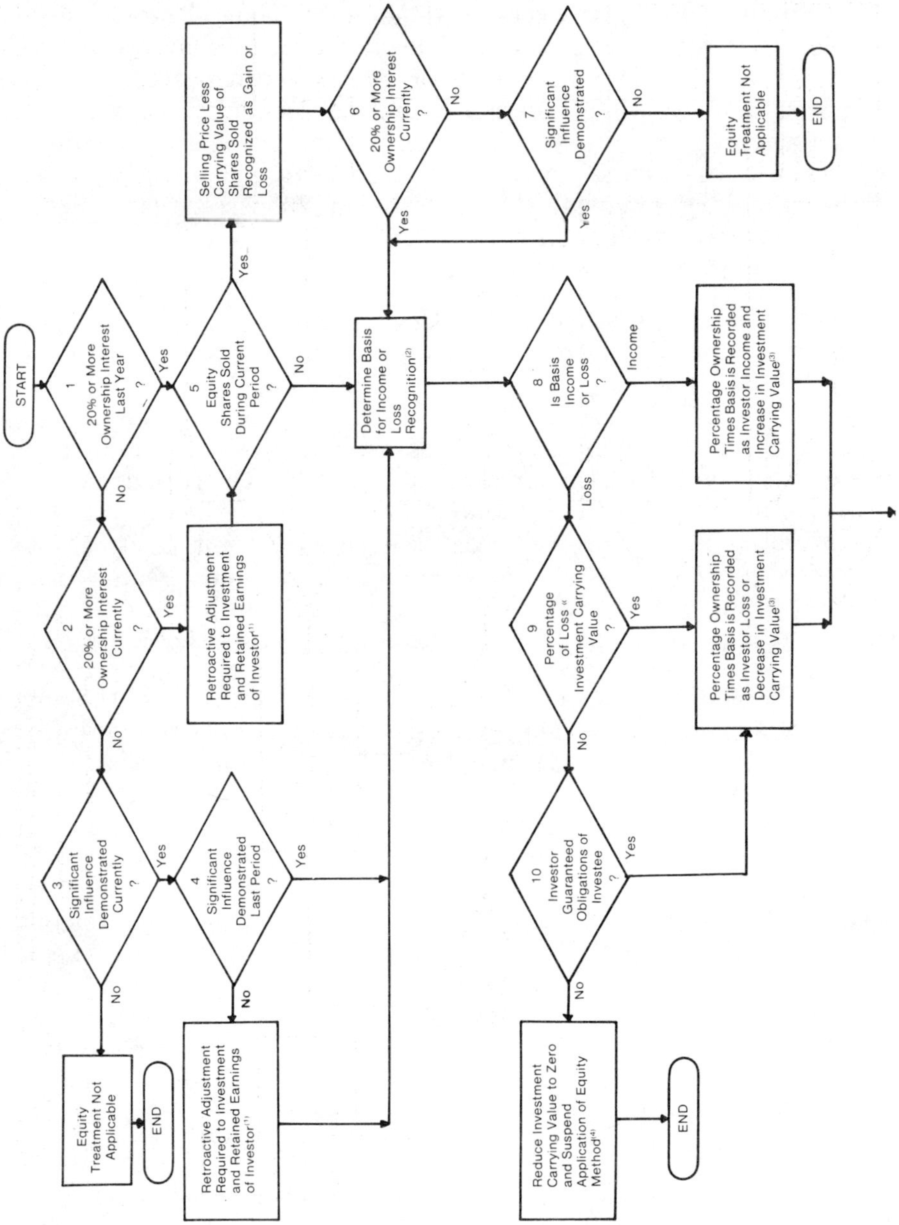
START
1 20% or More Ownership Interest Last Year ?
Yes
No
2 20% or More Ownership Interest Currently ?
Yes
No
Retroactive Adjustment Required to Investment and Retained Earnings of Investor(1)
3 Significant Influence Demonstrated Currently ?
Yes
No
Equity Treatment Not Applicable
END
4 Significant Influence Demonstrated Last Period ?
Yes
No
Retroactive Adjustment Required to Investment and Retained Earnings of Investor(1)
5 Equity Shares Sold During Current Period ?
Yes
No
Selling Price Less Carrying Value of Shares Sold Recognized as Gain or Loss
6 20% or More Ownership Interest Currently ?
Yes
No
7 Significant Influence Demonstrated ?
Yes
No
Equity Treatment Not Applicable
END
Determine Basis for Income or Loss Recognition(2)
8 Is Basis Income or Loss ?
Income
Loss
Percentage Ownership Times Basis is Recorded as Investor Income and Increase in Investment Carrying Value(3)
9 Percentage of Loss « Investment Carrying Value ?
Yes
No
Percentage Ownership Times Basis is Recorded as Investor Loss or Decrease in Investment Carrying Value(3)
10 Investor Guaranteed Obligations of Investee ?
Yes
No
Reduce Investment Carrying Value to Zero and Suspend Application of Equity Method(4)
END

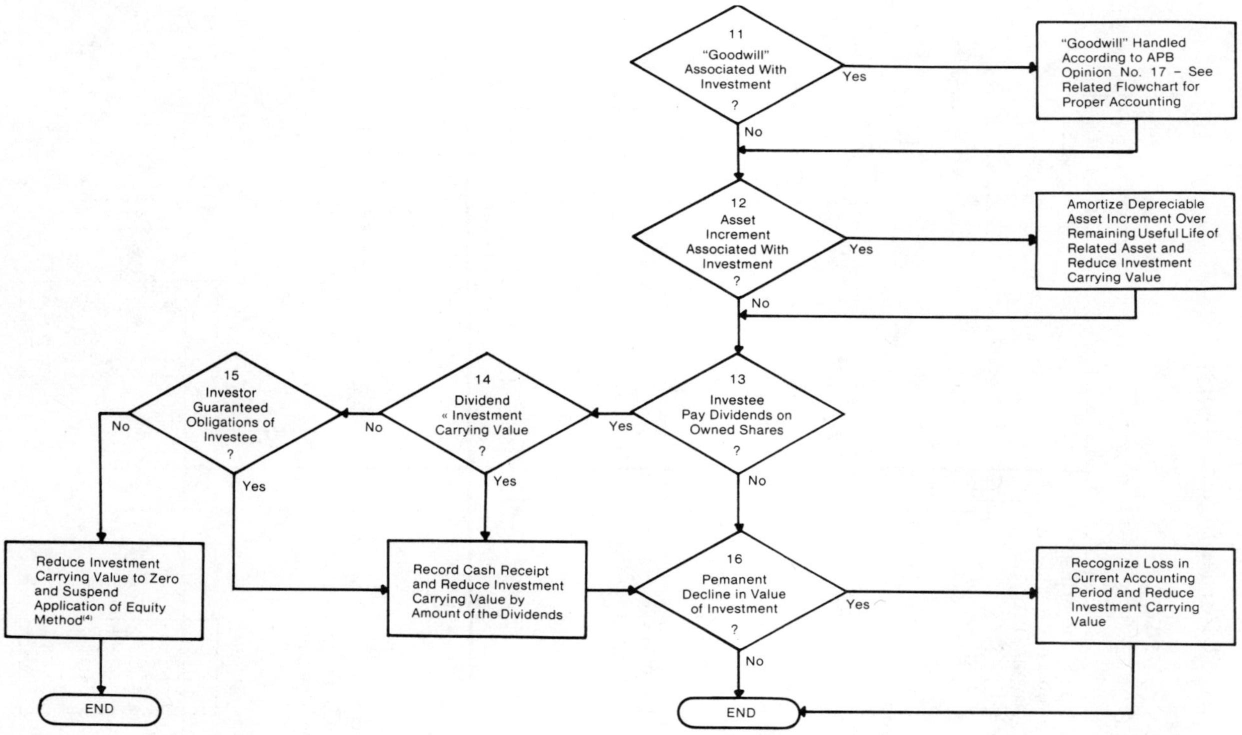

(1) Adjustment amount determined in a manner consistent with accounting for a step-by-step acquisition of a subsidiary.
(2) Basis for income recognition is equal to current investee income (loss) less any intercompany profits and less any cumulative preferred dividends.
(3) Extraordinary items and prior period adjustments are reported separately by investor if material.
(4) Subsequent losses will not be recorded. Subsequent income only recognized if it is in excess of accumulated losses.

Exhibit I

Percentage of Ownership

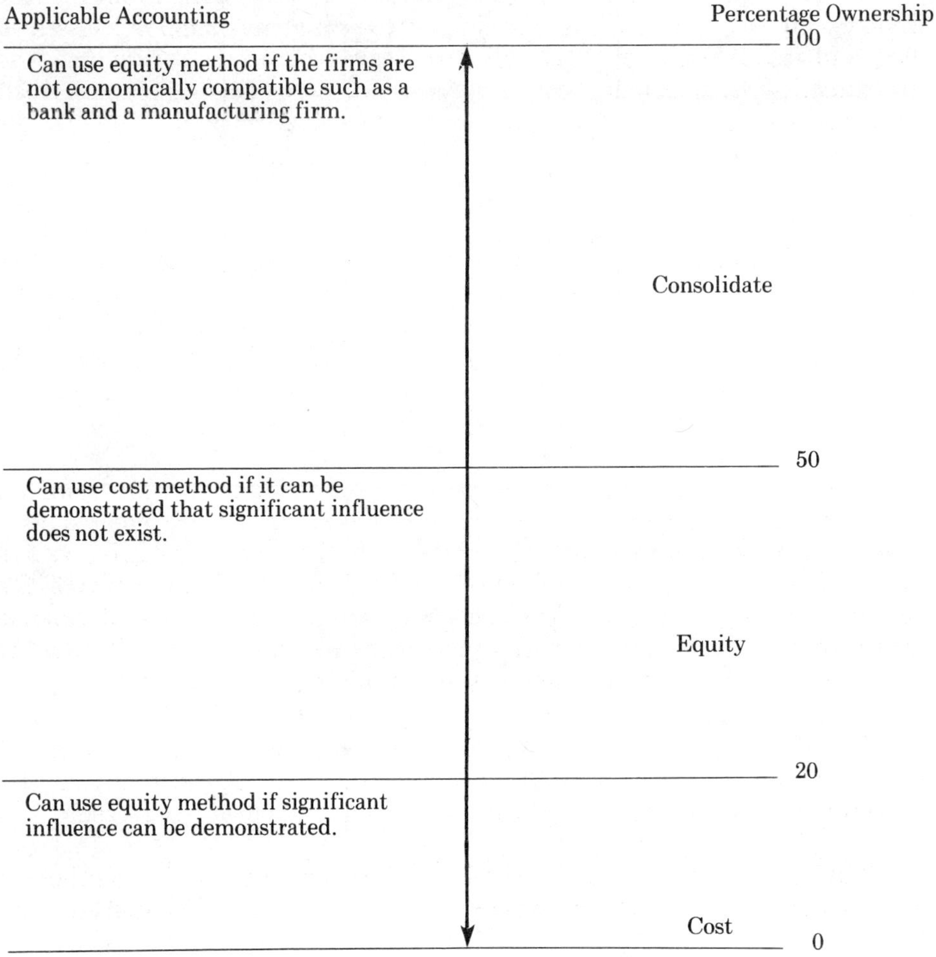
Applicable Accounting
Percentage Ownership
100
Can use equity method if the firms are not economically compatible such as a bank and a manufacturing firm.
Consolidate
50
Can use cost method if it can be demonstrated that significant influence does not exist.
Equity
20
Can use equity method if significant influence can be demonstrated.
Cost
0

equity treatment until its share of future income is equal to the share of losses that were not recognized. Therefore, the investor still must keep track of reported losses, even though such losses will not be recognized.

If the investor company has guaranteed any obligations of the investee or is committed to provide future financial support, losses in excess of investment carrying value may be recognized. In this case, the investment carrying value could become negative. The above described accounting procedures are shown in the Flowchart by the Blocks numbered 9 and 10.

The next major accounting problem shown on the Flowchart deals with the existence of "goodwill." Such an excess should be allocated to specific assets, allocated to assets and goodwill or allocated to goodwill. Subsequent to the allocation, the amount will be depreciated or amortized by charges to income. Any excess of book value over cost first should be assigned to non-current assets other than long-term marketable securities, and any unassigned excess should be amortized.

Under the equity method of accounting for investments in common stock, dividends received from the investee company are treated as a reduction in the investment value, rather than as income. Again, we are faced with the potential problem of receiving dividends in excess of the carrying value of the investment. If this were to happen, the dividends would be treated the same as the previously discussed losses. Flowchart Blocks 14 and 15 illustrate the accounting for dividends received.

The final accounting consideration relates to declines in the value of the investment. If a decline is determined to be permanent, the investment value should be reduced currently, and a loss recognized.

This general discussion of the Flowchart and the equity method of accounting should lay the foundation for the more detailed analysis that follows.

Technical Considerations of APB Opinion No. 18

From a technical accounting standpoint, Paragraph 19 of APB Opinion No. 18 provides the basic outline for applying the equity method. Because of its importance, Paragraph 19 is discussed in detail, with example material to illustrate the points made in each section of the paragraph. The reader is encouraged to make frequent references to the Flowchart in order that each technical consideration may be kept in perspective.

Paragraph 19a

Intercompany profits and losses should be eliminated until realized by the investor or investee as if a subsidiary, corporate joint venture or investee company were consolidated.

The treatment of unrealized intercompany profits and losses depends upon whether or not the transaction between the investor and investee is considered to be an "arm's length" transaction. Accounting Interpretation No. 1 of APB Opinion No. 18 states in Paragraph 3,

> When an investor controls an investee through majority voting interest and enters into a transaction with an investee which is not on an "arm's length" basis, none of the inter-company profit or loss from the transaction should be recognized in income by the investor until it has been realized through transactions with third parties.

In this particular case, any unrealized profits or losses would be eliminated in their entirety. To illustrate, assume Jar, Inc. holds a 75 percent ownership interest in the common shares of Book-It, Inc., an unconsolidated subsidiary. Assume that Jar, Inc. sold merchandise to Book-It, Inc. and recorded a gross profit of $50,000. It was determined that this was not an "arm's length" transaction. At the balance sheet date of Book-It, Inc., none of the merchandise purchased from Jar, Inc. had been sold. Therefore the entire $50,000 unrealized profit would be eliminated, and Book-It, Inc. would determine its net income on the basis of the new inventory cost.

Paragraph 4 of Accounting Interpretation No. 1 states,

> In other cases, it would be appropriate for the investor to eliminate intercompany profits in relation to the investor's common stock interest in the investee. In these cases, the percentage of intercompany profit to be eliminated would be the same regardless of whether the transaction is "downstream" (i.e., a sale by the investor to the investee) or "upstream" (i.e., a sale by the investee to the investor).

Therefore, where an "arm's length" transaction can be demonstrated between the investee and investor, only the proportional share of the unrealized profits or losses would be eliminated. Assume, for illustrative purposes, the same facts as above, except that Jar, Inc. holds a 25 percent (rather than 75 percent) ownership interest in Book-It, Inc. Ignoring income tax considerations, $12,500 of unrealized intercompany profits would be eliminated ($50,000 × .25 = $12,500). If we assume a 50 percent tax rate, the elimination would be calculated as follows:

Total unrealized profits	$50,000
Tax consequence of profits	25,000
After tax unrealized profits	$25,000
Proportionate share of profits (25%)	$ 6,250

In this case, the investor's net income would be reduced by $6,250. Had the sale been made "upstream," the investee would have reduced income by $25,000 and thereby reduced the investor's equity interest by $6,250 (25 percent of $25,000).

Paragraph 19b

A difference between the cost of an investment and the amount of underlying equity in net assets of an investee should be accounted for as if the investee were consolidated.

Assuming excess of cost over equity, the difference should be accounted for in one of the following manners:

(1) Allocated to specific assets, or

(2) Allocated to both assets and goodwill, or

(3) Allocated to goodwill.

To illustrate the application of Paragraph 19b, assume the following example: On January 1, 197A, Jar, Inc. purchased 1,000 shares (25 percent) of the 4,000 shares of Book-It, Inc. for $400,000 cash. The relevant values of Book-It, Inc., at acquisition date, are shown in Table I.

Table I

	Book Value	Fair Value
Nondepreciable assets	$ 400,000	$ 600,000
Depreciable assets (20 year life straight-line depreciation)	900,000	1,500,000
Total	$1,300,000	$2,100,000
Liabilities	$ 500,000	$ 500,000
Stockholders' equity	800,000	
Total	$1,300,000	

Situation 1—Allocation of Excess to Specific Assets

Cost of investment	$ 400,000
Book value of net assets purchased (25% × ($1,300,000 - $500,000))	200,000
Excess of cost over book value	$ 200,000

Asset Readjustment:

Allocated to nondepreciable assets: $600,000 fair value - $400,000 book value = $200,000 × 25% ownership	(50,000)
Allocated to depreciable assets: $1,500,000 fair value - $900,000 book value × 25% ownership	(150,000)
Unassigned excess	$ 0

Situation 2—Allocation of Excess to Both Assets and Goodwill

Assume the same information as in Situation 1 except the fair values of Book-It, Inc. were:

Nondepreciable assets	$ 500,000
Depreciable assets	1,200,000
Total	$1,700,000

The allocation would be made as follows:

Cost of investment	$ 400,000
Book value of net assets purchased (25% × $1,300,000 − $500,000)	200,000
Excess of cost over book value	$ 200,000

Asset Readjustment:

Allocated to nondepreciable assets: ($500,000 − $400,000 = $100,000 × 25%)	(25,000)
Allocated to depreciable assets: ($1,200,000 − $900,000 = $300,000 × 25%)	(75,000)
Unallocated excess = goodwill	$100,000

Situation 3—Allocation to Goodwill

Assume the same facts as in Situation 1, except that fair value is equal to book value at date of acquisition. The allocation would be made as follows:

Cost of investment	$400,000
Book value of net assets purchased (25% × $1,300,000 − $500,000)	200,000
Excess of cost over book value or goodwill	$200,000

The journal entries needed to record the purchase and subsequent amortization under each of the three situations are reflected in Table II, below. Note that goodwill is amortized in accordance with APB Opinion No. 17 (over the period benefited, not to exceed 40 years).

The only difference in the journal entries presented below is in the amount of amortization periodically charged against income. The difference in the amortization amounts is due to the different amortization periods effective under each situation.

The examples reflect the fact that the investment account contains elements other than the book value of assets purchased. Therefore, the investor is required to keep a record of the different elements in order properly to expense each item in the appropriate accounting period.

Table II

	Situation 1		Situation 2		Situation 3	
Purchase[a]						
Investment in Book-It, Inc.: Common Stock	400,000		400,000		400,000	
Cash		400,000		400,000		400,000
Amortization						
Equity in Earnings of Book-It, Inc., (Ordinary)	[b]7,500		[c]6,250		[d]5,000	
Investment in Book-It, Inc., Common Stock		7,500		6,250		5,000

[a] Note that the allocation process has no effect on the entry to record the investment.
[b] Allocated to depreciable assets \$150,000/20 year useful life = \$7,500.
[c] Depreciable assets \$ 75,000/20 year useful life = \$3,750
Goodwill \$100,000/40 years = 2,500
\$6,250

[d] Goodwill \$200,000/40 years = \$5,000

The various elements shown in Situation 2 may be reflected in a T-account as follows:

Investment in Book-It, Inc., Common Stock

Purchased Book Value	200,000	
Nondepreciable Asset Increment	25,000	
Depreciable Asset Increment	75,000	
Goodwill	100,000	
Total	400,000	

A problem arises when the investor has allocated a portion of the excess of cost over book value to assets that later are sold by the investee. The investor must adjust his share of the *unamortized* increment previously reflected in the investment account. To illustrate, assume the nondepreciable and depreciable assets as reflected in Situation 1 (allocation of \$50,000 to nondepreciable, and \$150,000 to depreciable, assets), above, are sold for a gain of \$400,000 and a loss of \$200,000, respectively, after the investment has been owned for two years. The investor's share of the gain or loss would be reflected in the investment account as shown in Table III, below:

Table III

ALLOCATION TO ASSETS

	Nondepreciable		Depreciable	
Investor's share of investee gain or (loss)—25%		$100,000		$ (50,000)
Asset increment	$50,000		$150,000	
Amortization (2 years)	0		[a](15,000)	
Unamortized increment		50,000		135,000
Gain or (loss) reported by investor		$ 50,000		$(185,000)

[a] $150,000/20 years: $7,500 × 2 = $15,000

Situations 1, 2 and 3 are concerned with instances when cost exceeds the fair value of the net assets purchased. If the fair value of the net assets purchased exceeds the cost, "negative goodwill" exists. This excess is used to reduce the long-term assets other than long-term marketable securities. If the long-term assets are reduced to zero, the remaining portion of the "negative goodwill" is a deferred credit and is amortized over the period benefited, not to exceed 40 years in accordance with APB Opinion No. 17.

Paragraphs 19c and 19d

The investment(s) in common stock should be shown in the balance sheet of an investor as a single amount, and the investor's share of earnings or losses of an investee(s) should ordinarily be shown in the income statement as a single amount except the investor's share of extraordinary items and its share of prior-period adjustments reported in the financial statements of the investee in accordance with APB Opinion No. 9 (now APB Opinion No. 30 and SFAS No. 16) should be classified in a similar manner unless they are immaterial in the income statement of the investor.

APB Opinion No. 30 greatly expanded income statement presentations by requiring disclosure of disposal of segments of businesses, in addition to the extraordinary items. APB Opinion No. 20 requires disclosure of the cumulative effect of accounting changes in the income statement as a separate line item. To illustrate Paragraphs 19c and 19d, as amended by APB Opinion Nos. 20 and 30 and SFAS No. 16, assume that Jar, Inc. purchased 1,000 shares (25 percent) of the 4,000 shares of Book-It, Inc. for $400,000 on January 1, 197A. During 197A, Jar, Inc.'s income from continuing operations was $500,000. The tax rate is 50 percent. Book-It, Inc.'s income statement is reflected below:

Income from continuing operations (after taxes)		$200,000
Discontinued operations		
Income (loss) from operations of discontinued segment (net of tax)	$(20,000)	
Loss on disposal of segment, including provision for operating losses during phase-out period (net of tax)	(10,000)	(30,000)
Income before extraordinary items and cumulative effect of accounting change		$170,000
Extraordinary Items:		
Loss due to expropriation of plant (net of tax)		(40,000)
Income before accounting change		$130,000
Cumulative effect of change in accounting principle		30,000
Net Income		$160,000

Jar, Inc.'s income statement would be constructed as illustrated below:

Jar, Inc.
Income Statement
For the Year Ended December 31, 197A

Income before nonoperating items	$500,000	
Nonoperating items:		
Equity in continuing operations of Book-It, Inc. ($200,000 × .25)	50,000	
Income from continuing operations before tax	$550,000	
Provision for income tax	275,000	
Income from continuing operations		$275,000
Discontinued operations:		
Equity in earnings (loss) of discontinued segment of Book-It, Inc. (less income taxes of $375) [a]	(4,625)	
Equity in loss on disposal of discontinued segment of Book-It, Inc. (less taxes of $188)	(2,312)	(6,937)
Income before extraordinary items and accounting changes		$268,063
Extraordinary Items:		
Equity in loss due to expropriation of plant of Book-It, Inc. (net of tax of $750)		(9,250)
Income before accounting changes		$258,813
Accounting Changes:		
Equity in cumulative effect of a change in accounting principle of Book-It, Inc. (net of tax of $563)		6,937
Net Income		$265,750

[a] $20,000 × 25% (ownership) = $5,000 × 85% (dividend deduction) = $4,250.
$5,000 − $4,250 = $750 subject to income tax.
$750 × 50% = $375.

For an in depth study of taxes on undistributed earnings of investee companies, see Topic 5 on income tax allocation. Topic 7, on earnings per share, illustrates the proper per share disclosure of the above amounts.

Subparagraphs e, f, g and h of Paragraph 19 have not been covered because they are self-explanatory and do not present any new or complex subject matter. See the text of the Opinion for these subparagraphs.

Paragraph 19i

An investor's share of losses of an investee may equal or exceed the carrying amount of an investment accounted for by the equity method plus advances made by the investor. The investor ordinarily should discontinue applying the equity method when the investment (and net advances) is reduced to zero and should not provide for additional losses unless the investor has guaranteed obligations of the investee or is otherwise committed to provide further financial support for the investee. If the investee subsequently reports net income, the investor should resume applying the equity method only after its share of that net income equals the share of net losses not recognized during the period the equity method was suspended.

To illustrate this paragraph, assume that on January 1, 197A, Jar, Inc. purchased 1,000 shares (25 percent) of the outstanding voting common stock of Book-It, Inc. for $400,000—which is $100,000 in excess of the book value of Book-It's net assets. The $100,000 can be related to specific depreciable assets with a remaining useful life of 20 years. Book-It uses straight-line depreciation for all assets. The results of operations for Book-It for the years 197A through 197G are reflected in Table IV.

Table IV

	Net Income (Loss)
197A	$ (500,000)
197B	(1,100,000)
197C	(500,000)
197D	200,000
197E	400,000
197F	600,000
197G	800,000

Assuming that Jar, Inc. has guaranteed obligations of Book-It, Inc., the investment account, equity in earnings of investee and supporting calculations are reflected in Table V.

Assuming that the investor *has not* guaranteed obligations of the investee or otherwise *is not* committed to provide further financial support for the investee, the investor should discontinue applying the equity method when the investment and net advances are reduced to zero. The investor should not resume the equity method until the investor's share of investee earnings, subsequent to the date the investment is reduced to zero, is equal to the losses not recognized during the period the equity method was suspended. This is illustrated in Table VI.

The following computation relative to Table VI illustrates the cumulative loss that must be recovered after Book-It, Inc. earns net income again in year 197D and also reflects the year in which Jar, Inc. would resume applying the equity method.

Investment	$ 400,000
197A operating loss	(125,000)
197B operating loss	(275,000)
197C operating loss	(125,000)
Asset increment	(100,000)
Loss to be recovered from future earnings before equity method resumed	$(225,000)
197D operating income	50,000
197E operating income	100,000
Unrecovered loss 1/1/197F	$ (75,000)
197F operating income	150,000
Operating income in excess of accumulated losses	[a]$ 75,000

[a] Resume equity method in year 197F.

Subparagraph j of Paragraph 19, relative to income tax allocation, has been superseded by APB Opinion Nos. 23 and 24, and will be discussed in detail in Topic 5.

Paragraph 19k

When an investee has outstanding cumulative preferred stock, an investor should compute its share of earnings (losses) after deducting the investee's preferred dividends, whether or not such dividends are declared.

To illustrate this paragraph, assume that Jar, Inc. purchased 1,000 shares (25 percent) of the 4,000 outstanding shares of Book-It, Inc. for $400,000, on January 1, 197A. During 197A and 197B, Book-It, Inc. had earnings (losses) of $400,000 and ($200,000) respectively. No dividends were declared in 197A or 197B. A partial stockholders' equity section for Book-It appears as follows:

Preferred stock ($200 par, cumulative, 8%, 1,000 shares)	$200,000
Common stock ($100 par, 4,000 shares outstanding)	400,000

Table VII reflects Jar, Inc.'s share of Book-It's earnings after considering preferred dividends.

Table V

	January 1 197A	197A	197B	197C	197D	197E	197F	197G
Beginning Investment Balance	$400,000	$400,000	$270,000	($10,000)	($140,000)	($95,000)	0	$145,000
Equity in Earnings of Book-It, Inc.		(125,000)	(275,000)	(125,000)	50,000	100,000	150,000	200,000
Amortization of Asset Increment		(5,000)	(5,000)	(5,000)	(5,000)	(5,000)	(5,000)	(5,000)
Income (loss) Recognized		(130,000)	(280,000)	(130,000)	45,000	95,000	145,000	195,000
Ending Investment Balance		$270,000	$(10,000)	(140,000)	(95,000)	0	145,000	340,000
Remaining Book Value Purchased	$300,000	$175,000	(100,000)	(225,000)	(175,000)	(75,000)	75,000	275,000
Asset Increment	100,000	95,000	90,000	85,000	80,000	75,000	70,000	65,000
Total Investment	$400,000	$270,000	$(10,000)	$(140,000)	$(95,000)	0	$145,000	$340,000

Year	Income (Loss)		% of Ownership		Investor Share of Earnings
197A	$ (500,000)	X	25	=	$(125,000)
197B	(1,100,000)	X	25	=	(275,000)
197C	(500,000)	X	25	=	(125,000)
197D	200,000	X	25	=	50,000
197E	400,000	X	25	=	100,000
197F	600,000	X	25	=	150,000
197G	800,000	X	25	=	200,000

The asset increment would be amortized at the rate of $5,000 per year ($100,000/20 years = $5,000).

Table VI

	January 1 197A	197A	197B	197C	197D	197E	197F	197G
Beginning Investment Balance	$400,000	$400,000	$270,000	0	0	0	0	$ 75,000
Equity in Earnings of Book-It, Inc.		(125,000)	(175,000)	0	0	0	75,000	200,000
Amortization of Asset Increment		(5,000)	(95,000)	0	0	0	0	0
Income (loss) Recognized		(130,000)	(270,000)	0	0	0	0	0
Ending Investment Balance		$270,000	0	0	0	0	$ 75,000	$275,000
Remaining Book Value Purchased	$300,000	$175,000	0	0	0	0	$ 75,000	$275,000
Asset Increment	100,000	95,000	0	0	0	0	0	0
Total Investment	$400,000	$270,000	0	0	0	0	$ 75,000	$275,000

Year	Income (Loss)		% of Ownership		Investor Share of Earnings
197A	$ (500,000)	X	25	=	$(125,000)
197B	(1,100,000)	X	25	=	(275,000)
197C	(500,000)	X	25	=	(125,000)
197D	200,000	X	25	=	50,000
197E	400,000	X	25	=	100,000
197F	600,000	X	25	=	150,000
197G	800,000	X	25	=	200,000

The asset increment would be amortized at the rate of $5,000 per year ($100,000/20 years = $5,000).

Table VII

Year	Income (Loss)	Preferred Dividends	Income (Loss) After Preferred Dividends	% of Ownership	Jar, Inc.'s Share of Book-It's Income (Loss) After Preferred Dividends
197A	$ 400,000	[a]$16,000	$ 384,000	25	[b]$ 96,000
197B	$(200,000)	16,000	(216,000)	25	(54,000)

[a] $200 par × .08 = $16 × 1,000 shares = $16,000
[b] Consideration must be given to preferred dividends whether declared or not.

Therefore, Jar, Inc., after considering the preferred dividends, would report earnings of $96,000 in 197A, instead of $100,000 ($400,000 × 25%), and would report a loss of $54,000 in 197B, instead of $50,000 ($200,000 × 25%).

Paragraph 19l

An investment in voting stock of an investee company may fall below the level of ownership described in paragraph 17 ... and the investor may thereby lose the ability to influence policy, as described in that paragraph. An investor should discontinue accruing its share of the earnings or losses of the investee for an investment that no longer qualifies for the equity method. . . . The investment account should not be adjusted retroactively under the conditions described in this subparagraph. However, dividends received by the investor in subsequent periods which exceed his share of earnings for such periods should be applied in reduction of the carrying amount of the investment.

Once the investor's ownership interest falls below 20 percent, or if it is determined that significant influence is not exerted, the investor must discontinue application of the equity method and start applying the cost method. A change from the equity method to the cost method is illustrated by the following example. Assume that Jar, Inc. purchased 1,000 shares (25 percent) of the 4,000 outstanding shares of Book-It common stock for $400,000 on January 1, 197A. The purchase price was $100,000 in excess of the fair value of the net assets at that date. The $100,000 "goodwill" is to be amortized over a 40-year period, because the period to be benefited cannot be determined. Table VIII reflects the operations of Book-It, Inc. for the years 197A through 197F. Assume that, on January 1, 197C, Book-It, Inc. sold 2,667 shares of common stock to other companies, thereby reducing the ownership interest of Jar, Inc. from 25 percent to 15 percent. This sale would require a switch from the equity to the cost method for Jar, Inc. The income recognized by Jar, Inc., and the balance in the investment account, are shown in Table IX.

Table VIII

Year	Income (Loss)	Dividends
197A	$100,000	$ 70,000
197B	200,000	150,000
197C	75,000	60,000

Year	Income (Loss)	Dividends
197D	15,000	20,000
197E	(20,000)	10,000
197F	(10,000)	5,000

Table IX

Year	Income Recognized by Jar, Inc.	Dividends Recognized by Jar, Inc.	Goodwill Amortization	Investment Account Balance
Jan. 1				
197A	0	0	0	$400,000
197A	[a]$ 25,000	[b]$ 17,500	[c]$ 2,500	405,000
197B	50,000	37,500	2,500	415,000
197C	[d]11,250	9,000	0	415,000
197D	2,250	3,000	0	[e]415,000
197E	(3,000)	1,500	0	413,500
197F	(1,500)	750	0	412,750

[a] $100,000 × 25% = $25,000
[b] $70,000 × 25% = $17,500
[c] $100,000/40 years = $2,500
[d] Percentage ownership is now 15%
[e] No change in investment account because the change was made January 1, 197C to the cost method and cumulative earnings exceed cumulative dividends.

It is necessary for the investor to keep a record of the cumulative earnings and cumulative dividends from the time of change from the equity to the cost method, because the investor must reduce the investment account by the amount that the cumulative dividends exceed the cumulative earnings from the time of the change. However, the amount of the reduction is limited to the *dividends paid* in the year that the cumulative dividends exceed cumulative earnings. This is illustrated by Table X, which also provides support for the investment account balance for years 197E and 197F.

The year 197E is the first year in which cumulative dividends exceed cumulative earnings. The excess of cumulative dividends over cumulative earnings since the change from equity to cost is $3,000, but the investment reduction is only $1,500—the amount of the dividends received in 197E. The reduction in the investment account is treated in a prospective manner, i.e., the account is reduced in current and future periods, but limited only to the amount of dividends paid in those periods.

Table X

Jar, Inc.'s Share of Cumulative Earnings and Dividends of Book-It, Inc. from 197C-197F and Investment Reduction

Year	Earnings	Cumulative Earnings	Dividends	Cumulative Dividends	Excess of Cumulative Dividends Over Cumulative Earnings	Investment Reduction	Excess of Cumulative Dividends Over Cumulative Earnings After Investment Reduction
197C	$11,250	$11,250	$ 9,000	$ 9,000	0	0	0
197D	2,250	13,500	3,000	12,000	0	0	0
197E	(3,000)	10,500	1,500	13,500	$ 3,000	[a]$ 1,500	$ 1,500
197F	(1,500)	9,000	750	14,250	5,250	750	3,000

[a] Investment reduction is limited to dividends received.

Paragraph 19m

An investment in common stock of an investee that was previously accounted for on other than the equity method may become qualified for use of the equity method by an increase in the level of ownership. ... The investment, results of operations (current and prior periods presented), and retained earnings of the investor should be adjusted retroactively in a manner consistent with the accounting for a step-by-step acquisition of a subsidiary.

Paragraph 19n

The carrying amount of an investment in common stock of an investee that qualifies for the equity method of accounting as described in subparagraph (m) may differ from the underlying equity in net assets of the investee. ... If the investor is unable to relate the difference to specific accounts of the investee, the difference should be considered to be goodwill and amortized over a period not to exceed forty years, in accordance with APB Opinion No. 17.

To show the impact of these two paragraphs, assume that on January 1, 197A, Jar, Inc. purchased 600 shares (15 percent) of the outstanding common shares of Book-It, Inc. for $240,000. The fair value of the net assets purchased (15 percent) on this date was $180,000. In addition, Jar, Inc. was able to purchase an additional 400 shares (10 percent) of the common shares outstanding on January 1, 197C, for $160,000. The fair value of the net assets purchased (10 percent) was $120,000 at the date of acquisition. Book-It's earnings and dividends for the years 197A through 197D are shown in Table XI.

Table XI

BOOK-IT'S

Year	**Earnings**	**Dividends**
197A	$100,000	$40,000
197B	150,000	50,000
197C	100,000	40,000
197D	175,000	60,000

Based upon the information in Table XI, the following journal entries would be required.

Jan. 1, 197A	Investment in Common Stock of Book-It, Inc.	240,000	
	Cash		240,000
	Purchase of 600 shares (15%) of Book-It common stock		
Dec. 31, 197A	Cash	6,000	
	Dividend Revenue		6,000
	To record Jar, Inc.'s share of 197A dividends ($40,000 × 15%)		

Dec. 31, 197B	Cash	7,500	
	Dividend Revenue		7,500
	Jar, Inc.'s share of 197B dividend ($50,000 × 15%)		
Jan. 1, 197C	Investment in Common Stock of Book-It, Inc.	160,000	
	Cash		160,000
	Purchase of 400 shares (10%) of Book-It common stock		
Jan. 1, 197C	Investment in Common Stock of Book-It, Inc.	21,000	
	Prior Period Adjustment-Change From Cost to Equity Method of Accounting		21,000
	To record change from cost to equity method		

1 Year	2 Jar, Inc.'s Share of Earnings	3 Jar, Inc.'s Share of Dividends	4 Goodwill Amortization	(1-2-3) Addition to Retained Earnings and the Investment Account
197A	[a]$15,000	[b]$ 6,000	[c]$1,500	$ 7,500
197B	22,500	7,500	1,500	13,500
	$37,500	$13,500	$3,000	$21,000

Cash			10,000	
Dec. 31, 197C Investment in Common Stock of Book-It, Inc.			12,500	
Equity in Earnings of Book-It, Inc.				22,500
To record Jar, Inc.'s share of earnings for 197C				
Earnings		$25,000	($100,000 × 25%)	
Dividends	$10,000		($ 40,000 × 25%)	
Amortization of goodwill		(2,500)		
	$10,000	$22,500		
$60,000/40 years =		$ 1,500		
$160,000-$120,000 = $40,000/40 years =		1,000		
		$ 2,500		

Cash			15,000	
Dec. 31, 197D Investment in Common Stock of Book-It, Inc.			26,250	
Equity in Earnings of Book-It, Inc.				41,250
To record Jar, Inc.'s share of earnings for 197D				
Earnings		$43,750	($175,000 × 25%)	
Dividends	$15,000		($ 60,000 × 25%)	
Amortization of goodwill		(2,500)		
	$15,000	$41,250		

[a] $100,000 × 15% = $15,000
[b] $40,000 × 15% = $6,000
[c] $240,000 − $180,000 = $60,000/40 years = $1,500

This completes the discussion of the major provisions of Paragraph 19. Paragraph 20 of the Opinion identifies the disclosure requirements for investments carried on the equity method. The disclosure required can be divided into four major categories as follows:

(1) The investor should disclose the name, percentage ownership, accounting policy and any difference between investment carrying value and the equity in the net assets of the investee for each investment accounted for under the equity method.

(2) For investments, other than subsidiaries, where a market price is available, the aggregate value of each investment should be shown.

(3) For unconsolidated subsidiaries and other investments of less than 50 percent ownership interest, the investor should supply summary information concerning the investee's assets, liabilities and results of operations, if material. This information should be presented in the notes to the financial statements.

(4) Any material effects of possible conversion of convertible securities, exercise of options, and warrants or any other contingent issuances of an investee should be disclosed in the notes to the financial statements.

The Notes to the Financial Statements relative to investments of Kaiser Industries Corporation are shown in Exhibit II, and show the disclosure offered for the years 1973 and 1974.

Exhibit II

Kaiser Industries Corporation (Dec)

Consolidated Balance Sheets

	1974	1973
	(thousands of dollars)	
Investments	$401,913	$355,110
Consolidated Statements of Net Earnings		
Earnings from continuing operations before equity in earnings of unconsolidated companies, minority interest and extraordinary items	$ 16,443	$ 44,163
Equity in earnings of unconsolidated companies, less taxes of $6,816 and $3,981	47,521	28,825
Earnings from continuing operations before minority interest and extraordinary items	$ 63,964	$ 72,988

Financial Review

Summary of Significant Accounting Policies

Principles of Consolidation—The accompanying consolidated financial statements include the accounts of Kaiser Industries Corporation and its majority owned subsidiaries, principally 58 percent owned Kaiser Steel Corporation and its consolidated subsidiaries (principally Kaiser Resources Ltd., a Canadian corporation 59 percent owned by Kaiser Steel). Intercompany transactions and accounts and minority interest in net earnings have been eliminated. Investments in less-than-majority-owned Kaiser Aluminum & Chemical Corporation, Kaiser Cement & Gypsum Corporation, Hamersley Holdings Limited, National Steel and

	—Ownership—		—December 31, 1974—			—December 31, 1973—		
	Number of Shares	Percent of Outstanding Shares	Carrying Value	Quoted Market Value	Market Value Over (Under) Carrying Value	Carrying Value	Quoted Market Value	Market Value Over (Under) Carrying Value
Kaiser Aluminum	7,336,952	38%	$255,577	$ 92,629	$(162,948)	$222,838	$145,822	$(77,016)
Kaiser Cement:								
Common	2,257,113	37	31,569	11,003	(20,566)	30,673	18,339	(12,334)
Preferred	50,000	19	2,601	1,050	(1,551)	2,601	1,413	(1,188)
Hamersley (owned by Kaiser Steel)	68,679,750	28	73,800	131,178	57,378	71,830	117,442	45,612
			363,547	$235,860	$(127,687)	327,942	$283,016	$(44,926)
National Steel and Shipbuilding		50	16,400			6,492		
Other companies			21,966			20,676		
Total			$401,913			$355,110		

The market value of Kaiser Aluminum and Kaiser Cement is based on the closing price on the New York Stock Exchange as of December 31. The market value of Hamersley is based on the closing price on the Melbourne Stock Exchange on December 31 converted to U.S. dollars at the December 31 rate of exchange. No public market exists for the shares of National Steel and Shipbuilding or the other companies.

Shipbuilding Company and certain other companies are accounted for by the equity method. Accordingly the accompanying consolidated financial statements include the Corporation's share of undistributed earnings and other capital changes of these companies.

Investments (thousands of dollars)

Under the equity method of accounting, the carrying value of these investments, shown in the above table, has been adjusted to include the Corporation's cumulative share of undistributed earnings or losses and other capital changes of each company but does not reflect fluctuations in the market value of the holdings.

The market value of the parent company's 58 percent holdings of Kaiser Steel common stock of $83,583,000 and $62,441,000 (based on closing bid prices in the over-the-counter market) was less than the carrying value by $128,255,000 and $115,002,000 at December 31, 1974 and 1973, respectively.

As noted previously, in May 1973, Kaiser Steel sold 15 million of its Hamersley shares reducing its ownership from 34 percent to 28 percent. Conzinc Riotinto of Australia Limited owns 54 percent of Hamersley's stock.

The aggregate market value of the above investments, including Kaiser Steel, fluctuates and might not be realizable upon sale at any particular time. At December 31, 1974, the total market value of the parent company's holdings in Kaiser Aluminum, Kaiser Steel and Kaiser Cement exceeded the aggregate tax basis of those holdings by approximately $143,000,000.

Summary financial information for the principal unconsolidated companies which are accounted for by the equity method follows:

	Kaiser Aluminum		Kaiser Cement		Hamersley		National Steel and Shipbuilding	
	1974	1973	1974	1973	1974	1973	1974	1973
				(thousands of dollars)				
Balance Sheets—December 31								
Current assets	$ 799,417	$ 617,680	$ 75,709	$ 63,161	$ 97,967	$134,650	$ 41,074	$ 32,244
Investments	396,567	391,737	22,762	16,349	366	366	—	—
Property, plant and equipment —net	832,656	787,912	129,380	123,193	640,948	628,745	23,049	17,147
Other assets	28,711	16,837	3,588	2,527	49,964	45,898	—	—
	$2,057,351	$1,814,166	$231,439	$205,230	$789,245	$809,659	$ 64,123	$ 49,391
Current liabilities	$ 452,210	$ 394,124	$ 31,303	$ 28,934	$ 81,859	$ 72,490	$ 25,324	$ 36,408
Long-term debt	709,110	626,131	80,177	60,464	300,906	355,710	21,000	—
Deferred income taxes	146,000	127,900	16,101	14,592	150,891	132,746	—	—
Stockholders' equity	750,031	666,011	103,858	101,240	255,589	248,713	17,799	12,983
	$2,057,351	$1,814,166	$231,439	$205,230	$789,245	$809,659	$ 64,123	$ 49,391
Retained earnings free for dividends under the most restrictive financing covenant	$ 82,000		$ 5,100		$ 15,900		none	
Results of Operations for the Year Ended December 31								
Sales and operating revenues	$1,735,501	$1,280,731	$193,101	$169,725	$317,732	$245,753	$182,683	$119,730
Earnings before interest and taxes	235,658	124,459	14,664	18,666	77,550	69,954	10,774	13,205
Interest	60,310	55,821	6,110	4,726	28,018	30,361	699	—
Income taxes	71,000	24,100	869	4,208	18,356	15,898	5,259	6,619
Net earnings	104,348	44,538	7,685	9,732	31,176	23,695	4,816	6,586

Net earnings of Kaiser Aluminum in 1973 include a net gain of $5,700,000 on the sale of its interest in a Japanese aluminum fabricating firm and equity of $2,590,000 in 50 percent owned United International Shipping Corporation's net gain on sale of two ships.

At December 31, 1974, Hamersley had deferred $26,111,000 in losses resulting from exchange rate fluctuations. These losses will be charged to earnings as Hamersley's long-term debt is repaid.

Of National Steel and Shipbuilding's 1974 long-term debt, $7,500,000 was owed to Kaiser Industries and $7,500,000 to the other stockholder, Morrison-Knudsen Company, Inc. The company's 1974 results reflect an anticipated net loss of $2,242,000 recorded in the third quarter, on a fixed price contract for four vessels.

Except for dividends and interest from unconsolidated companies, the corporation's equity in earnings of those companies is not available to Kaiser Industries for its separate purposes.

A summary of the equity in the earnings of unconsolidated companies, and the dividends and interest received for the years ended December 31, 1974 and 1973 follows:

	1974 Equity In Earnings	1974 Dividends and Interest Received	1974 Equity In Undistributed Earnings	1973 Equity In Earnings	1973 Dividends and Interest Received	1973 Equity in Undistributed Earnings
			(thousands of dollars)			
Kaiser Aluminum	$39,046	$ 6,420	$32,626	$16,083	$ 3,668	$12,415
Kaiser Cement	2,145	1,254	891	2,949	1,254	1,695
Hamersley	8,755	6,785	1,970	6,353	7,781	(1,428)
National Steel and Shipbuilding	2,707	299	2,408	3,293	5,000	(1,707)
Other companies	1,684	15	1,669	4,128	14	4,114
	54,337	$14,773	$39,564	32,806	$17,717	$15,089
Less applicable income taxes	6,816			3,981		
	$47,521			$28,825		

Source: *Accounting Trends and Techniques*, Copyright © 1975 by the American Institute of Certified Public Accountants, Inc., pp. 144-146.

SFAS No. 12 (December 1975) Accounting for Certain Marketable Securities

Note: This Standard does not apply to not-for-profit organizations, mutual life insurance companies or employee benefit plans. However, FASB Interpretation No. 10 concludes that SFAS No. 12 applies to personal financial statements prepared in accordance with GAAP.

SFAS No. 12 applies to most marketable equity securities carried on the cost method, i.e., to those signifying ownership interest of less than 20 percent and absence of significant influence over the operating policies of the investee company. Standard No. 12 defines a marketable equity security as follows:

> ... any instrument representing ownership shares (e.g., common, preferred, and other capital stock), or the right to acquire (e.g., warrants, rights, and call options) or dispose of (e.g., put options) ownership shares in an enterprise at fixed or determinable prices. The term does not encompass preferred stock that by its terms either must be redeemed by the issuing enterprise or is redeemable at the option of the investor, nor does it include treasury stock or convertible bonds.
>
> *Marketable,* as applied to an equity security, means an equity security as to which sales prices or bid and ask prices are currently on a national securities exchange (e.g., those registered with the Securities and Exchange Commission) or in the over-the-counter market. FASB Interpretation No. 16 provides additional guidance in the determination of marketable and non-marketable securities.

The general accounting principle promulgated by this Standard is that the defined equity securities should be shown on the financial statements at lower of aggregate cost or market. New methods of determining both the cost and market value of equity securities have been offered. Paragraph 8 of the Standard states that "the carrying amount of a marketable equity securities portfolio shall be the lower of its aggregate cost or market value, determined at the balance sheet date." [1] This paragraph introduces the concept of using security portfolios in the process of determining lower of cost or market.

A starting point in applying SFAS No. 12 is the division of all defined securities into a current and a noncurrent portfolio. This can be seen in Block 2 of the Flowchart. If a classified balance sheet is not prepared, all defined equity securities are considered to be noncurrent.

---

[1] FASB Interpretation No. 13 deals with the proper accounting for securities when the parent and subsidiary(ies) have different balance sheet dates. The aggregate portfolio amounts (cost and market) will be determined at the balance sheet date of each individual subsidiary and combined with the parent at its balance sheet date.

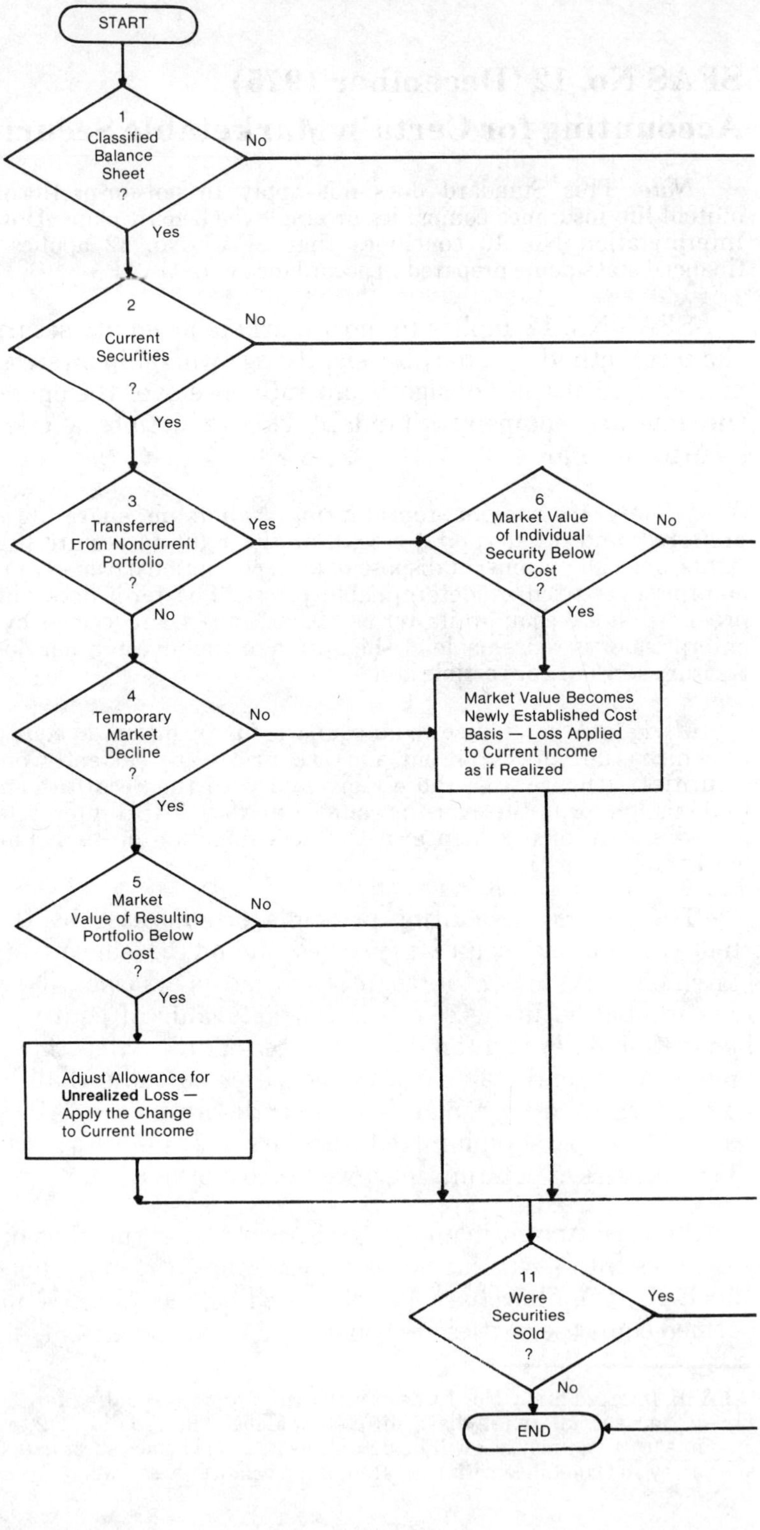
START
1
Classified
Balance
Sheet
?
No
Yes
2
Current
Securities
?
No
Yes
3
Transferred
From Noncurrent
Portfolio
?
Yes
No
6
Market Value
of Individual
Security Below
Cost
?
No
Yes
4
Temporary
Market
Decline
?
No
Yes
Market Value Becomes
Newly Established Cost
Basis — Loss Applied
to Current Income
as if Realized
5
Market
Value of Resulting
Portfolio Below
Cost
?
No
Yes
Adjust Allowance for
Unrealized Loss —
Apply the Change
to Current Income
11
Were
Securities
Sold
?
Yes
No
END

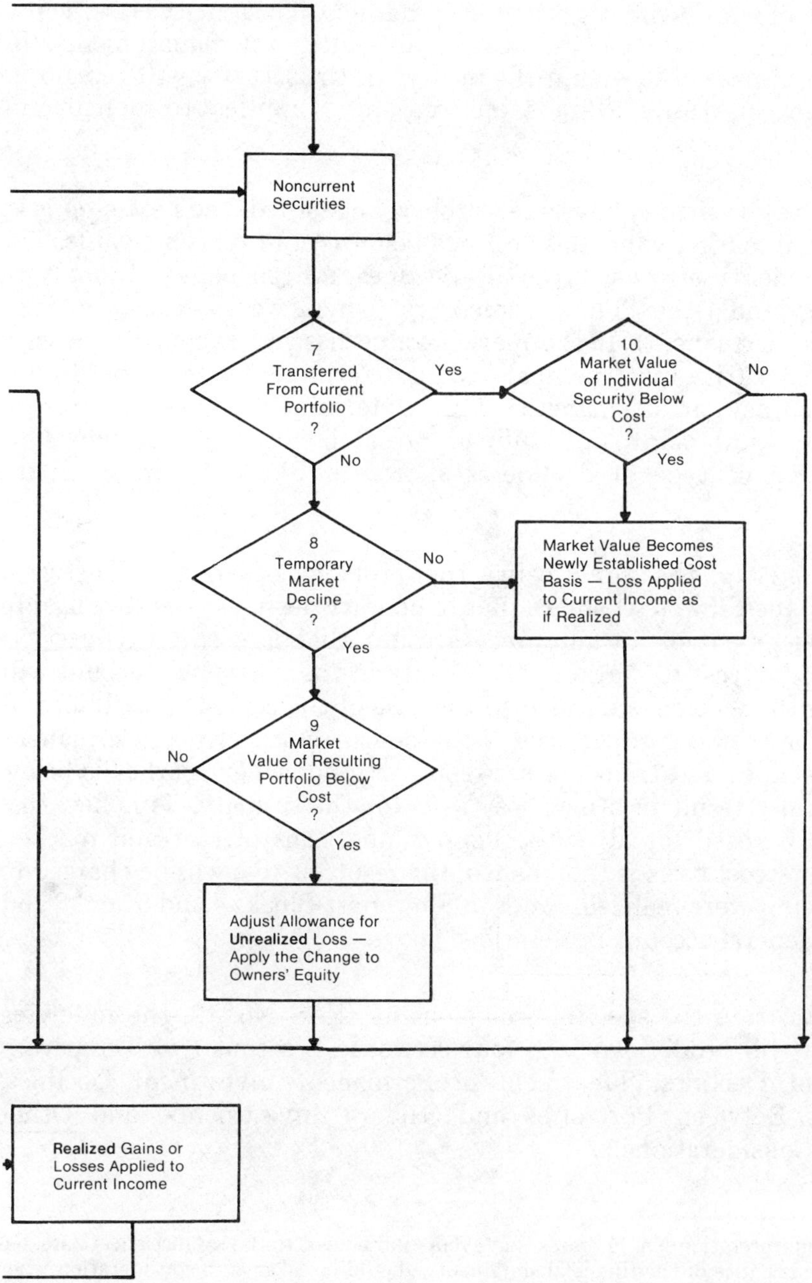
Noncurrent Securities
7 Transferred From Current Portfolio ?
Yes
No
10 Market Value of Individual Security Below Cost ?
No
Yes
8 Temporary Market Decline ?
No
Yes
Market Value Becomes Newly Established Cost Basis — Loss Applied to Current Income as if Realized
9 Market Value of Resulting Portfolio Below Cost ?
No
Yes
Adjust Allowance for **Unrealized** Loss — Apply the Change to Owners' Equity
Realized Gains or Losses Applied to Current Income

The determination of the current/noncurrent classification is related to the intent of management. If management intends to dispose of the security within the normal operating cycle or one year, whichever is longer, the security would be classified as current and placed in the current portfolio. Subsequent classifications are not contingent upon realization of management's intent. For example, if a security classified as current is not sold during the year, as intended, but management still intends to dispose of it within the next year, the security will remain in the current portfolio. The same reasoning applies to noncurrent securities.

After the securities have been properly classified, the next step is to determine if market value has declined below cost or carrying value. The Standard identifies two types of declines for purposes of analysis: Temporary and Other Than Temporary (which we shall subsequently refer to as Permanent). If the market value has fallen below cost, each individual security must be analyzed to determine whether the decline was temporary or permanent. This determination is a matter of managerial judgment not subject to strict interpretation. The classification of type of decline is shown in Blocks 4 and 8 of the Flowchart.[2]

Ignoring for the time being the problem of transfers between portfolios, the Flowchart shows that temporary declines generally lead to the establishment of an allowance account that is used to reduce the portfolio from cost to market. The change in the allowance account will appear on the income statement in the case of the current portfolio, and on the balance sheet in the case of the noncurrent portfolio. Permanent market declines and transfers between portfolios when market is below cost generally result in a new cost basis for the security. This new cost basis will be used for all subsequent comparisons of cost and market. When a new cost basis is established, the resulting loss will be charged to income as if it were realized. Refer to Flowchart Blocks 4 and 5, and 8 and 9, for the general accounting described above.

To illustrate the specific provisions of SFAS No. 12, the following discussion will be divided into four sections: Treatment of Temporary Investment Declines, Treatment of Permanent Investment Declines, Transfers Between Portfolios and Sale of Investments, and Other Material Considerations.

---

[2]FASB Interpretation No. 11 states that events subsequent to the balance sheet date, but prior to the issuance of the financial statements, should be taken into consideration when determining the nature of the decline.

Treatment of Temporary Investment Declines

When the decline of market below cost is considered to be *temporary,* its impact is assessed on an aggregate portfolio basis by comparing total market with total cost. The aggregate value by which market is below cost is recognized as an *unrealized* loss and an adjustment to the valuation allowance account. Once the portfolio is written down to market, it may be written back up as a result of subsequent recovery in the market value of the securities in the portfolio. However, the "write-up" can never exceed the amount required to restore the portfolio to its cost basis. In the case of temporary declines, the historical cost basis will never be changed and will remain intact for all comparisons of cost and market.

Table I shows the security portfolios for a hypothetical company for a period of three years. Amounts in the Table will be used to illustrate the accounting for temporary declines in the values of the portfolios. It can be assumed that the company prepares a classified balance sheet and that the placement of the individual securities into the current and noncurrent portfolios is correct.

The current portfolio will be examined first. For the year 197A, aggregate market is $3,000 less than aggregate cost. Remember that, for temporary declines, the difference between cost and market of individual securities is not considered; the fact that Security 2 shows a market value above cost is not relevant to the decision process. The $3,000 decline in the current portfolio will be recognized as an *unrealized* loss because the securities have not been sold to an outside party. The journal entry needed to record the unrealized loss is:

Net unrealized loss on current marketable equity securities	3,000	
Valuation allowance for unrealized loss on current marketable equity securities		3,000

The net unrealized loss would be reflected in the income statement for the year 197A as a non-operating item before income from continuing operations. The valuation allowance account is a contra asset, and will be shown as a reduction from the current marketable equity security account.

The noncurrent portfolio shows a $16,000 unrealized loss for the year 197A. The required journal entry would be similar to that presented above, with the proper notation that the loss was being recorded for the noncurrent portfolio. The following entry would be appropriate:

Table I

Information on Equity Securities with a Classified Balance Sheet for 197A-197C (Calendar years)—Temporary Investment Decline

	197C			197B			197A		
	Cost	Market	Unrealized Gain (Loss)	Cost	Market	Unrealized Gain (Loss)	Cost	Market	Unrealized Gain (Loss)
CURRENT PORTFOLIO									
Security 1	[1]$ 25,000	$ 27,000	$ 2,000	$ 50,000	$ 51,000	$ 1,000	$ 50,000	$ 45,000	$ (5,000)
2	30,000	31,000	1,000	30,000	28,000	(2,000)	30,000	32,000	2,000
3	148,000	148,000	-	-	-	-	-	-	-
Total Current Portfolio	$203,000	$206,000	$ 3,000	$ 80,000	$ 79,000	$ (1,000)	$ 80,000	$ 77,000	$ (3,000)
NONCURRENT PORTFOLIO									
Security 3	-	-	-	$150,000	$145,000	$ (5,000)	$150,000	$135,000	$(15,000)
4	$ 60,000	$ 63,000	$ 3,000	60,000	63,000	3,000	60,000	64,000	4,000
5	40,000	38,000	(2,000)	40,000	37,000	(3,000)	40,000	35,000	(5,000)
Total Noncurrent Portfolio	$100,000	$101,000	$ 1,000	$250,000	$245,000	$ (5,000)	$250,000	$234,000	$(16,000)

[1] Sold one-half of Security 1 for $30,000.

Net unrealized loss on noncurrent marketable equity securities	16,000	
Valuation allowance for unrealized loss on noncurrent marketable equity securities		16,000

The net unrealized loss on noncurrent securities is *not* closed to income, as is the case with the current portfolio, but is reflected in the stockholders' equity section of the balance sheet, below retained earnings but prior to treasury stock.[3] This is a major difference between the accounting for temporary declines in the current versus noncurrent portfolios. The valuation allowance is a contra asset, and is used to reduce noncurrent marketable equity securities to market.

In year 197B, Table I reflects a market recovery in the current portfolio. The $1,000 unrealized loss is the amount that should be reflected as the balance in the valuation allowance. Therefore, the adjusting entry for 197B would be $2,000 ($3,000 previous balance − $1,000 current balance) and is shown below:

Valuation allowance for unrealized loss on current marketable equity securities	2,000	
Net unrealized gain on market recovery of current marketable equity securities		2,000

The net unrealized gain recorded in year 197B is shown on the income statement in the nonoperating section before income from continuing operations. The valuation allowance, with its current balance of $1,000, would reduce the cost basis of the securities from $80,000 to the market value of $79,000.

During 197B, the noncurrent portfolio also reflected a market recovery of $11,000 ($16,000 − $5,000). The entry to adjust the allowance account at the end of 197B is:

Valuation allowance for unrealized loss on noncurrent marketable equity securities	11,000	
Net unrealized loss on noncurrent marketable equity securities		11,000

Keep in mind that, in 197A, the decline of $16,000 was recorded as an unrealized loss and was shown on the balance sheet. Therefore, the entry in 197B is an adjustment to the unrealized loss account, rather than an unrealized gain. This marks another major difference in the accounting for securities in the current versus noncurrent portfolios. In effect, the entry for the noncurrent portfolio is merely a reversal of the entry used to record the initial decline.

3 FASB Technical Bulletin No. 79-19 states that changes in the valuation allowance reflected in the equity section of a subsidiary or investee company should be used to adjust the investment account and equity section of the parent or investor company.

At the end of year 197C, the market value of the current portfolio is higher than cost. SFAS No. 12 allows a write-up only to the original cost basis; therefore, the amount of the entry for 197C is limited to $1,000. This is the amount needed to eliminate the valuation allowance, in order that the securities will be reported at cost on the financial statements. The necessary entry for 197C to adjust the current portfolio would be:

Valuation allowance for unrealized loss on current marketable equity securities	1,000	
Net unrealized gain on market recovery of current marketable equity securities		1,000

With this entry, the balance in the allowance account becomes zero and will have no affect on the 197C balance sheet. However, the unrealized gain will appear on the income statement in 197C as previously discussed.

The noncurrent portfolio at the end of 197C shows that market is above cost. The same rule, prohibiting a write-up of the portfolio above cost, applies. Therefore, the balance in the allowance account of $5,000 ($16,000 balance at the end of 197A – $11,000 reduction from the 197B adjusting entry) must be eliminated as follows:

Valuation allowance for unrealized loss on noncurrent marketable equity securities	5,000	
Net unrealized loss on noncurrent marketable equity securities		5,000

This entry not only eliminates the valuation allowance, but also reduces the net unrealized loss account to zero.

During 197C, other transactions took place that have not been discussed. Specifically, Security 3 was transferred from the noncurrent to the current portfolio, and $25,000 (one-half) of Security 1 was sold. These two items will be discussed in the section dealing with transfers and sales of investments.

Treatment of Permanent Investment Declines

SFAS No. 12 refers to declines in investment value that are "other than temporary." Throughout the remainder of the section, these declines will be referred to as "permanent." In addition, the Standard does not address the concept of permanent declines in the current portfolio. Accounting for permanent declines in the current portfolio should be handled in accordance with Accounting Research Bulletin (ARB) No. 43, Chapter 3A, Paragraph 9, and is not discussed in this section. (The relevant section of ARB No. 43 states, "In the case of marketable securities where market value is less than cost by a substantial amount and it is evident that the decline in market value is not due to a mere temporary condition, the amount to be included as a current asset should not exceed the market value.")

A permanent decline in market value below cost of securities in the noncurrent portfolio results in a new cost basis being established. This new cost basis then will be used for all future comparisons of cost and market. For permanent declines, the new cost basis is established on an individual security basis, rather than on an aggregate basis, and will be used in the determination of any gains or losses for accounting purposes upon ultimate disposition of the security.

Table II provides the information to illustrate the accounting for permanent declines in the noncurrent portfolio. The current portfolio information presented will be used as example material at a later time.

At the end of 197A, market was below cost for both Security 3 and Security 5, while market was above cost for Security 4. Permanent declines are handled on an individual security basis; therefore, the total realized loss is equal to $17,000 ($10,000 loss for Security 3 + $7,000 loss for Security 5). The journal entry to reflect this unrealized loss would be:

Realized loss on noncurrent marketable equity securities	17,000	
Marketable equity securities—Security 3		10,000
Marketable equity securities—Security 5		7,000

Note that the loss account has been labeled "realized," even though the securities have not been sold. The realized loss would be shown on the income statement in the nonoperating section before income from continuing operations. The noncurrent marketable securities were written-down directly, and a new cost basis was established. The new cost basis for Security 3 is $100,000 ($110,000 – $10,000 write-down), and the cost basis of Security 5 is $23,000. These new cost bases will be carried forward to year 197B, and will be used in future market/cost comparisons.

At the end of year 197B, a market recovery occurred in Security 3 and Security 5, and market now is above cost. Since the write-down in 197A created a new cost basis, it is not acceptable to write marketable securities up above the cost basis. As a result, no journal entry is required in 197B.

Table II

Information on Equity Securities with a Classified Balance Sheet for 197A-197C (Calendar years)— Permanent Investment Decline

CURRENT PORTFOLIO

	197C			197B			197A		
	Cost	Market	Unrealized Gain (Loss)	Cost	Market	Unrealized Gain (Loss)	Cost	Market	Unrealized Gain (Loss)
Security 1	$ 40,000	$ 41,000	$ 1,000	$ 40,000	$ 40,000	-	$ 40,000	$ 35,000	$ (5,000)
2	20,000	18,000	(2,000)	20,000	19,000	$ (1,000)	20,000	21,000	1,000
3	100,000	105,000	5,000	-	-	-	-	-	-
Total Current Portfolio	$160,000	$164,000	$ 4,000	$ 60,000	$ 59,000	$ (1,000)	$ 60,000	$ 56,000	$ (4,000)

NONCURRENT PORTFOLIO

	197C			197B			197A		
	Cost	Market	Unrealized Gain (Loss)	Cost	Market	Unrealized Gain (Loss)	Cost	Market	Unrealized Gain (Loss)
Security 3	-	-	-	$100,000	$107,000	$ 7,000	$110,000	$100,000	$(10,000)
4	$ 50,000	$ 46,000	$(4,000)	50,000	51,000	1,000	50,000	52,000	2,000
5	23,000	27,000	4,000	23,000	25,000	2,000	30,000	23,000	(7,000)
Total Noncurrent Portfolio	$ 73,000	$ 73,000	$ -	$173,000	$183,000	$ 10,000	$190,000	$175,000	$(15,000)

At the end of year 197C, Security 4 reflects a decline in market value of $4,000, and this decline is viewed as permanent in nature. The entry to record this loss in value is:

Realized loss on noncurrent marketable equity securities	4,000	
Marketable equity securities—Security 4		4,000

The handling of the loss is the same as discussed above.

As indicated earlier, Tables I and II show information relating to both the transfer and sale of securities in year 197C. A discussion of the proper accounting for these transactions follows.

Transfers Between Portfolios and Sale of Investments

Transfers from one portfolio to another are made at lower-of-cost-or-market, determined on an individual security basis. If a transfer is made at a time when market is less than cost, a new cost basis is established, and a loss is charged against current income as if it were realized.

Refer back to Table I, which was used to illustrate temporary declines, and note that, during 197C, Security 3 was transferred from the noncurrent to the current portfolio. At the time of the transfer, the cost basis of the security was $150,000, and the market value was $148,000. Application of the rules stated above would require the company to recognize a $2,000 loss ($150,000 – $148,000) on the date of transfer. The appropriate journal entry would be:

Loss on transfer between noncurrent and current portfolios	2,000	
Marketable equity securities—current	148,000	
Marketable equity securities—noncurrent		150,000

The loss resulting from the transfer would be charged against current income in the nonoperating section of the income statement. Security 3 now would have a new cost basis of $148,000, and would be carried at that amount in the current portfolio.

Table II, dealing with permanent declines, reveals that, in 197C, Security 3 was transferred from the noncurrent to the current portfolio at a time when the newly adjusted cost basis was $100,000, and the market value was $105,000. Since the market was above cost on the date of transfer, no loss will be recognized. The security would be transferred at cost. The correct entry to effect the transfer is shown below:

Marketable equity securities—current	100,000	
Marketable equity securities—noncurrent		100,000

As indicated earlier, one-half ($25,000) of Security 1 was sold during 197C for $30,000 cash. The entry to record the sale is very straight forward and is given below:

Cash	30,000	
Marketable equity securities—current		25,000
Gain on sale of marketable equity securities		5,000

There would be no adjustment to the valuation allowance as a result of the sale. Adjustments to the valuation allowance account are made at the balance sheet date in the form of an adjusting entry.

Other Material Considerations

Paragraph 22 of SFAS No. 12 deals with income tax implications of accounting for the defined equity securities. The Paragraph states:

> Unrealized gains and losses on marketable securities, whether recognized in net income or included in the equity section of the balance sheet, shall be considered as timing differences, and the provisions of APB Opinion No. 11, "Accounting for Income Taxes", shall be applied in determining whether such net unrealized gain or loss shall be reduced by the applicable income tax effect.

This statement deals with *unrealized* gains and losses on unsold securities in both the current and noncurrent portfolios. Refer to APB Opinion No. 11 in Topic 5 for the applicable accounting.

It is important to note that SFAS No. 12 does not speak to the question of *realized* losses associated with unsold securities. It can be assumed, to be consistent, that these losses should be treated as timing differences. The primary reason for this assumption relates to the fact that losses on unsold securities are not recognized for tax purposes until the security is sold.

Paragraph 14 applies to businesses with specialized industry accounting practices for marketable equity securities. These industries include "investment companies, brokers and dealers in securities, stock life insurance companies, and fire and casualty insurance companies." SFAS No. 12 does not require any deviation from specialized industry practices, with the exception of entities carrying marketable equity securities at cost. Now, such entities must carry securities at the lower of aggregate cost or market, as defined by the Standard.

Disclosure Requirements

Paragraph 12 of the Standard specifies the disclosure requirements for marketable equity securities. These requirements can be divided into three broad categories as follows:

(1) The investor should disclose the total cost and market value of the marketable equity securities, as of the balance sheet date. If a

classified balance sheet is prepared, this information should be presented by portfolios (current and noncurrent).

(2) Gross unrealized gains and losses must be presented, divided between current and noncurrent portfolios.

(3) The net realized gains and losses, basis for determination of the gains and losses, and changes in valuation allowances must be presented.

Information from the 1976 Annual Report of UV Industries, Inc. is presented in Exhibit I. The information shows the financial presentation of marketable equity securities and Note 3 to the Financial Statements, which explains the Company's accounting for these securities. The Note is of interest because it goes into some detail about the gains and losses, both realized and unrealized, relating to the securities.

Exhibit I
UV Industries, Inc. (Dec)

	1976	($000)	1975
Marketable equity securities (Note 3)	$3,387		$2,775

Note 3: Marketable Equity Securities—In accordance with Statement No. 12 of the Financial Accounting Standards Board, the current and noncurrent portfolios of marketable equity securities are carried at the lower of cost or market. Marketable equity securities consisted of the following:

	Cost	Market (in thousands)	Unrealized Gain (Loss)
December 31, 1975:			
Current	$1,646	$ 116	$(1,530)
Noncurrent	$4,735	$2,775	$(1,960)
December 31, 1976:			
Noncurrent	$4,333	$3,387	$ (946)

To reduce the carrying value of the current marketable equity securities portfolio to market, which was lower than cost at December 31, 1975, a valuation allowance in the amount of $1,530,000 was established with a corresponding charge to income at that date. To reduce the carrying amount of the noncurrent marketable equity securities portfolio to market, which was lower than cost at December 31, 1975, a valuation allowance in the amount of $1,960,000 was established by a charge to stockholders' equity representing the net unrealized loss. During 1975 realized losses of $299,000 on the sale of marketable equity securities were included in the determination of net income.

During 1976 the Company sold its current marketable equity securities portfolio realizing a loss of $1,561,000 and reversed against that loss the $1,530,000 allowance established in 1975.

On January 21, 1976 the Company entered into an agreement under which it may sell, over a three year period at a minimum aggregate price of $3,040,000, all of its holdings in Phoenix Steel Corporation which are included in the noncurrent portfolio. The Common Shares, representing 11.6% of the total outstanding shares of Phoenix, are valued at $2,470,000 which represents the present value of the current minimum aggregate price at December 31, 1976 assuming that no shares will be sold in 1977. As a result of the agreement the Phoenix warrants held at December 31, 1975 were sold for $250,000 during 1976, resulting in a realized loss of $152,000, which has been included in the determination of net income. Since these warrants were sold, the valuation allowance established at December 31, 1975 has been reversed.

The cost of securities sold was based on the average cost of all units held at the time of such sales.

Source: *Accounting Trends & Techniques,* Copyright © 1977 by the American Institute of Certified Public Accountants, Inc., p. 143.

Topic 3

Nonmonetary Assets

Detail Contents

APB Opinion No. 29 (May 1973) Accounting for Nonmonetary Transactions

Flowchart and General Discussion

Before a meaningful discussion of APB Opinion No. 29 can be started, it is important to define several terms that have special meaning for purposes of the Opinion. While it is always difficult to convey the significance of a term in words, the definitions below (from APB Opinion No. 29, Paragraph 3), along with the example material presented later in the discussion, should give the reader an appreciation of the terms:

1. *Monetary Assets and Liabilities.* Those assets and liabilities whose value is expressed in a fixed amount of purchasing power, e.g., cash, receivables and payables.

2. *Nonmonetary Assets and Liabilities.* Those assets and liabilities whose value is not expressed in a fixed amount of purchasing power, e.g., inventories, land and equipment.

3. *Exchange Transaction.* A transfer between two entities. Each entity receives a benefit in the form of an asset, and each entity gives up an asset or incurs a liability.

4. *Nonreciprocal Transfers.* One-directional transfers. They involve a transfer of assets *or* a receipt of assets or services, but not both. The payment of a property dividend by an entity to its stockholders would be an example of a nonreciprocal transfer.

5. *Productive Assets.* Assets used in the production process, e.g., equipment, buildings, land and investments accounted for using the equity method.

6. *Similar Productive Assets.* Assets used in the production process that "are of the same general type, that perform the same function or that are employed in the same line of business."

APB Opinion No. 29 specifies the accounting for exchange transactions and nonreciprocal transfers of nonmonetary assets and liabilities. The Opinion also covers exchanges and transfers that are primarily, but not exclusively, nonmonetary transactions. An exchange transaction or nonreciprocal transfer may include nonmonetary assets and liabilities, as well as a "small" amount of monetary assets or liabilities. The amount of the monetary assets or liabilities involved in the transaction is referred to as "boot."

Paragraph 4 of the Opinion identifies five specific transactions that are exempt from the general provisions of the Opinion. These transactions include the following:

(1) Business combinations reported in accordance with APB Opinion No. 16. (See Topic 11 for a detailed analysis of business combinations including APB Opinion No. 16.)

(2) Nonmonetary asset transfers between companies under the same control.

(3) Exchange of capital stock for nonmonetary assets or services.

(4) Receipt or issuance of stock resulting from a stock split or stock dividend.

(5) Involuntary conversion of nonmonetary assets to monetary assets with a subsequent reinvestment in nonmonetary assets. FASB Interpretation No. 30 states that, when an enterprise has an involuntary conversion of a nonmonetary asset to a monetary asset, the general provisions of APB Opinion No. 29 *do not* apply. The gain or loss resulting from the involuntary conversion must be recognized currently. However, if the involuntary conversion resulted in damage or destruction to the asset, and the amount to be received cannot be determined, the provisions of SFAS No. 5 are applicable. (See Topic 6 for a complete discussion of SFAS No. 5.) The gain or loss that must be recognized currently will be disclosed in accordance with the provisions of APB Opinion No. 30. (See Topic 1 for a detailed discussion of APB Opinion No. 30.)

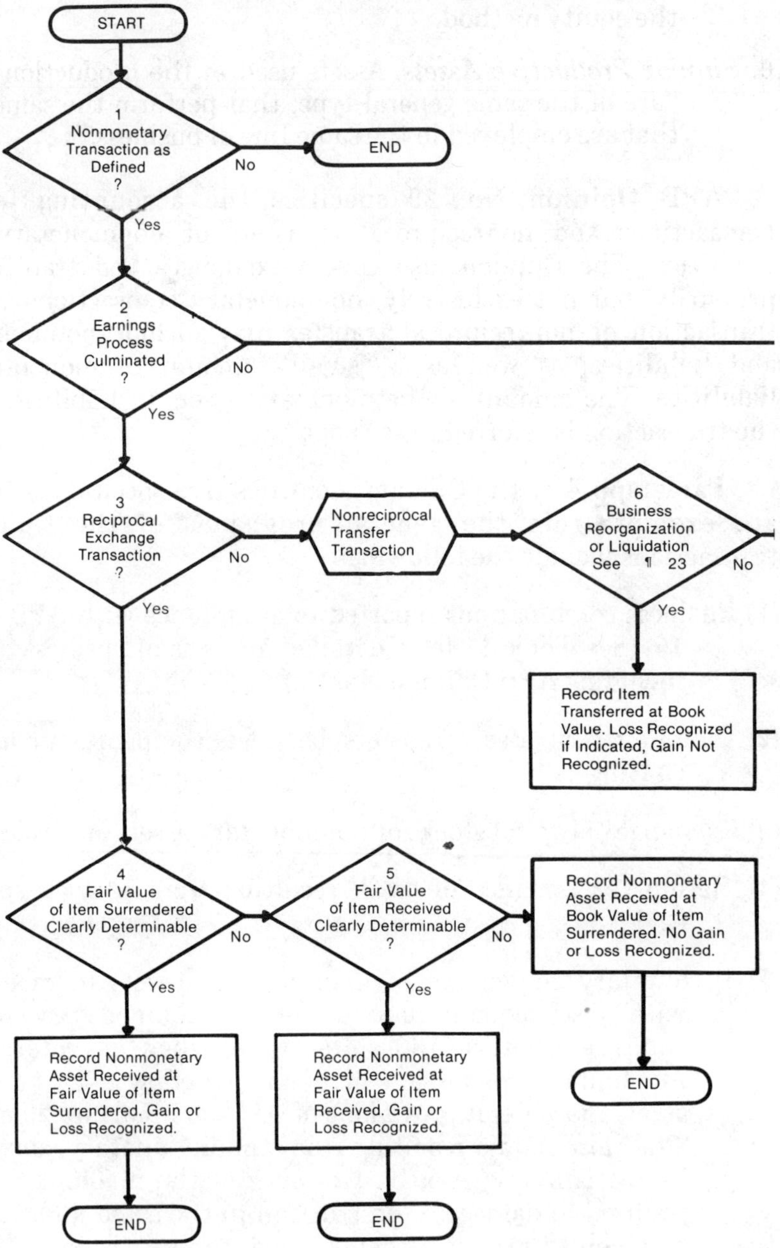
START
1
Nonmonetary
Transaction as
Defined
?
No
END
Yes
2
Earnings
Process
Culminated
?
No
Yes
3
Reciprocal
Exchange
Transaction
?
No
Nonreciprocal
Transfer
Transaction
6
Business
Reorganization
or Liquidation
See ¶ 23
No
Yes
Record Item
Transferred at Book
Value. Loss Recognized
if Indicated, Gain Not
Recognized.
Yes
4
Fair Value
of Item Surrendered
Clearly Determinable
?
No
5
Fair Value
of Item Received
Clearly Determinable
?
No
Record Nonmonetary
Asset Received at
Book Value of Item
Surrendered. No Gain
or Loss Recognized.
END
Yes
Record Nonmonetary
Asset Received at
Fair Value of Item
Surrendered. Gain or
Loss Recognized.
END
Yes
Record Nonmonetary
Asset Received at
Fair Value of Item
Received. Gain or
Loss Recognized.
END

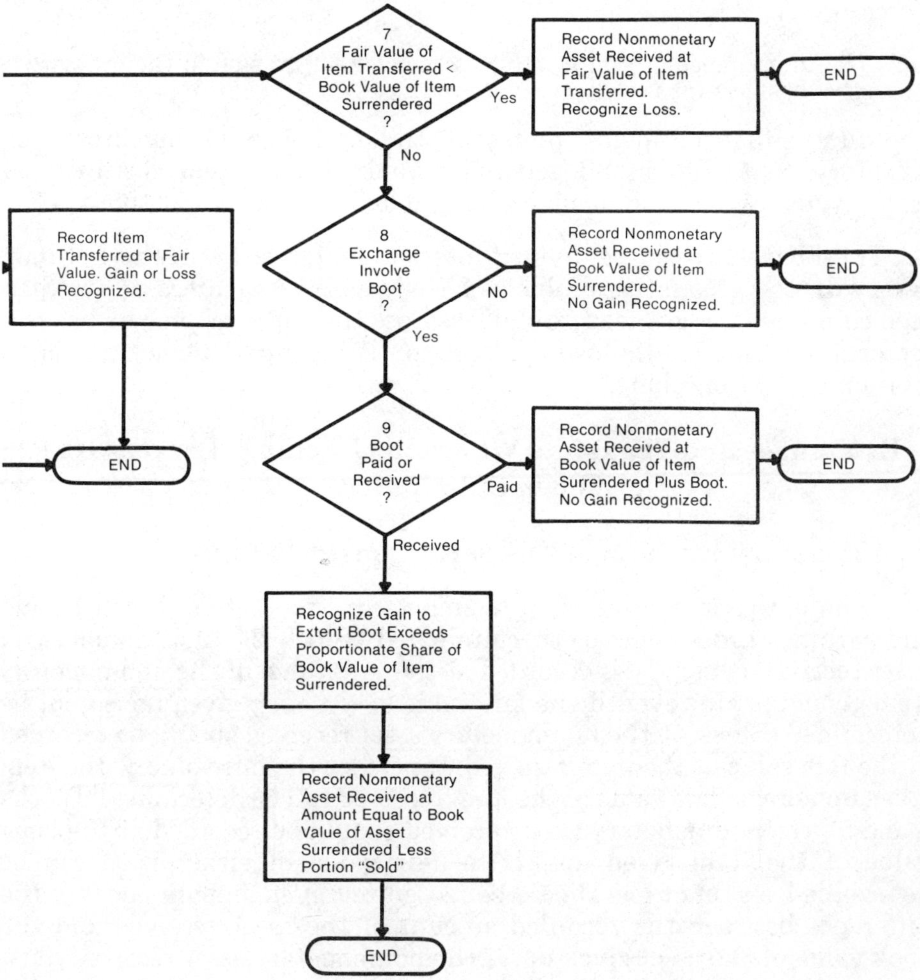
7
Fair Value of Item Transferred < Book Value of Item Surrendered ?
Yes
No
Record Nonmonetary Asset Received at Fair Value of Item Transferred. Recognize Loss.
END
Record Item Transferred at Fair Value. Gain or Loss Recognized.
8
Exchange Involve Boot ?
No
Yes
Record Nonmonetary Asset Received at Book Value of Item Surrendered. No Gain Recognized.
END
END
9
Boot Paid or Received ?
Paid
Received
Record Nonmonetary Asset Received at Book Value of Item Surrendered Plus Boot. No Gain Recognized.
END
Recognize Gain to Extent Boot Exceeds Proportionate Share of Book Value of Item Surrendered.
Record Nonmonetary Asset Received at Amount Equal to Book Value of Asset Surrendered Less Portion "Sold"
END

With this introduction to the terms used in the Opinion, the reader should be able to understand the essential features of the Flowchart and example material. The basic accounting for nonmonetary exchanges or transfers depends on whether or not the earnings process has been culminated as a result of the transaction. The Opinion (Paragraph 21) identifies two situations where it is assumed that the earnings process has *not* been culminated.

> [1] An exchange of a product or property held for sale in the ordinary course of business for a product or property to be sold in the same line of business to facilitate sales to customers other than the parties to the exchange. . . .
>
> [2] An exchange of a productive asset not held for sale in the ordinary course of business for a similar productive asset. . . .

The first situation might represent the exchange of inventory for inventory; and the second generally would be an item classified as property, plant and equipment, exchanged for a similar productive asset.

The Flowchart can be divided into two major sections: the left half deals with the accounting problems faced when the earnings process has been culminated, and the right half assumes the earnings process has *not* been culminated. The following discussion is organized along this major division in the Flowchart.

Exchanges and Transfers Where the Earnings Process Has Been Culminated

Nonmonetary Exchanges—General Considerations

If an entity is involved in a nonmonetary transaction (Block 1), and the earnings process has been culminated (Block 2), the nonmonetary asset received generally is recorded at the fair value of the nonmonetary item given up. However, if the fair value of the item given up cannot be determined (Block 4), the nonmonetary asset received should be recorded at the fair value of the item received. If neither the fair value of the item given up nor the fair value of the item received can be determined (Blocks 4 and 5), the nonmonetary asset received should be recorded at the book value of the item given up. If the fair value of either item can be determined, a gain or loss should be recognized in an amount equal to the difference between the recorded amount of the asset received and the book value of the asset given up. If the nonmonetary asset received must be recorded at the book value of the item given up, no gain or loss results. The asset received takes on the book value of the asset given up.

A "small" amount of boot (cash or other monetary consideration) may be given or received in connection with a nonmonetary exchange.

The fact that boot is involved does not change the general principle that the asset received should be recorded at the fair value of the item given up. If the fair value of the item given up cannot be determined, the decision process described above should be followed.

The Opinion does not define the meaning of "small" as it relates to the boot given or received. The question that must be answered by the accountant's judgment is, "What is the maximum boot that can be given or received in an exchange transaction and still have that transaction qualify as a nonmonetary exchange?" Certainly, if the boot were to approach 50 percent of the total fair value, the transaction could not be classified as nonmonetary.

The determination of fair value in an exchange transaction can pose difficult problems for the accountant. The Opinion provides some guidance in the determination of fair value. Paragraph 25 of the Opinion indicates that the following information may be considered in the determination of fair value:

(1) Estimated realizable values in cash transactions of the same or similar assets;

(2) Quoted market prices;

(3) Independent appraisals; and

(4) Estimated fair values of assets or services received in exchange.

It is not appropriate to use estimated fair value in an exchange transaction unless the fair value can be estimated within reasonable limits. Fair value is not estimated within reasonable limits if "major uncertainties exist about the realizability of the value that would be assigned to an asset" (APB Opinion No. 29, Paragraph 26). As indicated above, if it is not appropriate to use fair value, the asset received should be recorded at the book value of the item given up.

Nonmonetary Exchanges—Technical Considerations

To illustrate the technical aspects of nonmonetary exchanges where the earnings process is assumed to have culminated, assume that Book-It, Inc. exchanged a piece of equipment that had an appraised value of $30,000 for inventory to be resold. The equipment had a cost basis of $100,000; and, at the date of exchange, accumulated depreciation was $75,000. The exchange of equipment for inventory represents an exchange of dissimilar assets, and, therefore, it is assumed that the earnings process has been culminated. In this example, the fair value of the item surrendered is known to be $30,000, and this amount should be used to record the value of the inventory received. The next step is to determine if there is a gain or loss on the transaction that must be recognized. The gain or loss is determined by comparing the fair value of the asset given up with the book value of that asset, and is computed as follows:

Cost of Equipment	$100,000
Less: Accumulated Depreciation	75,000
Book Value of Equipment	$ 25,000
Fair Value of Equipment	30,000
Gain on Exchange	$ 5,000

Because the fair value assigned to the asset received is greater than the book value of the asset given up, a gain resulted from the exchange. The entry to record the exchange of equipment for inventory would be as follows:

Inventory	30,000	
Accumulated Depreciation—Equipment	75,000	
Equipment		100,000
Gain on Nonmonetary Exchange		5,000

The preceding example depicted a situation where the fair value of the item surrendered in the exchange transaction was known. In many nonmonetary exchanges, the fair value of the item given up may not be known, or the fair value of the item received may be more evident than the fair value of the item given up. To illustrate this situation, assume the same facts as in the above example, except that the fair value of the equipment is not known and the normal selling price of the inventory items was $20,000. In this case, the value assigned to the inventory received would be $20,000, and the gain or loss would be determined as follows:

Cost of Equipment	$100,000
Less: Accumulated Depreciation	75,000
Book Value of Equipment	$ 25,000
Fair Value of Inventory	20,000
Loss on Exchange	$ 5,000

The fair value of the inventory received is less than the book value of the equipment; therefore, a loss will be recognized. The entry required to record the exchange in this case would be:

Inventory	20,000	
Accumulated Depreciation—Equipment	75,000	
Loss on Nonmonetary Exchange	5,000	
Equipment		100,000

Yet another situation exists where both the fair value of the item given up and the fair value of the item received *cannot* be determined within reasonable limits. To illustrate this situation, assume that Book-

It, Inc. exchanged inventory with a book value of $50,000 for a parcel of land. The fair value of neither item is reasonably determinable. In this case, the land would be recorded at the book value of the inventory and no gain or loss could result. Note that this situation represents an exchange of a productive asset for inventory, which would be deemed as dissimilar assets. It is assumed that the earnings process has been culminated, yet no gain or loss resulted. The entry to reflect the exchange would be:

Land	50,000	
Inventory		50,000

The three preceding examples involved exchanges of nonmonetary assets where no boot was given or received. To show the effect of the boot on a nonmonetary exchange, assume that Book-It, Inc. exchanges equipment with a fair value of $100,000, plus $10,000 in cash, for some inventory items. The equipment given up has a cost basis of $95,000; and, at the date of the exchange, accumulated depreciation of $20,000 has been recorded. The assets exchanged are dissimilar (equipment and cash for inventory), and it is assumed that the earnings process has been culminated. The inventory acquired should be recorded at the fair value of the items given up ($100,000 + $10,000). The calculation of gain or loss on the exchange is shown below.

Fair Value of Equipment	$100,000
Cash Paid	10,000
Total Fair Value of Assets Surrendered	$110,000
Book Value of Equipment ($95,000—$20,000)	(75,000)
"Book Value" of Cash	(10,000)
Gain on Exchange	$ 25,000

Since the fair value ($110,000) assigned to the asset received is greater than the book value ($85,000) of the assets given up, a gain on the exchange will be recognized. The entry required to record the exchange transaction is as follows:

Inventory	110,000	
Accumulated Depreciation—Equipment	20,000	
Equipment		95,000
Cash		10,000
Gain on Nonmonetary Exchange		25,000

Because the "fair value" of the cash paid always is equal to the "book value," a boot paid in cash will not affect the determination of the gain or loss. However, if the boot were paid in some other monetary asset, such as a receivable, there could be a difference between fair value and book value that would impact the gain or loss.

Nonreciprocal Transfers—General Considerations

If an entity enters into a nonmonetary transaction (Block 1) where the earnings process has culminated (Block 2), and if the transaction does not qualify as an exchange transaction (Block 3), it will be classified as a nonreciprocal transfer between owners or between an owner and another entity. Nonreciprocal transfers include property dividends to owners, gifts from municipalities, gifts to other entities, and reacquisitions of an enterprise's stock by transfer of nonmonetary assets rather than cash.

Generally, nonmonetary items involved in a nonreciprocal transfer should be recorded at their fair value, and any resulting gain or loss would be recognized. The gain or loss is measured by the difference between the fair value and the book value of the nonmonetary asset transferred. However, there are exceptions to this general rule. The exceptions include nonreciprocal transfers of nonmonetary assets to owners in "a spin-off or other form of reorganization or liquidation or in a plan that is in substance the rescission of a prior business combination" (Block 6—APB Opinion No. 29, Paragraph 23). For these exceptions, the item(s) transferred should be accounted for at book value, rather than at fair value. If it can be demonstrated that the item transferred has suffered an impairment in value below book value, it would be appropriate to recognize a loss on the transfer. However, it is never appropriate to recognize a gain from these nonreciprocal transfers considered to be exceptions to the general rule.

Nonreciprocal Transfers—Technical Considerations

To illustrate the technical aspects of accounting for nonreciprocal transfers, assume that Book-It, Inc. distributes its investment in the shares of Speculation Company as a property dividend to existing stockholders. The investment in Speculation Company was accounted for using the cost method. The stock to be distributed currently is selling for $75,000 and has a book value to Book-It, Inc. of $60,000.

This transaction involves a nonmonetary asset (investment); and, because it is not the exchange of inventory for inventory or of similar productive assets, it is assumed that the earnings process has been culminated. Since this is a one-way transfer, the transaction cannot be classified as an exchange transaction. Therefore, the transaction must represent a nonreciprocal transfer. Because the investment is carried on the cost basis, the transaction should be accounted for using fair value of the item transferred. In this particular case, the recorded value of the dividend should be $75,000. The difference between the fair value ($75,000) and the book value ($60,000) of the stock represents a gain of $15,000 to be recognized. Based upon this information, the following journal entries are required.

Investment in Speculation Company Stock	15,000	
Gain Due to Market Increase of Investment		15,000
Retained Earnings	75,000	
Property Dividend Payable		75,000
Property Dividend Payable	75,000	
Investment in Speculation Company Stock		75,000

Had the investment in Speculation Company been carried on the equity basis, rather than on the cost basis, the transaction would have been treated as a spin-off, and book value would have been the appropriate accounting value to use.

A second example of a nonreciprocal transfer would result from the following set of assumptions. Book-It, Inc. wants to construct a plant in the town of Rogers. To induce Book-It to locate in Rogers, the city government has agreed to donate land with a fair value of $200,000 to the company for use as a plant site. To secure the land, Book-It agreed that it will hire at least 100 residents of Rogers in the next five years. This example represents a nonreciprocal transfer (only Book-It, Inc. received an asset) with a performance agreement. The presence of a performance agreement does not alter the general rule for recording nonreciprocal transfers. Therefore, Book-It would record the value of the plant site at $200,000. The following journal entry is needed to record the transfer:

Land Held for Future Plant Site	200,000	
Contributed Capital—Plant Site Donation		200,000

This last example completes the discussion of nonmonetary exchanges and nonreciprocal transfers where the earnings process has been culminated. The remaining discussion will center on the problems of accounting for nonmonetary exchanges where the earnings process is *not* culminated.

Nonmonetary Exchanges Where the Earnings Process Is Not Culminated

Recall that the earnings process would not be culminated if the exchange involved inventory for inventory, or similar productive assets. To help organize the discussion of these types of transactions, exchanges not involving boot will be discussed first, followed by exchanges that involve boot.

Nonmonetary Exchanges Not Involving Boot

For nonmonetary transactions (Block 1) where the earnings process is not culminated (Block 2), the first test to be conducted is a determination if the exchange will result in a loss. A loss on an exchange would be indicated if the fair value of the item transferred were less than the book value of the item given up (Block 7). In those cases where a loss is indicated, the nonmonetary asset received should be recorded at the fair value of the item transferred, and the loss should be recognized in full.

To illustrate this point, assume that Book-It, Inc. exchanges inventory with a recorded value of $150,000 for other inventory that has a current selling price of $135,000. Because this is an exchange of inventory for inventory, it is assumed that the earnings process is not culminated. In this situation, the first step is to determine if the exchange will result in a loss. Since the fair value of the inventory received is less than the book value of the inventory surrendered, a loss of $15,000 ($150,000 – $135,000) is indicated and must be recognized. The entry necessary to record this exchange of inventory is as follows:

Inventory	135,000	
Loss on Nonmonetary Exchange	15,000	
Inventory		150,000

If the nonmonetary exchange does not indicate a loss, and there is no boot involved in the transaction (Block 8), the nonmonetary asset received should be recorded at the book value of the item surrendered. If the asset received is assigned the book value of the asset given up, no gain will result (and the possibility of a loss has been ruled out) (Block 7). To illustrate this accounting, assume that Book-It, Inc. exchanges Equipment A, which is used in the productive process, for similar Equipment B. Both pieces of equipment are of the same general type and perform identical functions. Equipment A has a cost basis of $100,000; and, at the date of exchange, accumulated depreciation of $50,000 had been recorded. Equipment A currently has a fair market value of $75,000. Equipment B also has a fair market value of $75,000.

Since this is an exchange of similar productive assets, it is assumed that the earnings process has not culminated. The first step is to determine if the exchange transaction indicates a loss. The fair market value of the asset transferred ($75,000) is greater than the book value of $50,000 ($100,000 – $50,000); and therefore a gain, not a loss, is indicated. Because the exchange does not culminate the earnings process, the gain cannot be recognized, and the asset received is recorded at the book value of the asset given up. The entry required to reflect this exchange transaction is as follows:

Equipment B	50,000	
Accumulated Depreciation—Equipment A	50,000	
Equipment A		100,000

Equipment B now has a depreciable cost basis of $50,000, which is the book value of Equipment A.

Nonmonetary Exchanges Involving Boot

When a company enters into a nonmonetary transaction (Block 1) where the earnings process is not culminated (Block 2) and boot is involved, the test to determine if a loss is indicated (Block 7) is still applicable. Once it has been determined that a loss is not indicated, the accounting for the transaction depends on whether the company paid or received the boot (Block 9).

The entity paying the boot is required to record the asset received at an amount equal to the monetary consideration paid, plus the book value of the item surrendered. Accordingly, a gain would not be recognized on this type of exchange. As before, if a loss is indicated, it should be recognized in full at the date of the exchange.

The entity receiving the boot is considered to have "sold" a portion of the asset exchanged; and, therefore, the earnings process has culminated on the portion of the asset sold. Because the earnings process has culminated on this portion of the asset, it is appropriate to recognize a gain. The gain is limited to the extent that the boot received exceeds the proportionate share of the asset sold. The asset received by the entity is recorded at an amount equal to the book value of the item surrendered, less the portion of the book value sold. Any indicated losses would be recognized in full.

To illustrate the technical aspects of nonmonetary exchanges involving monetary consideration, assume that Book-It, Inc. and Jar, Inc. exchange similar productive nonmonetary assets. Book-It surrenders Equipment A and $5,000 cash for Equipment B, which is held by Jar, Inc. Specific information about the two pieces of equipment is shown in Exhibit I.

Exhibit I

Exchange Assumptions

	Equipment A (Book-It, Inc.)	Equipment B (Jar, Inc.)
Cost	$100,000	$90,000
Accumulated Depreciation	20,000	15,000
Book Value	$ 80,000	$75,000
Fair Market Value	$ 65,000	$70,000

Because similar productive assets were exchanged, it is assumed that the earnings process has not culminated. The first test is to determine if a loss on the exchange is indicated. Considering Book-It, Inc. first, the loss would be determined as follows:

Book Value of Equipment	$80,000
Book Value of Cash	5,000
Total Book Value	$85,000
Fair Value of Equipment Surrendered	(65,000)
Fair Value of Cash Surrendered	(5,000)
Loss on Exchange	$15,000

Since the fair value ($70,000) of the items surrendered is less than the book value ($85,000) of the equipment and cash, a loss of $15,000 is indicated. When a loss is indicated, the value assigned to the nonmonetary asset received is the fair value ($70,000) of the items surrendered. The loss must be recognized in full. The entry necessary to record the exchange is:

Equipment B	70,000	
Accumulated Depreciation—Equipment A	20,000	
Loss on Nonmonetary Exchange	15,000	
Equipment A		100,000
Cash		5,000

In the situation described above, the reader can see that the asset received must be recorded at fair value because generally accepted accounting principles prohibit recording assets at more than fair value on the date of the transaction.

Next, an analysis of the effect of the transaction on Jar, Inc. must be made. For the same reasons stated above, the earnings process is assumed not to have culminated, and the loss test must be applied. The determination of the loss would be accomplished as follows:

Book Value of Equipment Surrendered	$75,000
Fair Value of Equipment Surrendered	70,000
Loss on Exchange	$ 5,000

Since fair value is less than book value, a loss is indicated on the exchange. The value of the nonmonetary asset received should be equal to its fair value of $65,000. The $5,000 loss should be recognized in full. The necessary journal entry is presented below.

Cash	5,000	
Equipment A	65,000	
Accumulated Depreciation—Equipment B	15,000	
Loss on Nonmonetary Exchange	5,000	
Equipment B		90,000

The preceding example illustrated the accounting for a nonmonetary exchange where a loss was indicated. To depict a similar exchange where a gain is present, assume that Book-It, Inc. and Jar, Inc. exchange similar productive assets. Book-It exchanges Equipment A and $5,000 cash for

Equipment B, which is held by Jar, Inc. Specific information relating to the two pieces of equipment is shown in Exhibit II below.

Exhibit II

Exchange Assumptions

	Equipment A (Book-It, Inc.)	Equipment B (Jar, Inc.)
Cost	$100,000	$ 90,000
Accumulated Depreciation	20,000	15,000
Book Value	$ 80,000	$ 75,000
Fair Market Value	$ 95,000	$100,000

Again, the first step is to determine if a loss is indicated. Turning first to Book-It, Inc., note that the fair value of $95,000 is greater than the book value of $80,000; therefore, no loss is indicated. Because Book-It is the payer of the boot, no gain can be recognized on the exchange (Block 9). The asset received, Equipment B, is recorded at an amount equal to the book value of the asset surrendered, Equipment A, plus the boot paid. In this particular case, the amount assigned to Equipment B would be calculated as follows:

Book Value of Asset Surrendered	$80,000
Cash Paid	5,000
Amount Assigned to Equipment B	$85,000

The following journal entry is required on the books of Book-It, Inc. to record the nonmonetary exchange.

Equipment B	85,000	
Accumulated Depreciation—Equipment A	20,000	
Equipment A		100,000
Cash		5,000

For Jar, Inc., note that the fair market value of $100,000 is greater than the $75,000 book value of the asset. Therefore, no loss is indicated. On the contrary, a gain is indicated; and Jar, Inc., as recipient of the boot, must recognize a portion of the gain. The amount of gain to be recognized is determined by the following formula:

$$G = MC - \left[\left(\frac{MC}{MC + FAR}\right)(BV)\right]$$

Where: G = Gain to be recognized.
MC = Monetary consideration received.
FAR = Fair value of asset received (or, if more clearly determinable, the fair value of the asset surrendered).
BV = Book value of the asset surrendered.

Using this formula and the information given above, the gain to be recognized is calculated as follows:

$$G = \$5{,}000 - [(\frac{\$5{,}000}{\$5{,}000 + \$95{,}000})\ (\$75{,}000)]$$

$$G = \$1{,}250$$

The expression MC/MC+FAR is used to determine the percentage of the book value of the asset considered to be sold.

Next, the amount to be recorded as the value of the asset received must be calculated, using a similar formula. The formula used for this purpose is presented below.

$$A = BV - [(\frac{MC}{MC + FAR})\ (BV)]$$

Where: A = Amount recorded for the asset received.
BV = Book value of asset surrendered.
MC = Monetary consideration received.
FAR = Fair value of asset received (or, if more clearly determinable, the fair value of the asset surrendered).

Using this formula and the related information, the amount to be used for the asset received can be calculated as follows:

$$A = \$75{,}000 - [(\frac{\$5{,}000}{\$5{,}000 + \$95{,}000})\ (\$75{,}000)]$$

$$A = \$71{,}250$$

Based upon the information generated from the two formulas, the following journal entry is required by Jar, Inc. to record the exchange:

Equipment A	71,250	
Accumulated Depreciation—Equipment B	15,000	
Cash	5,000	
Equipment B		90,000
Gain on Nonmonetary Exchange		1,250

With this entry, the discussion and illustrations of accounting for nonmonetary transactions is complete. Additional consideration will be given to the income tax implications of APB Opinion No. 29, as well as to the required disclosures.

Income Tax Considerations

A difference may exist between the financial reporting and tax reporting of gains and losses on nonmonetary transactions. Any difference is considered to be a timing difference and is accounted for in accordance with the provisions of APB Opinion No. 11. (See APB Opinion No. 11 in Topic 5 for a detailed analysis of accounting for tax timing differences.)

Disclosure Requirements

The disclosure requirements of APB Opinion No. 29 are minor in nature and include the following items:

(1) A description of the nature of the nonmonetary transactions, as well as of the accounting basis used for the transferred assets, must be disclosed; and

(2) Gains and losses on nonmonetary exchanges must be disclosed.

SFAS No. 34 (October 1979) Capitalization of Interest Cost

This pronouncement represents a significant departure from previous accounting practices. In the past, interest costs were generally treated as period costs by most non-utility companies. Under normal conditions it was not considered proper to capitalize interest cost and treat that cost as part of the cost of the asset acquired or constructed. Utility companies have been routinely capitalizing interest costs, as well as the cost of equity funds, for the past 40 years. The primary purpose of interest capitalization for utility companies was to increase the rate base and thereby the return on assets. The rate base becomes higher because interest is considered to be a component of the historical cost of the assets placed in service. The interest costs that were charged to the asset account would be amortized and charged to income over the life of the asset. Thus, in the long run, interest would be charged to income over the life of the asset rather than in the year the costs were incurred. This practice has the tendency to smooth income.

The task force selected to study the problem of interest capitalization was faced with an environment in which several different alternatives were available for the treatment of interest costs. Some companies considered all interest to be period costs and accordingly charged the entire amount of the interest incurred to income in the current accounting period. Still other companies followed the practice of capitalizing the cost of debt in certain selected circumstances but did not capitalize the cost of equity funds (this policy led to a partial capitalization of interest costs). Finally, some companies, primarily utilities, were capitalizing both the cost of debt and the imputed cost of equity capital. The question studied prior to the release of SFAS No. 34 was whether or not it was acceptable for non-utility companies to capitalize the cost of debt and/or equity capital as a normal part of the cost of assets acquired or constructed. If the practice was deemed to be appropriate, the next issue was to determine under what circumstances these costs should be capitalized.

As a result of the findings of the task force and the position papers of interested parties, the FASB concluded that in certain defined circumstances it would be appropriate to capitalize the cost of *debt*, and it was not appropriate to capitalize the cost of equity capital. The basis for this conclusion can be found in Appendix B to the Statement.

Defining Some Important Terms

In order to narrow the circumstances under which interest capitalization would be deemed appropriate, the FASB defined certain key terms in Statement No. 34. Some of the terms are defined below and others will be introduced during the discussion of the flowchart that follows.

1. *Interest Cost.*[1] The term interest cost is meant to include the following:

(a) interest on obligations having an explicit interest rate,

(b) interest imputed on certain types of payables as described in APB Opinion No. 21, *Interest on Receivables and Payables* (see Topic 6 for a complete discussion of APB Opinion No. 21),

(c) interest associated with capital leases as defined in SFAS No. 13, *Accounting for Leases* (see Topic 8 for a discussion of this Statement).

2. *Qualifying Asset.* A qualifying asset is one for which interest capitalization is appropriate. Paragraph 9 of the Statement defines qualifying assets as:

(a) "Assets that are constructed or otherwise produced for an enterprise's own use (including assets constructed or produced for the enterprise by others for which deposits or progress payments have been made)"

(b) "Assets intended for sale or lease that are constructed or otherwise produced as discrete projects (e.g., ships or real estate developments)."

---

[1] Statement No. 34 does not address the issue of compound interest. Some authors, relying on the "Basis for Conclusions," have interpreted compound interest to be consistent with the Statement. We do not agree with this interpretation and look forward to some guidance from the FASB. If you interpret the Statement differently, we would appreciate your comments.

3. *Capitalization Period.* The capitalization period represents the length of time during which it is appropriate to capitalize interest on a qualifying asset. This time period encompasses all the activities required to bring a qualifying asset to the condition and location necessary for its intended use. A problem is created for accountants because the capitalization period may include several fiscal periods or merely a part of one fiscal period. Interest capitalization will require the same type of allocations as accountants often make for other costs that do not coincide with a company's accounting period. The point to remember in the technical examples that appear later in this section is that interest capitalization may require certain estimations and/or allocations depending upon the circumstances faced in a given case.

The capitalization period does not begin until three conditions have been met. These conditions include:

(1) Expenditures for a qualifying asset have been made,

(2) Activities that are necessary to get the asset ready for its intended use are in progress, and

(3) Interest costs are being incurred.

Remember that all three of these conditions must be met before it is appropriate to begin the capitalization of interest.

The capitalization period ends when a qualifying asset is substantially complete and ready for its intended use. More will be said about the capitalization period during the discussion of the flowchart.

4. *Capitalization Rate.* The amount of interest to be capitalized during any given accounting period is determined by multiplying the "capitalization rate" times the *average accumulated expenditures* made on a qualifying asset. The amount of the average accumulated expenditures would be determined from the beginning of the capitalization period until the date the asset was complete and ready for use. Recall from the previous discussion that interest may be capitalized for more than one accounting period if the qualifying asset is not ready for its intended use.

If an enterprise borrowed money specifically for the construction or production of a qualifying asset, the rate of interest on the specific borrowing should be used as the capitalization rate for the qualifying asset in question. If the company incurred no specific new borrowing for the qualifying asset, the weighted average rate of interest on all borrowed funds should be used as the capitalization rate. A more refined definition of the capitalization rate will be given during the discussion of the flowchart.

5. *Expenditures.* Paragraph 16 of the Statement defines expenditures as the amounts spent "for the qualifying asset that have required the payment of cash, the transfer of other assets, or the incurring of a liability on which interest is recognized (in contrast to liabilities, such as trade payables, accruals, and retainages on which interest is not recognized)." The important point to remember is that an expenditure is not made by merely acquiring a qualifying asset; the method of payment also must be examined. For example, if the company is constructing an asset that qualifies for interest capitalization, and some materials are acquired for construction on "net-60" credit terms, an expenditure has not been made because cash has not been paid and the items purchased were acquired through the creation of a trade payable. The expenditure would be made when the payable was eliminated through the transfer of an asset in settlement of the account.

With this introduction to some of the key terms of SFAS No. 34, attention may be turned to an examination of the flowchart. The flowchart is designed to demonstrate how each of the terms defined above impact the accountant's decision-making process.

Flowchart and General Discussion

The first step in the decision-making process is for the accountant to determine if the asset acquired or constructed by the enterprise is one that qualifies for interest capitalization, i.e., a qualifying asset (Block 1). A description of qualifying assets has been given previously and no additional discussion is necessary. Once it has been determined that the enterprise has a qualifying asset, the next step is to see if the capitalization period has begun. Identification of the proper capitalization period is a complex process and requires several blocks in the flowchart. Before it is appropriate to capitalize interest in the current accounting period, three conditions must be met. First, the enterprise must have undertaken "activities" that are necessary to make the qualifying asset ready for its intended use (Block 2). The word "activities" is meant to encompass a broad range of functions that relate to the asset. Paragraph 17 of the Statement states that the word should include "all steps required to prepare the asset for its intended use." In addition to physicial construction, the following items are considered activities for purposes of meeting the first condition:

1. Administrative and technical activities during the preconstruction stage, such as the development of plans or the process of obtaining permits from governmental authorities.

2. Activities undertaken after construction has begun in order to overcome unforeseen obstacles, such as technical problems, labor disputes, or litigation.

Obviously, the word "activities" includes work during the preconstruction stage, work during the construction phase, and some post-construction work. Certainly the construction of a nuclear power plant would involve substantial costs of obtaining governmental permits and costs relating to unforeseen obstacles.

The second condition that must be met before interest capitalization is appropriate is that the enterprise has incurred expenditures in connection with a qualifying asset (Block 3). If an enterprise has ceased activities or expenditures on a qualifying asset, no interest should be capitalized in that particular accounting period. When activities and expenditures have started again, interest capitalization may resume. If the activities or expenditures have been suspended for a *brief* period of time, and it is reasonable to assume that both of these items will continue in the very near future, interest capitalization should not be discontinued during this period of time.

The third condition that must be met is that the enterprise must have incurred interest costs during the current accounting period (Block 4). If the enterprise has incurred no interest costs, capitalization of interest would not be appropriate. The interest costs incurred by the enterprise need not be related to the expenditures or activities in the current period. For purposes of meeting this condition, the enterprise must have incurred interest costs relating to any debt instrument, even if the funds obtained through the issuance of the instrument were not used for purposes of acquiring or constructing a qualifying asset.

When all three of the conditions listed above have been met, the start of the interest capitalization period has been signaled. Once the beginning of the capitalization period has been identified, the next step in the accounting process is to determine the end of the capitalization period for accounting purposes. Recall that the actual capitalization period runs from the date the activities described above occur until the qualifying asset is substantially complete and ready for its intended use. This time period may cover several accounting periods; however, the accountant must determine the amount of interest to capitalize in the current accounting period. This is a classic allocation problem and presents the practitioner and student with several very interesting computational and implementation problems. If interest has been capitalized in the previous accounting period (Block 5), then the capitalization period will begin at the start of the current accounting period. If interest has *not* been capitalized in the previous accounting period, the capitalization period will begin on the date when the three conditions discussed above have been met, i.e., activities undertaken, expenditures made, and interest costs incurred.

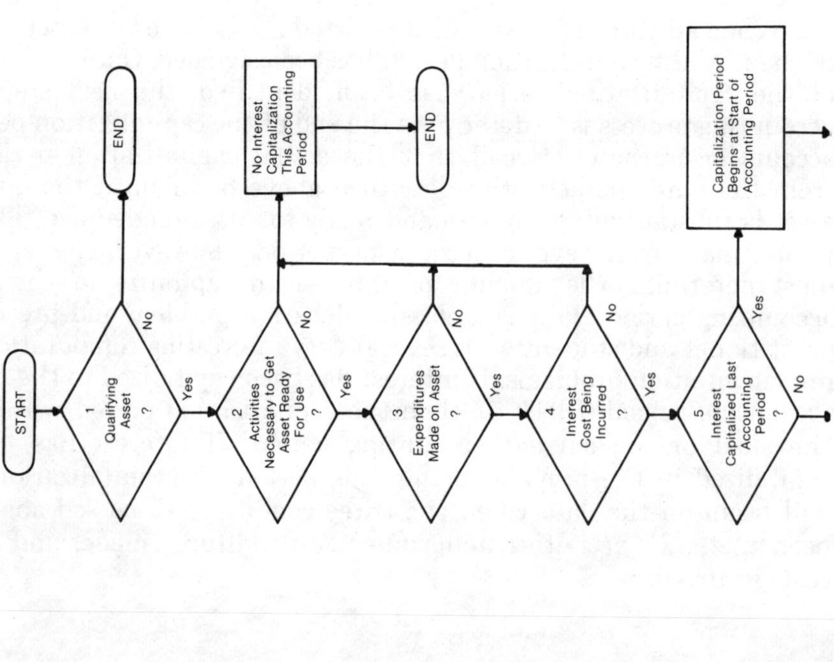
START
1 Qualifying Asset ?
No
END
Yes
2 Activities Necessary to Get Asset Ready For Use ?
No
No Interest Capitalization This Accounting Period
END
Yes
3 Expenditures Made on Asset ?
No
Yes
4 Interest Cost Being Incurred ?
No
Yes
5 Interest Capitalized Last Accounting Period ?
Yes
Capitalization Period Begins at Start of Accounting Period
No

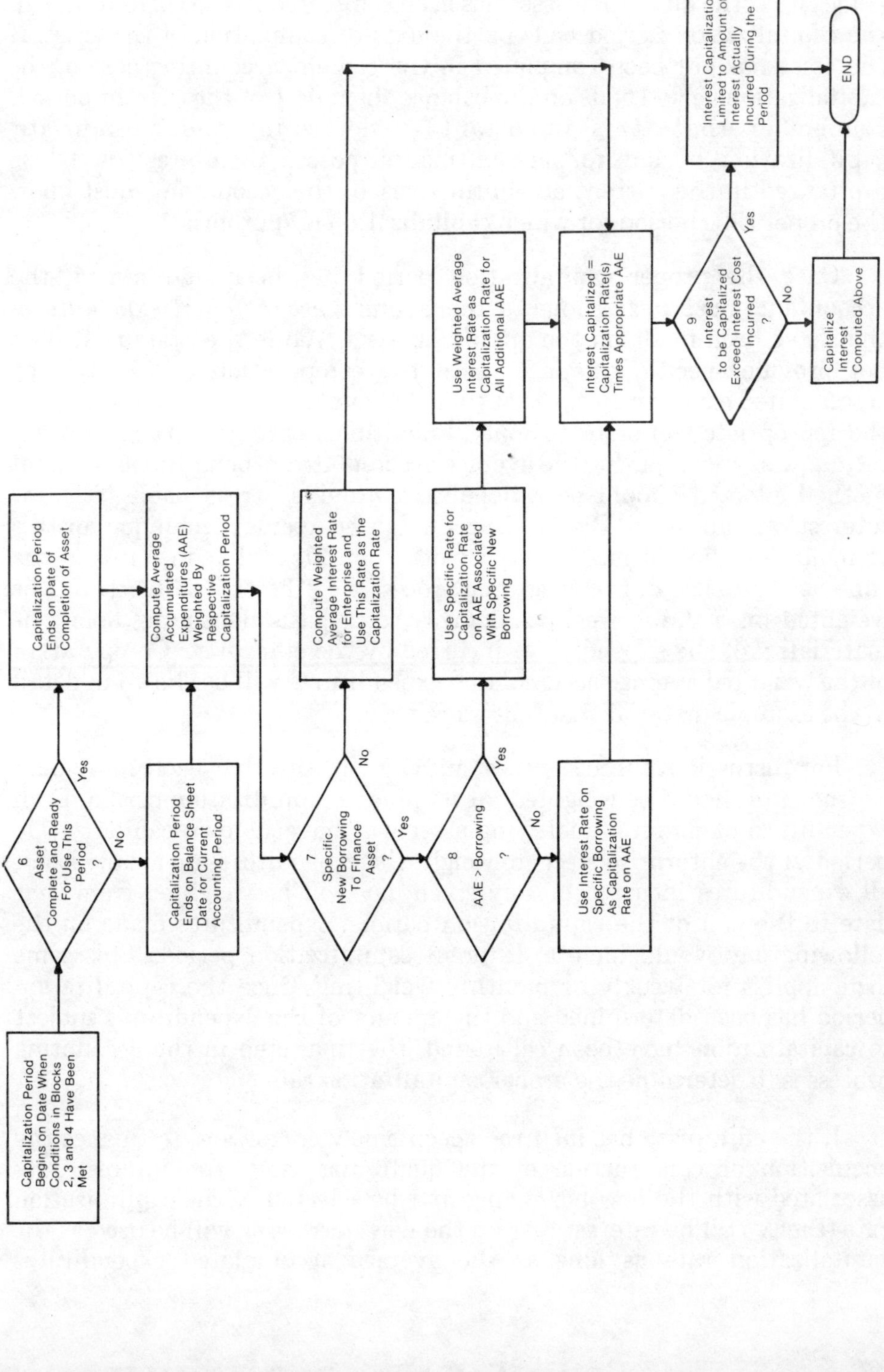
Capitalization Period Begins on Date When Conditions in Blocks 2, 3 and 4 Have Been Met
6 Asset Complete and Ready For Use This Period ?
Yes
No
Capitalization Period Ends on Date of Completion of Asset
Capitalization Period Ends on Balance Sheet Date for Current Accounting Period
Compute Average Accumulated Expenditures (AAE) Weighted By Respective Capitalization Period
7 Specific New Borrowing To Finance Asset ?
No
Yes
Compute Weighted Average Interest Rate for Enterprise and Use This Rate as the Capitalization Rate
8 AAE > Borrowing ?
Yes
No
Use Specific Rate for Capitalization Rate on AAE Associated With Specific New Borrowing
Use Weighted Average Interest Rate as Capitalization Rate for All Additional AAE
Use Interest Rate on Specific Borrowing As Capitalization Rate on AAE
Interest Capitalized = Capitalization Rate(s) Times Appropriate AAE
9 Interest to be Capitalized Exceed Interest Cost Incurred ?
Yes
No
Interest Capitalization Limited to Amount of Interest Actually Incurred During the Period
Capitalize Interest Computed Above
END

To identify the end of the capitalization period for current accounting purposes it is necessary to determine if the asset has been substantially completed and made ready for use in the current period (Block 6). If the qualifying asset has been completed in the current period, the capitalization period ends on the date of completion of the asset. If the asset has not been completed in the current accounting period, the capitalization period ends on the balance sheet date of the current period. Remember that it is important to determine the appropriate capitalization period for accounting purposes. If interest is to be capitalized in the current accounting period, the accountant must know the proper time period for which capitalization is appropriate.

Once the proper capitalization period has been determined, the accountant must next compute the *average accumulated expenditures* that have been made on the qualifying asset. While the Statement does not provide specific guidance as to the computation of the average accumulated expenditures, the authors believe that a weighted average is the appropriate technique to apply. Practitioners are free to choose other techniques for computing the average accumulated expenditures; the final method adopted should be rational and provide a reasonable basis for interest capitalization. By selecting a weighted average technique for this computation the authors have provided some flexibility in terms of the time period to use in the weighting process, i.e., the expenditures may be weighted on a daily, weekly, monthly, etc., basis depending upon the materiality of the expenditures incurred by the enterprise. Computation of the weighted average accumulated expenditures will be shown in detail in the example material that follows.

For discussion purposes, it is sufficient to say that each individual expenditure should be weighted for its *unique* capitalization period. Each expenditure made on a qualifying asset will have its own capitalization period. If the enterprise elects to weight the expenditures on a daily basis, all expenditures incurred on any given day will be weighted from that date to the end of the capitalization period. Expenditures made on the following day would have a different capitalization period. This same logic applies for weekly or monthly weighting. Once the capitalization period has been determined and the amount of the expenditures subject to capitalization have been calculated, the final step in the accounting process is to determine the proper capitalization rate.

If the enterprise has incurred specific new borrowings to finance the acquisition or construction of the qualifying asset, the interest rate associated with the new borrowing *may* be selected as the capitalization rate (Block 7). The interest rate on the new borrowing will be used as the capitalization rate as long as the average accumulated expenditures associated with the new borrowing *do not* exceed the amount of the new borrowing (Block 8). If the average accumulated expenditures exceed the amount of the new borrowing, the enterprise will have two capitalization rates. The rate of interest on the new borrowings will be used as the capitalization rate for the average accumulated expenditures associated with the new borrowing and the weighted average interest rate from all borrowings will be used as the capitalization rate for all other average accumulated expenditures. In this case, it is necessary for the enterprise to compute the weighted average interest rate on all borrowings.

If the enterprise has not incurred any new borrowing specifically for the purpose of financing the qualifying asset, the weighted average interest rate will be used as the capitalization rate (Block 7). Paragraph 12 of the Statement indicates that the interest to be capitalized should be an amount that "theoretically could have been avoided if expenditures for the asset had not been made." This conclusion leads the authors to believe that the weighted average interest rate should be reflective of the current interest costs the enterprise *might* incur if it borrowed funds to finance the acquisition of the qualifying asset. Therefore, some judgment is required when calculating the weighted average interest rate. This interest rate must reflect only current interest rates if the requirements of Paragraph 12 are to be met.

Once the capitalization period has been determined, the average accumulated expenditures calculated, and the capitalization rate(s) identified, the final step in the computational process is to compute the interest to be capitalized. When this amount has been computed, the final decision in the accounting process involves a comparison of the interest capitalized with the actual interest costs incurred during the period (Block 9). The amount of interest that may be capitalized during any accounting period is limited to the amount of interest actually incurred. If the amount of interest capitalized is less than the actual interest incurred, there are no further decisions or entries to be made. If the amount of interest capitalized is greater than the interest incurred, the amount capitalized must be adjusted to the amount of interest incurred. In this case all interest incurred will be capitalized and there will be no interest charged to income.

This general discussion of the flowchart has been helpful in gaining an understanding of the nature of the interest capitalization process. However, as will be seen in the technical material that follows, many new and difficult accounting problems must be solved before a complete understanding of the process can be obtained.

Technical Considerations Involved in the Interest Capitalization Process

To illustrate the specific computational and accounting problems associated with interest capitalization, four separate examples will be fully developed. Information relating to the first example is listed in Exhibit I.

Exhibit I
Interest Capitalization Assumptions—Example 1

1. Maddan, Inc., a December 31 year-end company, was involved in several long-term construction or asset purchase activities during 198A.

2. On January 1, 198A, a $500,000 advance payment was made to Clair Company for equipment to be delivered to Maddan on July 1, 198A. The equipment was delivered as scheduled and the final $500,000 payment was made on that date. Maddan, Inc. borrowed the $500,000 advance payment and the $500,000 final payment. The rate of interest associated with these borrowings was 12 percent.

3. On April 1, 198A, construction was started on an addition to the current plant facilities. The addition was to be completed on March 1, 198B, at an estimated cost of $10,000,000. Cash payments made during 198A relating to the construction project were as follows:

May 1, 198A	$1,200,000
July 1, 198A	400,000
August 1, 198A	900,000
October 1, 198A	5,000,000
November 1, 198A	600,000
	$8,100,000

Maddan had established a line of credit for the construction project that allowed the company to borrow up to $10,000,000 anytime during 198A and 198B. The rate of interest associated with the line of credit was 13 percent.

4. Total interest costs incurred during 198A amounted to $500,000.

The first problem associated with the material presented in Exhibit I is to determine if the assets described are "qualifying assets" as defined in Statement No. 34. The equipment purchased on July 1, 198A is a qualifying asset because it is an asset that was produced by an outside entity for Maddan's use, and thus qualifies under Paragraph 9(a) of the Statement. Just because an enterprise has acquired a qualifying asset does not mean that interest will be capitalized. Before it is appropriate to capitalize interest, the accountant must determine if the qualifying asset meets the conditions specified for the capitalization period to begin. The plant facilities being constructed for Maddan's use also qualify under Paragraph 9(a). In this particular example, both of the assets described are qualifying assets.

The next step in the analysis of this example is to determine if the conditions needed for interest capitalization have been met. Maddan has undertaken activities necessary to make both assets ready for their intended use, i.e., the construction or purchase of the asset has begun. In addition, Maddan has incurred expenditures in connection with both of the assets *and* the company has incurred interest during the current accounting period. All three of the conditions necessary to begin the capitalization of interest have been met.

Next, the proper capitalization period must be determined. This is a complex problem and will be discussed in some detail. Because the acquisition of both assets was started this accounting period, no interest was capitalized last period. The capitalization period will begin on a qualifying asset on the date the three conditions described above have been met (activities undertaken, expenditures incurred and interest incurred).

In the case of the equipment acquired on July 1, 198A, the capitalization period begins on January 1, 198A, and ends on July 1, 198A, the date the asset was delivered and made ready for its intended use. Thus the capitalization period for the equipment is one-half of the current accounting period (January 1 through July 1, 198A).

Concentrating on just the equipment for the next few moments, the next step in the accounting process is to compute the average accumulated expenditures. Each individual expenditure must be weighted from the date it was incurred until the end of the capitalization period. The $500,000 expenditures made on January 1, 198A, has been outstanding from the beginning of the capitalization period to the end of the period (6 months) and should be weighted accordingly. The $500,000 final payment was made on the date the equipment was delivered and made ready for use. The average accumulated expenditures would be computed as follows:

Date of Expenditure [a]	Amount [a]	Capitalization Period [b]	Average Expenditure
January 1	$500,000	6/12	[c] $250,000
July 1	500,000	0/12	—0—
			$250,000

[a] See Exhibit I, Item 2.
[b] Period from date of expenditure to July 1, 198A.
[c] $500,000 × 6/12 = $250,000.

After the amount of the average accumulated expenditures have been computed, the appropriate capitalization rate must be selected. Since Maddan entered into a specific new borrowing agreement for the acquisition of the equipment, the capitalization rate *may* be the rate of interest associated with the new borrowing. The average accumulated expenditures of $250,000 are less than the amount of the new borrowing of $1,000,000, therefore, the 12 percent interest rate on the borrowing should be used as the capitalization rate.

The final step in the computational process is to calculate the amount of interest to capitalize in relation to the equipment. The calculation would be made as follows:

Average Accumulated Expenditures	$250,000
Capitalization Rate	× 12%
Interest to be Capitalized	$ 30,000

The journal entries to record the progress payment on January 1, 198A would be as follows:

Progress Payment on Constructed Asset	500,000	
Cash		500,000

The journal entry to record the final payment for the equipment of July 1, 198A would be:

Progress Payment on Constructed Asset	500,000	
Cash		500,000

The journal entry to record the interest to be capitalized and to transfer the asset into service would be:

Equipment	1,030,000	
Progress Payment on Constructed Asset		1,000,000
Interest Incurred		30,000

The authors believe that it is essential for an enterprise to use an interest suspense or clearing account as a result of SFAS No. 34. The account "Interest Incurred" is such a suspense account. All interest incurred during the period should be charged to the suspense account instead of interest expense. The account will be cleared by debits to either an asset account (as shown above) or to interest expense and a credit to the suspense account. This type of accounting facilitates the allocation procedures required by the Statement. The use of a suspense account should prove very beneficial if the enterprise prepares interim financial statements and capitalizes interest in the interim period.

This last set of journal entries completes the analysis of the equipment described in Exhibit I. The remaining item requiring analysis is the expansion of the existing plant facilities of Maddan. Once again, the company has undertaken activities to make the asset ready for its intended use, made expenditures in connection with the plant facilities, and incurred interest during the period. Since all three conditions required for interest capitalization have been met, interest capitalization is appropriate in the current accounting period (198A). Because there was no interest capitalized on the plant construction last period, the capitalization period begins on the first date that all the conditions described above have been met.

In this case, there will be a different capitalization period for each individual expenditure incurred. When thinking about the capitalization period it is important to remember that each individual expenditure has its own unique capitalization period. These differing capitalization periods will impact the computation of the average accumulated expenditures on the project. Since the construction has not been completed by the end of the current accounting period, the capitalization period for all expenditures will end on the balance sheet date (December 31, 198A).

In the computation of the average accumulated expenditures relating to the plant facilities each individual expenditure will be weighted from the date it was incurred to the balance sheet date. For example, the first expenditure was incurred on May 1, 198A and amounted to $1,200,000. This expenditure must be weighted from May 1 to December 31, 198A, or a period of eight months. The computation of the average accumulated expenditures for the plant facilities is shown below:

Date of Expenditure [a]	*Amount* [a]	*Capitalization Period* [b]	*Average Expenditure*
May 1, 198A	$1,200,000	8/12	[c]$ 800,000
July 1, 198A	400,000	6/12	200,000
August 1, 198A	900,000	5/12	375,000
October 1, 198A	5,000,000	3/12	1,250,000
November 1, 198A	600,000	2/12	100,000
	$8,100,000		$2,725,000

[a] See Exhibit I, Item 3.
[b] Period from date of expenditure to December 31, 198A.
[c] $\$1,200,000 \times 8/12 = \$800,000$.

Once the average accumulated expenditures have been calculated, the next step is to determine the proper capitalization rate(s). Maddan's line of credit for the construction of the plant facility represents a specific new borrowing intended to finance the asset. The amount of the new borrowing ($8,100,000) is more than the amount of the average accumulated expenditures ($2,725,000), therefore, the capitalization rate will be the 13 percent associated with the line of credit. The amount of interest capitalized in connection with the plant facilities in 198A would be computed in the following manner:

Average Accumulated Expenditures	$2,725,000
Capitalization Rate	× 13%
Interest Capitalized	$ 354,250

The journal entry necessary to record the interest computed above would be:

Construction in Progress-Plant Facility	354,250	
Interest Incurred		354,250

The balance in the "Construction in Progress-Plant Facility" account at December 31, 198A is $8,454,250 ($8,100,000 expenditures + $354,250 interest).

The total amount of interest capitalized during 198A was $384,250 ($354,250 on Plant Facility + $30,000 on Equipment). The total amount of interest incurred in 198A by Maddan was $500,000. Therefore, the interest incurred was greater than the interest capitalized and no adjustment to the amounts capitalized is required. The balance in the "Interest Incurred" account at December 31, 198A is $115,750 ($500,000 incurred − $384,250 capitalized). Since no additional interest will be capitalized in 198A, the balance in the suspense account would be cleared through a charge to interest expense for the period. The journal entry necessary to clear the suspense account at the end of the accounting period would be:

Interest Expense	115,750	
Interest Incurred		115,750

Of the $500,000 interest incurred during 198A, $384,250 has been capitalized as part of the cost of qualifying assets, and $115,750 has been charged to income as interest expense.

The assumptions established for this first example were designed to be relatively straight-forward. The primary concerns of the material were to introduce the concept of the capitalization period, the computation of the average accumulated expenditures, and the selection of the appropriate capitalization rate where the enterprise financed the construction or purchase of the asset through the issuance of new borrowings. There are several complicating factors that have not been discussed. The second example is designed to introduce some additional new concepts and computations required of accountants under the provisions of SFAS No. 34. The new decision requirements introduced in the second example deal with the following problems:

(1) Interest capitalization on land

(2) The impact of issuing noninterest bearing notes in exchange for qualifying assets

(3) Selection of the proper capitalization rate when qualifying assets are purchased with the proceeds from the sale of stock

(4) Accounting for interest to be capitalized when the amount of interest capitalized exceeds the amount of interest actually incurred during the period.

Specific information about the Example 2 assumptions is shown in Exhibit II.

Exhibit II

Interest Capitalization—Example 2

1. Tract Development Corporation, a December 31 year-end company, was involved in certain construction and development activities during 198B.

2. A parcel of land was purchased on January 1, 198B, for $3,000,000 cash. The land is being held for a future plant site. During 198B, no activities were performed on the land to make it ready for its intended use.

3. On April 1, 198B, the company purchased another parcel of land for $5,000,000 cash and a noninterest bearing note for $4,000,000. The note is to be repaid in full at the end of 10 years. Tract would normally have to pay 10 percent for similar financing. The land purchased was to be subdivided and sold as developed lots in the near future. Tract incurred the following *cash* expenditures during 198B for the development of the land.

May 1, 198B	$120,000
July 1, 198B	300,000
December 1, 198B	48,000
	$468,000

The land development was incomplete on December 31, 198B.

4. Tract contracted for the construction of a building for its use on July 1, 198A. Estimated total expenditures were $4,000,000, which were financed through the issuance of common stock. The building is to be constructed on a site purchased on July 1, 198A, for $500,000 cash. Actual cash expenditures for the building during 198A and 198B were:

July 1, 198A	$ 100,000
September 1, 198A	300,000
December 1, 198A	400,000
February 1, 198B	500,000
March 1, 198B	400,000
May 1, 198B	500,000
July 1, 198B	800,000
	$3,000,000

The building was completed and ready for use on August 1, 198B.

5. In addition to the financing discussed above, Tract's debt structure on December 31, 198B is presented below:

Debt	*Interest Rate*
$ 500,000	10%
50,000	5%
1,000,000	11%
2,000,000	12%
$3,550,000	

6. Total interest incurred by Tract during 198B amounted to $598,500.

Because the assumptions for Example 2 are complex and detailed, each asset will be discussed individually and a summary of all the assets will be prepared at the end of the discussion.

To begin the analysis of the information presented in Example 2, consider the land purchased on January 1, 198B, for $3,000,000 cash. Technically the land may be considered a qualifying asset, however, there will be no interest capitalization in the current accounting period because no activities are in progress to make the land ready for its intended use. If some activities were under way and expenditures were incurred in connection with the land, interest capitalization would be proper because Tract Development did incur interest during the accounting period. Since interest will not be capitalized on the land in the current period, no further consideration will be given to this asset.

The next asset, described in Item 3, is the land purchased on April 1, 198B, that is to be subdivided and sold as developed lots. This land is a qualifying asset as defined in Paragraph 9(b) of the Statement. Tract is in the process of making the land ready for its intended use, has incurred expenditures in connection with the property, and has incurred interest costs during the current accounting period. Once it has been determined that interest capitalization is proper, the next step in the accounting process is to determine the appropriate capitalization period for the asset.

The capitalization period for the land begins on April 1, 198B because that is the first date on which (1) activities were underway to develop the property, (2) expenditures have been incurred in connection with the purchase price and development activities, and (3) Tract has incurred interest during the period of $598,500. The capitalization period ends on December 31, 198B, because at the balance sheet date the development of the land was still not complete. Therefore, the capitalization period runs from April 1 to December 31, 198B.

Once the capitalization period has been determined, the next step is to compute the average accumulated expenditures relating to the land. The first problem encountered in the computation is related to the issuance of the $4,000,000 noninterest bearing note. Paragraph 2 of Statement No. 34 specifies that the provisions of APB Opinion No. 21—*Interest on Receivables and Payables*—applies in the process of interest capitalization. The noninterest bearing note issued for land would fall under the provisions of APB Opinion No. 21 (see Topic 6 for a detailed discussion of APB Opinion No. 21). With this in mind, Tract Development would have to pay 10 percent interest for financing similar to the noninterest bearing note and no information is available about the fair value of the land or the market value of the note. Under these circumstances, it is appropriate to use the 10 percent interest rate to *impute* interest on the note. The $4,000,000 face amount of the note must be divided into its principal and interest elements. This calculation is made below:

Face Amount of the Note	$4,000,000
Present Value Factor for $1 for 10 Years at 10 Percent—Appendix A	× .38554
Principal Amount of the Note	$1,542,160

The principal amount of the note is equal to $1,542,160, therefore, the interest component would be equal to $2,457,840 ($4,000,000 Face Amount less $1,542,160 Principal Amount). Once the principal component of the note has been determined, the amount of the average accumulated expenditures may be calculated.

Each individual expenditure associated with the land will be weighted in the computation from the date the expenditure is incurred to the balance sheet date (the end of the capitalization period). The computation of the average accumulated expenditures for 198B is shown below:

Date of Expenditure [a]	*Amount* [a]	*Capitalization Period* [b]	*Average Expenditure*
April 1, 198B (Principal Amount of Note)	$1,542,160	9/12	[c] $1,156,620
April 1, 198B (Cash Downpayment)	5,000,000	9/12	3,750,000
May 1, 198B	120,000	8/12	80,000
July 1, 198B	300,000	6/12	150,000
December 1, 198B	48,000	1/12	4,000
	$7,010,160		$5,140,620

[a] See Exhibit II, Item 3.
[b] Period from date of expenditure to December 31, 198B.
[c] $\$1,542,160 \times 9/12 = \$1,156,620$.

Note that each expenditure has been weighted from the date it was incurred to the end of the accounting period. Because the expenditures were incurred on the first of each month, the authors have decided to use a monthly weighting for the expenditures. If the expenditures had been incurred at various times during the month and the amounts were material, a daily or weekly weighting may be appropriate. This is a judgment that management must make.

The entry to record the original purchase of the land would be:

Land Under Development	[a] 6,542,160	
Discount on Notes Payable	2,457,840	
Notes Payable		4,000,000
Cash		5,000,000

[a] $5,000,000 cash down payment + $1,542,160 principal of note = $6,542,160.

While there would have been three separate journal entries to record the development expenditures incurred in connection with the land, the entry below represents a summary of all three of those entries and has been prepared for illustration purposes only.

Land Under Development	[b] 468,000	
Cash		468,000

[b] $120,000 + $300,000 + $48,000 = $468,000.

The balance in the "Land Under Development" account prior to interest capitalization is $7,010,160 ($6,542,160 + $468,000) and appears in the schedule showing the computation of the average accumulated expenditures.

Now that the proper amounts have been recorded for the land, the next step is to select the proper capitalization rate(s). The $4,000,000 face amount noninterest bearing note represents a specific new borrowing in connection with the land. The $5,000,000 cash downpayment and the $468,000 development expenditures incurred during the period will be capitalized at the weighted average interest rate because no new borrowings were incurred to finance these expenditures.

Average accumulated expenditures in an *amount equal to the principal amount* of the noninterest bearing note will be capitalized at the rate of 10 percent; the rate used to impute interest. Average accumulated expenditures in excess of the amount specified above will be capitalized at the weighted average capitalization rate. Before the computation of the interest to be capitalized in this particular example can be completed it is necessary to calculate the weighted average capitalization rate. The authors' computation of this rate is shown below:

Selected Debt [a]	*Interest Rate* [a]	*Interest Cost*
$ 500,000	10%	$ 50,000
1,000,000	11%	110,000
2,000,000	12%	240,000
$3,500,000		$400,000

[a] See Exhibit II, Item 5.

The weighted average capitalization rate would be computed by dividing the total interest cost on the *selected* debt by the amount of the debt. In the above example, the weighted average capitalization rate is equal to 11.43 percent ($400,000/$3,500,000). The reader should note that the authors have omitted the $50,000, 5 percent debt listed in Exhibit II from the computation of the weighted average capitalization rate. Statement No. 34 requires that the accountant exercise judgment in determining the debt to include and exclude in the calculation of the proper weighted average capitalization rate, and the authors believe that the $50,000, 5 percent debt represents an obsolete interest rate that does not reflect the realities of any current borrowing by Tract. The objective of the computation is to attempt to estimate a reasonable measure of the acquisition cost of the asset by determining the interest cost that could be *avoided* if the asset had not been purchased and developed. The authors feel that inclusion of the $50,000, 5 percent debt would distort the determination of the weighted average capitalization rate. Judgments similar to this will have to be made in most cases where the weighted average capitalization rate must be calculated.

Now that the two interest rates associated with the acquisition and development of the land have been determined, the amount of interest to be capitalized may be computed. This computation is shown below:

Average Accumulated Expenditures	$5,140,620
Average Accumulated Expenditures Equal to Principal Amount of the Noninterest Bearing Note	1,156,620
Average Accumulated Expenditures in Excess of the Principal Amount of the Note	$3,984,000

While the principal amount of the new borrowing ($1,542,160) is in excess of the average accumulated expenditures associated with the new borrowing ($1,156,620), the difference between these two amounts cannot be used to apply to other average accumulated expenditures. The reason for this is that the note was issued only for the purchase price of the land and cannot be used for the payment of development expenditures. The remainder of the purchase price of the land was paid for in cash and this amount did not come from a new borrowing. The 10 percent interest rate on the noninterest bearing note will be used as the capitalization rate for the average accumulated expenditures associated with the principal amount of the note and the weighted average interest rate will be used as the capitalization rate for all other average accumulated expenditures. The computation of the interest to be capitalized in connection with the land development is shown below:

Average Expenditure	*Capitalization Rate*	*Interest Capitalization*
$1,156,620	10%	$115,662
3,984,000	11.43%	455,371
$5,140,620		$571,033

Remember that the reason for the use of two capitalization rates was the fact that the average accumulated expenditures exceeded the amount of the specific new borrowing associated with the purchase price of the land.

The journal entry necessary to capitalize the interest relating to the land would be as follows:

Land Under Development	571,033	
Interest Incurred		571,033

The "Interest Incurred" account is a clearing account that facilitates the accounting problems encountered in Statement No. 34. The interest capitalized above does not exceed the actual interest incurred by the company of $598,500, however, if any additional interest is to be capitalized the entry just completed may require an adjustment. This part of the accounting process will be addressed in the summary part of the analysis.

The final assets that need to be analyzed from the Example 2 material are the building that is currently being constructed for Tract and the land that was purchased as the site for the building. The building and land are both qualifying assets because they represent assets that are being constructed by an outside enterprise for use by Tract. It is appropriate to capitalize interest on the land and building because, (1) activities are currently underway to make the assets ready for their intended use, (2) expenditures have been incurred on both the land and the building, and (3) Tract has incurred interest during the current accounting period. Since interest capitalization is proper, the next step is to determine the capitalization period for the assets.

The capitalization period for the building being constructed begins on January 1, 198B, because interest has been capitalized during 198A and the construction was not complete on December 31, 198A. During 198B, construction is still in progress, expenditures are being made and interest is being incurred by Tract. The capitalization period ends on August 1, 198B, the date the building is completed and ready for its intended use. Now that the proper capitalization period has been determined, the average accumulated expenditures may be computed.

The average accumulated expenditures during 198B are calculated below. Remember that each individual expenditure must be weighted for the length of time it has been outstanding during the capitalization period.

Date of Expenditure[a]	*Amount*[a]	*Capitalization*[b] *Period*	*Average Expenditure*
July 1, 198A (Land Purchase)	$ 500,000	7/12	[c] $ 291,667
July 1, 198A	100,000	7/12	58,333
September 1, 198A	300,000	7/12	175,000
December 1, 198A	400,000	7/12	233,333
February 1, 198B	500,000	6/12	250,000
March 1, 198B	400,000	5/12	166,667
May 1, 198B	500,000	3/12	125,000
July 1, 198B	800,000	1/12	66,667
	$3,500,000		$1,366,667

[a] See Exhibit II, Item 4.
[b] Period from January 1, 198B or date of expenditure to August 1, 198B.
[c] $500,000 × 7/12 = $291,667.

Two important points need to be made about the calculations shown above. First, interest will be capitalized on the land that was purchased on July 1, 198A. The interest associated with the land expenditure *will not* be charged to the land account, instead, it will be added to the cost of the facility that is constructed on the land. Second, the expenditures for 198A are included as part of the base for computation of the interest to be capitalized in 198B. Statement No. 34 requires the accountant to compute the average *accumulated* expenditures, and these would include expenditures incurred in prior accounting periods. However, the capitalization period relating to these expenditures would run only from the beginning of the current accounting period (January 1, 198B) to the date the assets are completed and made ready for use (August 1, 198B).

Once the capitalization period has been identified and the average accumulated expenditures have been calculated, the proper capitalization rate(s) must be selected. Since the land was acquired for cash and the construction of the building is being financed through the sale of stock, no specific new borrowing can be related to the expenditures incurred. Because no new borrowing can be identified, the weighted average capitalization rate is the appropriate rate to use. The weighted average capitalization rate has been previously calculated to be 11.43 percent. The amount of interest to be capitalized on the plant construction for 198B would be:

Average Accumulated Expenditures	$1,366,667
Weighted Average Capitalization Rate	× 11.43%
Interest Capitalization on Plant Facility	$ 156,210

Some of the expenditures associated with the plant site and facilities were recorded in 198A. While there would have been several entries to record the 198B expenditures, a summary of the entries is shown below:

Progress Payments on Construction	[a] 2,200,000	
Cash		2,200,000

[a] $500,000 + $400,000 + $500,000 + $800,000.

Finally, the journal entry to record the interest capitalization on the land and plant facilities for 198B would be:

Progress Payments on Construction	156,210	
Interest Incurred		156,210

At this point in the accounting process it is necessary to summarize the information developed during the analysis of the information from Example 2. Total interest capitalized is equal to $727,243 ($571,033 from the purchase of the land to be subdivided + $156,210 from the building facilities constructed for Tract). The total interest incurred during 198B was $598,500 as shown in Exhibit II. The interest capitalized of $727,243 *exceeds* the interest actually incurred during the period of $598,500. Paragraph 15 of the Statement prohibits the capitalization of interest in excess of the amount of interest incurred during the period. The total amount of interest to capitalize is *limited* to $598,500. In this case, it is necessary to correct the journal entries previously made.

When the interest capitalized exceeds the interest incurred, an additional allocation problem is created. The interest capitalized must be allocated to the various assets that qualify for capitalization on some rational basis. The Statement provides no specific guidance in the implementation of the allocation process, but it would seem logical to allocate the interest on the basis of the relative value of the interest that was capitalized. While other allocation procedures may be acceptable, e.g., on the basis of the average accumulated expenditures on the assets involved, the authors believe that the process described above is rational and systematic. In the case of the Example 2 material, the allocation would be accomplished as follows:

Interest Capitalized on Land to be Subdivided	$571,033
Interest Capitalized on Land and Plant Facilities	156,210
Total Interest Capitalized	$727,243

$$\frac{\$571{,}033}{\$727{,}243} \times \$598{,}500 = \$469{,}944 \text{ Allocate to Land Development}$$

$$\frac{\$156{,}210}{\$727{,}243} \times \$598{,}500 = \$128{,}556 \text{ Allocate to Land and Plant Facility}$$

As a result of the above allocation process an adjusting journal entry is required to properly state the amount of interest capitalized. In the case of the land development interest of $571,033 has been capitalized and only $469,944 should be capitalized. The difference of $101,089 should be used to reduce the account "Land Under Development." For the land and plant facility, interest of $156,210 has been capitalized and $128,556 should have been capitalized. The difference of $27,654 should be used to reduce the account "Progress Payments on Construction." As a result of the allocation process the following journal entry is needed to restate the interest capitalized:

Interest Incurred	128,743	
Land Under Development		101,089
Progress Payments on Construction		27,654

This completes the discussion and analysis of the Example 2 material. The reader may wish to take a few minutes to review both the information given in Exhibit II and the solution offered on the preceding pages before moving on to the next example. The Example 2 material was much more complex than Example 1 and may require some additional time to digest. The third example is designed to extend the reader's understanding of Statement No. 34.

The information about Example 3 is outlined in Exhibit III. Specifically the Example is designed to illustrate the following problem areas:

(1) Temporary interruptions in the construction process of a qualifying asset

(2) Accounting for self-constructed qualifying assets where the construction costs exceed the fair market value of the asset constructed

(3) Accounting for the discontinuation of a land development project

(4) Distinction between "cost incurred" and "expenditure" as defined in the Statement.

Exhibit III

Interest Capitalization—Example 3

1. Dyer, Inc., a December 31 year-end company, was involved in several specific construction and purchase activities during 198A.

2. On January 1, 198A, the company began construction on a new coal burning generator designed to reduce its utility costs. When completed the generator would provide all electrical needs of Dyer. The company was forced to shut down construction of the generator from May 1, 198A to June 1, 198A, as the result of a governmental injunction that grew out of public concern about the pollution potential of the generating facility. This interruption was considered only temporary in nature. Construction materials for the entire project were purchased on January 1, 198A for $400,000 cash. Other cash expenditures during 198A were as follows:

February 1, 198A	$100,000
March 1, 198A	150,000
April 1, 198A	200,000
May 1, 198A	150,000
June 1, 198A	200,000
	$800,000

The generator was completed and placed in service on July 1, 198A. Dyer financed the construction of the generator through the use of a line of credit that allowed the company to borrow any amount up to $1,500,000 throughout 198A. The line of credit carried an interest rate of 12 percent. The generator could be constructed by an outside contractor for a purchase price of $1,150,000.

3. On April 1, 198A, Dyer purchased land that cost $1,000,000 with the intent of subdividing the parcel and selling it as developed lots. A note was issued for the entire purchase price of the land. The note bears interest at the rate of 11 percent, which is assumed to be a reasonable interest rate for this type of project. Dyer incurred costs of $20,000 on April 1, 198A, and $30,000 on May 1, 198A, relating to the development of the property. The company financed the expenditures by borrowing funds with a stated interest rate of 13 percent. On June 1, 198A, Dyer determined that it was not economically feasible to develop the land for sale as lots, so the company discontinued the development project. Dyer decided to retain the land as a possible future plant site.

4. On November 1, 198A, Dyer began construction on a new piece of equipment. Materials for the construction cost $150,000 and were purchased on November 1 on credit terms of "net-90 days" (no interest). Labor costs of $25,000 were incurred during November and paid on December 1, 198A. Additional labor costs were incurred during December in the amount of $40,000, and were paid on January 1, 198B. In addition to the materials described above, Dyer purchased materials on November 1, for $50,000. In payment of this purchase the seller required that Dyer sign a 10 percent, 90-day note for the entire purchase price.

5. Total interest costs incurred during 198A amounted to $210,500.

6. Dyer computed its weighted average capitalization rate to be 12.2 percent.

Since this Example contains several different assets, the analysis of the information presented will be on a piecemeal basis taking one asset at a time. Towards the end of the analysis, information about each individual asset will be summarized to determine if the total interest capitalized is less than the interest costs incurred by Dyer during 198A.

The analysis will start with the coal burning generator described in Item 2 of the Exhibit. The generator is a qualifying asset according to the provisions of Paragraph 9(a) of the Statement. The capitalization period for this asset begins on January 1, 198A because that is the first date that (1) activities are underway on the construction project, (2) expenditures have been made for construction materials, and (3) interest has been incurred by Dyer. The capitalization period ends on July 1, 198A, because this is the date the generator is complete and ready for use. Interest capitalization would not be suspended during the month of May because the interruption in construction is deemed to be temporary in nature. Interest capitalization will be suspended only when there has been a prolonged or permanent interruption in the construction or purchase of a qualifying asset, i.e., an extended period of time when no activities were being carried out and no expenditures were being made in connection with the project.

Once the capitalization period has been determined, the average accumulated expenditures must be calculated. This computation is shown below. Remember that each individual expenditure must be weighted from the date it was incurred to the end of the capitalization period.

Date of Expenditure [a]	*Amount* [a]	*Capitalization Period* [b]	*Average Expenditure*
January 1, 198A	$ 400,000	6/12	[c] $200,000
February 1, 198A	100,000	5/12	41,667
March 1, 198A	150,000	4/12	50,000
April 1, 198A	200,000	3/12	50,000
May 1, 198A	150,000	2/12	25,000
June 1, 198A	200,000	1/12	16,667
	$1,200,000		$383,334

[a] See Exhibit III, Item 2.
[b] Period from date of expenditure to July 1, 198A.
[c] $400,000 × 6/12 = $200,000

Since the average accumulated expenditures of $383,334 do not exceed the $1,200,000 amount of new borrowing, the interest rate associated with the line of credit will become the capitalization rate. The final step in the accounting process is to compute the amount of interest to capitalize. This computation is shown below:

Average Accumulated Expenditures	$383,334
Capitalization Rate	× 12%
Interest to be Capitalized	$ 46,000

While there would have been several journal entries during 198A to record the expenditures associated with the generator, the entry below represents a summary of those entries.

Construction in Progress—Generator	1,200,000	
Cash		1,200,000

The journal entry required to capitalize the interest relating to the generator would be as follows:

Construction in Progress—Generator	46,000	
Interest Incurred		46,000

The amount of interest capitalized thus far does not exceed the interest incurred during the accounting period. However, if the total interest capitalized exceeds the interest incurred some adjustment will be required for the entry above. This comparison will be made in the summary phase of the analysis.

Before the amount shown in the "Construction in Progress—Generator" account can be transferred to the "Equipment" account and placed in service, the cost of the asset ($1,246,000) must be compared with the fair market value of the generator. Based upon the information in Exhibit III, the fair value of the generator as measured by the price quote from an outside contractor is $1,150,000. Since the fair market value is $96,000 ($1,246,000 – $1,150,000) less than the amount currently recorded in the "Construction in Progress" account, a loss must be recognized in the period of construction. The loss will be equal to the $96,000 necessary to reduce cost to market value. Paragraph 19 of the Statement requires that interest be capitalized during the construction period even though cost will exceed fair market value of the asset. As a result of this requirement, the entry necessary to transfer the amount currently in "Construction in Progress" to the proper "Equipment" account would be:

Equipment	1,150,000	
Provision to Reduce Construction Cost to Fair Value	96,000	
Construction in Progress—Generator		1,246,000

The "Provision to Reduce Construction Cost to Fair Value" account should be shown on the income statement as a line item in the nonoperating section. Another point must be made about the construction of the generator. Materials for the entire construction of the generator were purchased on January 1, 198A for cash. This expenditure is weighted from the date of purchase *rather than* the date the materials were actually used on the project.

The second asset to be considered from the Example 3 material is the purchase of land for subdivision and development. The land is a qualifying asset for at least part of the year because it was purchased for the purpose of development. However, when development was discontinued on June 1, 198A, the land no longer qualified for interest capitalization. The capitalization period for the land development project begins on April 1, 198A because that is the first date that (1) activities were undertaken to develop the property, (2) expenditures have been made on the land, and (3) interest was incurred by Dyer, Inc. The capitalization period ends on June 1, 198A, because this is the date that Dyer determined that it was not economically feasible to continue the development of the land. When it was decided that the land would be held for a future plant site the amount of the expenditures incurred represent an investment rather than an inventory item. Interest capitalization is not considered proper for assets classified as investments. In the case of the land, the interest capitalization period runs from April 1, 198A to June 1, 198A.

The next step in the accounting process is to compute the average accumulated expenditures on the land while it was a qualifying asset. The computation of the average accumulated expenditures is shown below and remember that each individual expenditure must be weighted from the date it was incurred to the end of the capitalization period.

Date of Expenditure [a]	*Amount* [a]	*Capitalization Period* [b]	*Average Expenditure*
April 1, 198A (Purchase Price)	$1,000,000	2/12	[c] $166,667
April 1, 198A (Development Cost)	20,000	2/12	3,333
May 1, 198A	30,000	1/12	2,500
	$1,050,000		$172,500

[a] See Exhibit III, Item 3.
[b] Period from date of expenditure to June 1, 198A.
[c] $1,000,000 × 2/12 = $166,667.

Both the purchase of the tract of land and the payment of the development costs were made through specific new borrowings. The purchase price of the *land* was financed through the issuance of an 11 percent note, and the development costs were financed by borrowed funds bearing interest at the rate of 13 percent. Since the amount of the new borrowings ($1,050,000) is greater than the amount of the average accumulated expenditures ($172,500), the interest rates on the new borrowings will be used as the capitalization rates. The 11 percent interest rate will be used for the average accumulated expenditures associated with the purchase price of the land, and the 13 percent interest rate will apply to the average accumulated expenditures associated with the development costs. The computation of the interest to be capitalized during 198A on the land development project is shown below:

Type of Expenditure	*Average Expenditure*	*Capitalization Rate*	*Interest Capitalized*
Land-Purchase Price	$166,667	11%	[a] $18,333
Development Cost	3,333	13%	433
Development Cost	2,500	13%	325
	$172,500		$19,091

[a] $166,667 × 11% = $18,333

A summary of the journal entries necessary to record the initial purchase of the land, the subsequent development expenditures, and interest capitalization would be:

Land Under Development	1,069,091	
Cash		1,050,000
Interest Incurred		19,091

At this point in the analysis it is not known if the interest capitalized is greater than the interest incurred by Dyer in the current accounting period. As a consequence, the journal entry shown above may require some adjustment during the summary phase of the analysis.

Because Dyer, Inc. discontinued development of the land on June 1, 198A, and decided to hold it as a possible future plant site, the company must transfer the balance in the "Land Under Development" account to an appropriate investment account. The land is no longer held for development and is therefore no longer a qualifying asset. The cost basis of the land is now $1,069,091, even though the original purchase price was only $1,000,000. The journal entry to transfer the balance in the "Land Under Development" account would be:

Land Held for Plant Site	1,069,091	
Land Under Development		1,069,091

The reader should be aware of the fact that in the case of the land development two different capitalization rates were used. It would not be unusual to find multiple interest rates from specific new borrowings being used as capitalization rates.

Attention is now turned to the last asset from the Example 3 material. Dyer, Inc. is in the process of constructing a piece of equipment for its own use. This is a qualifying asset as defined in Paragraph 9(a) of the Statement. The capitalization period for the equipment begins on November 1, 198A because that is the first date that (1) activities have been started to construct the asset, (2) expenditures have been made in connection with the project, and (3) interest has been incurred by Dyer. The capitalization period ends on December 31, 198A, because this is the balance sheet date and construction has not been completed. After the capitalization period has been determined, the average accumulated expenditures may be calculated. This calculation is shown below:

Date of Expenditure [a]	*Amount* [a]	*Capitalization Period* [b]	*Average Expenditure*
November 1, 198A	$50,000	2/12	[c] $ 8,333
December 1, 198A	25,000	1/12	2,083
	$75,000		$10,416

[a] See Exhibit III, Item 4.
[b] Period from date of expenditure to December 31, 198A.
[c] $50,000 × 2/12 = $8,333.

Recall from Exhibit III that the following costs were incurred by Dyer in connection with the construction project:

Materials (Purchased on net-90 day basis)	$150,000
Labor for November (Paid December 1, 198A)	25,000
Labor for December (Paid January 1, 198B)	40,000
Materials (Purchased by issuing note payable)	50,000
	$265,000

Of the $265,000 total costs incurred in connection with the project, only $75,000 qualify as "expenditures" according to the provisions of Statement No. 34. For purposes of interest capitalization, an "expenditure" exists when cash has been paid, an asset transferred, or a liability incurred that requires the recognition of interest. In the case of the materials purchased on November 1, 198A on a net-90 day basis, no payment will be made until the end of January 198B; therefore, the cost cannot be considered an expenditure. The labor costs incurred during December were not paid until January 198B, and cannot be included in the expenditures for purposes of interest capitalization. The labor costs for November were actually weighted from December 1, 198A, the date of payment. The materials that were purchased on November 1, 198A, by issuing a note payable qualify as expenditures because the liability created bears interest. Now that the average accumulated expenditures have been computed, the next step in the capitalization process is to select the proper capitalization rate(s).

For the information being analyzed, two capitalization rates will be used. The expenditure for the acquisition of materials on November 1, 198A, was accomplished by issuing a 10 percent note payable. The 10 percent rate will be applied to the average accumulated expenditures associated with the $50,000 purchase of materials. No specific new borrowing is related to the labor costs paid on December 1, 198A; therefore, the company's weighted average capitalization rate of 12.2 percent applies to these expenditures. The computation of the interest to be capitalized is shown below:

Type of Expenditure	*Average Expenditure*	*Capitalization Rate*	*Interest Capitalized*
Materials purchased	$ 8,333	10%	$ 833
Labor costs	2,083	12.2%	254
	$10,416		$1,087

The journal entry to record the interest to be capitalized would be:

Construction in Progress—Equipment	1,087	
Interest Incurred		1,087

Once again, two capitalization rates were used to determine the proper amount of interest to be capitalized. The analysis of all assets listed in the Example 3 material has been completed and one final test is required.

The final step is to compare the interest capitalized in connection with all the assets listed above with the actual interest incurred by Dyer, Inc. during 198A. The summary below shows the amount of interest that has been capitalized.

Qualifying Asset	*Interest Capitalized*
Generator Construction	$46,000
Land Development	19,091
Equipment Construction	1,087
	$66,178

The actual interest incurred by Dyer in 198A amounted to $210,500 (see Exhibit III), which is in excess of the amount of interest capitalized; therefore, no adjustment is required to the journal entries prepared for each asset. The final entry required by Dyer is to clear the suspense account "Interest Incurred." The balance in the suspense account is $144,322 ($210,500 actual interest costs – $66,178 interest capitalized) and must be closed to interest expense for 198A. The entry to accomplish this would be:

Interest Expense	144,322	
Interest Incurred		144,322

This last entry completes the analysis of the Example 3 material. The fourth, and final, example is designed to demonstrate some refinements of Statement No. 34. Specifically, the last example will deal with interest capitalization on certain leasing transactions and with the problem of project completion in stages rather than as one discrete event. The information about the final example is listed in Exhibit IV.

Exhibit IV
Interest Capitalization—Example 4

1. Eagle, Inc., a December 31 year-end company, signed a lease agreement on January 1, 198A, requiring the payment of $100,000 at the beginning of each of the next five years. Eagle's incremental borrowing rate is 12 percent which is approximately equal to the lessor's implicit rate on the leased property. The property has a fair market value of $403,735 and an estimated economic life of five years. Eagle depreciates

similar owned property on the straight-line basis. The equipment was installed on January 1, 198A, and Eagle made the first lease payment on this date; however, problems soon developed with the installation and Eagle could not use the equipment until April 1, 198A.

2. Eagle contracted with Hayes Company to construct an apartment complex consisting of 10 units with a total estimated cost of $1,000,000. Hayes began construction on January 1, 198A, and completed two of the 10 units on August 1, 198A. Eagle was able to rent these two units during the month of August. The remaining units were still not completed at December 31, 198A. Advance payments were made by Eagle for the units under construction in the following amounts:

March 1, 198A	$150,000
May 1, 198A	150,000
June 1, 198A	170,000
July 1, 198A	180,000
September 1, 198A	80,000
December 1, 198A	70,000
	$800,000

Of the payments made between March 1 and July 1, 198A, $200,000 represents payments for the two units that have been completed. These payments were incurred uniformly during the period, i.e., at the rate of $50,000 for each payment made. Eagle obtained a loan from a local bank in connection with the construction project. The borrowing bears interest at the rate of 12 percent.

3. Eagle contracted with Owens Contractor, Inc. to construct a plant facility consisting of three separate processes: (1) a metal stamping process facility, (2) a cleaning and painting process facility, and (3) an assembly facility. The production facility requires that the incoming metal be stamped first, then sent to the cleaning and painting facility, and finally to the assembly room. The estimated cost of the facility is $3,000,000. Construction was started by Owens Contractor on January 1, 198A. The metal stamping facility was completed on September 1, 198A; however, the cleaning and painting and assembly facilities were not completed by December 31, 198A. Advanced payments were made by Eagle to Owens in the following amounts:

January 1, 198A	$ 200,000
March 1, 198A	500,000
June 1, 198A	500,000
September 1, 198A	400,000
November 1, 198A	360,000
	$1,960,000

Eagle obtained a bank loan to finance the construction of the plant facility and is required to pay 13 percent on the borrowed funds.

4. Interest costs incurred during 198A amounted to $245,600.

5. For the sake of simplicity, the land that would be associated with the apartment complex in (2) above and the land portion of the plant facility in (3) above have been ignored. Detailed information about interest capitalization on land was shown in the Example 2 material and need not be repeated in this Example.

Once again, the analysis of the information in Exhibit IV will be carried out on each individual asset and a summary of the individual considerations will be prepared towards the end of the discussion. The first asset identified in the Exhibit is the leased property, and the analysis will begin by examining the terms of the lease agreement in detail.

The lease agreement creates a unique problem for Eagle, Inc. in the interest capitalization process. Since the lease described in Item 1 of the Exhibit is a capital lease, an obligation on which interest accrues is created on January 1, 198A, the date of the lease agreement (see Topic 8 for a complete discussion of lease accounting). Since Eagle was not able to use the property until April 1, 198A, the leased asset is a qualifying asset as defined by Statement No. 34. The capitalization period begins on January 1, 198A, because this is the first date that (1) activities have begun in connection with the leased property, (2) expenditures have been made in the form of the lease payment, and (3) Eagle has incurred interest costs. The capitalization period ends on April 1, 198A, the date the equipment is ready for its intended use. The capitalization period will be for three months of 198A. Before the average accumulated expenditures can be computed, the entry to record the capital lease property and related obligation must be made. The journal entry is shown below:

Leased Property Under Capital Lease	403,735	
Obligation Under Capital Lease		403,735

The amount recorded as the leased asset and obligation is the present value of the minimum lease payments required by the lease agreement. The calculation of this amount is shown below:

Lease Payment	$100,000
Present Value Factor for an Annuity Due at 12% for 5 Years (Appendix A)	4.03735
Present Value of the Minimum Lease Payment	$403,735

The present value of the minimum lease payment is equal to the fair value of the leased asset at the inception, and is used to record the leased asset and obligation. The discount rate of 12 percent is used because it is equal to Eagle's incremental borrowing rate and the rate implicit in the lease.

Given the journal entry to record the capital lease, the average accumulated expenditures would be calculated as follows:

Total Expenditures—January 1, 198A	$403,735
Capitalization Period (January 1—April 1)	× 3/12
Average Accumulated Expenditures	$100,934

Expenditures, as defined in the Statement, are made when cash is paid, assets transferred or liabilities incurred that normally bear interest. In the case of the leased asset, the obligation of $403,735 was incurred on January 1, 198A, and this obligation bears interest at the rate of 12 percent. The expenditure for 198A is equal to $403,735, the amount of the lease obligation.

Now that the average accumulated expenditures have been computed, the proper capitalization rate must be determined. Eagle, Inc. assumed a specific new borrowing in connection with the leased property, i.e., the lease obligation, and since this amount is greater than the average accumulated expenditures of $100,934, the 12 percent interest rate implicit in the lease will be used as the capitalization rate. The computation of the interest to be capitalized is shown below:

Average Accumulated Expenditures	$100,934
Capitalization Rate	× 12%
Interest to be Capitalized	$ 12,112

The journal entry necessary to record the interest would be:

Leased Property Under Capital Lease	12,112	
Interest Incurred		12,112

Since it is not yet known if the interest capitalized on all qualifying assets will exceed the amount of interest actually incurred, this journal entry may require some adjustment in the summary phase of the analysis. The next asset to be reviewed is the apartment complex under construction. Remember that the land portion of the project has been intentionally left out of the analysis in order to simplify the accounting process.

In connection with the apartment project, two units were completed and placed in service before the entire complex was completed. This is an example of a qualifying asset being completed in stages rather than all at one time. The construction of the apartment complex is a qualifying asset as specified in Paragraph 9(a) of the Statement. The new problem created in this example is that Paragraph 18 of the Statement requires that interest capitalization cease on the part of the asset that has been substantially completed as long as the use of the asset is not dependent upon the completion of the entire project. In this example there will be one capitalization period for the two units completed during 198A and another capitalization period for the uncompleted units.

The capitalization period for all of the units begins on March 1, 198A, because this is the first date that (1) activities were started on the apartment complex, (2) expenditures in the form of advanced payments were made by Eagle to Hayes Company, and (3) interest was incurred by Eagle. Even though construction began on January 1, 198A, the capitalization period did not begin on this date because no expenditures have been made. The capitalization period ends on two different dates. For the two units completed during 198A, the capitalization period ends on August 1, 198A, the date the units were placed in service. For the eight units that were not completed during 198A, the capitalization period ends on December 31, 198A, the balance sheet date of Eagle.

After the capitalization periods have been determined, the average accumulated expenditures may be computed. The expenditures on the apartment complex must be divided between the completed units and the uncompleted units. Recall from the information in Exhibit IV that the $200,000 total expenditures associated with the completed units were incurred at the rate of $50,000 for each of the following dates: March 1, May 1, June 1, and July 1, 198A. The remainder of the expenditures made on these dates were associated with the uncompleted units. The computation of the average accumulated expenditures for the two completed units would be as follows:

Date of Expenditure [a]	*Amount* [a]	*Capitalization Period* [b]	*Average Expenditure*
March 1, 198A	$ 50,000	5/12	[c] $20,833
May 1, 198A	50,000	3/12	12,500
June 1, 198A	50,000	2/12	8,333
July 1, 198A	50,000	1/12	4,167
	$200,000		$45,833

[a] See Exhibit IV, Item 2.
[b] Period from date of expenditure to August 1, 198A.
[c] $50,000 × 5/12 = $20,833.

The computation of the average accumulated expenditures relating to the eight units that were not completed during 198A would be accomplished as follows:

Date of Expenditure [a]	*Total Expenditure* [a]	*Applicable to Completed Units*	*Applicable to Uncompleted Units*	*Capitalization Period* [b]	*Average Expenditure*
March 1	$150,000	$ 50,000	$100,000	10/12	[c] $ 83,333
May 1	150,000	50,000	100,000	8/12	66,667
June 1	170,000	50,000	120,000	7/12	70,000
July 1	180,000	50,000	130,000	6/12	65,000
September 1	80,000	-0-	80,000	4/12	26,667
December 1	70,000	-0-	70,000	1/12	5,833
	$800,000	$200,000	$600,000		$317,500

[a] See Exhibit IV, Item 2.
[b] Period from date of expenditure to December 31, 198A.
[c] $100,000 × 10/12 = $83,333.

The average accumulated expenditures for the completed and uncompleted units have been calculated, and the next step is to determine the appropriate capitalization rate to apply to these expenditures.

Eagle financed the expenditures on the apartment complex through a specific new borrowing. The bank loan bears interest at the rate of 12 percent. Since the average accumulated expenditures of $363,333 ($45,833 + $317,500) do not exceed the $800,000 amount of the new borrowing, the interest rate associated with the bank loan will be used as the capitalization rate for both the completed and the uncompleted units. The computation of the amount of interest to be capitalized in connection with the construction of the apartment complex is shown below:

	Completed Units	Uncompleted Units	Total
Average Accumulated Expenditures	$45,833	$317,500	$363,333
Capitalization Rate	× 12%	× 12%	× 12%
Interest Capitalization	$ 5,500	$ 38,100	$ 43,600

The journal entry to record the capitalization of interest and the cost of the completed units would be:

Rental Property—Apartment	205,500	
Cash		200,000
Interest Incurred		5,500

The journal entry to record the capitalization of interest and the costs of the uncompleted units would be:

Progress Payments on Constructed Assets	638,100	
Cash		600,000
Interest Incurred		38,100

Once again, it is not known if the amount of interest capitalized on all assets exceeds the amount of interest incurred by Eagle during the current accounting period. The journal entries made above may require some adjustment in the summary phase of the analysis. The final asset to be considered is the plant facility being constructed.

The plant facility is a qualifying asset according to Paragraph 9(a) of the Statement. The plant is being constructed to produce a product by a sequential process. The metal stamping process is complete and ready for use, but cannot be used until the entire plant is complete. No single process will stand alone. Paragraph 18 of the Statement requires that interest capitalization continue on the *entire* asset until all processes are complete and ready for use. Accounting for interest capitalization on the construction of the plant will *not* require the determination of two or more separate capitalization periods as was the case with the apartment complex.

The capitalization period begins on January 1, 198A, because this is the first date that (1) activities were started to construct the facility, (2) expenditures were made on the plant in the form of advanced payments to Owens Contractors, and (3) Eagle, Inc. has incurred interest costs. The capitalization period ends on December 31, 198A, the balance sheet date of the company. The construction of the entire facility is not complete at December 31, 198A. Once the capitalization period has been determined, the average accumulated expenditures may be computed. The computation would be made as follows:

Date of Expenditure [a]	Expenditure [a]	Capitalization Period [b]	Average Expenditure
January 1, 198A	$ 200,000	12/12	[c] $ 200,000
March 1, 198A	500,000	10/12	416,667
June 1, 198A	500,000	7/12	291,667
September 1, 198A	400,000	4/12	133,333
November 1, 198A	360,000	2/12	60,000
	$1,960,000		$1,101,667

[a] See Exhibit IV, Item 3.
[b] Period from date of expenditure to December 31, 198A.
[c] $200,000 × 12/12 = $200,000.

As in all previous examples, each individual expenditure must be weighted for the length of time it has been outstanding during the capitalization period. Now that the average accumulated expenditures have been calculated, the proper capitalization rate must be selected.

Eagle has financed the construction of the plant through a specific new borrowing at the bank. Since the average accumulated expenditures of $1,101,667 are less than the amount of the new borrowings of $1,960,000, the rate of interest on the new borrowing will be used as the capitalization rate. The computation of the interest to be capitalized would be made as follows:

Average Accumulated Expenditures	$1,101,667
Capitalization Rate	× 13%
Interest to be Capitalized	$ 143,217

A summary journal entry to record the costs of the plant facility and the interest capitalization would be:

Progress Payments on Constructed Asset	2,103,217	
Cash		1,960,000
Interest Incurred		143,217

After this entry has been made it is time to summarize the results of the interest capitalization on the various assets in Exhibit IV. The total interest capitalized is computed below:

Leased Property	$ 12,112
Completed Apartment Units	5,500
Uncompleted Apartment Units	38,100
Plant Facility	143,217
Total Interest Capitalized	$198,929

The total interest incurred by Eagle during 198A amounted to $245,600 as shown in Exhibit IV. The total amount of interest incurred of $245,600 exceeds the total amount of interest capitalized of $198,929; therefore, the interest capitalization shown in the various journal entries will not require adjustment.

The final problem to be solved in connection with the information in Exhibit IV is to clear the suspense account "Interest Incurred." The balance in the account is $46,671 ($245,600 incurred – $198,929 capitalized) and will be closed to interest expense at December 31, 198A. The journal entry to clear the suspense account would be:

Interest Expense	46,671	
Interest Incurred		46,671

As a result of this entry it is now known that Eagle has capitalized interest of $198,929 during 198A, and expensed interest of $46,671 during the same period.

This completes the analysis of all four examples relating to interest capitalization. However, there are some additional matters that must be mentioned before the discussion of Statement No. 34 is complete.

Other Considerations

The Board, in Paragraph 23 of the Statement, states that if interest capitalization is applied to interim reports prior to December 16, 1979, all interim periods of the fiscal year should be restated to reflect the effects of capitalization. The Board provides no guidance in this area; however, APB Opinion No. 28 (see Topic 12 for a complete discussion of Interim Reporting) states that the interim period should apply the same accounting principles that were applied in the last annual period (with certain modifications). Interest capitalization in the interim period may present a serious problem in the computation of the weighted average capitalization rate. The authors feel that using an effective weighted rate, where it is required, would be an appropriate procedure. Applying this effective rate to the year-to-date average accumulated expenditures and subtracting previous interest capitalized during the current fiscal year appears to be a procedure that will meet the requirements of interim reporting.

In making the transition to SFAS No. 34, if assets that qualify for interest capitalization existed at the beginning of the fiscal year in which the transition is made, interest should be capitalized from the beginning of the year. If interest has been capitalized on qualifying assets using a method different from that described in SFAS No. 34, no adjustment is necessary, but SFAS No. 34 should be applied in all future periods. If interest has been capitalized on assets that *do not* qualify under the SFAS No. 34, no adjustment is necessary, but interest capitalization should be discontinued after the enterprise adopts the Statement.

Disclosures

Paragraph 21 of the Statement specifies the disclosure requirements during the period of interest capitalization. These disclosures include:

1. The amount of interest incurred and expensed, if no interest is capitalized during the current period, and

2. The total amount of interest incurred and the amount capitalized, if any interest has been capitalized in the current period.

Topic 4

Intangibles (Including Research and Development)

Detail Contents

APB Opinion No. 17 (August 1970)
Intangible Assets

APB Opinion No. 17 specifies procedures to be followed in accounting for the costs of intangible assets acquired from others or developed internally. Prior to the issuance of this Opinion, there were two basic types of intangibles for accounting purposes: those having a limited life, and those having a life that was not readily determinable. Intangibles with a limited life were amortized, but those intangibles whose useful life could not be determined were not amortized until such time as a useful life could be determined. In practice, most intangibles that did not have a limited life never were amortized. These previous practices were changed by APB Opinion No. 17.

The primary controversy in accounting for intangibles centered around the handling of "goodwill." Goodwill may be internally generated through excellent management of an enterprise, or as a result of above-average earnings, or it may be purchased as part of the cost of acquiring a group of assets, such as in a business combination. (See APB Opinion No. 16, "Business Combinations" in Topic 11 for a complete discussion of accounting for the cost of purchased goodwill. Also consult APB Opinion No. 18 in Topic 2 for the proper accounting of goodwill when the equity method is used to account for investments.) APB Opinion No. 17 addresses the problem of accounting for both internally generated goodwill and goodwill acquired through a purchase transaction.

The previous classification of intangibles into those with limited life and those lacking a limited life was abandoned by this Opinion. Instead, intangibles were classified as to those having a specific identity and those that lacked specific identity. Goodwill would fall into the latter category.

Flowchart and General Discussion—Purchased Intangibles

The Flowchart of APB Opinion No. 17 identifies the process of assigning costs to intangible assets and the subsequent accounting for those intangibles.

Intangible assets that are purchased (Block 1) may be purchased either individually (Block 6) or as part of a group of assets acquired. If the intangible asset is purchased individually, it should be capitalized and amortized over its expected useful life, using the straight-line method of amortization. (The straight-line method of amortization is not required if the company can demonstrate that some other method is more appropriate.) If it is not possible to determine the useful life of the intangible, it should be amortized over a period not to exceed 40 years. When, in rare cases, the useful life of the intangible is greater than 40 years, it still should be amortized over the 40-year period.[1]

The amount to be capitalized for an intangible asset purchased singly is the amount of cash paid. If the intangible was not acquired for cash, the cost assigned to the intangible would be equal to the fair value of the asset(s) given up or the present value of any liability incurred. If stock is issued to acquire the intangible, the cost would be equal to the fair value of the intangible asset received.

Intangible assets that may be purchased individually include patents, copyrights, trademarks and the like. Because these assets may be purchased individually, they have a specific identity. In the case of patents and copyrights, a *legal* life has been specified by the government. These items would be amortized over their legal life or useful life, whichever is shorter, providing the amortization period does not exceed 40 years. Since trademarks have no such legal life, they would be amortized over their useful life or 40 years, whichever is shorter.

Intangible assets also may be purchased as part of a group of assets or as the result of a business combination. If this is the case, the first step in the accounting process is to isolate those assets—both tangible and

---

[1] When acquiring a savings and loan or similar institution, the fair value assigned to accounts with the capacity to generate future income or business or payments made relating to the nature of the territory served will be excluded from goodwill. Such amounts will be established as separate intangible assets and amortized in accordance with the provisions of APB Opinion No. 17. The reader is encouraged to consult FASB Interpretation No. 9 for complete details.

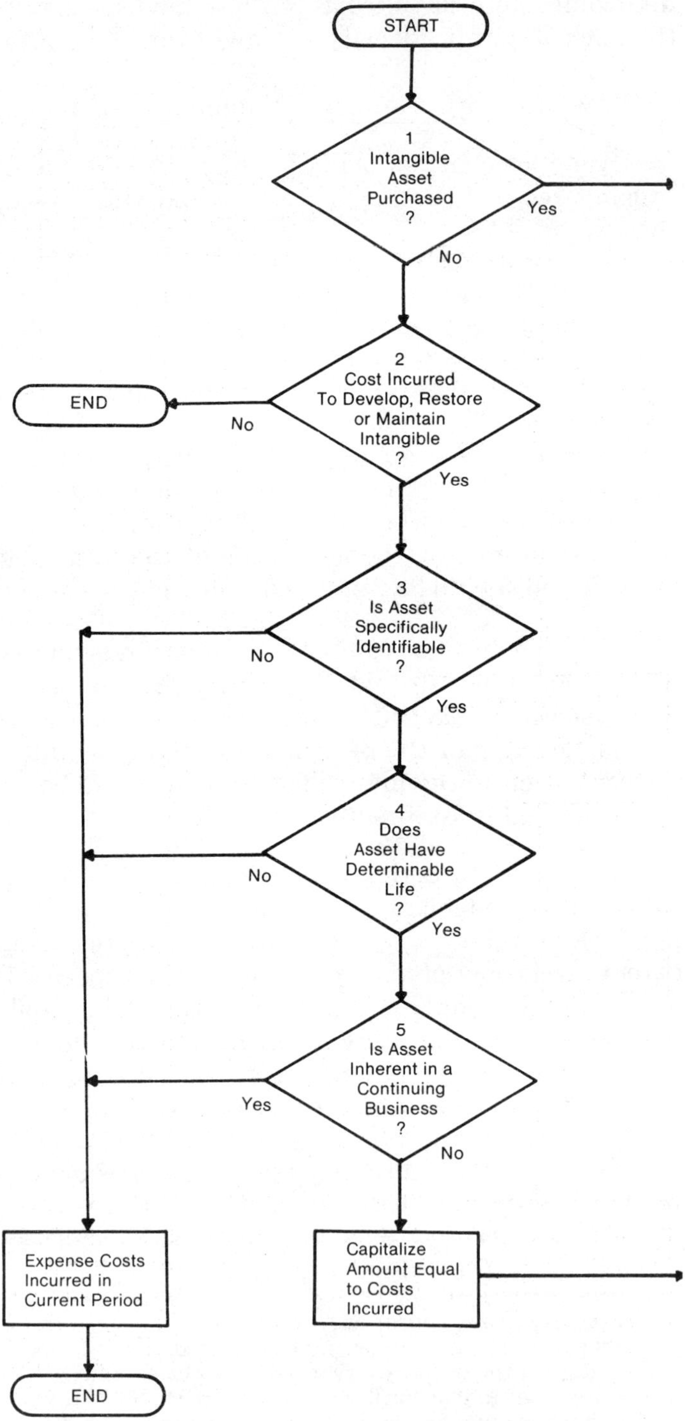
START
1
Intangible
Asset
Purchased
?
Yes
No
2
Cost Incurred
To Develop, Restore
or Maintain
Intangible
?
END
No
Yes
3
Is Asset
Specifically
Identifiable
?
No
Yes
4
Does
Asset Have
Determinable
Life
?
No
Yes
5
Is Asset
Inherent in a
Continuing
Business
?
Yes
No
Expense Costs
Incurred in
Current Period
Capitalize
Amount Equal
to Costs
Incurred
END

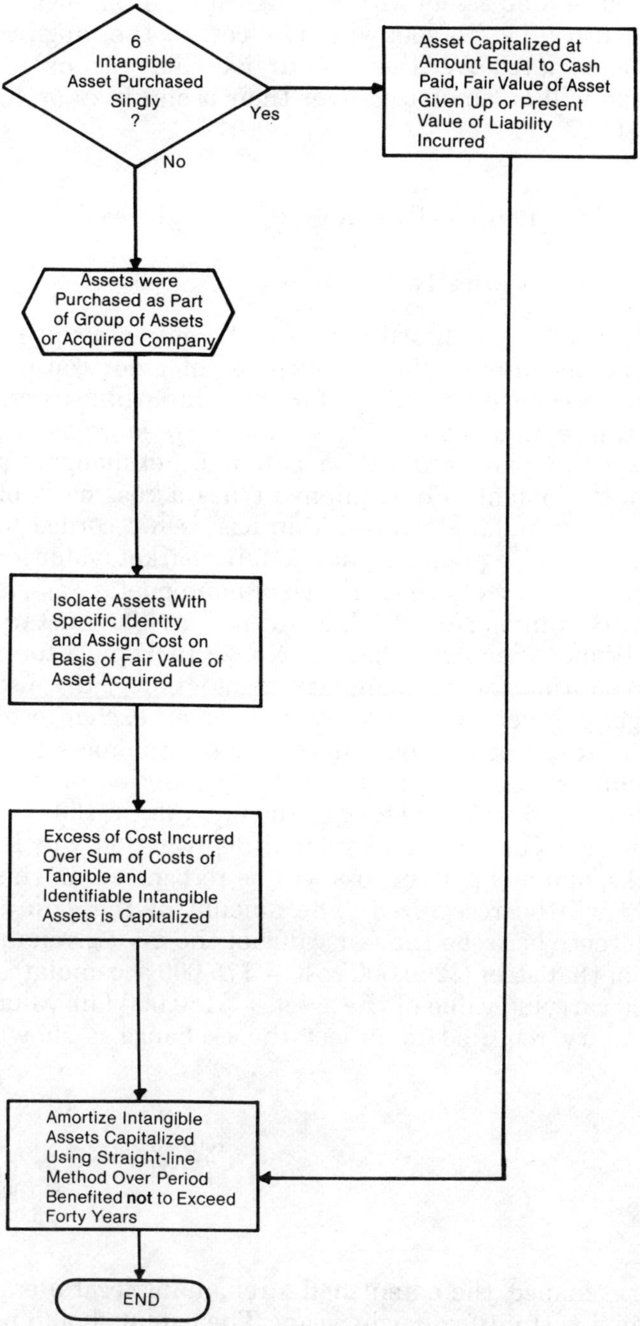
6
Intangible
Asset Purchased
Singly
?
Yes
No
Asset Capitalized at Amount Equal to Cash Paid, Fair Value of Asset Given Up or Present Value of Liability Incurred
Assets were Purchased as Part of Group of Assets or Acquired Company
Isolate Assets With Specific Identity and Assign Cost on Basis of Fair Value of Asset Acquired
Excess of Cost Incurred Over Sum of Costs of Tangible and Identifiable Intangible Assets is Capitalized
Amortize Intangible Assets Capitalized Using Straight-line Method Over Period Benefited not to Exceed Forty Years
END

intangible—that have a specific identity. The total cost paid to acquire the assets should be assigned to the specifically identifiable assets on the basis of their fair values. After this has been done, any costs in excess of the fair values of the identifiable assets will be assigned to an intangible asset lacking specific identity, i.e., to goodwill. The cost of the tangible assets acquired will be depreciated over their useful lives. The cost of the intangible assets acquired will be amortized over their useful lives or 40 years, whichever is shorter.

Technical Considerations—Purchased Intangibles

Intangibles Purchased Individually

When an intangible asset is purchased for cash, the only accounting problem is to determine the useful life for purposes of amortization. However, there are some accounting problems for those intangible assets acquired in a noncash transaction. To illustrate some of these problems, assume that Technology Company acquired a patent by exchanging a piece of equipment for the patent. The equipment has a cost basis of $200,000, and $75,000 of accumulated depreciation has been recorded to the date of the transfer. The equipment has a fair market value of $160,000. This transaction represents an exchange of nonmonetary assets and the provisions of APB Opinion No. 29, "Accounting for Nonmonetary Transactions," are applicable. (See APB Opinion No. 29 in Topic 3 for a detailed analysis of accounting for nonmonetary transactions.) Because this is not an exchange of inventory for inventory, or an exchange of similar productive assets, it can be assumed that the earnings process has culminated; and any gain or loss resulting from the transaction may be recognized. The patent received will be valued at the fair value ($160,000) of the equipment given up. The asset and related depreciation will be removed from the books, and any gain or loss will be recognized. In this case, a gain of $35,000 will be recognized. The amount of the gain is determined by the difference between the fair value of the asset given up and the carrying value of that asset ($200,000 cost – $75,000 accumulated depreciation = $125,000 carrying value of the asset – $160,000 fair value = $35,000 gain). The entry required to reflect the exchange is shown below:

Patent	160,000	
Accumulated Depreciation	75,000	
Equipment		200,000
Gain on Asset Transfer		35,000

At the date of the exchange, the patent had a remaining legal life of 15 years and an estimated useful life of eight years. The patent should be amortized over an eight-year period, using the straight-line method. The following entry shows the amortization for the first year of the patent:

Amortization Expense—Patent	20,000	
Patent		20,000

In this example, the amount of the amortization was charged directly to the patent account. It is just as acceptable to establish an accumulated amortization account as a contra asset to the patent account.

For purposes of the next example, assume that Technology Company, Inc. issues 5,000 of its $10 par value stock for a patent with an estimated fair value of $120,000. The stock currently is selling for $30 per share. The exchange of stock for a nonmonetary asset is exempt from the provisions of APB Opinion No. 29, and the value assigned to the stock should be the fair value of the asset received. In this case, the patent would be recorded at its fair value of $120,000, even though the fair value of the stock given up is $150,000 (5,000 shares × $30 per share). The journal entry to record the exchange is shown below:

Patent	120,000	
Common Stock		50,000
Contributed Capital in Excess of Par		70,000

The cost of the patent would be amortized over its remaining legal life or its useful life, whichever is shorter. The journal entry to record the amortization was shown above and will not be repeated here.

To illustrate a situation where a decision must be made as to the period of time necessary to amortize an intangible asset, assume that Intangible, Inc. purchased a patent, with a remaining life of 15 years, for $300,000. This particular patent was purchased by Intangible because it competed with one (with a remaining useful life of five years) already owned by the company. Intangible never intends to use the patent purchased. Since Intangible made the purchase only to eliminate competition, the purchase will be amortized over the remaining life of the patent already owned, which is five years. The annual amortization is $60,000 ($300,000/5 years).

Intangibles Purchased as Part of a Group of Assets

To illustrate the accounting for intangible assets acquired as part of a group of assets, assume that, on January 1, 197A, Technology Company purchases all of the assets and assumes all of the liabilities of Spaceage Company. The purchase price agreed upon is $1,000,000 cash. The information shown below lists the cost and fair value of the assets and liabilities of Spaceage on the date of the transaction.

	Cost	Fair Value
Total Tangible Assets	$1,300,000	$ 950,000
Identifiable Intangible Assets:		
Patents	100,000	25,000
Trademark	200,000	400,000
Total Tangible and Identifiable Intangible Assets	$1,600,000	$1,375,000
Liabilities Assumed	(400,000)	(400,000)
Net Tangible and Identifiable Intangible Assets	$1,200,000	$ 975,000

Technology Company paid $1,000,000 for net tangible and identifiable intangible assets with a total fair value of $975,000. The difference between the cost ($975,000) assigned to the assets acquired and the total purchase price ($1,000,000) is the cost to be assigned to an unidentifiable intangible asset, i.e., to goodwill. Therefore, the amount of goodwill resulting from this purchase transaction is $25,000. The entry shown below is representative of the type of entry that would be made to reflect the transaction:

Tangible Assets	950,000	
Patents	25,000	
Trademark	400,000	
Goodwill	25,000	
Liabilities		400,000
Cash		1,000,000

This is not the actual entry that would be made, since the make-up of the tangible assets and liabilities was not given. The patents, trademark and goodwill all will be amortized over their useful lives (not to exceed 40 years). The entry to record the amortization already has been shown. Notice that APB Opinion No. 17 requires the amortization of goodwill in the same manner as used for any other intangible asset.

Flowchart and General Discussion—Internally Generated Intangibles

In addition to purchasing intangible assets, a company may incur costs to develop, restore or maintain an intangible. It should be kept in mind that some of these types of costs may, in fact, be research and development costs and subject to the provisions of SFAS No. 2, "Accounting for Research and Development Costs." (See SFAS No. 2 in this Topic for a complete discussion of the proper accounting for research and development costs.) All costs referred to in the subsequent discussion are costs other than those of research and development.

For the costs incurred in connection with internally generated intangible assets to be capitalized (Block 2), they first must meet three specific conditions. First, the costs must be related to an intangible asset that can be specifically identified, such as legal fees in connection with obtaining a patent (Block 3). Next, the identifiable asset must have a determinable life (Block 4). Finally, the intangible must not be one that is inherent in a going concern and related to the enterprise as a whole (Block 5—APB Opinion No. 17, Paragraph 24). Internally created goodwill would fail to meet all three of these conditions because it is not specifically identifiable, it lacks a determinable life and it is inherent to a going concern. Therefore, the costs associated with the "creation" of goodwill never may be capitalized as an asset.

An example of costs that would meet all three of the conditions specified above would be the costs incurred to defend a patent held by the company. These costs would be identified with the patent, have a determinable life, and not be related to the enterprise as a whole. The costs to defend a patent should be capitalized and amortized over the remaining legal life or useful life of the patent, whichever is shorter. These costs were incurred to restore or maintain the intangible asset—patents.

Other Considerations

The costs assigned to intangible assets should be reviewed periodically. If the review indicates that there has been a material decrease in the expected future benefits to be derived from the intangible, a write-down may be necessary. Such a write-down would *not* be considered an extraordinary item. (APB Opinion No. 30 prohibits classification of a write-down of intangibles as an extraordinary item. See Topic 1 for a detailed analysis of APB Opinion No. 30.) Normally, it will be treated as an operating item or as a line item in the nonoperating section of the income statement.

A review of the account also may indicate that there has been a change in the estimated useful life of the intangible. If this is the case, the change should be handled on a prospective basis, i.e., by changing the amortization expense in current and subsequent periods.

The amortization of goodwill is not deductible for income tax purposes and creates a permanent difference, rather than a timing difference. No deferred taxes should be recognized for this difference. For all other intangibles, any difference between the amortization for financial accounting purposes and that for tax purposes results in a timing difference; and the provisions of APB Opinion No. 11, "Accounting for Income Taxes," are applicable. (See Topic 5 for a complete analysis of APB Opinion No. 11.)

Retroactive restatement of all financial statements presented for periods prior to the effective date of the Opinion (November 1, 1970) is required.

The information shown below was taken from the 1976 Annual Report of Cadence Industries Corporation, and shows the line-item "Intangible Assets—net" and the related footnotes. Footnote 1 indicates the Company's accounting policy for goodwill. Footnote 4 presents detailed information about the composition of the intangible assets of the Company.

Cadence Industries Corporation (Dec)

	1976	1975
Intangible Assets—net (Notes 1 and 4)	$26,011,000	$26,367,000

Note 1 (*in part*): *Summary of Significant Accounting Policies:*

Intangibles—Cost in excess of net assets of companies acquired prior to November 1, 1970, is not being amortized since there is no present indication of any impairment in the value of these intangibles. The cost of intangible assets acquired after October 31, 1970, amounting to $4,264,000 (net of amortization) at December 31, 1976, is being amortized on a straight-line basis over their estimated lives, but not exceeding forty years.

Note 4: Intangible Assets—Intangible assets (net of amortization) relate to the following activities:

	1976	1975
Publishing and publishing services	$11,494,000	$11,904,000
Pharmaceutical products	4,583,000	4,529,000
Mail order marketing	4,337,000	4,337,000
Theatres	5,597,000	5,597,000
	$26,011,000	$26,367,000

The Hudson merger (Note 1) resulted in an increase in intangibles of $116,000 before amortization.

Source: *Accounting Trends and Techniques,* Copyright © 1977 by the American Institute of Certified Public Accountants, Inc., p. 147.

SFAS No. 2 (October 1974)
Accounting for Research and Development Costs

Flowchart and General Discussion

SFAS No. 2 establishes the policy of requiring an enterprise to expense research and development costs as incurred. Prior to the issuance of this Statement, companies followed a wide variety of practices. Some companies capitalized all research and development costs and amortized the costs over some future period. Other companies expensed some types of research and development costs and capitalized others. For those costs that were capitalized, the amortization period selected usually was arbitrary. The primary impact of SFAS No. 2 is that similar research and development costs now will be treated in the same manner, thereby providing a degree of comparability between financial statements of different enterprises.

Two major decisions are required in assessing research and development activities. First, a decision must be made as to whether a particular activity is considered research or development, as defined in the Statement. For those activities determined to be research and development, the second decision involves the proper recognition of the costs associated with the activity. Some types of research and development costs will be charged to income as incurred, while other costs (e.g., those for physical facilities used in the research and development process) will be capitalized and charged to current and future periods through amortization.

The Flowchart identifies the major decisions that must be made in determining which specific costs will be expensed as research and development costs and which costs will be capitalized. The costs capitalized may become research and development costs in some future period.

The Statement (Paragraph 8(a)) defines research as a "planned search or critical investigation aimed at discovery of new knowledge with the hope that such knowledge will be useful in developing a new product or service or a new process or technique or in bringing about a significant improvement to an existing product or process." The definition adopted in the Statement is based, in large part, on the definition of research used by the National Science Foundation. Development is defined (Paragraph 8(b)) as the "translation of research findings or other knowledge into a plan or design for a new product or process or for a significant improvement to an existing product or process whether intended for sale or use." The definition of development specifically *excludes* the following types of activities:

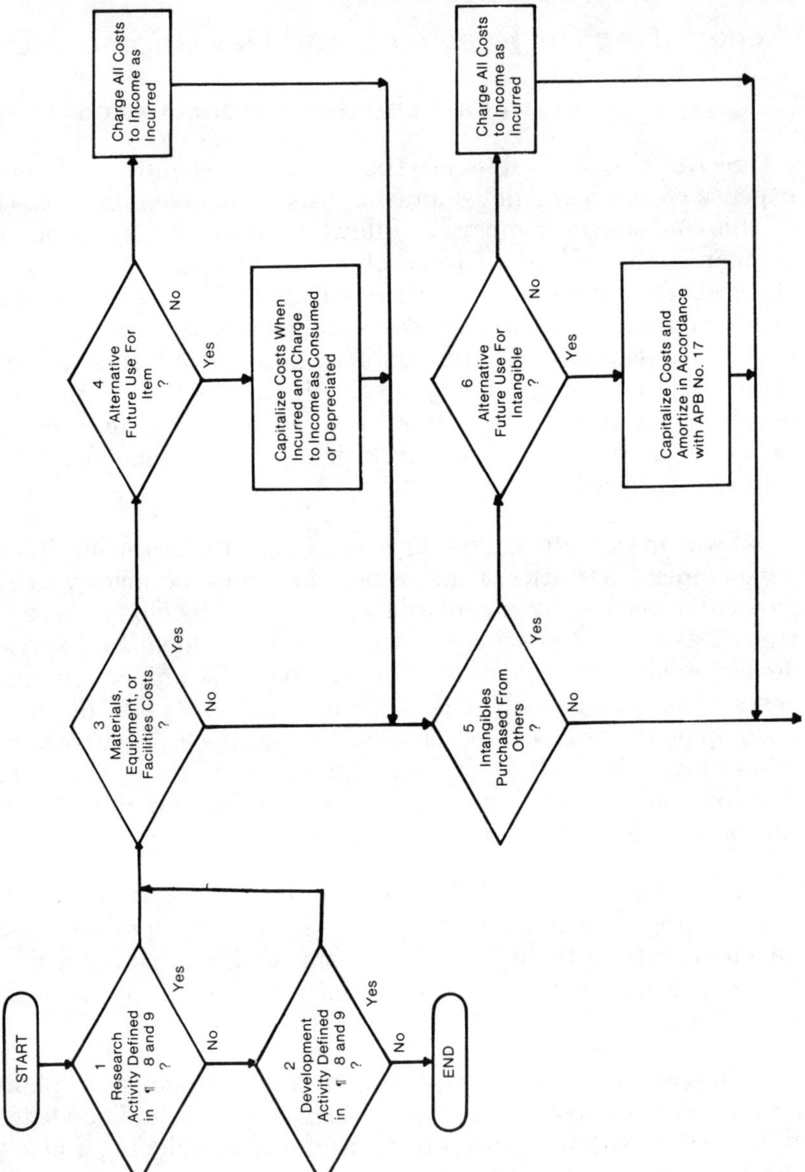
START
1
Research
Activity Defined
in ¶ 8 and 9
?
Yes
No
2
Development
Activity Defined
in ¶ 8 and 9
?
Yes
No
END
3
Materials,
Equipment, or
Facilities Costs
?
Yes
No
4
Alternative
Future Use For
Item
?
Yes
No
Charge All Costs
to Income as
Incurred
Capitalize Costs When
Incurred and Charge
to Income as Consumed
or Depreciated
5
Intangibles
Purchased From
Others
?
Yes
No
6
Alternative
Future Use For
Intangible
?
Yes
No
Charge All Costs
to Income as
Incurred
Capitalize Costs and
Amortize in Accordance
with APB No. 17

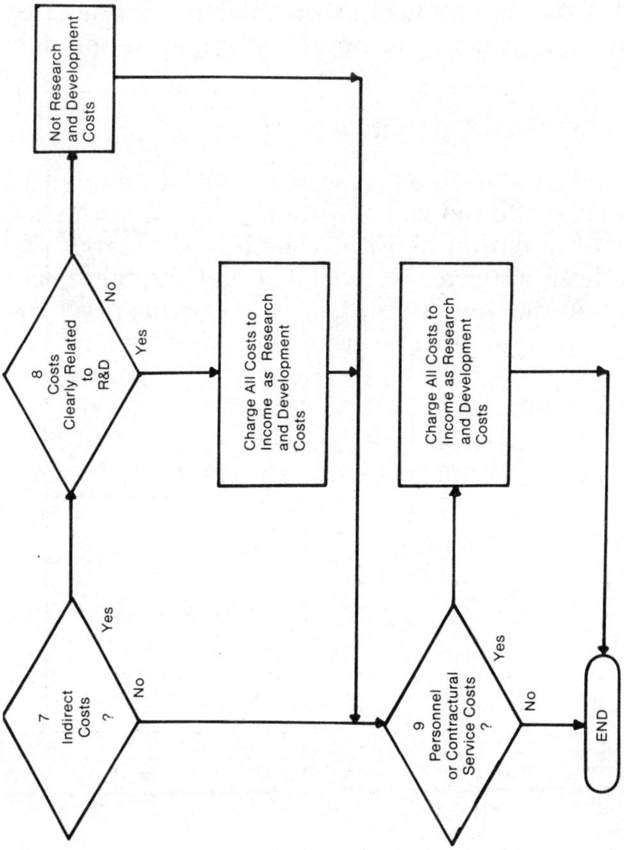
7
Indirect
Costs
?
Yes
No
8
Costs
Clearly Related
to
R&D
Yes
No
Not Research
and Development
Costs
Charge All Costs to
Income as Research
and Development
Costs
9
Personnel
or Contractural
Service Costs
?
Yes
No
Charge All Costs to
Income as Research
and Development
Costs
END

(1) Routine alterations of existing products or manufacturing processes, even if the alteration represents an improvement in the product or process; and

(2) Market research or market testing activities.

If the Statement had merely defined research and development, management would have been allowed wide latitude in the classification of costs. In effect, the determination of what constitutes research and development would have been a matter of judgment and the Statement might or might not have had much of an influence on existing practices. However, Paragraph 9 of the Statement specifically identifies certain activities that are considered research and development for purposes of the Statement, and Paragraph 10 identifies activities that are *not* considered to represent research and development. The activities identified in these two paragraphs have been listed in Exhibit I.

Exhibit I

Identifying Research and Development Activities

Activities Considered to be Research and Development in Paragraph 9	Activities Not Considered to be Research and Development in Paragraph 10
1. Laboratory research aimed at discovery of new knowledge.	1. Engineering follow-through in an early phase of commercial production.
2. Searching for applications of new research findings or other knowledge.	2. Quality control during commercial production including routine testing of products.
3. Conceptual formulation and design of possible product or process alternatives.	3. Trouble-shooting in connection with break-downs during commercial production.
4. Testing in search for or evaluation of product or process alternatives.	4. Routine, on-going efforts to refine, enrich or otherwise improve upon the qualities of an existing product.
5. Modification of the formulation or design of a product or process.	5. Adaptation of an existing capability to a particular requirement or customer's need as part of a continuing commercial activity.
6. Design, construction, and testing of pre-production prototypes and models.	6. Seasonal or other periodic design changes to existing products.
7. Design of tools, jigs, molds, and dies involving new technology.	7. Routine design of tools, jigs, molds, and dies.
8. Design, construction, and operation of a pilot plant that is not of a scale economically feasible to the enterprise for commercial production.	8. Activity, including design and construction engineering, related to the construction, relocation, rearrangement, or start-up of facilities or equipment other than pilot plants and facilities or equipment whose sole use is for a particular research and development project.
9. Engineering activity required to advance the design of a product to the point that it meets specific functional and economic requirements and is ready for manufacture.	9. Legal work in connection with patent applications or litigation, and the sale or licensing of patents.
10. To the extent that the acquisition, development or improvement of a process by an enterprise for use in its selling or administrative activities does not include costs for computer software.[1]	10. To the extent that the acquisition, development or improvement of a process by an enterprise for use in its selling or administrative activities includes costs for computer software.[1]

[1] For a more complete explanation, see FASB Interpretation No. 6 and FASB Technical Bulletin No. 79-2.

When faced with a specific cost, the first step in the decision process is to determine if the cost is related to research and development, as defined in the Statement (Blocks 1 and 2). If the cost is determined to be part of research and development, proper accounting depends upon the type of cost incurred. If the cost represents materials, equipment or facilities that will be used in the research and development process (Block 3), and if these items have no alternative future use (Block 4), the costs will be considered research and development costs and should be expensed in the current period. This means that the cost of certain physical assets will be expensed as incurred rather than capitalized. If the materials, equipment or other facilities have an alternative future use, their costs should be capitalized. The costs of materials used in the current period, along with the current period depreciation applicable to the equipment and facilities, will be research and development costs and will be expensed in the current period.[2]

If the costs incurred represent an amount paid to some other enterprise or individual for the purchase of an intangible asset (Block 5), and if the intangible has no alternative future use (Block 6), the costs will be expensed in the current period. An intangible would have no alternative future use if it were purchased for a specific research and development project, and could be used in no other project, or if it had no general use to the enterprise other than in the particular project. If the intangible had some alternative future use, it would be capitalized and amortized in accordance with the provisions of APB Opinion No. 17, "Intangible Assets." (See APB Opinion No. 17 in this Topic for a detailed analysis of accounting for intangible assets.) The amortization expenses for the current period would be classified as research and development costs, and would be charged against current income.

If the costs represent indirect costs (Block 7), and if those costs clearly are related to research and development type activities (Block 8), they should be considered research and development costs, and should be expensed in the current period. Research and development costs may include allocated indirect costs, but only if the costs are specifically identified with research and development activities.

The final category of costs represents personnel services or contractual services provided by others (Block 9). All of these types of costs are research and development costs and should be charged to expense as incurred. The contractual service costs referred to above represent services provided by some other organization for the company.

---

[2] FASB Interpretation No. 4 deals with the appropriate accounting for R&D related "assets" acquired in a purchase business combination. The provisions of SFAS No. 2 apply to the fair value of these R&D assets.

It is a common practice to "farm out" part or all of a research project to an organization with expertise in a particular area.

If the enterprise provides research and development work for another organizaton under a contractual arrangement, costs incurred under the contract *do not* represent research and development, as defined in the Statement. In this case, the enterprise conducting the research and development work would be doing so as a routine part of its revenue producing activities.

Technical Considerations

To illustrate the technical considerations of accounting for research and development costs, the assumptions in Exhibit II will be used.

Exhibit II

Assumptions for Research and Development Costs

1. R&D, Inc. was involved in research and development Project Number 3 during the year 197C. The Company's year-end is December 31.
2. $1,000,000 of materials were used by R&D, Inc. in Project Number 3 during 197C.
3. A patent was acquired at a cost of $100,000 on January 1, 197C for use in Project Number 3. The patent will have alternative future uses. It has a useful life of 10 years.
4. Equipment was acquired on January 5, 197C, at a cost of $30,000, for use in Research Project Number 3. The equipment has a useful life of five years, with no residual value. It has no alternative uses. Straight-line depreciation is used on all equipment.
5. Salaries of persons directly involved in Research Project Number 3 were $500,000 for 197C.
6. Equipment was acquired on July 1, 197C at a cost of $1,500,000 for use in Research Project Number 3. The equipment has a 10-year useful life with no residual value. It can be used in other research and development activities and other activities not classified as research and development.
7. Consulting fees paid to persons or entities outside the firm for research and development projects amounted to $50,000.

8. Overhead allocated to research and development activities was $15,000. This was considered to be a reasonable allocation.

Given the information in Exhibit II, above, the research and development costs for 197C may be computed. The research and development costs are presented in Table I.

Table I

Research and Development Costs

Situation	Research and Development Cost
Material Used	$1,000,000
Amortization of Patent ($100,000/10 Years)	10,000
Equipment Purchased on January 5	30,000
Personnel Salaries	500,000
Depreciation of Equipment Purchased on July 1 ($1,500,000/10 Years)	150,000
Consulting Fees	50,000
Overhead Allocation	15,000
Total Research and Development Costs for Project Number 3	$1,755,000

As noted in Table I, the materials used, personnel salaries, consulting fees and overhead allocation were directly related to the Research Project and were incurred in 197C. These costs are research and development costs and are charged to income in 197C. The patent and the equipment purchased on July 1 have alternative uses after Project Number 3 is completed. Since the items have alternative uses, only the amortization of the patent of $10,000 and of the depreciation of $150,000 are considered research and development costs for 197C and accordingly charged to expense. The cost of the equipment purchased on January 5 was charged to research and development costs, instead of to depreciation for 197C, as the equipment will not have any alternative uses after Project Number 3 is completed.

Disclosures

The enterprise should disclose the total amount of research and development costs charged to income. If comparative financial statements are issued, total research and development costs charged to income should be disclosed for each period.

The disclosure may be made in the text of the income statement or in the footnotes to the financial statements.

Certain government-regulated companies may defer research and development costs, and additional disclosures are required for these companies. Consult Paragraph 14 of the Statement for specific disclosure requirements.

Topic 5

Income Taxes and Tax Credit

Detail Contents

APB Opinions and SFAS Statements

1.	APB Opinion No. 2	–Accounting for the "Investment Credit"
2.	APB Opinion No. 4	–Accounting for the "Investment Credit"
3.	APB Opinion No. 11	–Accounting for Income Taxes
4.	APB Opinion No. 23	–Accounting for Income Taxes–Special Areas
5.	APB Opinion No. 24	–Accounting for Income Taxes–Investments in Common Stock Accounted for by the Equity Method
6.	SFAS No. 31	–Accounting for Tax Benefits Related to U. K. Tax Legislation Concerning Stock Relief

FASB Interpretations

1.	FASB Interpretation No. 22	–Applicability of Indefinite Reversal Criteria to Timing Differences (Interpretation of APB Opinion Nos. 11 and 23)
2.	FASB Interpretation No. 25	–Accounting for an Unused Investment Tax Credit (Interpretation of APB Opinion Nos. 2, 4, 11 and 16)
3.	FASB Interpretation No. 29	–Reporting Tax Benefits Realized on Disposition of Investments in Certain Subsidiaries and Other Investees (Interpretation of APB Opinion Nos. 23 and 24)

Future Considerations of the FASB

1.	Exposure Draft	–Balance Sheet Classification of Deferred Income Taxes

This Exposure Draft, if issued, would serve as an amendment to APB Opinion No. 11. The proposed Statement deals with the proper classification of deferred income taxes in the balance sheet of the reporting entity. The Board proposes that the deferred taxes related to an asset or liability account should be classified in the same manner as the asset or liability. For example, if the asset that gave rise to the deferred taxes is classified as current, the related deferred taxes would also be classified as current on the balance sheet. In those cases where the tax deferral is not related to an asset or liability, the deferred tax account should be classified according to the expected date of reversal of the timing difference.

2. Proposed Interpretation —Application of Percentage Limitations in Recognizing Investment Tax Credits Under FASB Interpretation No. 25

This Proposed Interpretation, if issued, would serve as an interpretation to the previously issued FASB Interpretation No. 25. The Revenue Act of 1978 increased the percentage limitation for deducting the investment tax credit. The percentage limitation will continue to increase through 1982. For purposes of the "with-and-without" computation of tax expense, the statutory percentage limitations in effect for the year of the computation should be used. Additional investment tax credit to be recognized should be based on the statutory limitation applicable to the years in which previously recorded deferred tax credits are expected to reverse.

APB Opinion No. 2 (December 1962)
Accounting for the "Investment Credit"

and

APB Opinion No. 4 (Amending No. 2) (March 1964)
Accounting for the "Investment Credit"

Flowchart and General Discussion

APB Opinion No. 2 specifies a single acceptable method of accounting for the investment tax credit. This method is referred to as the "cost reduction method," or the deferral method. Subsequent to the issuance of this Opinion, the Securities and Exchange Commission issued Accounting Series Release No. 96, indicating that, while the method of accounting for the investment tax credit identified in APB Opinion No. 2 was acceptable, an alternative method, known as the "tax reduction method," was also acceptable for SEC reporting purposes. The cost reduction method advocated by Opinion No. 2 never gained wide acceptance. Many practitioners preferred the tax reduction method. In an effort to settle the controversy created by the SEC and accounting practitioners, the Accounting Principles Board issued Opinion No. 4, which accepted the tax reduction method as an alternative to the cost reduction method. The Board still maintained that the cost reduction method was preferable for financial reporting purposes.

As a result of this series of events, there now are two acceptable methods of accounting for the investment tax credit. Management is free to choose between the cost reduction and the tax reduction methods. Each method has a different impact on the balance sheet and income statement in any given year, but, in the long-run, the effects are identical. The situation is similar to selecting straight-line or accelerated depreciation.

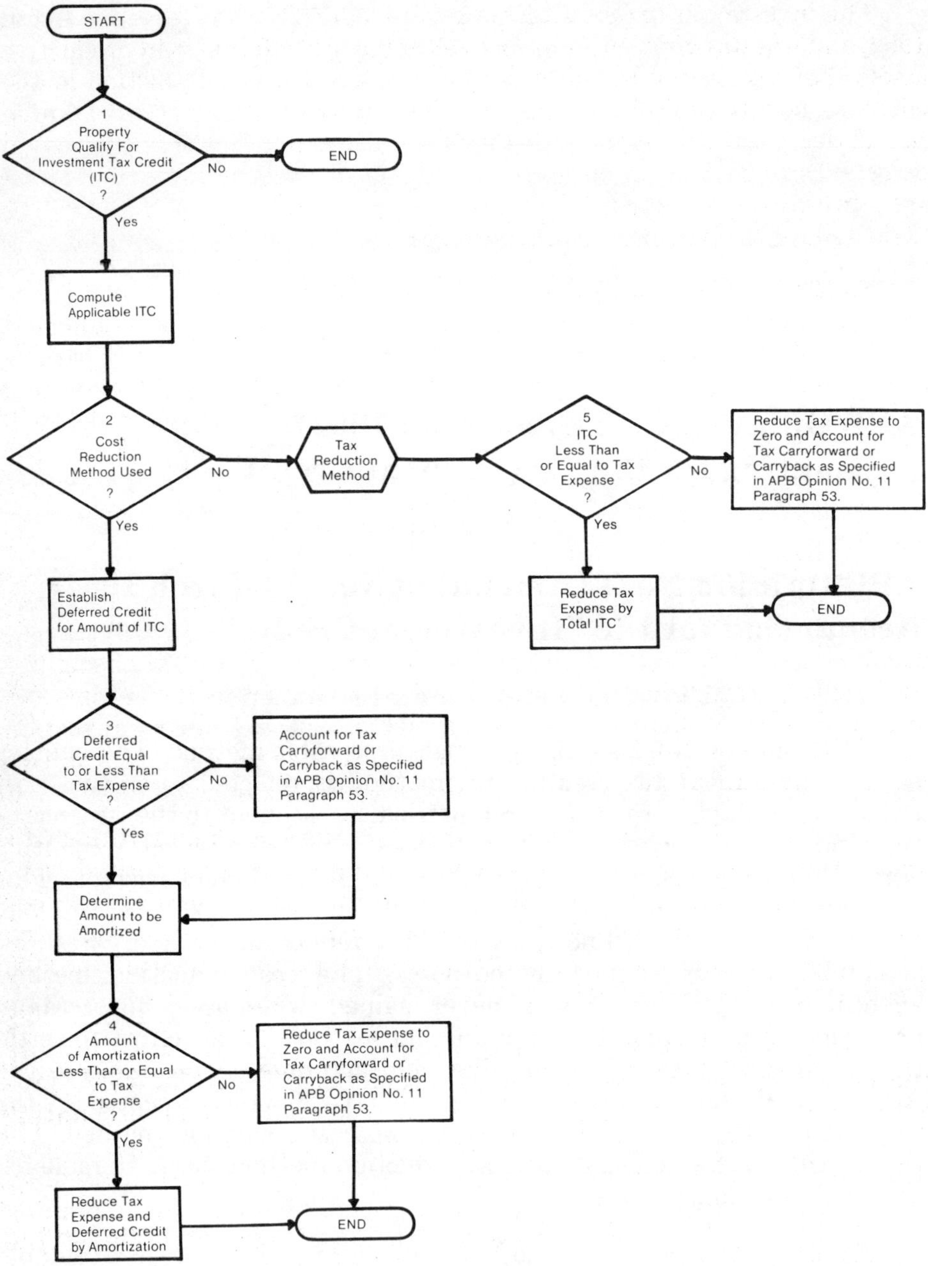
START
1 Property Qualify For Investment Tax Credit (ITC) ?
No
END
Yes
Compute Applicable ITC
2 Cost Reduction Method Used ?
No
Tax Reduction Method
5 ITC Less Than or Equal to Tax Expense ?
No
Reduce Tax Expense to Zero and Account for Tax Carryforward or Carryback as Specified in APB Opinion No. 11 Paragraph 53.
Yes
Reduce Tax Expense by Total ITC
END
Yes
Establish Deferred Credit for Amount of ITC
3 Deferred Credit Equal to or Less Than Tax Expense ?
No
Account for Tax Carryforward or Carryback as Specified in APB Opinion No. 11 Paragraph 53.
Yes
Determine Amount to be Amortized
4 Amount of Amortization Less Than or Equal to Tax Expense ?
No
Reduce Tax Expense to Zero and Account for Tax Carryforward or Carryback as Specified in APB Opinion No. 11 Paragraph 53.
Yes
Reduce Tax Expense and Deferred Credit by Amortization
END

The investment tax credit first was introduced in the Revenue Act of 1962, and was designed as an incentive for business to invest in productive assets. For tax purposes, the investment tax credit is a reduction in the current taxes payable by a company. The amount of the credit allowed has varied over the years, but today the rate is 10 percent of the cost of qualified property with an economic life of seven years or more. There are limitations on the total dollar amount of the credit that may be deducted for tax purposes in any one year.

For financial accounting purposes, the cost reduction method treats the investment tax credit as a reduction in the cost of the equipment acquired. The amount of the credit is not used to reduce the cost basis of the property for accounting purposes, but is treated as a contra asset or a deferred credit. The investment tax credit established is amortized each period, as a reduction in income tax expense, in relation to the benefits received from the use of the asset, i.e., over the useful life of the asset acquired. The effects of the credit are recognized over the life of the asset and not just in the year the asset was purchased.

The tax reduction method, most commonly referred to as the flow-through method, treats the entire investment tax credit as a reduction in income tax expense in the year the asset is acquired. The entire benefit of the credit is recognized in one year. This is similar to the income tax treatment of the credit. The primary advantage of the tax reduction method is that it will increase income in the year an asset is acquired, while the cost reduction method recognizes the tax saving gradually.

The Flowchart identifies the major decisions required for the application of either the cost reduction or the tax reduction method. Once it has been determined that the acquired asset qualifies for the investment tax credit (Block 1), and the amount of the credit has been determined, the next major decision is to determine which of the two accounting methods is used by the company (Block 2).

Assume that an enterprise has income enough to allow it to utilize the entire investment tax credit applicable to the current year. This assumption will be released later, so that additional accounting considerations may be discussed. If the cost reduction method is used (Block 2), a deferred credit account will be established, or increased, by the amount of the investment tax credit. At the end of the accounting period, the company will determine the proper amortization of the deferred credit. The amount to be amortized usually is determined by the same method used to depreciate the acquired asset, since the investment tax credit must be amortized over the life of that asset. The current period's amortization will be used to reduce the deferred credit account and to reduce the income tax expense. Remember that income tax expense is the amount of tax, whether paid currently or not, that is applicable to the income produced in the current period. If the enterprise uses the tax reduction method, income tax expense would be reduced by the total amount of the investment tax credit. As long as the income tax expense exceeds the investment tax credit, the accounting is quite straightforward.

Now release the assumption concerning the income generated during the period. There may be instances when the income tax expense is not sufficient to absorb the entire amount of the applicable investment tax credit. In this case, the enterprise must deal with an investment tax credit *carryforward* or *carryback.* The carryforward or carryback represents the amount of the investment tax credit that could not be utilized in the current period. (For a complete discussion of tax carryforwards and carrybacks, consult APB Opinion No. 11 in this Topic.) If the accounting results in the recognition of a *carryback,* the company will recognize the effects of the carryback in the current year as a claim for refund of taxes paid. However, if a *carryforward* is produced, no accounting recognition is given to the carryforward unless the company is certain that enough income will be produced in future periods to make the realization of the carryforward almost certain.

Technical Considerations

To illustrate accounting for both the cost reduction and tax reduction methods, the assumptions listed in Exhibit I will be used.

Exhibit I

Investment Tax Credit

1. On January 1, 197A, Taxsaver Company, Inc. purchased a piece of equipment that cost $200,000 and has an estimated useful life of eight years. The equipment is to be depreciated, using the straight-line method with a zero salvage value.
2. The equipment qualifies for the maximum investment tax credit of 10 percent.
3. Accounting income before taxes for the year ended December 31, 197A is $100,000. Taxable income is also equal to $100,000, and the tax rate applicable is 48 percent.
4. Taxsaver Company has had no deferred tax items since beginning business several years ago.

The property acquired qualifies for the investment tax credit of 10 percent, or $20,000 ($200,000 × .10). Assume that Taxsaver uses the cost reduction method of accounting for the investment tax credit. A deferred credit will be established for the amount of the investment tax credit.

The first step is to determine if the transaction will result in an investment tax credit carryforward or carryback. To make this determination, income tax expense must be compared with the amount of the investment tax credit. This comparison is shown below:

Net Income Before Income Taxes	$100,000
Tax Rate	× .48
Income Tax Expense	$ 48,000
Investment Tax Credit	20,000
Excess of Expense over Tax Credit	$ 28,000

The investment tax credit is less than income tax expense, so it appears that no carryforward or carryback will be recognized. The income taxes payable for 197A would be determined as follows:

Taxable Income	$100,000
Tax Rate	× .48
Income Taxes Payable Before Credits	$ 48,000
Investment Tax Credit	(20,000)
Income Taxes Payable	$ 28,000

For tax purposes, the investment tax credit is treated as a reduction in taxes payable in the year the asset is acquired, subject to certain limitations. Based upon the information developed above, the entry required to record the income tax expense, deferred credit and income taxes payable would be:

Income Tax Expense	48,000	
Deferred Investment Tax Credit		20,000
Income Taxes Payable		28,000

Next, the entry to amortize the investment tax credit must be prepared. The investment tax credit will be recognized over the life of the asset, using the straight-line method of amortization. The amount of the amortization for 197A would be $2,500 ($20,000/8 years). The amount of the amortization is less than the income tax expense for the period, and therefore the entire amount of the amortization will be recognized. The entry to record the amortization is shown below:

Deferred Investment Tax Credit	2,500	
Income Tax Expense		2,500

As a result of the entries prepared above, the income tax expense for 197A will be $45,500 ($48,000 – $2,500). The balance in the deferred investment tax credit account is $17,500 ($20,000 – $2,500). The deferred investment tax credit account may be treated as a contra asset account in property, plant and equipment, but more commonly is carried as a deferred credit.

Notice that the investment tax credit did not affect the cost basis of the equipment purchased. Depreciation expense recorded on the asset during 197A would be $25,000 ($200,000/8 years).

Assume the same facts as in the preceding example, except that the company uses the tax reduction method of accounting for the investment tax credit. Because the investment tax credit of $20,000 is less than the income tax expense of $48,000, the entire tax credit will be used to reduce the tax expense. The entry required to record the impact of the investment tax credit and the taxes payable for 197A would be:

Income Tax Expense	28,000	
Income Taxes Payable		28,000

Under the cost reduction method, income tax expense will be reduced by $2,500 for each of the next seven years. Under the tax reduction method, the entire investment tax credit was recognized in 197A and no subsequent reductions in income tax expense will occur.

Partial income statements for 197A under the cost reduction and the tax reduction methods are compared below:

	Cost Reduction Method	**Tax Reduction Method**
Net Income Before Income Taxes	$100,000	$100,000
Income Tax Expense	45,500	28,000
Net Income	$ 54,500	$ 72,000

This example was used to illustrate the basic accounting for the investment tax credit. To demonstrate a more complex situation, assume that the facts listed in Exhibit I are the same, except that net income before income taxes and taxable income for 197A are equal to $15,000, and the applicable tax rate is 22 percent.

Assuming that Taxsaver Company uses the cost reduction method to account for the investment tax credit, a deferred credit account must be established. The comparison of the investment tax credit with income tax expense is shown below:

Net Income Before Income Taxes	$15,000
Tax Rate	× .22
Income Tax Expense	$ 3,300
Investment Tax Credit	20,000
Excess of Tax Credit Over Expense	$16,700

In this case, the investment tax credit exceeds the income tax expense for the period, and the company must account for a carryforward or a carryback. Assume the company earned substantial income in previous years, and that the excess credit will be treated as a carryback to claim a refund for taxes paid in those years. The computation of the taxes payable for 197A is shown below:

Taxable Income	$15,000
Tax Rate	× .22
Income Taxes Payable Before Credits	$ 3,300
Investment Tax Credit Applicable to 197A	(3,300)
Income Taxes Payable	$ 0
Investment Tax Credit	$20,000
Investment Tax Credit Used	3,300
Investment Tax Credit Carryback	$16,700

There are no taxes currently payable, and the investment tax credit carryback will be used as a claim for refund of taxes paid in previous years. The entry required to record the income tax expense for the year, the carryback and the deferred credit is as follows:

Income Tax Expense	3,300	
Receivable for Refund of Taxes	16,700	
Deferred Investment Tax Credit		20,000

The next entry is to record the amortization of the deferred investment tax credit of $2,500. The amortization of the deferred credit is less than the income tax expense of $3,300, so there are no further problems with carrybacks. The entry to record the amortization would be:

Deferred Investment Tax Credit	2,500	
Income Tax Expense		2,500

As a result of these entries, the income tax expense applicable to the 197A income would be $800. When the refund is received from the government, the receivable will be eliminated. The remaining investment tax credit of $17,500 ($20,000 – $2,500) will be amortized at the rate of $2,500 for the next seven years.

If Taxsaver Company had been using the tax reduction method, instead of the cost reduction method, the following entry would be required to reflect the facts stated above:

Receivable for Refund of Taxes	16,700	
Refund of Prior Year's Taxes		16,700

The receivable would be eliminated when payment of the refund was received. The refund account would be treated as "negative tax expense" in the 197A income statement. The basic concept of the tax reduction method is that the benefits of the investment tax credit should be shown in the year the asset was acquired, so the refund account will increase reported income for the year.

Partial income statements for 197A under the second set of assumptions are shown below:

	Cost Reduction Method	Tax Reduction Method
Net Income Before Income Taxes	$15,000	$15,000
Income Tax Expense	(800)	
Refund of Prior Year's Taxes		16,700
Net Income	$14,200	$31,700

Please note that the difference in net income under the first set of assumptions was $17,500 ($72,000 tax reduction – $54,500 cost reduction), and that the same difference exists under the second set of assumptions ($31,700 tax reduction – $14,200 cost reduction = $17,500). The $17,500 is the unamortized balance in the deferred investment tax credit account, and it represents the net difference in accounting treatment under the two methods.

Assuming that Taxsaver Company paid no taxes in previous years or that the taxes paid were not sufficient to absorb the full $16,700, the Company would have to treat all or part of the amount as a carryforward. Accounting recognition is not given to carryforwards in the current period unless the company is "assured beyond any reasonable doubt" that the benefits of the carryforward will be received (APB Opinion No. 11, "Accounting for Income Taxes," Paragraph 46). For a complete discussion and illustration of accounting for tax carryforwards, refer to APB Opinion No. 11, "Accounting for Income Taxes."

Disclosures

The method used to account for investment tax credits must be disclosed; and the amounts involved also should be disclosed, if material. The Notes to the Financial Statements relative to the investment tax credit for Amsted Industries Incorporated and Pennwalt Corporation are shown in Exhibits I and II, respectively, and present disclosures for the years 1975 and 1976. Note that Amsted Industries Incorporated, Exhibit I, uses the flow-through method, while Pennwalt Corporation, Exhibit II, uses the cost reduction or deferral method.

Exhibit I

Amsted Industries Incorporated (Sep)

Notes to Consolidated Financial Statements

Accounting Policies (in part)—Investment tax credits are accounted for on the "flow-through" method, which recognizes the benefit in the year the assets which gave rise to the credit are placed in service.

Income Taxes—The provisions for taxes on income from continuing operations consist of the following:

	1976	1975
Current federal taxes, less investment tax credits of $1,357,000 in 1976 and $733,000 in 1975	$26,854,000	$30,268,000
Foreign income taxes	2,635,000	3,043,000
State income taxes	2,522,000	2,964,000
Deferred taxes	968,000	907,000
Provision for taxes on income	$32,979,000	$37,182,000

Source: *Accounting Trends and Techniques,* Copyright © 1977 by the American Institute of Certified Public Accountants, Inc., p. 269.

Exhibit II

Pennwalt Corporation (Dec)

Pennwalt Accounting Policies

Investment Credit—Investment credit is recognized for financial reporting purposes as a reduction of the Federal income tax provision over the life of applicable assets. The unamortized accumulated investment credit is included in accumulated depreciation.

Notes to Consolidated Financial Statements

Income Tax and Investment Credit—The provision for Federal and other income taxes includes:

	1976	1975
	(Thousands of Dollars)	
Federal	$17,873	$10,531
Foreign	7,370	6,008
State and local	3,088	1,375
Total current provision	28,331	17,914
Deferred	5,017	4,292
Investment tax credit, net	1,019	1,939
	$34,367	$24,145

Total income tax expense of $34,367,000 in 1976 and $24,145,000 in 1975, were different than the amounts at the statutory Federal income tax rate due to the following reasons:

	1976	1975
Statutory Federal income tax rate	48.0%	48.0%
Income taxes of foreign subsidiaries	5.8	(0.2)
All other items, net	(4.2)	(4.5)
Effective income tax rate	49.6%	43.3%

Deferred income tax expense is primarily related to the excess of tax over book depreciation. Deferred taxes are not provided on the undistributed earnings of foreign subsidiaries because of the Company's intention to reinvest such undistributed earnings. At December 31, 1976, the cumulative amount of such undistributed earnings was $49,000,000.

Amortization of the investment credit amounted to $989,000 in 1976 and $860,000 in 1975, and the unamortized accumulated investment credit is $6,881,000 at December 31, 1976.

Source: *Accounting Trends and Techniques,* Copyright © 1977 by the American Institute of Certified Public Accountants, Inc., p. 272.

APB Opinion No. 11 (December 1967) Accounting for Income Taxes

Introduction

Income for financial accounting purposes is determined through the application of generally accepted accounting principles. Income for tax purposes is determined through the application of the rules and regulations contained in the Internal Revenue Code and the rules specified by various other taxing authorities. The reasons lying behind generally accepted accounting principles are different from the reasons supporting the various provisions specified by taxing authorities. For example, depreciation expense for financial accounting purposes represents a rational and systematic allocation of the cost of an asset over its estimated useful life, but depreciation deductions for tax purposes may be designed to serve as an incentive for investment in new assets. The manner in which revenues and expenses are recognized for accounting and tax purposes may not always be the same. Due to the nature of the measurement, there is likely to be some difference between accounting income and taxable income.

One difference between accounting income and taxable income is due to the time period in which revenues and expenses are recognized. For example, an item of revenue may be included in the determination of accounting income in the current period, but not included in taxable income until some future period. The revenue item will be taxed, but it will not be taxed in the current period. This type of difference is referred to as a "timing" difference. Timing differences are defined in APB Opinion No. 11 (Paragraph 13(e)) as "differences between the periods in which transactions affect taxable income and the periods in which they enter into the determination of pretax accounting income." An important characteristic of a timing difference is that it will reverse or "turn around" in some future period and thereby no longer be considered a difference between financial income and taxable income. Timing differences result from any of the following situations:

1. Revenues or gains are included in taxable income *later* than they are included in accounting income. An example would be the recognition of income from long-term construction projects on the

completed contracts basis for tax purposes, and on the percentage of completion basis for accounting purposes.

2. Expenses or losses are deducted in the determination of taxable income *later* than they are deducted for financial accounting purposes. For example, a company may estimate warranty costs for accounting purposes and deduct actual warranty costs for tax purposes.

3. Revenues or gains are included in taxable income *earlier* than they are included in accounting income. Rent collected in advance may have to be included in taxable income of the current period, but may be recognized when earned for accounting purposes.

4. Expenses or losses are deducted in the determination of taxable income *earlier* than they are deducted for financial accounting income. Depreciation expense may be recorded, using the straight-line method for accounting purposes and the double declining balance method for tax purposes.

Another reason for a difference between accounting income and taxable income is that certain items may be included in accounting income but *never* included in taxable income, or vice versa. Such an item is referred to as a "permanent" difference and is defined (APB Opinion No. 11, Paragraph 13(f)) as a "difference between taxable income and pretax accounting income arising from transactions that, under applicable tax laws and regulations, will not be offset by corresponding differences or 'turn around' in other periods." Once an item is classified as a permanent difference, it always will be considered a permanent difference. Examples of permanent differences would include interest from tax-free municipal obligations, amortization of goodwill, and certain nondeductible expenses, e.g., expenses in excess of some stated maximum amount.

APB Opinion No. 11 addresses the question of proper accounting treatment of both timing and permanent differences. There are two major views regarding the proper accounting for these items. One view, known as partial allocation, states that income tax expense recorded for financial accounting purposes should be the taxes that are payable in that accounting period. Under this view of accounting for income taxes, if an item of revenue is included in financial income in the current period but will be recognized for tax purposes in a future period, income tax expense should not be recorded on the revenue item because no taxes will be paid on the amount in the current period. The only exception to this general rule would be if the company experienced a material *nonrecurring* difference between financial income and taxable income. Under partial allocation, income tax expense should be recognized on this nonrecurring item if it can be determined that taxes will be paid in the near future. For example, a company may have one installment sale involving a material amount of money. Income is recognized for accounting purposes at the date of the sale, but will be included in taxable income as collections are made. If this transaction is considered to be material and nonrecurring, income tax expense would be based upon accounting, rather than tax, income.

The other view of accounting for income taxes is known as comprehensive allocation. Under this view, income tax expense of the current period should be based upon income taxes associated with accounting income (excluding amounts for permanent differences), even if the amounts will not be paid in the current period. Comprehensive allocation views income tax expense as the amount that eventually will be paid on the income generated in the current period. Income tax expense should include the tax effect of all items included in the determination of accounting income.

APB Opinion No. 11 adopted comprehensive allocation as the proper method to record income tax expense for financial accounting purposes. Given this action, the Board had to decide upon the accounting treatment afforded timing and permanent differences. Timing differences affect more than one accounting period, and the treatment given to these items is referred to as *Interperiod* tax allocation, i.e., the process of allocating taxes between periods. The income tax expense recorded during an accounting period must give proper recognition to all items representing timing differences. Recognition (in income tax expense) of timing differences will give rise to deferred income taxes. Permanent differences *do not* affect future accounting periods and would not enter into the process of interperiod tax allocation.

The deferred taxes resulting from timing differences may be viewed in three different ways. The difference between income tax expense and the income taxes payable may be viewed as a liability for taxes payable or as a prepaid account, depending upon the direction of the difference. This is referred to as the "liability" method of accounting for the difference. The second view accounts for the difference between income tax expense and income taxes payable as either a deferred credit or a deferred charge, depending upon the direction of the difference. The last view, the "net of tax method," uses either the liability or deferred method to calculate the tax effects of the timing differences. The tax effects are then used in the valuation of related assets and liabilities. The Board elected the use of the second view for interperiod tax allocation. This method is referred to as the "deferred" method.

Examples of Accounting for Timing Differences

To illustrate the process of comprehensive tax allocation, assume a company purchases a depreciable asset for $1,000,000. The asset has a useful life of 10 years and an estimated salvage value of $100,000. The company has elected to use straight-line depreciation for accounting purposes and double declining balance depreciation for income tax purposes. The tax rate applicable to the company is 48 percent. Assume further that this is the only item that will give rise to a timing difference, i.e., all other items of revenue and expense are the same for accounting and tax purposes. Table I shows the depreciation recorded for accounting purposes, and the depreciation deducted for tax purposes, over the life of the asset. In addition, the Table shows the computation of the tax effect of the difference between the accounting expense and the tax deduction.

Table I

Asset Depreciation

Year	Depreciation for Accounting Purposes	Depreciation for Tax Purposes	Timing Difference	Current Deferred Income Taxes	Total Deferred Income Taxes
1	[a]$ 90,000	[b]$ 200,000	[c]$ 110,000	[d]$ 52,800	$ 52,800
2	90,000	160,000	70,000	33,600	86,400
3	90,000	128,000	38,000	18,240	104,640
4	90,000	102,400	12,400	5,952	110,592
5	90,000	81,920	(8,080)	(3,878)	106,714
6	90,000	65,536	(24,464)	(11,743)	94,971
7	90,000	52,429	(37,571)	(18,034)	76,937
8	90,000	41,943	(48,057)	(23,067)	53,870
9	90,000	33,554	(56,446)	(27,094)	26,776
10	90,000	[e]34,218	(55,782)	(26,776)	-0-
Total	$ 900,000	$ 900,000	-0-	-0-	

[a] $1,000,000 cost — $100,000 salvage value = $900,000/10 years.
[b] $1,000,000 × 20% = $200,000.
[c] $200,000 — $90,000 = $110,000.
[d] $110,000 × 48% tax rate = $52,800.
[e] Rounded so that the total depreciation equals $900,000.

As indicated in Table I, the total depreciation over the life of the asset is the same, regardless of the method used. Over the life of the asset, the expenses for accounting purposes will be the same as the deductions for tax purposes. The problem of interperiod tax allocation is accounting for income tax expense and income taxes payable in each individual year.

Assume that financial accounting income and taxable income both were equal to $500,000 before consideration of the depreciation charge for Year 1. The following computation would be required to determine income tax expense and income taxes payable in that year:

	Accounting Income	Taxable Income
Income Before Depreciation	$ 500,000	$ 500,000
Depreciation for Year 1	(90,000)	(200,000)
Net Income	$ 410,000	$ 300,000
Tax Rate	× .48	× .48
Income Tax Expense	$ 196,800	
Income Taxes Payable		$ 144,000

Given this information and the computations shown in Table I, the journal entry to record the income taxes for Year 1 would be:

Income Tax Expense	196,800	
Income Taxes Payable		144,000
Deferred Income Taxes		52,800

The credit balance in the Deferred Income Taxes account would continue to grow until Year 5, when the timing difference reverses and begins to draw down the credit balance in the account. Assuming there were no other timing differences, the journal entry in Year 5 would require a debit to deferred income taxes for $3,878. From that year forward, the account would continue to be reduced.

The initial accumulation of the deferred credits and subsequent reduction can be shown graphically.

Exhibit I

Graph of Depreciation Charges

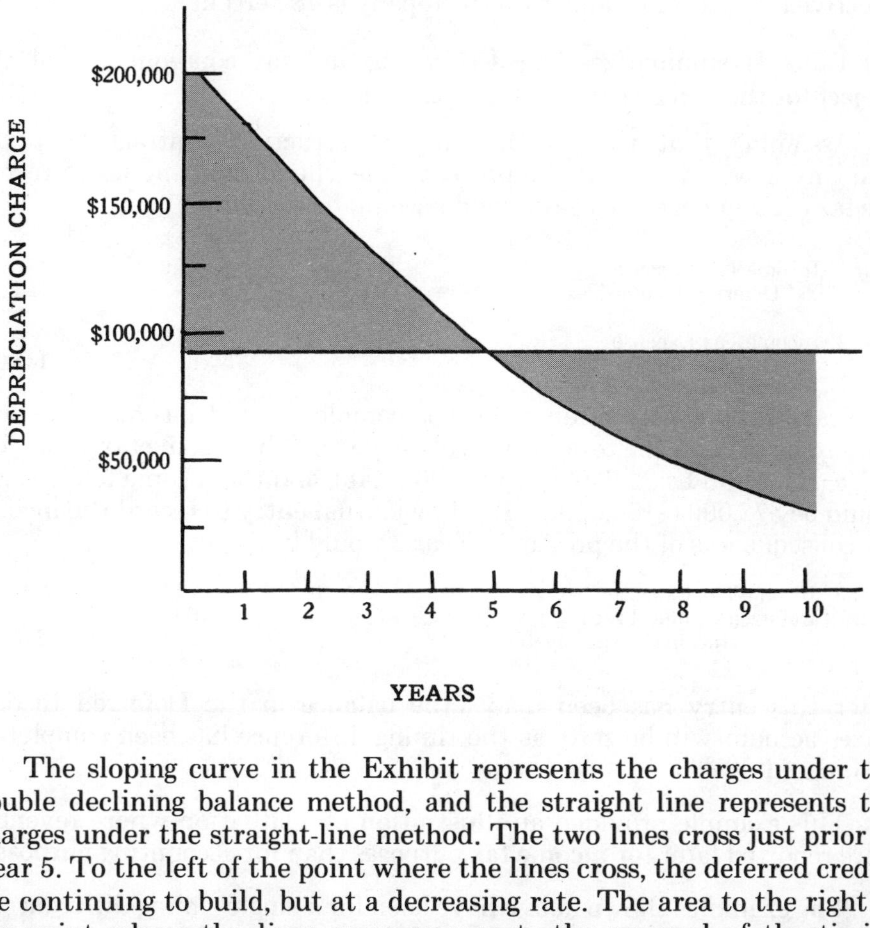

The sloping curve in the Exhibit represents the charges under the double declining balance method, and the straight line represents the charges under the straight-line method. The two lines cross just prior to Year 5. To the left of the point where the lines cross, the deferred credits are continuing to build, but at a decreasing rate. The area to the right of the point where the lines cross represents the reversal of the timing difference. The reversal will continue until Year 10, when the difference is zero.

The example of straight-line depreciation for accounting purposes and double declining balance method for tax purposes is representative of a situation where expenses are deducted earlier for tax purposes than for accounting purposes. To illustrate a situation where revenues are recognized differently for accounting and taxable income, assume a company has just entered into a long-term construction contract to build a dam. The company estimates that it will require three years to complete the project, at a total cost of $3,000,000. The contract price of the dam is $3,500,000, thus a profit of $500,000 will be earned on the project, if costs go according to estimates. The company elects to use the percentage of completion method of accounting for the contract, for accounting purposes, and the completed contracts method for tax purposes. The effective tax rate applicable to the company is 48 percent.

Table II summarizes the accounting and tax consequences of the project for the three-year construction period.

Assuming that this is the only construction contract that the company is working on at the present time, the journal entries to record the tax consequences in Years 1 and 2 would be as follows:

Year 1	Income Tax Expense	24,000	
	Deferred Income Taxes		24,000
Year 2	Income Tax Expense	144,000	
	Deferred Income Taxes		144,000

In Year 3, the construction project is completed; and income taxes will have to be paid on the total profits of $500,000. The income taxes payable in Year 3 would be $240,000 ($500,000 × .48), and the income tax expense would be $72,000 ($150,000 × .48). The journal entry to record the income tax consequences of the project in Year 3 would be:

Year 3	Income Tax Expense	72,000	
	Deferred Income Taxes	168,000	
	Income Taxes Payable		240,000

After this entry has been made, the balance in the Deferred Income Taxes account will be zero, as the timing difference has been completely eliminated.

This example provided an illustration of a situation where revenues were reported later for income tax purposes than for accounting purposes.

The examples shown above have been for a single timing difference. A company may have several timing differences in a particular year: some of the timing differences may originate in the year, and some of the differences may reverse in the same year. When this situation occurs, the Opinion allows the grouping of similar types of timing differences for the purposes of calculating the increase or decrease in the deferred income tax account. The two most common methods of grouping are known as the "gross-change method" and the "net-change method."

When using the gross-change method, timing differences that originate in the current period enter into the computation of deferred taxes, using the tax rate in effect in the current period; and reversals of a timing difference enter into the computation at the rate that was in effect when the difference originated. Current tax rates are used for originating differences, and prior year tax rates are used for reversals.

Table II

Long-Term Construction Project

Year	Costs Incurred This Period	% Complete This Period	Accounting Income	Taxable Income	Difference	Deferred Income Taxes
1	$ 300,000	10%	[a]$ 50,000	-0-	$ 50,000	[b]$ 24,000
2	1,800,000	60%	300,000	-0-	300,000	144,000
3	900,000	30%	150,000	$500,000	(350,000)	(168,000)
Total	$3,000,000	100%	$500,000	$500,000	$ -0-	$ -0-

[a] $500,000 × .10 = $50,000.
[b] $50,000 × .48 = $24,000.

Under the net-change method, the change in deferred taxes uses the current rate for both originating and reversing items. In practice, the net-change method is computed based upon taxable income before considering timing differences and taxable income after considering timing differences, and the difference between the two values represents the change in the deferred taxes for the period. This is referred to as the "with and without timing differences method."

To illustrate the computation of increases or decreases in the deferred income tax account using the gross-change and net-change methods, assume that a company is faced with the following situation:

Accounting Income Before Taxes	$56,000
Originating Timing Difference:	
Tax Depreciation in Excess of Book Depreciation	(8,000)
Reversing Timing Difference:	
Book Depreciation in Excess of Tax Depreciation	1,000
Taxable Income	$49,000

The tax rate in effect when the reversing item was originated was 50 percent, and the current tax rates are 22 percent on the first $25,000 of income and 47 percent on all income in excess of $25,000. Based upon this information, income taxes payable in the current period would be:

Taxable Income	Tax Rate	Taxes Payable
$25,000	22%	$ 5,500
24,000	47%	11,280
$49,000		$16,780

Income tax expense under the gross-change method would be determined as follows:

Accounting Income Before Taxes	$56,000
Reversing Timing Difference:	
Book Depreciation in Excess of Tax Depreciation	1,000
Income Without Considering Timing Difference	$57,000

	Accounting Income	Tax Rate	Income Tax Expense
	$25,000	22%	$ 5,500
	32,000	47%	15,040
	$57,000		$20,540
Reversal ($1,000 × 50%)			(500)
			$20,040

The increase in deferred income taxes for the period is equal to the difference between the income tax expense ($20,040) and the income taxes payable ($16,780), which is $3,260. Notice that, under the gross-change method, the reversing items are determined using the tax rate in effect when the item originated.

Under the net-change method, the income taxes payable would be the same, but there will be a difference in the income tax expense for the current period. When using this method, all timing differences, both originating and reversing items, are handled at the current tax rate. The computation of the income tax expense for the period is as follows:

Accounting Income	Tax Rate	Income Tax Expense
$25,000	22%	$ 5,500
31,000	47%	14,570
$56,000		$20,070

The increase in the deferred income taxes for the period is equal to the difference between the income tax expense ($20,070) and the income taxes payable ($16,780), and amounts to $3,290. The information below summarizes the difference between the gross-change and net-change method in this case:

	Income Tax Expense	Income Taxes Payable	Deferred Income Taxes
Gross-Change Method	$20,040	$16,780	$3,260
Net-Change Method	20,070	16,780	3,290

To more clearly illustrate the technique of using the "with and without timing differences" method of determining the increase or decrease in the deferred income tax account, assume the following information for the Years 197B and 197A:

	197B	197A
Accounting Income Before Taxes	$18,000	$37,000
Originating Timing Difference:		
Excess of Tax Over Book Depreciation	(12,000)	(10,000)
Taxable Income	$ 6,000	$27,000

The tax rates applicable to the company are 22 percent on the first $25,000 of income and 47 percent on all income in excess of $25,000. The computation of the income taxes payable and income tax expense (the with and without method) is shown below:

	Taxable Income	Tax Rate	Income Taxes Payable
Income Taxes Payable 197A:	$25,000	22%	$ 5,500
	2,000	47%	940
	$27,000		$ 6,440
Income Taxes Payable 197B:	$ 6,000	22%	$ 1,320

	Accounting Income	Tax Rate	Income Tax Expense
Income Tax Expense 197A:	$25,000	22%	$ 5,500
	12,000	47%	5,640
	$37,000		$11,140
Income Tax Expense 197B:	$18,000	22%	$ 3,960

In 197A, the deferred income tax account increased by $4,700 ($11,140 expense − $6,440 payable); and, in 197B, the account increased by $2,640 ($3,960 expense − $1,320 payable). If the short-cut approach had been used, the deferred income taxes would have increased by $4,700 in 197A ($10,000 timing difference × .47) and by *$5,640* in 197B ($12,000 timing difference × .47). The calculation of the deferred income taxes, using this approach, in 197B would have been wrong. An increase was based on the assumption that the maximum tax rate of 47 percent applied to the timing difference. This assumption was not warranted by the facts.

The "with and without" method does not compute the tax effect of the timing difference directly, but treats the deferral as the difference between the income tax expense and the income taxes payable. The short-cut method used earlier computes the tax effect on the individual timing difference that may yield inappropriate results under certain circumstances.

The gross-change method, which assumes a with and without treatment, is probably the correct method to use, from a theoretical point of view, because it applies the proper prior period tax rate to reversals in the deferred tax account. However, from a practical point of view, the net-change method, which also assumes a with and without treatment, would be considered preferable, because of the ease of computation.

This completes the discussion of timing differences. The second major area covered by APB Opinion No. 11 deals with the tax treatment of operating losses.

Tax Consequences of Operating Losses

Under existing provisions of the Internal Revenue Code, a corporation that suffers a net operating loss for tax purposes is allowed to use the loss to reduce income that was taxed in prior years, and, in some cases, to reduce future income for tax purposes. If the corporation has earned profits in preceding years, the net operating loss may be "carried back" three years to reduce income previously taxed and may result in a refund due to the corporation in the current year of the loss. If the corporation has not earned profits in the past, and therefore, has not paid taxes, the net operating loss can be "carried forward" for seven years to reduce any income that would be taxed in those years. In this case, the corporation would receive a future benefit as the result of the net operating loss incurred in the current period. This treatment of net operating losses for tax purposes is referred to as loss carrybacks and loss carryforwards.

APB Opinion No. 11 addressed the problem of *accounting* for the loss carrybacks and carryforwards. Remember that the reason for the carrybacks and carryforwards is the tax treatment afforded such items; the accounting problem is to determine when to give proper recognition to these items for financial reporting purposes. It is possible for a corporation to report net income for financial accounting purposes, yet show a net operating loss for tax purposes. A net operating loss is defined by the provisions of the Internal Revenue Code, not by generally accepted accounting principles.

The Opinion concludes (Paragraph 12(c)) that "the tax effects of operating loss carrybacks should be allocated to the loss period. The tax effects of operating loss carryforwards usually should not be recognized until the period of realization." For there to be any "tax effects" of an operating loss carryback, the corporation must have reported taxable income in years prior to the loss year. This being the case, the corporation may use the current period net operating loss to reduce income previously taxed and may claim a refund for overpayment of taxes.[1]

To illustrate the accounting for a net operating loss carryback, assume that a corporation has incurred a net operating loss of $75,000, in 197D, and that the net loss for accounting purposes also is equal to $75,000, i.e., there are no timing differences or permanent differences between accounting and tax loss. The corporation reported taxable income in previous years as follows:

197A	$25,000
197B	40,000
197C	10,000
	$75,000

Assuming that the tax rate in effect for the entire period is 48 percent, the corporation would have paid taxes in years 197A, 197B and 197C of $36,000 ($75,000 × .48). The net operating loss in 197D may be carried back for three years, so the company would be entitled to a refund of all taxes paid in years 197A through 197C. The entire net operating loss then would be used in the current period.

[1] The provisions of this Opinion that permit the recognition of the tax benefit of an operating loss carryforward when future realization is assured *do not* apply to recognition of an used investment tax credit, according to the provisions of FASB Interpretation No. 25.

The journal entry necessary to reflect the tax effects of the net operating loss carryback would be:

Tax Refund Receivable	36,000	
Tax Effect of Loss Carryback		36,000

The receivable would be classified as a current asset, and the tax benefits of the net operating loss would reduce the reported loss on the current period income statement. The tax effect of the loss carryback would be shown in the following manner on the 197D income statement:

Net Loss Before Taxes	$(75,000)
Tax Effect of Loss Carryback	36,000
Net Loss	$(39,000)

As a practical matter, if the previously reported taxable income had been greater than the current period net operating loss, the company should carry back the loss to the oldest period first. This is done so as not to lose the tax benefits that could be received from the oldest period.

There are at least two situations that can create a loss carryforward. First, the corporation may not have had any taxable income in the three preceding years; therefore, no refund could be claimed. Second, the current period net operating loss might exceed the taxable income reported in the three previous years. For example, in the situation above, if the current period net operating loss had been $100,000, the corporation would have used $75,000 as a carryback to years 197A through 197C, and been faced with a carryforward of the unused portion of the net operating loss.

The Opinion concludes that, in normal cases, the tax effects of a loss carryforward will not be recognized for accounting purposes until the benefits of the carryforward are realized. Before a company can benefit from a loss carryforward, it must earn income that is taxable. As this income is earned, the carryforward can be used to reduce taxable income and thereby reduce future taxes payable. However, if the company does not earn taxable income in future years, there will be no benefit from the loss carryforward. The reasoning of the Board is that the company should wait until income is generated, and the benefits of the loss carryforward can be measured, before any accounting treatment is given to the carryforward. As the tax benefits of the carryforward are realized in future years, the effects should be reported as an extraordinary item on the income statement in the year the benefits are received.

An exception to this general accounting rule is made in the case where the company can demonstrate that the tax effects of the loss carryforward are "assured beyond any reasonable doubt" (APB Opinion No. 11, Paragraph 45). In this case, the benefits of the loss carryforward will be recognized in the current loss period in a manner similar to that shown for loss carrybacks. The tax effect of the loss carryforward is *not* considered an extraordinary item when this condition is met.

To illustrate the proper accounting for a loss carryforward, assume that a corporation incurs a net operating loss of \$100,000 in its first year of operation. The loss cannot be carried back, since this is the initial year of operation; therefore, it must be treated as a carryforward. Because the company is new, it is not safe to assume that the tax effects of the carryforward are assured beyond any reasonable doubt. No accounting recognition will be given to the carryforward in the loss year. Assume that, in the second year of operation, the company earns income of \$175,000 for both accounting and tax purposes. Since the company will pay taxes in the second year of operations, the carryforward can be used to reduce taxable income and the related taxes to be paid. The effects of the carryforward will be reported in the current period income statement as an extraordinary item. The current tax rate applicable to the company is 47 percent. Income tax expense for the year is equal to \$82,250 (\$175,000 accounting income × .47). Income taxes payable would be determined as follows:

Taxable Income Before Carryforward	\$175,000
Net Operating Loss Carryforward	(100,000)
Taxable Income	\$ 75,000
Tax Rate	× .47
Income Taxes Payable	\$ 35,250

The tax effect of the loss carryforward is equal to the difference between the income tax expense (\$82,250) and the income taxes payable (\$35,250), which amounts to \$47,000 (\$100,000 carryforward × .47). The journal entry required to record the taxes for the second year of operation would be:

Income Tax Expense	82,250	
Tax Effect of Loss Carryforward		47,000
Income Taxes Payable		35,250

A partial income statement for the company is shown below:

Net Income Before Taxes and Extraordinary Item	\$175,000
Income Taxes	82,250
Net Income Before Extraordinary Item	\$ 92,750
Extraordinary Item:	
Tax Effect of Loss Carryforward	47,000
Net Income	\$139,750

If the company could demonstrate that the realization of the tax effects of the loss carryforward was assured beyond any reasonable doubt, accounting recognition would be given to the carryforward in the loss year. The future tax benefits of the carryforward are \$47,000 (\$100,000 ×

.47) based upon current tax rates. Because tax rates may change, or because different levels of income will be taxed differently, the $47,000 must be viewed as an *estimate* of the future benefits to be derived from the carryforward. The journal entry to record the tax effects of the carryforward would be:

Estimated Future Benefits of Loss Carryforward	47,000	
Tax Effect of Loss Carryforward		47,000

The estimated future benefits account would be classified as an asset, and the tax effect account would be used to reduce the reported loss in the current period. A partial income statement for the company at the end of its first year of operations would be:

Net Loss Before Taxes	$(100,000)
Tax Effect of Loss Carryforward	47,000
Net Loss	$(53,000)

The asset account representing the estimated future benefits of the loss carryforward would be reduced as the benefits are received for tax purposes. Recall that the company earned income of $175,000 for both accounting and tax purposes in the second year of operations. In this year, the company will receive the tax benefits of the loss carryforward. Under the conditions described above, the journal entry in the second year to record the taxes would be:

Income Tax Expense	82,250	
Estimated Future Benefits of Loss Carryforward		47,000
Income Taxes Payable		35,250

The asset account has now been eliminated from the books of the company. A partial income statement for the second year of operations is presented below:

Net Income Before Taxes	$175,000
Income Taxes	82,250
Net Income	$ 92,750

Over the two-year period, the results will be the same; however, income or loss reported in each individual year will be different. The results of the different treatment of the carryforward are shown below:

	Realization Not Assured	**Realization Assured**
First Year	$(100,000)	$(53,000)
Second Year	139,750	92,750
Total	$ 39,750	$ 39,750

Intraperiod Income Tax Allocation

To this point, the discussion has been concerned with interperiod tax allocation. APB Opinion No. 11 also deals with the problem of intraperiod tax allocation. Intraperiod tax allocation refers to the process of allocating the income taxes to items that have individual tax consequences and are reported separately on the income statement or in the balance sheet. The Board concluded that taxes associated with these items should be reported in the same section of the financial statements as the item itself. The tax consequences of these items should be directly related to the item. Extraordinary items and prior periods adjustments should be reported on a "net of tax basis," i.e., the gross amount of the item should be reduced or increased by the taxes relating to the item. APB Opinion No. 30, "Reporting the Results of Operations," requires that gains or losses from the disposal of a business segment be reported on a net of tax basis; and APB Opinion No. 20, "Accounting Changes," requires that the cumulative effect of the change be reported net of tax. (See Topic 1 for a detailed coverage of APB Opinions No. 30 and 20.)

Disclosures

The following disclosures are required by Paragraph 63 of the Opinion:

1. The amount and date of expiration of any loss carryforward;

2. Any significant amount of other unused deductions or credits and the date when they expire; and

3. Explanation of any significant differences between pretax income and income tax expense that are not apparent to the statement user.

In addition, the Board recommends that companies disclose the difference between income for accounting purposes and taxable income. This could be done through the use of a reconciliation of the two accounts.

The income tax disclosures on the 1976 and 1975 Income Statement and in the related Note to the Financial Statements of J.P. Stevens & Co., Inc. and Johnson & Johnson are shown below. Both presentations show the detail breakdown of the current provision for income taxes.

J. P. Stevens & Co., Inc. (Oct)

	1976		1975
		($000)	
Income before taxes on income	$73,743		$36,498
Estimated taxes on income—Note G	32,600		16,600
Net income	$41,143		$19,898

Note G: Estimated Taxes on Income—Estimated taxes on income consist of:

	1976	1975
Income taxes currently payable:		
Federal and foreign	$31,440,000	$13,060,000
State	4,400,000	2,100,000
Investment tax credits	(5,000,000)	(2,170,000)
	30,840,000	12,990,000
Deferred Federal income taxes	1,760,000	3,610,000
	$32,600,000	$16,600,000

A reconciliation of the consolidated effective tax rate with the statutory 48% Federal income tax rate follows:

	1976	1975
Consolidated effective tax rate	44.2%	45.5%
Investment tax credits	6.8	5.9
State income taxes, net of Federal income tax benefit	(3.1)	(3.0)
Other, net	.1	(.4)
	48.0%	48.0%

Source: *Accounting Trends & Techniques,* Copyright © 1977 by the American Institute of Certified Public Accountants, Inc., p. 268.

Johnson & Johnson (Dec)

	1976	($000)	1975
Earnings before provision for taxes on income	$361,544		$318,822
Provision for taxes on income (Note 5)	156,168		135,004
Net earnings	$205,376		$183,818

Notes to Consolidated Financial Statements

Note 1 (in part): Summary of Significant Accounting Policies

Income Taxes—Domestic investment tax credits and certain international tax incentives are deferred. The deferred amount is amortized as a reduction of the provision for taxes on income over the estimated lives of the related assets.

The Company intends to continue to reinvest its undistributed international earnings to expand its international operations. Therefore no tax has been provided to cover the repatriation of such undistributed earnings. At January 2, 1977, the cumulative amount of undistributed international earnings for which the Company has not provided United States income taxes was approximately $200,000,000.

Note 5: Income Taxes—Income tax expense consists of:

(Dollars in Thousands) Year 1976	U.S.	International	Total Provision For Taxes on Income
Federal and international			
Currently payable	$63,728	78,902	142,630
Net tax effect—timing differences	(2,356)	4,079	1,723
Net deferred investment tax credit	2,139	—	2,139
Domestic state and local	9,676	—	9,676
	$73,187	82,981	156,168
Effective tax rate	40.5%	45.9%	43.2%
Year 1975			
Federal and international			
Currently payable	$54,760	64,246	119,006
Net tax effect—timing differences	(683)	4,749	4,066
Net deferred investment tax credit	3,255	—	3,255
Domestic state and local	8,677	—	8,677
	$66,009	68,995	135,004
Effective tax rate	42.2%	42.5%	42.3%

Source: *Accounting Trends & Techniques,* Copyright © 1977 by the American Institute of Certified Public Accountants, Inc., p. 268.

APB Opinion No. 23 (April 1972) Accounting for Income Taxes—Special Areas

and

APB Opinion No. 24 (April 1972) Accounting for Income Taxes—Investments in Common Stock Accounted for by the Equity Method (Other than Subsidiaries and Corporate Joint Ventures)

Flowchart and General Discussion

When APB Opinion No. 11, "Accounting for Income Taxes," was issued, the Board intentionally deferred certain areas of income tax accounting until a future date. The areas deferred were considered specialized areas of income tax accounting. APB Opinions No. 23 and 24 are the result of further deliberation by the Board on these specialized areas. It is logical to discuss both of the Opinions at the same time because the provisions of APB Opinion No. 23 are directly related to some of the provisions of APB Opinion No. 24. Separating the two Opinions would create a great deal of redundancy. The special areas covered by the two Opinions are:[1]

(1) Parent company accounting for income taxes relating to undistributed earnings of a subsidiary or permanent corporate joint venture;

(2) Investor company accounting for income taxes relating to undistributed earnings of an investee company, accounted for using the equity method;

(3) Income tax accounting relating to bad debt reserves of savings and loan associations; and

(4) Income tax accounting relating to policyholders' surplus of stock life insurance companies.

The Flowchart will be used as each of the special areas identified above is discussed. The Flowchart organizes the provisions of both Opinions in order that the reader may obtain an overview of the decision-making and accounting processes involved.

While the Opinions make a distinction between a subsidiary and a permanent corporate joint venture, the accounting requirements are the same and they will be treated together in the discussion.

Investments in Subsidiaries and Corporate Joint Ventures

The central issue addressed by the Opinions is the income tax accounting for undistributed earnings of subsidiaries and corporate joint ventures (Block 1). Undistributed earnings of these companies are equal to the difference between the parent company's percentage shares of the reported earnings and the dividends distributed. Under the equity method of accounting for investments in subsidiaries and corporate joint ventures, the parent company recognizes income as earned by the subsidiary or joint venture, rather than as it is received. (APB Opinion No. 18 in Topic 2 details the analysis of accounting for investments using the equity method.) Therefore, the parent would recognize income based upon the entire reported income, whether distributed or undistributed. The income thus recognized would be included in the parent company's income and enter into the computation of the income tax expense of the parent. However, income is not recognized for tax purposes until such time as the dividends are received. The issue raised by the Opinions is:

---

[1] FASB Interpretation No. 22 identifies railroad grading and tunnel boring as timing differences for which the provisions of APB Opinion No. 11 are applicable. The provisions of APB Opinion No. 23 *do not* apply to these timing differences.

Should the undistributed earnings of the subsidiary or corporate joint venture be treated as a permanent difference or as a timing difference for the purposes of income tax allocation?

A timing difference exists when a difference between financial accounting income and tax income occurs in one accounting period and turns around or reverses in one or more subsequent accounting periods. For example, if a company uses accelerated depreciation for tax purposes, and straight-line depreciation for accounting purposes, taxable income will be less than accounting income in the early years of the asset's life, and greater than accounting income in the later years of the asset's life. However, the depreciation over the life of the asset will be the same; and, therefore, income reported for accounting and tax purposes will be the same. When a timing difference exists, income tax allocation as specified in APB Opinion No. 11 is appropriate.

A permanent difference is a difference in financial accounting income and taxable income that results from transactions that will not reverse in subsequent periods. For example, interest on municipal securities generally is not taxable, but is included in the determination of accounting income. Accounting and tax income will always be different by the amount of the interest, i.e., the difference will never reverse. Tax allocation is not appropriate for permanent differences.

Normally, undistributed earnings of a subsidiary or corporate joint venture should be treated as a timing difference in the computation of income tax expense by the parent company. The reason for this treatment is based upon the assumption that eventually all earnings will be paid to the parent in the form of dividends. An exception to this general rule exists if there is evidence to indicate that the subsidiary or joint venture has permanently invested or will permanently invest the undistributed earnings (Block 3), or will pay out the undistributed earnings in the form of a tax-free liquidation (Block 4). The determination of whether a company intends to indefinitely postpone the payment of undistributed earnings is largely a matter of managerial judgment. (See APB Opinion No. 23, Paragraph 12, for some guidance on the question of indefinite postponement.)

When it has been determined that a subsidiary or joint venture intends to indefinitely postpone the payment of undistributed earnings (either in part or in total), the amount so determined should be treated as a permanent difference, rather than as a timing difference, and no tax allocation will be required.

When the amount of undistributed earnings that is to be considered as a timing difference has been determined, deferred taxes will be

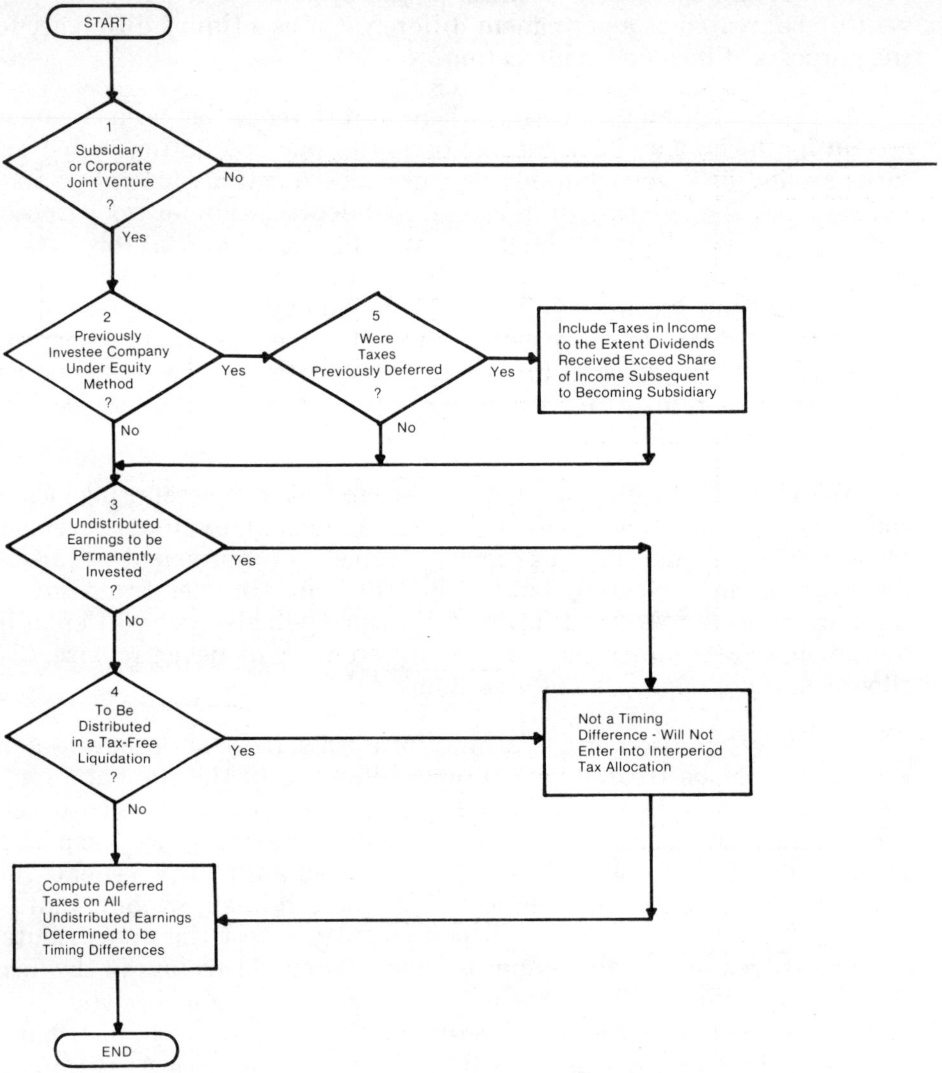

recorded on that amount. The computation of the deferred taxes assumes that all undistributed earnings so identified will be distributed in the form of dividends, and that the parent company will take full advantage of all possible tax credits, deductions and planning alternatives. For example, dividends received from certain qualifying corporations are subject to an 85 percent deduction from taxable income. If it is assumed that the parent will take full advantage of all tax credits, and if the corporation paying the dividends qualifies, only 15 percent (100% – 85%) of the dividends will be included in the computation of the deferred taxes.

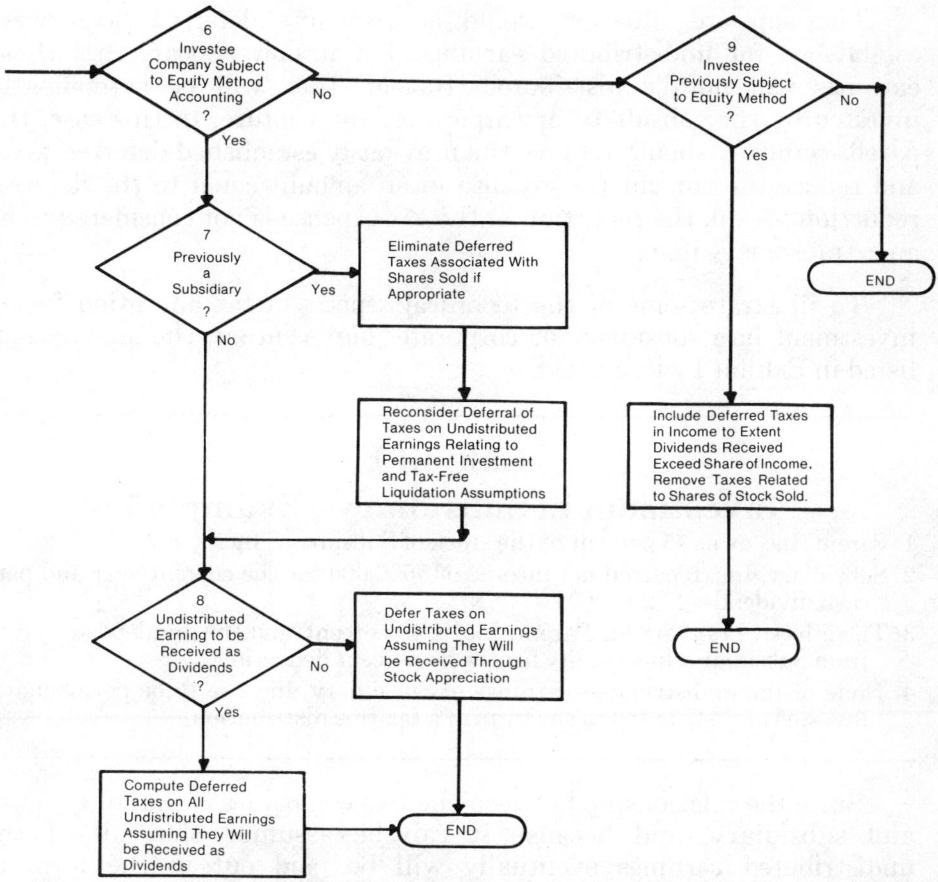

The parent company's equity in the losses of a subsidiary or corporate joint venture should be handled in accordance with the provisions of Paragraphs 44 through 50 of APB Opinion No. 11. (See APB Opinion No. 11 in this Topic for a discussion of operating loss carryforwards and carrybacks.)

If it had been assumed previously that part or all of the undistributed earnings would be indefinitely postponed, and it now appears that these earnings will be distributed in the form of dividends, deferred taxes must be established in the current period. The tax expense associated with the deferral is *not* classified as an extraordinary item.

The opposite situation would occur where deferred taxes were established for undistributed earnings, but it now appears that those earnings will not be distributed. Rather, they will be permanently invested by the subsidiary or corporate joint venture. In this case, the parent company should remove the previously established deferred taxes and reduce the current tax expense in an amount equal to the deferral reduction. Again, the reduction in the tax expense is not considered to be an extraordinary item.

To illustrate some of the technical aspects of tax allocation for an investment in a subsidiary or corporate joint venture, the assumptions listed in Exhibit I will be used.

Exhibit I

Investment in Subsidiary—Example 1

1. Parent, Inc. owns 75 percent of the stock of Subsidiary, Inc.
2. Subsidiary, Inc. reported net income of $500,000 for the current year and paid cash dividends of $200,000.
3. The effective tax rate for Parent, Inc. is 48 percent, and the dividends received from Subsidiary, Inc. qualify for the 85 percent deduction.
4. None of the undistributed earnings of Subsidiary, Inc. are to be permanently invested or distributed in the form of a tax-free distribution.

Since the relationship between the two companies is that of a parent and subsidiary, and because it can be assumed that all of the undistributed earnings eventually will be paid out in the form of dividends, Parent, Inc. will have to determine the amount of the timing difference inherent in the facts and allocate taxes on that amount. The first step is to determine the amount of the undistributed earnings of Subsidiary, Inc. that are subject to interperiod tax allocation. The determination of Parent, Inc.'s share of the undistributed earnings of Subsidiary, Inc. is shown below:

	Reported by Subsidiary, Inc.	Parent, Inc. % of Ownership	Parent, Inc. Equity
Net Income	$500,000	75	$375,000
Dividends	(200,000)	75	(150,000)
Undistributed Earnings	$300,000		$225,000

Based upon this information, Parent, Inc. would prepare the following schedule to record income tax expense, income taxes payable and the deferred income taxes associated with the undistributed earnings of Subsidiary, Inc.:

Table I

Current Period Tax Computations

	Income Tax Expense	Income Tax Payable	Deferred Income Taxes
Parent's Equity in Subsidiary's Earnings	$375,000		
Parent's Share of Subsidiary's Dividends		$150,000	
Parent's Share of Undistributed Earnings			$225,000
Dividend Deduction Reciprocal[a]	× 15%	× 15%	× 15%
Amount Available for Taxes	$ 56,250	$ 22,500	$ 33,750
Tax Rate	× 48%	× 48%	× 48%
Total	$ 27,000	$ 10,800	$ 16,200

[a] Since the dividend deduction is 85 percent, taxes will be paid on 15 percent of the dividends received.

As indicated in the Table, Parent, Inc. will accrue taxes on its equity in the earnings of Subsidiary, Inc. It is assumed that the total $375,000 will be paid to Parent, Inc. in the form of dividends, so the company can exclude 85 percent of the amount from the tax computation. Income taxes are payable on the amount of dividends received, subject to the 85 percent deduction. The total dividends received first are reduced by 85 percent, and taxes payable are computed on the remainder. Because it was assumed that all undistributed earnings will be paid in the form of dividends, the deduction also applies to the $225,000. Deferred income taxes are recorded on the amount of the undistributed earnings of Subsidiary, Inc.

Parent, Inc. would record the following journal entry to reflect the tax consequences of the earnings and dividends of Subsidiary, Inc.:

Income Tax Expense	27,000	
Income Taxes Payable		10,800
Deferred Income Taxes		16,200

The deferred income taxes will be reduced as the undistributed earnings of Subsidiary, Inc. are distributed to Parent, Inc. as dividends. It is interesting to note that the effective tax rate used in the computations in Table I was 7.2 percent (100% − 85% = 15% × 48% = 7.2%). The use of this rate is the result of the assumption that the parent company will use all available tax credits, deductions and planning alternatives.

The preceding example provided an illustration designed to introduce the concept of deferred income taxes on undistributed earnings of a subsidiary. To illustrate some of the other points discussed earlier, a more complex example is constructed, using the assumptions listed in Exhibit II.

Exhibit II

Investment in Subsidiary—Example 2

1. Parent, Inc. has owned 65 percent of the stock of Subsidiary, Inc. for a number of years.
2. Subsidiary, Inc. reported net income of $1,000,000 for the year ended December 31, 197C, and paid dividends of $400,000 during the year.
3. Parent, Inc. has a 48 percent tax rate and is allowed an 85 percent dividend deduction on dividends received from subsidiaries.
4. $100,000 of Subsidiary, Inc.'s undistributed earnings are to be permanently invested by the Company.
5. $75,000 of Subsidiary, Inc.'s undistributed earnings in 197A were assumed to be permanently invested, and no deferred taxes were calculated. It now is assumed that the $75,000 will be distributed in the form of dividends in the near future.
6. $50,000 of Subsidiary, Inc.'s undistributed earnings in 197B that were to be distributed in the form of dividends (and for which deferred taxes had been recorded) now are assumed to be permanently invested, and will not be distributed in the form of dividends.

This example offers some interesting problems not included in the first example. To begin analysis, it is necessary to determine Parent, Inc.'s equity in the undistributed earnings of Subsidiary, Inc. The computation is as follows:

	Reported by Subsidiary, Inc.	Parent, Inc. % of Ownership	Parent, Inc. Equity
Net Income	$1,000,000	65	$650,000
Dividends	(400,000)	65	(260,000)
Undistributed Earnings	$ 600,000		$390,000

The $390,000 represents Parent, Inc.'s equity in the total undistributed earnings of Subsidiary, Inc. However, $100,000 of the undistributed earnings of Subsidiary, Inc. is assumed to be permanently invested by the Company and not available for the payment of dividends. It is therefore necessary to adjust the total undistributed earnings for the amount assumed to be permanently invested. The computation below shows this adjustment:

Undistributed Earnings Before Adjustment	$390,000
Undistributed Earnings to be Permanently Invested ($100,000 × .65)	(65,000)
Undistributed Earnings Subject to Tax Allocation	$325,000

Undistributed earnings assumed to be permanently invested by the subsidiary are viewed as permanent differences and do not enter into the computation of income tax allocation. In this case, the $325,000 of undistributed earnings represents the earnings that eventually will be paid in the form of dividends, and is subject to tax allocation.

There are two additional problems facing Parent, Inc. in the computation of the proper amount of tax expense, taxes payable and deferred income taxes. First, there is the $75,000 from 197A that was assumed to be permanently invested by Subsidiary, Inc. and not subject to tax allocation. In 197C, it is known that the assumption was incorrect and that the $75,000 will be distributed in the form of dividends in the near future. Since it is assumed that the amount will be distributed, deferred taxes must be established in the current period by Parent, Inc. Parent, Inc.'s share of the $75,000 is equal to $48,750 ($75,000 × .65), and this amount will enter into the computation of the deferred income taxes for 197C. The second problem deals with the $50,000 of undistributed earnings from 197B that were assumed to be available for distribution as dividends. Naturally, deferred taxes were computed on the $50,000. In 197C it is determined that the $50,000 will be permanently invested by Subsidiary, Inc. and will not be available for payment as dividends. For this amount, the recorded deferred taxes should be removed by Parent, Inc., with a corresponding reduction in the income tax expense in the current period. Parent, Inc.'s share of the $50,000 amount is equal to $32,500 ($50,000 × .65), and will be excluded from the computation of deferred income taxes.

All of the items presented in Exhibit II have been analyzed, and Parent, Inc. now may prepare a schedule to determine the income tax expense, income taxes payable and deferred income taxes resulting from the earnings and dividends of Subsidiary, Inc. Table II summarizes the necessary computations.

Table II

Current Period Tax Computations

	Income Tax Expense	Income Taxes Payable	Deferred Income Taxes
Parent's Equity in Subsidiary's Earnings	$650,000		
Parent's Share of Subsidiary's Dividends		$260,000	
Parent's Share of Undistributed Earnings			$390,000
Parent's Share of Undistributed Earnings to Be Permanently Invested	(65,000)		(65,000)
Undistributed Earnings of Prior Years No Longer Permanently Invested	48,750		48,750
Undistributed Earnings of Prior Years Now Assumed to Be Permanently Invested	(32,500)		(32,500)
Total	$601,250	$260,000	$341,250
Dividend Deduction Reciprocal[a]	× 15%	× 15%	× 15%
Amount Available for Taxation	$ 90,188	$ 39,000	$ 51,188
Tax Rate	× 48%	× 48%	× 48%
Total	$ 43,290	$ 18,720	$ 24,570

[a] Since the dividend deduction is 85 percent, taxes will be paid on 15 percent of the dividends received.

Based upon this information, Parent, Inc. would prepare the following journal entry to reflect the tax consequences of the earnings of Subsidiary, Inc.:

Income Tax Expense	43,290	
Income Taxes Payable		18,720
Deferred Income Taxes		24,570

Separate entries could have been made for the consequences of the adjustments for prior years' undistributed earnings. The entry presented above represents the net tax consequences of all items, and the reader may wish to separate the entry into its component parts.

This last example completes the discussion of income tax accounting for subsidiary and corporate joint venture undistributed earnings.

Investee Company Accounted for Using the Equity Method

The undistributed earnings of an investee company, accounted for using the equity method (generally, ownership interest of 20 to 50 percent) (Block 6), will give rise to a difference between financial accounting income and taxable income of the investor company. The investor company recognizes its proportionate share of the earnings of the investee as the earnings are reported, rather than as received in the form of dividends. For tax purposes, the investor company recognizes income from its investment in the investee company as dividends are received. Dividends received generally are less than reported earnings of the investee company. Accordingly, the financial accounting income of the investor will be greater than the investor's taxable income. The undistributed earnings of the investee company (reported income, less dividends distributed) should be treated as a timing difference for purposes of income tax allocation.

The appropriate tax rate to use in the allocation process depends upon whether the investor company expects to realize the undistributed earnings in the form of dividends (Block 8) or through stock appreciation upon the ultimate sale of the investment. If the investor company expects to receive the undistributed earnings in the form of stock appreciation, the appropriate tax rate would be the capital gains rate, provided the securities qualify for capital gains treatment.

Since the difference between the equity in the earnings of the investee company and the dividends received is to be treated as a timing difference, tax allocation, using the procedures described in APB Opinion No. 11, is appropriate. Deferred taxes will be established for the undistributed earnings, using the appropriate effective tax rate after giving consideration to all possible tax credits, deductions and planning alternatives. If the investee company should incur a loss, the investor's share of the loss should be handled in accordance with Paragraphs 44 through 50 of APB Opinion No. 11.

A significant difference in accounting for the undistributed earnings of an investee company and a subsidiary lies in the fact that, for investee companies, it is inappropriate to assume any permanent investment or distribution of earnings in the form of a tax-free liquidation. For an investment in an investee company, accounted for using the equity method, all undistributed earnings are assumed to be distributable, either as dividends or through stock appreciation. The investor company is not faced with the problem of determining the disposition of undistributed earnings.

To illustrate the basic tax allocation process involved when the investment is accounted for using the equity method, the assumptions listed in Exhibit III will be used.

Exhibit III

Investment Using Equity Method—Example 1

1. Investor, Inc. owns 40 percent of the common stock of Investee, Inc.
2. Investee, Inc. reported income of $750,000 during the current year and paid dividends of $300,000.
3. Investor, Inc. has an effective tax rate of 48 percent, and the dividends received from Investee, Inc. qualify for the 85 percent dividend deduction.
4. Investor, Inc. assumes that all undistributed earnings will be received in the form of dividends, and there are no plans to sell any of the shares of Investee, Inc.

Because Investor, Inc. owns 40 percent of the common stock of Investee, Inc., the investment should be accounted for using the equity method. Investee, Inc. did not distribute all earnings during the current period; thus, Investor, Inc. must use interperiod tax allocation procedures for the undistributed earnings of Investee, Inc. The computation below shows the determination of Investor, Inc.'s share of the undistributed earnings of Investee:

	Reported by Investee, Inc.	Investor, Inc. % of Ownership	Investor, Inc. Equity
Net Income	$750,000	40	$300,000
Dividends	(300,000)	40	(120,000)
Undistributed Earnings	$450,000		$180,000

During the current year, Investor, Inc. recognized $300,000 as equity in the earnings of Investee, Inc. For tax purposes, only the $120,000 of dividends received will be considered as income. The undistributed earnings are subject to tax allocation. Table III shows the computation of the income tax expense, income taxes payable and deferred income taxes as a result of the reported earnings of Investee, Inc.

Table III

Current Period Tax Computations

	Income Tax Expense	Income Taxes Payable	Deferred Income Tax
Investor's Equity in Investee's Earnings	$300,000		
Investor's Share of Investee's Dividends		$120,000	
Investor's Share of Undistributed Earnings			$180,000
Dividend Deduction Reciprocal[a]	× 15%	× 15%	× 15%
Amount Available for Taxes	$ 45,000	$ 18,000	$ 27,000
Tax Rate	× 48%	× 48%	× 48%
Total	$ 21,600	$ 8,640	$ 12,960

[a] Since the dividend deduction is 85 percent, taxes will be paid on 15 percent of the dividends received.

Investor, Inc. will prepare the following journal entry to record the tax consequences of the earnings, dividends and undistributed earnings of Investee, Inc. during the year:

Income Tax Expense	21,600	
Income Taxes Payable		8,640
Deferred Income Taxes		12,960

The deferred taxes will be reduced as the undistributed earnings of Investee, Inc. are paid out in the form of dividends.

The next example has been developed as a comprehensive illustration of accounting for income taxes of an investee company when the equity method is used. Exhibit IV lists the assumptions used in the example.

Exhibit IV

Investment Using Equity Method—Example 2

1. Investor, Inc. owns 35 percent of the common stock of Investee, Inc. At the date of purchase of the shares, Investor, Inc. paid $200,000 in excess of the fair value of the net assets and treated this amount as goodwill. Goodwill is being amortized over a 40-year period, in accordance with the provisions of APB Opinion No. 17.
2. Investee, Inc. reported net income of $1,500,000 during the current year and paid dividends of $500,000.
3. Investor, Inc. has an effective tax rate of 48 percent, and the dividends received from Investee, Inc. qualify for the 85 percent dividend deduction.
4. After careful analysis, Investor, Inc. estimates that $300,000 of the current year's undistributed earnings of Investee, Inc. will be realized through the sale of shares of stock. The effective tax rate applicable to the gain on the sale

of the stock is 25 percent. The remaining undistributed earnings of Investee, Inc. are expected to be received in the form of dividends in the near future.

Because Investor, Inc. owns 35 percent of the common stock of Investee, Inc., the investment qualifies for equity method accounting. The undistributed earnings of Investee, Inc. are subject to interperiod income tax allocation. To determine the amount of undistributed earnings subject to tax allocation, the following computations are necessary:

	Reported by Investee, Inc.	Investor, Inc. % of Ownership	Investor, Inc. Equity
Net Income	$1,500,000	35	$ 525,000
Dividends	(500,000)	35	(175,000)
Undistributed Earnings	$1,000,000		$ 350,000

The $350,000 represents Investor, Inc.'s equity interest in the undistributed earnings of Investee, Inc. However, it was determined that $300,000 of Investee, Inc.'s total undistributed earnings will be realized in the form of stock appreciation upon sale of shares, rather than in the form of dividends. The amount realized through appreciation in the value of the investment is to be taxed at a different rate than dividend income. It is necessary to adjust Investor, Inc.'s equity in the undistributed earnings of Investee, Inc. as a result of this situation. The following computations show the adjustment required:

Investor, Inc.'s Equity in Total Undistributed Earnings	$350,000
Investor, Inc.'s Equity in Undistributed Earnings Realized Through Stock Appreciation ($300,000 × 35%)	(105,000)
Investor, Inc.'s Equity in Undistributed Earnings to be Realized in the form of Dividends	$245,000

The $105,000 determined above will be taxed at the 25 percent rate.

Another adjustment to earnings is required in this example. Investor, Inc. is using the equity method of accounting for its investment in Investee, Inc. As part of that accounting, the $200,000 of goodwill is being amortized at the rate of $5,000 per year ($200,000/40 years). The amortization of goodwill represents a permanent difference between accounting income and tax income. Goodwill must be amortized for accounting purposes, but is not deductible for income tax purposes. Because the amount of amortization is a permanent difference, it is not subject to tax allocation and must be removed as part of the determination of income. This adjustment is made in Table IV, which shows the computation of income taxes for the earnings, dividends and undistributed earnings of Investee, Inc.

Table IV

Current Period Tax Computation

	Income Tax Expense	Income Taxes Payable	Deferred Income Taxes
Investor, Inc.'s Equity in Earnings	$525,000		
Investor, Inc.'s Equity in Dividends		$175,000	
Investor, Inc.'s Equity in Undistributed Earnings			$350,000
Goodwill Amortization	(5,000)		(5,000)
Investor, Inc.'s Equity in Earnings to be Taxed at Capital Gains Rate	(105,000)		(105,000)
Elimination of Goodwill	5,000		5,000
Total	$420,000	$175,000	$245,000
Dividend Deduction Reciprocal[a]	× 15%	× 15%	× 15%
Amount Available for Taxation	$ 63,000	$ 26,250	$ 36,750
Tax Rate	× 48%	× 48%	× 48%
Total	$ 30,240	$ 12,600	$ 17,640
Taxes Related to Undistributed Earnings Taxed at Capital Gains Rate ($105,000 × 25%)	26,250	-0-	26,250
Total	$ 56,490	$ 12,600	$ 43,890

[a] Since the dividend deduction is 85 percent, taxes will be paid on 15 percent of the dividends received.

The following journal entry would be made by Investor, Inc. to reflect the tax consequences of the income, dividends and undistributed earnings of Investee, Inc. in the current year:

Income Tax Expense	56,490	
Income Taxes Payable		12,600
Deferred Income Taxes		43,890

The deferred income taxes will be reduced when dividends are received or when shares of stock of Investee, Inc. are sold.

Accounting for income taxes when a company has a change in ownership interest in a subsidiary, corporate joint venture or investee company is another subject area covered in the Opinions. Accounting problems relating to changes in ownership interest will be discussed next.

Decreases in Ownership Interest

A parent company's percentage ownership of a subsidiary may fall below 50 percent, and the company then would be considered as an investee company, subject to the equity method of accounting for the investment. The percentage ownership in an investee company or corporate joint venture may fall below 20 percent, and the investment then would no longer qualify for equity method accounting. In either of these cases, accounting for income taxes by the parent or investor company would change from the practices previously followed.[2]

Decrease in Ownership Interest of a Subsidiary

If the ownership interest in a subsidiary or permanent corporate joint venture decreases, so that the investment can no longer be considered a subsidiary, but does qualify for equity accounting (Block 7), new income tax accounting procedures are required. Deferred taxes should be calculated on the investor's share of the undistributed earnings of the investee company from the date the former subsidiary became an investee company, i.e., from the date of change in ownership interest. The procedures to be used from the date of change in ownership interest are the same as those previously described for an investee company qualifying for equity accounting treatment. Special accounting treatment may be required for deferred taxes recorded during the time the company was classified as a subsidiary.

If deferred taxes have been recorded for the undistributed earnings prior to the date the subsidiary became an investee company, these taxes may have to be removed from the books of the investor company. If the decrease in ownership interest was due to the disposition of shares of stock, deferred taxes related to the disposition should be removed from the deferred income tax account and included in income in the period of disposition.

The deferred taxes relating to the percentage of ownership retained by the investor company would be included in income only when, and if, the dividends received from the investee company (from the date of change of ownership interest) exceed the investor's equity in the earnings of the investee. The total amount of deferred taxes included in income in this manner may not exceed the amount of taxes previously deferred while the company was treated as a subsidiary.

Deferred taxes may not have been recorded while the company was classified as a subsidiary because the undistributed earnings were

---

[2] An investor company may realize a tax benefit relating to the difference between the accounting basis and tax basis of shares sold. FASB Interpretation No. 29 states that such tax benefits should be classified in the same manner as the gain or loss resulting from the disposition of shares, i.e., in continuing operations, extraordinary items or disposal of a business segment.

assumed to be permanently invested by the subsidiary or were expected to be distributed in the form of a tax-free liquidation. Because the company is no longer considered a subsidiary, permanent investment of undistributed earnings and tax-free liquidations no longer are considered in the tax allocation process. Therefore, deferred taxes must be recorded in the period of change of ownership interest on these amounts. The deferred taxes will be based on the percentage of ownership retained by the investor company.

Decrease in Ownership Interest of an Investee Company

The ownership interest in an investee company may decrease so that it no longer qualifies for equity method accounting (Block 9). The investment now would be accounted for using the cost method. Under the cost method, income is recognized when it is received in the form of dividends. Since income is *not* recognized when earned by the investee company, there is no recognition given to undistributed earnings. There will be no difference between financial accounting income and tax income as a result of the cost method, so no deferred taxes will be recorded.

The deferred taxes that were recorded on the undistributed earnings when the investee company qualified for equity method treatment may have to be removed from the books of the investor company. If the change in ownership interest was due to the disposition of shares of stock of the investee company, the deferred taxes associated with the undistributed earnings relating to the shares should be removed from the deferred tax account and included in income in the period of disposition.

The deferred taxes associated with the undistributed earnings relating to the ownership interest *retained* by the investor company would be included in income only when, and if, the dividends received from the investee company exceed the investor's equity in the earnings from the date of change in ownership interest. The total amount of deferred taxes included in income in this manner cannot exceed the deferred taxes recorded while the investee company qualified for equity method treatment.

Decrease in Ownership Interest—An Example

There are several possible examples that could be developed to illustrate the accounting for income taxes after there has been a change in ownership interest. Since many of the procedures are the same, one example should be sufficient to gain an understanding of the general problem. The assumptions listed in Exhibit V will be used to illustrate the accounting required when the ownership interest decreases to the point that a subsidiary company becomes an investment qualifying for equity method accounting.

Exhibit V

Decrease in Ownership Interest

1. From January 1, 197A, until January 1, 197C, Book-It, Inc. owned 60 percent of the common stock of Jar, Inc. and accounted for the company as a subsidiary.
2. On January 1, 197C, Book-It, Inc. sold 20 percent of the common shares it owned in Jar, Inc., and retained a 40 percent ownership interest.
3. From January 1, 197A, until January 1, 197C, Jar, Inc. reported income of $1,000,000 and paid no dividends. The total undistributed earnings were assumed to be distributable in the form of dividends in future periods.
4. The tax rate in effect during this period for Book-It, Inc. was 50 percent, and dividends that would have been received from Jar, Inc. qualify for the 85 percent dividend deduction. Book-It recorded $45,000 of deferred taxes on the undistributed earnings of Jar, Inc.
5. Jar, Inc. reported income of $500,000 for the year ended December 31, 197C, and paid dividends of $50,000 during the year.
6. Book-It, Inc. assumes that all of the undistributed earnings in 197C will be realized through the distribution of dividends in future periods.

Jar, Inc. qualified as a subsidiary from January 1, 197A, until January 1, 197C. Because Book-It, Inc. retained only a 40 percent ownership interest after January 1, 197C, Jar, Inc. qualifies as an investment, under the equity method, from that date forward. Since the decrease in ownership interest changed the classification of the investment for accounting purposes, it is necessary to determine if any of the $45,000 of deferred taxes should be removed from the books of Book-It, Inc. The change in ownership interest was due to the disposition of stock, so the deferred taxes relating to the shares sold must be removed. The computation of the amount to be removed is shown below:

Deferred Taxes Previously Recorded	$45,000
Percentage of Ownership Interest Sold	× 20%
Deferred Taxes to be Removed	$ 9,000

The entry required by Book-It, Inc. to remove the deferred taxes is shown below:

Deferred Income Taxes	9,000	
Income Tax Expense		9,000

Because the dividends received in 197C did not exceed the reported income, no further adjustment is required to the deferred taxes previously recorded. Now, the computation of the taxes for the current period can be made. The method used is the same as that described earlier for investee companies that qualify for equity method accounting. The computation of Book-It, Inc.'s equity in the undistributed earnings of Jar, Inc. for 197C would be determined as follows:

	Reported by Jar, Inc.	Book-It Inc. % of Ownership	Book-It, Inc. Equity
Net Income	$500,000	40	$200,000
Dividends	(50,000)	40	(20,000)
Undistributed Earnings	$450,000		$180,000

Table V shows the computation of taxes for the current period, based upon Book-It, Inc.'s equity in earnings, dividends and undistributed earnings of Jar, Inc.

Table V

Current Period Tax Computation

	Income Tax Expense	Income Taxes Payable	Deferred Income Taxes
Book-It's Equity in Earnings	$200,000		
Book-It's Equity in Dividends		$ 20,000	
Book-It's Equity in Undistributed Earnings			$180,000
Dividend Deduction Reciprocal[a]	× 15%	× 15%	× 15%
Amount Available for Taxation	$ 30,000	$ 3,000	$ 27,000
Tax Rate	× 50%	× 50%	× 50%
Total	$ 15,000	$ 1,500	$ 13,500

[a] Since the dividend deduction is 85 percent, taxes will be paid on 15 percent of the dividends received.

Based upon this information, the following journal entry would be made by Book-It, Inc. for 197C:

Income Tax Expense	15,000	
Income Taxes Payable		1,500
Deferred Income Taxes		13,500

When this entry is combined with the entry to remove the deferred taxes previously recorded, income tax expense in 197C would be $6,000 ($15,000 – $9,000), and deferred taxes would be $4,500 ($13,500 – $9,000). The two entries could have been made in combined form, but were shown separately for purposes of illustration.

Increase in Ownership Interest

The percentage of ownership may increase, so as to change the classification of the investment from an investee company, accounted for using the equity method, to a subsidiary (Block 2). When this situation occurs, new income tax accounting procedures are required. From the date of change in ownership interest, the parent company is to defer taxes on all undistributed earnings of the subsidiary that are not assumed to be permanently invested or distributable in the form of a tax-free liquidation. This accounting procedure has been described earlier.

Deferred taxes recorded under the equity method while the company was classified as an investee may have to be removed from the books of the parent company after the date of change in ownership interest. If, after the date the company became a subsidiary, the parent company's share of dividends exceeds its equity in earnings of the subsidiary, deferred taxes relating to the excess should be removed (Block 5). The total deferred taxes included in income in this manner cannot exceed the amount of taxes previously deferred.

The accounting required in this situation is very similar to the accounting required when there has been a decrease in ownership interest. Refer back to the previous example for accounting details.

Disclosures

The disclosures required for subsidiaries and permanent corporate joint ventures are specified in Paragraph 14 of APB Opinion No. 23, and are listed below:

1. The total undistributed earnings for which deferred taxes have *not* been computed should be disclosed;

2. If the undistributed earnings are going to be permanently invested or distributed in a tax-free liquidation, this fact should be stated.

Bad Debt Reserves of Savings and Loan Associations

Savings and loan associations are required by regulatory authority to allocate a percent of earnings to bad debt reserves for financial accounting purposes. This is required as a means of protecting depositors. The Internal Revenue Service also allows the savings and loan to allocate a percent of earnings to bad debt reserves for tax purposes. However, the amount allowable for tax purposes differs from the amount required by the regulatory authority. Since the portion of income allocated to bad debt reserves differs for accounting income and tax income, a proper determination of the nature of the difference is required. APB Opinion No. 23 recognized the fact that the difference may never reverse, depending upon the situation. Since the difference can result in an indefinite reversal, savings and loan associations normally should not compute deferred taxes on the amount. An exception would be if the savings and loan expected to reduce the bad debt reserves associated with taxable income. In this case, it would be appropriate to defer taxes on the reduction, with a corresponding charge to tax expense in the period when the decrease is expected. The charge to income tax expense should not be treated as an extraordinary item.

The disclosures required relating to the bad debt reserves are specified in Paragraph 24 of APB Opinion No. 23, and are listed below:

1. The bad debt reserves for which deferred taxes have *not* been computed; and

2. A description of why the bad debt reserves are provided, and a statement that taxes may be payable if the reserves are not used for the purpose specified.

Policyholders' Surplus of Stock Life Insurance Companies

Stock life insurance companies are allowed to reduce tax income by a specific amount, calculated on a formula basis, and to use this amount as policyholders' surplus. The amount used as policyholders' surplus may be included in tax income of subsequent years, if the insurance company decides to "(a) distribute policyholders' surplus to stockholders as dividends, (b) transfer amounts from policyholders' surplus to shareholders' surplus designated for tax purposes as available for any business purpose, or (c) take, or if it fails to take, certain other specified actions (none of which usually occur)" (APB Opinion No. 23, Paragraph 26).

The allocation of tax income to policyholders' surplus creates a difference in financial accounting income and tax income. Because this difference may never reverse, a possible indefinite reversal exists. The stock life insurance company normally should not defer taxes on the difference between financial accounting income and tax income due to policyholders' surplus. If, however, the stock life insurance company expects to reduce the policyholder's surplus, the company should defer tax on the reduction, with a corresponding charge to tax expense in the period in which it is determined that a decrease is expected. The charge to income tax expense *should not* be treated as an extraordinary item.

The disclosures relative to policyholders' surplus of stock life insurance companies are specified in Paragraph 29 of APB Opinion No. 23 and are listed below:

1. The policyholders' surplus for which deferred tax has not been computed; and

2. A description of the handling of policyholders' surplus for tax purposes, and a statement that tax may be payable on the surplus if the insurance company performs certain actions.

Example Disclosures

Information from the footnotes to the 1976 Annual Report of Corning Glass Works is presented below. Note 3 relates to Taxes on Income and clearly shows the taxes on income of the parent company and taxes on "unremitted earnings" of associated companies. The last paragraph of the Note describes the accounting treatment given to undistributed earnings of subsidiaries and associated companies.

Corning Glass Works (Dec)

Statement of Accounting Policies

Taxes on income—Certain charges, primarily provisions for furnace repairs, employe benefits, inventories and depreciation, are not deductible in the tax return for the period in which they are recognized as expenses in the financial statements; certain income from equity basis companies and foreign subsidiaries is included in net income when it is earned but is not taxed until received by Corning (timing differences). In computing income tax expense for a period, the company deducts these charges and includes this income in the periods in which they are recognized in the financial statements rather than in the period in which they are included in the tax return (deferred tax accounting).

Corning and its subsidiaries and associated companies provide income taxes on their earnings at applicable rates. Additional U.S. federal income taxes which would be payable by Corning upon remittance of subsidiaries' earnings to the parent company are provided to the extent that future remittance is anticipated. In general, it is expected that 50% of Corning's share in the earnings of subsidiaries and associated companies will be remitted and 50% will remain invested indefinitely.

Investment tax credits are deferred for financial statement purposes and used to reduce income tax expense in equal installments over the lives of the related properties.

Notes to Consolidated Financial Statements

Note 3: Taxes on Income—Income tax expense is reported in the Consolidated Statements of Income and Retained Earnings in these segments:

Dollars in thousands	**1976**	**1975**
Taxes on income	$51,874	$7,723
Taxes provided in equity in earnings of associated companies	1,109	1,471
Tax expense for the year	$52,983	$9,194

The 1975 effective tax rate varies from the U.S. statutory rate of 48% because of the relative importance of investment tax credits, earnings of the company's domestic international sales corporation, dividend income and other permanent differences between book and taxable income.

Income tax expense for the year is provided for current or future payment to the following taxing authorities:

Dollars in thousands	**1976**	**1975**
U. S. federal	$40,999	$5,435
Foreign governments	6,018	2,416
State and municipal	5,966	1,343
	$52,983	$9,194

Income tax expense for the year is reconciled to taxes payable in the tax returns as follows:

Dollars in thousands	**1976**	**1975**
Tax expense for the year	$52,983	$9,194
Timing differences		
(See Statement of Accounting Policies)	(5,067)	(1,102)
Investment credits allowed in the current tax return (more) less than amortization of credits allowed in prior years	224	(1,752)
Taxes payable in the tax returns	$48,140	$6,340

Corning provides U. S. federal income tax on the earnings of subsidiaries and associated companies to the extent they are expected to be remitted. Taxes have not been provided on accumulated unremitted earnings of $69,500,000 at January 2, 1977 and $47,000,000 at December 28, 1975, which are expected to remain invested indefinitely. It is estimated that U.S. federal income taxes (after foreign tax credits and dividend exclusions) which would be payable if these earnings were remitted were $15,000,000 at January 2, 1977, and $11,152,000 at December 28, 1975. Changes in the two years in net deferred tax timing differences related to taxes other than U.S. federal were minor.

Source: *Accounting Trends & Techniques,* Copyright © 1977 by the American Institute of Certified Public Accountants, Inc., p. 274-275.

SFAS No. 31 (September 1979) Accounting for Tax Benefits Related to U.K. Tax Legislation Concerning Stock Relief

Introduction

This Statement is highly specialized in nature and relates to recent changes in the tax laws of the United Kingdom (U.K.). The Statement identifies the financial accounting nature of what is known in the U.K. as the "stock relief" section of the tax laws. The term "stock" used in the U.K. is what we would label as *inventory,* so it may be helpful to think of the word "inventory" each time the word "stock" appears. In general, the U.K. tax law permits certain tax benefits, depending upon whether or not a company's inventory increased or decreased during the current period. While this is an oversimplification of the law, it does get at the heart of the issue addressed in SFAS No. 31. The basic question addressed in the Statement was whether the "stock relief" was to be treated as a timing difference or as a permanent difference for financial accounting purposes. The Board concluded that the tax benefits of the "stock relief" section of the law should be treated as a timing difference by U.K. companies that prepare financial statements on the basis of U.S. generally accepted accounting principles. The Board based its conclusion on the fact that there is a potential for recapture of the "stock relief" tax benefit, and that such recapture would be the same as the reversal of any timing difference.

The specifics of the U.K. tax law state that a company may deduct from taxable income an increase in the carrying value of its inventories, and that decreases in the carrying value of the inventory would be a reversal of the tax benefit for purposes of determining taxable income. The Board feels that the tax benefit of the "stock relief" should serve as a timing difference as long as there is the potential for recapture, i.e., a decrease in the carrying value of the inventory. The U.K. tax law sets a six-year period for recapture of the tax benefit; therefore, as long as it is reasonable to assume that the tax benefit will be recaptured within a six-year period, it should be viewed as a timing difference. Of course, if it is not probable that the tax benefit will be recaptured, the tax benefit should not be deferred. The U.K. law specifies that any recapture of the tax benefit should be handled on a LIFO basis. As an example, Footnote 4 to Paragraph 1 states that, "a decrease in inventory in 1978-1979 would first be offset against any 'stock relief' claimed in 1977-1978."

This general introduction should prove sufficient to an understanding of the technical material presented in the following section.

Technical Considerations

To illustrate the computational and accounting aspects of SFAS No. 31, the information in Exhibit I has been developed.

Exhibit I

U.K. Stock Relief Tax Legislation

1. Newman, Inc., a December 31 year-end company, is a United Kingdom enterprise that reports its financial information in accordance with U.S. generally accepted accounting principles.

2. Financial accounting income before income tax considerations is presented below:

198A—$200,000

198B—$190,000

198C—$225,000

3. Changes in Newman's inventories were as follows:

198A—$10,000 increase

198B—$15,000 increase

198C—$6,000 decrease

4. In 198D, Newman, Inc. determined that it was probable that the tax benefit of any "stock relief" would be recaptured prior to the end of the relevant six-year period.

5. The tax rate for Newman from 198A through 198D is 50 percent.

Since Newman, Inc. is a United Kingdom enterprise reporting its financial information in accordance with U.S. generally accepted accounting principles, a "stock relief" (inventory) deduction may be appropriate. Newman, Inc. realized a $10,000 increase in the carrying value of its inventories during 198A, and, since it is probable that the stock relief will be recaptured within the relevant time period, a stock relief deduction is allowed in 198A.

Because the tax benefit of the stock relief deduction is to be treated as a timing difference, "Income Taxes Payable" will be reduced in 198A by an amount equal to the tax effect of the stock relief deduction. The "Deferred Taxes" account will be established in an amount equal to the the tax effect of the stock relief deduction. The stock relief deduction is equal to the increase in inventory during the current period.

After analyzing the situation for 198A, Newman now may prepare a schedule to determine income tax expense, income tax payable and the deferred taxes. Table 1 summarizes the necessary computations.

Table 1
Tax Computations for 198A

	Income Tax Expense	*Income Tax Payable*	*Deferred Taxes*
Income Before Taxes	$200,000	$200,000	-
Increase in Inventory	-	(10,000)	$10,000
Total	$200,000	$190,000	$10,000
Tax Rate	X .50	X .50	X .50
Total	$100,000	$ 95,000	$ 5,000

The reader can see that the stock relief deduction of $10,000 reduced "Income Tax Payable" and increased the "Deferred Tax" account by an after-tax amount of $5,000. Based upon the information developed in Table 1, Newman would prepare the following journal entry to record taxes for 198A:

Income Tax Expense	100,000	
Income Tax Payable		95,000
Deferred Income Tax		5,000

The stock relief deduction was treated just as any other timing difference for financial accounting purposes (See APB Opinion No. 11 in this Topic for a complete discussion of timing differences). The assumption implicit in the treatment of the timing difference is that the amount will reverse out (be recaptured) in future periods, and the balance in the deferred tax account will decline.

Turning attention to 198B, notice that the carrying value of inventories increased by another $15,000. Once again, Newman qualifies for a stock relief deduction. This is because the inventory increased, *and* it is probable that the stock relief deduction will be recaptured within the appropriate time period.

Newman prepared Table 2 to compute the income tax expense, income tax payable and deferred income taxes for 198B.

Table 2

Tax Computations for 198B

	Income Tax Expense	*Income Tax Payable*	*Deferred Taxes*
Income Before Taxes	$190,000	$190,000	
Increase in Inventory	-	(15,000)	$15,000
Total	$190,000	$175,000	$15,000
Tax Rate	X .50	X .50	X .50
Total	$ 95,000	$ 87,500	$ 7,500

As in 198A, Newman may use the information in Table 2 to prepare the journal entry to record income taxes in 198B.

Income Tax Expense	95,000	
Income Tax Payable		87,500
Deferred Income Tax		7,500

At the end of 198B, the "Deferred Income Tax" account has a credit balance of $12,500 ($5,000 from 198A + $7,500 from 198B).

In 198C, the carrying value of inventory decreased. When this occurs, Newman has had a recapture of at least part of the previous stock relief deductions taken. When a recapture occurs, the company must apply a LIFO basis to the recapture. Accordingly, the tax effect of the inventory decrease in 198C will first be applied to the stock relief deduction taken in 198B. If this amount of recapture proves insufficient, additional recapture is available from 198A.

Given this information, Newman has prepared Table 3 to compute income tax expense, income tax payable and deferred income taxes for 198C.

Table 3
Tax Computations for 198C

	Income Tax Expense	*Income Tax Payable*	*Deferred Taxes*
Income Before Taxes	$225,000	$225,000	
Decrease in Inventory	-	6,000	($6,000)
Total	$225,000	$231,000	($6,000)
Tax Rate	X .50	X .50	X .50
Total	$112,500	$115,500	($3,000)

As a result of the recapture of a portion of the stock relief deduction, part of the previously established deferred taxes will now be reversed. The journal entry necessary in 198C to reflect the taxes of Newman would be as follows:

Income Tax Expense	112,500	
Deferred Income Tax	3,000	
Income Tax Payable		115,500

On the basis of additional information in 198D, Newman determined that the remaining stock relief deduction established in 198A and 198B will not be recaptured before the six-year expiration date. Once this information is known, the remaining deferred tax relating to the deduction should be reversed out and included as a part of the current period tax expense. The amount of deferred tax to be reversed would be determined as follows:

Stock Relief Deduction—198A	$ 5,000
Stock Relief Deduction—198B	7,500
Total	$12,500
Recapture of Stock Relief—198C	3,000
Stock Relief Deduction Not Recaptured	$ 9,500

The journal entry necessary to reverse out the stock relief deduction would be:

Deferred Income Tax	9,500	
Income Tax Expense		9,500

The entry completely removes the effect of the stock relief deductions established in prior years. The balance in the deferred tax account would be zero.

As discussed previously, when the stock relief deduction becomes available and taxes are not deferred because the deduction will not be recaptured before the six-year expiration period, no timing difference exist. However, when the benefit is not recognized and, at a later date, it is determined that it is probable that the benefit could be recaptured, it becomes necessary to establish deferred taxes in the period in which the determination is made. The amount of the deferred taxes should be equal to the stock relief deduction that *could have been* established originally. The corresponding side of the journal entry would be a debit to "Income Tax Expense" in the period in which the determination was made.

If a company prepares interim period financial statements, the stock relief tax benefit should serve as an adjustment to the effective tax rate used in computing the interim period taxes. This adjustment should be made in the first interim period in which the stock relief tax benefit becomes available.

Topic 6

Equities

Detail Contents

APB Opinions and SFAS Statements

1. APB Opinion No. 14	–Accounting for Convertible Debt and Debt Issued with Stock Purchase Warrants
2. APB Opinion No. 21	–Interest on Receivables and Payables
3. APB Opinion No. 25	–Accounting for Stock Issued to Employees
4. APB Opinion No. 26	–Early Extinguishment of Debt
5. SFAS No. 4	–Reporting Gains and Losses from Extinguishment of Debt
6. SFAS No. 5	–Accounting for Contingencies
7. SFAS No. 6	–Classification of Short-Term Obligations Expected to be Refinanced
8. SFAS No. 11	–Accounting for Contingencies–Transition Method

FASB Interpretations

1. FASB Interpretation No. 8	–Classification of a Short-Term Obligation Repaid Prior to Being Replaced by a Long-Term Security (Interpretation of SFAS No. 6)
2. FASB Interpretation No. 14	–Reasonable Estimation of the Amount of a Loss (Interpretation of SFAS No. 5)
3. FASB Interpretation No. 28	–Accounting for Stock Appreciation Rights and Other Award Plans (Interpretation of APB Opinion Nos. 15 and 25)

FASB Technical Bulletins

1. FASB Technical Bulletin No. 79-3	–Subjective Acceleration Clauses in Long-Term Debt Agreements

Future Considerations of the FASB

1. Exposure Draft	–Accounting for Compensated Absences

This proposed Statement of Financial Accounting Standard is concerned with the appropriate accounting for paid absences such as vacation pay, paid holidays, sick leave, etc. The proposed accounting treatment would require an enterprise to establish a liability and expense equal to the expected amount that will be paid in the current period for services performed by employees. This accounting treatment will require employers to estimate future payments for compensated absences and allocate the amount to the accounting period in which the services of the employees are performed.

2. Proposed Interpretation —Applicability of APB No. 21 to Television Film License Agreements

This proposed interpretation states that receivables and payables resulting from agreements involving television film licenses would be accounted for using the provisions of APB Opinion No. 21. If the agreement is for longer than one year, and there is no interest rate stated or the stated rate is not reasonable, an interest rate should be imputed.

APB Opinion No. 14 (March 1969)

Accounting for Convertible Debt and Debt Issued with Stock Purchase Warrants

Flowchart and General Discussion

APB Opinion No. 14 deals with the problem of accounting for securities that contain both debt and equity elements. Securities with features of both debt and equity provide the safeguard of debt—periodic interest payments—and allow the holder to participate in the long-term growth of the company by converting the debt security to an equity interest. Some securities may be debt during their entire life, and be retired as debt. Other securities may begin as debt instruments and eventually be converted into an equity interest. Still other securities may begin as debt instruments and, at some time, be divided into a debt *and* equity interest.

The Flowchart is designed around the three types of debt securities identified in the Opinion. The types of securities identified contain both debt and equity features and include (1) convertible debt, (2) debt with non-detachable stock purchase warrants, and (3) debt with detachable stock purchase warrants. The basic thrust of the Opinion is to determine when it is appropriate to account for the debt and equity elements of these securities on an individual basis.

The discussion that follows will treat separately each of the securities specifically identified in the Opinion.

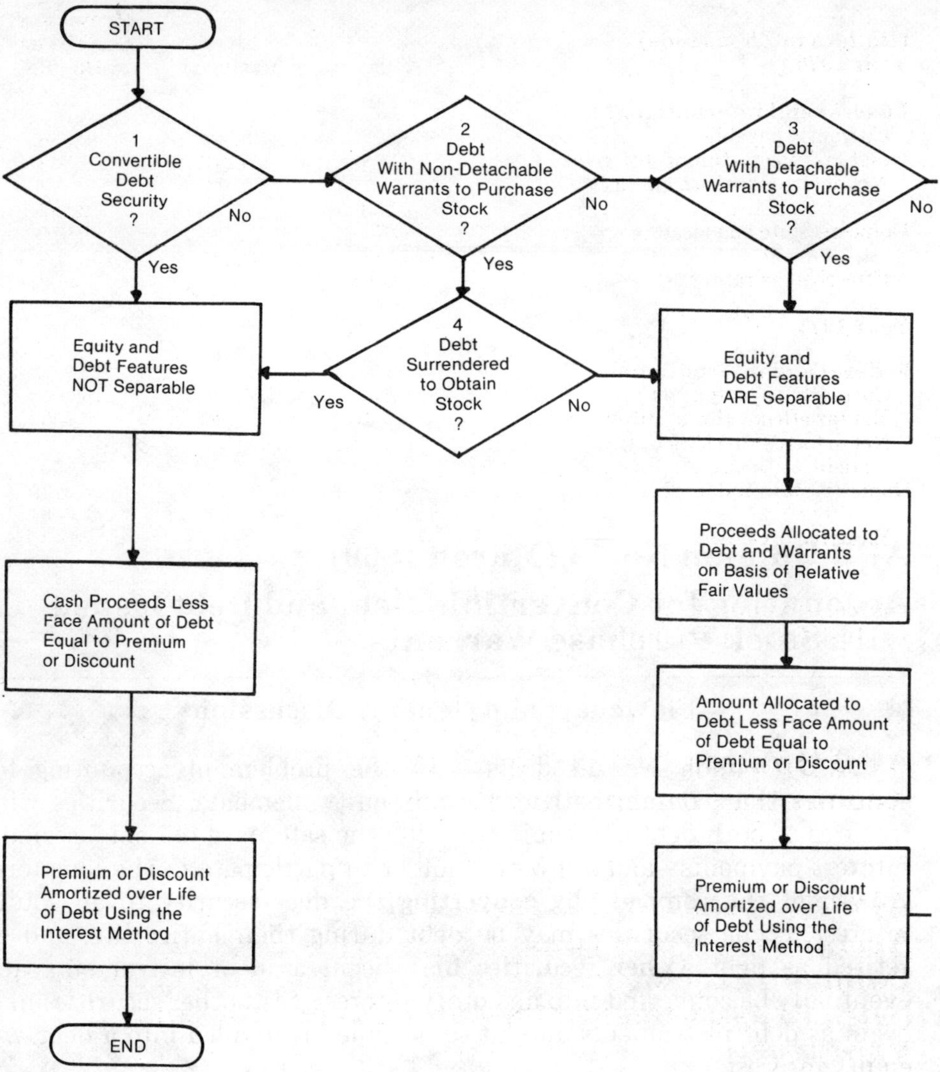
START
1 Convertible Debt Security ?
No
Yes
2 Debt With Non-Detachable Warrants to Purchase Stock ?
No
Yes
3 Debt With Detachable Warrants to Purchase Stock ?
No
Yes
Equity and Debt Features NOT Separable
4 Debt Surrendered to Obtain Stock ?
Yes
No
Equity and Debt Features ARE Separable
Proceeds Allocated to Debt and Warrants on Basis of Relative Fair Values
Cash Proceeds Less Face Amount of Debt Equal to Premium or Discount
Amount Allocated to Debt Less Face Amount of Debt Equal to Premium or Discount
Premium or Discount Amortized over Life of Debt Using the Interest Method
Premium or Discount Amortized over Life of Debt Using the Interest Method
END

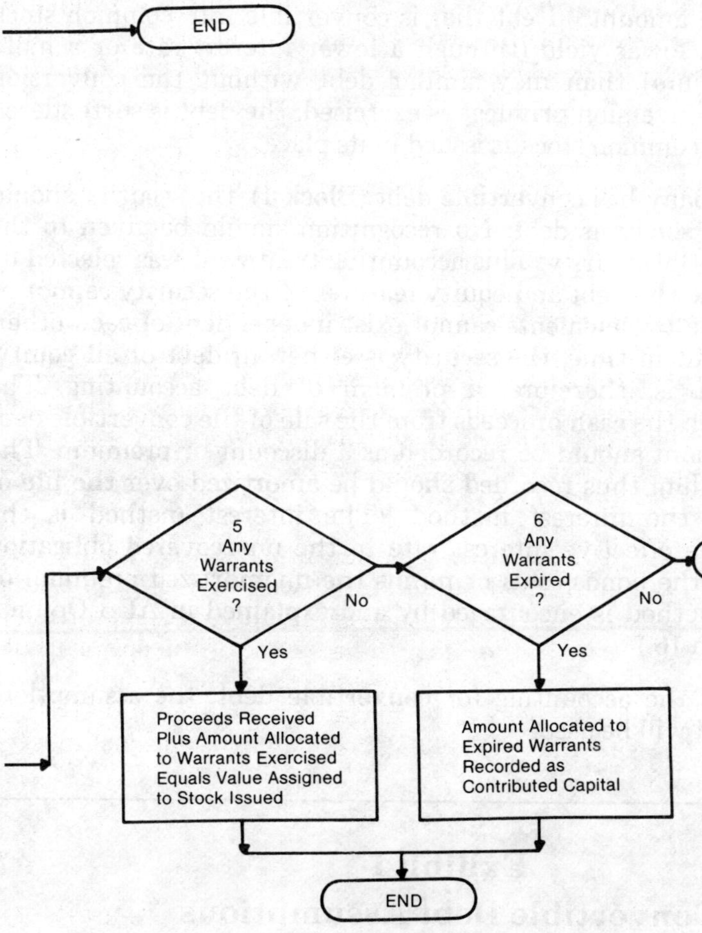
END
5
Any
Warrants
Exercised
?
No
Yes
6
Any
Warrants
Expired
?
No
Yes
END
Proceeds Received
Plus Amount Allocated
to Warrants Exercised
Equals Value Assigned
to Stock Issued
Amount Allocated to
Expired Warrants
Recorded as
Contributed Capital
END

Convertible Debt

Convertible debt is defined (APB Opinion No. 14, Paragraph 3) as "debt securities which are convertible into common stock of the issuer or an affiliated company at a specified price at the option of the holder and which are sold at a price or have a value at issuance not significantly in excess of the face amount." Debt that is convertible into common stock may be sold at a lower yield (through a lower interest rate or a more substantial premium) than may similar debt without the conversion privilege. If the conversion privilege is exercised, the debt is surrendered to the issuer, and common stock is issued in its place.

When a company has convertible debt (Block 1), the security should be accounted for solely as debt. No recognition should be given to the equity feature of the security. This accounting treatment was selected by the Board because the debt and equity features of the security cannot be separated, i.e., the two elements cannot exist independent of each other. At any given point in time, the security is either all debt or all equity. Convertible debt is, therefore, a problem of debt accounting. The difference between the cash proceeds from the sale of the convertible debt and the face amount should be recorded as a discount or premium. The discount or premium thus recorded should be amortized over the life of the debt, using the interest method. (The interest method is the application of the effective interest rate to the unrecovered obligation balance—face of the bonds, plus or minus the unamortized premium or discount. This method is encouraged by and explained in APB Opinion No. 12, Paragraph 16.)

To illustrate the accounting for convertible debt, the assumptions listed in Exhibit I will be used.

Exhibit I

Convertible Debt Assumptions

1. On January 1, Seller Company, Inc. issued 1,000, five-year, 10 percent, $1,000 face value convertible bonds.
2. Interest is payable semiannually on January 1 and July 1.
3. Each $1,000 bond is convertible into 20 shares of $10 par value common stock. On January 1, the market price of the common stock is $45 per share.
4. Due to the conversion privilege, the bonds were priced to yield eight percent.

The bonds will be sold at a premium, because the effective yield is less than the stated rate. For this particular example, it is necessary to calculate the proceeds from the sale. The proceeds will be equal to the net present value of the bonds, i.e., the present value of the interest annuity plus the present value of the face amount. The present value of the bond may be calculated using the following formula:

$$PVB = (FV \times SR)(A) + (FV)(P)$$

Where:	PVB	=	Present value of the bonds (cash proceeds).
	FV	=	Face value of the bonds.
	SR	=	Stated interest rate per interest payment period.
	A	=	Present value of an annuity, using the effective interest rate per interest payment period
	P	=	Present value of $1, using the effective interest rate per interest payment period.

For the example bonds, there are 10 interest payment periods (5 years × 2 interest payments per year = 10 payments); therefore, the stated interest rate to be used in the above formula will be five percent (10 percent/2) and the effective rate will be four percent (8 percent/2). Remember that the interest rates must be expressed as a rate per interest payment period. With this in mind—and using 8.11090 as the present value factor for an ordinary annuity for 10 periods at four percent, and .67556 as the present value factor for $1 for 10 periods at four percent—the formula will provide the following result:

$$PVB = (\$1{,}000{,}000 \times .05)(8.11090) + (\$1{,}000{,}000)(.67556) = \$1{,}081{,}105$$

The difference between the proceeds of $1,081,105 and the $1,000,000 face amount of the bonds is recorded as the premium on the bonds. The entry to record the issuance of the convertible bonds is as follows:

Cash	1,081,105	
Bonds Payable		1,000,000
Premium on Bonds		81,105

If, in the above example, the proceeds were known, but the effective interest rate was not known, the formula could be used on a trial-and-error approach to determine the effective interest. This is a very time-consuming task, and one that can be handled quite easily through the use of a computer program.

Once the bond proceeds have been determined, a premium amortization schedule similar to Table I may be prepared. Table I itemizes the cash interest paid, interest expense, premium amortization and bond carrying value for each interest payment period. The interest method has been used to amortize the bond premium.

Table I

Schedule of Interest and Premium Amortization

	Period	Cash Interest	Interest Expense	Premium Amortization	Carrying Value of Bonds
Initial Value	-	-	-	-	$1,081,105
	1	a$ 50,000	b$ 43,244	c$ 6,756	d1,074,349
	2	50,000	42,974	7,026	1,067,323
	3	50,000	42,693	7,307	1,060,016
	4	50,000	42,401	7,599	1,052,417
	5	50,000	42,097	7,903	1,044,514
	6	50,000	41,781	8,219	1,036,295
	7	50,000	41,452	8,548	1,027,747
	8	50,000	41,110	8,890	1,018,857
	9	50,000	40,754	9,246	1,009,611
	10	50,000	*40,389	9,611	e1,000,000
		$500,000	$418,895	$81,105	

a $1,000,000 × 5% = $50,000.
b $1,081,105 × 4% = $43,244.
c $50,000 — $43,244 = $6,756.
d $1,081,105 — $6,756 = $1,074,349.
e Represents the maturity value of the bonds at the end of five years.
* Rounded.

Using the information in Table I, the journal entry required on July 1, (the first interest payment period) would be:

Interest Expense	43,244	
Premium on Bonds	6,756	
Cash		50,000

To complete the example, assume that, just after the third interest payment, all the bonds were converted into common stock. At the time of conversion, the bonds have a carrying value of $1,060,016. Each bond will be converted into 20 shares of $10 par value common stock, so 20,000 (1,000 × 20) shares of common will be issued for the bonds. Assuming that market value is equal to book value, the journal entry to record the conversion would be as follows:

Bonds Payable	1,000,000	
Premium on Bonds	60,016	
Common Stock (20,000 shares × $10 par)		200,000
Contributed Capital in Excess of Par		860,016

The debt securities have now all been converted into equity. If only part of the bonds had been converted, a proportionate share of the premium would have been removed from the account.

Debt with Non-Detachable Stock Purchase Warrants

A review of the Flowchart indicates that debt with non-detachable stock purchase warrants (Block 2) will be treated as either convertible debt or as debt with detachable stock purchase warrants. The appropriate treatment of the security is determined by whether or not the debt must be surrendered to obtain the stock (Block 4). If the debt must be surrendered, the security will be accounted for as if it were convertible debt. Accounting for convertible debt has been discussed above. If the debt does not have to be surrendered to obtain the stock, the security will be accounted for in the same manner as debt with detachable stock purchase warrants. Accounting for debt with detachable stock purchase warrants is discussed in the following section.

Debt with Detachable Stock Purchase Warrants

Generally, detachable warrants may be removed from the debt and used to purchase shares of stock, or they may be sold to a third party interested in acquiring shares. The debt and warrants usually trade separately in the market. This means that the two are independent securities that carry individual values. If a company has debt with detachable stock purchase warrants, APB Opinion No. 14 requires that separate recognition be given to the value of the debt and the warrants (Block 3). The value to be assigned to the debt and equity elements of the security is based on the relative fair values of the debt and warrants. Because the two trade separately, the relative fair values may be determined. However, in some cases, the fair values may have to be estimated.

The total proceeds from the sale of the securities should be allocated to the debt and warrants on the basis of actual or estimated fair market values. The portion of the proceeds that is allocated to the warrants is considered to be paid-in or contributed capital of the company. An account, such as "Stock Warrants Outstanding," should be used to record the value assigned to the warrants. The difference between the proceeds allocated to the debt and the face of the debt should be recorded as a discount or premium. The discount or premium is amortized over the life of the debt, using the interest method.

As the warrants are exercised, the value assigned to the stock issued is equal to the proceeds allocated to the warrants exercised, plus any additional proceeds received from the exercise of the warrants (Block 5). Unexercised warrants generally expire after a period of time (Block 6). The amount allocated to warrants that have expired is considered to be paid-in or contributed capital of the company. Warrants may be allowed to expire because there is no economic advantage to be gained from their exercise.

To illustrate the accounting for debt with detachable stock purchase warrants, the assumptions listed in Exhibit II will be used.

Exhibit II

Assumptions for Debt with Detachable Stock Purchase Warrants

1. On January 1, Seller Company, Inc. issued 200, four-year, 10 percent, $1,000 face value bonds with detachable warrants.
2. Interest is paid annually on December 31.
3. Each $1,000 bond has a detachable warrant that can be used to purchase one share of Seller Company, Inc. common stock for $50. The par value of the common stock is $30 per share.
4. The debt with detachable warrants was priced to yield 11 percent.
5. At the time of sale, it is estimated that the bonds would sell for $958.975, independent of the warrants, and that the warrants would sell for $10, independent of the bonds.

The proceeds from the sale may be calculated using the preceding formula. The formula—using 3.10245 as the present value factor for an ordinary annuity for four periods at 11 percent and .65873 as the present value factor for $1 for four periods at 11 percent—will yield the following results:

$$PVB = (\$200{,}000 \times .10)(3.10245) + (\$200{,}000)(.65873) = \$193{,}795$$

The proceeds now must be allocated to the debt and warrants on the basis of their relative fair market values. The first step in the process is to determine the total fair market value of the two securities. This is accomplished in the following manner.

Bonds (200 bonds × $958.975)	$191,795
Warrants (200 warrants × $10)	2,000
Total Fair Value	$193,795

In this example, the total value of the bonds and warrants is equal to the proceeds received from the sale. Therefore, allocation based on the relative fair values of each would provide results equal to their individual fair values, making it unnecessary to complete the allocation process.

The discount or premium on the bonds is determined by the difference between the proceeds allocated to the bonds and the face amount of the bonds. For this example, a discount would result because the effective yield is greater than the stated yield. The discount is calculated as follows:

Face Value of Bonds (200 bonds × $1,000)	$200,000
Proceeds Allocated to Bonds	191,795
Discount on Bonds	$ 8,205

Based upon this information, the following journal entry is required to record the issuance of the bonds and warrants.

Cash	193,795	
Discount on Bonds Payable	8,205	
Bonds Payable		200,000
Stock Warrants Outstanding		2,000

The discount of $8,205 is amortized over the life of the bonds, using the interest method. Since $2,000 of the proceeds were allocated to the warrants, the effective discount on the bonds was increased by $2,000. Without considering the warrants, the discount on the bonds would have been $6,205 ($200,000 – $193,795). With the allocation of the proceeds to the warrants, the discount is determined to be $8,205. This difference will affect the determination of the interest rate used to amortize the discount, using the interest method. The 11 percent interest rate used above resulted in the $6,205 discount, and cannot be used to amortize a discount of $8,205. The problem now is to determine the interest rate that will allocate the $8,205 discount over the life of the debt.

The correct interest rate may be determined by the trial-and-error method or by the use of a computer program. The trial-and-error method is very time-consuming because present value factors must be found for both an annuity and the present value of $1. When using the trial-and-error method, both A and P must be found for the equation. Determining the effective interest through the use of a computer program is an excellent way to solve this problem. The typical computer program is both efficient and quick in the solution of this type of problem.

The appropriate interest rate to use to amortize the discount in this example is 11.3318 percent. Once this rate has been determined, an amortization schedule similar to Table II can be developed. Table II summarizes the cash interest paid, interest expense, discount amortization, and the bond carrying value for the life of the security.

Table II

Schedule of Interest Expense and Discount Amortization

	Period	Cash Interest	Interest Expense	Discount Amortization	Carrying Value of Bonds
Initial Value	-	-	-	-	[a]$191,795
	1	[b]$20,000	[c]$21,734	[d]$ 1,734	[e]193,529
	2	20,000	21,930	1,930	195,459
	3	20,000	22,149	2,149	197,608
	4	20,000	22,392	2,392	[f]200,000
		$80,000	$88,205	$ 8,205	

[a] Proceeds allocated to the bonds.
[b] $200,000 × 10% = $20,000.
[c] $191,795 × 11.3318% = $21,734.
[d] $21,734 − $20,000 = $1,734.
[e] $191,795 + $1,734 = $193,529.
[f] Represents the maturity value of the bonds.

Using the information in Table II, the journal entry required for the first annual interest payment and discount amortization would be as follows:

Interest Expense	21,734	
Discount on Bonds Payable		1,734
Cash		20,000

Table II contains the information to prepare the above journal entry for each year of the life of the bonds.

To continue with the example, assume that 190 warrants were exercised for the purchase of 190 shares of common stock. The proceeds from the exercise of the warrants would be $9,500 (190 warrants × $50 exercise price). The following entry would be required to reflect the exercise of the warrants:

Cash	9,500	
Stock Warrants Outstanding	[a]1,900	
Common Stock		[b]5,700
Contributed Capital in Excess of Par		[c]5,700

[a] 190 warrants/200 warrants × $2,000 = $1,900.
[b] 190 common shares × $30 par value = $5,700.
[c] ($9,500 proceeds + $1,900 value of warrants) − ($5,700 amount assigned to common stock) = $5,700.

Assuming that the remaining warrants were allowed to expire, the journal entry shown below would be required.

Stock Warrants Outstanding	[a]100	
Contributed Capital from Warrants		100

[a] \$2,000 − \$1,900 = \$100.

In the above example, the proceeds received from the sale of the bonds were equal to the market value of the bonds and warrants. This is a simple example, designed to illustrate the basic accounting required for debt with detachable stock purchase warrants. For a more complex example, the assumptions listed in Exhibit III will be used.

Exhibit III
Assumptions for Debt with Detachable Stock Purchase Warrants

1. On January 1, Seller Company, Inc. issued 500, four-year, nine percent, \$1,000 face value bonds with detachable warrants.
2. Interest is paid annually on December 31.
3. Each \$1,000 bond has a detachable warrant that can be used to purchase one share of Seller Company, Inc. common stock for \$100. The par value of the common stock is \$75 per share.
4. The debt with detachable warrants was priced to yield eight percent.
5. At the time of sale, it is estimated that the bonds will sell for \$1,020, independent of the warrants; and that the warrants will sell for \$20, independent of the bonds.

Using the formula given, the following proceeds may be calculated:

$$PVB = (\$500{,}000 \times .09)(3.31213^{a}) + (\$500{,}000)(.73503^{b}) = \$516{,}561$$

[a] Present value factor for an ordinary annuity for four periods at eight percent. See Appendix A, Table II.
[b] Present value factor for \$1 for four periods at eight percent. See Appendix A, Table I.

These particular bonds were sold at a premium, because the effective yield of eight percent is less than the stated yield of nine percent. The proceeds of \$516,561 must be allocated to the bonds and warrants on the basis of their relative fair market values. The total fair values would be determined as follows:

Bonds (500 bonds × \$1,020 fair value)	\$510,000
Warrants (500 warrants × \$20 fair value)	10,000
Total Fair Value	\$520,000

Because there is a difference between the proceeds of \$516,561 and the total fair value of \$520,000, the proceeds must be allocated to the bonds and warrants. The allocation would be accomplished as follows:

Bonds ($510,000/$520,000 × $516,561)	$506,627
Warrants ($10,000/$520,000 × $516,561)	9,934
Total Proceeds Allocated	$516,561

The premium relating to the bonds may be determined, once the allocation process is complete. The premium is equal to the difference between the amount allocated to the bonds and the face amount of the bonds, and is calculated below:

Amount Allocated to Bonds	$506,627
Face Amount of Bonds	500,000
Premium on Bonds Payable	$ 6,627

Based upon the information generated above, the journal entry to record the issuance of the bonds would be as follows:

Cash	516,561	
Bonds Payable		500,000
Premium on Bonds Payable		6,627
Stock Warrants Outstanding		9,934

The premium will be amortized over the life of the bonds, using the interest method. As in the previous example, a new effective interest rate must be determined to properly amortize the premium. The appropriate rate to use in the amortization process is 8.5945 percent, and was determined by the use of a computer program. With the calculation of this rate, an amortization table may be prepared. Table III summarizes relevant information relating to the example bond issue.

Table III

Schedule of Interest Expense and Premium Amortization

Period	Cash Interest	Interest Expense	Premium Amortization	Carrying Value of Bonds
Initial Value -	-	-	-	[a]$506,627
1	[b]$ 45,000	[c]$ 43,542	[d]$ 1,458	[e]505,169
2	45,000	43,417	1,583	503,586
3	45,000	43,281	1,719	501,867
4	45,000	43,133	1,867	[f]500,000
	$180,000	$173,373	$ 6,627	

[a] Proceeds allocated to the bonds.
[b] $500,000 × 9% = $45,000.
[c] $506,627 × 8.5945% = $43,542.
[d] $45,000 − $43,542 = $1,458.
[e] $506,627 − $1,458 = $505,169.
[f] Represents the maturity value of the bonds.

The entry required for the first annual interest payment and premium amortization is presented below:

Interest Expense	43,542	
Premium on Bonds Payable	1,458	
Cash		45,000

Entries to record the exercise of warrants and the expiration of warrants would be similar to those presented above and need not be repeated.

No disclosure requirements are identified in the Opinion.

APB Opinion No. 21 (August 1971) Interest on Receivables and Payables

Flowchart and General Discussion

APB Opinion No. 21 specifies the accounting treatment for a receivable or payable when the present value and face amount are not equal. The Opinion applies to "receivables and payables which represent contractual rights to receive money or contractual obligations to pay money on fixed or determinable dates, whether or not there is any stated provision for interest" (APB Opinion No. 21, Paragraph 2). The following receivables and payables are specifically identified as being subject to the provisions of the Opinion:

(1) Secured and unsecured notes;

(2) Debentures, bonds and mortgage notes;

(3) Equipment obligations; and

(4) Some accounts receivable and payable.

Paragraph 3 of the Opinion identifies five specific receivables and payables that are exempt from the provisions of the Opinion. These include the following:

(1) Current receivables and payables arising from the normal course of business and on normal terms of trade;

(2) Amounts that will be applied to the future purchase price of property, goods or services;

(3) Amounts representing security for one party to a transaction, such as a security deposit;

(4) Cash lending activities of financial institutions such as banks and savings and loans; and

(5) Amounts from transactions between a parent and subsidiary companies or between subsidiaries of the same parent.

The Flowchart identifies the general accounting and reporting requirements established by APB Opinion No. 21. The decision blocks have been numbered for referencing in the discussion below. The receivables and payables identified as being subject to the provisions of

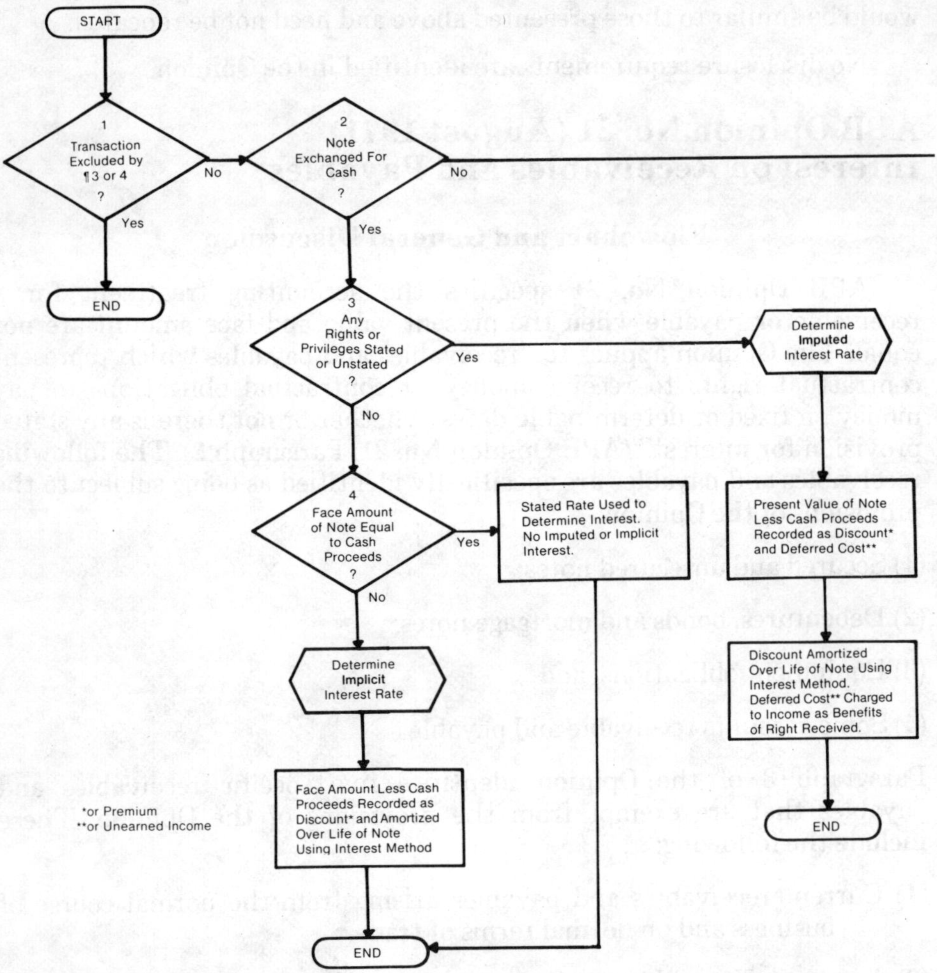
START
1
Transaction Excluded by ¶3 or 4
?
No
Yes
END
2
Note Exchanged For Cash
?
No
Yes
3
Any Rights or Privileges Stated or Unstated
?
Yes
No
Determine Imputed Interest Rate
Present Value of Note Less Cash Proceeds Recorded as Discount* and Deferred Cost**
Discount Amortized Over Life of Note Using Interest Method. Deferred Cost** Charged to Income as Benefits of Right Received.
END
4
Face Amount of Note Equal to Cash Proceeds
?
Yes
No
Stated Rate Used to Determine Interest. No Imputed or Implicit Interest.
Determine Implicit Interest Rate
Face Amount Less Cash Proceeds Recorded as Discount* and Amortized Over Life of Note Using Interest Method
END
*or Premium
**or Unearned Income

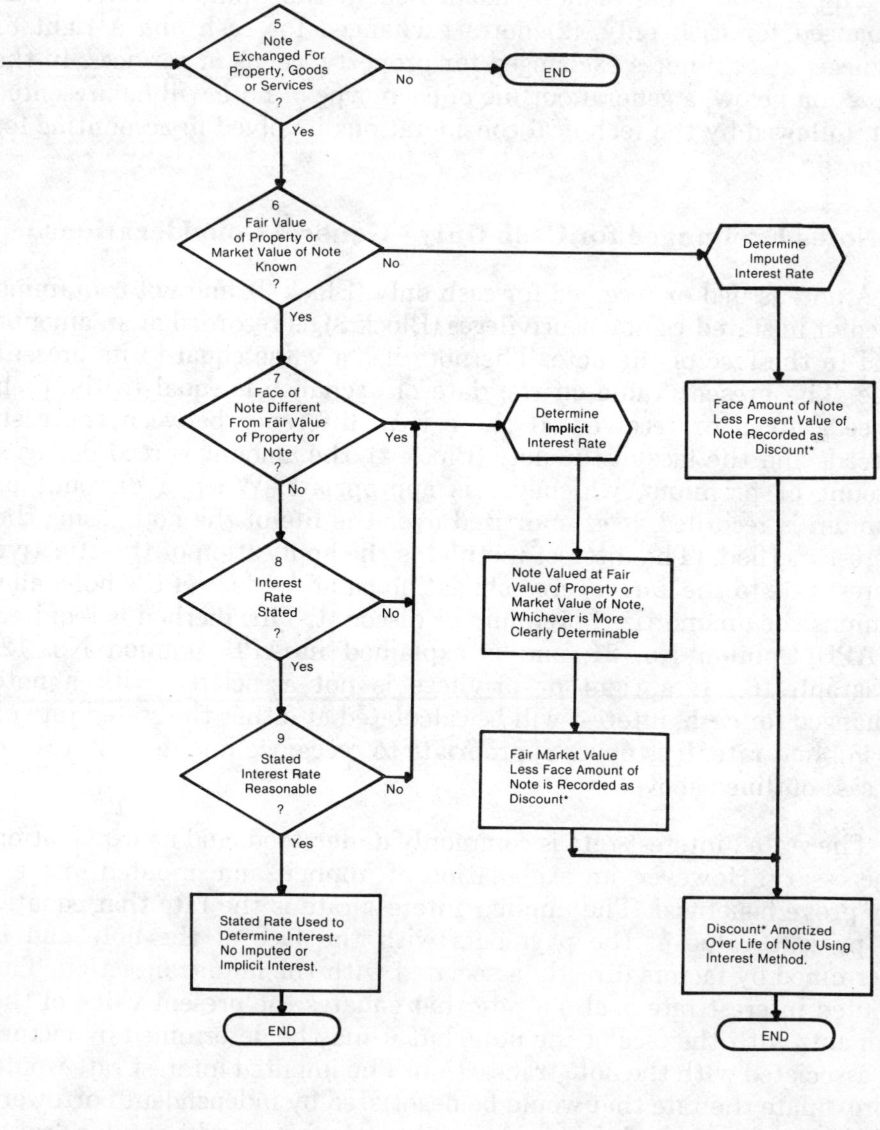
5
Note
Exchanged For
Property, Goods
or Services
?
No
END
Yes
6
Fair Value
of Property or
Market Value of Note
Known
?
No
Determine
Imputed
Interest Rate
Yes
7
Face of
Note Different
From Fair Value
of Property or
Note
?
Yes
Determine
Implicit
Interest Rate
Face Amount of Note
Less Present Value of
Note Recorded as
Discount*
No
8
Interest
Rate
Stated
?
No
Note Valued at Fair
Value of Property or
Market Value of Note,
Whichever is More
Clearly Determinable
Yes
9
Stated
Interest Rate
Reasonable
?
No
Fair Market Value
Less Face Amount of
Note is Recorded as
Discount*
Yes
Stated Rate Used to
Determine Interest.
No Imputed or
Implicit Interest.
Discount* Amortized
Over Life of Note Using
Interest Method.
END
END

the Opinion will be referred to as "notes" in the remainder of this discussion.

The general types of notes identified in the Opinion are (1) notes exchanged for cash only, (2) notes exchanged for cash *and* a right or privilege, and (3) notes exchanged for property, goods or services. In the discussion below, a general outline of each type of note will be presented first, followed by the technical considerations involved in accounting for the note.

Notes Exchanged for Cash Only—General Considerations

A note issued or received for cash only (Block 2), and not containing stated or unstated rights or privileges (Block 3), is recorded at an amount equal to the face of the note. The note has a value equal to its present value. The present value on the date of exchange is equal to the cash proceeds given or received. If there is a difference between the cash proceeds and the face of the note (Block 4), the amount is recorded as a discount or premium, whichever is appropriate. When a discount or premium is recorded, it is amortized over the life of the note, using the interest method. (The interest method is the application of the effective interest rate to the unrecovered obligation balance—face of the note, plus or minus the unamortized premium or discount. This method is required by APB Opinion No. 21, and is explained in APB Opinion No. 12, Paragraph 16.) If a right or privilege is not associated with a note exchanged for cash, interest will be calculated at either the stated rate or the implicit rate. It is never appropriate to recognize imputed interest in the case outlined above.

The stated interest rate is commonly understood, and no explanation is necessary. However, an explanation of implicit and imputed interest may prove beneficial. The implicit interest rate is the rate that equates the present value of the payments with the face of the note and is determined by factors directly associated with the note transaction. The imputed interest rate is also a rate that equates the present value of the payments with the face of the note, but it may be determined by factors not associated with the note transaction. The imputed interest rate would approximate the rate that would be negotiated by independent borrowers and lenders for a note having similar characteristics and a similar degree of risk. Implicit interest always may be determined mathematically, but imputed interest requires judgment on the part of the accountant.

Where a note is issued solely for cash (no rights or privileges associated with the note), the implicit interest rate will be used to determine interest if the face is different than the proceeds. If the face of the note is equal to the proceeds, and the interest rate is zero, no interest will be recognized from the transaction. It is appropriate to have a true non-interest bearing note under the provisions of APB Opinion No. 21.

Notes Exchanged for Cash Only—Technical Considerations

To illustrate the technical aspects of a note issued or received for cash only, assume that Borrower, Inc. borrows $10,000 from Lender Company, with no stated interest. The agreement requires Borrower, Inc. to repay $10,000 at the end of four years. There are no rights or privileges associated with the agreement.

By following the Flowchart, it can be determined that the stated rate of interest should be used to determine interest expense or income in the example. This note qualifies as a true non-interest bearing note, because the face amount ($10,000) is not greater than the proceeds ($10,000). The Opinion prohibits *imputing* interest where a note is exchanged for cash only; therefore, no interest will be recognized over the four-year period. The journal entries necessary to record the note for Borrower, Inc. and Lender Company are shown below and are quite simple:

Borrower, Inc.

Cash	10,000	
Notes Payable		10,000

Lender Company

Notes Receivable	10,000	
Cash		10,000

Since interest will not be recognized on this note, the only other entry required is for the payment of the principal amount at the end of the four-year period. The entries would be merely a reversal of the ones shown above.

This first example represents a very straightforward exchange of a note for cash only. A more complex example is presented below. In this case, assume that Borrower, Inc. borrows $300,000 from Lender Company, and that once again there is no stated interest rate. The agreement requires Borrower, Inc. to repay $710,210 at the end of 10 years. There are no rights or privileges associated with the agreement.

Because the face amount of the note ($710,210) is greater than the cash proceeds ($300,000), the *implicit* interest rate must be determined. Since Borrower, Inc. is receiving only $300,000 in cash and is required to repay $710,210, interest of $410,210 ($710,210 − $300,000) is implicit in the transaction.

At inception of the agreement, Borrower, Inc. and Lender Company should record the note at its face amount and recognize the implicit interest as a discount on the note. The following entries reflect the proper accounting at the date of the transaction:

Borrower, Inc.

Cash	300,000	
Discount on Notes Payable	410,210	
Notes Payable		710,210

Lender Company

Notes Receivable	710,210	
Cash		300,000
Discount on Notes Receivable		410,210

While the total interest has been determined above, the implicit rate of interest has yet to be determined. To calculate the implicit rate, one may use the trial-and-error method, a computer program or the procedure outlined below.

The following formula will provide the *present value factor* that is associated with the effective interest rate implicit in the transaction:

$$F = \frac{C}{N}$$

Where: F = Present value factor of $1
C = Cash proceeds received or given on exchange
N = Face of the note

Using this formula and the information given above, the following answer is generated:

$$F = \frac{\$300,000}{\$710,210}$$

$$F = .42241$$

The answer of .42241 represents the present value factor for $1 for 10 periods at a yet-to-be-determined interest rate. Given this information, turn to the present value table for $1, Appendix A, Table 1. Start in the 10 periods row, and go across the columns until the factor of .42241 is found. This present value factor corresponds to an interest rate of nine percent. Therefore, nine percent is the effective interest rate that will be used to recognize interest expense or income, using the interest method. It is important to note that the exact present value factor may not always be found in the table. The user may be required to interpolate an interest rate between two factors. This was not an installment note. In the case of installment notes, it will be necessary to use an annuity table, rather than merely a present value table. Even with these restrictions, the technique described above is more efficient than the trial-and-error method.

Once the effective rate has been determined, an amortization schedule can be prepared. Table I shows the amortization necessary for the example.

Table I
Discount Amortization Schedule

Period	Discount Amortization	Carrying Value of Note
Initial Value		$ 300,000
1	[a]$ 27,000	[b]327,000
2	29,430	356,430
3	32,079	388,509
4	34,966	423,475
5	38,113	461,588
6	41,543	503,131
7	45,282	548,413
8	49,357	597,770
9	53,799	651,569
10	58,641	[c]710,210
	$ 410,210	

[a] $300,000 × 9% = $27,000
[b] $300,000 + $27,000 = $327,000
[c] Amount equals the face of the note at maturity

Even though the note is non-interest bearing, implicit interest will be recognized. The entries to record the first year's amortization of the discount are as follows:

Borrower, Inc.

Interest Expense	27,000	
Discount on Notes Payable		27,000

Lender Company

Discount on Notes Receivable	27,000	
Interest Income		27,000

Amounts for subsequent amortization are found in Table I.

Notes Exchanged for Cash and a Right or Privilege—General Considerations

A note may be exchanged for cash and also have a stated or unstated right or privilege associated (Block 3). For example, a company may loan money to a major supplier with no stated interest, but with a provision that the supplier allow the company to purchase products in the future at less than the prevailing market price. Obtaining this right may be the primary reason for the loan. If such a right or privilege exists, recognition must be given to the value of the right by establishing a discount or premium on the note. In this case, the discount or premium is not the result of implicit interest, but must be the result of imputed interest. The user must impute interest associated with the right by using an assumed interest rate. The imputed interest rate is based largely on judgments made by the user, but the Opinion does provide some guidance in the selection of an appropriate rate. According to the Opinion (Paragraph 13), the rate should be "at least equal to the rate at which the debtor can obtain financing of a similar nature from other sources at the date of the transaction." The selection of the rate may be influenced "by the credit standing of the issuer, restrictive covenants, the collateral, payment and other terms pertaining to the debt, and, if appropriate, the tax consequences to the buyer and seller" (APB Opinion No. 21, Paragraph 13). The selection of the appropriate imputed interest is discussed in detail in Paragraphs 13 and 14 of the Opinion.

Once the appropriate rate has been selected, the present value of the note is calculated. The difference between the present value of the note and the face amount is the discount or premium. In most cases, the face of the note is equal to the amount disbursed or received; therefore, it is necessary to establish a deferred asset or unearned income account to offset the discount or premium recorded.

The discount or premium is amortized over the life of the note, using the interest method. The imputed interest rate is used in the amortization process. The deferred asset or unearned income account is amortized over the life of the note in proportion to the benefits received from the right or privilege. For example, for the right described above, the lender would amortize the deferred asset to cost of goods sold, based on the relationship between the current period purchases and the estimated total purchases from the supplier over the life of the note. The supplier would amortize the unearned income, based on the relationship between the current sales to the customer and estimated total sales over the life of the note.

Notes Exchanged for Cash and a Right or Privilege—Technical Considerations

To illustrate the somewhat complex technical aspects of accounting for a note exchanged for cash and a right or privilege, assume that Lender Company loans $3,000,000 to Borrower, Inc., a supplier of products to Lender Company. The $3,000,000 is to be repaid in four years, with no interest. Borrower, Inc. agrees to allow Lender Company to purchase merchandise at less than prevailing market prices during the next four years. Assume further that Borrower, Inc. would have to pay 12 percent interest for similar financing.

By reference to the Flowchart (Block 3), one can see that interest must be imputed on this loan agreement. For this example, the imputed interest rate was given at 12 percent. The right to purchase merchandise at less than the prevailing market price must be given accounting recognition. To accomplish this, the present value of the note must be determined, using the imputed interest rate. Because this is a lump-sum payment, the present value of $1 must be used (See Appendix A, Table I).

The present value factor for four periods at 12 percent is .63552, which leads to the following computation:

$$\$3{,}000{,}000 \times .63552 = \$1{,}906{,}560$$

The present value of the note is therefore $1,906,560, and the difference between the face of the note ($3,000,000) and the present value is the imputed interest of $1,093,440.

Given this information, the entries required at the date the loan agreement was consumated are as follows:

Borrower, Inc.

Cash	3,000,000	
Discount on Notes Payable	1,093,440	
Notes Payable		3,000,000
Unearned Income		1,093,440

Lender Company

Deferred Cost of Purchases	1,093,440	
Notes Receivable	3,000,000	
Cash		3,000,000
Discount on Notes Receivable		1,093,440

The next step involves the determination of the proper amortization of both the discount and the unearned income and deferred cost of purchases. The discount is amortized using the interest method, but the unearned income and deferred cost of purchases are amortized using the relationship between annual purchases/sales of merchandise and total expected purchases/sales of merchandise. The expected purchases/sales of merchandise, for purposes of the example, are presented in Table II below:

Table II

Schedule of Purchases/Sales

Year	Purchases/Sales
1	$ 500,000
2	600,000
3	800,000
4	1,000,000
Total	$2,900,000

Table III develops the calculation necessary to amortize the discount, as well as the amortization of the unearned income and deferred cost of purchases.

Table III

Amortization Schedule for Note Exchanged for Cash and a Right

Period	Deferred Cost or Unearned Income Amortization	Deferred Cost or unearned income Balance	Discount Amortization	Carrying Value of Note
Initial Value		$1,093,440	-	$1,906,560
1	[a]$ 188,524	[b]904,916	[c]$ 228,787	[d]2,135,347
2	[e]226,229	678,687	256,242	2,391,589
3	[f]301,639	377,048	286,991	2,678,580
4	[g]377,048	—0—	*321,420	[h]3,000,000
	$1,093,440		$1,093,440	

[a] \$500,000/\$2,900,000 × \$1,093,440 = \$188,524.
[b] \$1,093,440 − \$188,524 = \$904,916.
[c] \$1,906,560 × 12% = \$228,787.
[d] \$1,906,560 + \$228,787 = \$2,135,347.
[e] \$600,000/\$2,900,000 × \$1,093,440 = \$226,229.
[f] \$800,000/\$2,900,000 × \$1,093,440 = \$301,639.
[g] \$1,000,000/\$2,900,000 × \$1,093,440 = \$377,048.
[h] Amount represents the face of the note at the maturity date.
* Rounded.

Information from Table III is used to prepare the required journal entries for Year 1:

Borrower, Inc.

Unearned Income	188,524	
Sales		188,524
Interest Expense	228,787	
Discount on Notes Payable		228,787

Lender Company

Cost of Goods Sold	188,524	
Deferred Cost of Purchases		188,524
Discount on Notes Receivable	228,787	
Interest Income		228,787

In the example just completed, several assumptions were made to limit the complexity of the problem. Mention of some complicating factors needs to be made at this point. These additional considerations do not change the basic accounting presented above, but the reader should be aware of them.

Since the effective interest rate is imputed, it is possible for the borrower and lender to have a different perception of the lender's borrowing rate. If this were the case, the borrower and lender would use a different interest rate to determine the value of the right or privilege. By using a different rate, different amounts may be charged to sales and cost of sales over the life of the note.

In addition to this problem, the periodic amortization of the right or privilege by the lender and the borrower may not be the same. This would be the case where the two parties had different expectations concerning the total and annual sales/purchases between them. Thus, the combination of using different imputed interest rates and also different estimations of sales/purchases may complicate the analysis necessary to arrive at a correct solution to the problem.

Notes Exchanged for Property, Goods or Services— General Considerations

In most cases, a note issued or received for property, goods or services (Block 5) is valued at the present value of the consideration given or, if more clearly determinable, the present value of the consideration received. The consideration exchanged for the property, goods or services (hereafter referred to as property) consists of two components. One component is the purchase price in an arm's length cash transaction. The second component is the interest factor or the return to the seller for accepting the note instead of receiving cash at the time the exchange is made. If the fair value of the property (or market value of the note) is known (Block 6), the transaction may involve the use of the stated rate or the implicit rate, but interest may not be imputed. Assuming these values are known, if the face of the note is equal to the fair value of the property (Block 7), if the note contains a stated interest rate (Block 8) and if the stated rate is reasonable (Block 9), no new accounting problems are created in the Opinion. Traditional accounting treatment of the note would be applicable. However, if any of these conditions are not met, special accounting treatment is required.

If the fair value of the property or the market value of the note is known, any implicit interest in the exchange can be determined and a discount or premium established for the difference between the fair value of the property and the face of the note. If, however, the fair value of the property and the market value of the note are not known, interest must be imputed. The fair value of the property must be determined by using the imputed interest rate. The discount or premium established by imputing the interest or by recognizing the implicit interest is amortized, using the interest method over the life of the note. Generally, the use of imputed interest is a last resort for the accountant.

Notes Exchanged for Property, Goods or Services—Technical Considerations

To illustrate the accounting for a note exchanged for property, assume that Borrower, Inc. purchased equipment from Lender Company and was unable to pay cash. Lender Company agreed to accept Borrower's five-year non-interest bearing note, with payments of $54,114 payable at the end of each year. The total amount to be repaid is $270,570 (5 × $54,114). Lender Company normally purchases the equipment for $150,000, and resells it for $200,000.

Since the fair value of the property ($200,000) is known, the only applicable interest rates are the stated rate or the implicit rate. The face amount of the note ($270,570) is greater than the fair value of the property; therefore, this note requires the calculation of implicit interest. Borrower, Inc. is receiving equipment with a fair value of $200,000, but is required to pay $270,570, so there is $70,570 ($270,570 – $200,000) interest implicit in the transaction. The entries below are required to record the note at the date the agreement is consumated:

Borrower, Inc.

Equipment	200,000	
Discount on Notes Payable	70,570	
Notes Payable		270,570

Lender Company

Notes Receivable	270,570	
Sales		200,000
Discount on Notes Receivable		70,570
Cost of Goods Sold	150,000	
Inventory		150,000

The discount of $70,570 must be amortized over the life of the note, using the appropriate effective interest rate. The effective interest rate necessary to amortize the discount is unknown and must be computed. The *present value factor* corresponding to the effective interest rate is determined using the following formula:

$$F = \frac{P}{C}$$

Where: F = Present value factor for an annuity
P = Fair value of property or market value of the note
C = Periodic cash payment

Based upon the information in the example transaction, the formula yields the following results:

$$F = \frac{\$200,000}{\$\ 54,114} = 3.69590$$

The answer of 3.69590 represents the present value factor for an ordinary annuity for five years at a yet-to-be-determined interest rate. Turn to the present value table for an ordinary annuity, Appendix A, Table II. Start in the five periods row, and go across the columns until the factor of 3.69590 is found. This present value factor corresponds to an interest rate of 11 percent. Eleven percent is the effective rate that will be used to amortize the discount.

Once the appropriate implicit interest rate has been determined, an amortization schedule may be prepared. Table IV shows the calculation of the amortization of the discount for the example note.

Table IV

Schedule of Discount Amortization And Principal Repayment

Period	Principal Payment	Discount Amortization	Reduction in Note Carrying Value	Carrying Value of Note
Initial Value	-	-	-	$200,000
1	$ 54,114	[a]$ 22,000	[b]$ 32,114	[c]167,886
2	54,114	18,467	35,647	132,239
3	54,114	14,546	39,568	92,671
4	54,114	10,194	43,920	48,751
5	54,114	5,363	48,751	-0-
	$270,570	$ 70,570	$200,000	

[a] $200,000 × 11% = $22,000.
[b] $54,114 − $22,000 = $32,114.
[c] $200,000 − $32,114 = $167,886.

Based upon the information generated in Table IV, the entries to reflect the discount amortization and the note principal reduction for Year 1 of the note are presented below:

Borrower, Inc.

Notes Payable	54,114	
Interest Expense	22,000	
Discount on Notes Payable		22,000
Cash		54,114

Lender Company

Cash	54,114	
Discount on Notes Receivable	22,000	
Notes Receivable		54,114
Interest Income		22,000

This completes the example of accounting for a note exchanged for property where the interest is *implicit* in the transaction. To illustrate a situation where interest is not implicit in the contract, but must be *imputed,* assume that Borrower, Inc. purchased equipment from Lender Company. Lender agrees to accept a non-interest bearing note for the equipment, with annual year-end payments of $150,000 for six years. Assume that Borrower, Inc. normally would have to pay 12 percent for a similar financing arrangement. Due to the unique nature of the property, its fair market value is not known. The market value of the note cannot be determined, but the cost of the equipment to Lender is $500,000.

Since neither the fair market value of the equipment nor the market value of the note is known, interest on the loan must be imputed to determine the present value of the note. The present value calculation would be based on the 12 percent interest rate that Borrower, Inc. would have to pay for similar financing. The present value of the note (using the 4.11141 present value factor for an ordinary annuity for six periods at 12 percent) would be determined as follows:

$$\$150{,}000 \times 4.11141 = \$616{,}712$$

The difference between the present value of the note ($616,712) and the total payments of $900,000 ($150,000 × 6) is the imputed interest on the note ($900,000 − $616,712 = $283,288 imputed interest). The entries required to record the note and equipment are as follows:

Borrower, Inc.

Equipment	616,712	
Discount on Notes Payable	283,288	
Notes Payable		900,000

Lender Company

Notes Receivable	900,000	
Equipment		500,000
Discount on Notes Receivable		283,288
Gain on Sale of Equipment		116,712

The gain on the sale is a residual value, resulting from the fact that the seller of the equipment did not know the fair market value of the equipment sold.

The next step involves the amortization of the discount, using the interest method. Table V shows the principal reduction, discount amortization and carrying value of the note, using the imputed interest rate of 12 percent.

Table V

Schedule of Discount and Principal Amortization

	Period	Principal Payment	Discount Amortization	Reduction in Note Carrying Value	Carrying Value of Note
Initial Value	-	-	-	-	$616,712
	1	$150,000	[a]$ 74,005	[b]$ 75,995	[c]540,717
	2	150,000	64,886	85,114	455,603
	3	150,000	54,672	95,328	360,275
	4	150,000	43,233	106,767	253,508
	5	150,000	30,421	119,579	133,929
	6	150,000	16,071	133,929	-0-
		$900,000	$283,288	$616,712	

[a] $616,712 × 12% = $74,005.
[b] $150,000 — $74,005 = $75,995.
[c] $616,712 — $75,995 = $540,717.

The entries required to amortize the discount and record the principal reduction are the same as shown in the previous example, except for the amounts, and will not be repeated at this point.

The preceding two examples illustrated the accounting for a non-interest bearing note. However, the situation could occur where the note had a stated interest rate, but the stated rate was considered to be unreasonable in light of the transaction. To illustrate this situation, assume that Borrower, Inc. purchased equipment from Lender Company and issued a note, instead of cash. Assume that Lender Company paid $300,000 for the equipment, and that Borrower, Inc. agrees to a 12 percent note for $500,000. The note is to be paid in full at the end of five years. Borrower, Inc. normally would have to pay 10 percent interest for similar financing, and it is determined that the 12 percent stated rate is clearly unreasonable.

When it has been determined that the stated interest rate is unreasonable, the appropriate rate may be an implicit rate or an imputed rate. If the fair value of the property or the market value of the note are known, implicit interest will be calculated; otherwise, interest must be imputed. For purposes of this example, assume that the fair value of the property and the market value of the note are not known. Therefore, interest will have to be imputed at the 10 percent rate (the rate assumed to be reasonable). The present value of the note may be calculated using the following formula:

$$PVN = (MV \times SR)(PVA) + (MV)(PV)$$

Where:
PVN = Present value of the note
MV = Maturity value of the note
SR = Stated interest rate
PVA = Present value factor for an annuity, using the imputed rate
PV = Present value factor for $1, using the imputed rate

Given the information in the above example—and using 3.79079 as the present value factor for an ordinary annuity for five periods at 10 percent and .62092 as the present value factor for $1 for five periods at 10 percent—the formula would provide the following results:

$$PVN = (\$500{,}000 \times .12)(3.79079) + (\$500{,}000)(.62092) = \$537{,}907$$

The difference between the present value of the note ($537,907) and the total proceeds ($500,000) is the discount or premium. In this case, the amount is a premium of $37,907.

The entries to record the note at inception of the agreement are as follows:

Borrower, Inc.

Equipment	537,907	
Notes Payable		500,000
Premium on Notes Payable		37,907

Lender Company

Notes Receivable	500,000	
Premium on Notes Receivable	37,907	
Equipment		300,000
Gain on Sale of Equipment		237,907

After determining the appropriate present value, an amortization schedule similar to Table VI can be prepared.

Table VI

Schedule of Interest and Premium Amortization

Period	Stated Interest	Interest Expense or Income	Premium Amortization	Carrying Value of Note
Initial Value	-	-	-	$537,907
1	[a] $ 60,000	[b] $ 53,791	[c] $ 6,209	[d] 531,698
2	60,000	53,170	6,830	524,868
3	60,000	52,487	7,513	517,355
4	60,000	51,736	8,264	509,091
5	60,000	50,909	9,091	[e] 500,000
	$300,000	$262,093	$37,907	

[a] $500,000 × 12% = $60,000.
[b] $537,907 × 10% = $53,791.
[c] $60,000 − $53,791 = $6,209.
[d] $537,907 − $6,209 = $531,698.
[e] Represents the maturity value of the note.

Using the information in Table VI, the journal entries required for Year 1 to record the interest payment and premium amortization would be as follows:

Borrower, Inc.

Interest Expense	53,791	
Premium on Notes Payable	6,209	
Cash		60,000

Lender Company

Cash	60,000	
Interest Income		53,791
Premium on Notes Receivable		6,209

With this set of entries, the discussion and illustration of accounting for interest on receivables and payables is completed. Additional consideration will be given to the income tax implications of APB Opinion No. 21, as well as to the required disclosures.

Income Tax Considerations

A difference may exist between the financial and tax reporting of interest expense and interest income when implicit or imputed interest must be used. Any difference is considered to be a timing difference and is to be handled in accordance with provisions of APB Opinion No. 11. (See APB Opinion No. 11 in Topic 5 for a detailed analysis of accounting for tax timing differences.)

Disclosure Requirements

The disclosure requirements of APB Opinion No. 21 are minor in nature and include the following items:

(1) The discount or premium should be shown as a contra or adjunct account to the related receivable or payable; and

(2) The effective interest rate should be specified, and any unamortized issue costs should be carried as an asset properly classified as a deferred charge.

The "Other assets" section of the 1974 and 1975 balance sheets of Fields Plastics and Chemicals, Inc. is presented below. Note 5 to the financial statements discloses the fact that the Company imputed interest on its six percent note. The imputed interest rate was nine percent.

Fields Plastics and Chemicals, Inc. (Apr)

	1975	1974
Other assets:		
Long-term notes receivable (Note 5)	$601,244	$647,558

Note 5: Long-term Notes Receivable—Long-term notes receivable consisted of the following:

	April 30, 1975	1974
6% note, due $3,333 monthly through May 1, 1975 and $5,606 monthly level payment which includes interest through May 1, 1988 (a)	$609,583	$649,583
Less unamortized discount based on imputed interest of 9%	92,629	102,739
	516,954	546,844
4½% notes, due $29,623 annually (including interest) through January 15, 1980	130,603	153,378
Totals	647,557	700,222
Less current portion	46,313	52,664
	$601,244	$647,558

(a) Secured by machinery and equipment sold. The lease rental agreement and the note are pledged as collateral for the five year note payable to the bank.

Source: *Accounting Trends and Techniques,* Copyright © 1976 by the American Institute of Certified Public Accountants, Inc., p. 120.

APB Opinion No. 25 (October 1972) Accounting for Stock Issued to Employees

Flowchart and General Discussion

Many companies have set up plans that allow employees to purchase shares of stock in the company. The plan may be designed as a method for the corporation to raise capital and allow employees to become owners, or it may be designed as a way to provide employees with additional compensation. Prior to the issuance of APB Opinion No. 25, accounting for employee stock option and stock purchase plans was determined by the provisions of Accounting Research Bulletin No. 43 (ARB No. 43).

ARB No. 43 took a "traditional" view of these plans, because, at the time, many such stock purchase plans were quite simple in nature. The plan usually would give an employee the right to purchase a specified number of shares of stock at a specified price within some specified time period. If the price to be paid for the stock was equal to the fair value of the stock on the date the employee received the right to purchase the shares (date of grant), there were few accounting problems. If the price to be paid for the stock was less than the fair value of the stock on the date of grant, the difference was viewed as compensation to the employee, and certain accounting procedures were to be followed in handling the compensation. The date of grant of the rights to employees was selected as the central date of importance for accounting purposes. At the date of grant, the measurement of the amount of compensation was determined.

Over the years, employee stock option and purchase plans became more sophisticated. The traditional approach of ARB No. 43 simply was not applicable to some of these more sophisticated plans. These new types of plans, generally referred to as "variable plans," involve the issuance of stock to employees based upon future events. The number of shares to be issued and/or the price to be paid for those shares may not be known at the date of grant. While ARB No. 43 still applies to the traditional type of employee stock option and stock purchase plans, APB Opinion No. 25 was issued to indicate proper accounting for some of the more highly developed plans.

The Flowchart of APB Opinion No. 25 indicates the decisions required to properly classify the type of stock option or purchase plan under review. Once the plan has been properly classified, the Flowchart indicates (in general terms) the necessary accounting. The employee stock option or stock purchase must be classified as either "compensatory" or "noncompensatory." Generally, a noncompensatory plan may be thought of as a method for the corporation to raise capital by selling stock to its employees. A compensatory plan is viewed as a technique to provide employees with compensation in excess of their salaries.

For a given plan to be classified as a noncompensatory plan, it must meet the following four conditions, which are outlined in the Flowchart:

(1) Participation in the plan is open to most full-time employees who have met limited employment qualifications (Block 1);

(2) The number of shares of stock that a participating employee may purchase is based on a percentage of salary, or each employee may be able to purchase an equal share (Block 2);

(3) The exercise period for the options is reasonable (Block 3); and

(4) The difference between the exercise price and the market price is no greater than the discount allowed on stock offered to the public (Block 4).

If the plan fails to meet all four of these criteria, it will be classified as compensatory. There are different accounting requirements for compensatory and noncompensatory plans. Because the accounting for noncompensatory plans is somewhat easier than the accounting required for compensatory plans, the discussion will start with noncompensatory plans.

Noncompensatory Stock Option and Stock Purchase Plans

The reason for the classification as "noncompensatory" is that the plan involves no compensation to the employees who receive the right to purchase shares of stock. The price to be paid for the shares is

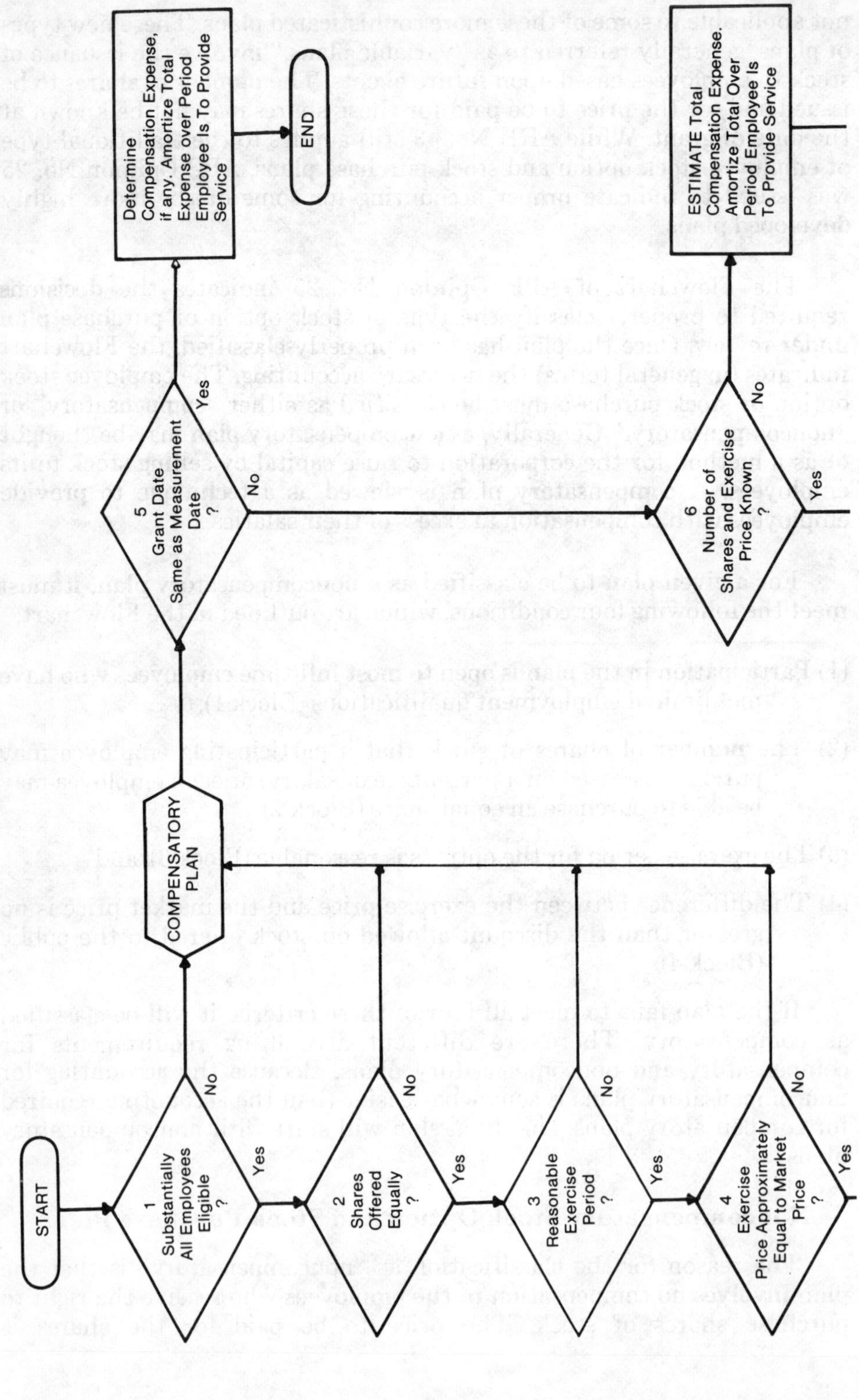
START
1 Substantially All Employees Eligible ?
Yes
No
2 Shares Offered Equally ?
Yes
No
3 Reasonable Exercise Period ?
Yes
No
4 Exercise Price Approximately Equal to Market Price ?
Yes
No
COMPENSATORY PLAN
5 Grant Date Same as Measurement Date ?
Yes
No
Determine Compensation Expense, if any. Amortize Total Expense over Period Employee Is To Provide Service
END
6 Number of Shares and Exercise Price Known ?
Yes
No
ESTIMATE Total Compensation Expense. Amortize Total Over Period Employee Is To Provide Service

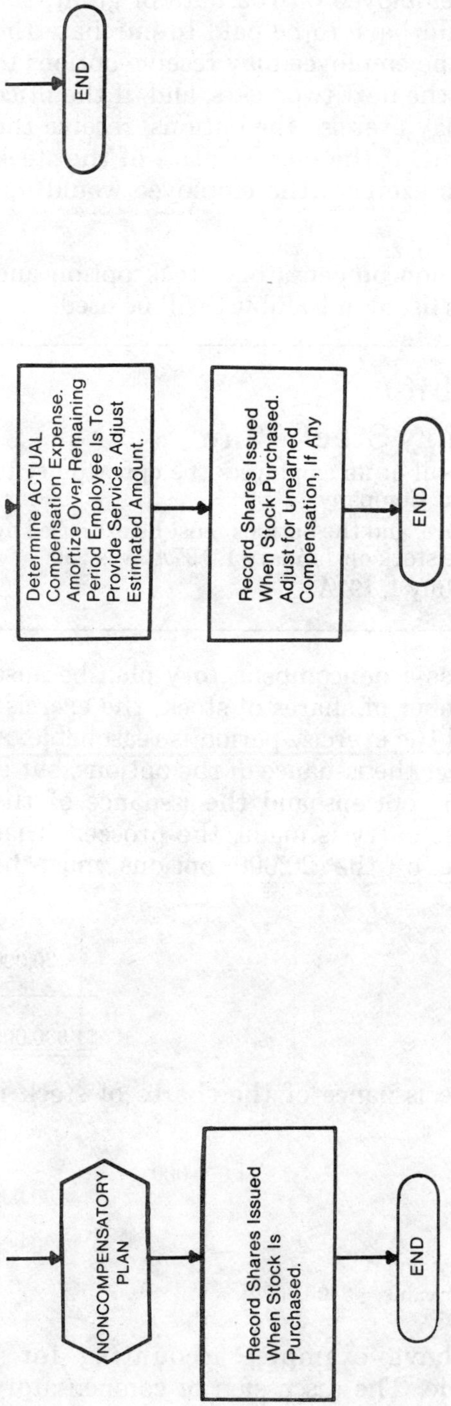
END
Determine ACTUAL Compensation Expense. Amortize Over Remaining Period Employee Is To Provide Service. Adjust Estimated Amount.
Record Shares Issued When Stock Purchased. Adjust for Unearned Compensation, If Any
END
NONCOMPENSATORY PLAN
Record Shares Issued When Stock Is Purchased.
END

approximately equal to the market price of the stock on the date of grant. If the rights were exercised by the employee on the date of grant, the price paid would be about what would have to be paid to purchase the stock in the open market. However, the employee may receive options to purchase the shares any time within the next two years; and, if the price of the stock goes up, the employee may exercise the options, receive the shares and sell them to realize a profit. If the market price of the stock falls below the price to be paid upon exercise, the employee would not exercise the right.

To illustrate the accounting for noncompensatory stock option and stock purchase plans, the assumptions listed in Exhibit I will be used.

Exhibit I

Noncompensatory Stock Plan

1. On January 1, 197A, Option, Inc. gave all of its employees the opportunity to buy 5,000 shares of $10 par stock in the Company.
2. The stock can be purchased at $50 a share, and the options must be exercised by April 1, 197B. The market price of the stock on January 1, 197A, was $50.
3. 20,000 stock options were exercised on July 1, 197A.

The stock option plan qualifies as a noncompensatory plan because each employee can buy an equal number of shares of stock, the exercise price is equal to the market price and the exercise period is reasonable. A journal entry is not necessary to reflect the issuance of the options, but is required to show the exercise of the options and the issuance of the additional shares of stock. Before the entry is made, the proceeds that will be received upon the exercise of the 20,000 options must be calculated:

Number of Options	20,000
Option Price	× $50
Proceeds Received Upon Exercise of the Options	$1,000,000

The receipt of the proceeds and the issuance of the shares of stock is recorded below:

Cash	1,000,000	
Common Stock		[a]200,000
Contributed Capital in Excess of Par		[b]800,000

[a] 20,000 shares × $10 par value = $200,000.
[b] $1,000,000 proceeds − $200,000 par value = $800,000.

As can be seen from the above example, accounting for a noncompensatory plan is quite simple. The discussion of compensatory plans will add a great deal to the complexity of the basic accounting illustrated in this example.

Compensatory Stock Option and Stock Purchase Plans

If a stock option plan does not meet the four criteria to be classified as noncompensatory, the plan will be classified as compensatory in nature. The classification may be somewhat misleading because compensation may or may not accrue to the corporation issuing the shares of stock. Keep in mind that this discussion is based on the viewpoint of the corporation issuing the stock, and not on the viewpoint of the individual employee receiving the shares.

Any compensation under this type of plan will be determined on the measurement date. The date is the first date that *both* the number of options to be granted (or the number of shares to be received) *and* the exercise price are known (Block 5). Compensation expense to the issuing corporation will be equal to the excess of the market price of the shares over the exercise price on the measurement date. Therefore, for compensation to become an accounting consideration, the market price of the stock must exceed the exercise price on the measurement date. When it has been determined that there is compensation associated with the options, the amount of the compensation expense should be amortized over the time period for which benefits from the employee's services will be received. The time period over which the employee is to provide benefits to the company may be identified in the plan, or it may be inferred.

Accounting problems may exist in the determination of the total compensation expense associated with the plan, and this would create problems in recording the periodic amortization. Under traditional plans, the number of shares to be issued and the price per share are known at the date of grant, and there are few problems in determining the compensation expense involved. However, under some of the more popular variable plans, the number of shares to be issued and/or the exercise price may not be known at the date of grant (Block 6). The date of measurement would not be the same as the date of grant. Some variable plans relate the number of shares to be issued to the future market price of the company's stock or to a certain future earnings level. When faced with this situation, the total compensation expense will not be known at the date of grant, yet the appropriate amortization period may be from the date of grant to the last date available for exercise of the options.

To properly illustrate the complexities involved in determining the compensation expense under a variable plan, Chart I has been prepared.

Chart I

Variable Stock Plan

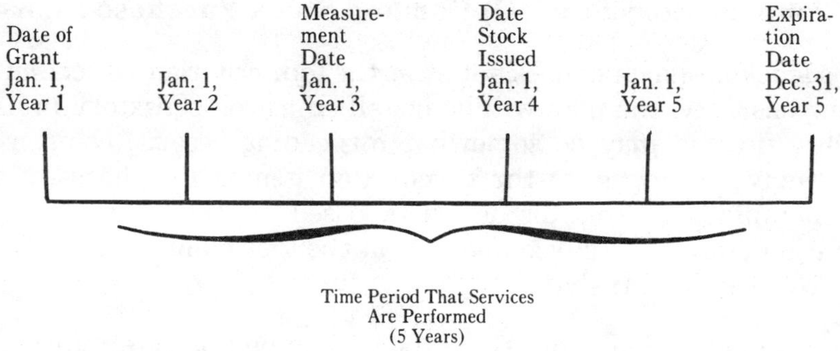

As indicated in the Chart, the proper time period for the amortization of the compensation expense, i.e., the time period in which the company will benefit from services of the employee, is from January 1, Year 1, to December 31, Year 5 (a total of five years). The problem created is that the total amount of compensation expense cannot be determined until January 1, Year 3, because this is the first date that both the number of shares to be issued and the exercise price are known. Therefore, total compensation expense must be estimated on the date of grant and amortized in Years 1 and 2.

The estimated amount of compensation expense is based upon the year-end market price of the stock, i.e., one estimate will be made at the end of Year 1, and used to determine the necessary amortization for the period, and another estimate of total compensation expense will be made at the end of Year 2. Since the determination of compensation expense is based on an estimate, any adjustment to the estimate would be accounted for in accordance with APB Opinion No. 20. (See APB Opinion No. 20 in Topic 1 for a detailed analysis of changes in accounting estimates.)

By referring back to the Chart, notice that the stock was issued on January 1, Year 4, which is before the total services of the employee have been performed. If shares of stock are issued before the total compensation expense has been allocated to income, part of the cost assigned to the stock issued represents amounts that should be charged to income in future periods as compensation expense. An account such as "Unearned Compensation from Stock Options" should be established for the amount of compensation relating to services to be performed in the future. This account will be amortized through charges to compensation expense as the services of the employees are provided.

FASB Interpretation No. 28, "Accounting for Stock Appreciation Rights and Other Variable Stock Option or Award Plans," is consistent with the discussion to this point. However, the Interpretation indicates that, if the period of time over which the employee is to perform services is not stated in the plan, the service period *may* be the vesting period. The vesting period may be inferred as the time from the date of grant to the date the options or rights become exercisable. If the options or rights are issued for services performed prior to the date of grant, the compensation should be charged to income as an expense in the period of the grant.

To illustrate the technical aspects of compensatory plans, the assumptions in Exhibit II will be used.

Exhibit II
Compensatory Plans—Traditional

1. On January 1, 197A, Option, Inc. granted stock options to its five vice presidents. Each vice president received 4,000 options with the right to purchase 4,000 shares of common stock at $45 per share any time between January 1, 197A, and December 31, 197E. Option, Inc. has a year-end of December 31.
2. The market price of the stock on January 1, 197A, was $50 per share. The par value of the stock is $20. All of the options were exercised on December 31, 197E.
3. The period over which services are to be rendered is assumed to be five years.

The first step is to determine the measurement date. The measurement date is January 1, 197A, because on this date both the number of shares that can be purchased (20,000) (4,000 × 5) *and* the option price ($45) can be determined. Once the measurement date has been determined, the total compensation expense can be computed, as shown below:

Market Price on Measurement Date	$ 50
Option Price	(45)
Compensation Expense per Share	$ 5
Total Options (4,000 × 5)	20,000
Compensation Expense per Share	× $5
Total Compensation Expense	$100,000

After determining the total compensation expense, the last calculation required is that which allocates the total compensation over the time period that services are performed. This computation is presented below:

Total Compensation Expense	$100,000	
Time Period Services are Performed	÷ 5	Years
Annual Compensation Expense	$ 20,000	

Based upon this information, the journal entries required at the date of grant and to record the amortization of the compensation expense in Year 1 would be:

Deferred Compensation on Stock Options	100,000	
Common Stock Options Outstanding		100,000
Compensation Expense	20,000	
Deferred Compensation on Stock Options		20,000

At the end of the first year, the accounts "Deferred Compensation On Stock Options" and "Common Stock Options Outstanding" will appear in the stockholder's equity section of the balance sheet in the following manner:

Common Stock Options Outstanding	100,000	
Less: Deferred Compensation on Stock Options	[a]80,000	20,000

[a] $100,000 − $20,000 = $80,000.

By the end of the fifth year, December 31, 197E, the deferred compensation on stock options will have been completely amortized. If the options are exercised on this date, the following entry is required.

Cash	[a]900,000	
Common Stock Options Outstanding	100,000	
Common Stock		[b]400,000
Paid-In Capital in Excess of Par		[c]600,000

[a] 20,000 options × $45 option price = $900,000.
[b] 20,000 shares × $20 par value = $400,000.
[c] 20,000 shares × ($45 − $20) = $500,000 + $100,000 = $600,000.

The illustration presented above is relatively straightforward. However, if complexities—such as a measurement date later than date of grant, or the exercise of options before compensation expense has been amortized—are added, the computations become more difficult. To illustrate these complexities, the assumptions in Exhibit III will be used.

Exhibit III

Compensatory Plans—Variable

1. On January 1, 197A, Option, Inc., a December 31 year-end company, granted stock options to its five vice presidents. Each vice president received 10,000 options, with the right to purchase 10,000 shares of common stock at a price equal to 90 percent of the quoted market price on the date the earnings per share of the company exceed $2.25. The options may be exercised any time after this date. The options expire on December 31, 197E.
2. The earnings per share of the company first exceeded $2.25 on December 31, 197C. The par value of the stock is $20. The options were exercised on January 1, 197D.
3. The quoted market prices of the stock were:

   December 31, 197A- $52

   December 31, 197B- $54

   December 31, 197C- $55
4. The period over which the services are to be rendered is assumed to be five years.

Because the earnings per share did not exceed $2.25 until December 31, 197C, the measurement date is different from the date of grant. In this case, total compensation expense must be estimated at the end of each year, and this total will be used for purposes of amortization. The amortization period is from January 1, 197A, to December 31, 197E, or five years. The determination of the compensation expense to be reported in year 197A is determined as follows:

Market Price December 31, 197A	$ 52.00	
Estimated Option Price (90% × $52)	46.80	
Estimated Compensation Expense Per Share	$ 5.20	
Total Shares That Can Be Purchased	50,000	
Estimated Compensation Expense Per Share	× 5.20	
Total Estimated Compensation Expense	$260,000.00	
Number of Years Service is to be Provided	÷ 5	Years
Estimated Annual Compensation Expense	$ 52,000.00	

Given the preceding information, the following journal entries can be made at December 31, 197A:

Deferred Compensation on Stock Options	260,000	
Common Stock Options Outstanding		260,000
Compensation Expense	52,000	
Deferred Compensation on Stock Options		52,000

Since the measurement date has not been determined at this point, there may be future adjustments to the Deferred Compensation on Stock Options and Common Stock Options Outstanding accounts.

To determine the compensation expense to be reported in 197B, the procedures applied in 197A are used. The compensation expense is computed as follows:

Market Price December 31, 19B	$ 54.00	
Estimated Option Price (90% × $54)	48.60	
Estimated Compensation Expense Per Share	$ 5.40	
Total Shares That Can Be Purchased	50,000	
Estimated Compensation Expense Per Share	× 5.40	
Total Estimated Compensation Expense	$270,000	
Compensation Expense Charged to 19A	− 52,000	
Remaining Estimated Compensation Expense	$218,000	
Number of Years of Service Remaining	÷ 4	Years
Estimated Annual Compensation Expense	$ 54,500	

Based on this computation, the following journal entry is required on December 31, 197B:

Compensation Expense	54,500	
Common Stock Options Outstanding		10,000
Deferred Compensations on Stock Outstanding		44,500

The amounts used in the journal entry for Common Stock Options Outstanding and Deferred Compensation on Stock Options were determined in the following manner:

Common Stock Options Outstanding:

Total estimated compensation expense at December 31, 197B	$270,000
Total estimated compensation expense at December 31, 197A	260,000
Adjustment to Common Stock Options Outstanding	$ 10,000

Deferred Compensation on Stock Options:

Total compensation expense at December 31, 197A		$260,000
Compensation expense for 197A		52,000
Balance in Deferred Compensation account at December 31, 197A		$208,000
Total estimated compensation expense at December 31, 197B	$270,000	
Compensation expense for 197A and 197B ($52,000 + $54,500)	106,500	
Balance in Deferred Compensation account at December 31, 197B		163,500
Necessary reduction in Deferred Compensation account		$ 44,500

The adjustment to compensation expense should be treated as a change in an accounting estimate, in accordance with the provisions of APB Opinion No. 20.

The measurement date in this example is December 31, 197C, since this is the first date on which the option price can be determined. The number of shares to be issued upon exercise of the options has been known since the date of grant. The computation of the *actual* compensation now can be made.

Market Price December 31, 197C	$55,00	
Option Price (90% × $55)	49.50	
Actual Compensation Expense Per Share	$ 5.50	
Total Shares That Can Be Purchased	50,000	
Actual Compensation Expense Per Share	× 5.50	
Total Actual Compensation Expense	$275,000	
Compensation Expense Charge to 197A and 197B ($52,000 + $54,500)	106,500	
Remaining Actual Compensation Expense	$168,500	
Number of Years of Service Remaining	÷ 3	Years
Actual Annual Compensation Expense	$ 56,167	

The necessary adjustments to the Common Stock Options Outstanding and the Deferred Compensation on Stock Options accounts would be computed as follows:

Common Stock Options Outstanding:

Total actual compensation expense	$275,000
Total estimated compensation expense on December 31, 197B	270,000
Adjustment to Common Stock Options Outstanding	$ 5,000

Deferred Compensation on Stock Options:

Balance in Deferred Compensation Account at December 31, 197B		$163,500
Total actual compensation expense at December 31, 197C	$275,000	
Compensation expense for 197A - 197C ($52,000 + $54,500 + $56,167)	162,667	
Balance in Deferred Compensation Account at December 31, 197C		112,333
Necessary reduction in Deferred Compensation Account		$ 51,167

Given the preceding computations, the journal entry required at December 31, 197C would be:

Compensation Expense	56,167	
Common Stock Options Outstanding		5,000
Deferred Compensation on Stock Options		51,167

Since the actual compensation expense is known, the amortization for years 197D and 197E also will be $56,167. No further adjustments will be necessary.

On January 1, 197D, the date the stock was issued, the total compensation to the employees had not been charged to income. It is expected that the employees will provide two more years of service for the company. Part of the total amount assigned to the stock issued actually represents unearned compensation, and should be treated as such in the balance sheet. The entry to record the issuance of the stock would be:

Cash	[a]2,475,000	
Common Stock Options Outstanding	275,000	
Unearned Compensation From Stock Options	[b]112,333	
Common Stock		[c]1,000,000
Paid-In Capital in Excess of Par		[d]1,750,000
Deferred Compensation on Stock Options		112,333

[a] 50,000 Shares × $49.50 Option Price = $2,475,000.
[b] Equal to remaining balance in Deferred Compensation on Stock Option account.
[c] 50,000 Shares × $20 = $1,000,000.
[d] ($2,475,000 Proceeds + $275,000 Compensation Expense) − $1,000,000 = $1,750,000.

At the end of both 197D and 197E, the following journal entry is necessary to amortize the compensation expense to income:

Compensation expense	56,167	
Unearned Compensation from Stock Options		56,167

This completes the discussion of the example.

The Opinion identifies certain modifications to the basic measurement principles shown above. These modifications apply only in special fact situations. The reader should refer to Paragraph 11 for information relating to the required modifications.

Income Tax Considerations of Compensatory Plans

Generally, an enterprise issuing stock under a compensatory stock purchase plan is allowed certain deductions for income tax purposes. The deduction for compensation expense is equal to the income reported by the employee receiving the stock. This deduction is allowed in the period in which the employee includes the income received in his/her taxable income. This situation creates two problems for the enterprise issuing the stock. First, a timing difference may exist if the compensation expense for financial accounting purposes is different from the allowable deduction for tax purposes in a given period. Second, there may be a difference between the total compensation expense recorded for accounting purposes and the total amount of compensation expense considered deductible for income tax purposes. This is true because the compensation expense recorded for accounting purposes is determined on the measurement date, and the expense deductible for tax purposes is determined on the date the employee includes the compensation in his/her income. These dates normally are not the same, and the price of the stock may change from one date to the next, thereby causing a difference in total compensation expense.

The difference in compensation expense that represents a timing difference should be treated in accordance with the provisions of APB Opinion No. 11. (See Topic 5 for a detailed analysis of the treatment of timing differences as described in APB Opinion No. 11.) The portion that represents the difference between the total compensation for accounting and tax purposes is similar to a permanent difference but *is not* treated as a permanent difference.

The treatment accorded the differences in total compensation expense depends on whether the difference causes taxable income to be more or less than accounting income. If the difference causes taxable income to be less than accounting income, the tax effect of the difference should be used to increase paid-in capital of the issuing corporation. If the difference causes taxable income to be more than accounting income, the tax effect of the difference is treated as a reduction of paid-in capital of the corporation. The reduction in paid-in capital is limited to the extent that the tax effect of similar items was used to increase the account in prior transactions. The Opinion does not provide guidance in the situation where there have been no previous increases in paid-in capital, or where paid-in capital is not sufficient to absorb the entire tax effect reduction. If such a situation were to arise, it seems that the most logical approach would be to reduce retained earnings for the tax effect of the difference not used to reduce paid-in capital.

Disclosures

Paragraph 15 of ARB No. 43, Chapter 13, Section B, provides the appropriate disclosures relative to stock issued to employees. The disclosures are as follows:

(1) The current status of the stock plan. This would include the number of shares that would be issued upon exercise of all options, the exercise price of the options, and the number of shares to be issued, based upon the options exercisable at the balance sheet date.

(2) The number of shares issued and the price the employees paid, based on the options actually exercised during the accounting period.

The Notes to the Financial Statement of Easco Corporation are shown in Exhibit IV and present disclosures relating to stock options for 1976 and 1975.

Exhibit IV

Easco Corporation (Dec)

Notes to Consolidated Financial Statements

Note 1 (in part): Summary of Accounting Policies

Incentive Plan—The Company has a cash and nonqualified stock option incentive plan for key employees. It is the Company's policy to accrue estimated benefits as earned under the plan.

Note 4: Incentive Plans—The Company has three qualified stock option plans which were established in 1964, 1968 and 1973. All plans are substantially the same and at December 31, 1976 provided an aggregate of 89,746 shares for the granting of options to officers and other key employees of the Company and its subsidiaries at not less than 100% of the fair market value of the stock on the date of grant. The options expire five years from the date of grant. The following tabulation summarizes the changes in qualified stock options during 1975 and 1976:

	Number of shares under option	Average price per share
Outstanding at December 31, 1974	78,467	$13.78
Granted	—	—
Exercised	(231)	16.31
Cancelled or expired	(6,679)	12.82
Outstanding at December 31, 1975	71,557	13.86
Granted	4,460	19.05
Exercised	18,347	13.08
Cancelled or expired	4,351	16.28
Outstanding at December 31, 1976	53,319	$14.36

At December 31, 1976, options of 50,350 shares were exercisable and options for 36,427 shares could be granted under the various plans.

The Company terminated its deferred compensation unit plan effective December 31, 1975 and, with stockholders' approval in April, 1975, adopted a new executive compensation plan consisting of two programs, an executive cash incentive compensation program and a nonqualified incentive stock option program. The plan is effective from January 1, 1975 until December 31, 1984.

Under the executive cash incentive compensation program, a cash bonus fund is established each year if adjusted net income equals at least 15% of average shareholders' equity. The amount of cash appropriated to the fund and available for distribution will vary from 20% to 80% of the aggregate base salaries of all participants in the program for that year, depending on the level of the ratio of adjusted net income to average shareholders' equity. The charges to income in 1976 and 1975 relating to the cash bonus fund were $202,000 and $137,000 respectively.

The nonqualified incentive stock option program provides for the granting of options to officers and other key employees for the purchase of 111,410 shares of common stock, plus 36,427 shares authorized but not issued under the third and fourth qualified stock option plans. The option price per share shall not be less than 100% of the fair market value of the stock on the date granted reduced by the excess of the fair market value of the stock at the time the option is exercised over the fair market value of the stock at the date granted, but in no event less than zero. The options expire six years from the date of grant and only 20% of the options granted can be exercised each year, commencing the year following the year granted provided a 5% improvement in earnings, a 15% return on average shareholders' equity and other conditions of the program are met.

At December 31, 1975, options for 107,950 shares were outstanding. During 1976, 1,200 options were granted, 5,420 options were cancelled and 13,590 options were exercised at an average price per share of $1.24. At December 31, 1976, options for 89,140 shares were outstanding of which 18,590 and 17,900 became exercisable in 1976 and 1977 respectively. Compensation expense of $324,000 in 1976 and $412,000 in 1975 was charged to income under the plan.

Source: *Accounting Trends and Techniques,* Copyright © 1977 by the American Institute of Certified Public Accountants, Inc., p. 246.

APB Opinion No. 26 (October 1972) Early Extinguishment of Debt

General Discussion

APB Opinion No. 26 specifies the accounting treatment for the gain or loss resulting from the refunding of debt prior to its scheduled maturity date. A gain or loss is represented by the difference between the debt repurchase price and the carrying value of the liability. The face value of the debt must be adjusted for any unamortized discount or premium, as well as for unamortized debt issue costs, in the determination of its carrying value.

The repurchase of debt, before scheduled maturity, may be accomplished through the use of internally generated funds, funds obtained from the sale of equity securities or funds obtained from the sale of other debt securities. This latter type of repurchase is commonly referred to as debt refunding.

Prior to the issuance of APB Opinion No. 26, there was general agreement as to the proper accounting for gains or losses resulting from debt repurchased with internally generated funds and from the sale of equity securities. The gain or loss was recognized immediately. However, in the case of debt refunding, there were at least three options available for the treatment of gains or losses. The gain or loss could be amortized over the life of the *new* debt issue, amortized over the life of the *old* debt issue or recognized immediately upon repurchase.

In APB Opinion No. 26, the Board concluded that *all* extinguishments of debt, regardless of the source of funds, were essentially alike. The difference between the repurchase price and the carrying value of the debt refunded should be recognized immediately as a gain or loss. The gain or loss so recognized should be treated as an extraordinary item in accordance with SFAS No. 4, "Reporting Gains and Losses from Extinguishment of Debt." (See SFAS No. 4 for a complete discussion of classification and disclosures for gains and losses from extinguishment of debt.)

Technical Considerations

To illustrate the rather straightforward accounting required by the provisions of the Opinion, assume that Borrower Company has $20,000,000 outstanding in bonds that will mature in five years. At the date of refunding, there was $160,000 in unamortized bond premium and $20,000 in unamortized bond issue costs associated with the issue. Borrower Company was able to repurchase the bonds for $19,500,000. The $19,500,000 needed for the repurchase was obtained through the issue of $20,000,000 of new debt. The new bond issue was sold at 98. Since the old issue was retired before its scheduled maturity, the transaction is accounted for as an early extinguishment of debt.

The journal entry required to record the sale of the new bond issue is as follows:

Cash ($20,000,000 × .98)	19,600,000	
Bond Discount	400,000	
Bonds Payable		20,000,000

The proceeds received from this bond issue will be used to retire the old bond issue.

The journal entry required to record the retirement of the old bond issue is as follows:

Bonds Payable	20,000,000	
Bond Premium	160,000	
Bond Issue Costs		20,000
Cash		19,500,000
Gain on Early Extinguishment of Debt		640,000

The type of new debt issued to effect the refunding has no bearing upon the treatment of the gain or loss.

Disclosure Requirements

The gain or loss, if material, would appear in the current income statement as an extraordinary item, with related footnote disclosure, if needed. A partial income statement and Footnote 8 to the financial statements of Clarostat Mfg. Co., Inc. are shown below. The Company reported an extraordinary gain from early extinguishment of debt in 1975.

Clarostat Mfg. Co., Inc. (Dec)

	1975	1974
Income before extraordinary credit	$170,017	$454,917
Extraordinary credit (Note 8):		
Gain from early extinguishment of debt (less applicable income taxes of $50,000)	55,709	
Net income	$225,726	$454,917

Note 8: Extraordinary Credit—The $105,709 gain results from the negotiated settlement of a long-term obligation due to an officer-shareholder, collateralized by a second deed of trust on Solar real property and a chattel mortgage on the subsidiary's machinery and equipment. The reduced balance of $577,391 was paid in 1976.

Source: *Accounting Trends and Techniques,* Copyright © 1976 by the American Institute of Certified Public Accountants, Inc., p. 261.

SFAS No. 4 (March 1975) Reporting Gains and Losses From Extinguishment of Debt

General Discussion

SFAS No. 4 addresses the problem of proper disclosure of gains or losses resulting from the extinguishment of debt. The Statement applies to early extinguishment of debt, debt extinguished at maturity and debt extinguished after maturity. (See APB Opinion No. 26 for a complete discussion of accounting for gains and losses from early extinguishment of debt.)

In general, gains and losses resulting from the retirement of debt should be reported as an extraordinary item net of applicable taxes. Gains and losses reported in this manner must, in the aggregate, be material.

This general rule does not apply to gains and losses resulting from debt retirement required to fulfill sinking fund provisions. Gains and losses from sinking fund retirements would be aggregated and reported as a separate line-item of income from continuing operations. Serial debt does not qualify as fulfillment of sinking fund requirements; therefore, gains or losses resulting from serial debt retirement would fall under the general rule stated above.

For gains and losses classified as extraordinary, specific disclosure requirements are itemized in the Statement. These disclosures include the following:

(1) Nature of the retirement, with sources of funds used to retire the debt identified;

(2) Income taxes resulting from the gains and losses; and

(3) Earnings per share on the aggregated gains and losses, reported on a net of tax basis.

Technical Considerations

To illustrate the disclosure requirements of SFAS No. 4, assume that Borrower Company, Inc. reports income before non-operating items of $300,000, in a year when debt extinguishment is to be reported. Aggregate gains and losses from the retirement of debt to satisfy *sinking* fund requirements were $50,000. Aggregate gains and losses from the extinguishment of debt *not* related to sinking fund requirements were $100,000. The composition of the $100,000 aggregate gain is shown below:

	Gain (Loss)	Source of Funds
Early Extinguishment of 8% Bonds	$(25,000)	Internal
Early Extinguishment of 10% Convertible Bonds	140,000	Sale of Equity Securities
Extinguishment at Maturity Date of 9% Debt	(15,000)	Bond Issue
Aggregate Gain	$100,000	

In addition to the above items, Borrower Company reported the $50,000 cumulative effect of a change in an accounting principle. The change in accounting principle resulted in an increase in income. The tax rate applicable to all income during the period is 50 percent. Borrower Company had 500,000 shares of common stock outstanding during the period.

A partial income statement and related footnote disclosure for Borrower Company is presented below.

Partial Income Statement

Income before non-operating items	$300,000
Gain from extinguishment of debt to satisfy sinking fund requirements	50,000
Income before taxes, extraordinary item and cumulative effect	$350,000
Income taxes	175,000
Income before extraordinary item and cumulative effect	$175,000
Extraordinary item:	
Gain from extinguishment of debt (net of taxes of $50,000)(Note 1)	50,000
Income before cumulative effect	$225,000
Cumulative effect:	
Cumulative effect of change in accounting principle (net of taxes of $25,000)	25,000
Net Income	$250,000

Note 1: The Company was involved in the extinguishment of three debt issues during the year. Each extinguishment, along with related tax effect and the source of the funds used to affect the extinguishment, is presented in the schedule below:

Extinguishment	Gain (Loss)	Tax Effect	Source of Funds
1. Early Extinguishment of 8% Bonds	$(25,000)	$(12,500)	Internal
2. Early Extinguishment of 10% Convertible Bonds	140,000	70,000	Sale of Equity Securities
3. Extinguishment at Maturity Date of 9% Debt	(15,000)	(7,500)	Bond Issue
Aggregate Gain	$100,000	$ 50,000	

Earnings per share on the aggregate gain (net of applicable taxes) is $.10 ($50,000/500,000 common shares).

SFAS No. 5 (March 1975)
Accounting for Contingencies
and
SFAS No. 11 (December 1975)
Accounting for Contingencies—Transition Method

General Discussion

SFAS No. 5 identifies accounting principles and reporting requirements for contingencies. A contingency is defined in the Statement (Paragraph 1) as "an existing condition, situation or set of circumstances involving uncertainty as to possible gain or loss to an enterprise that will ultimately be resolved when one or more future events occur or fail to occur." Where a contingency may involve a gain, it is referred to as a "gain contingency"; and, where the possibility of a loss exists, the amount is referred to as a "loss contingency." The Statement provides new principles and procedures for the treatment of loss contingencies, but does not change existing practice relating to gain contingencies. SFAS No. 11 is an amendment to SFAS No. 5, and deals with the proper accounting for contingencies during the transition period.

SFAS No. 5 identifies different probabilities for the occurrence of a loss contingency. The probabilities range from "probable" to "reasonably possible" to "remote." It is helpful to think of the range of probabilities as a continuum:

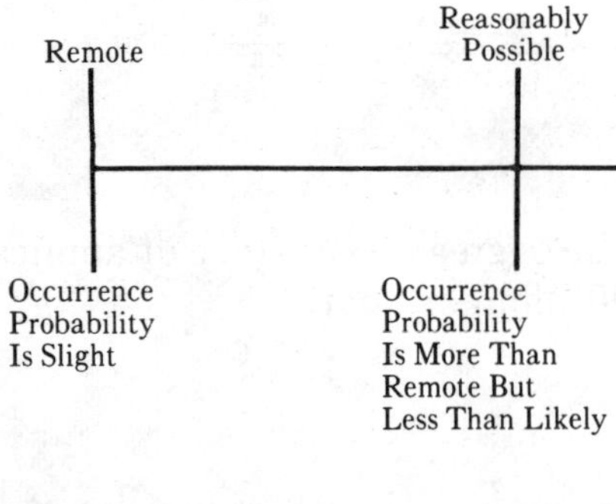

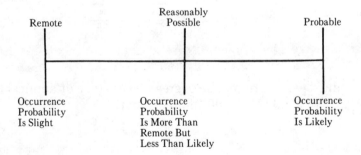

As indicated by the continuum, when a loss contingency exists, and it is determined that the probability of the future event occurring or failing to occur is slight, the loss contingency is referred to as remote. When the probability of the future event occurring is more than remote, but less than likely, the loss contingency is considered to be reasonably possible. It naturally follows that, when the probability of the occurrence of the future event is likely, the loss contingency is referred to as probable. The classification scheme is directly related to the accounting and disclosure requirements for the loss contingency.

The estimated amount of the loss from a loss contingency should be charged to income if the following two conditions are met (SFAS No. 5, Paragraph 8(a) and Paragraph 8(b)):

(1) Information available prior to issuance of the financial statements indicates that it is *probable* that an asset was impaired or a liability was incurred at the date of the financial statements, *and*

(2) The amount of the loss can be reasonably estimated.

Before the estimated loss resulting from the loss contingency can be charged to income, *both* of these conditions must be met. The first condition limits the accounting considerations to probable loss contingencies, i.e., to situations in which the future event is likely to occur. However, if the loss contingency is considered probable, but the amount of the loss cannot be reasonably estimated, there will be no charge to income. Loss contingencies that are considered reasonably possible, or that fail to meet one of the conditions specified above, generally will be disclosed in the footnotes to the financial statements. Loss contingencies that are remote generally will not require disclosures.

The Statement concludes that existing accounting practices regarding gain contingencies should be continued, i.e., contingencies are not recorded until such time as the gain is realized. While footnote disclosure of gain contingencies is allowed, care should be exercised in the disclosure, in order not to mislead the reader.

Appendix A of the Statement contains a list of several possible loss contingencies, along with a discussion of each item. The reader is encouraged to review the Appendix for details relating to each item covered. Exhibit I is a brief summary of some possible loss contingencies, demonstrating the appropriate accounting and disclosure requirements. A given loss contingency may be placed in one of three categories for accounting purposes:

(1) Those loss contingencies that typically are accrued, with a resulting charge to income,

(2) Those loss contingencies that should be accrued if they meet the two conditions stated above (contingency is classified as probable and amount of loss can be estimated), and

(3) Those loss contingencies for which accrual is unnecessary.

Exhibit I

Treatment of Certain Loss Contingencies

Contingency Losses Relative to:	Typically Accrued	Accrual[a] Possible	Accrual Unnecessary	Disclose	Not Disclosed
1. Collectibility of receivables	X			X[b]	
2. Obligations related to product warranties and product defects and customers premiums	X			X[b]	
3. Threat of expropriation		X		X[c]	
4. Litigation, claims and assessments		X		X[c]	
5. Guarantees of indebtedness of others		X		X	
6. Obligations of commercial banks under "standby letters of credit"		X		X	
7. Guarantees to repurchase receivables that have been sold		X		X	
8. Risk of loss or damage of enterprise property			X	X[c]	
9. Catastrophe losses of property and casualty insurance companies			X	X[c]	
10. General or unspecified business risks			X		X

[a] Accrual is required if *both* the loss contingency is probable and the amount of the loss can be reasonably estimated.
[b] Disclose through an accrual if both conditions are met, or through a footnote to the financial statements.
[c] No disclosure is necessary *unless* it is considered probable that a claim will be asserted and there is a reasonable possibility that the outcome will be unfavorable. If the occurrence is slight (remote) do not disclose.

For purposes of disclosure, a given loss contingency may be placed in one of three categories:

(1) Those that do not require disclosure in the footnotes to the financial statements,

(2) Those that do require disclosure in the footnotes, and

(3) Those that may require disclosure if certain conditions are met.

As indicated in Exhibit I, companies are not permitted to disclose loss contingencies relating to general or unspecified business risks. Generally, loss contingencies that meet one of the two criteria necessary for accrual, but fail to meet both, will be disclosed in the footnotes to the financial statements.

Other loss contingencies, such as litigation, claims and assessments, may be disclosed in the footnotes, if it is probable that a claim associated with these items will be asserted, and if there is a *reasonable possibility* of an adverse outcome. However, if the possibility of an adverse outcome is considered to be *remote,* no disclosure is required.

The Statement concludes that certain types of loss contingencies that have a remote possibility of resulting in an actual loss should be disclosed in the footnotes. These specifically identified loss contingencies include guarantees of indebtedness of others, obligations of commercial banks under "standby letters of credit" and agreements to repurchase receivables that have been sold.

The Statement continues to allow the appropriation of retained earnings for loss contingencies, but the appropriation must be included in the stockholders' equity section of the balance sheet. No portion of the appropriation is allowed to be charged to income.

Classification and Accounting—Loss Contingencies

To illustrate the specific provisions of SFAS No. 5, the assumptions listed in Exhibit II will be used.

Exhibit II
Loss Contingencies

1. Worldwide Enterprises, Inc. is in the process of preparing its financial statements for the year ended December 31, 197A. The statements will be issued on or about March 5, 197B.
2. At year-end, the company has estimated that its product warranty costs relating to items sold in 197A amount to $125,000. It is probable that customers will make claims for services in connection with products they purchased in 197A.
3. Worldwide is involved in three lawsuits relating to charges of patent infringement. The first suit was initiated on October 3, 197A, followed almost immediately by a second suit on October 8, 197A. The third suit was not initiated until January 27, 197B. The first suit was settled on February 18, 197B, and required the Company to pay $75,000 in damages. The third suit, initiated in 197B, also was settled on this date, and required the payment of damages amounting to $35,000. The second suit is considered to be a nuisance suit, and the likelihood of an adverse outcome is deemed to be remote.
4. Due to severe economic conditions in the industry in which Worldwide operates, the management wishes to accrue a loss contingency in the amount of $250,000. Management believes that this accrual will provide a more conservative income statement and balance sheet.
5. Because of political unrest in a foreign country in which Worldwide operates, management believes that there is a real threat of expropriation of its operations in that country. Other companies operating in the same foreign country recently have had their assets expropriated. The range of potential loss could be anywhere from $1,000,000 to as high as $4,000,000.

A description of the accounting and reporting requirements for each of these items will be given. First, the product warranty costs estimated on the basis of 197A sales should be accrued through a charge to income of that period. It is probable that a liability has been incurred in connection with the sales of 197A, and the amount of the liability can be reasonably estimated. The journal entry required to accrue the loss contingency would be:

Estimated Product Warranty Expenses	125,000	
Estimated Liability Under Product Warranty		125,000

The expense will appear as an operating expense in the 197A income statement, and the liability will appear on the 197A balance sheet.

The first lawsuit was initiated in 197A, but settled prior to the issuance of the financial statements. Under the provisions of SFAS No. 5, an accrual should be made for the loss contingency in the 197A financial statements. The entry to record the settlement would be similar to the entry shown above. However, the loss associated with the lawsuit may be classified as an extraordinary item (if it is unusual *and* infrequent) or as an unusual *or* infrequent item, or merely as an operating expense. If the settlement is considered to be an extraordinary, unusual or infrequent item, it should be accounted for following the provisions of APB Opinion No. 30, "Reporting the Results of Operations." (See Topic 1 for a complete discussion of APB Opinion No. 30.)

The second lawsuit is considered to be a nuisance suit, and the possibility of an adverse outcome has been assessed to be remote. No accrual or disclosure is required in this matter.

The third lawsuit was initiated in 197B (after the balance sheet date), but settled prior to the issuance of the financial statements. Because the action was not initiated in 197A, an accrual is not appropriate. Information relating to this lawsuit should be disclosed in the footnotes to the 197A financial statements of Worldwide, Inc.

The Statement expressly prohibits an accrual for general or unspecified business risks. Due to this fact, the loss contingency relating to the general economic conditions of the industry should not be accrued or disclosed. Worldwide may wish to appropriate retained earnings to reflect this loss contingency. Any appropriation made must be included in the stockholders' equity section of the 197A balance sheet and clearly labeled as an appropriation.

The last item deals with the threat of expropriation of certain foreign operations of Worldwide, Inc. Because assets of other companies doing business in the same foreign country have been expropriated, it is safe to assume that the loss contingency of Worldwide is probable. The estimate of probable loss ranges between $1,000,000 and $4,000,000, so there is some question as to whether or not the loss can be reasonably estimated. If the loss can be reasonably estimated, an accrual should be prepared for the loss contingency. FASB Interpretation No. 14, "Reasonable Estimation of the Amount of a Loss," provides guidance in the situation where a company has determined that the loss contingency is probable but is unable to estimate the probable amount of the loss. The Interpretation indicates that, where a range of potential loss can be determined, and no single value is more probable than any other value, the company should record the loss contingency at the lower limit of the range. In this case, Worldwide should accrue the loss contingency in the amount of $1,000,000.

The loss contingency established for the threat of expropriation probably would be classified as either an extraordinary item or an unusual or infrequent item in the 197A income statement of the Company. (See APB Opinion No. 30 in Topic 1 for proper treatment of extraordinary items and unusual or infrequent items.)

Accounting for Loss Contingencies During the Transition Period

SFAS No. 5 became effective for fiscal years beginning on or after July 1, 1975, and earlier application of the provisions of the Statement was encouraged. If adoption of the provisions of SFAS No. 5 resulted in an accounting change for a company, e.g., a change from expensing product warranty costs as incurred to full accrual of those costs, the change was to be treated as a "cumulative effect," which is described in APB Opinion No. 20 (see Topic 1). The cumulative effect would be reported in the income statement in the year of change, along with appropriate disclosures.

SFAS No. 11 changes the basic accounting during the transition period. This Statement requires retroactive restatement for as many periods as is deemed possible under the circumstances. If retroactive restatement of all prior period financial statements is not possible, the Statement (Paragraph 10) provides that "information presented shall be restated for as many consecutive periods immediately preceding the effective date of *FASB Statement No. 5* as is practical, and the cumulative effect . . . on retained earnings at the beginning of the earliest period restated . . . shall be included in determining net income of that period." However, if a company elects to apply the provisions of SFAS No. 5 prior to January 1, 1976, the company may apply the cumulative effect method to account for the change. Even though these companies may continue to use the cumulative effect method for the transition period, SFAS No. 11 encourages them to retroactively restate all financial statements presented.

Disclosures

For loss contingencies that are accrued, the company should disclose the nature of the accrual and, in some cases, the amount. The company may wish to disclose the amount of the accrual if such disclosure is required so as not to make the financial statements misleading. For loss contingencies not accrued, the company should disclose the nature of the contingency and, if possible, an estimate of the range of possible loss.

SFAS No. 6 (May 1975)

Classification of Short-Term Obligations Expected to be Refinanced

Flowchart and General Discussion

SFAS No. 6 is concerned with a rather common classification problem. The problem is: How should the accountant classify short-term obligations that management intends to refinance on a long-term basis? Normally, short-term obligations are thought of as current liabilities. Current liabilities generally are considered to be extinguished through a decrease in current assets or an increase in current liabilities. In other words, current liabilities require the use of working capital. If short-term obligations are expected to be refinanced, this is not the case. The current liability will be satisfied through the issuance of long-term debt, equity securities or other means. SFAS No. 6 concludes that, in certain cases, short-term obligations that normally are considered to be current liabilities may be excluded from the current portion of the balance sheet.

The short-term obligations referred to in the Statement may be thought of as debt that is due within one year, or within the operating cycle of the business if for a period longer than one year. Short-term obligations do not include obligations incurred in the normal course of generating revenues, e.g., accounts payable, accrued wages payable, etc.

The Flowchart of SFAS No. 6 illustrates the major provisions of the Statement. The left side of the Flowchart reflects the decisions required to determine if a given short-term obligation may be classified as other than a current liability, and the right side aids in the determination of the proper amount to be reclassified. The decision blocks have been numbered and will be referred to in the discussion that follows.

For the provisions of SFAS No. 6 to be applicable, the company must prepare a classified balance sheet (Block 1). (Certain industries have specialized accounting practices that preclude the preparation of classified balance sheets. In these cases, SFAS No. 6 would not be applicable.) If the company prepares a classified balance sheet, management must intend to refinance short-term obligations on a long-term basis before the accountant is faced with a classification problem. If management does not intend to refinance the short-term obligation, the entire amount should be classified as a current liability. Determining the intent of management has proved a significant problem in other pronouncements. For example, recall the problem of classifying an investment as current or noncurrent in SFAS No. 12 (see Topic 2 for details). This is not the case with Statement No. 6, however, because specific guidance is given in determining management's intent. Intent must be demonstrated by *either* a post-balance-sheet-date issuance of long-term debt or equity securities (Block 3) or the existence of a noncancelable financing agreement (Block 4). These are the only ways in which intent can be demonstrated.

Post-Balance-Sheet-Date Issuance

If, between the balance sheet date and the date of issuance of the financial statements to the public, the company issues long-term obligations or equity securities for the express purpose of refinancing short-term obligations, the short-term obligations may be classified as other than current at the balance sheet date. In the situation described above, the accountant is faced with a *fait accompli* as to the short-term obligations.[1]

The amount of the short-term obligations to be excluded from the current liability section of the balance sheet depends upon the dollar value of the long-term debt or equity securities issued (Block 9). The amount to be excluded is the lesser of the total short-term obligations refinanced or the long-term securities issued. If the long-term securities issued are greater in dollar amount than the short-term obligations, the total short-term obligations would be excluded from the current liability section of the balance sheet. However, if the dollar amount of the long-term securities is less than the short-term obligations to be refinanced, the amount excluded is limited to the amount of the long-term securities.

The amount excluded from the current liabilities may be classified under long-term debt or under a separate caption such as "Short-Term Obligations Expected to be Refinanced." When the separate caption option is selected, the amount should appear after current liabilities, but before long-term debt. If the reclassification is due to the issuance of equity securities, the short-term obligations *should not* be included in the stockholders' equity section of the balance sheet.

---

[1] FASB Interpretation No. 8 addresses the problem of using cash to repay short-term obligations and subsequently replacing the cash by issuing long-term debt. The Board concluded that short-term obligations retired in this manner should be classified as current, even though the proceeds from the sale of the long-term obligations are used to replace the cash involved in the retirement. The same rule applies for short-term obligations retired for cash and the cash replaced through the exercise of a financing agreement.

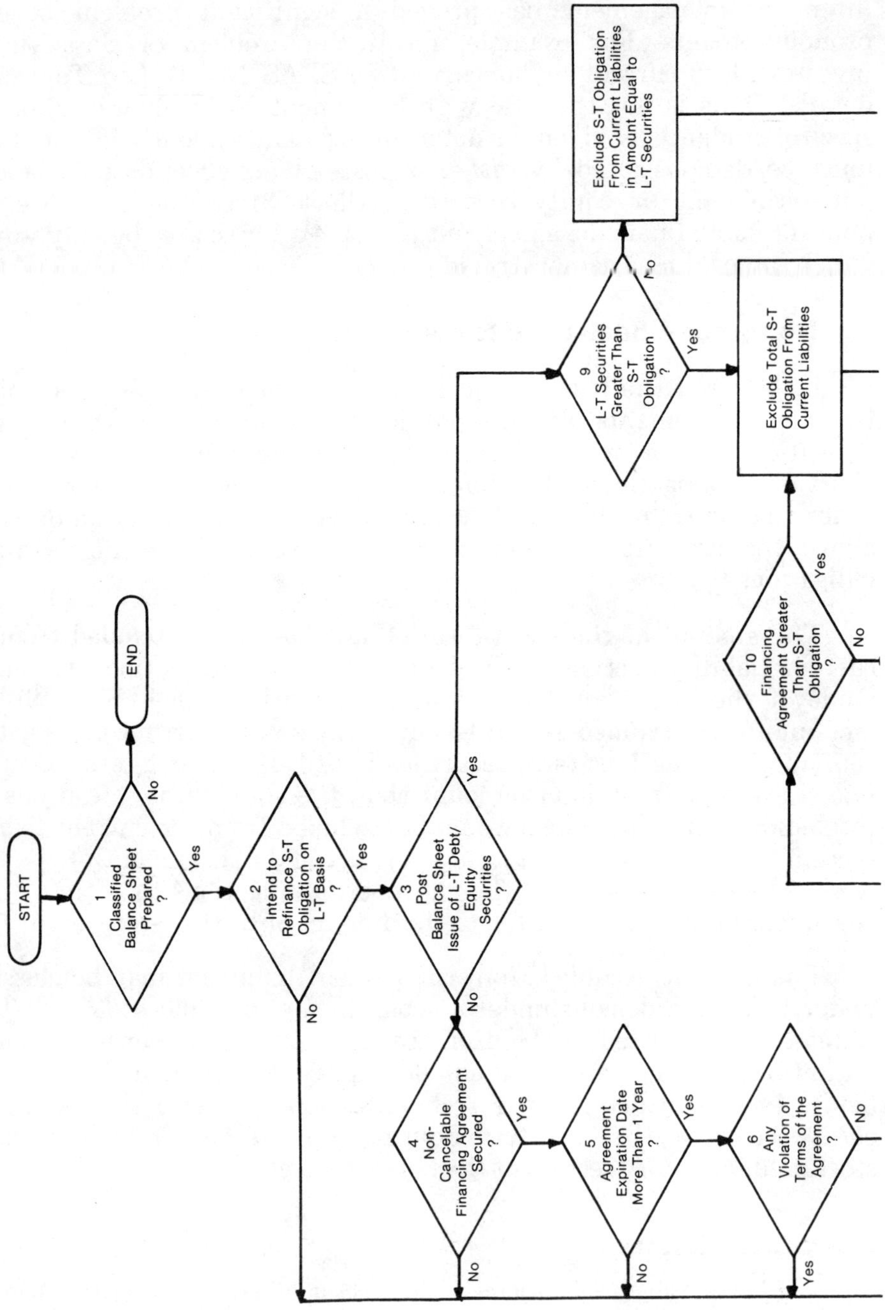
START
1 Classified Balance Sheet Prepared ?
Yes
No
END
2 Intend to Refinance S-T Obligation on L-T Basis ?
Yes
No
3 Post Balance Sheet Issue of L-T Debt/ Equity Securities ?
Yes
No
4 Non-Cancelable Financing Agreement Secured ?
Yes
No
5 Agreement Expiration Date More Than 1 Year ?
Yes
No
6 Any Violation of Terms of the Agreement ?
No
Yes
9 L-T Securities Greater Than S-T Obligation ?
Yes
No
Exclude S-T Obligation From Current Liabilities in Amount Equal to L-T Securities
Exclude Total S-T Obligation From Current Liabilities
10 Financing Agreement Greater Than S-T Obligation ?
Yes
No

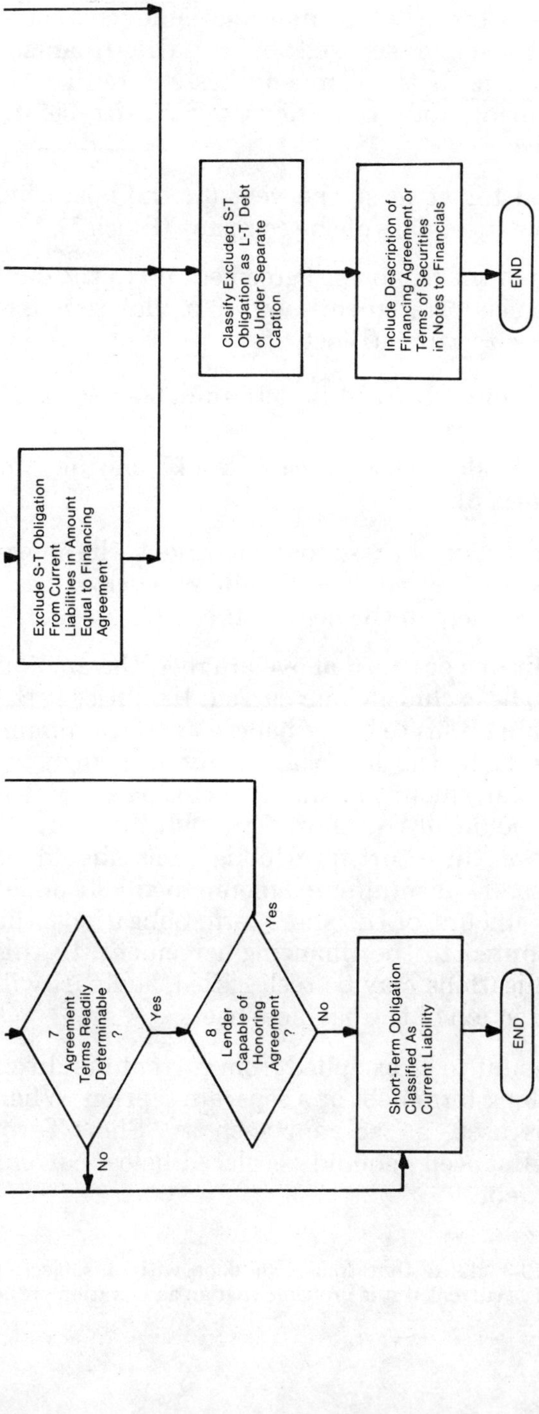
Exclude S-T Obligation From Current Liabilities in Amount Equal to Financing Agreement
Classify Excluded S-T Obligation as L-T Debt or Under Separate Caption
Include Description of Financing Agreement or Terms of Securities in Notes to Financials
END
7 Agreement Terms Readily Determinable ?
Yes
No
8 Lender Capable of Honoring Agreement ?
Yes
No
Short-Term Obligation Classified As Current Liability
END

Financing Agreement

If the company does not have a post-balance-sheet-date issuance of long-term obligations, the only other method available to demonstrate management intent is the existence of a noncancelable financing agreement. The agreement must be secured before the financial statements are issued to the public. If the company has entered into a noncancelable financing agreement, four conditions must exist before reclassification can be considered:

(1) The agreement must extend for at least one year (or the operating cycle) beyond the balance sheet date of the company (Block 5); [2]

(2) There must be no violations of the financing agreement up to the date of issuance of the financial statements; or, if a violation has occurred, a waiver has been secured (Block 6);

(3) The terms of the agreement must be readily determinable (Block 7); and

(4) The lender or prospective lender must be capable of honoring the financing agreement (Block 8).

If the agreement fails to meet any *one* of these four conditions, the short-term obligations must be classified as current liabilities, even though management intends to refinance them in the near future.

Provided that all the conditions outlined above are met, the amount of the short-term obligations to be excluded from current liabilities is the lesser of the total short-term obligations to be refinanced or the minimum amount expected to be available to the company under the financing agreement (Block 10). If the dollar amount of the financing agreement is greater than or equal to the amount of the short-term obligations to be refinanced, the total amount of the short-term obligations should be excluded from current liabilities. If the minimum amount available under the agreement is less than the amount of the short-term obligations, the amount to be reclassified is limited to the financing agreement. In this case, part of the short-term obligations may be reclassified, and part will remain in the current liability section of the balance sheet.

As indicated above, the amount to be excluded from current liabilities may be classified under either long-term debt or a separate caption. When the separate caption option is used, an account such as "Short-Term Obligations Expected to be Refinanced" should be placed below current liabilities but before long-term debt.

---

[2] FASB Technical Bulletin No. 79-3 states that long-term debt with a subjective acceleration clause may be reclassified as current if it is probable that an acceleration of the due date will occur

Additional Considerations

There are two additional considerations that must be discussed to gain a full understanding of SFAS No. 6. The basic thrust of the Statement deals with refinancing on a long-term basis; however, there are situations where short-term obligations may be continually replaced by new short-term obligations, with the short-term debt appropriately classified as long-term. This might be the case when a company makes use of a revolving credit agreement or a "stand-by" credit agreement. The Statement concludes (Paragraph 14) that "replacement of a short-term obligation with another short-term obligation after the date of the balance sheet but before the balance sheet is issued is not, by itself, sufficient to demonstrate an enterprise's ability to refinance the short-term obligation on a *long-term* basis" [emphasis added]. Before the short-term obligations may be classified as other than current, the revolving credit agreement or the "stand-by" credit agreement must meet the same conditions as any other financing agreement (see Blocks 4 through 8 of the Flowchart). If the conditions are met, it would be appropriate to consider reclassification.

The second consideration deals with the case where the amount that may be obtained under the financing agreement is subject to change. For example, the amount available under the agreement may be limited by the amount of collateral offered at any time, i.e., the amount of the loan agreement may be tied directly to the value of inventory. In cases where the amount available under the financing agreement changes, the amount that is used to determine the excludable amount would be a "reasonable estimate" of the minimum funds available from the date of maturity of the short-term obligations to the end of the fiscal year. For example, assuming that the funds available are linked to inventory, the maximum amount of the short-term obligation that could be reclassified would be the minimum inventory at any time during the year. If it is not possible to determine the amount available under the financing agreement, no reclassification is allowed.

Technical Considerations—Post-Balance-Sheet-Date Issuance

Exhibit I lists the refinancing assumptions that will be used to illustrate reclassification under a post-balance-sheet-date issuance of long-term obligations.

Exhibit I

Refinancing Assumptions

1. Jar, Inc. has a year-end of 12/31/7A, and prepares a classified balance sheet for issuance on or about April 10, 197B.

2. At 12/31/7A, Jar, Inc. has $10,000,000 of eight percent short-term obligations that mature on March 31, 197B.
3. Jar, Inc. intends to refinance the $10,000,000 on a long-term basis.
4. On March 30, 197B Jar, Inc. sold $12,000,000 of debenture bonds with the express purpose of using the proceeds to retire the short-term obligations. The debentures mature in five years and have a stated interest rate of nine percent.

Using the Flowchart to aid in the decision process, note that the first condition is met (Block 1), because Jar, Inc. prepares a classified balance sheet. Assumption 3 indicates that the Company intends to refinance the short-term obligations on a long-term basis; therefore, the second condition (Block 2) also is met. Assuming that $10,000,000 of the proceeds from the sale of the debentures were, in fact, used to retire the short-term obligations on March 31, 197B, the transaction would qualify as a post-balance-sheet-date issuance (Block 3). It is important to note that actual retirement of the short-term debt does not have to occur before issuance of the balance sheet. The maturity date of the short-term obligation might be after the release of the statements.

The next step in the process would be to compare the amount of the debt issue with the total amount of the short-term obligations refinanced (Block 9). The total amount ($12,000,000) of the debt issued is greater than the amount ($10,000,000) of the short-term obligations; therefore, the entire amount of the short-term obligations would be reclassified as other than current on the 12/31/7A balance sheet. Jar, Inc. could elect to classify the $10,000,000 as either "Long-Term Debt" or "Short-Term Debt Expected to be Refinanced". Appropriate disclosures will be illustrated later in this discussion.

Assuming that $8,000,000 of debentures were issued, rather than the original $12,000,000, and that the proceeds of $8,000,000 and $2,000,000 of internally generated cash were used to retire the short-term obligations, Jar, Inc. would reclassify only $8,000,000 of the short-term obligations. In this case, the company is limited by the amount of the debt that was issued to refinance the short-term obligations. The remaining $2,000,000 ($10,000,000 – $8,000,000) would continue to be classified as current liabilities.

For the final example, assume all information in Exhibit I is the same, except that the maturity date for the short-term obligations is May 1, 197B. In this case, the debentures will be sold on March 30, 197B, and the proceeds will be used to retire the short-term obligations on May 1, 197B. Assume that $10,000,000 of the proceeds from the sale of the debentures was used to make a temporary investment in government securities, and that the maturity date of the securities was May 1, 197B (the same as the maturity date of the short-term obligations). Based upon these assumptions, the $10,000,000 of short-term obligations would be reclassified as other than current if the temporary investment also was excluded from current assets.

This concludes the technical discussion of post-balance-sheet-date issuance of securities. The next section will deal with the technical considerations involved when the company has entered into a financing agreement for the purpose of refinancing short-term obligations.

Technical Considerations—Financing Agreements

Exhibit II lists the assumptions to be used in illustrating reclassification under a financing agreement. The assumptions are somewhat more complex than those presented above, because it is necessary to know the details of the agreement before any determination can be made about the propriety of reclassification.

Exhibit II
Refinancing Assumptions

1. Jar, Inc. has a year-end of 12/31/7A, and prepares a classified balance sheet for issuance on or about April 10, 197B.
2. At 12/31/7A, Jar, Inc. has $10,000,000 of eight percent short-term obligations that mature on August 15, 197B.
3. Jar, Inc. intends to refinance the $10,000,000 on a long-term basis.
4. Prior to April 10, 197B, Jar, Inc. entered into a financing agreement with a local bank that allows the company to borrow up to $12,000,000 at any time during the next two years. Any amount borrowed is due in full five years from the date the funds are received and bears interest at the rate of 11 percent.
5. It has been determined that the local bank is financially capable of honoring the agreement. The agreement may not be cancelled unless Jar, Inc. is in violation of any of the terms of the agreement.
6. As of April 10, 197B, there is no evidence of any violation of the provisions of the agreement.

The Flowchart may be used to aid in the decision-making process for this set of assumptions. Jar, Inc. issues a classified balance sheet (Block 1), and intends to refinance certain short-term obligations on a long-term basis (Block 2). The method of refinancing is through the use of a financing agreement. The terms of the agreement specify that it is noncancelable (Block 4), and assumption number 4 indicates that the term of the agreement is more than one year (Block 5). There are no known violations of the financing agreement as of April 10, 197B (Block 6), and the terms of the agreement are readily determinable, i.e., the amount, interest rate, lender and maturity date are all known (Block 7). Finally, it has been determined that the lending institution is capable of honoring the agreement (Block 8). Because the conditions in Blocks 4 through 8 have been met, reclassification of the short-term obligations is appropriate.

To determine the proper amount to be reclassified, it is necessary to compare the minimum amount available to Jar, Inc. under the financing agreement with the total amount of the short-term obligations expected to be refinanced. The amount available ($12,000,000) is greater than the amount of the short-term obligations ($10,000,000); therefore, it is appropriate to exclude the entire amount of the short-term obligations from the current liability section of the 12/31/7A balance sheet. Jar, Inc. may elect to classify the $10,000,000 as either "Long-Term Debt" or "Short-Term Obligations Expected to be Refinanced." If the latter is chosen, the amount should appear after current liabilities, but before long-term debt, on the balance sheet for 197A.

If, in the above example, the amount available under the financing agreement had been less than the amount of the short-term obligations that Jar, Inc. expected to refinance, the company would have been limited to excluding short-term obligations in the amount of the financing agreement. If this situation were to arise, part of the short-term obligations would be reclassified, and part would remain in the current liability section of the balance sheet.

A final example is presented below to illustrate the reclassification process when the amount available to the borrower under a financing agreement varies. Assume that all of the provisions listed in Exhibit II are the same, except that the financing agreement specifies that the Company may borrow up to 90 percent of the value of its trade accounts receivable. In this case, the amount available under the financing agreement will vary directly with the value of accounts receivable. Assume the company estimates that accounts receivable will reach a high of $15,000,000 in the first quarter of the year and a low of $10,000,000 in the third quarter of the year. The short-term obligations to be refinanced mature in the third quarter of the year. During this period the best estimate of the amount available under the financing agreement is $9,000,000 ($10,000,000 × .9). Therefore, only $9,000,000 of the short-term obligations may be reclassified on the 12/31/7A balance sheet.

Required Disclosures

If a company has excluded short-term obligations from current liabilities on the basis of the provisions of SFAS No. 6, it must disclose in the notes to the financial statements a general description of either the financing agreement or the debt or equity securities issued. Paragraph 36 of the Statement indicates that the disclosure should contain the amounts involved, a description of the financing agreement (including conditions and terms), restrictions imposed by the financing agreement and a description of the stock issued (including number of shares and amounts).

Presented below is the "Other Liabilities" section of the 1974 and 1975 balance sheet of Pratt & Lambert, Inc. Note F to the financial statements contains information concerning the refinancing of short-term obligations during this period.

Pratt & Lambert, Inc. (Dec)

	1975	1974
Other Liabilities (current maturities included in current liabilities):		
Long-term debt—notes payable to bank (Note F)	$1,800,000	$2,200,000
Deferred income taxes	205,519	187,303
Total other liabilities	$2,005,519	$2,387,303

Note F: Long-term Debt—On February 3, 1976, the company concluded a long-term financing arrangement with two banks whereby the company may borrow up to $4,000,000 through 1979 and an additional $3,000,000 through 1980 at an interest rate equal to ¼% over the prime rate. The loan is payable in annual amounts of $500,000, $1,000,000, $1,000,000 and $1,500,000 in 1980, 1981, 1982, and 1983 respectively, in equal quarterly installments. Any balance remaining is payable on December 31, 1983. The loan agreement contains, among other terms, various requirements which include the maintenance of consolidated working capital of at least $11,000,000 and shareholders' equity of at least $20,000,000.

On February 3, 1976, the company borrowed $3,000,000 under the above agreement which was used, in part, to repay short-term borrowing under its lines of credit ($200,000) and the notes payable under the term loan agreement ($1,600,000). Accordingly, these obligations have been classified as long-term debt in the accompanying balance sheet at December 31, 1975.

In addition, the agreement provides for demand line of credit borrowings of up to $3,000,000 at the bank's prime rate. The company is expected to maintain an average compensating balance, as determined by the bank ledger records, of 10% of its line of credit plus the balance owing on the amounts due under the long-term portion of the agreement.

Source: *Accounting Trends and Techniques,* Copyright © 1976 by the American Institute of Certified Public Accountants, Inc., p. 140.

Topic 7

Earnings Per Share

Detail Contents

APB Opinion No. 15 (May 1969)
Earnings Per Share

Note: See SFAS No. 21 in Topic 13 for a detailed analysis of the reporting of earnings per share in nonpublic entities.

Approach to Calculating Earnings Per Share

APB Opinion No. 15 provides guidelines for the calculation of earnings per share (EPS). At first reading, the Opinion appears to be rather general, and not overly difficult to apply. However, a more careful reading reveals a myriad of complex rules. Some are relatively easy to apply, while others are not. Overall, the Opinion is quite complex. In attempting to explain and analyze the Opinion, the basic problem is one of approach. The authors have elected to use a building block approach to the calculation of EPS. Each component part of the calculation will be broken down into its essential features and these features will be analyzed in detail. Once the reader comprehends a particular feature of the calculation, additional features will be added. The end product of this type of analysis is the ability to attack each important area of the earnings per share calculation and put the various pieces together into a complete computation of EPS. Much of what has been written about EPS has been either too general to be of any practical use or too detailed to apply to a wide variety of situations. The discussion and related example material should provide the reader with an in-depth understanding of the EPS calculation.

Flowcharts, diagrams and other materials will be provided for each section of the EPS calculation. An overall flowchart of the entire EPS process is too difficult to follow, and often is more confusing than helpful. The authors believe that several flowcharts and diagrams relating to a specific area of interest are more meaningful and useful to the reader.

The Corporate Capital Structure and Its Importance in the EPS Calculation

An excellent beginning for the discussion of EPS is identification of the type of capital structure the corporation has and, therefore, of the required EPS computations. The Opinion identifies two types of capital structures that are of importance to the computation of EPS. One type is referred to as a "simple" capital structure, and the other is known as a "complex" capital structure. The identification of a given capital structure as simple or complex depends upon the make-up of the equity securities on the right-hand side of the balance sheet.

Flowchart I shows the decision process required for proper classification of the capital structure of a corporation. The Flowchart introduces several new terms which will be defined. The reader may not fully appreciate the meaning of these terms at this stage of the discussion, but the terms will become familiar through use.

If the equity securities of a corporation consist only of common stock (Block 1), the capital structure will be classified as simple, and will lead to one type of EPS calculation. However, if the equity securities consist of common stock and "common stock equivalents," the capital structure may be either simple or complex (Block 2). A common stock equivalent is a security that gives the holder the right, through conversion or exercise, to obtain shares of common stock. These securities *are not* shares of common stock. They are rights to obtain stock if certain specified conditions are met. For example, stock options, warrants or their equivalent always are viewed as common stock equivalents, because they give the holder the right to obtain common shares. Convertible debt securities and convertible preferred stocks may be common stock equivalents if they meet certain tests that will be discussed later.

Another capital structure might consist only of common stock and "potentially dilutive securities," i.e., the capital structure would have no common stock equivalents. The capital structure of this corporation could *not* contain options, warrants or their equivalent, because these securities always are considered common stock equivalents. Recall from the above discussion that convertible debt or preferred stock may or may not be common stock equivalents. If a corporation has convertible debt or preferred stock that *fails* to meet the tests for classification as common stock equivalents, these securities become known as "potentially dilutive securities." A key part of the phrase used is "dilutive." For any security to be considered dilutive, it must have the effect of decreasing earnings

FLOWCHART I

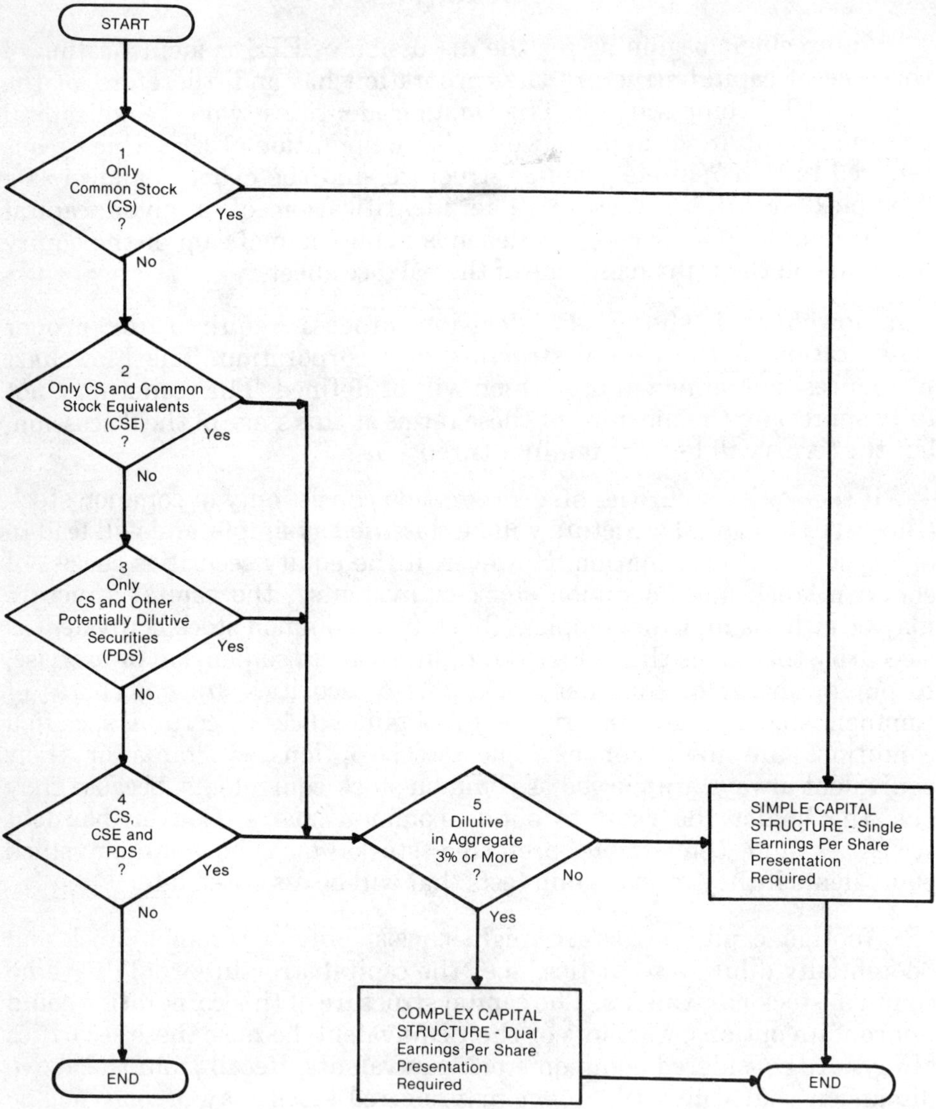
START
1
Only
Common Stock
(CS)
?
Yes
No
2
Only CS and Common
Stock Equivalents
(CSE)
?
Yes
No
3
Only
CS and Other
Potentially Dilutive
Securities
(PDS)
Yes
No
4
CS,
CSE and
PDS
?
Yes
No
END
5
Dilutive
in Aggregate
3% or More
?
No
Yes
SIMPLE CAPITAL
STRUCTURE - Single
Earnings Per Share
Presentation
Required
COMPLEX CAPITAL
STRUCTURE - Dual
Earnings Per Share
Presentation
Required
END

per share (or increasing a loss per share). That is to say that dilutive securities would reduce EPS below what would have been reported if the securities were not issued. The fact that the securities are referred to as "potentially" dilutive means that it is not known at this stage whether or not the securities *are* dilutive. That is something that will be determined in the process of computing EPS. If a corporation's capital structure is made up of common stock and potentially dilutive securities, it may be either a simple or a complex structure for purposes of APB Opinion No. 15 (Block 3).

Finally, a capital structure may contain common stock, common stock equivalents *and* potentially dilutive securities (Block 4). This is merely a combination of the elements described above. Again, such a capital structure may be either simple or complex.

The final test for the last three capital structures deals with the dilutive effect of the common stock equivalents and the potentially dilutive securities. For the capital structure to be classified as complex, the dilutive effect of these securities must be three percent or more of EPS in the aggregate (Block 5). That is, the presence of common stock equivalents and potentially dilutive securities must reduce EPS (or increase a loss per share) by at least three percent. If EPS is diluted by three percent or more, the capital structure is complex; and if the dilutive effect is less than three percent, the structure is classified as simple.

Before proceeding to the required reporting of EPS under a simple or complex capital structure, it is important to clear up some common misconceptions about the classification of a capital structure. First, many people believe that, if a corporation has common stock equivalents or potentially dilutive securities, the capital structure is complex. This is not true. The mere presence of these types of securities does not mean that the capital structure is complex; rather, it is the *dilutive* effect of these securities that leads to the proper classification. Another common error is to confuse nonconvertible debt and preferred stock with convertible debt and convertible preferred. Nonconvertible senior securities have nothing to do with the classification of the capital structure. A corporation may have many types of sophisticated nonconvertible senior securities and still have a "simple" capital structure for purposes of calculating EPS. The term "complex," as used in APB Opinion No. 15, has special meaning and is defined by reference to Blocks 2 through 5 on the Flowchart.

An enterprise with a simple capital structure, as defined above, is required to report only *one* earnings per share calculation. The Opinion (Paragraph 14) suggests that this calculation be referred to as "Earnings Per Common Share." If an enterprise has a complex capital structure, a *dual* presentation of earnings per share is required. If the capital structure contains common stock equivalents that are dilutive, the Opinion (Paragraph 15) suggests that one computation of earnings per share should be referred to as "Primary Earnings Per Share," and the second computation should be labeled "Fully Diluted Earnings Per Share." But if the complex capital structure contains no common stock equivalents *or* common stock equivalents that are not dilutive, the Opinion (Paragraph 16) suggests that the first computation of earnings per share should be entitled "Earnings Per Common Share—assuming no dilution," and the second computation should be referred to as "Earnings Per Common Share—assuming full dilution." The remainder of the discussion will focus on how to calculate the various amounts indicated above.

Unadjusted Earnings Per Share—A Starting Point

The basic formula for the calculation of earnings per share is net income, divided by number of common shares outstanding. This is a very simplistic notion of the concept of earnings per share, but is a helpful way to begin the analysis of unadjusted earnings per share.

For purposes of the following discussion, unadjusted earnings per share is defined as the computation of earnings per share, ignoring *all* common stock equivalents (options, warrants and their equivalent, and convertible securities classified as C.S.E.) and potentially dilutive securities (convertible debt and preferred that fail the tests necessary to be classified as common stock equivalents). From this point forward, options, warrants, convertible debt, convertible preferred stock, etc. will be referred to as "contingent equity issues." This is done to eliminate much of the description that would be needed in the absence of some shorthand term. By ignoring *all* contingent equity issues, much of the problem of computing earnings per share has been assumed away. However, it is necessary to do so at this point in order to begin the process of examining the components of earnings per share. Of course, all of the contingent equity issues will be discussed later in this section.

Unadjusted earnings per share (EPSU) is equal to net income available to common shareholders, divided by the weighted average number of common shares outstanding. Both the numerator and denominator of this equation are different from the basic formula given above, and therefore need to be analyzed in detail.

Calculation of Weighted Average Number of Shares—The Denominator

The first step in the calculation of EPSU is to compute the weighted average number of common shares outstanding for the period. Each share of common stock must be weighted for the portion of time it is outstanding during the period. Some shares of common stock may be outstanding for the entire year, and other shares may be outstanding for only a few months. The use of a weighted average takes this fact into consideration, whereas a simple average would ignore it. In the illustration below, it is crucial to remember that EPSU ignores all contingent equity issues.

To show the computation of the weighted average number of common shares outstanding during a time period, assume the facts listed in Exhibit I.

Exhibit I

Weighted Average Shares - General Example

1. Book-It, Inc. had 2,400,000 common shares outstanding on January 1, 197A and 3,000,000 shares outstanding on December 31, 197A (the end of the fiscal year).
2. Of these amounts, 2,300,000 common shares were outstanding during the entire year.
3. 600,000 shares were sold on June 1, 197A.
4. 100,000 shares were sold on July 1, 197A.
5. 100,000 shares were repurchased on October 1, 197A, to be held in the treasury. The repurchased shares were from the shares outstanding at the beginning of the year.

Table I below represents the computation of the weighted average number of common shares outstanding for 197A, based upon these assumptions.

Table I

Computation of Weighted Average Number of Shares Outstanding

Assumption from Exhibit I	Number of Shares (1)	Months Out-standing (2)	Fraction of Year (3)	Weighted Average Shares (1 × 3)
2	2,300,000	12	12/12	2,300,000
3	600,000	7	7/12	350,000
4	100,000	6	6/12	50,000
5	100,000	9	9/12	75,000
Weighted Average Shares Outstanding				2,775,000

The actual number of shares outstanding at the end of 197A is 3,000,000, compared with a weighted average number of shares outstanding of 2,775,000. The 100,000 shares of treasury stock repurchased were outstanding from January 1 through October 1 (nine months), and were weighted accordingly. The 2,400,000 shares outstanding at the beginning of the year were reduced by the number of treasury shares purchased to arrive at the 2,300,000 shares that were outstanding for the entire period. The shares issued during the period were weighted for the number of months each issue actually was outstanding during 197A.

An alternative approach to the weighting of the shares outstanding at the *beginning* of the year would have been to weight the 2,400,000 for the nine months all shares were outstanding, and then weight 2,300,000 (2,400,000 − 100,000 treasury shares) for the remaining three months of the year. If this approach were used, the following results would be obtained:

2,400,000 × 9/12 =	1,800,000
2,300,000 × 3/12 =	575,000
	2,375,000

The total weighted average shares of 2,375,000 are identical to combining assumptions 2 and 5 (2,300,000 + 75,000) from Table I. Regardless of the technique, the results will be the same.

Flowchart II identifies some additional adjustments that may be required in the calculation of the weighted average number of shares outstanding.

If, during the period under consideration, a business combination, accounted for as a pooling of interests, is consummated, the weighted average number of shares outstanding will have to be adjusted to give effect to the number of shares issued (Block 1). (See APB Opinion No. 16, "Business Combinations," in Topic 11 for a detailed analysis of accounting for business combinations accounted for as purchases and pooling of interests.) Appropriate weighting is required for the following items in connection with a pooling of interests:

(1) Shares issued in the pooling are weighted from the date of acquisition to the balance sheet date;

(2) Shares eliminated in the pooling are weighted from the beginning of the accounting period (or later, if issued later) to the acquisition date, after being restated in terms of the acquiring enterprise's stock; and

(3) Shares not eliminated in the pooling are assumed to be outstanding the entire period (or part of the period if issued after the start of the period) and should be weighted as such, after restating in terms of the acquiring enterprise's stock.

FLOWCHART II

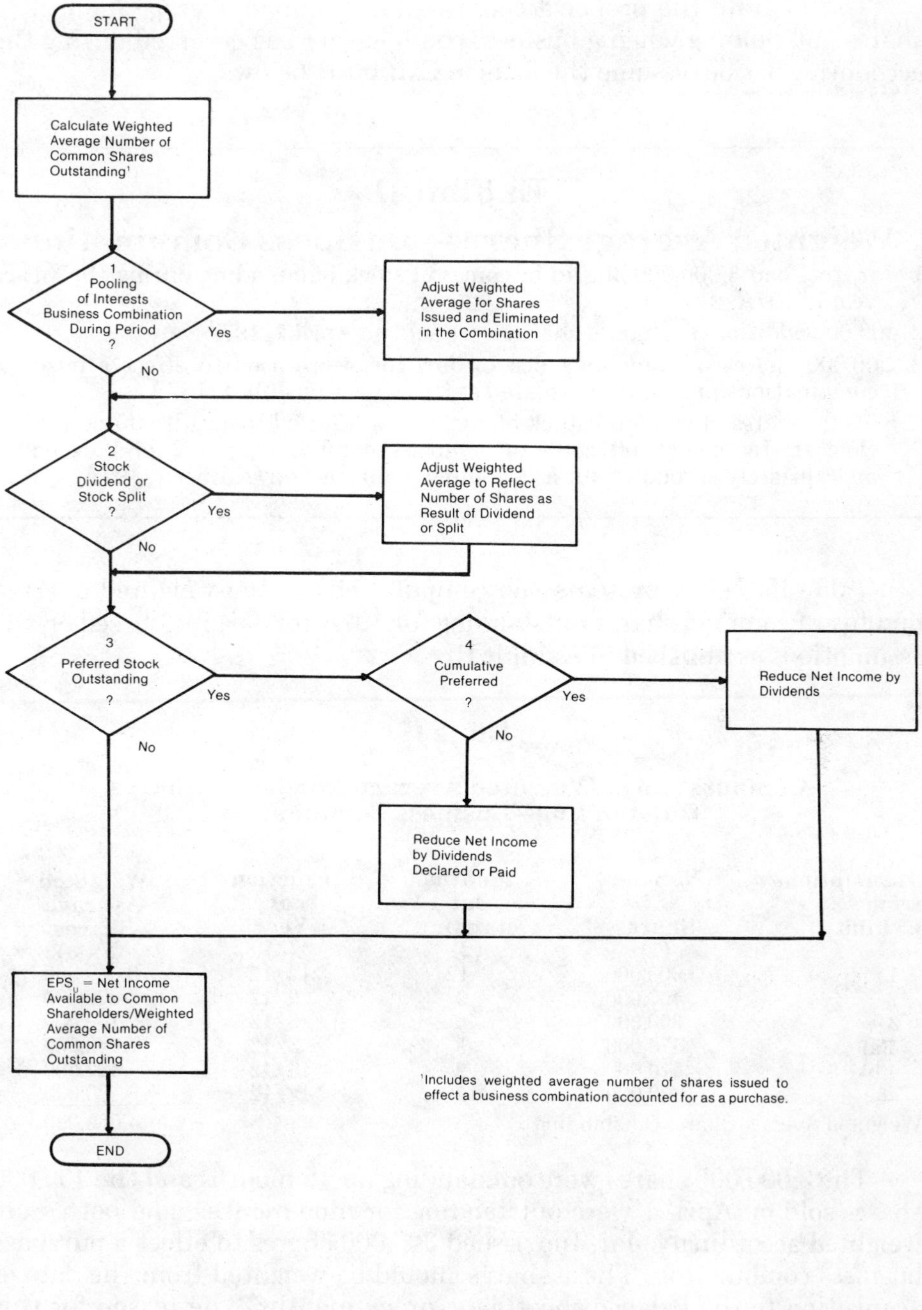

START
Calculate Weighted Average Number of Common Shares Outstanding[1]
1 Pooling of Interests Business Combination During Period ?
Yes
No
Adjust Weighted Average for Shares Issued and Eliminated in the Combination
2 Stock Dividend or Stock Split ?
Yes
No
Adjust Weighted Average to Reflect Number of Shares as Result of Dividend or Split
3 Preferred Stock Outstanding ?
Yes
No
4 Cumulative Preferred ?
Yes
No
Reduce Net Income by Dividends
Reduce Net Income by Dividends Declared or Paid
EPS$_u$ = Net Income Available to Common Shareholders/Weighted Average Number of Common Shares Outstanding
END

[1]Includes weighted average number of shares issued to effect a business combination accounted for as a purchase.

If the business combination was effected by a purchase, and common stock was issued in part or full consideration, the shares issued would be weighted from the date of acquisition to the balance sheet date.

To illustrate the proper accounting for weighted average number of shares outstanding when a business combination has occurred during the accounting period, assume the facts in Exhibit II below:

Exhibit II

Weighted Average Shares—Business Combination

1. Jar, Inc. had 3,000,000 shares of common stock outstanding during the entire year of 197A.
2. 400,000 additional common shares were sold on April 1, 197A.
3. 300,000 shares of common stock of Jar, Inc. were used to effect a business combination appropriately treated as a purchase on July 1, 197A.
4. 570,000 shares of common stock of Jar, Inc. were used to acquire 95 percent of Book-It, Inc.'s 300,000 common shares outstanding in a 2-for-1 exchange appropriately accounted for as a pooling of interest on October 1, 197A.

Table II below presents the computations of the weighted average number of common shares outstanding for 197A for Jar, Inc., based on the assumptions established in Exhibit II.

Table II

Computation of Weighted Average Number of Shares Outstanding—Business Combination

Assumptions from Exhibit II	Number of Shares (1)	Months Out-standing (2)	Fraction of Year (3)	Weighted Average Shares (1 × 3)
1	3,000,000	12	12/12	3,000,000
2	400,000	9	9/12	300,000
3	300,000	6	6/12	150,000
4(a)	570,000	3	3/12	142,500
4(b)	570,000	9	9/12	427,500
4(c)	30,000	12	12/12	30,000
Weighted Average Shares Outstanding				4,050,000

The 3,000,000 shares were outstanding for 12 months and the 400,000 shares sold on April 1 were outstanding for nine months, and both were weighted accordingly. Jar, Inc. issued 300,000 shares to effect a purchase business combination. These shares should be weighted from the date of acquisition to the balance sheet date, or six months. The reason for this weighting is that, in a purchase combination, income of the acquired company prior to the date of combination is not incorporated with the income of the acquiring company.

The shares issued to effect the pooling of interests require a more complex weighting. Jar, Inc. issued 570,000 of its common shares to effect the combination on October 1. These 570,000 shares were outstanding for three months and should be weighted accordingly. Jar, Inc. acquired 285,000 (300,000 × 95%) of the shares of the combining company. These shares had been outstanding on the books of the combining company from the beginning of the year until the date of combination. Because Jar, Inc. issued two of its shares for each share of the combining company, the 285,000 shares represent 570,000 (285,000 × 2) shares of Jar, Inc. stock. The 570,000 equivalent shares of Jar, Inc. stock should be weighted for the nine months prior to the combination. The reason for this weighting is that, in a pooling of interests, the income of the combining company is incorporated with the income of the combined company as if the combination took place at the beginning of the period. Therefore, the shares of Jar, Inc. are considered to be outstanding for the entire period (142,500 + 427,500 = 570,000). The last element of the pooling that needs to be considered is the 15,000 (300,000 × 5%) shares of the combining company stock that still are outstanding after the combination. These 15,000 shares represent 30,000 (15,000 × 2) shares of Jar, Inc. common stock. The 30,000 equivalent shares were outstanding for the entire year and are weighted accordingly.

The last adjustment to the denominator in the EPSU calculation is required when there has been a stock dividend or a stock split distributed during the period (Block 3). When the number of common shares outstanding changes as a result of splits or stock dividends, the weighted average number of shares should be adjusted to reflect the change. The adjustment should be on a retroactive basis for all periods presented. If the stock dividend or stock split occurs after the balance sheet date, but before the financial statements are issued, the adjustment still is required on a retroactive basis. The effects of stock dividends and stock splits and the computation of weighted average number of shares outstanding is illustrated, using the assumptions listed in Exhibit III.

Exhibit III
Assumptions for Weighted Average Shares—Splits and Dividends

1. Book-It, Inc. had 1,500,000 common shares outstanding during the entire year of 197C.
2. 300,000 additional common shares were sold on April 1, 197C.
3. 200,000 shares were sold on July 1, 197C.

4. Book-It, Inc. declared and paid a 10 percent stock dividend on September 1, 197C.
5. A 2-for-1 stock split occurred on January 15, 197D. The year end for Book-It is December 31, and the financial statements were not released until March 3, 197D.
6. The weighted average number of shares calculated for 197B, before considering any stock splits or dividends, was 1,200,000. Book-It is presenting comparative statements for 197C and 197B.

Table III below presents the computations of the weighted average number of common shares outstanding for 197C and 197B, based on the assumptions presented in Exhibit III.

Table III

Weighted Average Number of Shares Outstanding for 197C and 197B—Dividends and Splits

1. Computation of Weighted Average Shares for 197C

Assumptions from Exhibit III	Number of Shares (1)	Months Outstanding (2)	Fraction of Year (3)	Weighted Average Shares (1 × 3)
1	1,500,000	12	12/12	1,500,000
2	300,000	9	9/12	225,000
3	200,000	6	6/12	100,000
	Total weighted average shares before dividend and split			1,825,000
4	10% stock dividend (1,825,000 shares × 10%)			182,500
	Total weighted average shares before stock split			2,007,500
5	2-for-1 stock split			2,007,500
	Total weighted average shares outstanding			4,015,000

2. Computation of Weighted Average Shares for 197B

Weighted average shares outstanding for 197B (Assumptions)	1,200,000
10 percent stock dividend (1,200,000 × 10%)	120,000
Weighted average shares before split	1,320,000
2-for-1 stock split	1,320,000
Weighted average shares outstanding, retroactively restated for 197B	2,640,000

The computation of the weighted average number of shares *prior* to the stock dividend and split have been discussed at length in previous examples. By referring back to Exhibit III, recall that the stock dividend was distributed after the sale of additional shares was completed. The dividend will be paid on these additional shares. Therefore, the number of *weighted* shares issued in connection with the dividend is equal to 10 percent of the total weighted average number of shares (1,825,000) prior to the dividend. The dividend percentage would not apply to any increases or decreases in the number of shares *after* the date of record of the dividend. This requires an additional step in the calculation of the weighted average number of shares outstanding, i.e., the weighted average number of shares outstanding at the date of record for the stock dividend.

In this example, the stock split occurred after the end of the year, but prior to the financial statement release date. When this occurs, the weighted average shares must give recognition to the split *as if* the split had occurred in the period under consideration, in this case, 197C. The 2-for-1 split results in a doubling of the previously calculated weighted average number of shares outstanding of 2,007,500. The final total weighted average number of shares outstanding then is equal to 4,015,000. This number will be used as the denominator of the EPSU calculation.

Because Book-It, Inc. plans to present comparative financial statements for the years 197C and 197B, a restatement of the weighted average number of shares outstanding in 197B is required to reflect the distribution of the stock dividend and the stock split. The determination of the new weighted average number of shares for 197B will be made as if the dividend and split occurred at the end of 197B. At the end of 197B, Book-It, Inc. calculated the weighted average number of shares to be 1,200,000 for purposes of computing EPSU. Because the stock dividend occurred prior to the split, it must be considered first. The 10 percent stock dividend will add an additional 120,000 *weighted* shares to the previous total of 1,200,000. The stock split then is applied to this new total of 1,320,000, to give a total weighted average number of shares in 197B of 2,640,000. This is the value of the denominator that will be used to calculate EPSU for 197B.

This completes the discussion of items affecting the denominator in the unadjusted earnings per share computation. Remember that consideration has not been given to any contingent equity issues in the above examples. Attention now is directed to items that affect the numerator in the EPSU calculation.

Calculation of Net Income Available to Common Shareholders—The Numerator

The numerator of the equation for the calculation of EPSU may require adjustment for certain senior securities. The effects of debt securities already have been included in the numerator, i.e., interest expense has been deducted to arrive at the net income figure. However, there will be an adjustment necessary if the company has preferred stock outstanding (Block 3). Dividends on preferred stock are not shown on the income statement as a reduction in income, because such dividends are considered as distributions to equity holders. However, the earnings per share computation is based upon the *common* shares outstanding, and must be based upon income available to the common shareholders. Therefore, it is necessary to reduce reported net income by an amount equal to dividends on preferred stock. If the preferred stock is cumulative

(Block 4), net income is to be reduced by dividends indicated. If the preferred is noncumulative, net income will be reduced by dividends paid or declared. Remember that the discussion is about preferred dividends; cash dividends on common stock *are not* deducted from income in the computation of EPS.

To illustrate the adjustments to the numerator required for preferred stock outstanding, assume that Jar, Inc. had net income of $5,000,000 for the year 197C. The company has 100,000 shares of eight percent, $100 par value cumulative preferred stock outstanding during the year. Dividends have not been paid in 197C. The adjustment to reported net income is computed below:

Reported Net Income Before Adjustment	$5,000,000
Adjustment for Dividends ($100 par × 8% × 100,000 shares)	800,000
Net Income for EPSU Computation	$4,200,000

If the preferred stock had been noncumulative, there would be no adjustment to net income for purposes of the computation.

The example below is used to illustrate the complete calculation of EPSU by including items that affect both the numerator and the denominator.

Exhibit IV
Assumptions for Unadjusted EPS Calculation

1. Jar, Inc. had 5,000,000 shares of common stock outstanding during the entire year of 197A.
2. 500,000 shares of common stock were issued on July 1, 197A.
3. 400,000 shares of common stock were issued on October 1, 197A.
4. Jar, Inc. had 200,000 shares of 10 percent, $50 par cumulative preferred stock. All dividends have been paid, including the dividends for 197A.
5. Net income for the Company in 197A was $6,000,000.

Table IV shows the adjustments necessary to arrive at net income available for common shareholders and weighted average number of common shares outstanding for 197A.

Table IV

Computation of Numerator, Denominator for Unadjusted EPS

1. Computation of Numerator

Net Income	\$6,000,000
Preferred dividends paid (\$50 par × 10% × 200,000 shares)	1,000,000
Net Income available to Common Shareholders	\$5,000,000

2. Computation of Denominator

Assumptions from Exhibit IV	Number of Shares (1)	Months Outstanding (2)	Fraction of Year (3)	Weighted Average Shares (1 × 3)
1	5,000,000	12	12/12	5,000,000
2	500,000	6	6/12	250,000
3	400,000	3	3/12	100,000
Weighted Average Shares Outstanding				5,350,000

Unadjusted earnings per share is computed by dividing net income available to common shareholders by the weighted average number of common shares outstanding during the period. The computation is shown below:

$$\text{EPSU} = \frac{\$5{,}000{,}000}{5{,}350{,}000} = \$.935$$

With the calculation of unadjusted earnings per share, the first major building block in the process of computing earnings per share, in accordance with the provisions of APB Opinion No. 15, has been completed. The goal of this section has been to provide the reader with some essential background information that is necessary to proceed to the next section, which deals with contingent equity issues. Consideration of contingent equity issues will further complicate the determination of the numerator and denominator, as discussed above.

Contingent Equity Securities

For purposes of the following discussion, contingent equity securities are divided into three major categories: (1) options, warrants and their equivalent; (2) convertible securities; and (3) contingent agreements. Consideration first will be given to options, warrants and their equivalent. Since these securities may have a dilutive effect on EPS, the discussion below assumes that a dual presentation of EPS will be required. Whether a dual presentation will, in fact, be required is not known; however, making that assumption will aid in organizing the presentation. Further assume that the dual presentation required will include "Primary earnings per share" and "Fully diluted earnings per share." The discussion of options, warrants and their equivalent will be centered around their effect upon both primary and fully diluted EPS.

Options, Warrants and Their Equivalent—General Considerations

Options and warrants are securities that allow the holder to purchase shares of common stock for a specified price. The number of shares that may be purchased depends upon the terms of the option or warrant. Options, warrants and their equivalent are collectively referred to as common stock equivalents.

Paragraph 37 of the Opinion identifies some securities that are to be treated as warrants, and some special types of warrants. These securities, which are viewed as warrants, include:

(1) Convertible securities *requiring* a cash payment at the date of conversion;

(2) Convertible securities that *allow* a cash payment at the date of conversion;

(3) Warrants specifying that the proceeds from exercise *must* be used to retire debt or other securities;

(4) Warrants that *require* that debt of the issuing entity, instead of cash, be tendered as part or all of the total exercise price; and

(5) Warrants that *permit* the holder to tender cash or debt or other securities of the issuing entity in payment of the exercise price.

The unique feature of items 1 and 2 above is that the convertible security permits or requires the payment of cash upon conversion.

Normally, convertible securities do not require the payment of cash, but merely require that the security be surrendered. If cash is not permitted or required upon conversion, the security will not be included in items 1 and 2. Similarly, the unique feature of the *warrants* listed above relates to the method of payment of the exercise price, or the restricted use of the proceeds received upon exercise. While these securities are considered to be warrants, there are other items that are considered to be the equivalent of options or warrants. Securities considered to be the equivalent of options or warrants include (FASB, *Financial Accounting Standards—Original Pronouncements as of July 1, 1978,* "Unofficial Accounting Interpretations of APB Opinion No. 15," p. 602):

(1) Stock purchase agreements;

(2) Unpaid stock subscriptions;

(3) Deferred compensation plans requiring common stock issuance; and

(4) Stock appreciation rights and other variable stock options or awards.[1]

Common stock equivalents give the holder the right to become a common shareholder and, therefore, these securities represent an equivalent number of common shares that may be issued if the holder exercises his right. If certain tests are met, earnings per share is calculated on the *assumption* that the common stock equivalents are converted into actual common shares. The actual exchange into common shares has not taken place, but it is assumed that it has. Providing the tests are met, the holders of common stock equivalents are treated like common shareholders for purposes of the earnings per share computation.

Flowchart III outlines the major tests and related procedures to be followed to determine if common stock equivalents will be treated as if they were exercised for common stock, for purposes of the EPS calculation.

---

[1] FASB Interpretation No. 28 specifies that such stock appreciation rights and other variable stock option plan awards are considered to be common stock equivalents in the computation of earnings per share. When applying the treasury stock method, the "proceeds" are equal to the sum of the amount the employee must pay, the amount of compensation attributable to future services that has not been charged to expense, and any tax benefit that will be credited to capital. FASB Interpretation No. 31 modified FASB Interpretation No. 28 by requiring that the rights or awards that are payable in stock or *cash* be determined as common stock equivalents according to the terms most likely to be elected, based on the current fact situation existing at the end of the period. If the election appears to favor the payment of cash, the rights or awards are not considered common stock equivalents.

FLOWCHART III

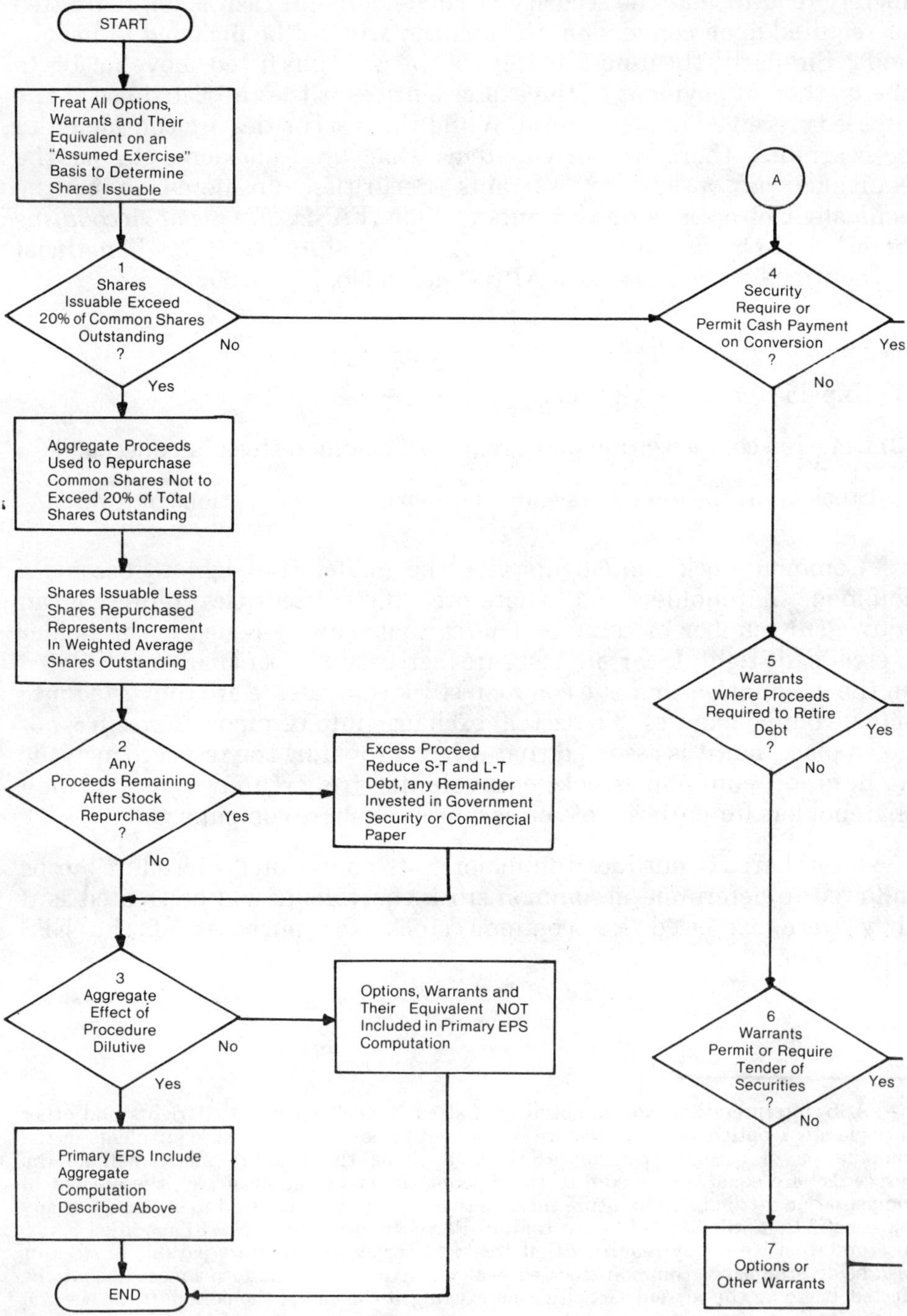

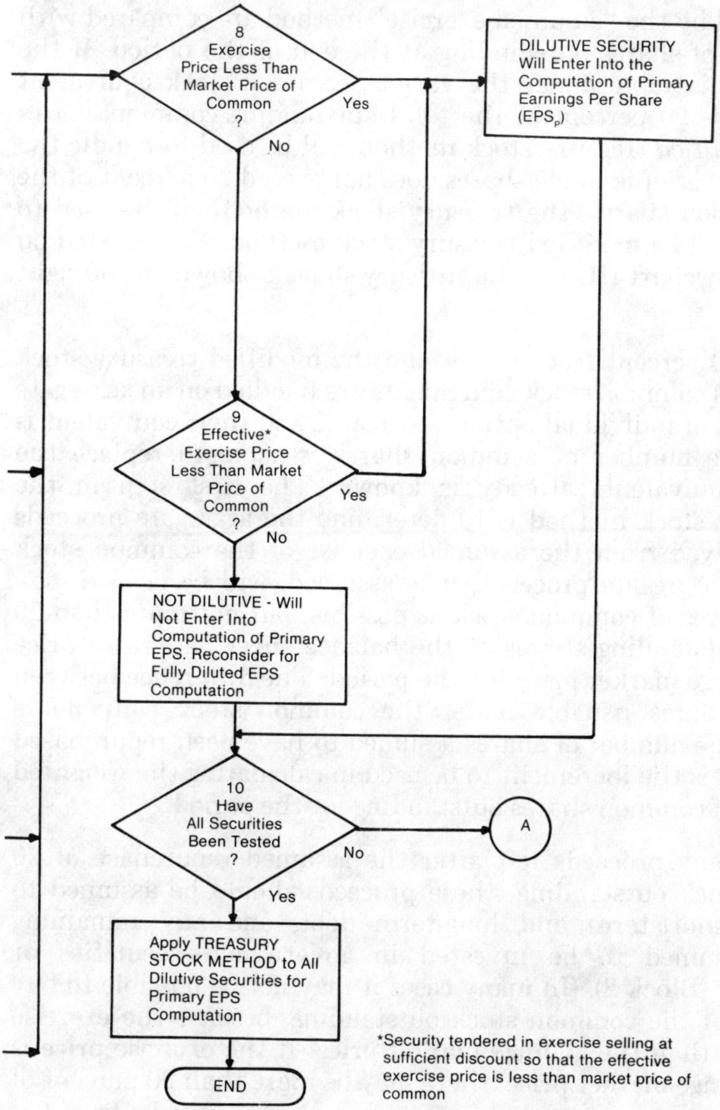
8
Exercise Price Less Than Market Price of Common ?
Yes
No
DILUTIVE SECURITY Will Enter Into the Computation of Primary Earnings Per Share (EPS_p)
9
Effective* Exercise Price Less Than Market Price of Common ?
Yes
No
NOT DILUTIVE - Will Not Enter Into Computation of Primary EPS. Reconsider for Fully Diluted EPS Computation
10
Have All Securities Been Tested ?
No
A
Yes
Apply TREASURY STOCK METHOD to All Dilutive Securities for Primary EPS Computation
END

*Security tendered in exercise selling at sufficient discount so that the effective exercise price is less than market price of common

To begin the process, all options, warrants and their equivalent must be identified. Once identified, all common stock equivalents are handled on an "assumed exercise" basis for the first major test. The "assumed exercise" method assumes that common stock equivalents *are exercised* and the applicable number of common shares are issued, either at the beginning of the accounting period or later if the common stock equivalents were issued later. After applying the "assumed exercise" method, the total number of common shares that would have to be issued if all common stock equivalents were exercised is known. The number of shares determined by the "assumed exercise" method are compared with the total number of shares outstanding at the end of the period. If the number of shares issuable under the various common stock equivalent agreements exceeds 20 percent of the total outstanding common shares (Block 1), the *modified* treasury stock method will be used to handle the shares. If the number of issuable shares does not exceed 20 percent of the outstanding common shares, the treasury stock method will be used to handle the shares. The modified treasury stock method is illustrated on the left side of Flowchart III, and the treasury stock is shown on the right side.

When the "20 percent test" *is* met and the modified treasury stock method is used, all common stock equivalents are handled on an aggregate basis, i.e., analysis of individual options, warrants and their equivalent is not required. The number of common shares issuable to replace the common stock equivalents already is known. The first step in the modified treasury stock method is to determine the aggregate proceeds that will be received from the assumed exercise of the common stock equivalents. The aggregate proceeds, it is assumed, will be used to buy back as many shares of common stock as possible, but not more than 20 percent of the outstanding shares at the balance sheet date, at a price equal to the average market price for the period. The difference between the number of shares issuable under the common stock equivalents agreements and the number of shares assumed to have been repurchased with the proceeds is the increment to be used in calculating the weighted average number of common shares outstanding for the period.

If there are any proceeds left after the assumed repurchase of 20 percent of the stock outstanding, these proceeds should be assumed to first eliminate short-term and long-term debt, and any remaining proceeds are assumed to be invested in government securities or commercial paper (Block 2). (In many cases it may not be possible to buy back 20 percent of the common stock outstanding, because the exercise price may be less than the average market price. If the exercise price is less than the average market price, there may be more than 20 percent of the shares outstanding represented by common stock equivalents; yet it still may not be possible to repurchase 20 percent of the stock, because of the difference between the exercise price and the average market price.)

The elimination of debt and investment in government securities or commercial paper would be assumed to have occurred at the beginning of the accounting period, or later if the debt had been issued after the beginning of the accounting period. The after-tax interest of the assumed debt elimination or government securities purchased is added to the numerator in the primary earnings computation.

If the application of the modified treasury stock method has a dilutive effect upon earnings per share, all common stock equivalents will be included in the calculation of *primary* earnings per share (EPSP). If the effects of the method are anti-dilutive, none of the common stock equivalents will be included in the calculation of primary earnings per share. When the "20 percent test" is met, the modified treasury stock method requires an *aggregate* computation for common stock equivalents.

When the shares issued, upon assumed exercise of the common stock equivalent, represent 20 percent or less of the outstanding common stock, the treasury stock method is used to handle the common stock equivalents. Under the treasury stock method, each common stock equivalent is handled on an individual basis to determine if it will enter into the computation of primary earnings per share. Only those common stock equivalents that are determined to be dilutive are considered in the EPSP computation.

Options, warrants and their equivalent are considered to be dilutive if either of the following conditions is met:

(1) The average market price exceeds the exercise price for substantially all (an 11-week period) of the three months prior to computation of EPS (Block 8);

(2) "The security which may be (or must be) tendered is selling at a price below that which it may be tendered under the option or warrant agreement and the resulting discount is sufficient to establish an effective exercise price below the market price of the common stock that can be obtained upon exercise." (APB Opinion No. 15, Paragraph 37)

(The Opinion *implies* that the options and warrants must be exercisable within five years of the balance sheet date and may be exercised currently if the holder desires.) If a common stock equivalent is found to be dilutive, it will be included in the calculation of EPSP; if it is not dilutive, it will be ignored.

The treasury stock method assumes that all dilutive common stock equivalents are exercised at the beginning of the period, or later if issued after the beginning of the period. The proceeds received, in excess of any required use of those proceeds, such as the retirement of debt, are assumed to be used to repurchase shares of common stock at the average market price for the period. The difference between the shares issuable under the common stock equivalents agreements and the number of shares repurchased with the proceeds represents the incremental number of shares in the determination of the weighted average shares outstanding.

If options, warrants and their equivalent *do not* meet the test for inclusion in the calculation of primary earnings per share, they still must be considered for the calculation of fully diluted earnings per share (EPSFD). Generally, if common stock equivalents are not included in the primary earnings per share computation, they will not be included in the fully diluted calculation. However, exceptions to this general rule do exist. When common stock equivalents *are included* in the EPSP computation, they must be reconsidered for the EPSFD computation. Recall that, for the EPSP computation, the exercise price of the common stock equivalents was compared with the *average* market price to determine if the security was dilutive. If the end of period market price is greater than the average market price, additional incremental shares will result. These incremental shares will be included in the calculation of EPSFD. If the average price is greater than the end of period price, no new computation is necessary and the same number of incremental shares will be used in both the primary and fully diluted EPS computations. The fully diluted computation is based upon a comparison of the end of period price with the exercise price, so as to obtain the maximum possible dilutive effect of the common stock equivalent.

Common Stock Equivalents—Effects on Primary EPS

The discussion above may have been difficult to follow, because of the technical nature of the treatment of common stock equivalents. The examples that follow will define more clearly any areas that proved hard to follow.

The impact of common stock equivalents on primary earnings per share and fully diluted earnings per share have been isolated in order to make the problem more manageable. To illustrate the effects of common stock equivalents on the computation of primary earnings per share, assume the facts listed in Exhibit V prevail.

Exhibit V

Options and Warrants - Example 1

1. Jar, Inc. has a December 31 year end. Earnings per share are to be calculated for the year ended December 31, 197C.
2. 1,500,000 common shares were outstanding for the entire year.

3. 50,000 warrants previously had been issued in 197A, with the holder receiving the right to purchase 50,000 common shares, at a price of $20 per share, any time after December 31, 197B.
4. The Company granted 200,000 stock options to a limited number of key employees on April 1, 197C. The options gave the holders the right to purchase 200,000 common shares, at a price of $22 per share, at any time after the date of grant.
5. The market price of Jar, Inc.'s common stock was above $22 per share for substantially all of 197C. Important average stock prices and the ending market price are presented below:

Average for the Year 197C	$24 per share
Average for April 1 to December 31, 197C	$25 per share
December 31, 197C ending market price	$30 per share

6. Jar, Inc. reported net income of $5,000,000 for the year ended December 31, 197C.

In reviewing these assumptions, notice that none of the options or warrants permits or requires the tendering of debt or other securities. Therefore, it will not be necessary to determine the "effective" exercise price. The total number of shares of common stock to be issued upon conversion of all options and warrants is 250,000 shares (50,000 under warrants, and 200,000 under the option agreement). The 250,000 shares that could be issued total less than 20 percent of all common shares outstanding at the end of the period (250,000/1,500,000 = 16.67 percent). The common stock equivalents do not meet the "20 percent test," and the treasury stock method will be used to determine any incremental shares.

Since the treasury stock method is to be used, each common stock equivalent must be tested separately to determine if it is dilutive. The average market price of the stock for 197C was $24 per share, which exceeded the $20 per share exercise price of the warrants. In addition, the market price of the stock was in excess of $22 per share for substantially all of 197C. Based upon these facts, the warrants are considered to be dilutive, and will enter into the calculation of EPSP. The next step is to determine the number of incremental shares resulting from the application of the treasury stock method. The following formula provides a short-cut approach to the calculation of the incremental shares:

$$S = \frac{MP - EP}{MP} \times NS$$

Where: S = Incremental shares
MP = Average Market price (or the greater of average or ending market price for fully diluted EPS)
EP = Exercise price of the option or warrant
NS = Number of shares issuable upon exercise of the option or warrant

This equation can be used only when the treasury stock method is applicable. It cannot be used if the options and warrants are anti-dilutive, or if the total number of issuable shares exceeds 20 percent of the outstanding common shares.

Based upon the information given in the example problem, the formula will provide the following results for the warrants:

$$S = \frac{\$24 - \$20}{\$24} \times 50{,}000 = 8{,}333$$

Therefore, 8,333 incremental shares will be added to the weighted average number of shares outstanding for the Company.

The 200,000 options will be considered next. The average market price per share applicable to the options is $25, which is the average price for the period of time the options were outstanding. The appropriate average market price exceeds the option price of $22 per share; and, therefore, the options also are considered to be dilutive for purposes of computing EPSP. The assumption is made, under the treasury stock method, that the options were exercised during the year, and that the proceeds from the exercise were used to repurchase common stock. The number of incremental shares to be added to the weighted average number of shares can be determined by using the formula given above. The results of the formula, when applied to the options, would be:

$$S = \frac{\$25 - \$22}{\$25} \times 200{,}000 = 24{,}000$$

Since the options were issued after the beginning of the year, they must be weighted for the appropriate period of time they have been outstanding. In this case the options were issued on April 1, 197C, and were outstanding for nine months during the period. The *weighted* incremental shares would be determined as follows:

$$24{,}000 \times 9/12 = 18{,}000$$

The 18,000 weighted shares will be added to the weighted average number of common shares outstanding during 197C.

All contingent equity issues in this example have been considered. The final step in the determination of the denominator for EPSP is to calculate the weighted average common shares outstanding during 197C. Since there were no new issues of common stock or purchases of treasury stock, the 1,500,000 common shares were outstanding all year.

The total weighted average number of common shares outstanding would be determined as follows:

Weighted Average Common Shares	1,500,000
Incremental Shares from Warrants	8,333
Weighted Incremental Shares from Options	18,000
Total Weighted Average Shares Outstanding	1,526,333

Because there is no preferred stock outstanding, the numerator of the EPSP will not be adjusted. The final step is to calculate EPSP. The calculation is shown below:

$$\text{EPSP} = \frac{\$5{,}000{,}000}{1{,}526{,}333} = \$3.28$$

Common Stock Equivalents—Effects on Fully Diluted EPS

Once primary earnings per share has been calculated, it is necessary to reconsider all options and warrants that were used or omitted from the primary calculation in the computation of fully diluted earnings per share. In the example problem given, all options and warrants were considered dilutive for the primary earnings per share computation. Therefore, any incremental shares used in the primary computation also will be used in the fully diluted computation. For purposes of fully diluted earnings per share, the exercise price of the warrants and options must be compared with the market price at the end of the period to determine if any additional incremental shares will be added to the fully diluted computation. Of course, if the average market price exceeds the end of period price, the average will be used, and no additional computations will be necessary.

By referring back to Exhibit V, notice that the December 31 market price is $30 per share, which is greater than the average market price of $24 per share for the warrants and $25 per share for the options. As a result, there will be some additional incremental shares for purposes of calculating fully diluted earnings per share. By using the equation given above, the following results are obtained for the warrants:

$$S = \frac{\$30 - \$20}{\$30} \times 50{,}000 = 16{,}667$$

For fully diluted earnings per share, there are 16,667 incremental shares as a result of the dilutive warrants. Since some incremental shares already are included in the primary calculation, only the additional incremental shares will be added. The additional incremental shares would be determined as follows:

Incremental Shares Using December 31 Market Price	16,667
Incremental Shares Using Average Market Price	8,333
Additional Incremental Shares to Be Added	8,334

The results for the options are shown below:

$$S = \frac{\$30 - \$22}{\$30} \times 200{,}000 = 53{,}333$$

The incremental shares using the year-end market price must be weighted for the nine months that the options were outstanding. Therefore, the weighted incremental shares would be 40,000 (53,333 × 9/12).

Incremental Shares Using December 31 Market Price	40,000
Incremental Shares Using Average Market Price	18,000
Additional Incremental Shares to Be Added	22,000

Based upon these computations, the total weighted average number of common shares outstanding for purposes of calculating fully diluted earnings per share would be determined as follows:

Number of Shares Used for Primary EPS Computation	1,526,333
Additional Incremental Shares for Warrants	8,334
Additional Incremental Shares for Options	22,000
Total Weighted Average Shares for Fully Diluted EPS Computation	1,556,667

Since there will be no change in the numerator, the computation of fully diluted earnings per share for Example 1 would be determined as follows:

$$EPSFD = \frac{\$5{,}000{,}000}{1{,}556{,}667} = \$3.21$$

Before a final determination can be made as to the proper presentation of EPS, it is necessary to see if the dilutive effect is three percent or more of unadjusted earnings per share (EPSU). If the dilutive effect is three percent or more, a dual presentation is required; if it is less than three percent, only unadjusted earnings per share will be reported.

To determine if the EPS calculations are dilutive by three percent or more, the fully diluted earnings per share (EPSFD) must be compared with unadjusted earnings per share, i.e., with earnings per share before consideration of any contingent equity issues. There is no preferred stock, so the numerator of EPSU will be equal to the reported net income of $5,000,000. There were no security issues or repurchase of treasury shares during the period, so the denominator of the EPSU equation will be the weighted average number of common shares outstanding of 1,500,000. Unadjusted earnings per share would be calculated as follows:

$$EPSU = \frac{\$5{,}000{,}000}{1{,}500{,}000} = \$3.33$$

The following equation can be used to determine the dilutive effect of the computations made above:

$$ADR = \frac{EPSFD}{EPSU}$$

Where: ADR = Aggregate Dilution Reciprocal
EPSFD = Fully Diluted Earnings per Share
EPSU = Unadjusted Earnings per Share

The formula provides the following repicrocal for the information in Example 1:

$$ADR = \frac{\$3.21}{\$3.33} = 96.4 \text{ percent}$$

Since 96.4 percent is less than 97 percent, a dual presentation of earnings per share is required. EPSP will be reported at $3.28, and EPSFD will be reported at $3.21.

The approach taken to the solution of the Example 1 problem was to determine common stock equivalents on an incremental basis. The example that follows utilizes the gross approach in the computation of fully diluted earnings per share.

Common Stock Equivalents—Effects on Primary EPS

The example just completed was relatively straightforward, although it did introduce several new concepts. To illustrate a more complex situation, the assumptions listed in Exhibit VI will be used.

Exhibit VI

Options and Warrants—Example 2

1. Book-It, Inc. has a December 31 year end. The period under consideration is January 1, 197D to December 31, 197D.
2. 2,000,000 common shares were outstanding on January 1, 197D.
3. 100,000 warrants were issued in 197B with the right to purchase 100,000 shares of common stock at a price of $30 per share any time after December 31, 197C. The warrants expire on December 31, 197E. The proceeds from the exercise of the options must be used to retire an eight percent, $2,500,025 note, payable on December 31, 197E. Book-It has a 52 percent tax rate.
4. 100,000 options were exercised on October 1, 197D. The options had been granted to a limited number of employees on April 1, 197C, with the right to purchase 100,000 shares of stock at a price of $28 per share.
5. 20,000 warrants that were issued in 197A were exercised on July 1, 197D for 20,000 shares of common stock. The warrants had an exercise price of $35 per share.
6. The market price was above $31 for all of 197D. The averages and period-end market prices for the time periods indicated below are:

Average for 197D	$35
Average from January 1 to October 1, 197D	$37
Average from January 1 to July 1, 197D	$34
July 1, 197D market price	$34
October 1, 197D market price	$36
December 31, 197D market price	$38

7. Net income for Book-It for 197D was $10,000,000.

The analysis begins, as before, with a determination of the number of shares that would be issued if all options and warrants outstanding were exercised. The warrants identified in Assumption 3 of Exhibit VI would require the issuance of 100,000 shares of common stock. The options in Assumption 4 were exercised in 197D and are part of the common stock outstanding, and thus no longer would represent a contingent equity security. The warrants identified in Assumption 5 also represent the exercise of a former contingent equity security and do not represent any issuable shares. Therefore, the shares that would be issued if all options and warrants were exercised amount to the 100,000 common shares from Assumption 3. This total must be compared with the total number of shares outstanding at the end of 197D for purposes of the "20 percent test." The number of shares outstanding on December 31, 197D is shown below:

Shares Outstanding at the Beginning of 197D	2,000,000
Issued Upon the Exercise of Options on October 1	100,000
Issued Upon the Exercise of Warrants on July 1	20,000
Total Shares Outstanding at December 31, 197D	2,120,000

The relationship between the number of shares issuable upon the exercise of all of the outstanding warrants and the total number of shares outstanding at the end of 197D is shown below:

$$\text{Percentage Relationship} = \frac{100{,}000}{2{,}120{,}000} = 4.7 \text{ percent}$$

The issuable shares represent 4.7 percent of the total number of shares outstanding. This is less than the 20 percent required to meet the "20 percent test"; therefore, the treasury stock method is applicable to the handling of the warrants for purposes of computing primary earnings per share.

The warrants are the only common stock equivalent outstanding at the end of the period. If they are to be included in EPSP they must be dilutive. To be dilutive, the exercise price—either actual or effective—must be less than the market price of the common stock for substantially all of the three month period preceding the calculation of EPSP. The average market price of the common stock was $35 per share for 197D, and the exercise price of the 100,000 warrants is $30 per share. Therefore, the warrants are considered to be dilutive and will be used in the EPSP computation.

The proceeds received from the exercise of the warrants must be used to retire the eight percent, \$2,500,025 note payable. Any proceeds in excess of \$2,500,025 will be used to repurchase common stock at the average market price. The proceeds of \$3,000,000 (100,000 warrants × \$30 per share) will be used to retire the \$2,500,025 debt, and the excess proceeds of \$499,975 (\$3,000,000 − \$2,500,025) are assumed to be used to repurchase common stock at the average market price of \$35 per share. The number of shares that can be repurchased with the excess proceeds is shown below:

$$\text{Number of Shares Repurchased} = \frac{\$499{,}975}{\$35} = 14{,}285$$

The difference between the number of shares issuable (100,000) and the number of shares that could be repurchased with the excess proceeds (14,285) represents the incremental number of shares that will be added to the weighted average number of shares in the denominator of the equation to calculate EPSP. The number of incremental shares to be added is equal to 85,715.

However, the assumed exercise of the warrants affects both the denominator *and* the numerator of the equation. Remember the assumption was that the eight percent debt would be retired with the proceeds from the exercise, and that the retirement would be treated as if it occurred at the beginning of 197D. Therefore, the interest expense in connection with the retired debt must be removed from the numerator of the equation. If the assumption is made that the debt is retired, then it is impossible to have any interest from the debt included in income.

The interest expense recorded in 197D for the debt assumed to be retired was \$200,002 (\$2,500,025 × 8%). This must be removed from the reported income for 197D. Interest is deductible for income tax purposes, and the fact that the company had interest expense reduced its tax liability. Therefore, it is necessary to remove the after-tax effect of the \$200,002 interest expense. The after-tax interest is computed using the following formula:

$$AI = I(1 - T)$$

Where: AI = Adjusted After-Tax Income
I = Period Interest Expense
T = Tax Rate

Based upon the information developed above, the formula provides the following results:

$$AI = \$200{,}002\,(1 - .52) = \$96{,}001$$

So $96,001 must be *added* to net income in an adjustment to the numerator of the EPSP equation.

The next problem to be addressed is the treatment given to the options that were exercised on October 1, 197D. At the end of the year, all the options were exercised and had to be included in the computation of the weighted average number of shares outstanding during 197D. However, the options were a contingent equity issue for part of 197D and had to be treated as such for the partial period. The options were outstanding for nine months in 197D, and the first step is to determine if they were dilutive during this period of time. The average market price for the partial period (January 1 through October 1) was $37 per share, and the exercise price of the options was $28 per share. Since the average market price was greater than the exercise price, the options were dilutive for the partial period and will enter into the calculation of EPSP. To determine the incremental shares to be added to the denominator, the following formula can be used:

$$S = \left(\frac{MP - EP}{MP} \times NS\right) \times PT$$

Where:
S = Incremental Shares
MP = Average Market Price per Share
EP = Exercise Price per Share of Options or Warrants
NS = Number of Shares Issuable Upon Exercise
PT = Partial Time Period

Application of the formula to the information given provides the following incremental shares:

$$S = \left(\frac{\$37 - \$28}{\$37} \times 100{,}000\right) \times 9/12 = 18{,}243$$

These 18,243 incremental shares will be added to the number of weighted average shares represented by the exercised options.

The options were exercised on October 1, 197D, and were considered as common stock outstanding for three months of 197D. The options resulted in a total of 100,000 common shares being issued. This represents 25,000 weighted common shares ($100{,}000 \times 3/12$). The 25,000 shares just determined will be added to the 18,243 incremental shares, to equal a total of 43,243 shares, which represents the common share effect of the options identified in Assumption 4. There is no adjustment to the numerator of the EPSP equation as a result of the exercise of the options.

The final contingent issue to be considered is the warrants identified in Assumption 5 of the problem. The treatment of the warrants is similar to the treatment given the options above. The average market price for the partial period (January 1 through July 1, 197D) was $34 per share, and the exercise price was $35 per share. Because the exercise price exceeded the average market price, the warrants are considered to be anti-dilutive during the partial period. The warrants will not be considered in the calculation of EPSP. This is a very unusual situation and was developed for illustrative purposes only.

The warrants were exercised on July 1, 197D for 20,000 common shares. The common shares were outstanding for six months and represent 10,000 weighted shares (20,000 × 6/12).

The analysis of the options and warrants now has been completed, and it is helpful to recap the results of the preceding computations to show their effect on the computation of EPSP.

	Increase (Decrease) In:	
	Numerator (Income)	Denominator (Shares)
Proceeds to Retire Debt	$ 96,001	85,715
100,000 Options Exercised	none	43,243
20,000 Warrants Exercised	none	10,000
Total	$ 96,001	138,958

The addition of the $96,001 to the $10,000,000 of reported net income gives a final numerator for primary earnings per share of $10,096,001. Since there were no issues or repurchases of common stock during the period, the denominator of the equation consists of the 138,958 shares from above, and the 2,000,000 shares that were outstanding all year, for a total of 2,138,958. The computation of EPSP is shown below:

$$\text{EPSP} = \frac{\$10{,}096{,}001}{2{,}138{,}958} = \$4.72$$

This same information now will be used to compute fully diluted earnings per share.

Common Stock Equivalents—Effects Upon Fully Diluted EPS

After primary earnings per share have been calculated, it is necessary to reconsider all options and warrants for the fully diluted earnings per share computation. If the end of period market price per share of the common stock is greater than the average market price per share, additional common shares will be added to the denominator of the EPSP equation. If the average market price per share is greater than the end of period market price, the incremental shares used in the EPSP computation will also be used in the EPSFD computation.

First consider the 100,000 warrants issued that required that the proceeds from exercise be used to retire the $2,500,025, eight percent note payable. With an exercise price of $30 per share, the total proceeds from the exercise of all warrants would be \$3,000,000. As computed in the EPSP calculation, the excess proceeds would amount to \$499,975. The ending market price per share of common stock was \$38, while the average for the year was \$35 per share. Since the end of period market price is greater than the average price during the period, the ending price will be used to determine the number of shares that could be repurchased with the excess proceeds. This is done in order to obtain the maximum possible dilution resulting from the issue of the warrants. The computation of the shares repurchased is shown below:

$$\text{Number of Shares Repurchased} = \frac{\$499{,}975}{\$38} = 13{,}157$$

The difference between the number of shares (100,000) issued upon exercise of the warrants and the number of shares (13,157) that could be repurchased with the excess proceeds is equal to the number of shares that will be included in the denominator of the EPSFD computation, along with the weighted average number of common shares. In this case, 86,843 shares will be added to the denominator of the EPSFD equation for the warrants.

The next item to be reconsidered is the 100,000 options that were exercised on October 1, 197D. The market price of the common stock was \$36 per share on October 1 (the end of the period for the options), and the average market price of common shares for the period January 1 through October 1 was \$37 per share. Because the end of period price was less than the average market price, no additional consideration is needed for the options. The 18,243 incremental shares calculated for the primary earnings per share computation also will be used in the fully diluted computation. The optioned common shares that were outstanding from October 1 through December 31, 197D, have a weighted number of shares equal to 25,000. The total number of shares included in the denominator from the options is 43,243 (25,000 + 18,243), which is the same total used in the primary earnings per share computation.

The final item to be reconsidered is the issue of 20,000 warrants that were exercised on July 1, 197D. There were no incremental shares from the partial period included in the primary earnings per share computation, because the exercise price of \$35 per share was greater than the average market price of \$34 per share. The conclusion was that the warrants were anti-dilutive.

When warrants or options are exercised during the year, they are included in the calculation of fully diluted earnings per share, even though they are anti-dilutive. The market price on the *date of exercise* is used to determine the number of shares that could have been purchased with the proceeds. The proceeds from the exercise of the 20,000 warrants was \$700,000 (20,000 × \$35 per share). The \$700,000 proceeds could have been used to repurchase 20,588 ($700,000/$34 market price per share) common shares on the exercise date. The difference between the 20,588 shares repurchased and the 20,000 shares issued represents 588 incremental shares that are anti-dilutive and that must be *deducted* from the weighted average shares outstanding.

From the EPSP computation, it was determined that the weighted shares represented by the exercise of the warrants was 10,000 (20,000 × $\frac{6}{12}$). Therefore, the number of shares to be included from the exercise of the warrants in the fully diluted earnings per share computation is 9,706 (10,000 – (588 × $\frac{6}{12}$)).

All options and warrants now have been reconsidered, and the recap below summarizes the results of the calculations to this point.

	Increase (Decrease) In:	
	Numerator (Income)	Denominator (Shares)
Warrants to Retire Debt	$ 96,001	86,843
100,000 Options Exercised	none	43,243
20,000 Warrants Exercised	none	9,706
Total	$ 96,001	139,792

The numerator of the fully diluted earnings per share equation will be the same as that used in the primary earnings per share computation—$10,096,001. The 139,792 shares shown above will be added to the 2,000,000 weighted average number of common shares outstanding to yield a denominator for the equation of 2,139,792. Fully diluted earnings per share is calculated below:

$$\text{EPSFD} = \frac{\$10{,}096{,}001}{2{,}139{,}792} = \$4.718$$

After completing all of the previous calculations, it is now time to determine if the common stock equivalents used in the computations are, in the aggregate, dilutive by three percent or more. If they are not dilutive by three percent or more, none of the above calculation will be used, and only one earnings per share presentation is required.

The extent of the dilution is measured by the relationship between the fully diluted earnings per share and the unadjusted earnings per share. Unadjusted earnings per share do not include any contingent equity issues. The weighted average number of common shares outstanding for purposes of computing the unadjusted earnings per share is determined as follows:

Shares Outstanding Entire Year	2,000,000
Weighted Shares from Exercise of Options	25,000
Weighted Shares from Exercise of Warrants	10,000
Total Weighted Average Shares Outstanding	2,035,000

Since there were no senior nonconvertible securities outstanding, there would be no adjustment to the reported net income of $10,000,000. The computation of the unadjusted earnings per share is shown below:

$$\text{EPSU} = \frac{\$10{,}000{,}000}{2{,}035{,}000} = \$4.91$$

Finally, the fully diluted earnings per share of $4.718 is divided by the unadjusted earnings per share of $4.91 to determine the aggregate dilution reciprocal (ADR). The computation is shown below:

$$\text{ADR} = \frac{\$4.718}{\$4.91} = 96.1 \text{ percent}$$

Since the aggregate dilution reciprocal is below 97 percent, the common stock equivalents are, in the aggregate, dilutive by three percent or more. Therefore, a dual presentation of earnings per share is required as follows:

Primary Earnings per Share	$4.72
Fully Diluted Earnings per Share	$4.718

Options, Warrants and Their Equivalent— The "20 Percent" Rule

In the two examples given above, the treasury stock method was used to handle options, warrants and their equivalent, because the number of shares that could be repurchased with the proceeds from the exercise of these items was less than 20 percent of the outstanding common stock. The assumptions listed in Exhibit VII provide an example where the "20 percent" test is met, and the modified treasury stock method must be used. Primary and fully diluted earnings per share will be discussed together, instead of being separated as in the previous examples. By now the reader should be familiar with the procedure required to handle contingent equity issues in the primary and fully diluted computations, and separate discussion is not necessary.

Exhibit VII

Options, Warrants and the "20 Percent" Rule

1. Book-It, Inc. has a December 31 year end and is preparing to calculate earnings per share for the year ended December 31, 197D.
2. 1,000,000 shares of common stock were outstanding during all of 197D.
3. 300,000 warrants were issued in 197A, giving the holders the right to purchase 300,000 shares of common stock, at a price of $50 per share, any time after December 31, 197B.

4. 25,000 warrants were issued on 197C, giving the holders the right to purchase 25,000 shares of common stock, at a price of $58 per share, any time after December 31, 197C.
5. The market price of the stock was above $51 per share for all of 197D. The average market price and the year-end market price of the common stock were equal to $53 per share.
6. Book-It, Inc. has $2,000,000 of eight percent short-term notes payable and $5,000,000 of seven percent long-term bonds payable. There is no other short- or long-term debt.
7. Book-It reported net income for 197D of $8,500,000. The tax rate applicable to the Company is 50 percent.

As with the two previous examples, the first step is to determine the number of issuable shares relating to the options and warrants. In this example, 325,000 common shares would be issued if the warrants and options all were exercised (300,000 from the 197A warrants and 25,000 from the 197C warrants). This total must be compared with the total number of common shares outstanding at the end of the period. The issuable shares represent 32.5 percent of the total shares outstanding (325,000/1,000,000 = 32.5 percent); therefore, the common stock equivalents meet the "20 percent" rule, and the modified treasury stock method will be used. Under the modified treasury stock method, all common stock equivalents are considered in the aggregate, rather than individually, to determine if they are dilutive.

Like the treasury stock method, the modified treasury stock method assumes that the proceeds from the exercise of the warrants will be used to repurchase shares of common stock at the average market price during the period. However, the number of common shares assumed to be repurchased must not exceed 20 percent of the total outstanding common stock at the end of the period. In this example, there were 1,000,000 common shares outstanding on December 31, 197D; therefore, no more than 200,000 (1,000,000 × 20%) shares may be treated as repurchased. If there are proceeds remaining after the repurchase of 20 percent of the shares outstanding, they will be assumed to be used to retire short-term debt of the company; if all the short-term debt is retired with the proceeds, the remainder will be used to retire long-term debt. Finally, if proceeds still remain after all short- and long-term debt has been retired, they will be invested in government securities or commercial paper.

The proceeds from the assumed exercise of the warrants is determined as follows:

300,000 Warrants × $50 Per Share Price	$15,000,000
25,000 Warrants × $58 Per Share Price	1,450,000
Total Proceeds from Exercise of Warrants	$16,450,000

With proceeds of $16,450,000, the company could repurchase 310,377 common shares at the average market price of $53 per share ($16,450,000/$53). However, under the modified treasury stock method, the company is limited to the repurchase of 200,000 common shares, i.e., 20 percent of the common shares outstanding. Given this limitation, the following computation is necessary:

Total Proceeds from Exercise of Warrants	$16,450,000
Repurchase of 200,000 Shares (200,000 × $53)	(10,600,000)
Excess Proceeds from Exercise	$ 5,850,000

The excess proceeds will be used to eliminate the short-term debt first. Book-It, Inc. has $2,000,000 of short-term notes payable that will be eliminated by the excess proceeds. After this has been done, the remaining proceeds amount to $3,850,000 ($5,850,000 – $2,000,000). The $3,850,000 remaining proceeds will be used to reduce the long-term debt of $5,000,000. The long-term debt assumed to be remaining after the reduction is equal to $1,150,000 ($5,000,000 – $3,850,000). There are no proceeds available to be invested in government securities or commercial paper, because the entire amount of the long-term debt was not eliminated.

The modified treasury stock method assumes that the debt is retired at the beginning of the year (or later if issued after the beginning of the year). If the debt is to be eliminated, the interest associated with the debt also must be eliminated. The following computation shows the interest expense associated with the debt assumed to be retired:

Short-Term Debt ($2,000,000 × 8%)	$160,000
Long-Term Debt ($3,850,000 × 7%)	269,500
Pre-Tax Interest to be Eliminated	$429,500

Since net income is reported on an after-tax basis, and the interest in this calculation is on a pre-tax basis, it is necessary to adjust the interest to an after-tax basis. The tax rate applicable to Book-It was given as 50 percent. By using the formula discussed earlier, the following after-tax adjustment is necessary:

$$\text{After-Tax Interest} = \$429{,}500\,(1 - .50) = \$214{,}750$$

The $214,750 will be added to the numerator for the earnings per share computation.

The adjustment required to the denominator of the equation is based upon the incremental shares resulting from the assumed exercise of the warrants. If all the warrants were to be exercised, 325,000 common shares would be issued. However, the proceeds from the exercise could be used to repurchase 200,000 common shares (due to the limitation), so there would be 125,000 incremental shares as a result of using the modified treasury stock method. These incremental shares will be added to the denominator of the earnings per share equation.

For purposes of the "20 percent" rule, the numerator of the earnings per share equation would be $8,714,750 ($8,500,000 net income + $214,750 interest adjustment), and the denominator would be 1,125,000 shares (1,000,000 shares outstanding the entire year + 125,000 incremental shares). Therefore, earnings per share under the "20 percent" rule would be computed as follows:

$$\text{EPS} = \frac{\$8{,}714{,}750}{1{,}125{,}000} = \$7.75$$

The last step is to determine if the earnings per share just calculated is dilutive, when compared to the unadjusted earnings per share. For purposes of calculating EPSU, there are no adjustments necessary to either the numerator or the denominator. This is true because no new shares were issued during the period and no treasury shares were acquired, and there is no preferred stock outstanding. The computation of EPSU is shown below:

$$\text{EPSU} = \frac{\$8{,}500{,}000}{1{,}000{,}000} = \$8.50$$

Because the earnings per share calculated under the modified treasury stock method is less than the EPSU, the warrants are considered to be dilutive in the aggregate. However, some of the common stock equivalents used may be anti-dilutive. An examination of the 25,000 warrants issued in 197C indicate that they are anti-dilutive, since the exercise price of $58 per share is greater than the average market price of $53 per share. The modified treasury stock method requires that all contingent equity issues be handled in the aggregate; and, obviously, the impact of the other warrants offset the anti-dilutive effect of the warrants issued in 197C.

Since the average market price per share is equal to the end of period market price, there would be no additional incremental shares for the fully diluted earnings per share computation. The $7.75 per share calculated above is both the fully diluted and primary earnings per share amount.

To determine the proper presentation of earnings per share, the aggregate dilution reciprocal must be computed. This computation is shown below:

$$\text{ADR} = \frac{\$7.75}{\$8.50} = 91.2 \text{ percent}$$

Since the ADR is below 97 percent, the common stock equivalents are, in the aggregate, dilutive by three percent or more, and a dual presentation of earnings per share is required. The following presentation would be appropriate for this example:

Primary Earnings Per Share	$7.75
Fully Diluted Earnings Per Share	$7.75

Had there been a difference between the average market price per share and the end of period market price per share, there might have been some additional incremental shares to be considered in the fully diluted earnings per share computation. However, this point has been covered in the two previous examples and was intentionally omitted from the example just concluded.

Options, Warrants and Their Equivalent—Variations in Stock Prices

One assumption made in all of the previous examples was that the average market price exceeded the exercise price for substantially all of the year. This avoided the problem of handling common stock equivalents in a situation where the value of the common stock varied widely from one time period to the next. In reality, the incremental number of shares resulting from the assumed exercise of common stock equivalents probably will be calculated on a quarter-by-quarter basis. In fact, if the average market price does not exceed the exercise price for substantially all of each of the four *quarters* of the year, the weighted average computation must be made on a quarter-by-quarter basis.

The assumptions listed in Exhibit VIII are designed to illustrate the computation of incremental shares from options and warrants on the quarter-by-quarter method.

Exhibit VIII

Options and Warrants in a Quarterly Computation

1. 200,000 warrants were issued prior to the current year, giving the holders the right to purchase 200,000 shares of common stock at $25 per share.
2. The following average market price and ending market price information is provided for each quarter of the current year:

Quarter	Average Market Price	Ending Market Price
1	$28	$30
2	$23	$26
3	$24	$23
4	$29	$28

3. The 200,000 shares issuable upon exercise of the warrants do not represent more than 20 percent of the outstanding common stock at the end of the year.

Because the shares issuable upon exercise of the warrants do not exceed 20 percent of the common shares outstanding, the treasury stock method of handling the warrants is appropriate. For purposes of computing primary earnings per share, the warrants will be considered to be dilutive if the average market price per share during the quarter is greater than the exercise price. If the warrants are not dilutive in any quarter, they will not be considered in the primary earnings per share computation. The equation for determining the number of incremental shares was given earlier, but will be repeated for convenience.

$$S = \frac{MP - EP}{MP} \times NS$$

Where: S = Incremental Shares
MP = Average Market Price (or the greater of average or ending market price for fully diluted EPS)
EP = Exercise Price of Options or Warrants
NS = Number of Shares Issuable upon Exercise

Table V shows the determination of whether the warrants are dilutive in a given quarter and, if dilutive, the number of incremental shares the warrants would represent. The computations in the Table apply only to the computation of primary earnings per share.

Table V

Incremental Shares for Primary EPS

Quarter	Are Warrants Dilutive	Computation		Incremental Shares
1	Yes	$\frac{\$28 - \$25}{\$28} \times 200{,}000$	= 21,429 × 3/12	5,357
2	No	None		-0-
3	No	None		-0-
4	Yes	$\frac{\$29 - \$25}{\$29} \times 200{,}000$	= 27,586 × 3/12	6,897
Total Incremental Shares				12,254

The average market price in the second quarter was $23 per share, which was less than the exercise price of $25 per share; thus, the warrants cannot be considered to be dilutive. In the third quarter, the average market price was $24 per share, which still is less than the exercise price, so the warrants also were excluded in this quarter.

When an option or warrant is found to be dilutive, the formula given yields the incremental shares for the entire year; the incremental shares must be weighted for the three-month period under consideration. The total incremental shares (12,254) will be added to the weighted average number of common shares outstanding, and this total will be used in the denominator of the primary earnings per share equation.

Once the number of incremental shares has been determined for the calculation of primary earnings per share, it is necessary to reconsider all of them for the fully diluted earnings per share computation. The number of incremental shares used in the EPSFD computation is based upon the end of period market price per share, rather than on the average price. However, if the average market price per share is greater than the end of period price, the average price will be used in the calcuation of EPSFD. During the first and second quarters of the year, the ending market price is greater than the average price; and, therefore, the end of period price will be used to determine the number of incremental shares for the first two quarters. In the third quarter, both the average market price per share and the end of period price are less than the exercise, so the warrants are considered anti-dilutive in the third quarter. In the fourth quarter, the average market price is greater than the end of period price, so the average market price will be used, rather than the ending market price. Table VI summarizes the computation of incremental shares for the fully diluted earnings per share calculation.

Table VI

Incremental Shares for Fully Diluted EPS

Quarter	Are Warrants Dilutive	Computation	Incremental Shares
1	Yes	$\frac{\$30 - \$25}{\$30} \times 200{,}000 = 33{,}333 \times 3/12$	8,333
2	Yes	$\frac{\$26 - \$25}{\$26} \times 200{,}000 = 7{,}692 \times 3/12$	1,923
3	No	none	-0-
4	Yes	$\frac{\$29 - \$25}{\$29} \times 200{,}000 = 27{,}586 \times 3/12$	6,897
Total Incremental Shares			17,153

The total incremental shares that will be added to the weighted average common shares outstanding for the computation of fully diluted earnings per share is 17,153. This is 4,899 (17,153 – 12,254) more shares than were used in the primary earnings per share computation.

This completes the discussion of material relating to the effect of options, warrants and their equivalent on the computation of earnings per share. The next section will deal with the effects of convertible securities on the EPS calculation.

Flowchart and General Discussion—Convertible Securities

Convertible securities are securities that may be exchanged for common stock, based upon some predetermined agreement. The most common types of convertible securities are convertible debt and convertible preferred stock. The issuing company uses the conversion privilege to make the security offering more attractive to the investor. The holder of the convertible security may become a common shareholder by "trading in" the debt or preferred stock for a specified number of common shares. These types of securities could have a dilutive effect upon earnings per share if converted. This is the reason they must be considered in the computation of earnings per share.

Flowchart IV depicts the classification and accounting process for convertible securities. A convertible security may be considered a common stock equivalent and included in the calculation of primary earnings per share, or it may fail the tests necessary to become a common stock equivalent and only be considered in the process of computing fully diluted earnings per share. For a convertible security to be classified as a common stock equivalent, it must be convertible currently or within five years from the balance sheet date (Block 1), and meet the "cash yield" test (Block 2). The cash yield test specifies that, for a convertible security to be classified as a common stock equivalent, its cash yield must be less than two-thirds of the bank prime interest rate at the date of *issuance.* The cash yield is equal to the annual cash interest or dividend, divided by the sales price of the security. The sales price of the security does not consider brokerage commissions, transfer taxes and other selling costs.

The cash yield test is performed on the date the security is issued. Once the security has been classified as a common stock equivalent, its status does not change. A security that previously has not been classified as a common stock equivalent later may become a common stock equivalent if another convertible issue (with identical provisions to the excluded security) is classified as a common stock equivalent on the date of issue (Block 4). If two securities have identical provisions, it would not be appropriate to classify one issue and not the other as a common stock equivalent.

If a convertible security fails to meet the cash yield test, and is not classified as a common stock equivalent, it will not be included in the computation of primary earnings per share. However, it may be considered again during the computation of fully diluted earnings per share. Be careful not to confuse convertible securities with convertible securities that permit or require a cash payment upon conversion. The latter are considered to be the equivalent of warrants for the purposes of calculating EPS.

FLOWCHART IV

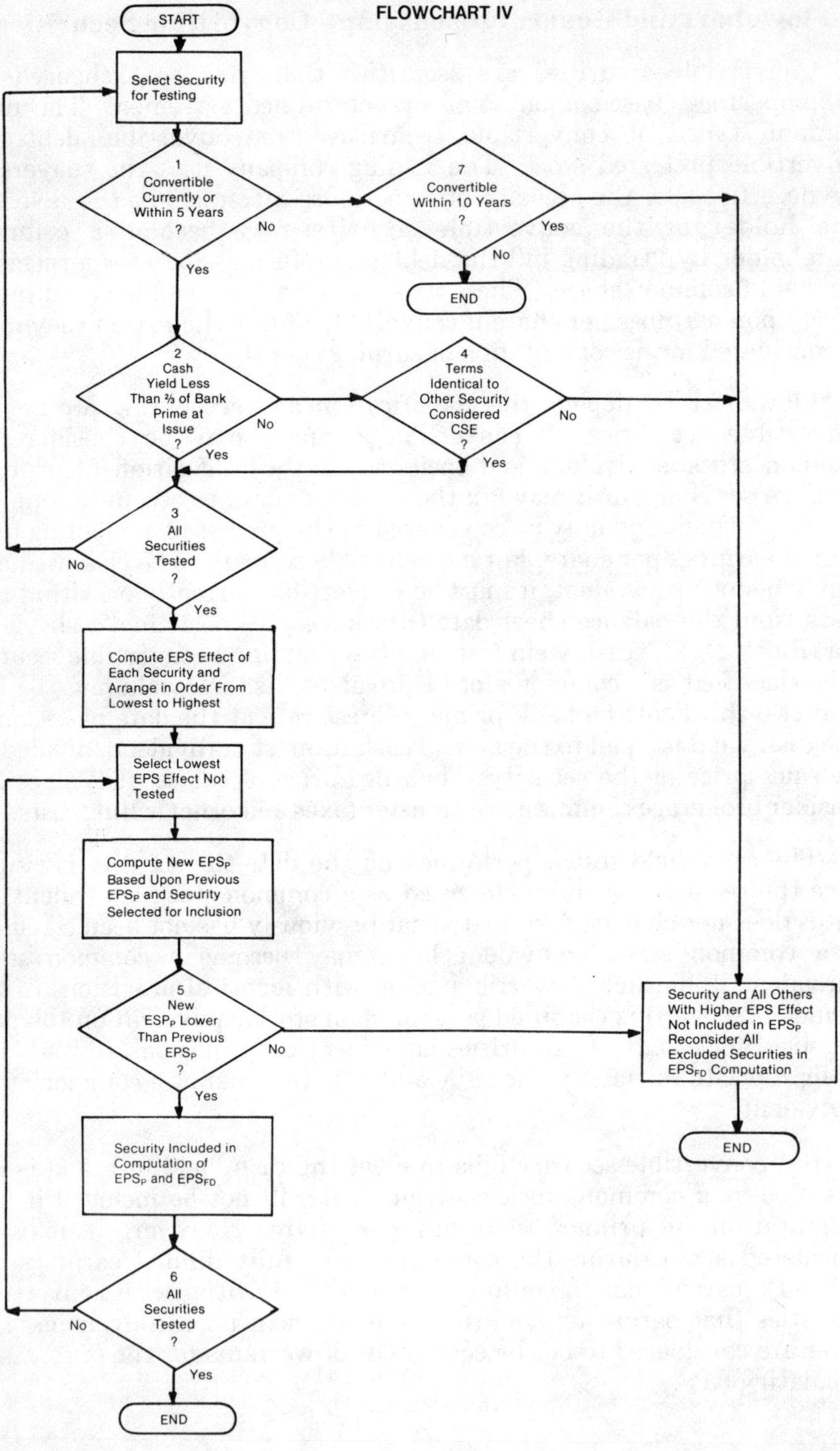

For a convertible security classified as a common stock equivalent to enter into the calculation of primary earnings per share, it must be dilutive. Convertible securities are the last items considered in the EPS computation. Options and warrants and contingent agreements already would have been considered prior to consideration of the convertible securities. (The effects of contingent agreements will be discussed in the next section. While they are important to the computation of earnings per share, *warrants, options* and *convertible securities* are of primary importance at this stage of the discussion.) The convertible securities must be dilutive in relation to the previous calculation of primary earnings per share. To be dilutive, the earnings per share effect of the convertible security must be less than the previously calculated primary earnings per share amount (Block 5). The earnings per share effect of a convertible security is determined by dividing the number of shares obtainable upon conversion into the annual dividend or after-tax interest associated with the security. If there is more than one convertible security, the earnings per share effect of each must be determined separately, and the test for dilution will begin with the security that has the lowest earnings per share. A new primary earnings per share will be computed, using the previous EPSP and the earnings per share effect determined to be the lowest. Each successive convertible security will be compared to the new primary earnings per share amount to determine if it is dilutive. The process continues on an individual security basis until all securities have been tested (Block 6).

When convertible debt is found to be a common stock equivalent that has a dilutive effect upon earnings per share, the number of shares issuable upon conversion are included in the denominator of the EPSP computation, using the "if converted" method. "If converted" method assumes that the debt was converted at the beginning of the year (or later if issued after the beginning of the year), and it is necessary to adjust the numerator of the equation for the after-tax effect of the interest expense recorded during the period. If there is a discount or premium associated with the convertible debt, it must be taken into consideration in the determination of interest expense and the after-tax effect of the expense.

It also is assumed that convertible preferred stock that is classified as a common stock equivalent and is dilutive was converted at the beginning of the period (or later if issued later). The number of common shares issuable upon conversion should be included in the denominator of the EPSP equation. There may be an adjustment necessary for the preferred dividend declared, paid or in arrears. In an earlier discussion, preferred dividends were deducted from net income to arrive at net income available for common shareholders. If the assumption is made that the preferred stock is converted into common shares, this deduction is not appropriate, and the preferred dividends must be added back to net income. If preferred dividends were not previously deducted from net income, no adjustment is required.

If a convertible security is used in the EPSP computation, it also will be used in the fully diluted calculation. Convertible securities that were not included in the EPSP computation must be reconsidered for the EPSFD computation. If the security is convertible within 10 years of the balance sheet date (Block 7) and is dilutive, using the same procedures described for the primary earnings per share computation, it will enter into the EPSFD computation. The adjustments necessary to the numerator and denominator for EPSFD would be determined in the same manner as would the adjustment for the EPSP computation.

Convertible Securities—Effects on Earnings Per Share

To illustrate the effects of convertible securities on the calculation of primary and fully diluted earnings per share, the assumptions listed in Exhibit IX will be used.

Exhibit IX

Convertible Securities—Example 1

1. Book-It, Inc. has a December 31 year end and is preparing to calculate earnings per share for the year ended December 31, 197E.
2. There were 4,000,000 shares of common stock outstanding during the entire year.
3. On July 1, 197C, Book-It sold $1,000,000 of eight percent convertible bonds at par. Each $1,000 bond is convertible into 100 shares of common stock at any time after December 31, 197C.
4. On January 15, 197D, the Company sold $500,000 of seven percent convertible debt at par. The debt is convertible into 125,000 shares of common stock any time after July 1, 197D.
5. On January 1, 197E, the Company sold 25,000 shares of eight percent, $50 par value, noncumulative convertible preferred stock at $40 per share. Each share of preferred stock is convertible into four common shares any time after January 1, 197E. No dividends have been declared or paid during 197E.
6. Book-It, Inc. reported net income of $10,000,000 for the year ended December 31, 197E. The Company's tax rate is 52 percent.
7. The bank prime rate of interest on certain key dates is shown below:

July 1, 197C	13%
January 15, 197D	12%
January 1, 197E	11%

A review of the convertible securities indicates that all issues are convertible currently and therefore may be included in the cash yield test. Table VII shows the determination of the cash yield for each of the convertible securities.

Table VII

Computation of Cash Yield

Security	Annual Cash Outflow	Sales Price	Cash Yield[a]
8% Bonds	[b]$ 80,000	$1,000,000	8%
7% Debt	[c]$ 35,000	$ 500,000	7%
8% Preferred	[d]$100,000	[e]$1,000,000	10%

[a] Cash Yield = Annual Cash Outflow/Sales Price.
[b] $1,000,000 par value × 8% stated rate = $80,000.
[c] $500,000 par value × 7% stated rate = $35,000.
[d] $50 par value × 8% stated rate = $4 per share × 25,000 shares = $100,000.
[e] 25,000 shares × $40 per share selling price = $1,000,000.

For the eight percent bonds and the seven percent debt, the selling price is equal to the par value. For this reason, the cash yield will be equal to the stated yield. The eight percent preferred cash yield is based upon the selling price of $40 per share, rather than upon the par value of $50 per share. The cash yield of each security must be compared to the bank prime interest rate on the date the security was sold. If the cash yield is less than two-thirds of the bank prime rate, the convertible security will be considered to be a common stock equivalent. Table VIII shows the determination of common stock equivalency for each security.

Table VIII

Classification of Convertible Securities

Security	Bank Prime Rate[a]	Two-Thirds of Prime Rate	Cash Yield	Common Stock Equiva-lent
8% Bonds	13%	8.67%	8%	Yes
7% Debt	12%	8.00%	7%	Yes
8% Preferred	11%	7.33%	10%	No

[a] At date of sale of security.

Only the eight percent bonds and the seven percent debt meet the cash yield test and may be considered in the computation of EPSP. The eight percent preferred will be reconsidered in the computation of ESPFD.

The two securities that qualified as common stock equivalents must be dilutive before they will enter into the computation of primary earnings per share. Because there is more than one security, the dilutive effect of each security must be determined individually. The earnings per share effect of each convertible security must be determined. The earnings per share effect for debt is calculated by dividing the number of shares issuable upon conversion into the after-tax interest expense adjustment. Table IX shows the calculation of the earnings per share effect for the two securities.

Table IX

Earnings Per Share Effect

Security	After-Tax Interest	Number of Shares Issued on Conversion	Earnings Per Share Effect[a]
8% Bonds	[b]$38,400	[c]100,000	$.384
7% Debt	[d]$16,800	125,000	$.1344

[a] After-tax interest/number of shares issued on conversion.
[b] $80,000 interest expense × (1 − .52) = $38,400.
[c] $1,000,000/$1,000 = 1,000 bonds × 100 shares per bond = 100,000 shares.
[d] $35,000 interest expense × (1 − .52) = $16,800.

The convertible security with the lowest earnings per share effect must be considered first; therefore, an analysis of the seven percent debt is required. To determine whether the seven percent debt is dilutive, primary earnings per share calculated prior to the inclusion must be compared with the primary earnings per share that will result from including the seven percent debt. If the latter EPSP is lower than the former, the debt is considered to be dilutive and is included in the primary earnings per share calculation.

Convertible securities are the last items to be considered in the earnings per share computation. Primary earnings per share after considering options, warrants and contingent agreements would be used as the initial value for comparison. Because there are no options, warrants or contingent agreements in this example, the initial primary earnings per share to be used would be the unadjusted earnings per share.

Since the preferred stock is noncumulative, and no dividends have been declared or paid in 197E, there will be no adjustment necessary to the reported earnings of $10,000,000. No additional common stock was sold or repurchased during 197E; thus, the weighted average number of common shares for the EPSU computation would be 4,000,000. The calculation of EPSU is shown below:

$$EPSU = \frac{\$10{,}000{,}000}{4{,}000{,}000} = \$2.50$$

The earnings per share effect of the seven percent debt is \$.1344, which is less than the EPSU of \$2.50; therefore, the seven percent debt is dilutive and will be considered in the primary earnings per share computation. The seven percent debt now is treated on an "if converted" basis, and a new primary earnings per share is calculated. The numerator of the new EPSP will be equal to \$10,016,800 (\$10,000,000 + \$16,800 after-tax interest adjustment). The denominator of the equation will be increased by the number of shares issuable upon conversion and will be equal to 4,125,000 shares (4,000,000 + 125,000 issuable shares). The new primary earnings per share is computed below:

$$EPSP = \frac{\$10{,}016{,}800}{4{,}125{,}000} = \$2.43$$

This new primary earnings per share amount will be used as the basis of the next comparison to determine the dilutive effect of the eight percent bonds.

The \$.384 earnings per share effect of the eight percent bonds is less than the \$2.43 new primary earnings per share, so the bonds are considered to be dilutive and will be included in the EPSP computation. The numerator of the EPSP equation is adjusted for the after-tax interest associated with the bonds and is equal to \$10,055,200 (\$10,016,800 + \$38,400). The denominator is increased by the number of shares issuable upon conversion and is equal to 4,225,000 shares (4,125,000 + 100,000). The new primary earnings per share is calculated below:

$$EPSP = \frac{\$10{,}055{,}200}{4{,}225{,}000} = \$2.38$$

Since there are no more convertible securities to be considered in the EPSP calculation, the \$2.38 is equal to the primary earnings per share. Had there been additional convertible securities, the \$2.38 would have served as the basis for the next comparison.

The final step in the process is to compute fully diluted earnings per share. All convertible securities included in the EPSP amount will be included in the EPSFD computation. The starting point for the computation of EPSFD is to use the numerator of \$10,055,200 and the denominator of 4,225,000 shares from the EPSP computation.

The only convertible security that needs to be reconsidered for the EPSFD computation is the eight percent preferred stock. If the preferred stock is dilutive, it will enter into the computation of EPSFD. To determine if the issue is dilutive, the earnings per share effect must be calculated, and compared to the EPSP amount. The annual dividend per share on the preferred stock is \$4 (\$50 par value × 8%). Each share of preferred stock may be converted into four shares of common stock, so the earnings per share effect on the preferred stock is \$1 (\$4 dividends/4 shares issuable stock upon conversion). The \$1 earnings per share effect of the preferred stock is less than the \$2.38 primary earnings per share; therefore, the issue is dilutive and will enter into the EPSFD computation on an "if converted" basis.

No dividends were declared or paid in 197E, and the preferred stock is not cumulative. There is no adjustment to the numerator of the equation for EPSFD. The 25,000 preferred shares may be converted into 100,000 common shares (25,000 × 4 common shares for each preferred share). The denominator of the EPSFD equation must be increased by the 100,000 issuable shares. The denominator will be equal to 4,325,000 after the adjustment (4,225,000 + 100,000). The computation of fully diluted earnings per share is shown below:

$$\text{EPSFD} = \frac{\$10{,}055{,}200}{4{,}325{,}000} = \$2.325$$

The aggregate dilution reciprocal is equal to 93 percent (\$2.325 EPSFD/\$2.50 EPSU), which means that the aggregate dilution is more than three percent and that a dual presentation of earnings per share is required.

The example just completed was designed to introduce the reader to the handling of convertible securities in the calculation of earnings per share. To illustrate a more complex situation, the assumptions in Exhibit X will be used.

Exhibit X

Convertible Securities—Example 2

1. Jar, Inc. has a December 31 year end, and is preparing to calculate earnings per share for the year ended December 31, 197F.
2. There were 6,000,000 shares of common stock outstanding during all of 197F.
3. On January 1, 197A, Jar, Inc. sold \$500,000 of a nine percent convertible debt at par. Each \$1,000 bond is convertible into 100 shares of common stock any time after January 1, 197A.
4. On July 15, 197C, the company sold a package of \$1,000,000 of eight percent \$100 par value convertible preferred stock and 75,000 shares of common stock, for a total amount of \$1,900,000. The estimated fair value of the

preferred stock at the date of sale was $1,020,000, and the fair value of the common stock was $980,000. The preferred stock is convertible into 80,000 shares of common stock any time after December 31, 197D.

5. On August 15, 197E, Jar, Inc. sold $500,000 of nine percent convertible debt for $499,000, after deducting brokerage commissions of $1,000. Each $1,000 bond is convertible into 100 shares of common stock any time after August 15, 197E.
6. On January 1, 197F, the company sold $300,000 face value six percent convertible bonds for $287,701. The bonds were priced to yield seven percent. Each $1,000 bond is convertible into 50 common shares any time after January 31, 197F.
7. On July 1, 197F, $800,000 of five percent convertible debt outstanding was converted into 10,000 shares of common stock.
8. Jar, Inc. reported net income of $6,080,000 for the year ended December 31, 197F. The Company's tax rate is 50 percent. Preferred dividends of $80,000 were paid during the year.
9. The bank prime interest rate on certain key dates is shown below:

January 1, 197A	14%
July 15, 197C	11%
August 15, 197E	10%
January 1, 197F	10%

All of the convertible securities are convertible currently or within five years of the balance sheet date and will enter into the cash yield test to determine if they represent common stock equivalents. The annual cash outflows associated with each of the convertible securities is shown in Table X below:

Table X

Cash Outflows

Security	Par or Face of Security	Interest Rate	Annual Cash Outflow[a]
9% Debt—1/1/197A	$ 500,000	9%	$ 45,000
8% Preferred	$ 1,000,000	8%	$ 80,000
9% Debt—8/15/197E	$ 500,000	9%	$ 45,000
6% Bonds	$ 300,000	6%	$ 18,000

[a] Cash Outflow = Par or Face of Security × Interest Rate.

To determine the cash yield, the annual cash outflow is compared to the selling price of the security. The sales price of all securities is given, except for the eight percent preferred stock. The preferred stock was sold in a package with common stock. The proceeds from the sale must be allocated to each security on the basis of its relative fair value on the date of sale. The calculation of the proceeds applicable to the preferred stock is shown below:

Fair Value of Preferred	$1,020,000
Fair Value of Common	980,000
Total Fair Value	$2,000,000

$$\frac{\text{Fair Value of Preferred}}{\text{Total Fair Value}} \quad \frac{\$1{,}020{,}000}{\$2{,}000{,}000} \times \$1{,}900{,}000 = \$969{,}000$$

On the basis of this allocation, $969,000 of the total proceeds will be assigned to the preferred stock.

Remember that the sales price for purposes of the cash yield test does not consider brokerage commissions, transfer taxes, etc., so the sales price of the nine percent debt issued August 15, 197E, is $500,000 ($499,000 + $1,000 brokerage fees).

Table XI shows the computation of the cash yield for all of the convertible securities.

Table XI

Computation of Cash Yield

Security	Annual Cash Outflow	Sales Price	Cash Yield[a]
9% Debt—1/1/197A	$ 45,000	$ 500,000	9%
8% Preferred	$ 80,000	$ 969,000	8.3%
9% Debt—8/15/197E	$ 45,000	$ 500,000	9%
6% Bonds	$ 18,000	$ 287,701	6.3%

[a] Cash Yield = Annual Cash Outflow/Sales Price

Next, the cash yield must be compared to two-thirds of the bank prime interest rate in effect on the date the securities were sold. Table XII provides the comparison and the determination of the common stock equivalency of each security.

Table XII

Determination of Common Stock Equivalents

Security	Prime Rate[a]	Two-thirds of Prime Rate	Cash Yield	Common Stock Equivalent
9% Debt—1/1/197A	14%	9.3%	9.0%	Yes
8% Preferred	11%	7.3%	8.3%	No
9% Debt—8/15/197E	10%	6.7%	9.0%	No
6% Bonds	10%	6.7%	6.3%	Yes

[a] At date of sale of security.

Table XII indicates that the nine percent debt issued on January 1, 197A, and the six percent bonds qualify as common stock equivalents, because their cash yield was less than two-thirds of the bank prime rate at the date of issue. However, take a minute to review and compare the nine percent debt securities issued on January 1, 197A, with the nine percent securities issued on August 15, 197E. Notice that the two issues have identical provisions. One qualified as a common stock equivalent, and the other did not. In this situation, both issues should be treated as common stock equivalents. So the nine percent debt issued on August 15, 197E, also will qualify as a common stock equivalent.

Before any of these securities can be used in the computation of primary earnings per share, they must be dilutive on an individual basis. The earnings per share effect of each issue must be calculated. The preferred stock does not qualify as a common stock equivalent, so the earnings per share effect in this example is determined by dividing the after-tax interest by the number of common shares issuable upon conversion.

Table XIII summarizes the computation of the after-tax interest for each issue.

Table XIII

Computation of After-Tax Interest

Security	Annual Cash Outflow	Adjust. for Discount Amortization	Expense	(1 - Tax Rate)	After-Tax Interest[a]
9% Debt—1/1/197A	$45,000	-0-	$45,000	.50	$22,500
9% Debt—8/15/197E	$45,000	-0-	$45,000	.50	$22,500
6% Bonds	$18,000	[b]$2,139	$20,139	.50	$10,070

[a] After-Tax Interest = Expense × (1—Tax Rate).
[b] $287,701 × 7% effective interest rate = $20,139 − $18,000 = $2,139.

One unusual item on the Table is the amortization of the discount associated with the six percent bonds. The bonds have a face value of $300,000, but were sold for $287,701, so as to yield an effective interest rate of seven percent to the investor. The discount amortized during the period raised the interest expense and must be included in the after-tax interest computation.

In addition to the three securities specifically identified as common stock equivalents, consideration must be given to the $800,000 of five percent convertible debt that was converted during 197F. In a case where convertible securities are converted during the year, the "if converted" method is applied to the partial period when the securities were still outstanding. The "if converted" method is used in the primary earnings per share calculation only if the securities are dilutive. The after-tax interest relating to this issue for the six months ended June 30, 197F (the day of conversion) is $10,000 ($800,000 × .05 = $40,000 × ½ = $20,000 × (1 − .50) = $10,000). The weighted number of shares issuable upon conversion are 5,000 (10,000 × $\frac{6}{12}$). Now that we have developed this information, Table XIV shows the computation of the earnings per share effect of the securities.

Table XIV

Computation of Earnings Per Share Effect

Security	After-Tax Interest	Number of Shares Issued on Conversion	Earnings Per Share Effect[a]
9% Debt—1/1/197A	$ 22,500	[b]50,000	$ .45
9% Debt—8/15/197E	$ 22,500	50,000	$ .45
6% Bonds	$ 10,070	[c]15,000	$ .67
5% Partial Period	$ 10,000	5,000	$2.00

[a] EPS Effect = After-tax interest/number of shares issuable on conversion.
[b] $500,000/$1,000 = 500 bonds × 100 shares per bond = 50,000 shares.
[c] $300,000/$1,000 = 300 bonds × 50 shares per bond = 15,000 shares.

The securities are arranged in order of their earnings per share effect, from the lowest ($.45) to the highest ($2.00). Now each security will be compared with the previous primary earnings per share to determine if it is dilutive. Since convertible securities are considered last in the earnings per share calculation, options, warrants and contingent agreements already will have been considered in the calculation of primary earnings per share. In the example, however, there were no options, warrants or contingent agreements, so all comparisons will be made on the basis of unadjusted earnings per share.

For purposes of calculating EPSU, all contingent equity issues are ignored. Reported net income of $6,080,000 must be reduced by the preferred dividends paid during the year, because the preferred stock is treated as if converted in the computation. The numerator or the EPSU equation would be $6,000,000 ($6,080,000 − $80,000 preferred dividends). Through the conversion of the five percent debt, 10,000 additional common shares were issued on July 1, 197F. These shares are to be weighted for the period of time outstanding and added to the weighted average number of common shares. The conversion represents 5,000 weighted shares (10,000 × $\frac{6}{12}$). The only other common shares outstanding during the year were the 6,000,000 shares. Thus, the denominator of the EPSU equation would be 6,005,000 shares. Unadjusted earnings per share is computed below:

$$\text{EPSU} = \frac{\$6{,}000{,}000}{6{,}005{,}000} = \$.999$$

The analysis of the earnings per share effect of the convertible securities classified as common stock equivalents begins with the nine percent debt issued on January 1, 197A. The earnings per share effect of \$.45 is less than the EPSU of \$.999; therefore, the securities are dilutive and will enter into the computation of primary earnings per share. Once this has been determined, a new EPSP must be calculated to include the convertible debt with the lowest earnings per share effect (the nine percent debt issued on January 1, 197A). The numerator of the EPSU equation will be increased by the after-tax interest of the debt, and the denominator will be increased by the number of shares issuable upon conversion. This is done because the assumption is made that the debt was converted at the beginning of the year. The computation of the new EPSP is shown below:

$$\text{EPSP} = \frac{\$6{,}000{,}000 + \$22{,}500}{6{,}005{,}000 + 50{,}000} = \frac{\$6{,}022{,}500}{6{,}055{,}000} = \$.995$$

The new EPSP includes the nine percent debt on an "if converted" basis, and will serve as the basis for determining if the other securities are dilutive.

The next security to consider is the nine percent debt issued on August 15, 197E. The adjustment to the numerator of the new EPSP equation would be the same as that made for the nine percent debt issued earlier. The second computation of EPSP is shown below:

$$\text{EPSP} = \frac{\$6{,}022{,}500 + \$22{,}500}{6{,}055{,}000 + 50{,}000} = \frac{\$6{,}045{,}000}{6{,}105{,}000} = \$.990$$

The second issue of nine percent debt was included in the EPSP calculation because its earnings per share effect of \$.45 was less than the new EPSP of \$.995.

The next convertible security to be considered is the six percent bond issue. Its earnings per share effect of \$.67 is less than the new EPSP, just calculated to be \$.990; therefore, it will be included in the determination of primary earnings per share. Still another EPSP computation is required to reflect the inclusion of the six percent debt. The computation is based upon the last EPSP calculation, and is shown below:

$$\text{EPSP} = \frac{\$6{,}045{,}000 + \$10{,}070}{6{,}105{,}000 + 15{,}000} = \frac{\$6{,}055{,}070}{6{,}120{,}000} = \$.989$$

The newest EPSP amount includes the nine percent debt issues of January 1, 197A, and August 15, 197E, and the six percent bonds on an "if converted" basis. The last security to be analyzed is the five percent debt that was converted during the current period. The earnings per share effect of the five percent debt is \$2.00 (Table XIV), which is greater than the latest EPSP amount of \$.989; therefore, the five percent debt is not dilutive and will not be included in the calculation of primary earnings per share.

All convertible securities now have been considered for the calculation of primary earnings per share. The next step is to calculate fully diluted earnings per share. Remember that, if a convertible security is used in the EPSP computation, it will be carried forward and used in the fully diluted computation. The calculation of fully diluted earnings per share starts with a numerator of \$6,055,070 and a denominator of 6,120,000 shares.

For purposes of computing fully diluted earnings per share, the eight percent preferred stock issue must be reconsidered, along with the five percent debt that was converted during the year. The eight percent preferred failed the cash yield test, and therefore was excluded from primary earnings per share, because it was not a common stock equivalent. The issue will be included in the calculation of fully diluted earnings per share if it is dilutive, i.e., if its earning per share effect is less than the EPSP amount of \$.989. The preferred issue pays an annual dividend of \$80,000 (\$1,000,000 × 8%). Each share of preferred is convertible into eight shares of common stock, and there are 80,000 common shares issuable upon conversion of the preferred. The earnings per share effect of the preferred issue is \$1.00 (\$80,000/80,000 common shares). The \$1 per share effect is greater than the EPSP amount, previously determined to be \$.989. For this reason, the preferred issue is anti-dilutive and will not be included in the computation of fully diluted earnings per share.

The last item to be considered is the five percent debt issue that was converted on July 1, 197F. The issue was not included in the primary earnings per share calculation because it was found to be anti-dilutive. However, for the computation of fully diluted earnings per share, any convertible security that was converted during the period and required a partial period adjustment is considered in the computation, whether dilutive or not. Table XIV indicates the after-tax interest and the number of shares issuable, properly weighted for the partial period of six months. The numerator of the fully diluted earnings per share equation will be increased by the \$10,000 after-tax interest, and the denominator will be increased by the 5,000 weighted shares issuable upon conversion. The computation of fully diluted earnings per share is shown below:

$$\text{EPSFD} = \frac{\$6{,}055{,}070 + \$10{,}000}{6{,}120{,}000 + 5{,}000} = \frac{\$6{,}065{,}070}{6{,}125{,}000} = \$.99$$

The inclusion of the anti-dilutive five percent debt issue increases the earnings per share from \$.989 to \$.99.

To complete the example, it is necessary to determine if, in the aggregate, the contingent equity issues are dilutive by three percent or more. This is determined by comparing the fully diluted earnings per share to the unadjusted earnings per share. The calculation of the aggregate dilution reciprocal is shown below:

$$\text{ADR} = \frac{\$.99}{\$.999} = 99 \text{ percent}$$

This means that the aggregate dilution of the convertible securities is only 1 percent (1 − .99); therefore, the company is considered to have a simple capital structure, and only a single earnings per share presentation is required. In the example, earnings per share will be reported at the unadjusted amount of $.999.

The purpose of this second example is two-fold: first, to introduce several new concepts in the calculation of earnings per share when a company has convertible equity securities; and, second, to illustrate that, even if a company has a complicated capital structure, a dual presentation of earnings per share is not always required. The dual presentation is not a function of the number or variety of the convertible securities, but rather of their *dilutive* effect.

The final item to be covered deals with contingent agreements. When computing earnings per share, consideration must be given to warrants, options and their equivalent *and* contingent agreements, before an analysis of convertible securities is begun. However, because of the complexity of the computations required for options, warrants and convertible securities, the authors moved the discussion of contingent agreements to the end of the section. Remember that the effects of contingent agreements must be determined before starting into convertible securities.

Contingent Agreements

[Paragraphs 88-92 of the AICPA Accounting Interpretation of APB Opinion No. 15 provides additional information about contingent agreements.]

For any one of several reasons, an enterprise may enter into an agreement that requires the issuance of shares of common stock if some future condition is realized. These types of agreements are referred to as contingent agreements because the consideration involved will be paid if some future event takes place, i.e., the consideration is contingent upon the future event. When the contingent agreement involves the issuance of common stock, it will affect the computation of earnings per share.

The shares of stock that are contingently issuable normally are classified as common stock equivalents and enter into the computation of primary earnings per share. The arrangement for distributing the stock generally does not affect the status of common stock equivalency. For example, the agreement may state that the stock will be issued only if the future condition is met, or it may require that the stock be placed in escrow and issued if the contingency is met (or returned to the company if the contingency is not met), or the stock may be issued with the stipulation that it be returned to the company if the future condition is not met. Regardless of the method of distribution, common stock involved in a contingent agreement generally will be considered to be common stock equivalents for purposes of calculating earnings per share.

There is an infinite variety of contingent agreements possible; and, obviously, the discussion cannot cover all types of contingent agreements. Three basic types of agreements will be discussed in this section. The first basic type of agreement requires that shares of common stock will be issued after the passage of a given time period. A second type of agreement specifies that shares of common stock will be issued, provided a certain level of earnings is achieved and maintained. The third basic type of agreement specifies that shares of common stock will be issued, depending upon the future market price of the stock. Each of these agreements will be discussed.

Contingent Agreements Involving the Passage of Time

If the contingent agreement specifies that a certain number of common shares will be issued after a given time period has elapsed, the contingent shares will be included in the computations of both primary and fully diluted earnings per share. The denominator of both equations will be increased by the number of common shares contingently issuable. There would be no adjustment to the numerator of either equation.

Contingent Agreements Involving Future Earnings

A contingent agreement of this type usually is involved in a business combination accounted for as a purchase. The acquiring company may specify that additional shares of stock will be issued if the acquired company maintains a certain earnings level or achieves a level of earnings higher than current earnings.

If the specified earnings level currently is being met, the contingently issuable shares will be included in both the primary and fully diluted earnings per share computations. The shares to be issued will be added to the denominator of each equation, and no adjustment will be required in the numerator of either equation. If the earnings level is not currently being met, the contingently issuable shares will not enter into the computations of primary earnings per share. However, the shares may enter into the computation of fully diluted earnings per share if their issuance would have a dilutive effect.

To illustrate the treatment of contingently issuable shares in an agreement specifying a certain earnings level, the assumptions listed in Exhibit XI will be used.

Exhibit XI

Contingent Agreement Involving Future Earnings

1. Book-It, Inc. reported net income of $1,500,000 for the year ended December 31, 197C and had 300,000 common shares outstanding during the entire year.
2. On January 1, 197C, Book-It acquired a wholly owned subsidiary in a business combination, properly accounted for as a purchase. As part of the agreement to combine, Book-It agreed to issue an additional 50,000 shares to the previous owners of the acquired company on December 31, 197D, if the acquired company's earnings exceeded $150,000 for each of the years 197C and 197D.
3. Book-It is preparing to compute earnings per share for 197C, and has determined that the earnings of the acquired company are $180,000 for the year ended December 31, 197C.

The shares are not issuable to the prior owners of the acquired company until December 31, 197D, but the $180,000 current earnings level of the acquired company is greater than the $150,000 required level. The earnings condition is met in 197C, and the contingently issuable shares will be included in the computations of both primary and fully diluted earnings per share. The 50,000 contingent shares are added to the 300,000 common shares outstanding during the entire year, to give a denominator of 350,000 shares for both primary and fully diluted earnings per share. There is no adjustment required to the numerator, so it will be equal to the $1,500,000 reported income of Book-It, Inc. The computation of primary earnings per share is shown below:

$$\text{EPSP} = \frac{\$1{,}500{,}000}{350{,}000} = \$4.29$$

Fully diluted earnings per share also are equal to $4.29.

If the reported income of the acquired company was $120,000, the earnings condition would not have been met, and the contingently issuable shares would not enter into the computation of primary earnings per share. Assuming the company reported income of $120,000, the calculation of primary earnings per share will be as follows:

$$EPSP = \frac{\$1{,}500{,}000}{300{,}000} = \$5.00$$

Using the same assumed earnings level, the contingently issuable shares will be included in the computation of fully diluted earnings per share. The 50,000 contingent shares will be added to the denominator as before, but, in this case, an adjustment to the numerator also is required. The adjustment is equal to the difference between the *required* earnings level and the current reported earnings level. This amount is determined below and will be added to the numerator of the fully diluted earnings per share computation.

Required Level of Earnings	$150,000
Reported Earnings	120,000
Adjustment to Numerator	$ 30,000

After the adjustment, the numerator of the equation is equal to $1,530,000 ($1,500,000 earnings of Book-It + $30,000 adjustment). The calculation of fully diluted earnings per share is as follows:

$$EPSFD = \frac{\$1{,}530{,}000}{350{,}000} = \$4.37$$

For the contingently issuable shares to be included in the fully diluted earnings per share amount, they must have a dilutive effect. In this example, primary earnings per share are $5.00, and fully diluted earnings per share are $4.37; thus, the contingent shares are dilutive and will be included in fully diluted earnings per share.

Since primary earnings per share are equal to unadjusted earnings per share in this example, the aggregate dilution reciprocal is equal to 87.4 percent ($4.37/$5.00), and a dual presentation of earnings per share is required.

Contingent Agreements Involving the Market Price of Stock

Contingent agreements may involve consideration based upon the future market price of common stock. A company might guarantee that the market price of its stock will reach a certain level by some future date, or it may guarantee that the market price of its stock will not fall below a certain level. If the guaranteed price is not realized, the company will issue additional shares of common stock.

To determine if the contingently issuable shares will be included in primary and fully diluted earnings per share, the end of period market price of the stock must be compared to the guaranteed value of the stock as specified in the agreement. If the comparison indicates that the guaranteed market price currently is not being met, the contingently issuable shares will be included in the denominator of both the primary and fully diluted earnings per share computations. If the guaranteed market value currently is being obtained, the contingently issuable shares will not be considered in the earnings per share computation.

To illustrate the treatment afforded contingent shares involved in an agreement concerning market price, the assumptions in Exhibit XII will be used.

Exhibit XII

Contingent Agreement Involving Market Price of Stock

1. Jar, Inc. reported income of $2,000,000 for the year ended December 31, 197B, and is preparing to calculate earnings per share.
2. On January 1, 197B, Jar, Inc. acquired a company through a business combination, properly accounted for as a purchase. As part of the agreement to combine, Jar, Inc. agreed to issue an additional 75,000 shares to the previous owners of the acquired company on December 31, 197C, if the market value of Jar, Inc. common stock fell below $45 per share.
3. Jar, Inc. had 500,000 shares of common stock outstanding during the entire year of 197B. The market price per share on December 31, 197B was $43.

Since the end of period market price of $43 is less than the guaranteed price of $45 per share, the contingently issuable shares will be included in the denominator of both the primary and fully diluted earnings per share computations. No adjustment to the numerator is required. The computation of primary earnings per share is shown below:

$$\text{EPSP} = \frac{\$2{,}000{,}000}{500{,}000 + 75{,}000} = \frac{\$2{,}000{,}000}{575{,}000} = \$3.48$$

In this example, fully diluted earnings per share would be the same as primary earnings per share.

This completes the discussion of contingent agreements. The next section identifies the required disclosures relating to earnings per share and provides illustrations of the disclosures.

Disclosures

The disclosures required by APB Opinion No. 15 are listed in AICPA Accounting Interpretation Number 100. The reader should consult this list, since it is comprehensive and concise.

The presentation of earnings per share by The American Ship Building Company and International Minerals & Chemical Corporation for 1976 and 1975 are shown below. The American Ship Building

Company was required to report a single earnings per share amount. Note 1 to the financial statements of the company discusses the computation of the weighted average number of shares outstanding, which includes a seven percent stock dividend and a one-for-two stock split. International Minerals & Chemical Corporation was required to disclose both primary and fully diluted earnings per share for both years. The footnote relating to the computation of earnings per share shows the determination of the weighted average number of shares used for the primary and fully diluted earnings per share denominators.

The American Ship Building Company (Sep)

	1976	1975
Net income (loss) per common share and common share equivalent (Note 1):		
Continuing operations	$1.78	$.19
Discontinued operations	(.21)	.37
Net income	$1.57	$.56
Average number of common shares and common share equivalents.	3,138,000	3,119,000

Note 1 (in part) Summary of Significant Accounting Policies.

Earnings Per Common Share and Common Share Equivalent—Earnings per common share and common share equivalent were computed by dividing net income, after providing for preferred dividend requirements, by the weighted average number of common shares and common share equivalents outstanding during the year (3,138,000 in 1976 and 3,119,000 in 1975). The calculation of average shares outstanding reflects 5% and 7% stock dividends issued during 1976 and 1975, respectively, and the declaration of a one-for-two stock split to be effected in the form of a dividend. This action was taken by the Board of Directors on November 23, 1976 and is distributable on January 14, 1977 to shareholders of record on December 6, 1976. All per share calculations including stock option information have been restated to reflect the Board's action. Earnings per common share on a fully diluted basis are substantially the same as primary earnings per share as presented.

International Minerals & Chemical Corporation (Jun)

	1976	1975
Earnings per common and common equivalent share:		
Primary		
Earnings before extraordinary item	$7.75	$ 9.91
Net earnings	7.75	10.17
Fully diluted		
Earnings before extraordinary item	7.39	8.90
Net earnings	7.39	9.13

Notes to Consolidated Financial Statements

Earnings per Common and Common Equivalent Share—Primary earnings per share are based on the weighted average number of common and common equivalent shares outstanding after recognition of preferred stock dividend requirements. Common equivalent shares include dilutive stock options and shares awarded under performance share plans.

Fully diluted earnings per share are based on primary earnings per share, adjusted for dilutive stock options at end of period market prices and for the assumed conversion of the 4% convertible subordinated debentures and Series preferred stock. In these computations, interest on those debentures (net of income tax effect) and dividends on Series preferred stock have been added to earnings applicable to common shares. Shares issuable on exercise of other options have been excluded from the computations as they would either have no effect or would be anti-dilutive. Shares used in the computations are as follows:

	1976	1975
Weighted average common shares—		
Outstanding	17,099,220	15,870,158
For stock options	125,156	176,825
For performance share plans	98,832	102,800
Total for primary earnings per share	17,323,208	16,149,783
Additional shares for conversion—		
4% debentures	437,177	948,888
Series preferred stock	542,191	1,116,470
Additional shares for stock options	7,525	10,721
Total for fully diluted earnings per share	18,310,101	18,225,862

Source: *Accounting Trends & Techniques,* Copyright © 1977 by the American Institute of Certified Public Accountants, Inc., pp. 293-294, and 297.

Topic 8

Leases

Detail Contents

2. FASB Technical Bulletin No. 79-11	–Effect of a Penalty on the Term of a Lease
3. FASB Technical Bulletin No. 79-12	–Interest Rate Used in Calculating the Present Value of Minimum Lease Payments
4. FASB Technical Bulletin No. 79-13	–Applicability of FASB Statement No. 13 to Current Value Financial Statements
5. FASB Technical Bulletin No. 79-14	–Upward Adjustment of Guaranteed Residual Values
6. FASB Technical Bulletin No. 79-15	–Accounting for Loss on a Sublease Not Involving the Disposal of a Segment
7. FASB Technical Bulletin No. 79-16	–Effect of a Change in Income Tax Rate on the Accounting for Leveraged Leases
8. FASB Technical Bulletin No. 79-17	–Reporting Cumulative Effect Adjustment from Retroactive Application of FASB Statement No. 13
9. FASB Technical Bulletin No. 79-18	–Transition Requirements of Certain FASB Amendments and Interpretations of FASB No. 13

SFAS No. 13 (November 1976)
Accounting for Leases,[1]

SFAS No. 17 (November 1977)
Accounting for Leases—Initial Direct Costs,

SFAS No. 26 (April 1979)
Profit Recognition on Sales-Type Leases of Real Estate,

SFAS No. 27 (May 1979)
Classification of Renewals or Extensions of Existing Sales-Type or Direct Financing Leases,

SFAS No. 28 (May 1979)
Accounting for Sales With Leasebacks, and

SFAS No. 29 (June 1979)
Determining Contingent Rentals

SFAS No. 13 is, perhaps, one of the more difficult pronouncements to understand and appreciate. The pronouncement itself is organized in such

[1] FASB Technical Bulletin No. 79-13 states that the provisions of SFAS No. 13 are applicable in the preparation of current value financial statements.

a manner as to make it very difficult for the reader to follow the flow of the decision process and the subsequent accounting. The following material will be divided into two main sections; the first section will be directed toward the lessee and the second toward the lessor. While this organization is different from that of the pronouncement, it is hoped that the reader will more readily see the similarities and differences in accounting for the lessee and the lessor.

Defining Some Important Terms

At the outset it is important to define some of the terms that will appear first in the Flowcharts and later in the example material presented. The pronouncement defines several terms: some will be defined below, and others will be introduced at a more appropriate time. The full meaning of each of these terms cannot be conveyed easily, but, with some explanation and the support of illustrations, the reader will have a good understanding of the specific meaning of the terms contained in SFAS No. 13.

1. *Minimum Rental Payment* (MRP). The MRP consist of the minimum payments required to be made under the lease agreement by the lessee to the lessor. The term indicates that additional payments above the minimum might be involved in the lease agreement, but most of the major decisions required are concerned with the MRP.

2. *Minimum Lease Payments* (MLP). The MLP may be different from the MRP; and, in some cases, it may be the same. The MLP always will include the MRP, but also can include other items, if specified in the lease. At this point, it is important to know that, in addition to the MRP, the MLP may include: [2]

(a) Guarantee of residual value by the lessee.[3] This represents an amount guaranteed by the lessee to the lessor for the estimated residual value of the asset at the end of the lease term.[4] If, at the termination of the lease, the actual residual value received by the

---

[2] Contingent rentals, as defined in SFAS No. 29, are generally *excluded* from the minimum lease payment amount. However, lease payments that relate to an index or rate, e.g., consumer price index or prime interest rate, are not considered contingent rentals and are included in the minimum lease payment. The amount to be included in the minimum lease payment is determined by the value of the rate or index at the inception of thc lease.

[3] FASB Interpretation No. 19 states that a guarantee by the lessee for "damage, extraordinary wear and tear or excessive usage" is not a guarantee of residual value.

[4] The lease term generally begins at the inception of the lease and ends when all potential obligations have been settled by the lessee. FASB Technical Bulletin No. 79-11 indicates that the lease term would include any periods for which failure to renew the lease would result in an economic penalty to the lessor.

lessor is less than the guaranteed residual value, the lessee may have to make up the deficiency by a payment to the lessor.

(b) Payment required for failure to renew or extend the lease. A penalty payment may be required of the lessee if the agreement specifies that the lease must be renewed or extended, or grants the lessee the right to renew or extend the lease. This part of the agreement is present to protect the rights of both the lessee and the lessor.

(c) Bargain purchase option payment. This represents a payment by the lessee to the lessor at the end of the lease term that will allow the lessee to obtain title to the leased property. The bargain purchase price usually is substantially below the estimated fair value of the property; therefore, it is reasonable to assume that the lessee will exercise the bargain purchase payment.

3. *Lessor's Implicit Interest Rate.* In general terms, this can be thought of as the lessor's rate of return on the leased property; more specifically, it is the rate of interest that will equate the present value of the MLP (after certain deductions) with the fair value of the leased property, less the investment tax credit at the inception of the lease.

4. *Lessee's Incremental Borrowing Rate.*[5] This is the rate of interest that the lessee would have to pay to borrow the funds necessary to purchase the leased property rather than enter into the lease agreement. This is an "opportunity cost" rate of interest, rather than a "real" interest cost. The determination of the incremental borrowing rate requires a series of reasoned judgments. Basically, the lessee is attempting to determine the terms of borrowing *if* the asset were purchased rather than leased.

With this introduction to the terms of SFAS No. 13, the reader should be able to understand the essential features of the Flowchart that follows.

Flowchart and Discussion of General Lease Agreement—Lessee

Flowchart 1 depicts the classification and accounting for general lease agreements from the standpoint of the lessee. The left side of the Flowchart deals with the problem of lease classification, and the right side addresses the major accounting problems. As before, the decision blocks have been numbered and will be referred to in this section.

---

[5] FASB Technical Bulletin No. 79-12 indicates that SFAS No. 13 does not prohibit the use of a secured borrowing rate as the incremental rate as long as the rate is reasonable and consistent with that rate normally used in the circumstances.

Lease Classification[6]

SFAS No. 13 identifies two types of leases from the viewpoint of the lessee: an operating lease and a capital lease. Accounting for an operating lease is not difficult and requires little explanation. Accounting for a capital lease, however, can be quite complex, and much of the example material is related to the accounting problems associated with a capital lease. The end product of SFAS No. 13 requires the lessee to treat a capital lease much like a purchased asset that was acquired by borrowing the necessary funds.

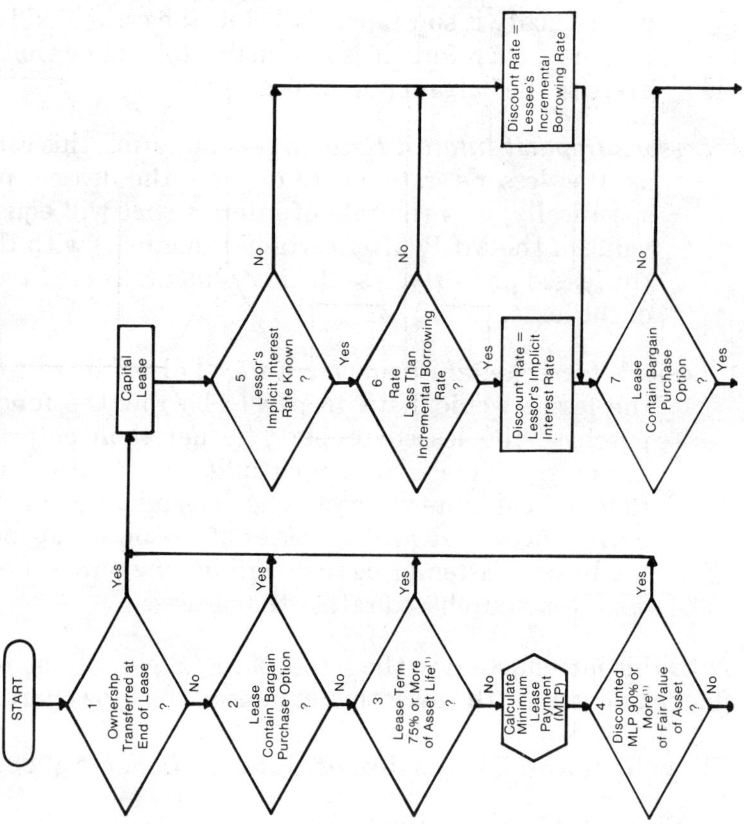

FLOWCHART 1
LESSEE - GENERAL

[6] FASB Interpretation No. 21 specifies that the "classification of a lease in accordance with the criteria of FASB Statement No. 13 shall not be changed as a result of a business combination unless the provisions of the lease are modified."

There are four major decisions that must be made before the lessee is able to determine if the lease will be classified as capital or operating. These decisions are shown in Blocks 1 through 4 of Flowchart 1. If any *one* of the decision criteria is met, the lease will be classified as capital in nature; and if *all* four of the decision criteria are *not* met, the lease will be considered to be operating. The first two decisions deal with transfer of ownership to the leased property. The first criterion is satisfied if the lease agreement specifies that title to the leased property will transfer to the lessee at the end of the lease term. If transfer of ownership is not

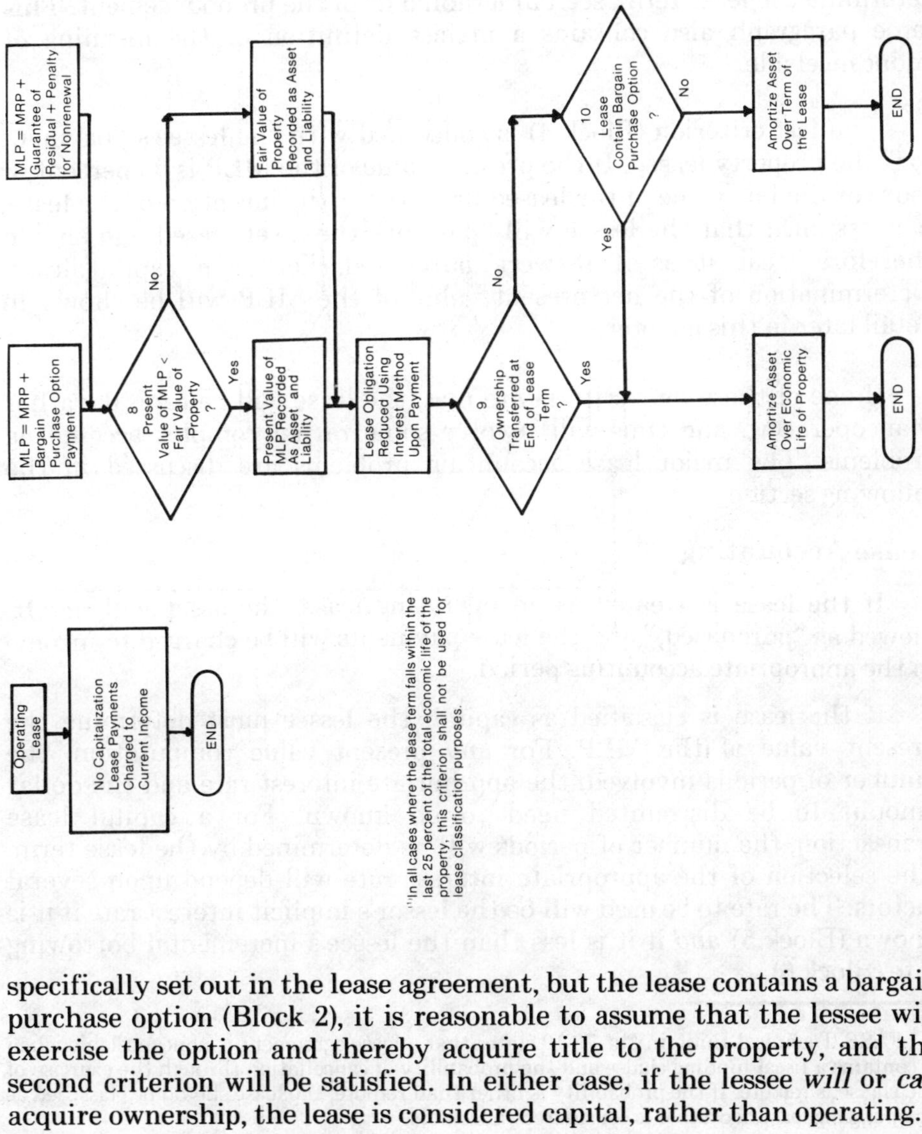

specifically set out in the lease agreement, but the lease contains a bargain purchase option (Block 2), it is reasonable to assume that the lessee will exercise the option and thereby acquire title to the property, and the second criterion will be satisfied. In either case, if the lessee *will* or *can* acquire ownership, the lease is considered capital, rather than operating.

The third criterion addresses the relationship between the lease term and the economic life of the leased property. The assumption is that, if the lessee makes substantial use of the property in terms of its economic life, the lessee has received the "privileges" of ownership, even if title does not transfer. Specifically, the criterion (Block 3) states that, if the lease term is 75 percent or more of the economic life of the property, the lease is considered capital. It is important to note that the lease must be *noncancelable*[7] and that the lease term may be longer than the time period specified in the lease agreement. For example, the lease term should include the periods covered by a renewal option. To properly determine the lease term, see Paragraph 5 (f) of the pronouncement. This same paragraph also contains a precise definition of the meaning of "noncancelable."

The last criterion (Block 4) is concerned with the lessee's "payment for" the property leased. If the present value of the MLP is 90 percent or more of the fair value of the leased property at the inception of the lease, it is assumed that the lessee will "pay for" the asset leased and should therefore treat it as if it were purchased, i.e., as a capital lease. Determination of the net present value of the MLP will be shown in detail later in this chapter.

If one of these four criteria are met, the lease will be capital, rather than operating, and thus will involve some rather complex accounting problems. The major lease accounting problems are discussed in the following section.

Lease Accounting

If the lease is treated as an operating lease, the asset will not be viewed as "purchased," and the lease payments will be charged to income in the appropriate accounting period.

If the lease is classified as capital, the lessee must determine the present value of the MLP. For any present value computation, the number of periods involved, the appropriate interest rate and the dollar amount to be discounted need to be known. For a capital lease transaction, the number of periods will be determined by the lease term. The selection of the appropriate interest rate will depend upon several factors. The rate to be used will be the lessor's implicit interest rate if it is known (Block 5) *and* if it is less than the lessee's incremental borrowing rate (Block 6).

---

[7] FASB Technical Bulletin No. 79-10 states that a lease agreement is noncancelable when it contains a fiscal funding clause and the probability of cancellation through the exercise of the clause is remote. If the probability is other than remote, the lease should be classified as an operating lease because it is considered cancelable.

Obviously, if the lessor's implicit rate is not known, the lessee's incremental rate must be used. The determination of the appropriate amount to use in the discounting process will depend on whether the lease contains a bargain purchase option (Block 7). If the lease does contain a bargain purchase option, the MLP will be equal to the MRP, plus the amount of the bargain purchase payment. For the present value computation, the MRP is an annuity and the bargain purchase option payment is a lump-sum payment at the end of the lease term. If present value tables are used, it will be necessary to have a table for the present value of $1 and the present value of an ordinary annuity of $1. (If payments are made at the beginning of each period, a table for the present value of an annuity due of $1 would replace the ordinary annuity table. Present value tables are provided in Appendix A.) If the lease does not contain a bargain purchase option, the MLP will be equal to the MRP, plus any guarantee of residual value and plus any penalty for nonrenewal of the lease. Again, the MRP is an annuity, and the other two items *generally* represent lump-sum payments at the end of the lease term.

As in the case of any purchased asset, the recorded value of the asset must not exceed the fair value at the date of acquisition. Therefore, it is necessary to record the asset "acquired" through the lease agreement at the lower of the present value of the MLP or the fair value of the leased property (Block 8). The liability owed to the lessor will be recorded at the same amount.

The lease obligation will be reduced as the lease payments are made, using the interest method. (The interest method is the application of the discount rate against the unrecovered obligation balance, and will be used extensively in this chapter. This method is required by SFAS No. 13, Paragraph 12, and is explained in APB Opinion No. 12, Paragraph 16.) The asset recorded will be amortized over its economic life, if ownership transfers or if there is a bargain purchase option (Blocks 9 and 10), or over the lease term, in the absence of either of these two provisions. The depreciation method used should be consistent with the method used for owned assets of a similar nature.

This general discussion has provided an overview for the detailed analysis that follows.

Technical Considerations for Lessee Accounting—General

To illustrate the specific provisions of SFAS No. 13 as they apply to the lessee, two examples follow:

Example I

Lease Assumptions

1. Lessee enters into a 10-year noncancelable lease that requires year-end payments of $53,000 ($3,000 of which represent executory costs).
2. Lessee's incremental borrowing rate is eight percent, and the lessor's implicit interest rate is unknown.
3. Ownership transfers to the lessee at the end of the lease term. The lease does not contain a bargain purchase option.
4. The leased property has a fair value of $340,000 and an estimated economic life of 12 years.

The major problems outlined in the above discussion deal with (1) proper classification of the lease, (2) determination of the appropriate interest rate for calculating the present value of the MLP, (3) determining the proper MLP and (4) selecting the proper amortization technique for the asset recorded and the related obligation. The technical aspects of the general discussion will be shown through the solution to the example problem presented.

The Example 1 lease qualifies as a capital lease. The lease agreement actually meets three of the four basic criteria, although only one criterion need be met. First, ownership to the property transfers to the lessee at the end of the lease term. Also, the lease term of 10 years is more than 75 percent of the asset's economic life (12 years × .75 = 9 years), and the present value of the MLP is more than 90 percent of the fair value of the leased property. The computation of the MLP is shown after selection of the proper interest rate.

Determination of the proper interest rate in this particular example is quite easy, because the lessor's implicit rate is not known. Therefore, the only possible rate to use in the discounting process is the lessee's incremental borrowing rate of eight percent.

Because the lease does not contain a bargain purchase option, the MLP will be equal to the MRP, plus any guaranteed residual value plus any penalty for nonrenewal. In the Example 1 lease, there is no guaranteed residual value or penalty for nonrenewal, so the MLP will be equal to the MRP. To calculate the proper MRP, the lessee must exclude executory costs, such as insurance, maintenance and taxes, from the required payments. In the example problem, $3,000 of the total MRP of $53,000 represent executory costs, and must be removed and treated as a separate component of the lease. The MLP therefore is equal to $50,000 per year.

We now have enough information to calculate the present value of the MLP, which is determined as follows:

Lease Payment Required	$ 53,000
Less: Executory Costs	3,000
	$ 50,000
Present Value Factor	[a]6.71008
Present Value of MLP	$335,504

[a] Present value factor for an ordinary annuity for 10 periods at eight percent, see Appendix A, Table II.

The fair value of the leased property is equal to $340,000, and 90 percent of the amount is $306,000. Therefore, the present value of the MLP ($335,504) is more than 90 percent of the fair value of the property ($306,000), and the fourth general criterion is met.

Once the lease has been identified as a capital lease, it is necessary to determine the proper amount to capitalize and record as a lease obligation. This determination involves a comparison of the present value of the MLP with the fair value of the leased property. The recorded value of the asset and the obligation will be the smaller of the two. In this particular case, the present value of the MLP is $335,504, and the fair value of the property is $340,000. Therefore, the appropriate amount to use would be $335,504 (the present value of the MLP). The journal entry necessary to record the asset and obligation at the inception of the lease would be:

Leased Property Under Capital Lease	335,504	
Obligation Under Capital Lease		335,504

The next major problem involves the amortization of the asset and the obligation. The lease obligation is amortized each interest payment period, using the interest method. Table I shows the complete determination of the amortization of the obligation and the classification of all lease expenses. It will prove beneficial to take a few minutes and recompute some of the values on the Table.

Table I

Lease Amortization and Expenses

Example 1

Amortization Schedule for Capital Lease

Period	Annual Payment	Annual Interest Expense	Obligation Reduction	Present Value of Obligation at year-end
Initial Value	-	-	-	$335,504
1	$ 50,000	a$ 26,840	b$ 23,160	c312,344
2	50,000	24,988	25,012	287,332
3	50,000	22,987	27,013	260,319
4	50,000	20,826	29,174	231,145
5	50,000	18,492	31,508	199,637
6	50,000	15,971	34,029	165,608
7	50,000	13,249	36,751	128,857
8	50,000	10,309	39,691	89,166
9	50,000	7,132	42,868	46,298
10	50,000	3,702	46,298	-0-
	$500,000	$164,496	$335,504	

Schedule of Recorded Expenses for Capital Lease

Period	Amortization	Interest	Executory Costs	Total	Annual Lease Payment
1	d$ 27,959	$ 26,840	$ 3,000	$ 57,799	$ 53,000
2	27,959	24,988	3,000	55,947	53,000
3	27,959	22,987	3,000	53,946	53,000
4	27,959	20,826	3,000	51,785	53,000
5	27,959	18,492	3,000	49,451	53,000
6	27,959	15,971	3,000	46,930	53,000
7	27,959	13,249	3,000	44,208	53,000
8	27,959	10,309	3,000	41,268	53,000
9	27,959	7,132	3,000	38,091	53,000
10	27,959	3,702	3,000	34,661	53,000
11	27,959			27,959	
12	*27,955			27,955	
	$335,504	$164,496	$30,000	$530,000	$530,000

a $335,504 × 8% = $26,840
b $50,000 — $26,840 = $23,160
c $335,504 — $23,160 = $312,344
d Assuming that straight-line depreciation is used for owned assets. ($335,504/12 years = $27,959).
* rounded.

By using Table I, we can determine that the proper accounting for the year-end payment of $53,000 would be as follows:

Obligation under Capital Lease	23,160	
Interest Expense	26,840	
Executory Costs	3,000	
Cash		53,000

At the end of the year, an adjusting entry is necessary to record the amortization of the leased property. Because ownership to the property transfers to the lessee at the end of the lease term, the asset should be amortized over the economic life of the property, using the depreciation method commonly used for similar owned assets. In the example problem, we will assume that straight-line depreciation is the appropriate method to use. The following adjusting entry would be required to complete the recording of lease expenses:

Amortization of Leased Property	27,959	
Accumulated Amortization - Leased Property		27,959

The Example 1 lease was designed to be relatively straight-forward, so that the basic considerations of capital lease accounting could be demonstrated. The following illustration, Example 2, is somewhat more complex and requires additional decisions and computations. A complete understanding of Example 1 is necessary before the reader proceeds to the next illustration.

Example 2
Lease Assumptions

1. The lessee enters into a five-year noncancelable lease that requires payments of \$100,000 at the beginning of each of the five years. The lease agreement further specifies that the lessee will guarantee the residual value of the property in the amount of \$10,000, which also is equal to the estimated residual value at the end of the lease term.
2. The lessee's incremental borrowing rate is eight percent and the lessor's implicit rate is known to be 10 percent.
3. The leased property has a fair value of \$423,196 and an estimated economic life of five years. The lessee depreciates similar assets using the straight-line method.
4. In the third year of the lease term, the estimated residual value declines to \$8,000.

On the face of these assumptions, the Example 2 lease qualifies as a capital lease. As will be shown, the lease agreement meets two of the four basic criteria for classification as a capital lease, either of which is sufficient to classify the lease as capital: first, the lease term of five years is more than 75 percent of the economic life of the leased property (5 years × .75 = 3.75 years); and, second, as the computations below will show, the present value of the MLP is more than 90 percent of the fair value of the leased property.

Selection of the proper interest rate to use in discounting the MLP requires a comparison of the lessee's incremental borrowing rate with the lessor's implicit rate, because both are known in this example. The lessee's incremental borrowing rate of eight percent will be used in this case, because it is less than the lessor's implicit rate.

As before, the lease does not contain a bargain purchase option and the MLP will be equal to the MRP, plus any guaranteed residual value and plus any penalty for nonrenewal. In the Example 2 lease, the MRP is equal to $100,000, and there is a guarantee of residual value of $10,000. To determine the present value of the MLP, the lessee must compute the present value of an annuity due (the MRP) and the present value of an amount (the guarantee of residual value). Determination of the present value of the MLP is as follows:

Lease Payment Required	$100,000	
Less: Executory Costs	-0-	
	$100,000	
Present Value Factor	[a]4.31213	
Present Value of Rental Payment		$431,213
Guarantee of Residual Value	$ 10,000	
Present Value Factor	[b].68058	
Present Value of Residual		6,806
Present Value of MLP		$438,019

[a] Present value factor for an annuity due for five periods at eight percent. See Appendix A, Table III.
[b] Present value factor for $1 for five periods at eight percent. See Appendix A, Table I.

The fair value of the leased property is equal to $423,196, and 90 percent of the amount is $380,876. Therefore, the present value of the MLP is more than 90 percent of the fair value of the leased property.

The present value of the MLP ($438,019) is greater than the fair value of the leased property ($423,196), so the leased property will be recorded at fair value of $423,196, the lesser of the two amounts. At the inception of the lease, the required journal entry would be:

Leased Property Under Capital Lease	423,196	
Obligation Under Capital Lease		423,196

Table II shows the computations for the amortization of the obligation and the asset, along with the determination of the expenses related to the lease transaction. There are several important points that need to be made about the computations shown in Table II. First, because the fair value of the leased property is recorded as the asset and obligation, the interest rate that must be used in the amortization of the obligation is the *lessor's implicit rate* of 10 percent. You will recall that the lessee's incremental borrowing rate was used to determine the present value of the MLP, but this amount was never used in the capitalization process. Therefore the eight percent rate will not be used when applying the interest method. The second major point about the Table is that, because the lease did not transfer ownership or contain a bargain purchase option, the asset recorded will be amortized over the lease term, rather than over the economic life of the property.

Table II

Lease Amortization and Expenses
Example 2

Amortization Schedule for Capital Lease

	Period	Annual Payment	Annual Interest Expense	Obligation Reduction	Present Value of Obligation at Year-End
Initial Value	-	-	-	-	$423,196
	1	$100,000	[a]$32,320	$ 67,680	355,516
	2	100,000	25,552	74,448	281,068
	3	100,000	18,107	81,893	199,175
	4	100,000	9,917	90,083	109,092
	5	100,000	[b]908	99,092	[c]10,000
		$500,000	$86,804	$413,196	

Schedule of Recorded Expenses for Capital Lease

Period	Amortiza-tion	Interest	Total	Annual Lease Payment
1	[d]$ 82,639	$32,320	$114,959	$ 100,000
2	82,639	25,552	108,191	100,000
3	[e]83,306	18,107	101,413	100,000
4	83,306	9,917	93,223	100,000
5	83,306	908	84,214	100,000
Payment for Residual Value				2,000
	$415,196	$86,804	$502,000	$ 502,000

[a] ($423,196 − $100,000) × 10% = $32,320
[b] Interest on the guaranteed residual value
[c] Guaranteed residual value
[d] $423,196 − $10,000 = $413,196/5 years = $82,639
[e] Annual depreciation expense

Annual depreciation expense	$ 82,639
Number of years prior to change in residual value	× 2
Accumulated depreciation	$ 165,278
Recorded value of leased property	$423,196
Accumulated depreciation	(165,278)
Revised estimated residual value	(8,000)
Amount remaining to depreciate	$ 249,918
Remaining useful life	÷ 3
Current depreciation	$ 83,306

Given this information, the entries to record the lease expenses for the first year would be as follows:

Obligation Under Capital Lease	67,680	
Interest Expense	32,320	
Cash		100,000
Amortization of Leased Property	82,639	
Accumulated Amortization—Leased Property		82,639

The last significant point in Table II relates to the $2,000 decline in residual value, which occurred in the third year of the lease term. This decline in residual value is a change in an accounting estimate and is treated in a prospective manner, as prescribed in APB Opinion No. 20. (See Topic 1 for a detailed analysis of APB Opinion No. 20, which includes accounting for changes in an accounting estimate.) The effect of the change in accounting estimate is charged to current and future periods. This is illustrated by the change in the amount of amortization of the asset account, from $82,639 in Year 2 to $83,306 in Year 3. In all future years, $83,306 will be charged to income as amortization.

The decline in residual value increased the ultimate cash outflow to the lessee by $2,000. Since the lessee guaranteed the residual value of $10,000, any decline would require the lessee to pay an amount equal to the decline to the lessor at the end of the lease term. The entry necessary to remove the asset and obligation balances at the end of the lease term would be as follows:[8]

Accumulated Amortization - Leased Property	415,196	
Obligation Under Capital Lease	10,000	
Leased Property Under Capital Lease		423,196
Cash		2,000

The $2,000 payment by the lessee to the lessor represents the decline in the residual value below the amount guaranteed.

Operating Leases

If a lease agreement fails to meet any of the lease criteria necessary to qualify as a capital lease, the accounting is quite simple. To illustrate, assume a five-year lease, with annual payments of $75,000. Further assume that the criteria necessary for classification as a capital lease are not met. The only entry that is necessary is the annual or periodic lease payment shown below:

Lease Rental Expense	75,000	
Cash		75,000

This completes the discussion of the technical aspect of accounting for general type leases. The remaining sections will deal with accounting problems associated with special lease situations faced by a lessee.

---

[8] Should the lessee terminate the lease agreement prior to the end of the lease term through a purchase of the property, FASB Interpretation No. 26 requires that the transaction be accounted for like a renewal or extension of a capital lease.

Flowchart and General Discussion of Sale-Leaseback Transactions

Accounting for sale and leaseback transactions has become somewhat complicated as a result of the issuance of SFAS No. 28—*Accounting for Sales with Leasebacks.* "Sale-leaseback transactions," according to SFAS No. 28, Paragraph 2, "involve the sale of property by the owner and a lease of the property back to the seller." In this type of transaction, one party is referred to as the "seller-lessee" and the other party to the transaction is referred to as the lessor. Statement No. 28 identifies three types of sale-leaseback transactions that are of importance from an accounting perspective. The first type of transaction is referred to as a "minor" leaseback because the seller-lessee retains only a minor interest in the property sold. The second type of sale-leaseback transaction is referred to as a "more than minor but less than substantially all" leaseback. While the wording associated with this type of sale-leaseback is cumbersome, it is very descriptive of the transaction and will be used throughout the remainder of this discussion. The last type of sale-leaseback transaction is referred to as a "substantially all" leaseback because the seller-lessee retains substantially all of the ownership interest in the property sold.

Flowchart 2 depicts the major decisions involved in classification and accounting for the three types of sale-leaseback transactions identified in SFAS No. 28. By following the information presented in the Flowchart, the reader should achieve an overview of the accounting treatment associated with the various sale-leaseback transactions.

Once it has been determined that a sale and leaseback transaction has occurred (Block 1), the next step in the decision-making process involves the comparison of the present value of the minimum lease payments required under the leaseback agreement with the fair market value of the property sold (Block 2). If the present value of the minimum lease payments is 10 percent or less of the fair value of the property sold, the transaction must be classified as a "minor" leaseback. If the present value of the minimum lease payments is greater than 10 percent, but less than 90 percent of the fair value of the property sold, the transaction must be classified as a "more than minor but less than substantially all" leaseback (Block 4). Finally, if the present value of the minimum lease payments is 90 percent or more of the fair value of the property sold, the transaction must be classified as a "substantially all" leaseback. Figure I clearly illustrates the classification problems shown in Flowchart Blocks 2 and 4.

FLOWCHART 2
SALE AND LEASEBACK

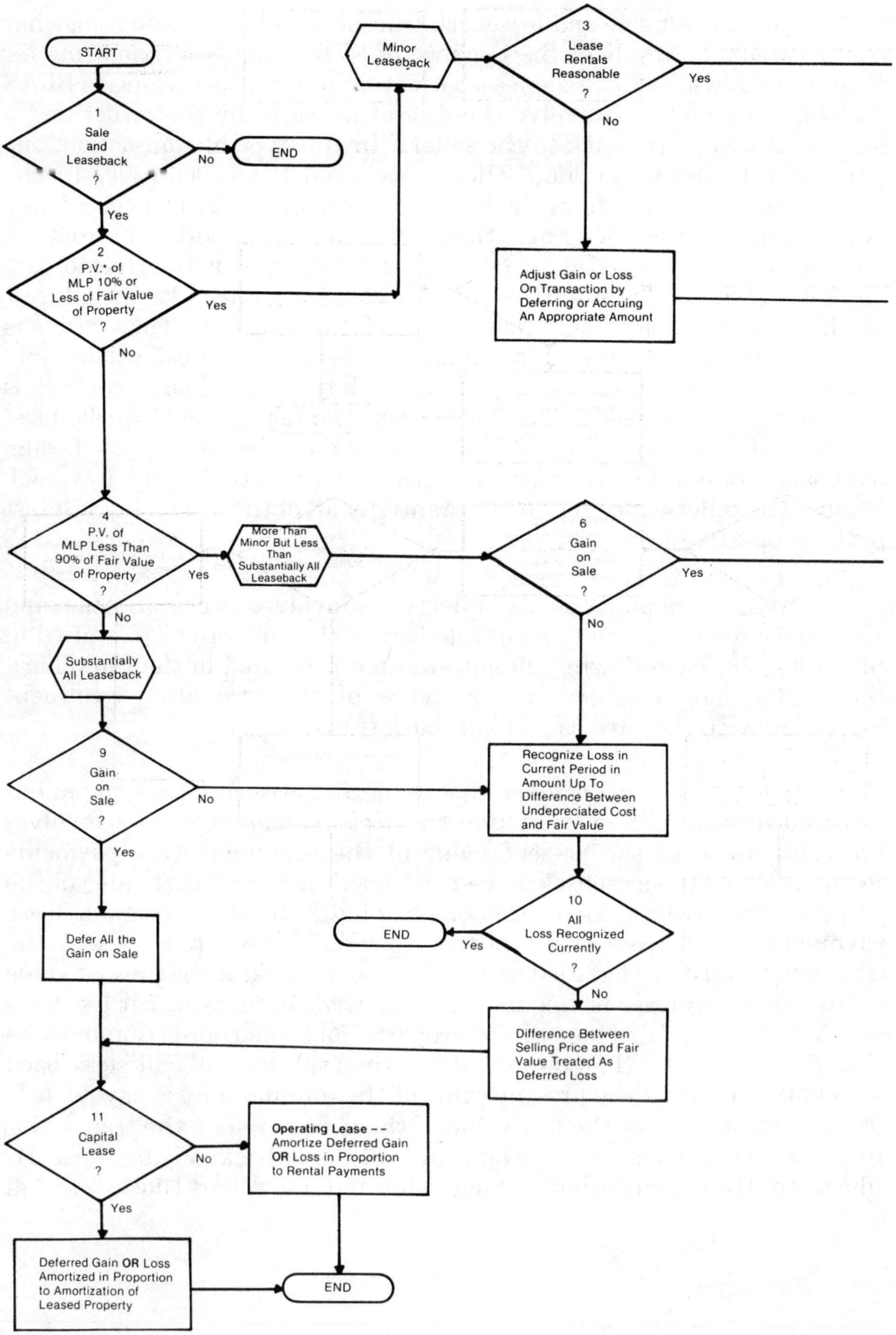

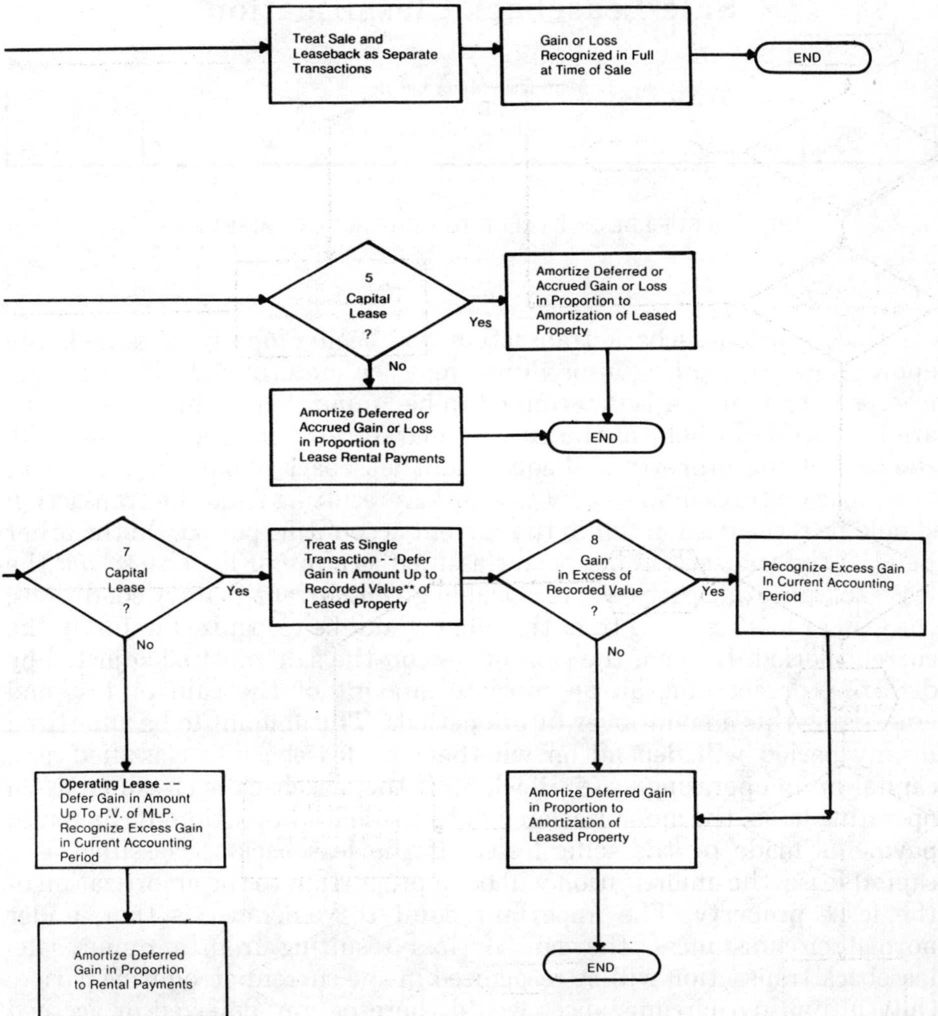

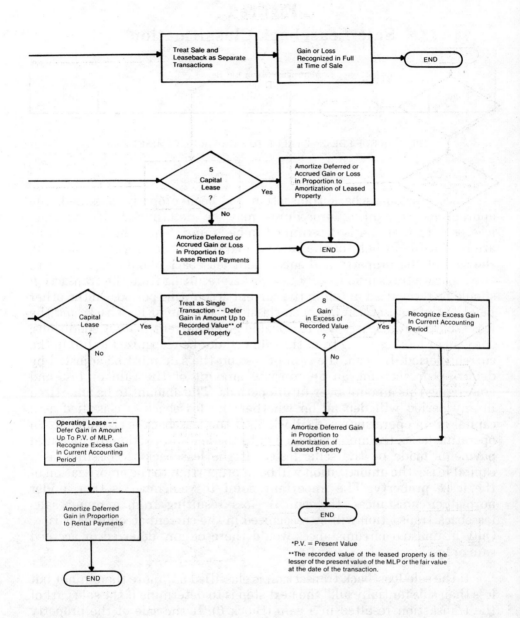

*P.V. = Present Value

**The recorded value of the leased property is the lesser of the present value of the MLP or the fair value at the date of the transaction.

Figure I
Sale-Leaseback Classification

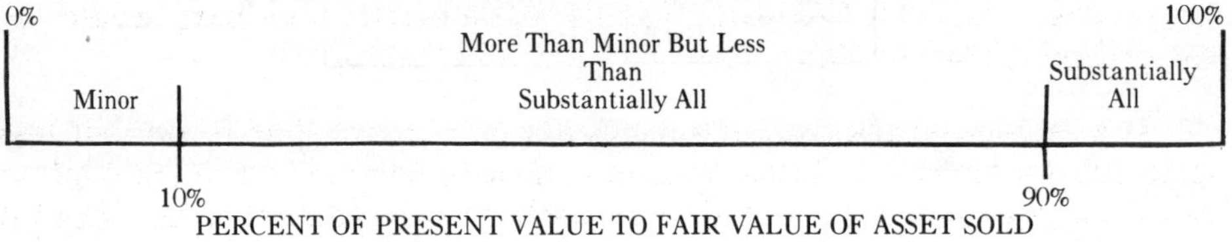

Once a sale-leaseback transaction has been properly classified, the appropriate accounting procedures may be determined. If the sale-leaseback transaction is determined to be "minor," and the lease rentals are reasonable in light of the current market for the property (Block 3), the sale of the property and subsequent leaseback should be treated as two separate transactions. Any gain or loss resulting from the transaction should be recognized in full in the current accounting period. On the other hand, if the transaction has been classified as a minor leaseback, *and* the lease rentals are clearly not reasonable given current market conditions, the gain or loss resulting from the sale will not be recognized in full in the current period. Instead, the gain or loss on the sale must be adjusted by deferring or accruing an appropriate amount of the gain or loss and amortizing this amount over future periods. The amount to be amortized in any period will depend on whether the leaseback is classified as a capital or an operating lease (Block 5). If the leaseback is classified as an operating lease, the amortization will be made in proportion to the rental payments made by the seller-lessee. If the leaseback is classified as a capital lease, the amortization will be in proportion to the amortization of the lease property. The important point to remember is that, under normal circumstances, the gain or loss resulting from a minor sale-leaseback transaction will be recognized in the current accounting period. Only in unusual circumstances would there be any deferred or accrued gain or loss.

If the sale-leaseback transaction is classified as "more than minor but less than substantially all," the next step is to determine if the sale part of the transaction resulted in a gain (Block 6). If the sale of the property results in a gain, and the leaseback meets the criteria for classification as a capital lease (Block 7), the sale and leaseback will be treated as a single transaction. The seller-lessee will defer all or part of the gain and amortize it in proportion to the amortization of the leased property. The amount of the gain that may be deferred is an amount equal to the recorded value of the property (recall from previous discussions that the recorded value of the property under a capital lease is the lesser of the present value of the minimum lease payment *or* the fair value of the property at the date of the lease agreement). If the total gain from the sale of the property is greater than the recorded value of the asset, the excess gain will be recognized in the current accounting period. In this latter case, part of the gain would be deferred, and part would be recognized in the current period.

If a sale-leaseback transaction results in a "more than minor but less than substantially all" leaseback, and the sale portion of the transaction results in a gain (Block 6), but the leaseback fails to qualify as a capital lease, the leaseback will be treated as an operating lease. In this case, it is appropriate to defer the gain in an amount up to the present value of the minimum lease payments associated with the leaseback agreement. Once again, if the gain on the sale exceeds the maximum amount that may be deferred, the excess gain should be recognized in the current accounting period. Any gain deferred should be amortized in proportion to the rental payments called for under the leaseback agreement.

In the cases discussed thus far, the "more than minor but less than substantially all" leaseback resulted in a gain on the sale portion of the transaction. Different accounting procedures are required in the cases where the sale results in a loss to the seller-lessee. When the sale-leaseback transaction results in a loss on the sale of the property (Block 6), the seller-lessee should recognize a loss in the current period in an amount up to the *difference* between the undepreciated cost of the property and its fair value. If the sales transaction results in a loss that exceeds the amount defined above, the seller-lessee should defer any excess loss. The excess loss will be equal to the difference between the selling price of the property and its fair value. The amortization of the deferred loss would depend on whether the leaseback is a capital or operating lease. If the leaseback qualifies for capital lease treatment, the deferred loss would be amortized in proportion to the amortization of the leased property. If the leaseback is to be treated as an operating lease, the deferred loss would be amortized in proportion to the rental payments made by the seller-lessee.

The final type of sale-leaseback results in a "substantially all" leaseback agreement. Recall that this type of leaseback results when the present value of the minimum lease payments are 90 percent or more of the fair value of the property subject to the agreement (Block 4). When a "substantially all" leaseback transaction occurs, and the sale portion of the transaction results in a gain (Block 9), the entire gain should be deferred. Once again, the amortization of the deferred gain will depend on whether the leaseback is treated as a capital lease or an operating lease. The deferred gain will be amortized in the same manner described for the "more than minor but less than substantially all" leaseback. If a "substantially all" leaseback transaction results in a loss on the sale portion of the transaction, the loss should be handled in the same manner described for the "more than minor but less than substantially all" leaseback transaction. Because this accounting has been described above it is not necessary to repeat the details.

This overview of the accounting requirements of SFAS No. 28 should serve as a solid introduction to the technical material that follows in the form of example material.

Technical Considerations of a Sale-Leaseback Transaction

To illustrate the technical provisions of SFAS No. 28, four comprehensive examples will be developed. Each example builds on the previous material, so it is important to review the examples in order. The assumptions used in the first example are set out below.

Example 1
Sale-Leaseback Assumptions

1. On January 1, 198A, Cites Corporation sold equipment to Sanders, Inc. for $12,000,000, and immediately leased the property back for a period of three years. The leaseback agreement requires Cites to make annual year-end rental payments of $400,000. Cites Corporation has a December 31 year end for accounting purposes.

2. The property subject to the sale-leaseback has a cost basis to Cites of $9,000,000, and an estimated economic life of 30 years. The fair market value of the property on January 1, 198A, was $12,000,000.

3. The seller-lessee's incremental borrowing rate is 10 percent, and the interest rate implicit in the leaseback agreement is known by Cites to be 12 percent. The leaseback agreement *does not* contain a bargain purchase option, and title to the property will be retained by Sanders at the end of the lease term.

4. The lease payments are considered reasonable in relation to the current market for similar types of property and similar lease terms.

The first step in the solution to this example is to recognize that the two companies have entered into a sale and leaseback agreement and, therefore, the provisions of SFAS No. 28 are applicable. The first major computational problem facing the accountant is to compute the present value of the minimum lease payments (MLP) required in the leaseback agreement. The purpose of this computation is to aid the accountant in the proper classification of the transaction. The present value of the MLP is calculated below:

Lease Payments Required	$400,000
Present Value Factor for an Ordinary Annuity for 3 Periods at 10 Percent (Appendix A)	× 2.48685
Present Value of MLP	$994,740

The present value of the MLP was calculated using the 10 percent incremental borrowing rate of Cites because the implicit rate of 12 percent is known and it is greater than the incremental borrowing rate.

In order to properly classify the leaseback, the present value of the MLP must be compared to the fair value of the property on the date of the leaseback agreement. The present value of the MLP is 8.3 percent of the fair value of the leased property ($994,740/$12,000,000 = 8.3 percent). Since the present value of the MLP is 10 percent or less of the fair market value of the property, the leaseback should be classified as "minor."

Now that the leaseback has been properly classified, the accountant must determine if the leaseback transaction will be treated as an operating or a capital lease. In this case, the leaseback is properly classified as an operating lease because (1) ownership does not transfer to Cites at the end of the lease term, (2) the leaseback does not contain a bargain purchase option, (3) the lease term is less than 75 percent of the economic life of the property (3 year lease term/30 year life = 10 percent), and (4) the present value of the MLP is less than 90 percent of the fair value of the leased property at the inception of the leaseback agreement. Therefore, the leaseback fails to meet any of the criteria necessary for classification as a capital lease.

Since the transaction is classified as a minor leaseback, and the lease payments are considered to be reasonable, no profit or loss resulting from the original sale will be deferred or accrued. The sale and leaseback must be treated as two separate transactions, and any gain or loss will be recognized in full in 198A, the period in which the sale took place. The gain on the sale of the equipment is computed below:

Selling Price	$12,000,000
Cost Basis	9,000,000
Gain on Sale	$ 3,000,000

The journal entry required on January 1, 198A, to record the sale portion of the sale-leaseback transaction is:

Cash	12,000,000	
Equipment		9,000,000
Gain on Sale-Leaseback		3,000,000

The "Gain on Sale-Leaseback" account would be classified on the income statement in accordance with the provisions of APB Opinion No. 30 (see Topic 1 for a complete analysis of APB Opinion No. 30).

Because the leaseback will be treated as an operating lease, the only entry required in connection with the leaseback is to record the year-end lease payment. The entry on December 31, 198A is shown below:

Lease Rental Payment	400,000	
Cash		400,000

This last entry completes the analysis of the first example material. The first example was designed to be straightforward and to serve as an introduction to the problems associated with a sale-leaseback transaction.

The second example is somewhat more complex than the first, and the assumptions relating to it are listed below.

Example 2
Sale-Leaseback Assumptions

1. On January 1, 198A, the Hunt Company, a December 31 year-end company, sold equipment with an estimated economic life of five years to the Thomas Company for $400,000 cash, and immediately leased the equipment from Thomas for four years. The leaseback agreement requires Hunt to pay $100,000 at the beginning of each of the next four years to Thomas Company.

2. The equipment involved in the sale and leaseback transaction has a cost to Hunt of $300,000, and a fair market value on the date of the sale of $400,000.

3. Hunt's incremental borrowing rate is 12 percent, and the rate implicit in the leaseback agreement is unknown.

4. Title to the equipment transfers to Hunt Company at the end of the lease term, and the company uses straight-line depreciation for similar owned assets.

After recognizing this as a sale-leaseback transaction, the first step in the accounting process is to determine the proper classification of the transaction. To accomplish this, the present value of the MLP must be computed. This calculation is shown below:

Lease Payment Required	$ 100,000
Present Value Factor for an Annuity Due for 4 Periods at 12 Percent (Appendix A)	× 3.40183
Present Value of MLP	$ 340,183

Next, the present value of the MLP must be compared to the fair value of the property sold. In this example, the present value of the MLP is 85 percent of the fair value of the equipment ($340,183 present value of MLP/$400,000 fair value of equipment = 85 percent). This sale-leaseback would be classified as "more than minor but less than substantially all" because the percentage relationship calculated above is more than 10 percent, but less than 90 percent, of the fair market value of the equipment.

After the sale-leaseback has been properly classified, the next step is to determine the type of lease involved in the transaction. The lease in this example must be classified as a capital lease because title to the property transfers to the seller-lessee at the end of the lease term. All or part of the gain will be deferred because the leaseback qualified as a capital lease and there is a gain on the sale portion of the transaction. The amount to be deferred may not exceed the recorded amount of the leased property, and the amount deferred should be amortized in proportion to the amortization of the leased asset. The reader should remember that these accounting procedures apply only if there is a *gain* associated with the sale portion of the sale-leaseback transaction. Other accounting procedures will be applied in cases where the sale results in a loss to the seller-lessee. If the amount of gain on the sale is greater than the recorded value of the property, this excess gain will be recognized in the current accounting period.

Before the amount of the gain to defer can be determined, the recorded value of the leased property must be computed. Under normal capital lease accounting, the recorded value of the property will be the smaller of the present value of the MLP or the fair market value of the asset on the date of the lease agreement. In this particular example, the present value of the MLP was calculated to be $340,183, which is less than the fair value of the property at the inception of the leaseback ($400,000). Therefore, the recorded value of the property will be $340,183. The maximum gain that could be deferred is limited to $340,183, the recorded value of the asset. The next step in the accounting process is to calculate the actual gain from the sale portion of the transaction. The amount of the gain is computed below:

Selling Price	$400,000
Cost Basis	300,000
Gain on Sale	$100,000

Since the gain on the sale of $100,000 is less than the recorded amount of the property ($340,183), the entire gain will be deferred, and the sale-leaseback will be treated as a single transaction. The entries necessary to record the initial sale and subsequent leaseback of the equipment are as follows:

Cash	400,000	
Equipment		300,000
Deferred Gain on Sale-Leaseback		100,000

Leased Property Under Capital Lease	340,183	
Obligation Under Capital Lease		340,183

Table I below shows the computation of the amortization schedule and the determination of the expenses to be recorded under the lease assumptions used in Example 2.

Table I
Amortization Schedule for Sale-Leaseback

Amortization Period	Annual Payment	Annual Interest Expense	Obligation Reduction	Present Value of Obligation at End of Year
Initial Value				$340,183
1	$100,000	a $28,822	$ 71,178	269,005
2	100,000	20,281	79,719	189,286
3	100,000	10,714	89,286	100,000
4	100,000	-0-	100,000	-0-
	$400,000	$59,817	$340,183	

Schedule of Recorded Expenses for Capital Lease

Period	Amortization	Deferred Gain	Amortization After Gain	Interest Expense	Total Expense
1	b $ 68,037	c $ 20,000	d $ 48,037	$28,822	$ 76,859
2	68,037	20,000	48,037	20,281	68,318
3	68,037	20,000	48,037	10,714	58,751
4	68,036	20,000	48,036	-0-	48,036
5	68,036	20,000	48,036	-0-	48,036
	$340,183	$100,000	$240,183	$59,817	$300,000

a $340,183 — $100,000 = $240,183 × .12 = $28,822.
b $340,183/5 years = $68,037.
c $100,000 gain/5 years = $20,000.
d $68,037 — $20,000 = $48,037.

Given the information generated in Table I, the entry for the first lease payment is presented below:

Interest Expense	28,822	
Obligation Under Capital Lease	71,178	
Cash		100,000

The final entry required is to amortize the leased asset and to amortize a portion of the deferred gain on the sale portion of the transaction. The gain should be amortized in proportion to the amortization of the leased property. Since the leased property is amortized using the straight-line method, the deferred gain should be amortized using the same accounting method. The amortization period should be that period considered appropriate for the leased asset (economic life of the property or the term of the lease). In this example, title to the property transferred to the seller-lessee at the end of the lease term, and the appropriate amortization period is the economic life of the asset. Given this information, the deferred gain should be amortized using the straight-line method over the economic life of the leased property. The journal entry necessary to record the depreciation of the leased asset and the amortization of the deferred gain would be as follows:

Amortization of Leased Property	48,037	
Deferred Gain on Sale-Leaseback	20,000	
Leased Property Under Capital Lease		68,037

Information required to make the journal entries for the remainder of the life of the property can be found in Table I.

Had the leaseback in this example been classified as an operating lease, the maximum gain that could have been deferred would be equal to the present value of the MLP, which may or may not be equal to the fair value of the property. The fair value of the leased property would be of no consequence in the case of an operating lease classified as "more than minor but less than substantially all."

This completes the analysis of the Example 2 material. This material required a more complex decision-making process on the part of the accountant. The next example will build on some of the material just presented.

Information about the third example is found below.

Example 3

Sale-Leaseback Assumptions

1. On January 1, 198A, Western Industries, a December 31 year-end company, sold equipment to Mills Company for $600,000, and immediately leased the equipment back for a period of five years. The leaseback agreement requires Western to make annual year-end rental payments of $158,278 for each of the next five years.

2. The equipment subject to the sale-leaseback has a cost basis to Western of $500,000, and an estimated useful life of five years. The fair market value of the equipment on January 1, 198A, is $600,000.

3. Western's incremental borrowing rate is 10 percent, and the lessor's implicit interest rate is not known.

4. The leaseback agreement is noncancelable, and ownership to the leased equipment transfers to Western at the end of the lease term.

Western uses the sum-of-the-years' digits method to depreciate similar owned assets.

After recognizing that the transaction between Western and Mills is a sale and leaseback, the next step is to properly classify the leaseback portion of the transaction. To accomplish this, the accountant must compute the present value of the MLP. This computation is shown below:

Lease Payments Required	$158,278
Present Value Factor for an Ordinary Annuity for 5 Periods at 10 Percent (Appendix A)	× 3.79079
Present Value of MLP	$600,000

The present value of the MLP must now be compared to the fair market value of the equipment to determine the proper classification of the leaseback. The present value of the MLP is 100 percent ($600,000/$600,000) of the fair value of the equipment. Therefore, the leaseback qualifies as a "substantially all" leaseback.

Once the leaseback has been properly classified, the next step is to determine the type of lease involved in the transaction. The lease described in Example 3 qualifies as a capital lease because ownership to the equipment transfers at the end of the lease term. Also, the lease term of five years is more than 75 percent of the economic life of the asset, and the present value of the MLP is more than 90 percent of the fair value of the leased property. Table II shows the computations of the amortization schedule and the determination of the expenses to be recorded under the lease assumptions specified. Meeting one of the four basic criteria is sufficient to classify the lease as a capital lease.

Table II
Amortization Schedule for Sale-Leaseback

Amortization Period	Annual Payment	Annual Interest Expense	Obligation Reduction	Present Value of Obligation at End of Year
Initial Value				$600,000
1	$158,278	[a] $ 60,000	$ 98,278	501,722
2	158,278	50,172	108,106	393,616
3	158,278	39,362	118,916	274,700
4	158,278	27,470	130,808	143,892
5	158,278	* 14,386	143,892	—0—
	$791,390	$191,390	$600,000	

Schedule of Recorded Expenses for Capital Lease

Period	Amortization	Deferred Gain	Amortization After Gain	Interest Expense	Total Expense
1	[b] $200,000	[c] $ 33,333	[d] $166,667	$ 60,000	$226,667
2	160,000	26,667	133,333	50,172	183,505
3	120,000	20,000	100,000	39,362	139,362
4	80,000	13,333	66,667	27,470	94,137
5	40,000	6,667	33,333	14,386	47,719
	$600,000	$100,000	$500,000	$191,390	$691,390

[a] $600,000 × .10 = $60,000.
[b] 5/15 × $600,000 = $200,000 for 198A.
[c] 5/15 × $100,000 = $33,333.
[d] $200,000 − $33,333 = $166,667.
* Rounded

Since the present value of the MLP is equal to the fair value of the equipment, the asset and obligation will be recorded at $600,000. The journal entries to record the initial sale and subsequent leaseback of the equipment are as follows:

Cash	600,000	
Equipment		500,000
Deferred Gain on Sale-Leaseback		100,000
Leased Property Under Capital Lease	600,000	
Obligation Under Capital Lease		600,000

The entire gain on the sale portion of the transaction was deferred because the leaseback was classified as "substantially all."

Because ownership of the equipment transfers to the seller-lessee at the end of the lease term, the asset will be amortized over its economic life of five years. The seller-lessee uses the sum-of-the-years' digits method to depreciate similar owned assets, and will use this method for assets recorded under capital lease agreements. The obligation is amortized using the interest method at the rate of 10 percent, the seller-lessee's incremental borrowing rate. The deferred gain must be amortized consistent with the amortization of the asset. The journal entries necessary to record the first annual leaseback payment and the amortization of the equipment and deferred gain would be as follows:

Obligation Under Capital Lease	98,278	
Interest Expense	60,000	
Cash		158,278
Amortization of Leased Property	166,667	
Deferred Gain on Sale-Leaseback	33,333	
Leased Property Under Capital Lease		200,000

The amortization of the deferred gain reduces the total amortization expense charged to income during the period. Rather than a direct reduction of the leased property account, as shown above, the accountant may elect to utilize an accumulated amortization account that would serve as a contra asset account.

This completes the analysis of the Example 3 material. All examples to this point have resulted in a gain to the seller-lessee, so the final example is designed to demonstrate the proper accounting when a loss results from the sale portions of a sale-leaseback.

The relevant information relating to the final example material is found below.

Example 4
Sale-Leaseback Assumptions

1. Johnson, Inc., a December 31 year-end company, sold equipment to the Great Northern Company on January 1, 198A, for $290,000, and immediately leased the property back for a period of four years. The leaseback agreement requires that Johnson make annual year-end rental payments in the amount of $100,000 for each of the next four years.

2. The equipment sold has an undepreciated cost basis to Johnson of $350,000, and an estimated economic life of five years. The fair value of the equipment on January 1, 198A, is $310,245.

3. Johnson's incremental borrowing rate is 11 percent, and the implicit rate used by Great Northern is unknown.

4. Johnson uses straight-line depreciation for similar owned assets.

Since the transaction is obviously a sale-leaseback agreement, the first step is to compute the present value of the MLP. This computation is shown below:

Lease Payment Required	$100,000
Present Value Factor for an Ordinary Annuity at 11 percent for 4 Periods (Appendix A)	× 3.10245
Present Value of MLP	$310,245

Next, the present value of the MLP must be compared to the fair market value of the leased equipment to determine the proper classification of the leaseback. The present value of the MLP is 100 percent ($310,245/$310,245) of the fair value of the leased equipment. Therefore, the leaseback qualifies as "substantially all."

The leaseback agreement in this example qualifies as a capital lease because the lease term of four years is more than 75 percent of the economic life of the equipment (4 years/5 years = 80%). The sale portion of the transaction results in a loss to the seller-lessee. The amount of the loss is computed below:

Selling Price of Equipment	$290,000
Cost Basis of Equipment	350,000
Loss on Sale of Equipment	$ 60,000

Because the leaseback results in a loss of $60,000, the next step is to determine if any of the loss will be deferred or if the entire loss will be recognized in the current period.

The amount of the loss that must be recognized in the current accounting period is equal to the difference between the undepreciated cost basis of the asset and its fair value. The computation of the amount of loss to be *recognized* in 198A is shown below:

Undepreciated Cost Basis of the Equipment	$350,000
Fair Market Value of Equipment	310,245
Loss Recognized in 198A	$39,755

Of the total loss of $60,000, only $39,755 will be recognized in the period of the sale. The difference of $20,245 ($60,000 total loss − $39,755 recognized loss = $20,245) will be deferred. The deferred loss will be amortized in proportion to the amortization of the leased property under the capital lease. In effect, the deferred loss represents a prepayment of lease payments relating to the leaseback. In this particular example, the deferred loss will be amortized over a period of four years using the straight-line method, because the leaseback is a capital lease and the straight-line method is used for similar owned assets.

The entries necessary to record the initial sales transaction and the related leaseback are as follows:

Cash	290,000	
Loss on Sale-Leaseback	39,755	
Deferred Loss on Sale-Leaseback	20,245	
Equipment		350,000
Leased Property Under Capital Lease	310,245	
Obligation Under Capital Lease		310,245

Table III shows the computation of the amortization schedule and the determination of the expenses to be recorded under the leaseback assumptions specified.

Table III
Amortization Schedule for Sale-Leaseback

Amortization Period	*Annual Payment*	*Annual Interest Expense*	*Obligation Reduction*	*Present Value of Obligation at End of Year*
Initial Value				$310,245
1	$100,000	[a] $34,127	$ 65,873	244,372
2	100,000	26,881	73,119	171,253
3	100,000	18,838	81,162	90,091
4	100,000	9,909	90,091	-0-
	$400,000	$89,755	$310,245	

Schedule of Recorded Expenses for Capital Lease

Period	*Amortization*	*Deferred Loss*	*Amortization After Loss*	*Interest Expense*	*Total Expense*
1	[b] $ 77,561	[c] $ 5,061	[d] $ 82,622	$34,127	$116,749
2	77,561	5,061	82,622	26,881	109,503
3	77,561	5,061	82,622	18,838	101,460
4	* 77,562	* 5,062	82,624	9,909	92,533
	$310,245	$20,245	$330,490	$89,755	$420,245

[a] $ $310,245 × .11 = $34,127.
[b] $ $310,245/4 years = $77,561.
[c] $ $20,245/4 years = $5,061.
[d] $ $77,561 ÷ $5,061 = $82,622.
* Rounded.

Because the leaseback agreement does not contain a bargain purchase option and the equipment title does not transfer to the seller-lessee at the end of the lease term, the equipment will be amortized over the life of the leaseback term using the straight-line method. The deferred loss must be amortized in a like manner. With the information provided in Table III, the entries to record the year-end lease rental payment and the amortization expense relating to the equipment and the deferred loss can be made. These entries appear below:

Interest Expense	34,127	
Obligation Under Capital Lease	65,873	
Cash		100,000
Amortization of Leased Property	82,622	
Deferred Loss on Sale-Leaseback		5,061
Leased Property Under Capital Lease		77,561

These last two entries complete the discussion and example material for sale and leaseback transactions for the seller-lessee. The next specialized area deals with real estate leasing. Much of the previous material will prove helpful during the discussion of leases involving real estate.

Flowcharts and Discussion of Leases Involving Real Estate—Lessee

Flowcharts 3 and 4 illustrate the classification and some of the accounting problems associated with real estate leases. All of the basic concepts discussed in the preceeding section apply to real estate leases; however, there are some cases where only a limited number of criteria apply or where additional computations may be required. The calculation of the MLP and the present value of the MLP for real estate leases is the same as previously discussed. The real estate flowcharts refer the reader back to the general flowchart (Flowchart 1) for specifics on the computation of the MLP.

As indicated in Flowcharts 3 and 4, there are four types of real estate lease transactions. These include leases involving: (1) land only, (2) land and building(s), (3) part of a building and (4) real estate and equipment. The discussion is organized to follow the Flowcharts. Of the four types of leases, only leases involving land and building(s) require the presentation of new example materials. The other types of real estate leases either are handled in the same way as are general leases or are merely an extension of the land and building(s) lease accounting.

Leases Involving Land Only

For leases involving land only, the relevant criteria are those dealing with transfer of ownership. If the ownership transfers *or* the lease contains a bargain purchase option, the lease will be classified as a capital lease (Blocks 2 and 3). In the absence of either of these two criteria, the lease will be accounted for as an operating lease. If classified as a capital

FLOWCHART 3
LESSEE - REAL ESTATE

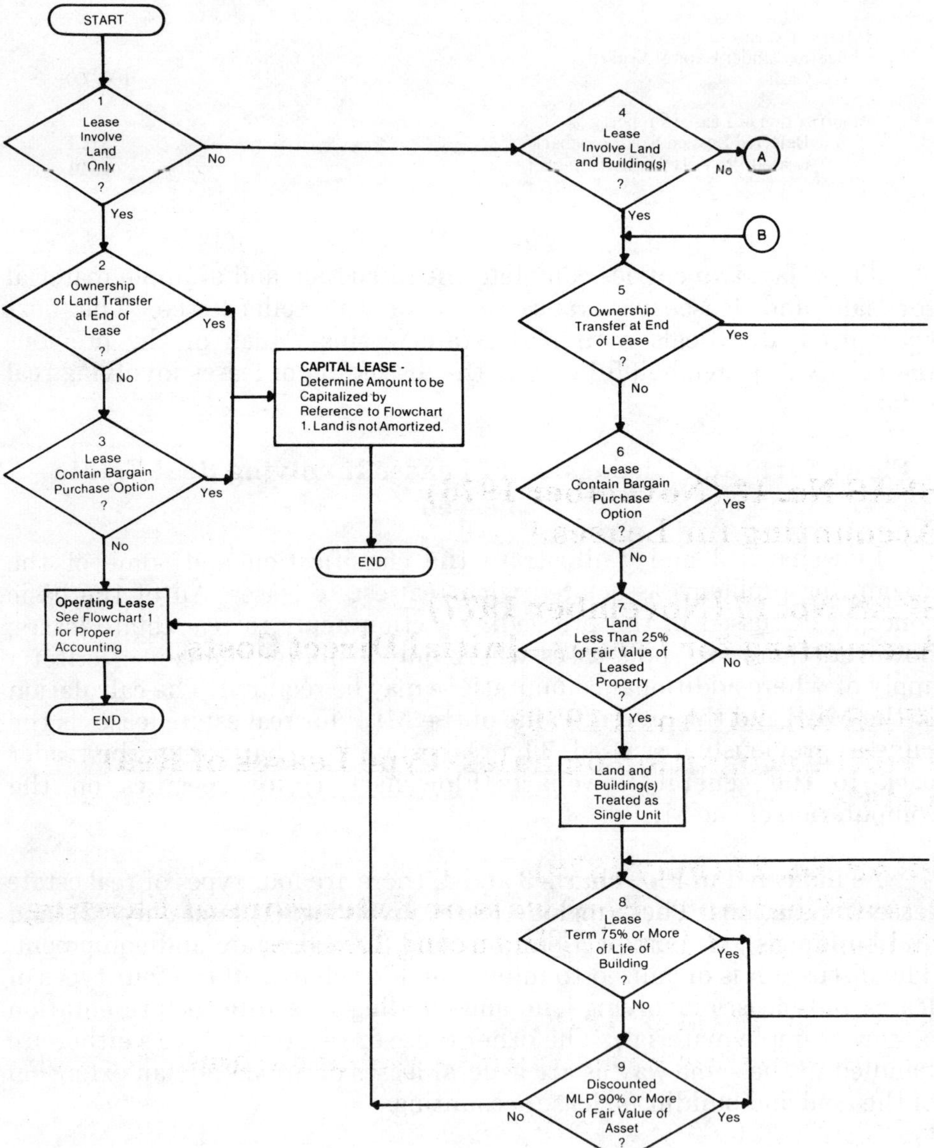

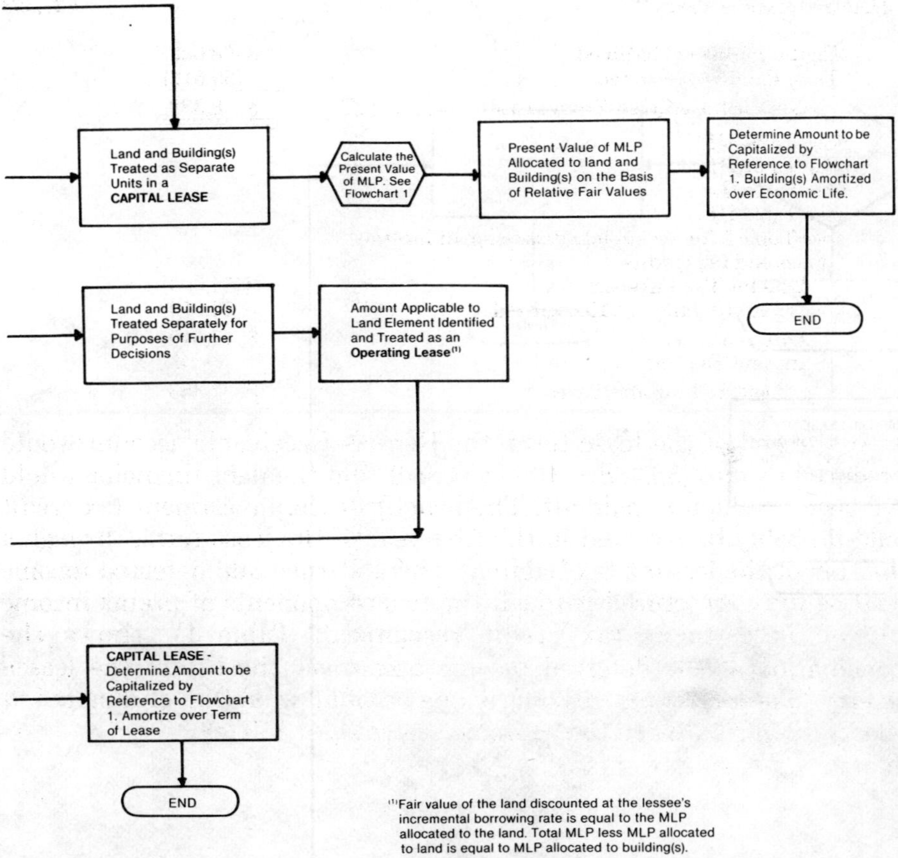

(1) Fair value of the land discounted at the lessee's incremental borrowing rate is equal to the MLP allocated to the land. Total MLP less MLP allocated to land is equal to MLP allocated to building(s).

FLOWCHART 4
LESSEE - REAL ESTATE

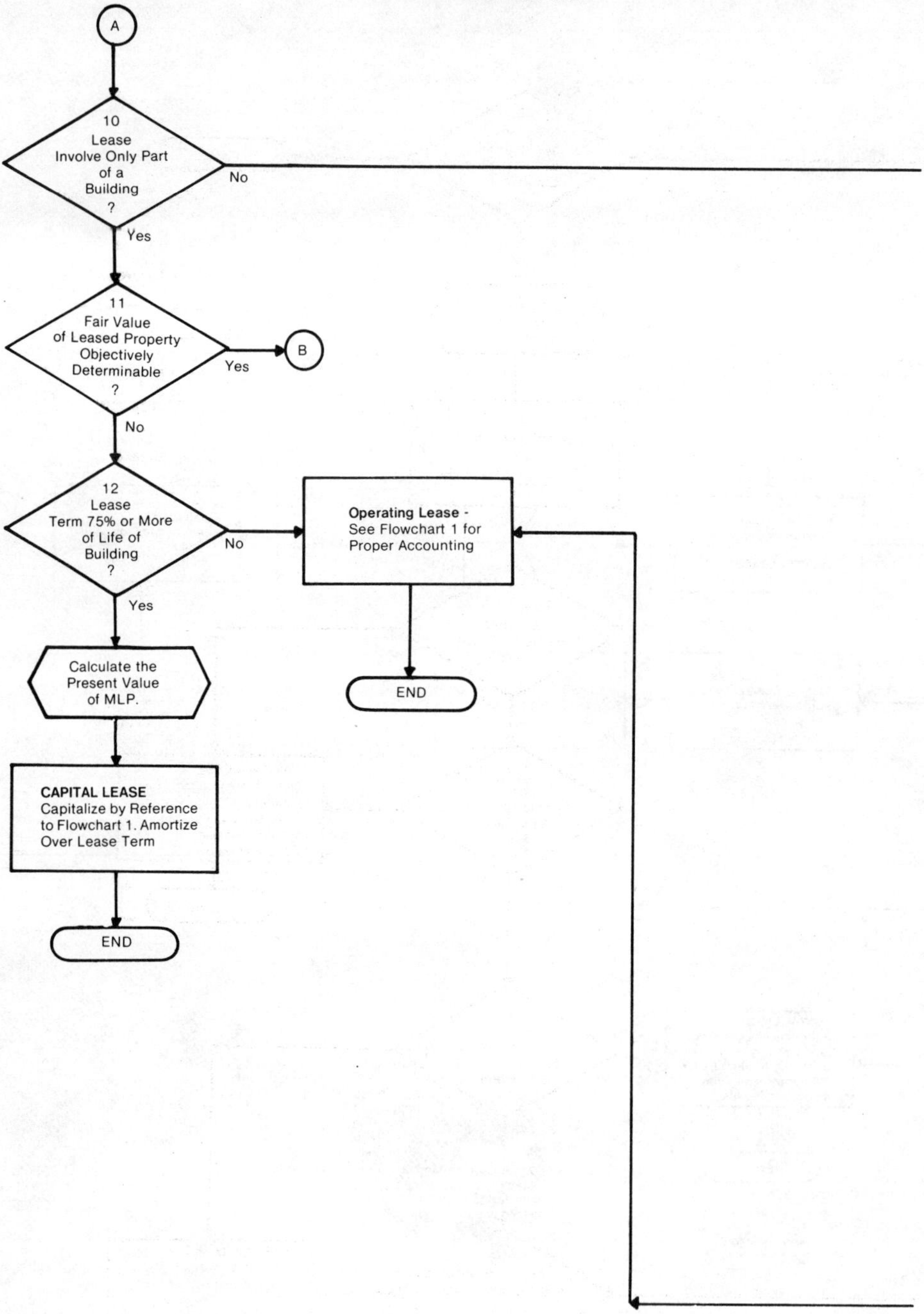

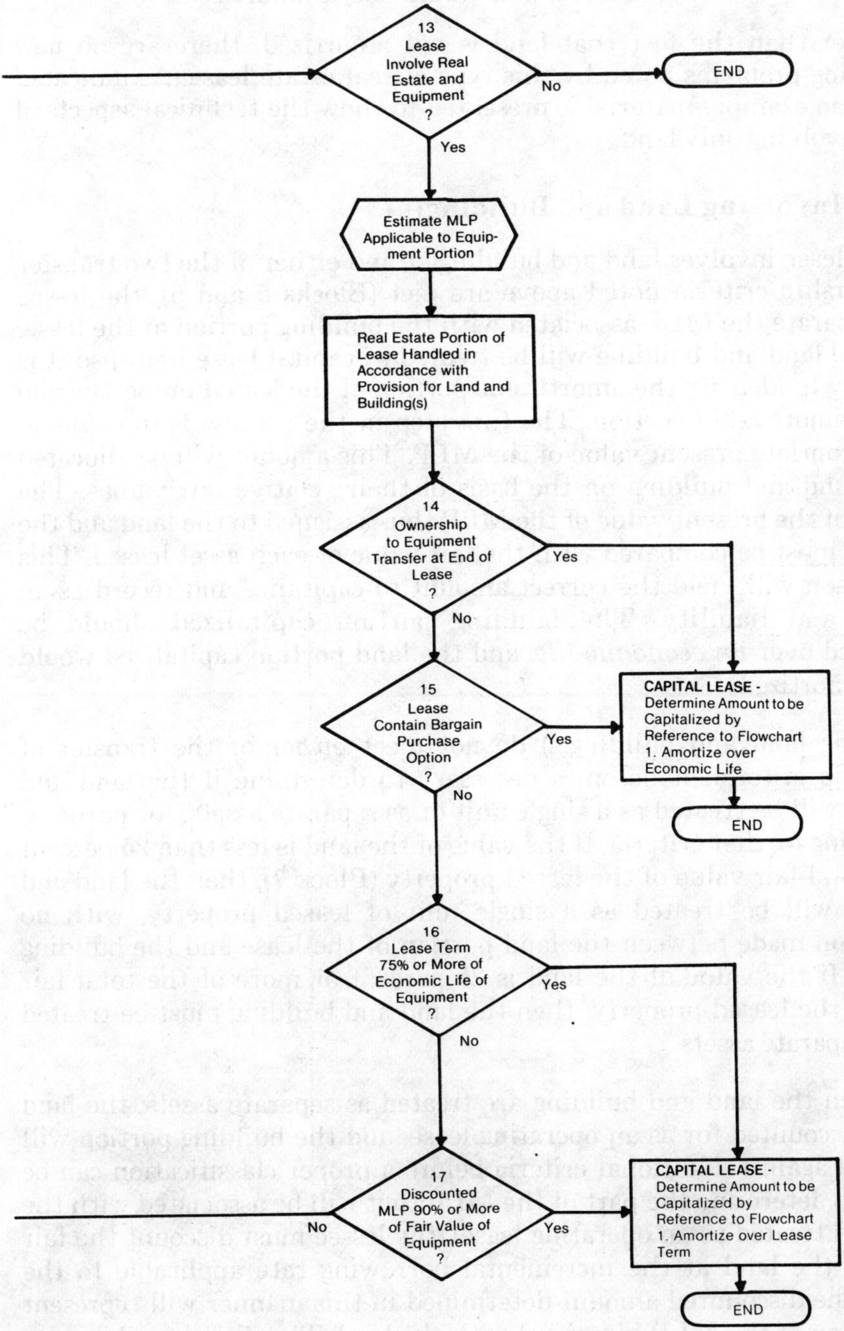
13
Lease
Involve Real
Estate and
Equipment
?
No
END
Yes
Estimate MLP
Applicable to Equip-
ment Portion
Real Estate Portion of
Lease Handled in
Accordance with
Provision for Land and
Building(s)
14
Ownership
to Equipment
Transfer at End of
Lease
?
Yes
No
15
Lease
Contain Bargain
Purchase
Option
?
Yes
No
CAPITAL LEASE -
Determine Amount to be
Capitalized by
Reference to Flowchart
1. Amortize over
Economic Life
END
16
Lease Term
75% or More of
Economic Life of
Equipment
?
Yes
No
17
Discounted
MLP 90% or More
of Fair Value of
Equipment
?
No
Yes
CAPITAL LEASE -
Determine Amount to be
Capitalized by
Reference to Flowchart
1. Amortize over Lease
Term
END

lease, the land should be capitalized at the lesser of the present value of the MLP or the fair value, with a corresponding liability for the same amount. The obligation will be reduced using the interest method over the term of the lease. Of course, land would not be amortized.

Other than the fact that land is not amortized, there are no new accounting problems posed by this type of real estate lease. As indicated earlier, no example material is presented to show the technical aspects of leases involving only land.

Leases Involving Land and Building(s)

If a lease involves land and building(s), and either of the two transfer of ownership criteria noted above are met (Blocks 5 and 6), the lessee must separate the MLP associated with the building portion of the lease. Both the land and building will be treated as capital lease items, so it is necessary to identify the amortizable portion of the leased property from the nonamortizable portion. The first step in the process is to compute the appropriate present value of the MLP. This amount will be allocated to the land and building on the basis of their relative fair values. The portion of the present value of the MLP thus assigned to the land and the building must be compared with the fair value of each asset leased. This comparison will yield the correct amount to capitalize and record as an asset(s) and liability. The building portion capitalized should be amortized over its *economic life,* and the land portion capitalized would not be amortized.

If the land and building(s) do not meet *either* of the transfer of ownership criteria, it becomes necessary to determine if the land and building will be treated as a single unit or as separate assets, for purposes of applying further criteria. If the value of the land is less than 25 percent of the total fair value of the leased property (Block 7), then the land and building will be treated as a single unit of leased property, with no distinction made between the land portion of the lease and the building portion. If the value of the land is 25 percent or more of the total fair value of the leased property, then the land and building must be treated as two separate assets.

When the land and building are treated as separate assets, the land will be accounted for as an operating lease, and the building portion will be tested against additional criteria before a proper classification can be made. To determine the part of the MLP that will be associated with the land (and treated as an operating lease), the lessee must discount the fair value of the land at the incremental borrowing rate applicable to the lessee. The discounted amount determined in this manner will represent the portion of the MLP identified with the land. The difference between the total MLP and the MLP attributed to the land will be the MLP associated with the building. The amount applicable to the building portion will be used to determine if the lease should be classified as operating or capital.

In cases where land and building are treated as a single unit or where the MLP associated with the building portion of a land and building lease has been determined, two additional criteria must be considered (Blocks 8 and 9). If *either* of the two criteria are met, the lease will be classified as capital; and, if neither criterion is met, it will be classified as operating. The first criterion is the 75-percent-of-economic-life decision, and the second is that the discounted value of the MLP is 90 percent or more of the fair value of the asset decision. (For a more explicit discussion of these two criteria, see Lease Classification.) The amount capitalized, if either criterion is met, will be amortized over the lease term.

Technical Considerations for Leases Involving Land and Building(s)

From an accounting standpoint, land and building(s) leases are, perhaps, the most complex type of real estate leases. The technical accounting and classification problems can be simplified by subdividing the land and building(s) category into four sections. The four sections are: (1) leases containing transfer of ownership or bargain purchase option provisions; (2) leases where the land element comprises less than 25 percent of the total fair value of the leased assets; (3) leases where the land element comprises 25 percent or more of the total fair value of the leased property; and (4) operating leases.

Leases Meeting the Transfer of Ownership Criteria

If the lease agreement meets either of the transfer of ownership criteria, the present value of the MLP must be divided into a land element and a building element. The Example 1 lease will be used to illustrate the separation of the two elements and the subsequent accounting. The Example 1 lease contains the following assumptions:

Example 1
Lease Assumptions—Land and Building Lease

1. The lessee enters into a five-year, noncancelable lease for land and renovated building that requires payments of $155,000 at the beginning of each of the five years. $5,000 of the payments are for executory costs. The lease specifies that ownership will transfer to the lessee at the end of the leased term.
2. The lessee's incremental borrowing rate is 11 percent, and the lessor's implicit rate is 10 percent.

3. The leased building has an estimated economic life of five years. The fair value of the land is $100,000, and the fair value of the building is $550,000 at the inception of the lease.
4. The lessee uses the straight-line depreciation method for all existing owned assets.

The present value of the MLP is determined as follows:

Rental Payments Required	$155,000
Less: Executory Costs	5,000
	$150,000
Present Value Factor	[a]4.16987
Present Value of MLP	$625,481

[a] Present value factor for an annuity due for five periods at 10 percent. See Appendix A, Table III. The lessor's implicit rate is used, because it is known and is less than the lessee's incremental borrowing rate.

Once the present value of the MLP has been determined, it is divided between the building and land elements, using the relative fair values at the inception of the lease. The disaggregation process is illustrated below:

Fair Value of the Land	$100,000
Fair Value of the Building	550,000
Total Fair Value of Leased Property	$650,000

MLP Allocated to Land =	$ 96,228	(100,000/650,000 × 625,481)
MLP Allocated to Building =	529,253	(550,000/650,000 × 625,481)
Total MLP	$625,481	

The present value of the MLP assigned to the land and to the building is less than the fair value of the respective assets, so the assets and obligation will be recorded at the present value of the MLP assigned. The entry to record the assets and obligation at inception of the lease is:

Leased Property Under Capital Lease-Land	96,228	
Leased Property Under Capital Lease-Building	529,253	
Obligation Under Capital Lease		625,481

The obligation would be reduced using the interest method, which has been described extensively in the preceeding pages. The entry to reduce the obligation and record the interest expense is the same as previously shown and will not be repeated here. Since ownership to the leased property transfers to the lessee at the end of the lease, the building will be amortized over its economic life. Land, of course, is not amortized. The entry to record the amortization of the building portion of the leased property is:

Amortization of Leased Property	105,851	
Accumulated Amortization of Leased Property - Building		105,851

The amount is determined on a straight-line basis as follows:

$529,253/5 years = $105,851.

Land Element Less than 25 Percent of Fair Value

A lease agreement for land and building(s) may be classified as a capital lease without a transfer of ownership or a bargain purchase option. When the land element of the leased property is less than 25 percent of the total fair value, land and building will be combined and treated as a single unit of leased property for purposes of testing further criteria. If the lease term is 75 percent or more of the economic life of the *building,* or if the present value of the MLP of the combined land and building is 90 percent or more of the combined fair value, the lease will qualify as a capital lease. If neither of these criteria is met, the lease will be classified as an operating lease.

To illustrate capital lease accounting, assume the same facts as in the Example 1 lease, except that ownership of the leased property *does not* transfer to the lessee at the end of the lease term. In the Example 1 lease, the fair value of the land is 15 percent of the total fair value of both land and building ($100,000/$650,000 = 15%). However, the lease term of five years is more than 75 percent of the economic life of the building (5 years × .75 = 3.75 years), and the present value of the MLP ($625,481) is more than 90 percent of the fair value of the combined land and building ($650,000 × .90 = $585,000). Since the lease agreement meets *at least one* of the criteria, it qualifies as a capital lease.

Because the fair value of the land element is less than 25 percent of the total fair value, the land and building are treated as a single unit under a capital lease. The single unit (both land and building) will be amortized over the lease term, using the straight-line method. The entries necessary at inception of the lease and the subsequent amortization are presented below (amortization of the lease obligation is not shown):

Leased Property Under Capital Lease	625,481	
Obligation Under Capital Lease		625,481
Amortization of Leased Property	[a]125,096	
Accumulated Amortization of Leased Property		125,096

[a] $625,481/5 years = $125,096 per year.

The amortization schedule for the obligation would be consistent with those previously shown.

Land Element 25 Percent or More of Fair Value

To illustrate the accounting for a land and building lease, where the fair value of the land element is 25 percent or more of the total fair value of the leased property, it is necessary to change two of the assumptions of the Example 1 lease: first, assume that ownership does not transfer to the lessee at the end of the lease term, and, second, assume that the fair value of the land is $200,000 and the fair value of the building is $450,000 at the inception of the lease. With these modified assumptions, the land element is now 31 percent of the total fair value of the leased assets ($200,000/$650,000 = 31%). The lease still qualifies as a capital lease, because the lease term of five years is more than 75 percent of the economic life of the building.

Since the lease is a capital lease, and the land element is 25 percent or more of the total fair value of the assets, the present value of the MLP must be divided between the land element and the building element. The procedure for dividing the MLP requires that the MLP associated with the land be determined by discounting the fair value of the land at the lessee's incremental borrowing rate. This is accomplished as follows:

$$\frac{\text{Fair Value of Land}}{\text{Present Value Factor}^{a}} \quad \frac{\$200{,}000}{4.10245} = \$48{,}751 \text{ MLP assigned to land}$$

a Present value factor for an annuity due at 11 percent for 5 periods. See Appendix A, Table III.

The difference between the MLP assigned to land and the total MLP will be the MLP assigned to the building. This amount would be determined as follows:

Rental Payment Required	$155,000
Less: Executory Costs	5,000
	$150,000
MLP Assigned to Land	(48,751)
MLP Assigned to Building	$101,249

Once the MLP associated with the building element has been calculated, the next step is to determine the present value of the MLP, using the implicit interest rate of 10 percent. The present value of the MLP is calculated below:

MLP Assigned to Building	$101,249
Present Value Factor	a4.16987
Present Value of MLP Assigned to Building	$422,195

a Present value factor for an annuity due at 10 percent for 5 periods. See Appendix A, Table III.

The present value ($422,195) of the MLP assigned to the building element is less than the fair value ($450,000) of the building; therefore, the building would be recorded at the present value of the MLP. The entry required at the inception of the lease would be:

Leased Property Under Capital Lease - Building	422,195	
Obligation Under Capital Lease		422,195

The land element would be treated as a separate *operating lease.*

The entry to record the first lease payment is shown below:

Lease Rental Expense - Land	[a]48,751	
Interest Expense	[b]32,095	
Obligation Under Capital Lease	[c]69,154	
Executory Costs	5,000	
Cash		155,000

[a] Annual lease payment assigned to land per above computation.

[b] ($422,195 − $101,249) × 10% = $32,095.

[c] $101,249 − $32,095 = $69,154.

The only amortization required would be for the building element of the lease. Assuming straight-line depreciation, the entry would be:

Amortization of Leased Property—Building	[a]84,439	
Accumulated Amortization of Leased Property - Building		84,439

[a] $422,195/5 years = $84,439 per year.

This last set of entries completes the illustrations of accounting for leases involving land and building(s). If any of the above lease examples had been classified as an operating lease, the only entry required would have been a record of the annual or interim rental expense.

Leases Involving Part of a Building

Where a lease agreement involves only part of a building, proper classification depends largely upon whether the lessee can determine the fair value of the leased asset (Block 11). If the fair value of the property can be *objectively* determined, the lessee would account for the lease as if it were the building portion of a lease involving land and building(s). (Refer back to the preceeding section for a complete discussion of proper classification and accounting for land and building(s) leases.) If the fair value *cannot* be determined, the only relevant criterion is the "75-percent-of-economic-life" test. If the lease term is 75 percent or more of the building's economic life, the lease will be classified as capital, and will be treated as if it were the building portion of a lease involving land

and building(s). If the lease qualifies as a capital lease under the "75-percent-of-economic-life" test, the asset recorded will be amortized over the lease term. The determination of the MLP and the amortization of the obligation are consistent with the method used for the general lease agreement (see Flowchart 1). If the fair value of the leased property is not known, *and* the lease term is less than 75 percent of the economic life of the building, the lease will be classified and accounted for as an operating lease.

Leases Involving Real Estate and Equipment

If the lease agreement involves both real estate and equipment, the lessee must separate the real estate portion of the MLP from the portion of the MLP applicable to the equipment. Paragraph 27 of SFAS No. 13 states that the separation "shall be estimated by whatever means are appropriate in the circumstances." It would appear that an allocation on the basis of fair values or appraisal values would be appropriate in most cases.

Once the allocation of the MLP has been completed, the real estate portion will be classified and accounted for according to the provisions specified for leases involving land and building(s). (Refer back to the section on land and building leases for a detailed discussion and illustrations.)

The portion of the MLP allocated to the equipment must meet one of the four basic criteria—ownership transfer, bargain purchase option, 75 percent or more of economic life, or discounted MLP 90 percent or more of fair value of the equipment—to be classified as a capital lease. If the equipment portion qualifies as a capital lease, the provisions described in Flowchart 1 would apply. If none of the four basic criteria are met, the lease is an operating lease.

When the equipment is classified as a capital lease, the asset recorded will be amortized over its economic life, if either of the two transfer-of-ownership criteria is met, and over the lease term, if neither of these criteria is met.

This completes the discussion and illustration of accounting for real estate leases. The last type of lease that needs to be explored is the *sublease.* Because a sublease involves accounting from the standpoints of both the lessee and the lessor, complete discussion of the topic will be deferred until after the lessor's accounting has been examined in full. For the time being, we will end the discussion of leases from the viewpoint of the lessee and will turn our attention to the lessor.

There are many new and interesting problems associated with the lessor's accounting for capital leases. These new problems result primarily from the more sophisticated classification of various types of capital leases, which requires the knowledge of new terminology.

Defining Some Additional Terms

Additional new terms that are important for a complete understanding of lessor accounting are defined below:

1. *Unguaranteed residual value:* The difference between the estimated residual value of the leased property and the amount of the guaranteed residual value.

2. *Initial direct costs:* "Those costs," according to SFAS No. 17, Paragraph 8, "incurred by the lessor that are directly associated with negotiating and consummating completed leasing transactions." These costs might include legal fees incurred, commissions paid, costs of credit investigations, etc. The important point to remember is that the costs must be associated with a *completed* lease agreement.

Flowcharts and Discussion of General Lease Agreement— Lessor Lease Classification

Flowchart 5 depicts the classification of various types of leases for the lessor, while Flowcharts 5A, 5B and 5C show the proper accounting treatment for the different types of capital leases.

You will recall from the discussion of the lessee that it is necessary to determine only if a particular lease is an operating or a capital lease to determine the appropriate accounting; however, in the case of the lessor, it also is necessary to determine the proper type of capital lease. SFAS No. 13 identifies three types of capital leases: sales-type, direct financing and leveraged. All three of these capital leases present different accounting problems to the lessor.

Flowchart 5, the classification flowchart, starts with the same four criteria as the lessee flowchart, and the decision process for these criteria is identical. If none of the four criteria (Blocks 1 through 4) are met, the lease would be classified as operating, and the accounting would be quite simple. If any one of the four criteria is met, there are two additional criteria that must be met before the lease will qualify as a capital lease. First, the lessor must be reasonably certain about the collectibility of the MLP (Block 5), *and* there must not be any important uncertainties associated with unreimbursable costs to be incurred by the lessor (Block

FLOWCHART 5
LESSOR - GENERAL CLASSIFICATION

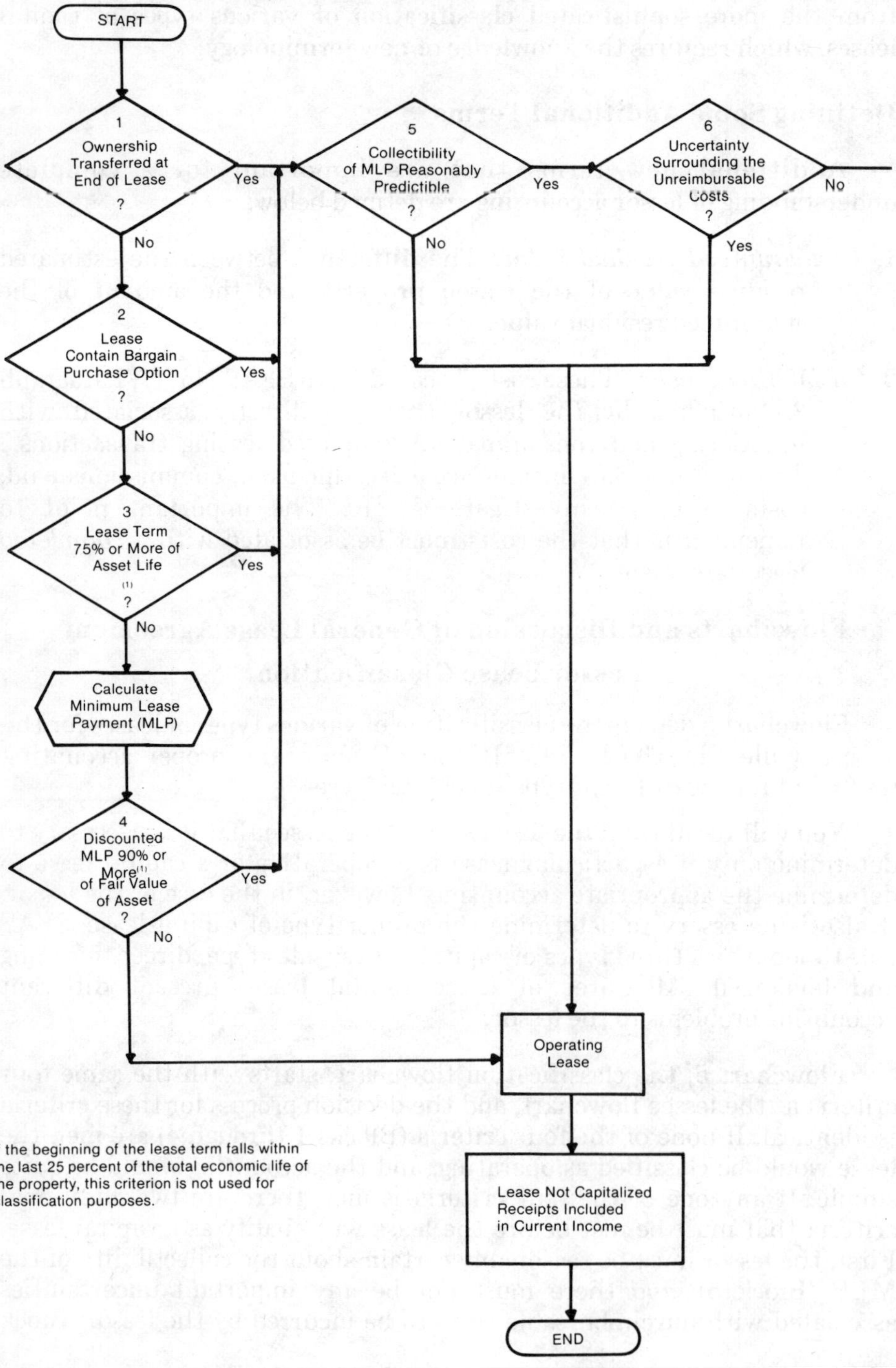

(1) If the beginning of the lease term falls within the last 25 percent of the total economic life of the property, this criterion is not used for classification purposes.

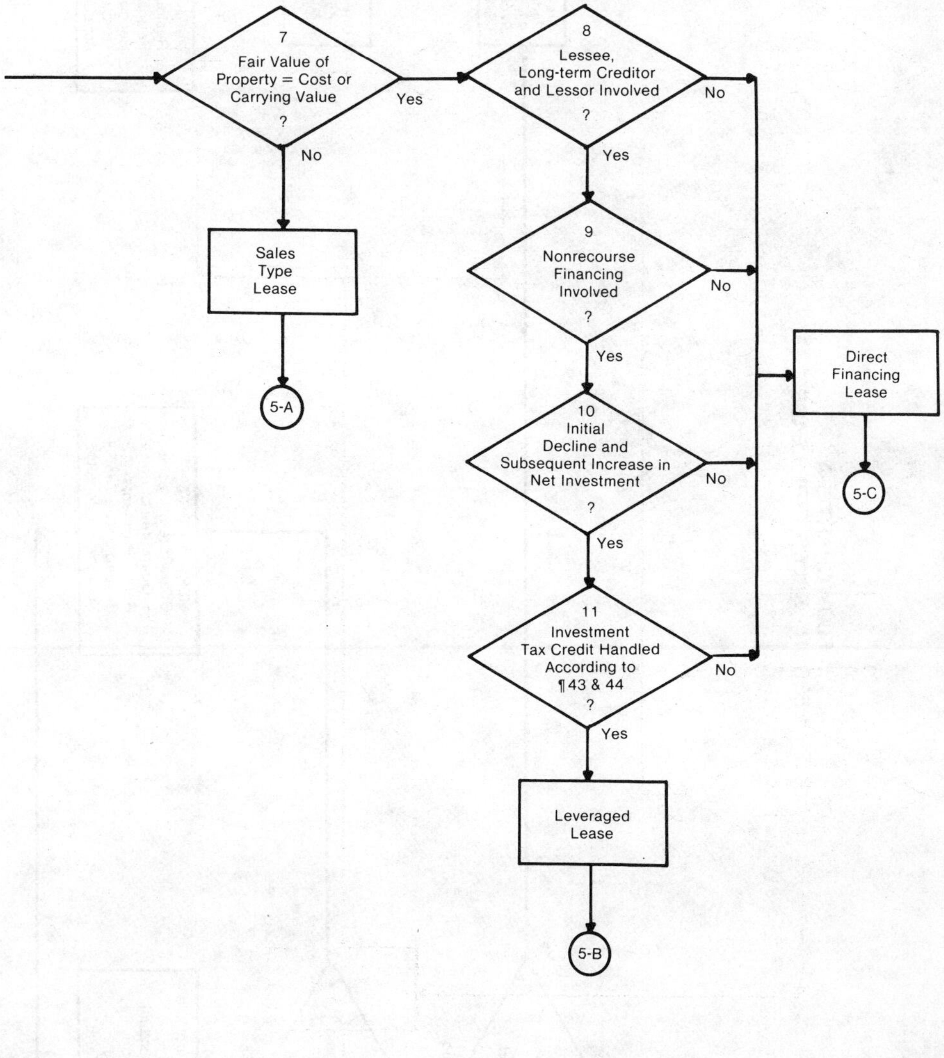
7
Fair Value of
Property = Cost or
Carrying Value
?
Yes
No
Sales
Type
Lease
5-A
8
Lessee,
Long-term Creditor
and Lessor Involved
?
No
Yes
9
Nonrecourse
Financing
Involved
?
No
Yes
10
Initial
Decline and
Subsequent Increase in
Net Investment
?
No
Yes
11
Investment
Tax Credit Handled
According to
¶43 & 44
?
No
Yes
Leveraged
Lease
5-B
Direct
Financing
Lease
5-C

FLOWCHART 5-A
LESSOR - SALES-TYPE LEASE

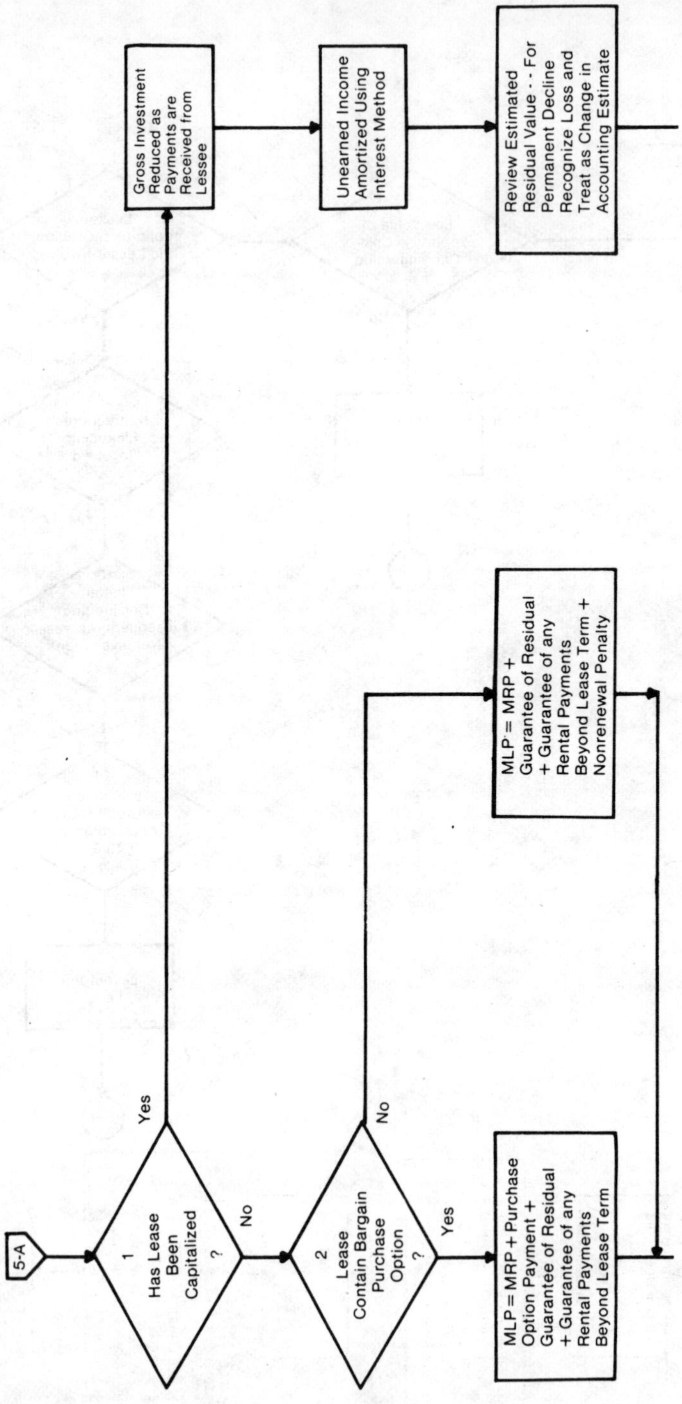

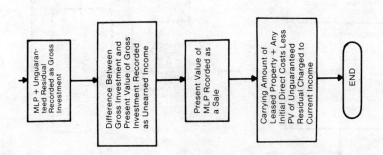

END
MLP + Unguaranteed Residual Recorded as Gross Investment
Difference Between Gross Investment and Present Value of Gross Investment Recorded as Unearned Income
Present Value of MLP Rcorded as a Sale
Carrying Amount of Leased Property + Any Initial Direct Costs Less PV of Unguaranteed Residual Charged to Current Income
END

FLOWCHART 5-B
LESSOR - LEVERAGED LEASE

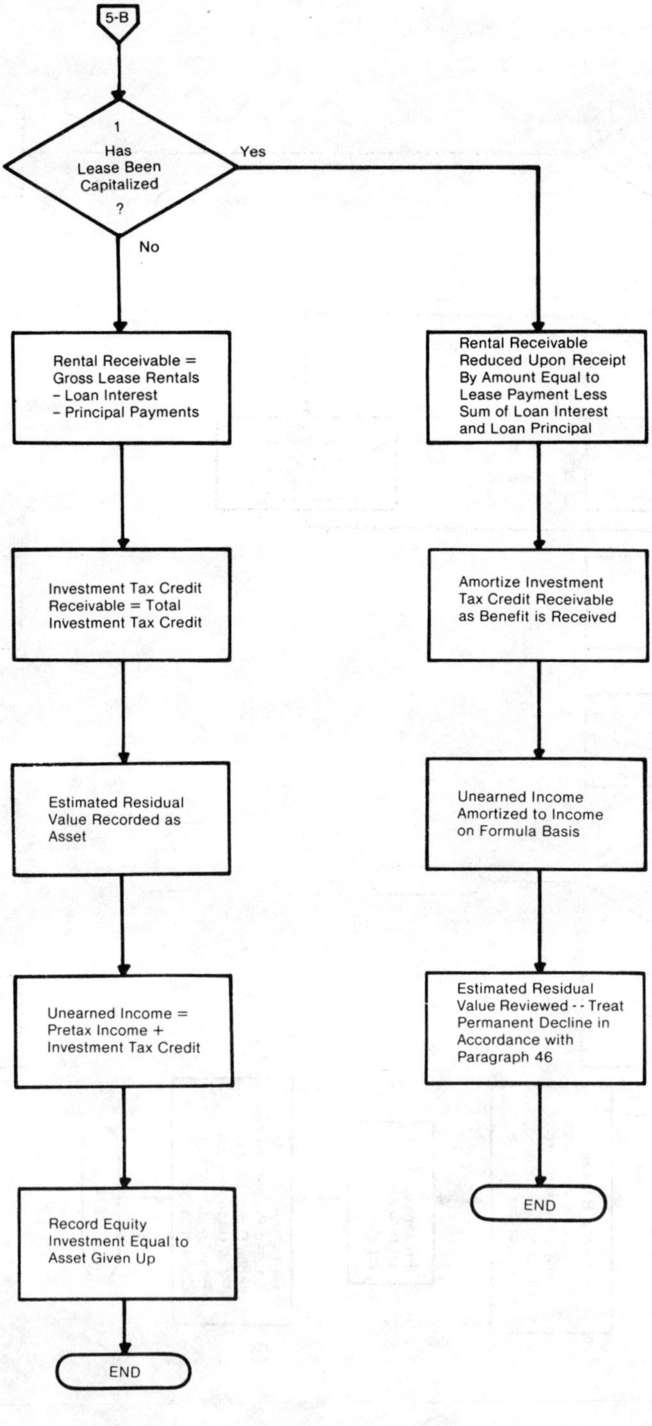

FLOWCHART 5-C
LESSOR - DIRECT FINANCING LEASE

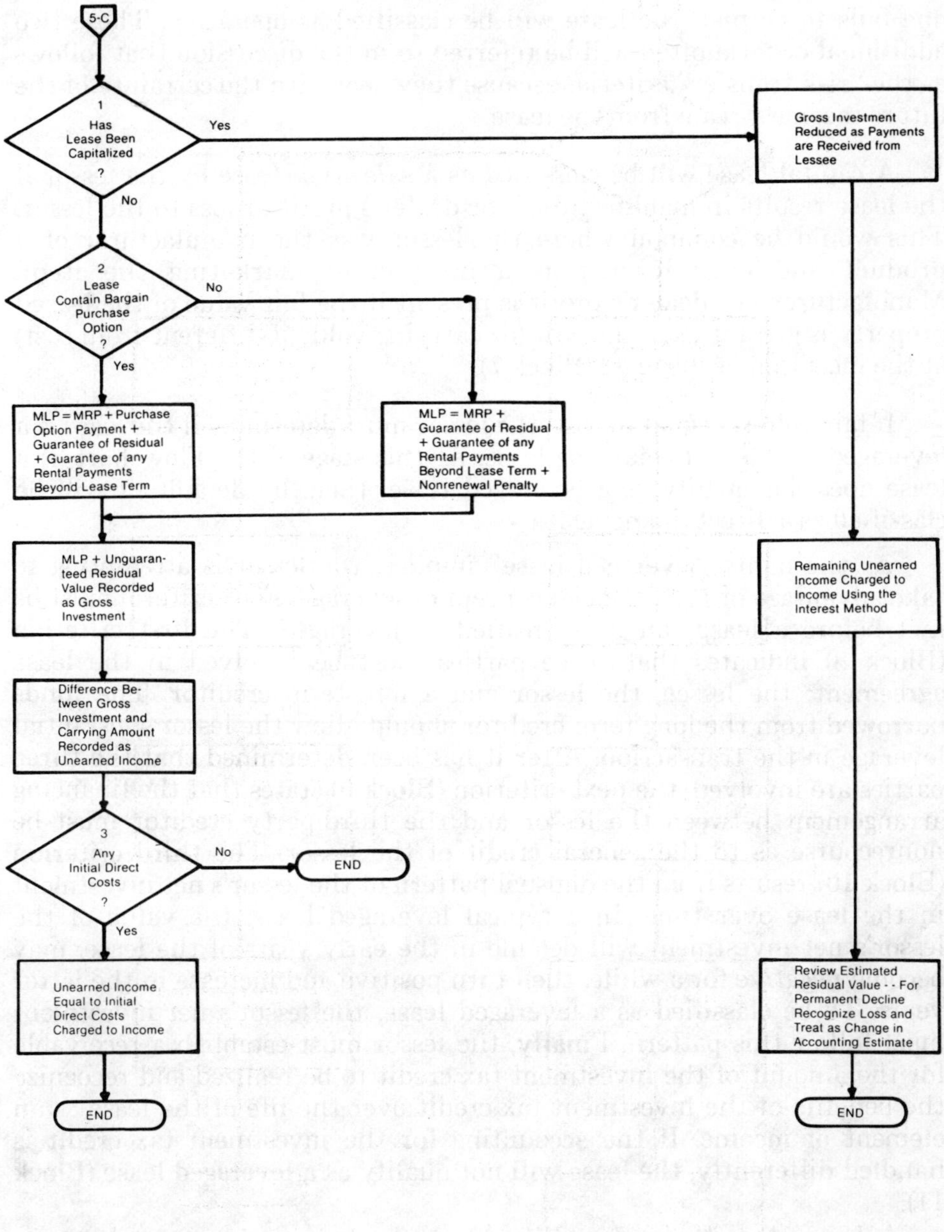

6). (See Paragraph 8(b) of SFAS No. 13 for an explanation of what may constitute important uncertainties relating to unreimbursable costs.) If *both* these criteria are met, the lease will be classified as capital; if either one fails to be met, the lease will be classified as operating. These two additional criteria often will be referred to in the discussion that follows as the "risk transfer" criteria, because they deal with the certainty of the future income stream from the lease.

A capital lease will be classified as a *sales-type* lease by the lessor if the lease results in manufacturer's or dealer's profit or loss to the lessor. This would be common where the lessor was the manufacturer of a product and used leasing as a method of marketing the item. Manufacturer's or dealer's profit is present if the fair value of the leased property is greater than the cost (or carrying value if different from cost) at the inception of the lease (Block 7).

If fair value is equal to cost, the lessor must determine if the lease is a leveraged or a direct financing lease. At this stage of the Flowchart, if a lease does not qualify as a leveraged lease, then, by default, it will be classified as a direct financing lease.

As the name "leveraged lease" implies, the lessor is attempting to take advantage of the financial concept of leverage. Four criteria must be met before a lease can be identified as leveraged. The first criterion (Block 8) indicates that three parties must be involved in the lease agreement: the lessee, the lessor and a long-term creditor. The funds borrowed from the long-term creditor should allow the lessor substantial leverage in the transaction. After it has been determined that the three parties are involved, the next criterion (Block 9) states that the financing arrangement between the lessor and the third-party creditor must be nonrecourse as to the general credit of the lessor. The third criterion (Block 10) results from the unusual pattern of the lessor's net investment in the lease over time. In a typical leveraged lease, the value of the lessor's net investment will decline in the early years of the lease, may become *negative* for a while, then turn positive and increase in the latter years. To be classified as a leveraged lease, the lessor's net investment must follow this pattern. Finally, the lessor must establish a receivable for the amount of the investment tax credit to be realized and recognize the benefits of the investment tax credit over the life of the lease as an element of income. If the accounting for the investment tax credit is handled differently, the lease will not qualify as a leveraged lease (Block 11).

A lease that does not qualify as a sales-type or leveraged lease is accounted for as a *direct financing* type lease. In the following sections, discussion of accounting for sales-type leases will be addressed first, followed by leveraged leases and direct financing leases.

Accounting for a Sales-Type Lease [9]

Once it has been determined that a particular lease is a sales-type lease, the lessor must capitalize the leased property as an investment. Proper accounting for both the date of inception of the lease and subsequent periods is shown in Flowchart 5A.

At the date of inception of the lease, the lessor must determine the proper value of the gross investment. The value of the gross investment depends on whether the lease agreement contains a bargain purchase option. If a bargain purchase option is specified, the MLP will be computed as follows (Block 2):

MLP = Minimum Rental Payments (MRP)
+Purchase Option Payment
+Guaranteed residual value (if any)
+Guarantee of any rental payments beyond the lease term (if any)

If the lease does not contain a bargain purchase option, the MLP will be determined as follows:

MLP = Minimum Rental Payments (MRP)
+Guaranteed residual value (if any)
+Penalty payment for nonrenewal (if any)
+Guarantee of any rental payments beyond the lease term (if any)

The appropriate MLP will be added to any unguaranteed residual value, and this total will constitute the lessor's gross investment in the lease.

The difference between the gross investment computed above, and the present value of the gross investment, will be recorded as *unearned income* resulting from a capital lease.

The final part of the initial accounting process is the recording of the sale and cost of sale of the property. As indicated in the Flowchart, the present value of the MLP would be recorded as the sales price, and the cost of the property sold would be determined as follows:

Cost of Sale = Carrying value of property
+Initial direct costs (if any)
−Present value of unguaranteed residual value (if any).

---

[9] SFAS No. 27, "Classification of Renewals or Extensions of Existing Sales-Type or Direct Financing Leases," identifies two problems in accounting for extensions or renewals. First, if an existing sales-type or direct financing lease is extended at or near the end of the original lease term, the classification criteria identified in the discussion apply. Second, if the renewal or extension occurs at some other time, the lease will be classified as a direct financing lease.

The difference between the sales price and the cost of the sale would represent the profit resulting from the sales-type lease.

In subsequent periods, the value of the gross investment would be reduced as lease payments are received. The unearned income would be recognized using the interest method. As a result, part of each lease receipt would be a recovery of investment, and the other part would be income from the lease of property.

Technical Considerations for a Sales-Type Lease

To illustrate the technical aspects of accounting for a sales-type lease, two example leases will be presented, along with solutions. The Example 1 lease assumptions are listed below.

Example 1
Lease Assumptions

1. The lessor enters into a five-year, noncancelable lease with a lessee that requires annual advance payments of $50,000. Title to the leased property does not pass to the lessee at the end of the lease term, and there is no bargain purchase option in the lease agreement.
2. The implicit interest rate is 10 percent.
3. The collectibility of the MLP is reasonably predictable, and there are no unreimbursable costs associated with the lease.
4. The cost of the leased property is $200,000, and the fair value at inception of the lease is $208,494. The property has an estimated economic life of five years and zero estimated residual value.

The lessor must begin by determining the proper classification of the lease. Since ownership does not transfer, and the lease does not contain a bargain purchase option, the lease agreement fails to meet the first two general criteria. However, the lease term of five years is more than 75 percent of the economic life of the leased property (five-year economic life $\times$ .75 = 3.75 years).

Because the third general criterion is met, *and* the collectibility of the MLP is reasonably certain and there are no unreimbursable costs associated with the lease, the Example 1 lease qualifies as a capital lease.

While not required for proper classification of the Example 1 lease, it should be noted that the lease agreement also meets the fourth general criterion. The present value of the MLP would be calculated as follows:

Required Rental Payments	$50,000
Present Value Factor	[a]4.16987
Present Value of MLP	$208,494

[a] Present value factor for an annuity due at 10 percent for 5 periods. See Appendix A, Table III.

The present value of the MLP ($208,494) is more than 90 percent of the fair value of the leased property at inception of the lease ($208,494 fair value × .90 = $187,645). The above computations show that the fourth general criterion also has been met.

Next, the lessor must determine the appropriate type of capital lease, i.e., sales-type, leveraged or direct financing. For the Example 1 lease, cost ($200,000) is different from fair value ($208,494); therefore, the lease properly is classified as a sales-type lease.

Because the lease does not contain a bargain purchase option, and there is no guarantee of residual value or penalty for nonrenewal or guarantee of rentals beyond the lease term, the MLP will be equal to the required minimum rental payments. The MLP is referred to as the lessor's gross investment in the lease, and is determined as follows:

Required Rental Payments	$50,000
Number of Annual Payments Required	× 5
Gross Investment in Lease	$250,000

The value of the gross investment will be recorded as an asset under a sales-type lease. In addition, a sale will be recorded in an amount equal to the present value of the gross investment. In the Example 1 lease, the present value of the gross investment is equal to the present value of the MLP ($208,494). The difference between the gross investment ($250,000) and the present value of the gross investment ($208,494) is recorded as unearned income under a capital lease. When a sale is recorded, it also is necessary to record the cost of the sale, which, in this case, is $200,000.

Given this information, the entry to record the capital lease at date of inception would be as follows:

Minimum Lease Payment Receivable	250,000	
Sales		208,494
Unearned Income		41,506
Cost of Goods Sold	200,000	
Inventory		200,000

It should be noted that, under a sales-type lease, there are two elements of profit; one from the sale of the property ($208,494 − $200,000 = $8,494) and the second from the financing of the sale through the lease agreement ($41,506 recognized over the five-year lease term).

Table I shows the computation of the lease amortization and the income recognition over the lease term.

Table I

Amortization Schedule for Example 1 Lease

	Period	Annual Payment	Annual Interest Income	Principal Reduction	Present Value of Principal
Initial Value	-	-	-	-	$208,494
	1	$ 50,000	[a]$15,849	[b]$ 34,151	[c]174,343
	2	50,000	12,434	37,566	136,777
	3	50,000	8,678	41,322	95,455
	4	50,000	4,545	45,455	50,000
	5	50,000	-0-	50,000	-0-
		$250,000	$41,506	$208,494	

[a] ($208,494 − $50,000) × 10% = $15,849.
[b] $50,000 − $15,849 = $34,151.
[c] $208,494 − $34,151 = $174,343.

The lease agreement requires advance rental payments (payment made at the beginning of each year); therefore, in Year 5, there would be no interest, because the last rental payment is made at the beginning of the year. Immediately after recording the investment in the lease, the lessor would record the receipt of the first rental payment and, at the end of Year 1, would record the income earned. The following entries reflect these two events.

Cash	50,000	
Minimum Lease Payment Receivable		50,000
Unearned Income	15,849	
Income From Capital Lease		15,849

Table I indicates the amounts that would be used for the above entries for the remainder of the lease term. At the end of the lease, the minimum lease payment receivable account would have a zero balance, and all of the unearned income would have been recognized.

The Example 1 lease served as an introduction to accounting for sales-type leases. The next example builds on the Example 1 lease, and incorporates more complex material.

The Example 2 lease assumptions are listed below. Note that many of the features of the Example 2 lease are the same as the Example 1 lease.

Example 2
Lease Assumptions

1. The lessor enters into a five-year, noncancelable lease with a lessee that requires annual advance payments of $50,000. Title to the leased property

does not pass to the lessee at the end of the lease term, and there is no bargain purchase option in the lease agreement.

2. The implicit interest rate is 10 percent.
3. The collectibility of the MLP is reasonably predictable, and there are no unreimbursable costs associated with the lease.
4. The cost of the leased property is $200,000, and the fair value at inception of the lease is $214,703. The property has an estimated economic life of five years and an unguaranteed residual value of $10,000.
5. The lessor incurred $5,000 of initial direct costs to consummate the lease agreement.

The Example 2 lease is also a capital lease, because the lease term of five years is more than 75 percent of the economic life of the property *and* because the collectibility of the MLP is reasonably predictable *and* there are no unreimbursable costs. The lease is a sales-type lease, because cost ($200,000) is not equal to fair value ($214,703) at the inception of the lease. The new variables added to this lease agreement are the unguaranteed residual value and the initial direct costs.

The gross investment in the lease is equal to the total rental payments required in the lease agreement, plus the unguaranteed residual value, and is computed below:

Annual Required Rental Payments	$ 50,000
Number of Rental Payments Required	× 5
Total Rental Payments	$250,000
Unguaranteed Residual Value	10,000
Gross Investment in Lease	$260,000

From the previous example, it is known that the difference between the gross investment and the present value of the gross investment is the amount of unearned income to be recognized over the lease term. The calculation of the present value of the gross investment would be as follows:

Annual Required Rental Payments	$ 50,000	
Present Value Factor	a4.16987	
Present Value of Rental Payments		$208,494
Unguaranteed Residual Value	$ 10,000	
Present Value Factor	b.62092	
Present Value of Unguaranteed Residual Value		6,209
Present Value of Gross Investment		$214,703

a Present value factor for an annuity due at 10 percent for five periods. See Appendix A, Table III.

b Present value factor for $1 at 10 percent for five periods. See Appendix A, Table I.

After this computation has been made, unearned income is determined to be $45,297 ($260,000 – $214,703). Note that the present value of the gross investment is equal to the fair value of the leased property at inception of the lease. To continue the initial entry required to record the gross investment, the amount of the sale has to be determined. The value of the sale is equal to the present value of the minimum rental payments, and was computed above to be $208,494.

The unguaranteed residual value affected both the computation of the gross investment and the present value of the gross investment. Both the unguaranteed residual value and the initial direct costs will affect the determination of cost of goods sold. Cost of sales is equal to the cost or carrying value of the leased property, plus any initial direct costs, less the present value of the unguaranteed residual value. The value of the cost of sales would be computed as follows:

Cost of Leased Property	$200,000
Initial Direct Costs	5,000
Present Value of Unguaranteed Residual Value	(6,209)
Cost of Goods Sold	$198,791

Based on the information developed above, the entries at inception of the lease would be:

Minimum Lease Payment Receivable	260,000	
Sales		208,494
Unearned Income		45,297
Inventory		6,209
Cost of Goods Sold	198,791	
Inventory		193,791
Cash		5,000

Notice that Inventory was reduced by $200,000 ($6,209 + $193,791 = $200,000) and that the initial direct costs were assumed to be fully paid in cash. The entries shown above are quite different from the basic entries made for the Example 1 lease. It is worth the reader's time to spend a few minutes analyzing and comparing the sets of entries under the Example 1 and Example 2 leases.

Once the initial entry to record the lease has been made, the lessor must prepare an amortization schedule to determine the income to be recognized in each of the five years of the lease term. Table II below develops the required information.

Table II

Amortization Schedule for Example 2

	Period	Annual Payment	Annual Interest Income	Principal Reduction	Present Value of Principal
Initial Value	-	-	-	-	a$214,703
	1	$ 50,000	b$16,470	c$ 33,530	d181,173
	2	50,000	13,117	36,883	144,290
	3	50,000	9,429	40,571	103,719
	4	50,000	5,372	44,628	59,091
	5	50,000	e909	49,091	f10,000
		$250,000	$45,297	$204,703	

[a] The initial value is the present value of the gross investment.
[b] ($214,703 — $50,000) × 10% = $16,470.
[c] $50,000 — $16,470 = $33,530.
[d] $214,703 — $33,530 = $181,173.
[e] Interest on the unguaranteed residual value.
[f] Unguaranteed residual value.

From the information in Table II, the lessor would make the following journal entries to record the first advance rental payment and to record income under the capital lease in the first year:

Cash	50,000	
Minimum Lease Payment Receivable		50,000
Unearned Income	16,470	
Income from Capital Lease		16,470

The amounts shown on Table II would be used for all subsequent entries involving receipt of rental payments and recognition of income.

Assuming that the estimated residual value turned out to be the actual residual value at the end of the lease, and that the lessor sold the property for $10,000, the following entry would be made:

Cash	10,000	
Minimum Lease Payment Receivable		10,000

Flowchart 5A indicates that the lessor must review the estimated residual value on a periodic basis and prepare an adjusting entry when it has been determined that there has been a permanent decline in the residual value. Illustration of accounting for a permanent decline in residual value will be deferred at this point, but will be shown in the accounting for direct financing leases. The accounting is identical and need not be repeated.

This completes the discussion and illustration of accounting for sales-type leases. Attention will now be focused on accounting for leveraged leases. Leveraged leases present many new and challenging problems, in the areas of both lease classification and lease accounting.

Accounting for Leveraged Leases

Flowchart 5B indicates the proper accounting for a lease classified as leveraged. The accounting at inception of the lease is shown on the left side of the Flowchart, and subsequent accounting is shown on the right.

At date of inception, the lessor will establish three asset accounts. First, a receivable will be set up for the gross rentals identified in the lease agreement, less the total principal and interest payments called for by the third-party creditor. Next, a receivable will be established for the total investment tax credit applicable to the leased property. Finally, the estimated residual value will be recorded as an asset. The lessor also will record the equity investment in the property, i.e., the funds committed to the property by the lessor. Given the nature of a leveraged lease, the lessor's equity investment always will be less than the cost of the property, because the third-party creditor also will be investing in the property. Unearned and deferred income will be recorded in an amount equal to the estimated pretax income expected to be earned, plus the investment tax credit to be received by the lessor.

In subsequent periods, the rental receivable will be reduced by the difference between the gross rental received and the total payment made to the third-party creditor. The investment tax credit receivable will be amortized as the benefits are received, usually in the year of inception. The unearned and deferred income will be recognized under a complex formula that requires the allocation of expected cash flows to income and to the investment made by the lessor. Income is recognized on the basis of the cash flows allocated to income. The examples that follow will demonstrate this allocation process.

Technical Considerations for a Leveraged Lease

For purposes of illustration, assume there is a lease agreement with the following characteristics:

Example 1
Lease Assumptions

1. Cost of the leased equipment is equal to $500,000. The equipment has an estimated residual value of $50,000, which will be realized at the end of the first year, after the termination of the lease.
2. The lessor finances the equipment by investing $100,000, and securing $400,000 worth of eight percent, 10-year nonrecourse financing from a third-party creditor. The financing agreement calls for payments of $59,612 to be made at the end of each year.
3. The lease term is 10 years and requires that lease payments of $68,000 be made at the end of each of the 10 years. The lessor is certain about the collectibility

of the lease payments and there are no unreimbursable costs associated with the lease agreement.

4. Relevant income tax information includes the facts that the equipment qualifies for the 10 percent investment tax credit, and that this credit will be retained by the lessor. The lessor elects the modified half-year convention and changes from double declining balance method to straight-line when appropriate. The ADR for the equipment is 10 years. It is assumed that the lessor's tax rate throughout the lease term will be 48 percent.[10]

The first problem is to determine the proper classification of the lease. Since ownership to the property does not pass, and the lease does not contain a bargain purchase option, the agreement fails to meet the first two criteria for a capital lease. However, the lease term is 10 years, and the economic life of the equipment also is 10 years; therefore, the lease meets the criterion that specifies that the lease term must be 75 percent or more of the economic life of the property. Further, assumption 3, above, indicates that there are no unreimbursable costs and that the lessor is certain of the collectibility of the lease payments. On the basis of these facts it can be determined that the lease is a capital lease.

The lease is not a sales-type because cost ($500,000) can be assumed to be equal to fair value, as the property was purchased and immediately leased. The lease appears to be a leveraged lease, because there are three parties involved and the financing secured by the lessor is nonrecourse. However, before it can be correctly classified, the pattern of the net investment must be determined. Assume that the lessor has agreed to account for the investment tax credit in accordance with SFAS No. 13, Paragraphs 43 (requiring a receivable for the amount of the credit) and 44 (requiring recognition as part of unearned and deferred income).

To begin the process of computing the value of the lessor's net investment in the equipment, it is necessary to calculate the expected taxable income from the lease and the expected cashflows. Table I, below, shows the computation of estimated taxable income; and Table II shows the expected cashflows.

---

[10] FASB Technical Bulletin No. 79-16 (revised) suggests that, if the lessor's tax rate changes, "the income effect of a change in the income tax rate should be recognized in the first accounting period ending on or after the date on which the legislation effecting a rate change becomes law."

Table I

Computation of Taxable Income

Year	Rentals Due	Deprecia-tion for Tax Purposes	Loan Interest Paid	Taxable Income (Loss)
1	$68,000	$(100,000)	[a]$(32,000)	$(64,000)
2	68,000	(80,000)	(29,791)	(41,791)
3	68,000	(64,000)	(27,405)	(23,405)
4	68,000	(51,200)	(24,829)	(8,029)
5	68,000	[b](25,800)	(22,046)	20,154
6	68,000	(25,800)	(19,041)	23,159
7	68,000	(25,800)	(15,795)	26,405
8	68,000	(25,800)	(12,290)	29,910
9	68,000	(25,800)	(8,504)	33,696
10	68,000	(25,800)	(4,419)	37,781
	$ 680,000	$ 450,000	$ 196,120	$ 33,880

[a] $400,000 × .08 = $32,000 interest element of payment.
[b] Change from DDB to straight-line depreciation.

Table II

Computation of Cash Flow

Year	Rentals and Residual Value	Loan Principal and Interest	Tax (Expense) or Credits	Investment Tax Credit	Cash Inflows (Outflows)
1	$68,000	$(59,612)	[a]$ 30,720	[b]$ 50,000	$ 89,108
2	68,000	(59,612)	20,060	-0-	28,448
3	68,000	(59,612)	11,234	-0-	19,622
4	68,000	(59,612)	3,854	-0-	12,242
5	68,000	(59,612)	(9,674)	-0-	(1,286)
6	68,000	(59,612)	(11,116)	-0-	(2,728)
7	68,000	(59,612)	(12,674)	-0-	(4,286)
8	68,000	(59,612)	(14,357)	-0-	(5,969)
9	68,000	(59,612)	(16,174)	-0-	(7,786)
10	68,000	(59,612)	(18,135)	-0-	(9,747)
11	50,000	-0-	-0-	-0-	50,000
	$730,000	$596,120	$ (16,262)	$ 50,000	$167,618

[a] 48% of taxable income or loss from Table I.
[b] 10% × $500,000 = $50,000.

The total cashflow of $167,618 will be allocated $100,000 to investment and $67,618 to income. The specific amounts to be allocated to investment and income in a particular year are calculated by use of the interest method. SFAS No. 13 states that allocations to *income* will be made only in those years when the net investment balance is positive. In years when the investment is negative, the entire cashflow will be allocated to the investment. This method of allocation causes a new problem in the implementation of the interest method.

After determining the cashflow, the next step is to determine the appropriate rate for the allocation process. Perhaps the most efficient method of estimating the rate is through the use of a computer program, but the rate also can be estimated on a trial-and-error basis. When the trial-and-error method is used, if the amount allocated to income is too high (more than $67,618 in this case), then the interest rate used is too high; and, conversely, if the amount allocated to income is too low (less than $67,618), then the interest rate is too low. The trial-and-error method can be very time-consuming, because the interest rate used in the allocation process has no obvious connection with the rate of return from the leased property.

For the Example 1 lease, the appropriate interest rate to use to allocate the cashflow to income in the years when the net investment is positive is 27.58 percent. Table III shows the proper allocation of the estimated cashflows to income and investment over the life of the leased property. It is certainly worth the reader's time to take a few minutes and recompute the values shown on the Table.

Table III

	ALLOCATION OF CASH FLOW TO INVESTMENT AND INCOME				INCOME RECOGNIZED ON BASIS OF CASH FLOW ALLOCATION		
End of Year	Cash Inflows and (Outflows)	Investment Balance	Allocate to Investment	Allocate to Income	Accounting Income Recognized	Income Tax Effect	Investment Tax Credit Recognized
-	-	$100,000	-	-	-	-	-
1	$ 89,108	38,472	$ 61,528	(1)$27,580	(2)$13,819	(3)$(6,633)	$20,394
2	28,448	20,635	17,837	10,611	5,317	(2,552)	7,846
3	19,622	6,704	13,931	5,691	2,851	(1,368)	4,208
4	12,242	(3,689)	10,393	1,849	926	(445)	1,367
5	(1,286)	(2,403)	(1,286)	-0-	-0-	-0-	-0-
6	(2,728)	325	(2,728)	-0-	-0-	-0-	-0-
7	(4,286)	4,701	(4,376)	90	45	(22)	67
8	(5,969)	11,967	(7,266)	1,297	650	(312)	959
9	(7,786)	23,054	(11,087)	3,301	1,654	(794)	2,441
10	(9,747)	39,159	(16,105)	6,358	3,186	(1,529)	4,701
11	50,000	-0-	39,159	*10,841	5,432	(2,607)	8,017
	$167,618	$ -0-	$100,000	$67,618	$33,880	$(16,262)	$50,000

* Rounded

(1) The appropriate rate to use to allocate the cashflows was determined through the use of a computer program and is equal to 27.58%. The allocation is based on the beginning investment balance and the income allocation is determined as follows:

$100,000 × .2758 = $27,580 Allocation to income; $89,108 — $27,580 = $61,528 Allocation to investment.

If the investment account balance is negative at the beginning of the year the entire allocation is to the investment account and no allocation is made to income.

(2) The income to be recognizzd for accounting purposes is determined as follows:

$$\frac{27{,}580}{67{,}618} = .40788 \times \$33{,}880 = \$13{,}819 \text{ Income recognized}$$

.40788 × $50,000 = $20,394 Investment Tax Credit recognized.

(3) 48% of the income recognized.

Table III shows that the value of the investment is declining in the early years of the lease, turns negative in Years 5 and 6, again becomes positive and continues to increase in the later years. This is the typical pattern described earlier and indicates that the Example meets this criteria (Block 10 of Flowchart 4) for a leveraged lease. Assuming that the lessor agrees to account for the investment tax credit, as described in Paragraphs 43 and 44, the lease would qualify as a leveraged lease.

Again referring to Table III, observe that, in Years 5 and 6, the entire cashflow is allocated to the investment account. This is because the value of the investment is $(3,689) at the *beginning* of Year 5 and is $(2,403) at the beginning of Year 6. Remember that the amounts shown in Table III are *end-of-year* balances, and that the allocation process is based upon the investment balance at the beginning of the year.

Table III also incorporates the calculation of income to be recognized in each year. The income recognized in a particular year is determined by multiplying the *total* pretax income by the percentage relationship between the cashflow allocated to that year and the total cashflow over the entire life. In Years 5 and 6, when no cashflow is allocated to income, no income can be recognized, because the numerator of the equation would be zero. The total income to be recognized can be found on Table I, and the total tax effect of that income and the investment tax credit can be found on Table II.

The following journal entries would be required, based upon the tables developed:

Inception of Lease:

Rentals Receivable	[a]83,880	
Investment Tax Credit Receivable	50,000	
Estimated Residual Value	50,000	
Cash		100,000
Unearned and Deferred Income		[b]83,880

[a] Total Rental Payments ($68,000 × 10)	$680,000
Debt Principal Repayment	(400,000)
Total Debt Interest Payment	(196,120)
Rental Receivable	$ 83,880

[b]Pretax Accounting Income	$ 33,880
Investment Tax Credit	50,000
Unearned and Deferred Income	$ 83,880

Receipt of Lease Rental and Payment of Debt:

Cash	8,388	
Rentals Receivable		[c]8,388
Income Taxes Payable	50,000	
Investment Tax Credit Receivable		50,000
Unearned and Deferred Income	13,819	
Income from Leveraged Lease		[d]13,819
Unearned and Deferred Income	20,394	
Investment Tax Credit Recognized		[e]20,394
Income Taxes Payable	[f]30,720	
Income Tax Expense	[g]6,633	
Deferred Income Taxes		[h]37,353

[c]

Rental Payment Received	$ 68,000
Debt Payment Incurred	(59,612)
Net Cash Received From Lease	$ 8,388

[d]See Table III.
[e]See Table III.
[f]See Table II.
[g]See Table III.
[h]See Topic 5 for a complete discussion of income taxes and tax credits.

Loss for Tax Purposes	$(64,000)
Accounting Income Recognized	13,819
Difference	$ 77,819
Income Tax Rate	× .48
Deferred Income Taxes	$ 37,353

At the end of the lease term, the Rentals Receivable account would be reduced to zero ($8,388 × 10 = $83,880), and the debt financing would have been completely paid-off. The benefit of the investment tax credit would probably be received in the first year of the lease term, through a reduction of the lessor's tax liability. The unearned and deferred income would be fully recognized through the two components of pretax income and the investment tax credit recognized. Table IV shows the reconciliation of the deferred income taxes over the life of the leased property. The estimated residual value account would be eliminated at the end of Year 11, when the equipment is sold for $50,000.

Table IV

Computation of Deferred Income Taxes

Year	Increase (Decrease) in Account	Account Balance
1	$37,353	$37,353
2	22,612	59,965
3	12,603	72,568
4	4,298	76,866
5	(9,674)	67,192
6	(11,116)	56,076
7	(12,653)	43,423
8	(14,045)	29,378
9	(15,380)	13,998
10	(16,606)	(2,608)
11	2,608	-0-

The major problem in accounting for a leveraged lease is understanding the process of allocating the estimated cashflows. Once this process is understood, the accounting becomes straightforward, and the problem of income recognition is solved.

Flowchart 5B indicates that the lessor must review the estimated residual value on a periodic basis and be prepared to account for a permanent decline in value. To illustrate the accounting for a permanent decline in the estimated residual value, assume the same facts as in Example 1, except that, at the start of Year 4, it is determined that the estimated residual value is only $20,000, rather than the original estimate of $50,000. Assume further that this decline in residual value also has resulted in a decline in the salvage value used for depreciation purposes. These two facts would require the lessor to revise the estimated pretax income and the cashflow previously prepared in Tables I and II.

This revised information means that depreciation for Years 5 through 10 would be $30,800, rather than the $25,800 indicated in Table I. Depreciation in Year 4 would not be affected, because double declining balance method ignores salvage value and the lessor has not yet changed from double declining balance to straight-line. This $5,000 decrease in pretax income ($25,800 – $30,800 = $(5,000)) for Years 5 through 10 also would change the estimated income tax effect of the earnings. Both of these elements, along with the changed cashflow, must be revised. Table V shows the effect of the change in residual value on these three amounts. The revised cashflow now will have to be allocated to income and investment, using the interest method. The revised pretax income and cashflow will result in a different pattern of income recognition. (Notice that pretax income is reduced by the $30,000 decline in residual value and that the revised cashflow is reduced by the after-tax consequences of the decline, i.e., $30,000 decline in residual − $14,400 tax effect = $15,600 decline in cashflow.)

Table V

Revised Estimates

Year	Taxable Income	Tax (Expense) or Credits	Cash Inflows (Outflows)
1	$(64,000)	$30,720	$ 89,108
2	(41,791)	20,060	28,448
3	(23,405)	11,234	19,622
4	(8,029)	3,854	12,242
5	15,154	(7,274)	1,114
6	18,159	(8,716)	(328)
7	21,405	(10,274)	(1,886)
8	24,910	(11,957)	(3,569)
9	28,696	(13,774)	(5,386)
10	32,781	(15,735)	(7,347)
11	-0-	-0-	20,000
	$ 3,880	$(1,862)	$152,018

Table VI develops the process of allocating the estimated cashflows to income and investment. Remember that cashflows will be allocated to income only in the years in which the net investment is positive. The appropriate interest rate to use in the allocation process is 27.55 percent. As indicated in Table VI, no cashflow is allocated to income in Years 5 through 8; therefore, no accounting income would be recognized in these years.

Table VI

End of Year	ALLOCATION OF CASHFLOW TO INVESTMENT AND INCOME: Cash Inflows or (Outflows)	Investment Balance	Allocate to Investment	Allocate to Income	INCOME RECOGNITION BASED ON CASHFLOW ALLOCATION: Accounting Income Recognized	Income Tax Effect	Investment Tax Credit Recognized
-	-	$100,000	-	-	-	-	-
1	$ 89,108	38,442	$ 61,558	[a]$27,550	[b]$2,054	[c]$ (986)	$26,481
2	28,448	20,584	17,858	10,590	790	(379)	10,179
3	19,622	6,633	13,951	5,671	423	(203)	5,451
4	12,242	(3,782)	10,415	1,827	136	(65)	1,756
5	1,114	(4,896)	1,114	-0-	-0-	-0-	-0-
6	(328)	(4,568)	(328)	-0-	-0-	-0-	-0-
7	(1,886)	(2,682)	(1,886)	-0-	-0-	-0-	-0-
8	(3,569)	887	(3,569)	-0-	-0-	-0-	-0-
9	(5,386)	6,517	(5,630)	244	19	(9)	235
10	(7,347)	15,659	(9,142)	1,795	134	(64)	1,725
11	20,000	-0-	15,659	*4,341	324	(156)	4,173
	$152,018	-0-	$100,000	$52,018	$3,880	$(1,862)	$50,000

* Rounded

[a] The appropriate rate to use to allocate the cashflows was determined through the use of a computer program and is equal to 27.55%. The allocation is based on the beginning investment balance and the income allocation is determined as follows:

$100,000 × .2755 = $27,550 allocation to income; $89,108 — $27,550 = $61,558 allocation to investment.

If the investment account balance is negative at the beginning of the year, the entire allocation is to the investment account and no allocation is made to income.

[b] The income to be recognized for accounting purposes is determined as follows:

$$\frac{\$27{,}550}{\$52{,}018} = .52962 \times \$3{,}880 = \$2{,}054 \text{ Income recognized}$$

$$.52962 \times \$50{,}000 = \$26{,}481 \text{ Investment tax credit recognized.}$$

[c] 48% of the income recognized.

Once the revised income allocation process is completed, the lessor can develop the information necessary to reflect the change in residual value that will be accounted for as a change in accounting estimate (see Topic 1 for a detailed analysis of APB Opinion No. 20, "Accounting Changes"). The lessor should determine the difference between the income that should have been recognized and the income actually recognized. It is important to keep in mind that the unearned and deferred income account contains two elements: pretax income, and the investment tax credit. Table VII below develops the information necessary to adjust for changes in the pretax income.

Table VII

Adjustment for Pretax Income

Year	Recognized (Table III)	Revised Income (Table VI)	Difference
1	$13,819	$2,054	$11,765
2	5,317	790	4,527
3	2,851	423	2,428
Income recognized	$21,987	$3,267	$18,720
Total Pretax Income	33,880	3,880	30,000
Future Pretax Income	$11,893	$ 613	$11,280

Table VII has isolated two elements in the required adjusting entry. The first is the $18,720 adjustment to pretax income, and the second is the $11,280 adjustment to the unearned and deferred income account.

Table VIII shows the difference between the investment tax credit that was recognized and the credit that should have been recognized under the assumption of the revised residual value.

Table VIII

Adjustment for Investment Tax Credit

Year	Investment Tax Credit Recognized (Table III)	Investment Tax Credit (Table VI)	Difference
1	$ 20,394	$ 26,481	$ 6,087
2	7,846	10,179	2,333
3	4,208	5,451	1,243
	$ 32,448	$ 42,111	$ 9,63

Table VIII has isolated the other element in the adjustment to unearned and deferred income. Sufficient information now is available to prepare the following adjusting journal entry to reflect the permanent decline in the estimated residual value of the equipment.

Unearned and Deferred Income	[a]20,943	
Pretax Income	18,720	
Investment Tax Credit Recognized		9,663
Estimated Residual Value		30,000

[a] The adjustment to unearned and deferred income consist of the pretax income of $11,280 plus the investment tax credit of $9,663.

A second adjusting entry is necessary to record the deferred tax consequences of the above entry. The required adjustment would be:

Deferred Income Taxes	[b]8,986	
Income Tax Expense		8,986

[b] $18,720 × .48 = $8,986.

Presented below is a reconciliation of the unearned and deferred income account:

	Unearned and Deferred Income	
	Before Adjust-ment	As Revised
Beginning Balance	$ 83,880	$53,880
Income Recognized (Table VII)	(21,987)	(3,267)
Investment Tax Credit (Table VIII)	(32,448)	(42,111)
	$ 29,445	$ 8,502
Adjustment Recorded	(20,943)	
Balance After Adjustment	$ 8,502	

Similar reconciliations could be prepared for the other accounts involved, but are not necessary at this point. For Years 4 through 11, income will be recognized, as reflected in Table VI, since the original allocation now is obsolete.

While the presence of initial direct costs complicates the accounting for other types of leases, such costs do not have a significant impact on the complexity of accounting for leveraged leases. If the lessor does incur initial direct costs under a leveraged lease, they merely reduce pretax income by the total amount and reduce cash flows by the after-tax effect in the first year of the lease. The allocation process, after recognition has been given to the initial direct costs, would be exactly the same as that described earlier.

This completes the discussion of leveraged leases. We now will turn our attention to accounting for direct financing leases, which will conclude the first major portion of the lessor classification and accounting.

Accounting for a Direct Financing Lease

Flowchart 5C shows the proper accounting for a direct financing lease, with accounting at date of inception on the left, and subsequent accounting on the right.

The gross investment in the lease is determined in much the same manner as for the sales-type lease, i.e., the value of the MLP depends on the existence of a bargain purchase option. The individual elements of the MLP are the same as those of the sales-type lease. The gross investment also is recorded at an amount equal to the MLP, plus any unguaranteed residual value. Unearned income is recorded as the difference between the gross investment and the cost or carrying amount of the leased property. If the lessor incurs any initial direct costs, the amount should be charged to income and also should reduce the balance in the unearned income account.

In subsequent periods, the interest method will be used to allocate the payments received to recovery of investment and unearned income. The basic differences between the sales-type and direct financing lease are in the recognition of manufacturer's or dealer's profits in a sales-type lease and in the handling of the initial direct costs in the direct financing lease. With these two exceptions, the basic accounting is very similar.

Technical Considerations for a Direct Financing Lease

To illustrate the technical aspects of accounting for a direct financing lease, four example leases will be developed. For a general understanding of direct financing lease accounting, the Example 1 lease assumptions are presented below:

Example 1
Lease Assumptions

1. The lessor enters into a five-year, noncancelable lease with a lessee that requires annual advance payments of $50,000. The lessor is certain about the collectibility of the MLP, and there are no unreimbursable costs associated with the lease.
2. The implicit interest rate is 10 percent.
3. Title to the leased property does not transfer to the lessee, and there is no bargain purchase option in the lease agreement.
4. The cost and the fair market value of the property is $208,494. The estimated residual value is zero, and the estimated economic life of the property is five years.

The Example 1 lease qualifies as a capital lease, because the lease term of five years is more than 75 percent of the economic life of the leased property (5 years × .75 = 3.75 years), and there are no material uncertainties about the unreimbursable costs, and the collectibility of the MLP is reasonably predictible. The lease cannot be a sales-type lease, because cost is equal to fair value of the leased property. It is not a three-party lease, and therefore will not qualify as a leveraged lease. The Example 1 lease must be a direct financing lease.

In addition to the above criteria, the lease agreement also meets the criterion concerning the discounted value of the MLP being 90 percent or more of the fair value of the property. The present value of the MLP is determined as follows:

Lease Payments Required	$ 50,000
Present Value Factor	[a]4.16987
Present Value of MLP	$208,494

[a] Present Value factor for an annuity due at 10 percent for 5 periods. See Appendix A, Table III.

The $208,494 present value of the MLP is more than 90 percent of the fair value of the leased property ($208,494 Fair Value × .90 = $187,645).

Under a direct financing lease, the asset recorded—called the gross investment in the lease—is equal to the *total* rentals receivable. In this case, the gross investment would be $250,000 ($50,000 × 5 = $250,000). The difference between the gross investment and the cost of the asset leased is recorded as unearned income, and would be determined as follows:

Gross Investment	$250,000
Cost of Asset Leased	208,494
Unearned Income	$ 41,506

Table I below shows the calculation of the lease amortization that is necessary to determine the pattern of income recognition.

Table I

Lease Amortization and Income—Lessor-Direct Financing

	Period	Annual Payment	Annual Interest Income	Principal Reduction	Present Value of Principal
Initial Value	-	-	-	-	a$208,494
	1	$ 50,000	b$15,849	c$ 34,151	d174,343
	2	50,000	12,434	37,566	136,777
	3	50,000	8,678	41,322	95,455
	4	50,000	4,545	45,455	50,000
	5	50,000	-0-	50,000	-0-
		$250,000	$41,506	$208,494	

a The cost and fair value of the property at the inception of the lease.
b ($208,494 — $50,000) × 10% = $15,849.
c $50,000 — $15,849 = $34,151.
d $208,494 — $34,151 = $174,343.

Because the lease requires advanced payments, the entry to record the asset at inception of the lease will be followed by the entry to record the receipt of the first payment and the recognition of income. The required entries are as follows:

Minimum Lease Payments Receivable	250,000	
Equipment		208,494
Unearned Income		41,506
Cash	50,000	
Minimum Lease Payments Receivable		50,000
Unearned Income	15,849	
Income from Capital Lease		15,849

For a direct financing lease, it should be noted that the lessor must calculate the present value of the MLP for *classification* purposes only. The present value of the MLP does not enter into the accounting for direct financing leases. The Example 1 lease illustrated the basic accounting for a direct financing lease. The Example 2 lease builds on the basic example by incorporating new variables into the computation of the lease payments receivable.

The assumptions of the Example 2 lease are given below:

Example 2
Lease Assumptions

1. The lessor enters into a five-year, noncancelable lease with a lessee that requires annual year-end payments of $30,000. The lessor is certain about the collectibility of the MLP, and there are no unreimbursable costs associated with the lease.
2. The implicit interest rate is 10 percent.

3. Title to the leased property does not transfer to the lessee, but the lease does contain a bargain purchase option with an option payment of $10,000, payable to the lessor at the end of the lease term.
4. The cost and the fair market value of the property each are $126,142 at the inception of the lease. The property has an estimated economic life of five years, and an *unguaranteed* residual value of $10,000 at the end of its useful life.

The new items for consideration are the bargain purchase option of $10,000, and the unguaranteed residual value of $10,000. Both of these amounts will influence the accounting for a direct financing lease.

The Example 2 lease qualifies as a capital lease because the lease agreement contains a bargain purchase option, there are no uncertainties regarding the unreimbursable costs and the collectibility of the MLP is predictable. Cost of the property is equal to fair value at inception of the lease; and, therefore, the Example 2 lease is not a sale-type lease. There are only two parties to the lease agreement, so the lease is not a leveraged lease. By process of elimination, the lease is a direct financing lease.

In addition to meeting the bargain purchase option criterion, the Example 2 lease also meets the "75-percent-of-economic-life" criterion. The lease term of five years is more than 75 percent of the economic life (5 years × .75 = 3.75 years). The calculation of the present value of the MLP, which is needed for lease classification purposes only, is shown below:

Lease Payment Required	$ 30,000	
Present Value Factor	[a]3.79079	
Present Value of Lease Payments		$113,724
Bargain Purchase Option Payment	$ 10,000	
Present Value Factor	[b].62092	
Present Value of Bargain Purchase Option		6,209
Present Value of MLP		$119,933

[a] Present Value factor for ordinary annuity at 10 percent for 5 periods. See Appendix A, Table II.
[b] Present Value factor for $1 at 10 percent for 5 periods. See Appendix A, Table I.

The present value of the MLP ($119,933) is more than 90 percent of the fair value of the leased property ($126,142 × .90 = $113,528), and the fourth basic criterion also is met. Note that the calculation of the present value of the MLP does not include the $10,000 unguaranteed residual value.

The gross investment in the lease is $170,000 and is determined as follows:

Lease Payments Required ($30,000 × 5)	$150,000
Bargain Purchase Option Payment	10,000
Unguaranteed Residual Value	10,000
	$170,000

The $170,000 gross investment is the recorded value of the asset under a direct financing lease. The difference between the gross investment and the cost of the leased property ($170,000 – $126,142 = $43,858) is recorded as unearned income. The entry at inception of the lease would be as follows:

Minimum Lease Payments Receivable	170,000	
Equipment		126,142
Unearned Income		43,858

Table II develops the amortization schedule necessary to determine the income to be recognized in Years 1 through 5.

Table II

Lease Amortization and Income—Lessor-Direct Financing

	Period	Annual Payment	Annual Interest Income	Principal Reduction	Present Value of Principal
Initial Value	-	-	-	-	[a]$126,142
	1	$ 30,000	[b]$12,614	[c]$ 17,386	[d]108,756
	2	30,000	10,876	19,124	89,632
	3	30,000	8,963	21,037	68,595
	4	30,000	6,860	23,140	45,455
	5	30,000	4,545	25,455	[e]20,000
		$150,000	$43,858	$106,142	

[a] Cost and fair value of the property.
[b] $126,142 × 10% = $12,614
[c] $30,000 — $12,614 = $17,386
[d] $126,142 — $17,386 = $108,756
[e] Represents an unguaranteed residual value of $10,000 and a bargain purchase option payment of $10,000.

The entry to record the first rental payment and the income for the year would be as follows:

Cash	30,000	
Minimum Lease Payments Receivable		30,000
Unearned Income	12,614	
Income from Capital Lease		12,614

As indicated in Table II, the $20,000 unamortized balance at the end of Year 5 represents the bargain purchase option payment of $10,000 and the unguaranteed residual value of $10,000. Assuming that the lessee exercises the bargain purchase option, the following entry would be required:

Cash	10,000	
Loss on Lease Transaction[a]	10,000	
Minimum Lease Payments Receivable		20,000

[a] Gains or losses on lease transactions are handled in accordance with APB Opinion No. 30. See Topic 1 for a detailed analysis of APB Opinion No. 30.

In this case, the loss of $10,000 is equal to the unguaranteed residual value of the asset. It is logical to assume that, if a lease contains a bargain purchase option, the lessor will have some unguaranteed residual value. This is true because the purchase option price is generally below fair value, so as to induce the lessee to exercise the option. In some lease agreements, it is possible to have a partial guarantee of residual value that would result in both a guaranteed residual value and some unguaranteed residual value. In this case, the gross investment would include both the guaranteed and unguaranteed residual values. The present value of the MLP will be affected by the guaranteed, but *not* by the unguaranteed residual.

The two examples presented above ignored the problem of initial direct costs. Since unearned income in an amount equal to the initial direct costs must be charged to income at the inception of the lease, the initial direct costs will affect the interest rate used to amortize the cost of the asset under a direct financing lease. To illustrate the accounting for direct financing leases where the lessor incurs initial direct costs, a third example is presented.

For purposes of the third example lease, assume a direct financing capital lease that requires $50,000 year-end payments over a five-year lease term, and an implicit interest rate of 10 percent. Also assume that the lessor incurred $4,943 of initial direct costs to consummate the lease agreement. The present value of the MLP is equal to the cost and fair value of the leased property at the inception of the lease.

Ignore, for the time being, the initial direct costs. The present value of the MLP and the unearned income would be determined as follows:

Annual Year-End Payment Required	$ 50,000
Present Value Factor	[a]3.79079
Present Value of Lease Payments[b]	$189,540
Gross Investment ($50,000 × 5)	$250,000
Present Value of Lease Payment	(189,540)
Unearned Income	$ 60,460

[a] Present Value factor for an ordinary annuity at 10 percent for five periods. See Appendix A, Table II.

[b] Remember that the present value of the MLP is also equal to the cost and fair value of the asset leased.

Unearned income, in an amount equal to the initial direct costs, must be charged to income. Therefore, the balance in the unearned income account, after the reduction for initial direct costs, would be $55,517 ($60,460 − $4,943 = $55,517). The lessor now must determine the rate of interest that will amortize the new unearned income over the term of the lease, using the interest method. The following formula will provide the *present value factor* corresponding to the new effective interest rate:

$$X = \frac{D + PVI}{P}$$

Where: X = Present value factor of an annuity
D = Initial direct costs
PVI = Present value of the gross investment
P = Periodic minimum rental payment

Given the information above, the formula would provide the following results:

$$X = \frac{\$4{,}943 + \$189{,}540}{\$50{,}000} = 3.88966$$

The answer of 3.88966 represents the present value factor for an ordinary annuity for five periods. Given this information, turn to the present value table for an ordinary annuity, Appendix A, Table II. Start in the five periods row, and go across the columns until the factor of 3.88966 is found. This present value factor corresponds to an interest rate of nine percent. This is the new effective interest rate that will be used to amortize the unearned income.

The exact present value factor may not always be found in the table. This may require the user to interpolate an interest rate between two factors. If the lease agreement is more complex than the one presented above, e.g., if the lease contained a guaranteed residual value or an unguaranteed residual value, the formula given above will not be adequate to provide an answer. In this case, the effective interest rate must be found by using the trial-and-error method or a computer program.

Once the new interest rate has been determined, an amortization schedule such as the one shown in Table III can be developed. The entries to record the initial direct costs might be as follows:

Initial Direct Costs Incurred	4,943	
Cash		4,943
Unearned Income	4,943	
Income from Capital Lease		4,943

Table III

Lease Amortization and Income—Lessor-Direct Financing

	Period	Annual Payment	Annual Interest Income	Principal Reduction	Present Value of Principal
Initial Value	-	-	-	-	[a]$194,483
	1	$ 50,000	[b]$17,503	[c]$ 32,497	[d]161,986
	2	50,000	14,579	35,421	126,565
	3	50,000	11,391	38,609	87,956
	4	50,000	7,916	42,084	45,872
	5	50,000	4,128	45,872	-0-
		$250,000	$55,517	$194,483	

[a] Total Lease Payments	$250,000
New Unearned Income	(55,517)
Present Value of Principal	$194,483
Original Unearned Income	$ 60,460
Initial Direct Costs	(4,943)
New Unearned Income	$ 55,517

[b] $194,483 × 9% = $17,503.
[c] $50,000 − $17,503 = $32,497.
[d] $194,483 − $32,497 = $161,986.

After the initial direct costs have been recorded, and the table of amortization prepared, the subsequent accounting will be identical to that previously described. The major new problem introduced was the determination of a new effective interest rate when the lessor incurs initial direct costs.

As indicated in Flowchart 5C, the lessor must periodically review the estimated residual value and be prepared to account for a permanent decline in the residual value. In the case of a permanent decline in the estimated residual value, a loss must be recognized, and the amortization of the unearned income must be treated as a change in an accounting estimate, in accordance with APB Opinion No. 20. (See Topic 1 for a complete analysis of APB Opinion No. 20, which includes changes in accounting estimates.)[11]

The fourth example lease is used to illustrate the accounting for a permanent decline in the estimated residual value. Assume the lessor has entered into a direct financing capital lease that requires five annual year-end payments of $100,000, with an implicit interest rate of 10 percent and an unguaranteed residual value of $20,000. The cost and fair market value of the property leased each are $391,497. Also assume that, at the beginning of the second year of the lease term, a permanent decline of

[11] If the residual value increases, the lessor is prohibited from recognizing it. In addition, FASB Technical Bulletin No. 79-14 states that the prohibition against recognizing residual value increases applies even if the amount is guaranteed.

$2,000 in the residual value occurred. The decline in the residual value will affect the unearned income over the life of the lease and the minimum lease payment receivable account. The calculation of the income adjustment is as follows:

Unguaranteed Residual Value	$20,000	
Present Value Factor (four remaining periods)	[a].68301	
Present Value of Unguaranteed Residual Beginning of Year 2		$13,660
Unguaranteed Residual Value - Revised	$18,000	
Present Value Factor	[a].68301	
Present Value of Revised Residual Value Beginning of Year 2		12,294
Unearned Income Adjustment		$ 1,366

[a] Present Value factor for $1 at 10 percent for four periods. See Appendix A, Table I.

The journal entry necessary to reflect the permanent decline in residual value is:

Loss on Decline in Estimated Residual Value	634	
Unearned Income	1,366	
Minimum Lease Payment Receivable		2,000

To illustrate the effect of the change in residual value on the capital lease amortization, Table IV is provided below.

Table IV

Lease Amortization and Income—Decline in Residual Value

	Period	Annual Payment	Annual Interest Income	Principal Reduction	Present Value of Principal
Initial Value	-	-	-	-	[a]$391,497
	1	$100,000	[b]$ 39,150	[c]$ 60,850	[d]329,281
	2	100,000	32,928	67,072	262,209
	3	100,000	26,221	73,779	188,430
	4	100,000	18,843	81,157	107,273
	5	100,000	10,727	89,273	[e]18,000
		$500,000	$127,869	$372,131	

[a] The cost and fair value of the leased property at the inception of the lease.
[b] $391,497 X 10% = $39,150
[c] $100,000 — $39,150 = $60,850
[d]

Cost and Fair Value at Inception of Lease	$391,497
Principal Amortization Period 1	(60,850)
Adjustment to Unearned Income for Change in Residual Value	(1,366)
Present Value of Principal in Year 2	$329,281

[e] Unguaranteed residual value at the end of Year 5.

Once the adjusting entry has been recorded, and a new amortization table prepared, subsequent accounting would be identical to that previously described. Table IV would be used for income recognition purposes for Years 2 through 5.

This completes the discussion of direct financing leases. The next section of this Topic will deal with real estate leasing from the viewpoint of the lessor.

Flowcharts and Discussion of Leases Involving Real Estate—Lessor

Flowcharts 6 and 7 illustrate the classification and accounting for real estate leases from the standpoint of the lessor. All of the basic classification and accounting concepts discussed previously apply to real estate leases. There are, however, certain cases where only a limited number of criteria apply or where additional computations may be required. The computation of the MLP, the gross investment and the present value of both is the same as discussed in the general lessor Flowcharts (Flowcharts 5, 5A, 5B, and 5C). Real estate leases involving initial direct costs or a permanent decline in the estimated residual value will be treated in a manner similar to that discussed in the preceeding sections. The real estate Flowcharts make reference to the general lessor Flowcharts for specifics on accounting procedures.

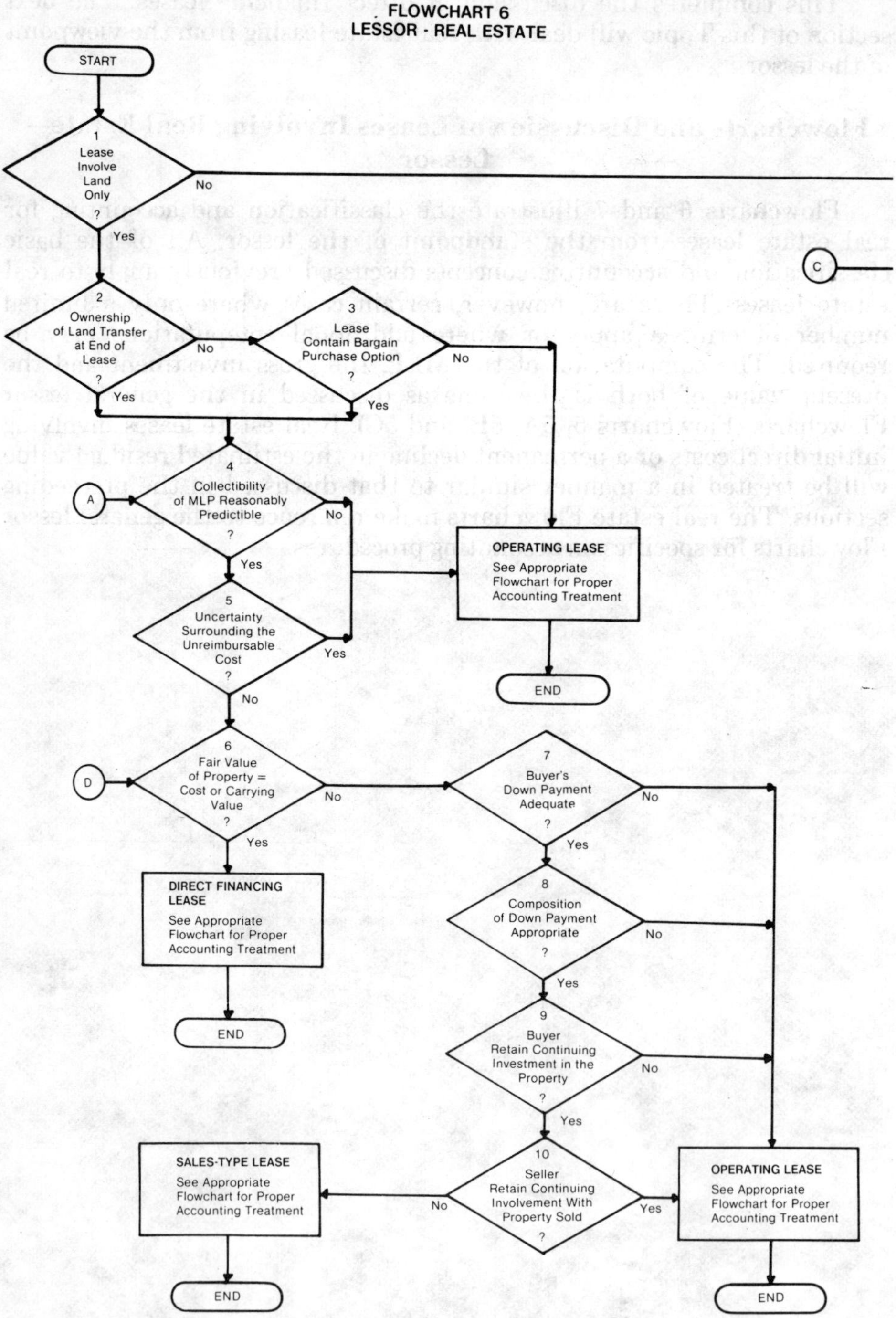
. FLOWCHART 6
LESSOR - REAL ESTATE
START
1
Lease
Involve
Land
Only
?
No
Yes
C
2
Ownership
of Land Transfer
at End of
Lease
?
No
Yes
3
Lease
Contain Bargain
Purchase Option
?
No
Yes
A
4
Collectibility
of MLP Reasonably
Predictible
?
No
Yes
OPERATING LEASE
See Appropriate
Flowchart for Proper
Accounting Treatment
5
Uncertainty
Surrounding the
Unreimbursable
Cost
?
Yes
No
END
D
6
Fair Value
of Property =
Cost or Carrying
Value
?
No
Yes
7
Buyer's
Down Payment
Adequate
?
No
Yes
DIRECT FINANCING
LEASE
See Appropriate
Flowchart for Proper
Accounting Treatment
8
Composition
of Down Payment
Appropriate
?
No
Yes
END
9
Buyer
Retain Continuing
Investment in the
Property
?
No
Yes
SALES-TYPE LEASE
See Appropriate
Flowchart for Proper
Accounting Treatment
10
Seller
Retain Continuing
Involvement With
Property Sold
?
No
Yes
OPERATING LEASE
See Appropriate
Flowchart for Proper
Accounting Treatment
END
END

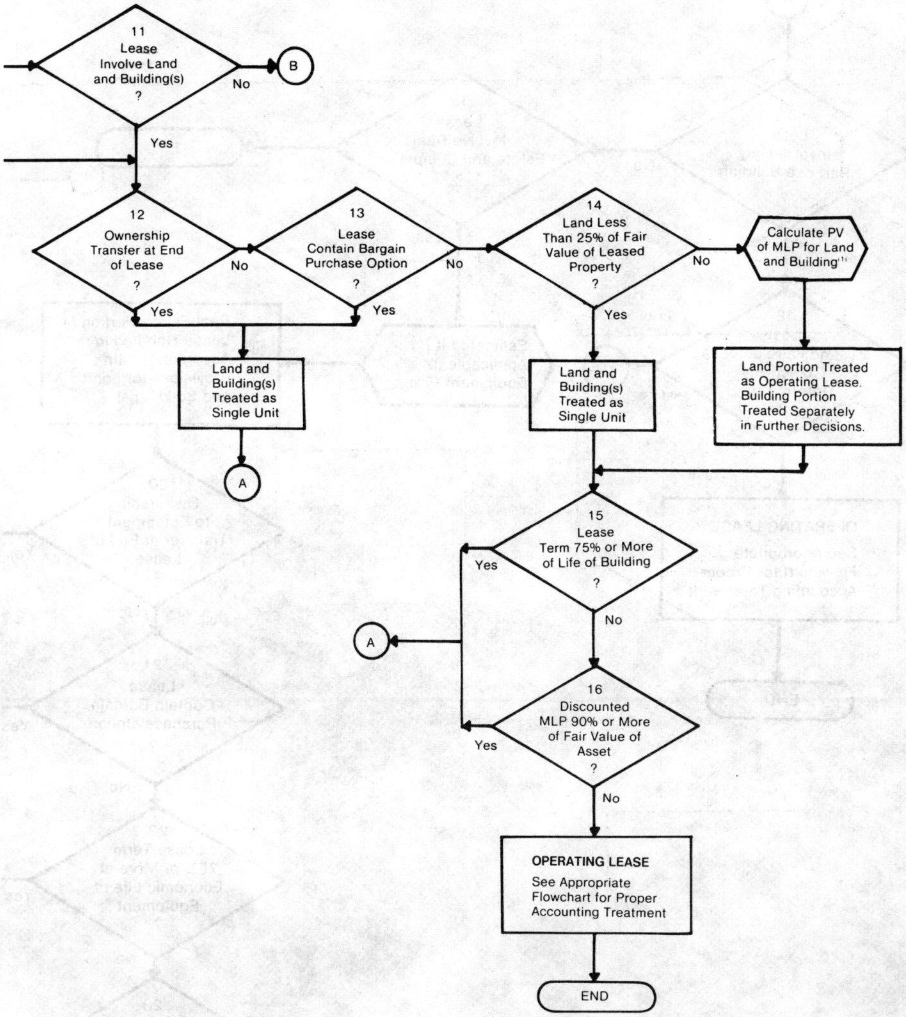

(1) Fair value of the land discounted at the lessee's incremental borrowing rate is equal to the MLP allocated to the land. Total MLP less MLP allocated to land is equal to MLP allocated to building(s).

FLOWCHART 7
LESSOR - REAL ESTATE

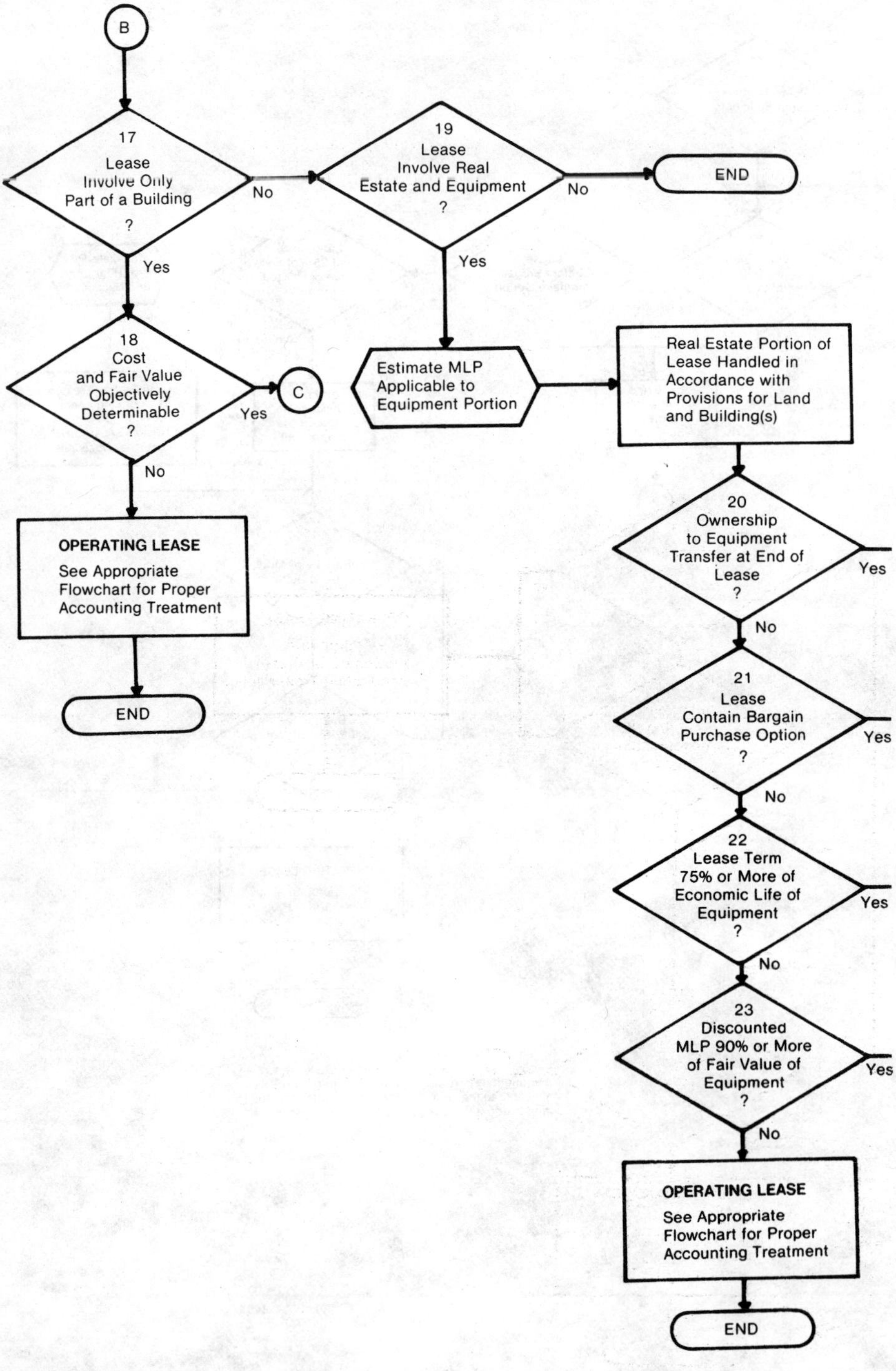

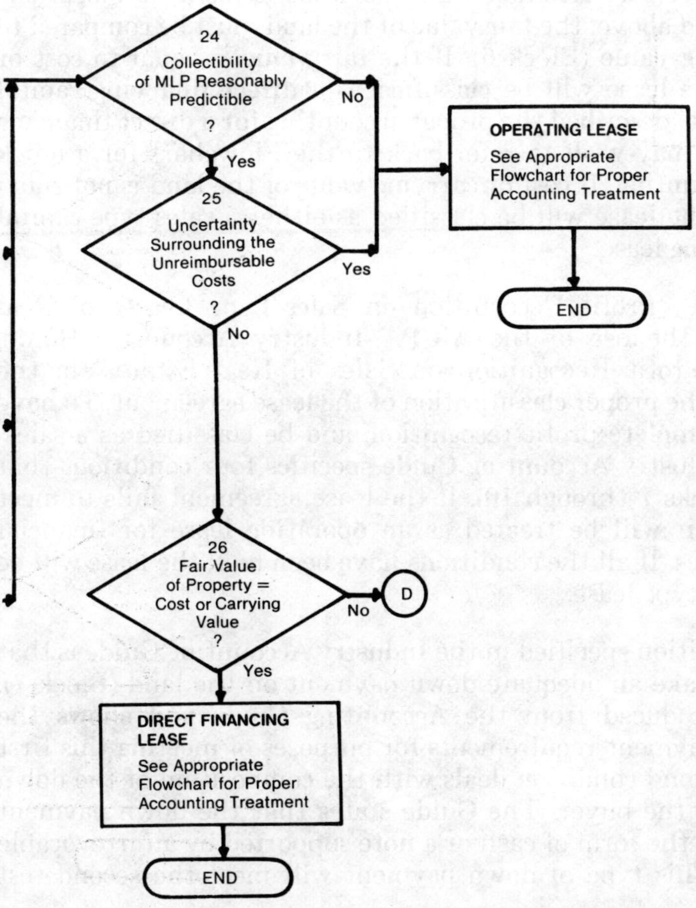
24
Collectibility of MLP Reasonably Predictible ?
No
Yes
OPERATING LEASE
See Appropriate Flowchart for Proper Accounting Treatment
END
25
Uncertainty Surrounding the Unreimbursable Costs ?
Yes
No
26
Fair Value of Property = Cost or Carrying Value ?
No
D
Yes
DIRECT FINANCING LEASE
See Appropriate Flowchart for Proper Accounting Treatment
END

The discussion that follows will include all four types of real estate leases (land only, land and building(s), part of a building, and real estate and equipment) covered in SFAS No. 13. However, new example material will be developed only for leases involving land and building(s). As discussed earlier, leases other than those involving land and building(s) are either handled in a conventional manner or are merely extensions of the land and building(s) category.

Leases Involving Land Only

When a lease involves land only, it may be classified as an operating, direct financing or sales-type lease. For the lease to be considered a capital lease, i.e., direct financing or sales-type, the agreement must meet one of the transfer-of-ownership tests (Blocks 2 or 3), and *both* of the risk-transfer tests (Blocks 4 and 5). If the lease agreement fails to meet one of the transfer-of-ownership tests and either of the risk-transfer tests, it will be treated as an *operating* lease for financial accounting purposes.

Once it has been determined that the lease agreement meets the conditions specified above, the fair value of the land must be compared to its cost or carrying value (Block 6). If the fair value is equal to cost or carrying value, the lease will be classified as a direct financing capital lease. Flowchart 5C described the proper accounting for a direct financing lease. The reader may wish to refer back to the Flowchart for a quick review of the accounting. If cost or carrying value of the land is not equal to its fair value, the lease will be classified as either a sales-type capital lease or an operating lease.

SFAS No. 26, "Profit Recognition on Sales-Type Leases of Real Estate," requires the use of the AICPA Industry Accounting Guide, "Accounting for Profit Recognition on Sales of Real Estate," in the determination of the proper classification of the lease agreement. To have immediate and complete profit recognition, and be classified as a sales-type lease, the Industry Accounting Guide specifies four conditions that must be met (Blocks 7 through 10). If the lease agreement fails to meet these conditions, it will be treated as an operating lease for financial accounting purposes. If all the conditions have been met, the lease will be handled as a sales-type lease.

The first condition specified in the Industry Accounting Guide is that the buyer must make an adequate down payment on the land (Block 7). Exhibit 1 is reproduced from the Accounting Guide and shows the minimum down payment requirements for purposes of meeting this first condition. The second condition deals with the composition of the down payment made by the buyer. The Guide states that the down payment should be made in the form of cash or a note supported by an irrevocable letter of credit. This type of down payment will meet the second test

(Block 8). The third condition specifies that the buyer must continue to increase his investment in the land each year after the down payment has been made. This condition requires the buyer to maintain a continuing investment in the land acquired through the lease agreement (Block 9). The fourth, and final, condition relates to the *seller's* continuing involvement with the land sold. Whenever a seller continues to be involved with the land, a question is raised as to whether or not the property has been "sold." The lease agreement should not be considered a sales-type lease if the seller's involvement carries the same kinds of risks as ownership of the property. In this case, the lease would be treated as an operating lease (Block 10). If the seller of the property meets all the conditions specified in the Industry Accounting Guide for immediate and complete profit recognition, the leased property will be treated as a sales-type lease. Accounting for a sales-type lease has been outlined in Flowchart 5A, and the reader may want to refer back to the Flowchart for details of the accounting process. When faced with a lease agreement involving land, the authors suggest that a copy of the Industry Accounting Guide (which contains Statement of Position 75-6 and 78-4) be obtained from the AICPA.

Exhibit 1
Minimum Down Payment Requirements

	Minimum Down Payment Expressed as a Percentage of Sales Value
Land:	
Held for commercial, industrial, or residential development to commence within two years after sale	[a] 20%
Held for commercial, industrial, or residential development after two years	[a] 25%
Commercial and Industrial Property:	
Office and industrial buildings, shopping centers, etc.:	
Properties subject to lease on a long-term lease basis to parties having satisfactory credit rating; cash flow currently sufficient to service all indebtedness	10%
Single tenancy properties sold to a user having a satisfactory credit rating	15%
All other	20%
Other Income-Producing Properties (hotels, motels, marinas, mobile home parks, etc.):	
Cash flow currently sufficient to service all indebtedness	15%
Start-up situations or current deficiencies in cash flow	25%
Multi-Family Residential Property:	
Primary residence:	
Cash flow currently sufficient to service all indebtedness	10%
Start-up situations or current deficiencies in cash flow	15%
Secondary or recreational residence:	
Cash flow currently sufficient to service all indebtedness	15%
Start-up situations or current deficiencies in cash flow	25%
Single Family Residential Property (including condominium or cooperative housing):	
Primary residence of the buyer	[b] 5%
Secondary or recreational residence	[b] 10%

[a] Not intended to apply to volume retail lot sales by land development companies.

[b] If collectibility of the remaining portion of the sales price cannot be supported by reliable evidence of collection experience, a higher down payment is indicated and should not be less than 60% of the difference between the sales value and the financing available from loans guaranteed by regulatory bodies, such as FHA or VA, or from independent financial institutions.

* * * * * *

This schedule cannot cover every type of real estate property. To evaluate down payments on other types of property, analogies can be made to the types of properties specified, or the risks of the particular property can be related to the risks of the properties specified.

Leases Involving Land and Building(s)

If a lease involves land and building(s), and *either* of the transfer-of-ownership criteria and *both* of the risk-transfer tests (Blocks 4, 5, 12 and 13) are met, the lease is classified as a capital lease, and the land and building(s) are treated as a single unit of leased property. If the lease fails to meet either of the two transfer-of-ownership criteria, it still may qualify for capital lease accounting if certain other conditions are met. Before these additional tests can be met, the lessor must determine the relative values of the land and building portions of the leased property. If the land portion of the leased property constitutes less than 25 percent of the total fair value, land and building(s) will be treated as a single unit of leased property for purposes of subsequent tests (Block 14). If the land element is 25 percent or more of the total value of the leased property, the lessor must separate the portion of the MLP applicable to land and to building and treat each as a separate unit of leased property.

When land and building(s) are treated as a single unit for purposes of subsequent testing, the lease term must be 75 percent or more of the economic life of the building, *or* the present value of the MLP must be 90 percent or more of the fair value of both the land and building (Blocks 15 and 16), and *both* risk-transfer tests must be met before the lease will qualify for capital lease treatment. When the land and building are treated as separate units of leased property, the land will be accounted for as an operating lease, and the building portion will be tested as indicated in the previous sentence.

To determine the portion of the MLP that will be associated with the land (and treated as an operating lease), the lessor must discount the fair value of the land at the incremental borrowing rate of the *lessee*. The discounted amount determined in this manner will represent the portion of the MLP identified with the land. The difference between the total MLP and the MLP attributed to the land will be the MLP associated with the building portion of the leased property. The amount thus associated with the building portion will be used to determine if the lease should be classified as operating or capital.

Once it has been determined that a lease is a capital lease, it must be classified as either a sales-type or direct financing lease. If cost or carrying value of the leased property is equal to fair value, the lease will be classified as direct financing; otherwise, it will be a sales-type lease. If the lease agreement meets none of the four general criteria, it will be treated as an operating lease. Also, if the lease meets *one* of the four general criteria but fails to meet *both* of the risk-transfer criteria, it will be treated as an operating lease.

Technical Considerations for Leases Involving Land and Building(s)

From an accounting standpoint, real estate leases involving land and building(s) can become quite complex. The complexity of the technical problems can be simplified by subdividing the land and building category into three sections: (1) leases meeting the transfer-of-ownership criteria, (2) leases where the land element comprises 25 percent or more of the total fair value of the leased property and (3) operating leases. The discussion that follows is organized around these three categories.

Leases Meeting the Transfer-of-Ownership Criteria

The Example 1 lease assumptions listed below are designed to show the accounting for a lease agreement that meets the transfer-of-ownership or bargain-purchase-option criteria.

Example 1
Lease Assumptions

1. The lessor enters into a five-year, noncancelable lease for land and building that requires annual payments of $78,000 at the beginning of each of the next five years. $3,000 of the payments is for executory costs. The lease specifies that ownership will transfer to the lessee at the end of the lease term.
2. The lessee's incremental borrowing rate is nine percent and the lessor's implicit rate is 10 percent.
3. The cost and fair value of the land is $100,000, and the cost and fair value of the building is $211,240 at the inception of the lease.
4. The collectibility of the MLP is reasonably predictable, and there are no unreimbursable costs associated with the lease.

Example 1 lease meets the criteria necessary for classification as a capital lease (ownership transfers, collectibility of the MLP is reasonably predictable and no unreimbursable costs). Because the lease meets the transfer-of-ownership criterion, the land and building are treated as a single unit of leased property for accounting purposes (the same accounting treatment will apply to land and building leases where the land element is less than 25 percent of the total fair value of the leased property). Because cost of the asset is equal to fair value at inception of the lease, the Example 1 lease is a direct financing lease. If necessary, refer back to Flowchart 5C for a review of accounting for direct financing leases.

The gross investment in the lease is $375,000 ($78,000 − $3,000 = $75,000 × 5 payments = $375,000), and the cost of the leased property is $311,240 ($100,000 for land + $211,240 for building). The difference between the gross investment and the cost of the leased assets is unearned income of \$63,760 (\$375,000 – \$311,240 = \$63,760). Given this information, the following journal entry to record the direct financing lease can be made:

Minimum Lease Payments Receivable	\$375,000	
Unearned Income		63,760
Land		100,000
Building		211,240

Because the entries to record the receipt of the rental payments and the recognition of income were discussed in detail in the section dealing with direct financing leases, they will not be repeated at this point.

Recall that, if the lease agreement does not transfer ownership or contain a bargain purchase option, land and building will be treated as a single unit if the land element is less than 25 percent of the total fair value. If, in this case, the lease qualifies for capital lease treatment, the accounting will be the same as that described above.

Lease Agreements Where Land Element is 25 Percent or More of Fair Value

If a lease agreement qualifies for capital lease accounting, and the land element is 25 percent or more of the fair value of both the land and building, the present value of the MLP must be divided into a land element and a building element. This accounting problem would develop if a lease agreement involving land and building failed to meet the transfer of ownership criteria, but the lease term was 75 percent or more of the economic life of the asset *or* the present value of the MLP was 90 percent or more of the fair value of the leased asset(s).

To illustrate this accounting problem, assume an Example 2 lease, with the same facts as in the Example 1 lease, except that ownership of the leased property does not transfer to the lessee, and the implicit interest rate is not known. When ownership to the leased property does not transfer, the lessor first must determine the relative fair values of the land and building elements of the lease. In this case, the land is more than 25 percent of the fair value of both land and building (\$100,000 fair value of land/\$311,240 total fair value = 32 percent). When the land element is 25 percent or more of the total fair value of the leased property, the land element and the building element will be treated as separate units of leased property.

Even though ownership does not transfer to the lessee, the Example 2 lease qualifies as a capital lease because the lease term of five years is more than 75 percent of the economic life of the building *and* the two risk-transfer criteria are met. Cost is equal to fair value of the property at inception of the lease; therefore, the Example 2 lease is a direct financing lease.

Since the lease is a capital lease, and the land element is 25 percent or more of the total fair value of the assets, the MLP must be divided between the land element and the building element. The procedure for dividing the MLP requires that the fair value of the land be discounted at the lessee's incremental borrowing rate to determine the portion of the MLP that will be associated with the land. This is accomplished as follows:

Fair Value of Land	$100,000	
		= $23,586
Present Value Factor[a]	4.23972	

[a] Present value factor for an annuity due at nine percent for five periods. See Appendix A, Table III.

The $23,586 will be the portion of the total MLP associated with the land element of the lease. The difference between the MLP assigned to the land and the total MLP will be the MLP assigned to the building portion of the lease. The difference is determined in the following manner:

Rental Payment Required	$ 78,000
Less: Executory Costs	3,000
	$ 75,000
MLP Assigned to Land	(23,586)
MLP Assigned to Building	$ 51,414

Once the MLP associated with the building element has been determined, the next step is to calculate the gross investment and unearned income. These two amounts are determined as follows:

MLP Assigned to Building	$ 51,414
Number of Lease Payments	× 5
Gross Investment in Lease	$257,070
Less: Fair Value of Building	211,240
Unearned Income	$ 45,830

Based upon the information developed above, the following entry would be required at inception of the lease:

Minimum Lease Payment Receivable	257,070	
Unearned Income		45,830
Building		211,240

The land element of the lease is treated as an operating lease. Income would be recognized as the periodic rental payment is received.

In order to amortize the unearned income over the lease term, using the interest method, the implicit interest rate relating to the building portion of the lease must be determined. In the absence of a computer program to calculate the interest rate, the following formula will provide the *present value factor* that corresponds with the new effective rate:

$$X = \frac{M - UI}{P}$$

Where: X = Present value factor of an annuity
M = Total minimum rental payments applicable to building
UI = Unearned income
P = Periodic minimum rental payment applicable to building.

Given the information above, the formula will provide the following results:

$$X = \frac{\$257{,}070 - \$45{,}830}{\$51{,}414} = 4.10861$$

The answer of 4.10861 represents the present value factor for an annuity due for five periods. Using Table III in Appendix A, move across the 5 periods row until a present value factor close to 4.10861 is found. The actual implicit interest rate is somewhere between 10 and 11 percent. To obtain the exact rate, it will be necessary to interpolate or to use the trial-and-error method. For the Example 2 lease, the implicit interest rate is 10.9069 percent, which was derived through the use of a computer program. Given this interest rate, Table I below shows the proper income recognition for the lease.

Table I

Lease Amortization Schedule

Period	Annual Rental	Annual Interest Income	Obligation Reduction	Present Value of Obligation at Year-End
Initial Value	-	-	-	[a]$211,240
1	$ 51,414	[b]$ 17,432	[c]$ 33,982	[d]177,258
2	51,414	13,726	37,688	139,570
3	51,414	9,615	41,799	97,771
4	51,414	5,057	46,357	51,414
5	51,414	-0-	51,414	-0-
	$257,070	$ 45,830	$211,240	

[a] Fair value and cost of building at inception of lease.
[b] ($211,240 − $51,414) × 10.9069% = $17,432.
[c] $51,414 − $17,432 = $33,982.
[d] $211,240 − $33,982 = $177,258.

The entry to record the first annual lease rental payment would be as follows:

Cash	78,000	
Minimum Lease Payment Receivable		51,414
Rental Income - Operating Lease		23,586
Executory Costs Clearing Account		3,000
Unearned Income	17,432	
Income from Capital Lease		17,432

Table I would be used for income recognition purposes under the capital lease for Years 1 through 5. The Example 2 lease completes the discussion of accounting for capital leases involving land and building(s).

Operating Leases

If any of the above lease examples had been classified as an operating lease, the only entry required would be the annual or interim rental income recognition. This was illustrated in the preceding section, for the land element of the Example 2 lease. We now turn to the next major area of real estate leasing, leases involving part of a building.

Leases Involving Part of a Building

A lease agreement may involve part of a building, such as an office or a complete floor(s) of a building. If both the fair value [12] and the cost (or carrying value, if different from cost) can be objectively determined (Block 18), the lessor would account for the lease as if it were the building portion of a lease involving land and building. If either the fair value or the cost cannot be objectively determined, the lease will be classified as an operating lease. If the lease qualifies as a capital lease, refer back to the preceding section on accounting for leases involving land and building for a complete technical review.

Leases Involving Real Estate and Equipment

If the lease agreement involves both real estate and equipment, the lessor must separate the real estate portion of the MLP from the portion of the MLP applicable to the equipment. Paragraph 27 of SFAS No. 13 states that the allocation "shall be estimated by whatever means are appropriate in the circumstances." It would appear that an allocation on the basis of fair values or appraisal values would be appropriate in most cases.

Once the allocation of the MLP to real estate and equipment has been accomplished, the real estate portion will be classified and accounted for in the manner specified for leases involving land and building(s). Refer to

[12] FASB Interpretation No. 24 states that independent appraisals of the leased property may be used as estimates of fair value for purposes of meeting the test shown in Block 18 of Flowchart 7.

the preceding discussion and technical review of land and building(s) for specifics.

The equipment must meet one of the four basic criteria (Blocks 20 through 23), and *both* of the risk-transfer criteria (Blocks 24 and 25), to be considered for capital lease treatment. The next step in the classification process is to compare the cost of the equipment with its fair value. If cost and fair value are equal, the equipment portion of the leased property will be treated as a direct financing lease. If cost and fair value are not equal, the lease will be classified as either a sales-type capital lease or an operating lease. Once again, the AICPA Industry Accounting Guide must be used to aid in the classification process. Refer back to the section of this discussion dealing with leases involving land only for an analysis of the conditions stated in the Guide. Look back to Flowcharts 5A and 5C for detailed information about accounting for sales-type and direct financing leases.

This concludes the discussion of lessor accounting for real estate leasing transactions. The next section of this Topic will address the problems of *sublease* classification and accounting. Subleases deal with accounting for both the lessor and the lessee, so the material examined above will be most helpful in the discussion that follows.

Subleases

The area of subleases is an excellent way to complete the technical discussion of SFAS No. 13, because subleases involve both lessee and lessor accounting. A sublease is defined in Paragraph 35(a) of the Statement as a transaction in which "the leased property is re-leased by the original lessee to a third party, and the lease agreement between the two original parties remains in effect." There are three parties involved in the sublease agreement: the original lessor, the original lessee/sublessor and the sublessee. To avoid any confusion that may result from the dual role played by the original lessee, i.e., both lessee and sublessor, we will consistently refer to this party as the sublessor in the discussion which follows.

Flowchart and Discussion of Subleases—Sublessor

Flowchart 8 depicts the lease classification problems inherent in the sublease process. This Flowchart refers the reader back to previous flowcharts for specific accounting treatment once the sublease has been properly classified. As indicated by the first major decision in Flowchart 8, the broad area of sublease accounting can be divided into two manageable sections: (1) when the sublessor is relieved of primary obligation under the original lease, and (2) when the sublessor is not relieved of such obligation. The left-hand column of Flowchart 8 addresses the former problem, and the rest of the Flowchart deals with the latter.

FLOWCHART 8
SUBLEASES

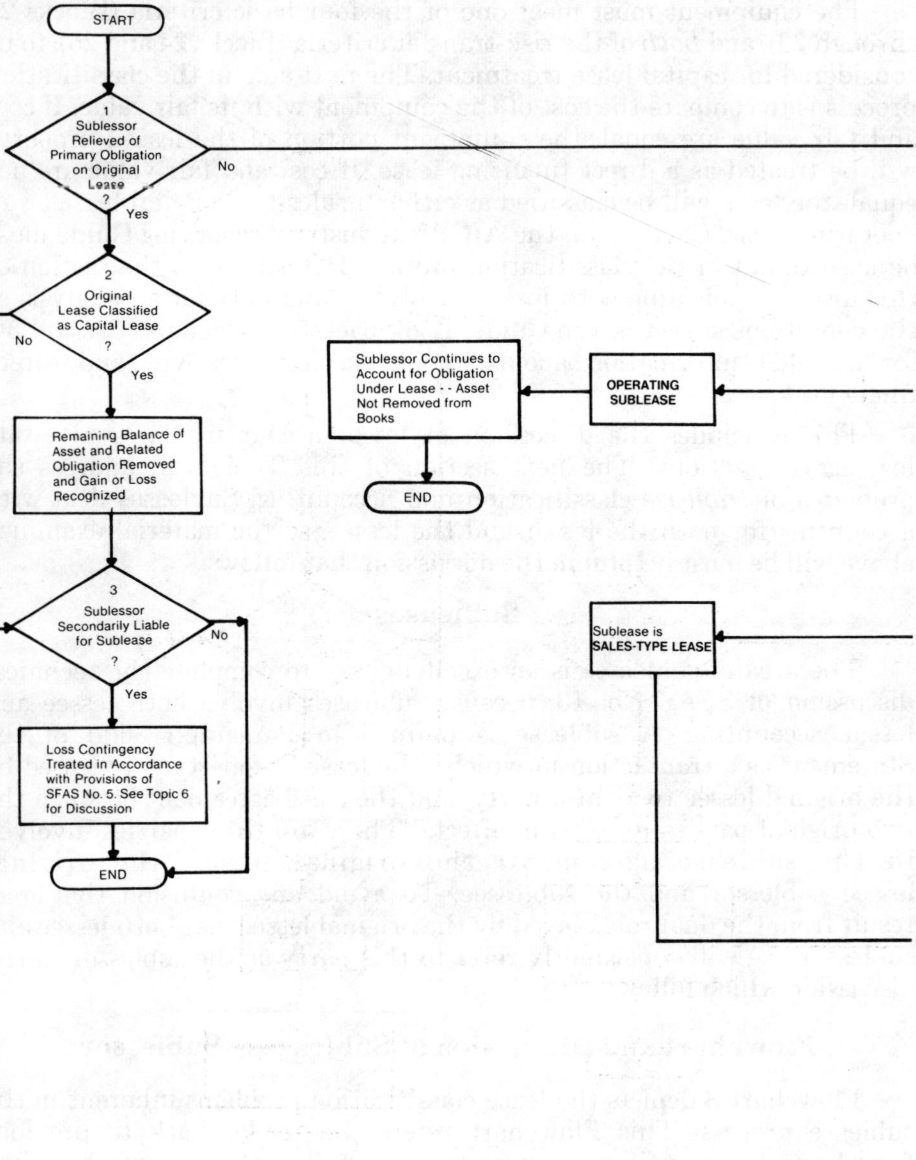

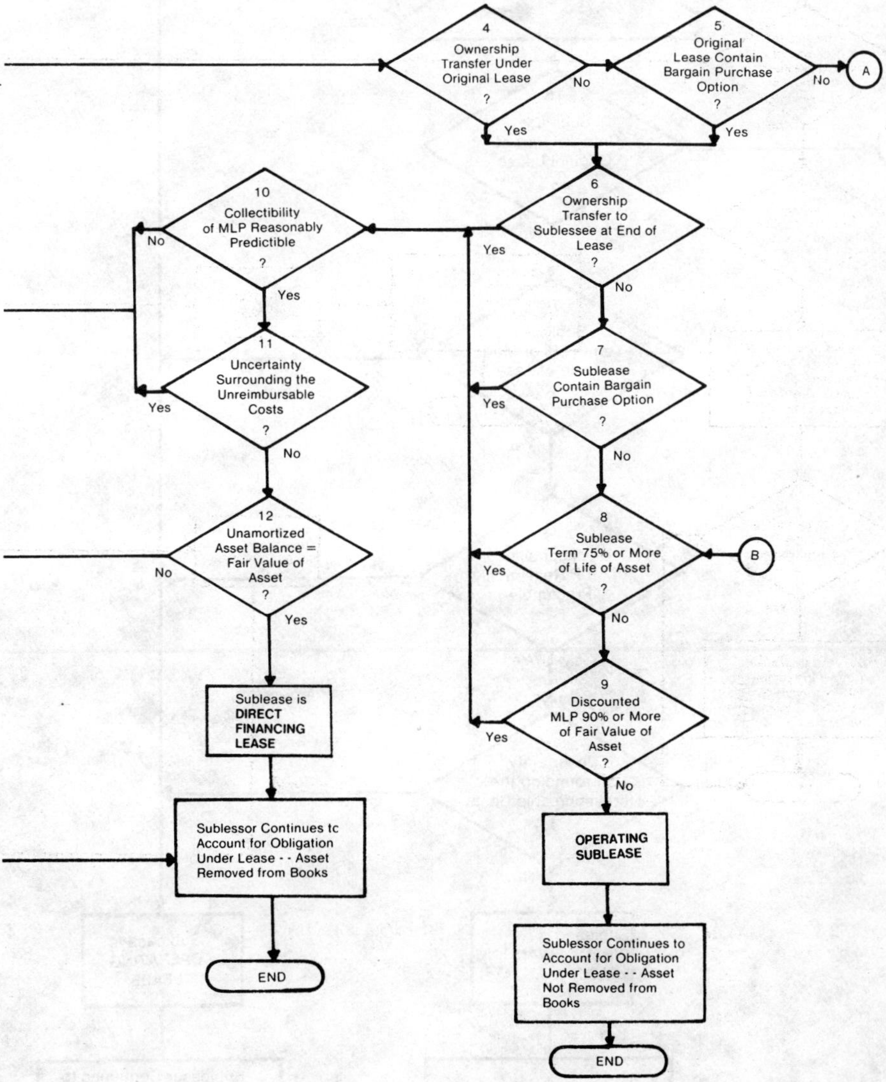
4
Ownership Transfer Under Original Lease ?
No
Yes
5
Original Lease Contain Bargain Purchase Option ?
No
Yes
A
6
Ownership Transfer to Sublessee at End of Lease ?
Yes
No
7
Sublease Contain Bargain Purchase Option ?
Yes
No
8
Sublease Term 75% or More of Life of Asset ?
Yes
No
B
9
Discounted MLP 90% or More of Fair Value of Asset ?
Yes
No
OPERATING SUBLEASE
Sublessor Continues to Account for Obligation Under Lease - - Asset Not Removed from Books
END
10
Collectibility of MLP Reasonably Predictible ?
No
Yes
11
Uncertainty Surrounding the Unreimbursable Costs ?
Yes
No
12
Unamortized Asset Balance = Fair Value of Asset ?
No
Yes
Sublease is DIRECT FINANCING LEASE
Sublessor Continues tc Account for Obligation Under Lease - - Asset Removed from Books
END

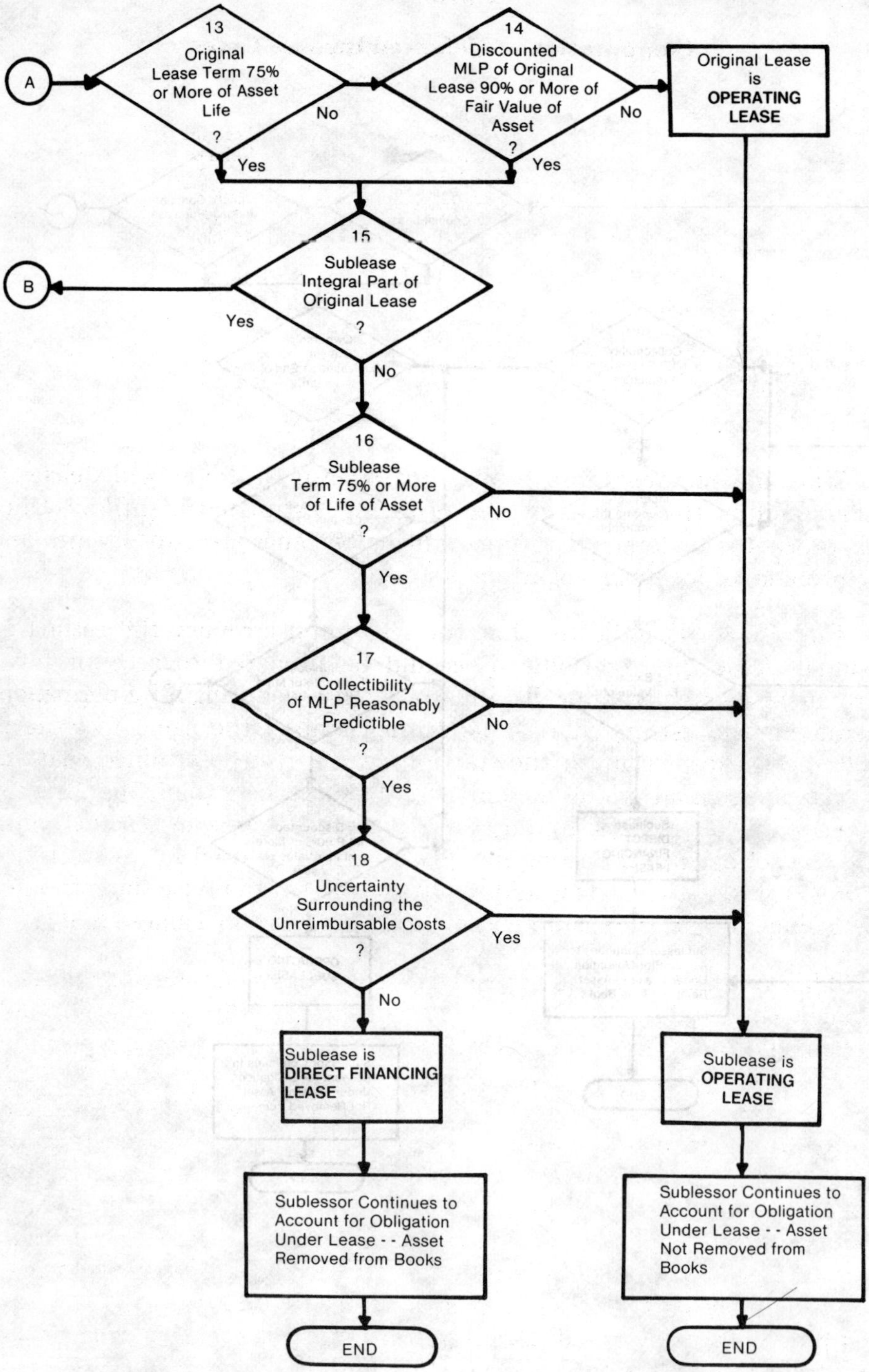
A
13
Original Lease Term 75% or More of Asset Life ?
No
Yes
14
Discounted MLP of Original Lease 90% or More of Fair Value of Asset ?
No
Yes
Original Lease is OPERATING LEASE
15
Sublease Integral Part of Original Lease ?
Yes
B
No
16
Sublease Term 75% or More of Life of Asset ?
No
Yes
17
Collectibility of MLP Reasonably Predictible ?
No
Yes
18
Uncertainty Surrounding the Unreimbursable Costs ?
Yes
No
Sublease is DIRECT FINANCING LEASE
Sublease is OPERATING LEASE
Sublessor Continues to Account for Obligation Under Lease - - Asset Removed from Books
Sublessor Continues to Account for Obligation Under Lease - - Asset Not Removed from Books
END
END

Accounting When the Sublessor Is Relieved of Primary Obligation

If the sublessor has been relieved of primary obligation under the original lease, *and* the original lease was classified as a capital lease by the sublessor (Block 2), both the asset and related obligation under the original lease must be removed from the books, and any gain or loss resulting from the removal must be recognized. Having been relieved of responsibilities under the original lease, the sublessor has no further accounting interest in the lease.

Regardless of the original lease classification (capital or operating), if the sublessor is secondarily liable under the sublease agreement, a loss contingency is created. In such a case, the sublessor would handle the contingency in accordance with the provisions of SFAS No. 5, "Accounting for Contingencies" (see Topic 6 for a detailed analysis of SFAS No. 5).

Technical Consideration When the Sublessor Is Relieved of Primary Obligation

The following example lease will be used to demonstrate the accounting for a sublease where the sublessor is relieved of primary obligation under the original lease and of secondary liability under the sublease.

Example 1

Lease and Sublease Assumptions

1. The original lease between the lessor and the sublessor was classified as a capital lease by the sublessor. It was a five-year, noncancelable lease that required annual year-end payments of $100,000. The leased property has an economic life of five years, and the sublessor uses the straight-line method for depreciation of similar owned assets.
2. The appropriate interest rate under the original lease was 10 percent.
3. The sublessor is relieved of primary obligation under the original lease and has no secondary liability for the sublease.
4. The property subject to the original lease was subleased by the sublessor at the beginning of the fourth year of the original lease term.

Based upon these assumptions, the sublessor has no further accounting responsibilities for the leased property, and it is appropriate to remove the leased asset and related obligation. Table I develops the amortization schedules used by the sublessor under the original lease. The computation of the present value of the MLP would be as follows:

Annual Rental Payments Required	$100,000
Present Value Factor	[a]3.79079
Present Value of MLP	$379,079

[a] Present value factor for an ordinary annuity at 10 percent for 5 periods. See Appendix A, Table II.

Under the terms of the original lease, the present value of the MLP was recorded as the value of the leased asset and related obligation.

Table I

Amortization Schedules—Original Lease

Amortization Schedule for Lease Obligation

	Period	Annual Payment	Annual Interest Expense	Obligation Reduction	Present Value of Obligation at Year-End
Initial Value	-	-	-	-	$379,079
	1	$100,000	[a]$ 37,908	[b]$ 62,092	[c]316,987
	2	100,000	31,699	68,301	248,686
	3	100,000	24,869	75,131	173,555
	4	100,000	17,355	82,645	90,910
	5	100,000	9,090	90,910	-0-
		$500,000	$120,921	$379,079	

Schedule of Amortization of Leased Asset

	Period	Amortization	Cumulative Amortization	Unamortized Asset Balance at Year-End
Initial Value	-	-	-	$ 379,079
	1	[d]$ 75,816	$ 75,816	303,263
	2	75,816	151,632	227,447
	3	75,816	227,448	151,631
	4	75,816	303,264	75,815
	5	*75,815	379,079	-0-
		$379,079		

[a] $379,079 × 10% = $37,908.
[b] $100,000 — $37,908 = $62,092.
[c] $379,079 — $62,092 = $316,987.
[d] Assuming straight-line depreciation is used for owned assets ($379,079/5 years = $75,816).
* Rounded.

At the date of inception of the sublease, the sublessor must determine the unamortized balance in the asset and obligation accounts and remove them from the books. At the beginning of Year 4, the unamortized obligation balance was $173,555, and the unamortized asset balance was $151,631. The difference between the two balances indicates that a $21,924 gain ($151,631 – $173,555 = $21,924) will be recognized. Given this information, the following journal entry is required at the date of inception of the sublease:

Accumulated Amortization of Leased Property	227,448	
Obligation Under Capital Lease	173,555	
Leased Asset Under Capital Lease		379,079
Gain on Capital Lease Transaction		[a]21,924

[a] Gains or losses on lease transactions are handled in accordance with APB Opinion No. 30. See Topic 1 for a detailed analysis of APB Opinion No. 30.

No further entries would be required by the sublessor. FASB Technical Bulletin No. 79-15 states that a *loss* on the sublease should be recognized if the recorded amount of the property exceeds the gross investment. In addition, FASB Interpretation No. 27 requires that, if a sublease is part of a disposal of a segment of a business, any loss on the sublease should be treated as part of the overall gain or loss on the disposal.

If the sublessor is secondarily liable under a capital lease or an operating lease, additional accounting or footnote disclosures, as required by SFAS No. 5, may be necessary.

Accounting When the Sublessor Is Not Relieved of Primary Obligation

The classification and accounting problems are much more interesting and complex when the sublessor is not relieved of primary obligation under the original lease agreement. When this occurs, the relationships between the parties to the lease and sublease become involved. First, there is the relationship between the original lessor and the sublessor (which has remained intact), and, next, there is the new relationship between the sublessor and the sublessee. One important point that should be kept in mind throughout the following discussion is that, if the sublessor is not relieved of primary obligation under the original lease, he must continue to account for the obligation that resulted if the original lease qualified as a capital lease; however, the unamortized balance of the leased asset will be removed. In effect, the sublessor is both lessee and lessor.

If, under the terms of the original lease, ownership transferred or there was a bargain purchase option (Blocks 4 and 5), the sublease will be classified as either a sales-type or direct financing capital lease or as an operating lease. For the *sublease* to qualify as a capital lease, it must meet *one* of the four general criteria (transfer of ownership, bargain purchase option, 75 percent of economic life or 90 percent of fair value [Blocks 6 through 9]) *and* both of the risk-transfer criteria (collectibility of MLP and no uncertainties about unreimbursable costs, Blocks 10 and 11). If the sublease qualifies as a capital lease, it will be classified as a sales-type lease if the unamortized asset balance is different from fair value of the asset. If the unamortized asset balance is equal to fair value, the lease will be classified as a direct financing lease. Finally, if *none* of the general criteria and risk transfer criteria are met, the sublease will be accounted for as an operating lease by the sublessor.

If the original lease did not transfer ownership or contain a bargain purchase option, the sublease still may qualify as a capital lease. If the *original* lease term was 75 percent or more of the economic life of the property, or if the discounted value of the MLP under the *original* lease was 90 percent or more of the fair value of the property, the sublessor is faced with two separate sets of classification problems.

First, when the sublease is an integral part of the original lease agreement (Block 15) the sublease must meet either the 75-percent-of-economic-life test *or* the discounted-MLP-90-percent-or-more-of-fair value test, *and* both of the risk-transfer tests, before it may be classified as a capital lease. If these tests are met, the sublease will be classified as either a sales-type or direct financing lease on the same basis as previously discussed. If the sublease fails these tests, it will be treated as an operating lease.

Second, when the sublease is *not* an integral part of the original lease agreement, it must meet the 75-percent-of-economic-life test and both of the risk-transfer tests to qualify as a direct financing lease. Note that, under these conditions, the sublease cannot be a sales-type lease. As before, if the sublease fails to meet these tests, it will be treated as an operating lease.

If the original lease failed to meet the four general criteria, it would have been classified as an operating lease. If the original lease was classified as operating, then the sublease would be classified the same.

Technical Considerations When the Sublessor Is Not Relieved of Primary Obligation

To illustrate the accounting aspects inherent in the situation where the sublessor is not relieved of primary obligation under the original lease agreement, it is necessary to develop assumptions for both the original lease and the sublease. Listed below are the assumptions relating to the original lease between the lessor and the sublessor.

Example 1
Lease Assumptions—Original Lease

1. The sublessor and lessor entered into a five-year, noncancelable lease that required annual year-end payments of $150,000.
2. Ownership to the property does not transfer at the end of the lease term, and the lease does not contain a bargain purchase option.

3. The sublessor's (original lessee's) incremental borrowing rate is 10 percent, and the lessor's implicit rate is not known.
4. The leased property has a fair value of $568,619. The estimated economic life is five years, and the estimated residual value is zero.

The original lease is a capital lease, because the lease term of five years is more than 75 percent of the economic life of the property (5 year economic life × .75 = 3.75 years). In addition, the present value of the MLP is more than 90 percent of the fair value of the property. This is shown through the following computations:

Fair Value of Property	$568,619
	× .90
90 Percent of Fair Value of Property	$511,757
Annual Rental Payment Required	$150,000
Present Value Factor	[a]3.79079
Present Value of MLP	$568,619

[a] Present value factor for an ordinary annuity at 10 percent for 5 periods. See Appendix A, Table II.

Therefore, the present value of the MLP of $568,619 is more than 90 percent of the fair value of the property ($511,757).

Table I prepares the amortization schedule used by the sublessor under the original lease agreement.

The sublessor (original lessee) would use the values shown on Table I to account for a capital lease as discussed in the section dealing with lessee accounting. The second set of assumptions listed below are those relating to the sublease agreement.

Example 1
Lease Assumptions—Sublease

1. At the beginning of the second year of the original lease, the sublessor entered into a four-year, noncancelable *sublease* with a sublessee. The sublease requires annual year-end payments of $150,000.
2. The sublessor is not relieved of primary obligation under the original lease agreement.
3. The implicit interest rate on the sublease is the rate that equates the present value of the lease payments with the unamortized asset balance. (The calculation of the implicit rate will be shown in the material that follows.) The sublessee's incremental borrowing rate is 11 percent, and the implicit rate is unknown to the sublessee.

Table I

Amortization Schedule for Original Lease

Schedule of Lease Amortization

	Period	Amortization	Annual Payment	Annual Interest Expense	Obligation Reduction	Present Value of Obligation at Year-End
Initial Value	-	-	-	-	-	$ 568,619
	1	[a]$ 113,724	$150,000	[b]$ 56,862	[c]$ 93,138	[d]475,481
	2	113,724	150,000	47,548	102,452	373,029
	3	113,724	150,000	37,303	112,697	260,332
	4	113,724	150,000	26,032	123,968	136,364
	5	*113,723	150,000	13,636	136,364	-0-
		$ 568,619	$750,000	$181,381	$568,619	

[a] Assuming that straight-line depreciation is used for owned assets ($568,619/5 years = $113,724).
[b] $568,619 × 10% = $56,862.
[c] $150,000 — $56,862 = $93,138.
[d] $568,619 — $93,138 = $475,481.
* Rounded.

4. Ownership does not transfer to the sublessee at the end of the lease term, and the sublease does not contain a bargain purchase option.
5. The collectibility of the MLP is reasonably predictable, and there are no unreimbursable costs associated with the sublease.

Neither the original lease nor the sublease allowed for the transfer of ownership, and neither contained a bargain purchase option. If we assume further that the sublease was not an integral part of the original lease, then the sublease must be either a direct financing lease or an operating lease. Because the sublease term of four years is more than 75 percent of the economic life of the property (5 year economic life × .75 = 3.75 years), and the two risk-transfer criteria are met, the sublease qualifies as a direct financing lease.

To begin the process of determining the implicit interest rate under the sublease agreement, the sublessor must determine the unamortized asset balance. The computation is shown below:

Capitalized Value of Leased Property (Table I)	$568,619
Year 1 Amortization (Table I)	(113,724)
Unamortized Asset Balance	$454,895

The difference between the $600,000 ($150,000 × 4 = $600,000) minimum rental payments (also called gross investment) required and the unamortized asset balance of $454,895 represents unearned income of the sublessor. In this example, the unearned income is $145,105 ($600,000 – $454,895). Next, the rate that will equate the rental payment stream with the unamortized asset balance must be determined.

For a relatively simple example, like the one presented, the following equation will compute the *present value factor* that can be used to determine the appropriate interest rate.

$$X = \frac{T - UI}{P}$$

Where:
X = Present value factor of an annuity
T = Total minimum rental payments required
UI = Unearned income
P = Periodic minimum rental payment

By applying the above information to this equation, we get the following results:

$$X = \frac{\$600{,}000 - \$145{,}105}{\$150{,}000} = 3.03263$$

The answer developed represents the present value factor for an ordinary annuity for four periods. Turn to the present value of an ordinary annuity table, Appendix A, Table II; move across the four-period row until the value 3.03263 is found. Notice that the exact value is not on the Table. However, it can be determined that the actual interest rate is between 12 and 13 percent. Using interpolation, we can see that the value is actually closer to 12 percent than to 13 percent. From this point forward, the trial-and-error method or a computer program must be used to achieve the exact answer. The correct implicit interest rate for this example is 12.0738 percent. This rate will be used to amortize the obligation of $454,895 and is illustrated in Table II.

Table II

Sublessor Amortization Schedule Under Sublease

Schedule of Lease Amortization

	Period	Payment	Annual Interest Income	Principal Reduction	Present Value of Principal
Initial Value	-	-	-	-	[a]$454,895
	2	$150,000	[b]$ 54,923	[c]$ 95,077	[d]359,818
	3	150,000	43,444	106,556	253,262
	4	150,000	30,578	119,422	133,840
	5	150,000	16,160	133,840	-0-
		$600,000	$145,105	$454,895	

[a] Unamortized lease asset balance at date of sublease.
[b] $454,895 × 12.0738% = $54,923.
[c] $150,000 — $54,923 = $95,077.
[d] $454,895 — $95,077 = $359,818.

Using both Tables I and II, the journal entries for the sublessor can be made for the original lease and the sublease. Recall that the sublessor must continue to account for the obligation under the original lease, as well as that under the new sublease. The journal entries required during Year 1 for the original lease are as follows (all amounts are from Table I):

Leased Asset Under Capital Lease	568,619	
Obligation Under Capital Lease		568,619
Interest Expense	56,862	
Obligation Under Capital Lease	93,138	
Cash		150,000
Amortization of Leased Property	113,724	
Accumulated Amortization-Leased Property		113,724

The first entry is to record the value of the leased property and related obligation under the original lease assumptions. The second entry is to record the first annual lease payment from the sublessor to the lessor, and the third entry is to record the amortization of the leased asset, assuming straight-line depreciation is used for similar owned assets.

The required journal entries for Year 2, the first year of the sublease, necessitate the use of both Tables I and II. The entry to record the payment for the second year from the sublessor to the lessor under the original lease is as follows (amounts from Table I):

Interest Expense	47,548	
Obligation Under Capital Lease	102,452	
Cash		150,000

For the sublease example, the sublessor would record the gross investment in the direct financing lease, remove the asset account and record the unearned income. The entry to accomplish this at date of inception of the sublease would be (amounts from Tables I and II):

Accumulated Amortization - Leased Property	113,724	
Minimum Lease Payments Receivable	600,000	
Unearned Income		145,105
Leased Property Under Capital Lease		568,619

The entry to record the receipt of the first lease payment from the sublessee and the recognition of income would be as follows:

Cash	150,000	
Minimum Lease Payments Receivable		150,000
Unearned Income	54,923	
Income from Sublease		54,923

The sublessor would need the information contained in both Tables I and II to determine the proper journal entries and amounts for Years 3 through 5. At the end of Year 5, both the original lease and the sublease will terminate, and no further accounting is required.

To complete the cycle of sublease accounting, information is developed below relating to proper classification and accounting from the viewpoint of the *sublessee.* The sublessee would use Flowchart 1 to classify the lease as capital or operating.

The Example 1 sublease qualifies as a capital lease for the sublessee, because the lease term of four years is more than 75 percent of the economic life of the asset (5-year economic life × .75 = 3.75 years).

Table III shows the amortization and expense schedule for the sublessee. The present value of the minimum lease payments is computed using the sublessee's incremental borrowing rate of 11 percent because the implicit rate is not known to the sublessee. The present value of the MLP is determined as follows:

Annual Rental Payments Required	$150,000
Less: Executory Costs	-0-
	$150,000
Present Value Factor	a3.10245
Present Value of MLP	$465,368

a Present value factor for an ordinary annuity at 11 percent for four periods. See Appendix A, Table II.

At inception of the sublease, the sublessee would record the asset and related obligation as follows:

Leased Asset Under Capital Lease	465,368	
Obligation Under Capital Lease		465,368

The payment of the first year-end lease payment and amortization of the leased asset would require the following entries:

Interest Expense	51,190	
Obligation Under Capital Lease	98,810	
Cash		150,000
Amortization of Leased Asset	116,342	
Accumulated Amortization-Leased Asset		116,342

Table III would be used by the sublessee to record expenses and amortization for Years 2 through 4 of the sublease.

This completes the discussion of subleases. The reader should now begin to see the differences and similarities that exist for lessee and lessor lease accounting.

The discussion of SFAS No. 13 will be concluded with the following section, dealing with required disclosures.

Disclosures Required for Lessee[13]

Paragraph 16 of the Standard specifies the disclosure requirements for the lessee. The disclosures can be divided into the following three categories:

1. A description of the leasing activities of the lessee, including such items as restrictions, purchase option payments, renewal payments and contingent rentals.

---

[13] During the transition period, FASB Technical Bulletin No. 79-17 suggests that the cumulative effect of the change to the provisions of SFAS No. 13 will be shown in income unless the period prior to the earliest year presented cannot be restated. In addition, FASB Technical Bulletin No. 79-18 indicates that amendments and interpretations should be applied retroactively unless SFAS No. 13 has been applied retroactively. the Technical Bulletin also states that "published annual financial statements" means financial statements that a company normally distributes to its share-holders on an annual basis.

Table III

Amortization and Expense Schedule—Sublessee

Schedule of Lease Amortization

	Period	Amortization	Annual Payment	Annual Interest Expense	Obligation Reduction	Present Value of Obligation At Year-End
Initial Value	-	-	-	-	-	$465,368
	1	[a]$116,342	$150,000	[b]$ 51,190	[c]$ 98,810	[d]366,558
	2	116,342	150,000	40,321	109,679	256,879
	3	116,342	150,000	28,257	121,743	135,136
	4	116,342	150,000	14,864	135,136	-0-
		$465,368	$600,000	$134,632	$465,368	

[a] Assuming that straight-line depreciation is used for owned assets ($465,368/4 years = $116,342).
[b] $465,368 × 11% = $51,190.
[c] $150,000 — $51,190 = $98,810.
[d] $465,368 — $98,810 = $366,558.

2. Capital leases require disclosure of: (a) the gross value of the assets leased, shown by major classes or combined with owned assets; (b) the minimum rental payments, less executory costs and interest, for each of the five years subsequent to the balance sheet date, and the aggregate payments for the years thereafter and (c) minimum sublease rentals and contingent rentals.

3. Operating leases require disclosure of: (a) the minimum rental payments for each of the five years subsequent to the balance sheet date, and the aggregate payments for years thereafter; (b) the aggregate amount of all future minimum rentals; and (c) lease expense for each income statement period. Separate disclosures are necessary for minimum rentals, contingent and sublease rentals.

The notes to the financial statements of The Pillsbury Company are presented in Exhibit I, and reflect the disclosures required of the lessee for the years 1976 and 1977.

Disclosures Required for Lessor[14]

Paragraphs 23 and 47 of the Standard specify the disclosure requirements for the lessor. These disclosures may be divided into the following four categories:

1. A description of the leasing activities of the lessor.

2. Direct financing and sales-type leases require disclosure of: (a) the composition of the investment account—including presentation of the minimum lease payments, executory costs, allowance for uncollectibles, unguaranteed residual values and unearned income—for each balance sheet date; (b) the minimum rental payments for each of the five years subsequent to the balance sheet date; (c) the amount of unearned income charged to income to compensate for the initial direct costs incurred and charged against income; and (d) any contingent rentals included in income.

3. The composition of the investment account for leveraged leases. This would include the presentation of the receivable, residual value, unearned and deferred income and deferred taxes.

4. Operating leases require disclosure of: (a) cost and carrying value of leased assets by major class of property and total accumulated depreciation; (b) minimum rental payments for each of the five years subsequent to the balance sheet date, and the aggregate

[14] See footnote 13, this Topic.

amount for years thereafter; and (c) contingent rentals for each income statement period.

The notes to the financial statements of The Pillsbury Company also are used to reflect the disclosures required for the lessor.

Exhibit I

The Pillsbury Company (May)

	1977	1976
Assets		
Net investment in direct financing leases (Note 6):		
Owned property, plant and equipment	$31,471,000	$26,496,000
Leased assets under capital leases	8,599,000	6,232,000
	$40,070,000	$32,728,000
Liabilities and Stockholders' Equity		
Long-term debt, noncurrent portion (Note 6):		
Restaurant subsidiaries (not guaranteed by The Pillsbury Company):		
Long-term debt	$143,212,000	$118,722,000
Obligations under capital leases	45,136,000	36,998,000
	188,348,000	155,720,000
Parent company and nonrestaurant subsidiaries:		
Long-term debt	64,731,000	64,763,000
Obligations under capital leases	5,541,000	6,623,000
	70,272,000	71,386,000
Total	$258,620,000	$227,106,000

Note 6: Leases—All noncancelable leases and subleases with an initial term greater than one year are included in this note and have been categorized as capital, direct financing or operating leases in conformity with the Definitions in Statement of Financial Accounting Standards No. 13, Accounting for Leases.

Commitments as Lessee

The Parent Company and nonrestaurant subsidiaries have leases for manufacturing, warehousing, administrative and transportation facilities and equipment with terms (including renewal options) ranging from one to 50 years. In addition, restaurant subsidiaries have leases covering restaurant properties with initial terms, in most cases, of 15 to 25 years which provide for one or more five-year renewal options.

Capital leases are concentrated in restaurant subsidiaries and cover primarily restaurant buildings. At May 31, 1977, Burger King and Steak and Ale were lessees under capital leases on 244 and 74 restaurant buildings, respectively. Capital leases of the Parent Company and nonrestaurant subsidiaries cover transportation and computer equipment and parts of several manufacturing facilities.

The following analysis represents property under capital leases at May 31:

	1977			1976		
	Total	Restaurant subsidiaries	Parent Company and nonrestaurant subsidiaries	Total	Restaurant subsidiaries	Parent Company and nonrestaurant subsidiaries
Buildings	$49,073,000	$40,226,000	$ 8,847,000	$44,780,000	$35,933,000	$ 8,847,000
Equipment	10,390,000	5,722,000	4,668,000	9,827,000	5,049,000	4,778,000
	59,463,000	45,948,000	13,515,000	54,607,000	40,982,000	13,625,000
Less accumulated amortization	(19,427,000)	(11,873,000)	(7,554,000)	(15,571,000)	(8,936,000)	(6,635,000)
	$40,036,000	$34,075,000	$ 5,961,000	$39,036,000	$32,046,000	$ 6,990,000

Amortization of property under capital leases was $4,710,000 and $4,264,000 in 1977 and 1976, respectively.

In addition to its capital leases, the Company is obligated under operating leases primarily for land in the restaurant subsidiaries, transportation equipment and grain handling and storage facilities. Total rental expense (including taxes, insurance and maintenance when included in rent) related to all operating leases (including those with terms less than one year) were as follows:

	Year ended May 31	
	1977	**1976**
Minimum rentals	$18,703,000	$15,341,000
Contingent rentals	833,000	871,000
Total	$19,536,000	$16,212,000

Minimum future obligations on leases in effect at May 31, 1977 are as follows for the periods ending May 31:

	Capital leases (In thousands)				Operating leases (In thousands)			
		Restaurant subsidiaries				Restaurant subsidiaries		
	Total	Used in operations	Subleased to franchises	Parent Company and nonrestaurant subsidiaries	Total	Used in operations	Subleased to franchises	Parent Company and nonrestaurant subsidiaries
1978	$ 11,019	$ 6,493	$ 1,428	$ 3,098	$ 19,416	$ 8,311	$ 1,823	$ 9,282
1979	8,997	5,991	1,425	1,581	13,874	7,823	1,831	4,220
1980	7,784	5,150	1,405	1,229	12,525	7,433	1,827	3,265
1981	6,844	4,744	1,368	732	11,473	7,319	1,816	2,338
1982	6,253	4,519	1,332	402	10,086	6,960	1,795	1,341
Later	69,827	52,403	11,773	5,651	103,876	72,302	17,535	14,039
Total minimum obligation (a)	110,724	79,300	18,731	12,693	171,260	110,148	26,627	34,485
Less executory costs	(2,948)	(1,524)		(1,424)	(9,530)			(9,530)
Net minimum obligation	107,776	77,776	18,731	11,269	(c)$161,730	$110,148	$26,627	$24,955
Less amount representing interest	(52,701)	(38,886)	(9,369)	(4,446)				
Present value of net minimum obligation	55,075	38,890	9,362	6,823				
Less current portion	(b)(4,398)	(2,662)	(454)	(1,282)				
Long-term obligation at May 31, 1977	$ 50,677	$36,228	$ 8,908	$ 5,541				
Long-term obligation at May 31, 1976	$ 43,621	$30,220	$ 6,778	$ 6,623				

(a) Minimum future obligations have not been reduced by minimum sublease rentals. In addition to minimum future obligations, contingent rentals may be paid under certain store leases on the basis of a percentage of sales in excess of minimum amounts. Contingent rentals amounted to $741,000 and $698,000 in 1977 and 1976, respectively.

(b) Included in current portion of long-term debt. Amounts so included for May 31, 1976 were Restaurant subsidiaries $2,556,000 and Parent Company and nonrestaurant subsidiaries $1,218,000.

(c) The present value of minimum future obligations under operating leases calculated on the Company's incremental borrowing rate at the inception of the leases are: Used in operations of Restaurant subsidiaries $57,630,000, subleased to franchises $14,314,000 and Parent Company and nonrestaurant subsidiaries $14,710,000.

The present values of minimum future obligations shown above are calculated based on interest rates (ranging from 5% to 15% with a weighted average of approximately 9.7%) determined to be applicable at the inception of the leases.

Interest expense on the outstanding obligation under capital leases was \$4,943,000 and \$4,583,000 in 1977 and 1976, respectively.

Investments as Lessor

At May 31, 1977, 406 restaurant buildings and land were leased by Burger King to franchisees. Of this number, 117 restaurant buildings were obtained through capital leases and 289 are owned while 164 parcels of land were obtained through operating leases and 242 are owned. The building leases are generally accounted for as direct financing leases while the land leases are accounted for as operating leases. Burger King also leases owned equipment to franchisees under direct financing leases.

Substantially all of the property leases provide for minimum rentals and contingent rentals, while equipment leases provide only for minimum rentals. Property is generally leased to franchisees for 15 years under leases which require the franchisee to pay real estate taxes and other operating expenses.

The following lists the net investment in direct financing leases (all attributable to Burger King) at May 31:

	1977			1976		
		Building and equipment			Building and equipment	
	Total	Owned	Leased	Total	Owned	Leased
Net minimum lease payments receivable (a)	$84,940,000	$66,419,000	$18,521,000	$69,449,000	$57,268,000	$12,181,000
Estimated unguaranteed residual value ...	4,276,000	3,310,000	966,000	2,226,000	1,772,000	454,000
Less unearned income	(45,853,000)	(35,699,000)	(10,154,000)	(36,654,000)	(30,812,000)	(5,842,000)
Net investment	43,363,000	34,030,000	9,333,000	35,021,000	28,228,000	6,793,000
Less current portion included in receivables	(3,293,000)	(2,559,000)	(734,000)	(2,293,000)	(1,732,000)	(561,000)
Net investment in direct financing leases	$40,070,000	$31,471,000	$ 8,599,000	$32,728,000	$26,496,000	$ 6,232,000

(a) Minimum lease payments do not include contingent rentals which were $4,319,000 in 1977 and $3,845,000 in 1976.

Owned assets, included in property, plant and equipment, leased to Burger King franchisees under operating leases at May 31 are as follows:

	1977	1976
Land and improvements	$24,413,000	$22,492,000
Buildings and improvements	5,441,000	4,378,000
Restaurant equipment	619,000	669,000
	30,473,000	27,539,000
Less accumulated depreciation	(3,109,000)	(1,755,000)
	$27,364,000	$25,784,000

The following is a schedule of minimum future rentals to be received under direct financing and operating leases in effect at May 31, 1977, for the periods ending May 31:

	Direct financing leases Total	Buildings and equipment Owned	Leased	Operating leases Total	Land Owned	Leased
1978	$ 8,199,000	$ 6,498,000	$ 1,701,000	$ 4,831,000	$ 2,862,000	$ 1,969,000
1979	8,166,000	6,469,000	1,697,000	4,742,000	2,801,000	1,941,000
1980	8,104,000	6,432,000	1,672,000	4,739,000	2,802,000	1,937,000
1981	7,996,000	6,366,000	1,630,000	4,716,000	2,802,000	1,914,000
1982	7,551,000	5,956,000	1,595,000	4,668,000	2,794,000	1,874,000
Later	44,924,000	34,698,000	10,226,000	28,651,000	15,799,000	12,852,000
Total (a)	$84,940,000	$66,419,000	$18,521,000	$52,347,000	$29,860,000	$22,487,000

(a) Minimum lease payments do not include contingent rentals which were $4,319,000 in 1977 and $3,845,000 in 1976.

Source: *Accounting Trends and Techniques,* Copyright © 1977 by the American Institute of Certified Public Accountants, Inc., pp. 182-184.

SFAS No. 22 (June 1978)
Changes in the Provisions of Lease Agreements Resulting from Refunding of Tax-Exempt Debt

Flowchart and General Discussion

SFAS No. 22 is an amendment to SFAS No. 13, "Accounting for Leases," and applies to a select type of lease agreement. Many governmental units or agencies[1] have issued tax-exempt obligations to finance the construction of physical facilities that are to be leased to a user entity. This type of lease agreement might be undertaken to attract new industry to a particular locale, or to finance community facilities, such as hospitals. The governmental unit becomes the lessor, and the user entity is the lessee in the lease agreement. Generally, the lease payments are set at an amount equal to the debt service costs, i.e., the lease payments would be equal to the principal and interest payments on the tax-exempt obligations.

In recent years, the lessor (governmental unit) often has refunded the obligations through the issue of a new obligation that contains more favorable terms. The economic advantage of the refunding may be passed through to the lessee in the form of lower lease payments. Such a refunding poses two problems from an accounting viewpoint. First, there has been a change in the terms of the lease agreement, and the provisions of SFAS No. 13 would be applicable. Second, the refunding may be viewed as an early extinguishment of debt, and the provisions of APB Opinion No. 26 would be applicable.

When there is a change in the terms of a lease agreement, Paragraphs 14(a) and 17(f)(i) of SFAS No. 13 are to be used to determine the proper accounting treatment. Where the revised lease agreement qualifies as a capital lease, these paragraphs specify that the asset recorded under the lease agreement, or the obligation recorded, should be adjusted for the amount of the change. A gain or loss resulting from a revision in the terms of a capital lease would not be recognized in the current period, but would be treated as an adjustment to the asset or liability account.

If the refunding is viewed as an early extinguishment of debt, the provisions of APB Opinion No. 26 specify that any gain or loss resulting from the extinguishment should be recognized currently.

---

[1] Certain property owned by a governmental unit or authority must meet additional specific criteria before classification as an operating lease. These criteria are listed in Paragraph 8 of FASB Interpretation No. 23.

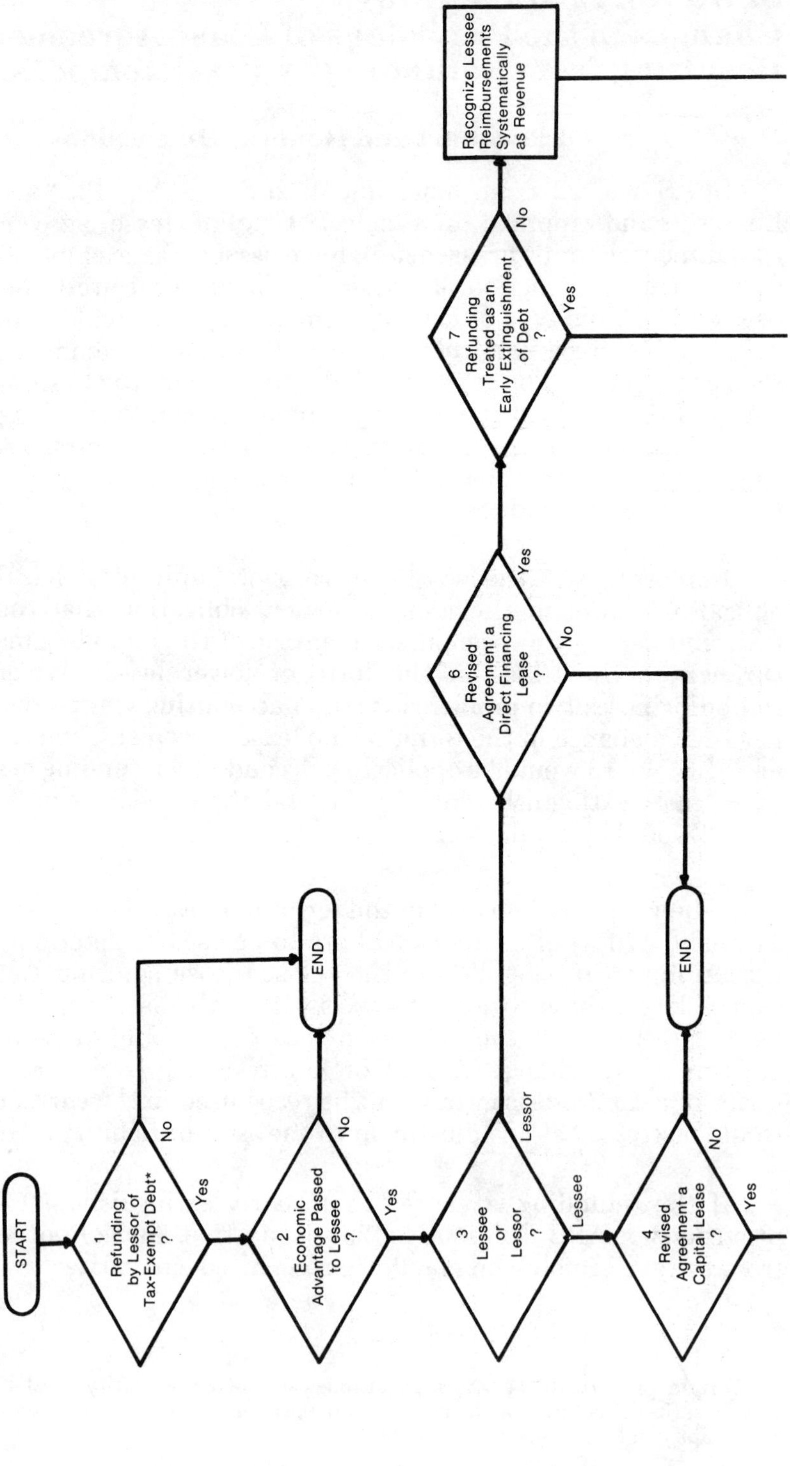
START
1
Refunding
by Lessor of
Tax-Exempt Debt*
?
Yes
No
END
2
Economic
Advantage Passed
to Lessee
?
Yes
No
3
Lessee
or
Lessor
?
Lessee
Lessor
4
Revised
Agreement a
Capital Lease
?
Yes
No
END
6
Revised
Agreement a
Direct Financing
Lease
?
Yes
No
7
Refunding
Treated as an
Early Extinguishment
of Debt
?
Yes
No
Recognize Lessee
Reimbursements
Systematically
as Revenue

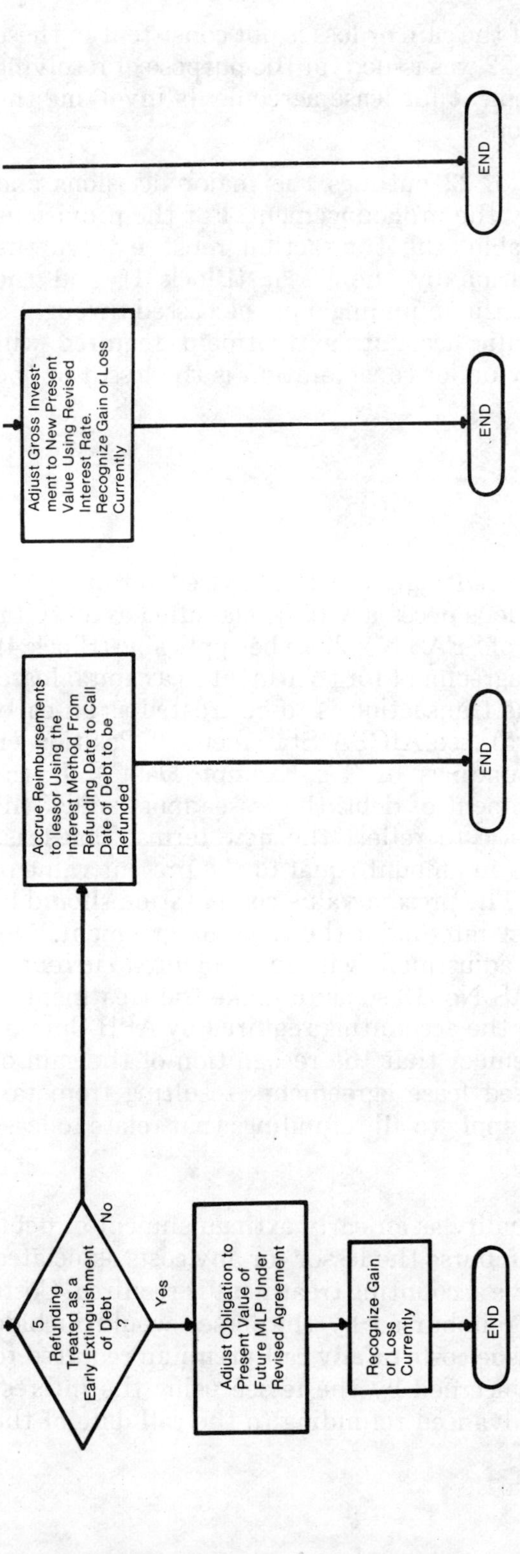

*Including an advanced refunding of tax-exempt debt.

The accounting treatment of the gain or loss is not consistent in these two pronouncements. SFAS No. 22 was issued for the purpose of resolving this conflict in accounting treatment for lease agreements involving the refunding of tax-exempt obligations.

The Flowchart of SFAS No. 22 outlines the major decisions and resultant accounting required by the pronouncement. For the provisions of SFAS No. 22 to be applicable, the transaction must involve the refunding of tax-exempt obligation by the lessor (Block 1), and the perceived economic advantage of the refunding must be passed through to the lessee (Block 2). The specific accounting treatment required will depend upon whether the entity under consideration is the lessor or the lessee (Block 3).

Lessee Accounting

The new lease agreement resulting from the revised terms of the refunding must meet the conditions necessary to be classified as a capital lease in order for the provisions of SFAS No. 22 to be applicable (Block 4). If the revised terms qualify the agreement for treatment as a capital lease, the lessee must determine if the transaction is to be treated as an early extinguishment of debt (Block 5) (see AICPA Statement of Position on "Accounting for Advance Refundings of Tax-Exempt Debt"). If the refunding is an early extinguishment of debt, the lessee must adjust the obligation under the capital lease to reflect the new terms. The lease obligation should be adjusted to an amount equal to the present value of the MLP under the new terms. The present value computation should be based upon the effective interest rate under the revised agreement. Any gain or loss resulting from the adjustment will be *recognized currently.* SFAS No. 22 has amended SFAS No. 13 so as to make the treatment of any gain or loss consistent with the accounting required by APB Opinion No. 26. It is important to remember that the recognition of the gain or loss is applicable only to revised lease agreements resulting from tax-exempt refunding, and does not apply to all refundings that relate to lease agreements.

If the refunding does not qualify as an early extinguishment of debt, but the lessee is obligated to reimburse the lessor for any costs associated with the refunding, an alternative accounting treatment is required. Costs of the refunding that may be reimbursed by the lessee would include unamortized discount or debt issue costs or any call premium required to be paid. These costs should be accrued by the lessee using the interest method, from the date of the advanced refunding to the call date of the obligations to be refunded.

Lessor Accounting

The revised lease agreement must be classified as a direct financing lease for the provisions of SFAS No. 22 to be applicable for lessor accounting. (Block 6). If the revised agreement is a direct financing lease, the lessor next must determine if the refunding is to be treated as an early extinguishment of debt (Block 7). When the refunding is classified as an early extinguishment of debt, the lessor should adjust the gross investment in the lease and the unearned income to reflect the new lease terms. Depending upon the terms of the revised agreement, the lessor may have to adjust both elements of the gross investment, i.e., the MLP receivable and the estimated residual value previously recorded. The amount of the adjustment is based upon the present value of the MLP receivable and the estimated residual value, using the interest rate applicable under the new agreement. The effect of the adjustment should be recognized as a gain or loss in the current accounting period.

If the refunding is not treated as an early extinguishment of debt, the lessor should "systematically" recognize any reimbursable costs as revenue. The period over which the reimbursable costs should be recognized is from the date of advanced refunding to the call date of the debt to be refinanced.

When the refunding is not to be treated as an early extinguishment of debt, the lessee and lessor are, in effect, systematically recognizing the gain or loss over future periods rather than in the current period.

Refunding of Tax-Exempt Debt Involving a Lease—An Example

To illustrate the technical aspects of SFAS No. 22, the assumptions listed in Exhibit I will be used.

Exhibit I

Assumptions for Refunding of Tax-Exempt Debt

1. Fastgrow City financed the construction of a $10,000,000 physical facility by issuing tax-exempt obligations. The debt bears interest at the rate of eight percent, and $1,000,000 in principal is to be repaid at the end of each of the next 10 years.
2. The City leased the facility to Lessee, Inc. for a period of 10 years. The lease payments were set equal to the loan principal and interest payments of the lessor. The lease was appropriately classified as a capital lease for the lessee and a direct financing lease for the lessor.
3. At the beginning of Year 3, Fastgrow City refunded the eight percent, $10,000,000 serial obligations by issuing five percent serial obligations that require a $1,012,500 principal payment at the end of each of the next eight years.

4. The refunding is treated as an early extinguishment of debt.
5. The economic advantage associated with the refunding (lower interest payments and therefore, lower lease payments) are passed through to Lessee, Inc.
6. The lease agreement under the revised terms is properly classified as a capital lease for the lessee and as a direct financing lease for the lessor.

The appropriate accounting for the lease transaction will be illustrated from the standpoint of both the lessee and the lessor.

Lessee Accounting

Based upon the assumptions listed above, the provisions of SFAS No. 22 apply to the transaction. Before the proper accounting for the lessee can be determined, it is necessary to calculate the balance in the obligation account of the lessee at the date of the refunding. The present value and fair value of the original leased property and obligation was $10,000,000. Table I shows the amortization of the $10,000,000 obligation under the original lease agreement.

Table I

Amortization of Lease Obligation

Period	Annual[a] Payment	Annual Interest Expense	Obligation Reduction	Obligation Balance End of Year
Initial Value				[b]$10,000,000
1	$ 1,800,000	[c]$ 800,000	[d]$ 1,000,000	[e]9,000,000
2	1,720,000	720,000	1,000,000	8,000,000
3	1,640,000	640,000	1,000,000	7,000,000
4	1,560,000	560,000	1,000,000	6,000,000
5	1,480,000	480,000	1,000,000	5,000,000
6	1,400,000	400,000	1,000,000	4,000,000
7	1,320,000	320,000	1,000,000	3,000,000
8	1,240,000	240,000	1,000,000	2,000,000
9	1,160,000	160,000	1,000,000	1,000,000
10	1,080,000	80,000	1,000,000	-0-
	$14,400,000	$4,400,000	$10,000,000	

[a] The annual payment is equal to the $1,000,000 principal payment plus the annual interest computed at 8 percent of the obligation balance.
[b] The $10,000,000 initial value is equal to the amount recorded as the lease obligation at the beginning of the lease term.
[c] $10,000,000 × .08 = $800,000.
[d] The annual principal payment.
[e] $10,000,000 − $1,000,000 = $9,000,000.

At the beginning of Year 3, the date of the refunding, the unamortized obligation balance is equal to $8,000,000. Since the economic advantage of the refunding is to be passed through to the lessee, and the revised lease agreement is classified as a capital lease, the lessee is required to adjust the lease obligation account. The amount of the adjustment will be recognized currently as a gain or loss, in accordance with the provisions of APB Opinion No. 26. The calculation of the gain or loss resulting from the revised lease terms is shown below:

Eight Percent Obligations to be Refunded	$8,000,000
Premium Required to Refund the Issue	100,000
Five Percent Obligation to be Issued	$8,100,000
Unamortized Obligation - Lessee	8,000,000
Loss on Lease Revision	$ 100,000

The premium required to refund the eight percent obligations is equal to the difference between the unamortized obligation balance for the eight percent debt of $8,000,000, and the face amount of the five percent refunding issue of $8,100,000 ($1,012,500 × 8 years = $8,100,000).

The journal entry necessary to reflect the loss and to adjust the balance in the lessee's obligation account would be:

Loss on Revised Lease Agreement	100,000	
Obligation Under Capital Lease		100,000

As a result of this adjustment, the new obligation balance will be $8,100,000, and will be reduced each period by the principal payment of $1,012,500. Interest will be recognized in subsequent periods, using the interest method. The new effective interest rate is five percent.

Table II shows the amortization of the lease obligation under the revised lease agreement.

Table II

Amortization of Lease Obligation Under Revised Agreement

Period	Annual[a] Payment	Annual Interest Expense	Obligation Reduction	Obligation Balance End of Year
Initial Value				[b]$8,100,000
3	$1,417,500	[c]$ 405,000	[d]$1,012,500	[e]7,087,500
4	1,366,875	354,375	1,012,500	6,075,000
5	1,316,250	303,750	1,012,500	5,062,500
6	1,265,625	253,125	1,012,500	4,050,000
7	1,215,000	202,500	1,012,500	3,037,500
8	1,164,375	151,875	1,012,500	2,025,000
9	1,113,750	101,250	1,012,500	1,012,500
10	1,063,125	50,625	1,012,500	-0-
	$9,922,500	$1,822,500	$8,100,000	

[a] The annual payment is equal to the $1,012,500 principal payment plus the annual interest computed at five percent on the obligation balance.
[b] The $8,100,000 initial value at the beginning of Year 3 is equal to the balance in the obligation account under the prior lease agreement, plus the $100,000 loss recognized as a result of the lease revision.
[c] $8,000,000 × .05 = $405,000.
[d] The annual principal payment.
[e] $8,100,000 − $1,012,500 = $7,087,500.

Notice that the economic advantage of the revised agreement has resulted in lower lease payments in each of the Years 3 through 10. Under the original agreement, the lease payment in Year 3 would have been $1,640,000. However, under the revised agreement, the required lease payment in Year 3 is $1,417,500.

This completes the discussion of the lessee accounting. Both Tables I and II also will be used in connection with the lessor accounting under the refunding.

Lessor Accounting

Fastgrow City, the lessor, must reduce the minimum lease payment receivable by an amount equal to the difference between the remaining principal and interest payments on the eight percent obligations and the five percent obligations. The principal and interest payments are computed from the date of refunding to the maturity date of the respective issues. By referring back to Table I, notice that Fastgrow City recorded the minimum lease payment receivable of $14,400,000, and unearned income of $4,400,000, at the inception of the original lease. At the beginning of Year 3, the date of the refunding, the minimum lease payment receivable would have been reduced by $3,520,000 ($1,800,000 in Year 1, and $1,720,000 in Year 2), and the unearned income account would have been reduced by $1,520,000 ($800,000 in Year 1, and $720,000 in Year 2). Therefore, the remaining balance in the minimum lease payment receivable is $10,880,000, and the balance in the unearned income account is $2,880,000, just prior to the refunding.

Table II shows that the total minimum lease payment receivable under the revised agreement will be $9,922,500, and the unearned income will be $1,822,500.

Given this information, the lessor could compute the amount of the adjustment required in the following manner:

	8 Percent Obligation	5 Percent Obligation	Difference
Principal Payment	$ 8,000,000	$8,100,000	$ 100,000
Interest Payment	2,880,000	1,822,500	(1,057,500)
Total	$10,880,000	$9,922,500	$(957,500)

The adjustment required to reflect the revised lease terms will reduce the unearned income account by $1,057,500, and the minimum lease payment receivable will be reduced by $957,500. The difference between these two amounts ($100,000), will be recognized as a *loss* on the refunding of debt *and* as a *gain* from the revised lease agreement. The entry to record the refunding of the debt is as follows:

Long-term Debt—8 Percent	8,000,000	
Loss on Refunding of Tax-Exempt Debt	100,000	
Long-term Debt—5 Percent		8,100,000

The entry required to reflect the revised lease agreement is as follows:

Unearned Income	1,057,500	
Minimum Lease Payment Receivable		957,500
Gain From Lease Revision		100,000

The amortization of the unearned income for Years 3 through 10 is shown in Table II, in the column for interest expense. The minimum lease payment receivable would be reduced each year by the amounts shown in the "Annual Payment" column of Table II.

SFAS No. 23 (August 1978) Inception of the Lease

General Discussion

SFAS No. 23 amends SFAS No. 13, "Accounting for Leases," in five specific areas. The intent of the amendments is to allow the lessee and the lessor to more fully reflect the economic conditions relating to the lease classification. The amendments all relate to events that are associated with the date of inception of the lease. Each of the five amendments will be discussed in detail below.

Amendment Relating to Date of Inception of the Lease

SFAS No. 13 specified that the date of inception of the lease is the *lease agreement date,* unless a commitment to lease the property has been made prior to the lease agreement. If such a commitment exists, the date of the commitment, rather than the agreement date, is considered the date of inception of the lease. The date of commitment is earlier than the date of lease agreement. SFAS No. 13 allowed one exception to the general rule stated above. This exception is for leased property that is to be purchased or constructed subsequent to the lease agreement or commitment date. For such leased property, the date of inception of the lease is not the lease agreement or commitment date, but the date of purchase of the property or the date the construction is completed.

The date of inception of the lease is important, because it is on this date that the classification of the lease is made. If an improper date of inception exists, the lease classification made on that date may not reflect the economic substance of the transaction.

SFAS No. 23 amended the lease inception date by removing the one exception permitted under SFAS No. 13. Even if property is to be purchased or constructed subsequent to the lease agreement or commitment date, the date of inception of the lease must be *either* the lease agreement or commitment date.

Amendment of the Risk-Transfer Criterion

For the lessor to classify a lease agreement as a capital lease, in accordance with the provisions of SFAS No. 13, the agreement must meet a risk-transfer test, in addition to other criteria. One part of the risk-transfer test specifies that "no important uncertainties surround the amount of unreimbursable costs yet to be incurred by the lessor under the lease" (SFAS No. 13, Paragraph 8(b)). SFAS No. 23 amends this test for property that is acquired or constructed subsequent to the date of the lease agreement or the commitment date. For this type of leased property, the risk-transfer test described above is to be applied on the date of acquisition of the property, if purchased, or on the date that construction is completed.

This risk-transfer test normally would be applied at the date of inception of the lease, which may be prior to the date of acquisition or completion of construction. However, SFAS No. 23 amends the date of the test, so that a clear determination of the status of the unreimbursable costs can be made.

Amendment Relating to the Determination of Fair Value of the Leased Property

Paragraph 10 of SFAS No. 13 requires that the lessee compare the present value of the minimum lease payments with the fair value of the leased property. The lesser of the two amounts should be recorded as the value of the leased property and the obligation under the capital lease. In addition, Paragraph 26(a)(i) of SFAS No. 13 makes reference to the use of fair value when the lease agreement involves both land and building(s). If a lease agreement involves both land and building(s), and also contains either a provision for transfer of ownership or a bargain purchase option, the lessee must account separately for the land and building elements. The separation of the land and building elements is made on the basis of the relative fair values of the two elements.

SFAS No. 23 amends the concept of fair value as it applies to Paragraph 10 and Paragraph 26(a)(i) of SFAS No. 13. Fair value must be adjusted for "a provision to escalate minimum lease payments for increases in construction or acquisition cost of the leased property or for increases in some other measure of cost or value . . . during construction or pre-acquisition period" (SFAS No. 23, Paragraph 8).

Amendment to Unguaranteed Residual Value

Paragraphs 17(a) and 18(a) of SFAS No. 13 specify that the lessor's gross investment in both a direct financing and a sales-type lease consists of the summation of the minimum lease payments and the unguaranteed residual value.

SFAS No. 23 amends these two paragraphs by specifying that the total residual value used to determine the amount of any unguaranteed residual value cannot be greater than the estimated residual value on the lease agreement or commitment date. However, an exception is provided to this amendment. If the agreement provides for the escalation of rental payments due to cost increases for leased property that is to be acquired at a later date or for property to be constructed, the effect of the increases are to be used in computing the estimated residual value.

Amendment to Estimated Residual Value in a Leveraged Lease Agreement

Paragraph 43(c) of SFAS No. 13 requires that, at the inception of a leveraged lease agreement, the lessor must record the estimated residual value of the leased property as an asset.

Paragraph 10 of SFAS No. 23 specifies that the amount of the estimated residual value recorded as an asset cannot exceed the residual value estimated at the lease inception date. An exception to this general rule is provided in SFAS No. 23. If the agreement provides for the escalation of rental payments, due to cost increases for leased property that is to be acquired at a later date or that is to be constructed subsequent to the lease inception date, the effect of the increases should be used in computing the estimated residual value.

Topic 9
Pensions

Detail Contents

This Exposure Draft deals with the accounting principles and reporting practices to be followed by defined benefit pension plans. APB Opinion No. 8 addressed the issue of accounting for the cost of pension plans, and the guidelines issued in this Exposure Draft identify the reporting responsibilities of the plan. The Exposure Draft indicated that GAAP would generally be followed in the preparation of the financial statements of the pension plan. The following financial statements are to be prepared by the plan's management: (1) statement of net assets available for benefits at the end of the period; (2) statement of changes in net assets available for benefits. In addition, the plan should disclose the actuarial present value of accumulated plan benefits as of the benefit valuation date, and information about the effects of certain factors affecting the year-to-year change in the actuarial present value of accumulated plan benefits.

This Exposure Draft deals with the adequacy of disclosure of pension plan information made by employers in their financial statements, and the accounting for post-retirement benefits. The proposal would group employers into two categories: those having only one defined benefit pension plan, and those with more than one such plan. Single plan employers would be required to disclose (a) the actuarial present value of accumulated plan benefits, (b) the actuarial present value of vested plan benefits, (c) net assets available for benefits and (d) description of significant actuarial assumptions and asset valuation methods used. For employers with more than one plan, the plans should be grouped as to those having an actuarial present value of accumulated plan benefits in excess of net assets available for benefits, and those having net assets available for benefits in excess of the actuarial present value of accumulated plan benefits. The disclosures described above then would apply to the aggregate amount of each group of plans.

Employers would also be required to disclose the following information about other post-retirement benefits: (a) a description of the benefits; (b) a description of the accounting policies currently followed; and (c) the cost of benefits included in determining net income for the period.

APB Opinion No. 8 (November 1966) Accounting for the Cost of Pension Plans

General Discussion and Definition of Terms

In recent years there has been a great deal of public concern about employee pension plans. This concern eventually led to the passage of the Employee Retirement Income Security Act of 1974 (ERISA), more commonly referred to as the Pension Reform Act. This law was primarily concerned with the financing of pension funds and protection of the rights of employees participating in a pension plan. Eight years prior to the enactment of this law, the Accounting Principles Board had issued Opinion No. 8, which dealt with the proper accounting recognition of the costs of pension plans. Prior to the issuance of APB Opinion No. 8, there existed a wide variety of methods used to account for pension fund costs. However, there was general agreement that pension costs should be accounted for using the accrual method.[1]

The Accounting Principles Board was convinced that the determination of the costs of a pension plan should be derived by using an "acceptable actuarial cost method." (There are several acceptable actuarial cost methods, including the unit credit method and projected benefit cost methods. Refer to Appendix A of the Opinion for a discussion of the assumptions made under each of these methods. The Opinion also

[1] FASB Interpretation No. 3 was issued shortly after the Pension Reform Act was passed. The interpretation concluded that while there may be some increase or decrease in the amount charged to pension costs during a period the Act did not impact the provisions of the Opinion. The concept of the maximum and minimum pension cost were still valid.

identifies those cost determination methods that are not considered acceptable for accounting purposes.) An actuarial cost method, according to APB Opinion No. 8, Appendix A, is a "technique used by actuaries for establishing the amount and incidence of annual actuarial cost of pension plan benefits." The Board concluded that the plan costs should be determined using an actuarial method. Generally, these methods take into consideration such items as employee turnover, mortality, normal retirement age, benefits to be paid upon retirement, etc. The actuarially determined costs usually are based upon a net present value concept, i.e., certain assumptions are made about earnings that will accumulate on funds invested in a pension plan.

Before proceeding with a discussion of the provisions of the Opinion, it is essential to define certain terms used in the Opinion that have a specific meaning for accounting purposes. A pension plan is defined in Paragraph 8 as "an arrangement whereby a company undertakes to provide its retired employees with benefits that can be determined or estimated in advance from the provisions of a document . . . or from the company's practices." A pension plan need not be represented by a formal written agreement to receive accounting recognition. A plan may be inferred from the practices of the company.

While there are several types of costs associated with a pension plan, the major costs may be identified as either "normal costs" or "past service costs." Normal costs, according to Appendix B of the Opinion, represent the "annual cost assigned, under the actuarial cost method in use, to years subsequent to the inception of a pension plan." Normal costs generally are thought of as the current period pension costs and are computed on a net present value basis. These costs may be considered to represent the retirement or other benefits earned by employees in the plan in the current accounting period. Past service costs, as defined in Appendix B, represent the "pension cost assigned, under the actuarial cost method in use, to years prior to the inception of a pension plan." Past service costs represent the retirement or other benefits earned by employees prior to adoption of the pension plan. For example, if an employee worked for a company for 20 years prior to the adoption of a pension plan, recognition should be given for the employee's past service. This recognition is referred to as the past service costs of the plan. A company is not required to give credit to employees for past service, but most do. The past service costs usually are based upon a net present value computation that assumes some earnings on funds invested in the plan. Some actuarial cost methods do not make a separate computation for past service costs, but include the past service costs in the normal costs. For example, the "individual level premium method" makes no distinction between past service costs and normal costs. Under this method, past service costs are considered part of normal costs (see APB Opinion No. 8, Appendix A).

Prior service costs are all costs associated with a pension plan prior to a valuation by an actuary. A precise definition of prior service costs is "pension cost assigned, under the actuarial cost method in use, to years prior to the date of a particular actuarial valuation" (APB Opinion No. 8, Appendix B). A pension plan may be in effect for several years and then be amended to provide additional or expanded benefits for employees. The increases or decreases in the prior service costs from the amendment are referred to as prior service increments. Prior service costs include past service costs, all normal costs (if any) charged to expense, interest on all costs and any additional costs (prior service increments) resulting from a new valuation. At the very inception of a pension plan where credit is given for past service cost, the prior service cost and the past service cost are the same.

APB Opinion No. 8 is concerned with the accounting recognition of expenses relating to pension plans and views any plan as a long-range commitment on the part of the company. The Opinion is not *directly* concerned with the funding of pension costs, but recognizes that the method of funding may influence the costs indirectly. Pension costs, both normal and past service, are based on a net present value computation that assumes that funds invested either internally or with a trustee will earn an assumed rate of return. The earnings on the pension fund are referred to as "interest" in the Opinion, even though the actual earnings may include items other than interest. When the amounts representing the net present value of normal costs and past service costs are invested in a fund, the value of the fund will grow by the amount of interest or other earnings from the invested funds. However, if these amounts are not invested in a pension fund, no earnings will be realized. From a net present value basis, the value of the pension fund will be deficient when amounts are needed to pay current employee retirement benefits. In this case, the company would be responsible for the past service costs, normal costs and the interest that *would have been earned* had the amounts been funded. The interest that would have been earned on invested funds is referred to as the "interest equivalent" or as "amounts equivalent to interest" in the Opinion.

With this basic introduction to some of the terms used in the Opinion, the discussion of the specific provisions can be started. New terms will be introduced and defined as the discussion develops.

Determination of the Maximum and Minimum Provision

The current provision for pension costs, i.e., the amount that will be charged to income in the current period, must be determined using an acceptable actuarial method *and* must fall within certain limits before it is considered appropriate by the Opinion. During any given year, the provision for pension costs cannot be less than a defined *minimum* amount, nor greater than a defined *maximum* amount. The use of a defined minimum and maximum prevents the current provision for pension costs from changing drastically from period to period. This notion is consistent with the Board's view of the long-run nature of pension costs.

The *minimum* pension provision for a particular year is equal to:

(1) Normal costs;

(2) An amount equivalent to interest on the unfunded prior service costs; and

(3) A provision for vested benefits (when certain conditions are met).

Normal costs have been fully explained above. The interest equivalent on the unfunded prior service costs recognizes the fact that, unless prior service costs are fully funded, the pension fund balance will not be sufficient to pay all of the actuarially determined benefits to current employees on retirement. The interest, i.e., earnings of the unfunded prior service costs, therefore should increase the current provision for pension costs. This is an example of how the funding of the pension costs influences the accounting determination of current costs.

Vested benefits are benefits whose payment is not contingent upon further employment. When an employee's benefits have vested in a pension plan, that employee will receive benefits, at some future date, from the plan, even if he/she is no longer employed by the company. The 1974 ERISA was very concerned with the treatment of vested benefits. While vested benefits may have to be considered in the determination of the minimum provision, this will occur only under unusual circumstances. A complete discussion of the impact of vested benefits will be postponed until the other elements of the minimum provision have been discussed.

The *maximum* pension provision for a particular year is equal to:

(1) Normal costs;

(2) Ten percent of past service costs—until fully amortized;

(3) Ten percent of prior service increments, i.e. the increases or decreases in prior service costs resulting from an amendment to the pension plan—until fully amortized; and

(4) An amount equivalent to interest on the difference between the total provision (since inception of plan) and the amounts actually funded (since inception of plan).

Normal costs are a part of both the minimum and the maximum provision. The next element of the maximum provision is somewhat difficult to explain from a logical point of view. Several different arguments have been presented for the handling of the past service costs of a pension plan. Some have argued that, since the costs are the result of services provided in years prior to the inception of the plan, the entire amount of the past service cost should be charged to retained earnings, as a prior period adjustment, in the year the plan is adopted. Others have argued that past service costs should be determined for each employee and charged to income for the period of time from the adoption of the plan to the retirement of the employee. As stated earlier, the Board concluded that the cost of pension plans is a long-run cost of doing business. It concluded that the past service costs should be spread over current and future periods, and not treated as a prior period adjustment. The dilemma facing the Board was to determine some reasonable time period for the recognition of past service costs. A 10-year period was selected (10 percent per year until fully amortized). It is difficult to determine the exact reasoning that went into the selection of the 10-year period, but the past service costs associated with a qualified pension plan may be deducted over a 10-year period for tax purposes. This tax provision may have had a substantial influence on the decision of the Board to adopt the 10-year amortization period. The third element in the maximum, i.e., 10 percent of the prior service increments, is directly related to the handling of the past service costs.

The final element in the maximum provision is the interest equivalent on the *difference* between the total provision for pension costs since inception of the plan and the amount funded since inception of the plan. This is interest on the difference between the expense recorded for accounting purposes and the amount actually invested in the pension fund. This interest equivalent is the result of the net present value computation of pension costs. If the actuarially determined amount of the provision is not funded in total, the pension fund will be deficient from an actuarial point of view, because the earnings of the fund are based upon the funding of all costs. The interest equivalent is an expression of difference between the assumed earnings of the fund and the actual earnings.

The interest equivalent used in the determination of the maximum provision should not be confused with the interest equivalent used to determine the minimum provision. They are not the same amounts. The interest included in the minimum provision is based on the *unfunded* prior service costs, while the interest used to determine the maximum provision is based on the difference between the amount of the provision and the amount of the funding. There are cases where no interest will be used in the minimum, or in the maximum. It is most important not to confuse these two concepts of interest equivalents.

The actuarially determined provision for pension costs recorded in any one period must fall between the minimum and the maximum. So long as it does, it will be used as the recorded provision. By saying that the actual recorded provision must fall between the maximum and the minimum, one should not infer that a company will use either the maximum or minimum amount in a given year. The maximum and minimum are designed to set limits on the amount of pension costs recorded in any period; they are not intended to be a computation of the actual provision. The provision is based upon an actuarial determination of the current period costs. The maximum and minimum are accounting measurements required by APB Opinion No. 8. The primary task of the accountant is to take information provided by an actuary or others and determine if the information provided is in correspondance with the provisions of APB Opinion No. 8. The problems presented by the Opinion are computational in nature.

In order to fully illustrate the provision of the Opinion, it will be necessary to develop several examples. The goal of most of the examples is to show the proper computation of the maximum and minimum, and to use this computation in the process of selecting the proper provision for the current period. The examples that follow begin with a very basic problem of accounting for pension costs and gradually increase in terms of difficulty, until all major points in the Opinion have been covered.

Determining the Propriety of the Provision for Pension Costs

To begin the technical discussion of pension costs, a basic example of pension accounting will be illustrated, using the assumptions in Exhibit I.

Exhibit I
Basic Pension Accounting

1. Jar, Inc. adopted a pension plan for its employees on January 1, 197A, the same day the company began business.
2. On December 31, 197A, the company's actuary determines that the normal costs for the period were $12,000.
3. The company funds all normal costs with the plan trustee. Funds deposited with the trustee are expected to earn interest at the rate of six percent.
4. The current period provision is determined to be $12,000, and there are no vested benefits associated with the plan.

Because the plan was adopted on the same day the company started operations, there are no past service costs associated with the plan. Also, there is no difference between the amount of the provision and the amount to be funded. Based on this information, it is not necessary for Jar, Inc. to calculate the maximum provision. There are no unfunded prior service costs and no vested benefits, so the company will not need to calculate the minimum provision.

The entry to record the provision for the current period would be:

Provision for Pension Costs	12,000	
Cash		12,000

The funds deposited with the trustee will earn interest at the compound rate of six percent. This example excluded any consideration of past or prior service costs in order to show the basic accounting for pension costs.

The next example is designed to illustrate the basic computation of the minimum and maximum provision. The assumptions in Exhibit II will be used to develop the required information about the plan.

Exhibit II

Pension Costs with No Funding of Past Service Costs

1. Jar, Inc. adopted a pension plan for its employees on January 1, 197A, several years after the Company began operations.
2. At the date of adoption of the plan, the company's actuary calculated the past service costs under the plan to be $250,000.
3. On December 31, 197A, the actuary calculated the normal costs for the year to be $10,000; and, on December 31, 197B, the actuary calculated normal costs of $10,500.
4. The company funds all normal costs with the trustee of the plan. Funds deposited with the trustee are assumed to earn six percent.
5. The provision for pension costs in 197A is determined to be $28,500, and in 197B to be $29,000.
6. Jar, Inc. does not plan to fund any of the past service costs, and the actuary has determined that there are no vested benefits associated with the plan.

Because there are past service costs associated with the plan, Jar, Inc. must calculate the maximum provision, to be sure that the indicated provision is less than this amount. Jar, Inc. has decided not to fund the prior service costs, so it will be necessary to calculate the minimum provision to be sure that the indicated provision is at least equal to the minimum. For the year ended December 31, 197A, the provision is given as $28,500. Before this amount can be recorded as the pension costs for 197A, the accountant must determine that it falls between the minimum and the maximum.

The computation of the maximum provision for 197A is shown below:

Normal Costs for 197A	$10,000
10 Percent of Past Service Costs	
($250,000 × .10)	25,000
10 Percent of Prior Service Increments	-0-
Interest Equivalents	-0-
Maximum Provision	$35,000

The normal costs were determined by the actuary, and the computation of 10 percent of the past service costs was quite straightforward. There were no prior service increments, since the plan had yet to be amended. There would be no interest equivalents in 197A, because the determination of the pension costs and funding was made at the end of the period. There would be no difference between the provision and the amount funded until the end of the year. The difference throughout the year was zero.

The determination of the amount of the past service costs was made at the beginning of 197A. Since there was no funding of the prior service costs, the minimum provision for 197A would be determined as follows:

Normal Costs for 197A	$10,000
Interest Equivalent on the Unfunded	
Prior Service Costs ($250,000 × .06)	15,000
Provision for Vested Benefits	-0-
Minimum Provision	$25,000

The interest equivalent on the prior service costs in 197A represents the amount of interest that would have been earned if the total prior service costs had been funded at January 1, 197A. Remember, at the beginning of the inception of the plan, both past service and prior service costs are the same. When computing the minimum, the term "prior service cost" will be used, even though it might consist only of the past service cost.

The indicated amount of the provision for 197A is $28,500, which falls between the maximum provision of $35,000 and the minimum provision of $25,000. The following journal entry would be required at the end of 197A to record the provision for pension costs:

Provision for Pension Costs	28,500	
Cash		10,000
Excess of Pension Expense Over Funding		18,500

The account, Excess of Pension Expense Over Funding, is classified as a liability in the balance sheet.

Note that the provision recorded was not the maximum or the minimum. These two values merely set limits upon the amount of the provision to be recorded. The $10,000 normal costs were funded with the trustee and will earn interest at the compound rate of six percent.

Exhibit II also provides information regarding the year 197B. The provision indicated is $29,000, and the minimum and maximum must be determined before recording the provision for 197B. The maximum provision would be calculated as follows:

Normal Costs for 197B	$10,500
10 Percent of Past Service Costs	
($250,00 × .10)	25,000
10 Percent of Prior Service Increments	-0-
Interest Equivalents ($18,500 × .06)	1,110
Maximum Provision	$36,610

The only differences between the maximum provision in 197A and the amount for 197B relate to the interest equivalents and the increased normal cost. The interest equivalent used in the computation of the maximum is based upon the difference between the provision and the funding. Recall that, in 197A, the difference was $18,500, which is the amount used in the computation of the interest equivalent for 197B. More will be said about the nature of the interest equivalent later in this discussion.

The minimum provision for 197B would be determined as follows:

Normal Costs for 197B		$10,500
Interest Equivalent on the Unfunded		
Prior Service Costs:		
Prior Service Costs from 197A	$250,000	
Interest Increment in 197A	15,000	
Prior Service Costs for 19B	$265,000	
Interest Rate	× .06	15,900
Provision for Vested Benefits		-0-
Minimum Provision		$26,400

Note that the $250,000 of prior service cost from 197A is the original past service cost. Remember that all the costs become prior service costs and that, after deducting the pension fund balance, the remainder is the unfunded prior service costs.

The factor that complicates the computation of the minimum provision is the interest equivalent. The unfunded prior service cost at January 1, 197A, amounted to $250,000, and interest equivalent for 197A was determined to be $15,000. Therefore, if Jar, Inc. had elected to fund the prior service costs at January 1, 197B, the Company would have to pay $265,000, i.e., the amount of the original past service cost plus the interest that could have been earned by the trustee. Using a six percent interest rate, $250,000 on January 1, 197A is equivalent to $265,000 on January 1, 197B. Based on this notion of compound interest, the interest equivalent used in the minimum provision for 197B will be six percent of the $265,000.

The provision indicated for 197B was $29,000, which is between the maximum of $36,610 and the minimum of $26,400. The journal entry to record the provision for pension costs in 197B would be:

Provision for Pension Costs	29,000	
Cash		10,500
Excess of Pension Expense Over Funding		18,500

Jar, Inc. elected to fund the normal costs of $10,500. The liability relating to the difference in the provision and funding is now equal to $37,000 ($18,500 from 197A and $18,500 from 197B).

If the maximum and minimum were to be determined for 197C, the interest equivalent used in the maximum would be based upon the $37,000 difference between the total provisions and total funding, and the interest equivalent used in the minimum would be based upon $280,900 ($265,000 at the start of 197B + $15,900 interest equivalent in 197B).

It sometimes is difficult to see the impact of the interest equivalents on the determination of the maximum and minimum provisions. To clearly illustrate this impact, Tables I and II have been developed, using some very limiting assumptions. Table I, Computation of the Maximum Provision, is prepared under the assumption that normal costs will be $10,000 for the next 10 years. In addition, it is assumed that the company *always* will record the maximum provision as the current pension costs, and that no past service costs will be funded. While these assumptions are very restrictive, they prove useful in the process of illustrating the concept of interest equivalents for the maximum provision.

In Table I, notice that the past service costs are fully amortized for accounting purposes at the end of 10 years. The interest equivalents calculated in the Table represent the amount that could have been earned if the *amortized amounts* of the past service cost ($25,000 per year) actually had been funded. This can be shown by the following computation:

Amount of Annual Annuity Assumed	$ 25,000
Present Value Factor for an Ordinary Annuity for 10 periods at six percent	13.1808
Amount of the Annuity	$329,520

The interest equivalent increases each year, due to the compounding of the interest on the difference between the total provision and the total funding. The maximum provision increases for the same reason. So, based upon the rather stabilizing assumptions made above, the major reason for changes in the maximum provision is the compound interest used to calculate the interest equivalent.

Table I

Computation of the Maximum Provision

Year	Normal Cost (a)	10% of Past Service Costs (b)	Interest Equivalent (c)=(g)×6%	Maximum Provision (d)=(a+b+c)	Funding (e)	Difference Between Provision and Funding: Current Period (f)	Difference Between Provision and Funding: Cumulative Total (g)=(g+f)
1	$ 10,000	$ 25,000	-0-	$ 35,000	$ 10,000	$25,000	$25,000
2	10,000	25,000	$ 1,500	36,500	10,000	26,500	51,500
3	10,000	25,000	3,090	38,090	10,000	28,090	79,590
4	10,000	25,000	4,775	39,775	10,000	29,775	109,365
5	10,000	25,000	6,562	41,562	10,000	31,562	140,927
6	10,000	25,000	8,456	43,456	10,000	33,456	174,383
7	10,000	25,000	10,463	45,463	10,000	35,463	209,846
8	10,000	25,000	12,591	47,591	10,000	37,591	247,437
9	10,000	25,000	14,846	49,846	10,000	39,846	287,283
10	10,000	25,000	17,237	52,237	10,000	42,237	329,520
	$100,000	$250,000	$79,520	$429,520	$100,000		

Remember that Table I was developed to illustrate the impact of the interest equivalent on the determination of the maximum provision, and is based upon some very restrictive assumptions. It is not likely that a company would develop such a table, because of the changes that might occur in the normal costs over a period of time, the periodic funding of past service costs, and several other factors. The authors do believe that the Table shows the effect of the interest equivalent in the computation of the maximum provision.

Table II, Computation of the Minimum Provision, also is based on the assumption that normal costs will remain at $10,000 per year for the next 10 years, and that all normal costs will be funded currently. In this example, there is no funding of prior service costs, so the balance of the unfunded prior service cost will continue to grow by the interest equivalent. Table II clearly demonstrates the compounding of interest. Notice that the minimum provision continues to increase each year, due to the compound interest used in the interest equivalent. The balance shown as the unfunded prior service cost at the end of Year 10 represents the unfunded past (prior) service cost of $250,000, plus the interest that could have been earned on this amount if it were funded at the date of adoption of the plan. The computation below shows the determination of the ending amount:

Amount of Unfunded Past (Prior) Service Costs	$250,000
Present Value Factor for the Amount of $1 for 10 Periods at Six Percent	1.79084
Amount of Unfunded Prior Service Costs	$447,710

Table II

Computation of the Minimum Provision

Year	Unfund-Normal Cost (a)	Interest on Unfund-ed Prior Service Cost (b)=(d)×6%	Minimum Provisions (c)=(a+b)	Unfunded Prior Service Cost (d)= (Balance + b)
Initial Value -	-	-	-	$250,000
1	$ 10,000	$ 15,000	$ 25,000	265,000
2	10,000	15,900	25,900	280,900
3	10,000	16,854	26,854	297,754
4	10,000	17,865	27,865	315,619
5	10,000	18,937	28,937	334,556
6	10,000	20,073	30,073	354,629
7	10,000	21,277	31,277	375,906
8	10,000	22,554	32,554	398,460
9	10,000	23,908	33,908	422,368
10	10,000	25,342	35,342	447,710
	$100,000	$197,710	$297,710	

While the past service costs have been fully *amortized* over the 10-year period, the unfunded prior service costs have increased to $447,710. In this example, if the funded normal costs had varied over the 10-year period, it would not affect the interest equivalent used in the computation of the minimum provision. Any increase or decrease in the normal cost would, of course, affect the total minimum provision.

The above example assumed that there would be no funding of the past service costs. To illustrate an example where *all* past service costs are funded at the date of adoption of the pension plan, the assumptions listed in Exhibit III will be used.

Exhibit III

Pension Costs with Total Funding of Past Service Costs

1. Jar, Inc. adopted a pension plan for its employees on January 1, 197A, several years after the company began operations.
2. At the date of adoption of the plan, the company's actuary calculated the past service costs under the plan to be $250,000. This amount was deposited with the trustee on January 1, 197A.
3. On December 31, 197A, the actuary calculated the normal costs for the year to be $9,500; and on December 31, 197B, the actuarially determined normal costs were $9,800.
4. The company funds all normal costs with the trustee of the plan at the end of each year. Funds deposited with the trustee are assumed to earn six percent interest.
5. The provision for 197A is determined to be $21,000, and the provision for 197B is determined to be $18,750.
6. There are no vested benefits associated with the pension plan.

Since there are past service costs associated with the plan, Jar, Inc. must calculate the maximum provision specified in APB Opinion No. 8. However, in this example, there will be no *unfunded* prior service costs or vested benefits, so the minimum provision will be equal to the normal costs for 197A and 197B. The actual provision recorded in 197A and 197B must be at least equal to the normal costs, but cannot exceed the yet to be determined maximum provision. The computation of the maximum provision for 197A is shown below:

Normal Costs for 197A	$ 9,500
10 Percent of Past Service Costs ($250,000 × .10)	25,000
10 Percent of Prior Service Increments	-0-
Interest Equivalent ($250,000 × .06)	(15,000)
Maximum Provision	$19,500

The unusual item in the calculation of the maximum amount is, once again, the interest equivalent. The past service costs were fully funded at the beginning of 197A, so the difference between the provision and the funding during 197A is equal to $250,000. In this example, the interest equivalent will *reduce* the maximum provision, because the funding exceeds the provision. An examination of the effects of this interest equivalent reduction will be shown later in this section.

The minimum provision is equal to the normal costs of $9,500, because there is no unfunded prior service cost or vested benefits.

The indicated provision for pension costs is equal to $21,000, which is greater than the maximum allowed under the provisions of APB Opinion No. 8. Therefore, the provision for 197A will be equal to the maximum provision of $19,500. The entry to record the funding of the past service costs at the beginning of 197A, and to record the provision at the end of the year are presented below:

Excess of Funding Over Pension Expense	250,000	
Cash		250,000
Provision for Pension Costs	19,500	
Cash		9,500
Excess of Funding Over Pension Expense		10,000

The difference between the provision and the funding of $10,000 reduced the excess of funding over pension expense account. The account is classified as an asset on the balance sheet. At the beginning of 197B, the difference between the provision and the funding is $240,000.

For 197B the minimum provision is equal to the normal costs of $9,800. The calculation of the maximum provision is shown below:

Normal Costs for 197B	$ 9,800
10 Percent of Past Service Costs ($250,000 × .10)	25,000
10 Percent of Prior Service Increments	-0-
Interest Equivalent ($240,000 × .06)	(14,400)
Maximum Provision	$20,400

The provision indicated for 197B is equal to $18,750, which falls between the minimum provision of $9,800 and the maximum provision of $20,400, so this amount will be recorded as the provision for 197B. The entry to record the provision is shown below:

Provision for Pension Costs	18,750	
Cash		9,800
Excess of Funding Over Pension Expense		8,950

Jar, Inc. funds the normal costs of $9,800. The balance in the excess of funding over pension expense account is now $231,050 ($240,000 – $8,950), and that figure will be used to determine the interest equivalent for 197C under the maximum provision.

When the past service costs are funded in full at inception of the pension plan, it is impossible to fully amortize the costs in a 10-year period. This is due to the fact that the interest equivalent serves to reduce the maximum allowable provision. If this situation occurs, the past service costs must be amortized over a period greater than 10 years. There is a popular misconception about the amortization of past service costs for accounting purposes. One often hears the statement that past service costs and prior service increments are amortized over 10 years. This is not what the Opinion states. The correct statement should be that past service costs are amortized at the rate of 10 percent per year *until fully amortized.* To illustrate this point, Table III has been developed.

Table III

Computation of the Maximum Provision

Year	Normal Cost (a)	10% of Past Service Costs (b)	Interest Equivalent (c)=(g)×6%	Maximum Provision (d)=(a+b+c)	Funding (e)	Difference Between Provision and Funding: Current Period (f)	Difference Between Provision and Funding: Cumulative Total (g)=(g+f)
Initial Value	-	-	-	-	-	-	$250,000
1	$ 10,000	$ 25,000	$ (15,000)	$ 20,000	$ 10,000	$(10,000)	240,000
2	10,000	25,000	(14,400)	20,600	10,000	(10,600)	229,400
3	10,000	25,000	(13,764)	21,236	10,000	(11,236)	218,164
4	10,000	25,000	(13,090)	21,910	10,000	(11,910)	206,254
5	10,000	25,000	(12,375)	22,625	10,000	(12,625)	193,629
6	10,000	25,000	(11,618)	23,382	10,000	(13,382)	180,247
7	10,000	25,000	(10,815)	24,185	10,000	(14,185)	166,062
8	10,000	25,000	(9,964)	25,036	10,000	(15,036)	151,026
9	10,000	25,000	(9,062)	25,938	10,000	(15,938)	135,088
10	10,000	25,000	(8,105)	26,895	10,000	(16,895)	118,193
11	10,000	25,000	(7,092)	27,908	10,000	(17,908)	100,285
12	10,000	25,000	(6,017)	28,983	10,000	(18,983)	81,302
13	10,000	25,000	(4,878)	30,122	10,000	(20,122)	61,180
14	10,000	25,000	(3,671)	31,329	10,000	(21,329)	39,851
15	10,000	25,000	(2,391)	32,609	10,000	(22,609)	17,242
16	10,000	18,277	(1,035)	27,242	10,000	(17,242)	-0-
	$160,000	$393,277	$(143,277)	$410,000	$160,000		

The Table is based on some restrictive assumptions, but these assumptions do not alter the basic point the authors wish to illustrate. The specific assumptions are that the normal costs are stable at $10,000 for the future, and that the company always records the maximum provision for pension costs.

An examination of Table III indicates that it takes 16 years to fully amortize the past service costs, even though the costs were fully funded at the date of adoption of the pension plan. Column (b) shows a total gross amortization of $393,277, but this amount is reduced by the $143,277 interest equivalent shown in Column (c). The net amortization is $250,000 ($393,277 – $143,277). Note that, for the Years 11 through 15, ten percent of the past service costs ($250,000 × .10) still are used to determine the maximum provision.

The interest equivalent decreases each year, because of the smaller difference between the total funding and the cumulative provision. As the interest equivalent decreases, the maximum provision increases. The maximum provision increases more each year, due to the compounding effect of the interest calculation.

Remember that past service costs are amortized at the rate of 10 percent per year until fully amortized. The actual amortization period may not be 10 years in all cases.

The two preceding examples have made extreme assumptions about the treatment of past service costs. In the first example, it was assumed that *no* funding of past service costs occurred; and, in the second example, it was assumed that *all* the past service costs were funded at the inception of the plan. The next example takes a more realistic look at the treatment of past service costs. The assumptions relating to the pension plan are listed in Exhibit IV.

Exhibit IV
Pension Costs with Partial Funding of Past Service Costs

1. Jar, Inc. adopted a pension plan for its employees on January 1, 197A, several years after the company began operations.
2. At the date of adoption of the plan, the company's actuary calculated the past service costs under the plan to be $250,000.
3. On December 31, 197A, the actuary calculated the normal costs for the year to be $12,000; and, on December 31, 197B, the actuarially determined normal costs were $12,900.
4. The company funds all normal costs with the trustee of the plan at the end of each year. In addition, the company has decided to fund the past service costs, at the rate of $18,000 per year, at the same time. Funds deposited with the trustee are assumed to earn six percent interest.

5. The provision for 197A is determined to be $36,000, and the provision for 197B is determined to be $36,475.
6. There are no vested benefits associated with the pension plan.

Since there are past service costs associated with the pension plan, Jar, Inc. will have to calculate the maximum provision, to make sure that the provision indicated does not exceed the maximum. Not all of the past service costs are funded currently, so the company also will have to calculate the minimum provision, to be sure that the indicated provision is not less than the minimum. The new element introduced into this example is the partial funding of the past service costs.

The maximum provision, as defined in APB Opinion No. 8, for 197A is determined as follows:

Normal Costs for 197A	$12,000
10 Percent of Past Service Costs ($250,000 × .10)	25,000
10 Percent of Prior Service Increments	-0-
Interest Equivalent	-0-
Maximum Provision	$37,000

Since the recognition of the pension costs and the funding of both normal and past service costs takes place at the end of the year, there is no interest equivalent for 197A. The minimum provision would be determined as follows:

Normal Costs for 197A	$12,000
Interest Equivalent on the Unfunded Prior Service Costs ($250,000 × .06)	15,000
Provision for Vested Benefits	-0-
Minimum Provision	$27,000

Because the funding of the past service costs takes place at the end of the year, there was $250,000 of unfunded prior service costs for the entire year 197A.

The provision of $36,000, falls between the maximum of $37,000 and the minimum of $27,000, and will be recorded as the provision for 197A. The entry to record the provision is as follows:

Provision for Pension Costs	36,000	
Cash		30,000
Excess of Pension Expense Over Funding		6,000

Jar, Inc. funded the normal costs of $12,000 and the past service costs of $18,000 with the trustee of the plan. The difference between the provision of $36,000 and the funding of $30,000 will be used to determine the interest equivalent under the maximum for 197B.

The computation of the maximum provision for 197B is shown below:

Normal Costs for 197B		$12,900
10 Percent of Past Service Costs ($250,000 × .10)		25,000
10 Percent of Prior Service Increments		-0-
Interest Equivalent ($6,000 × .06)		360
Maximum Provision		$38,260

The minimum provision for 197B is determined as follows:

Normal Costs for 197B		$12,900
Interest Equivalent on the Unfunded Prior Service Costs:		
Prior Service Costs from 197A	$250,000	
Interest Equivalent in 197A	15,000	
Funding of Prior Service Costs	(18,000)	
Unfunded Prior Service Costs	$247,000	
Interest Rate	× .06	14,820
Provision for Vested Benefits		-0-
Minimum Provision		$27,720

The computation of the minimum provision is somewhat more complex than that shown in the previous examples. This is due to the partial funding of the prior service costs. As noted previously, in the computation of the defined minimum, the past service costs become prior service costs for determination of the unfunded prior service costs. Notice that the prior service costs are increased by the interest equivalent determined in 197A, and then reduced by the $18,000 funding that took place at the end of 197A. If the minimum were to be computed for 197C, the $247,000 balance would be increased by the interest equivalent of $14,820, and reduced by the $18,000 funding at the end of 197B.

The indicated provision for 197B is $36,475, which falls between the maximum of $38,260 and the minimum of $27,720, and therefore will be recorded as the provision in 197B. The entry needed to record the provision in 197B would be:

Provision for Pension Costs	36,475	
Cash		30,900
Excess of Pension Expense Over Funding		5,575

The normal costs of $12,900 and the past service costs of $18,000 were funded at the end of the year. At the beginning of 197C, the difference between the provision and the funding is $11,575 ($6,000 from 197A and $5,575 from 197B), which will serve as the basis for computing the interest equivalent under the maximum provision for 197C.

Table IV was developed to illustrate the effects of partial funding on the determination of the maximum pension provision. Once again, the Table is based upon some limiting assumptions. The assumptions are that the normal costs remain constant at $10,000 for the next 10 years, that the company always records the maximum provision as the pension costs for the period and that the normal costs plus $18,000 of past service costs are funded at the end of each year. These assumptions have been made so that the effect of the partial funding can be isolated.

The Table shows that the interest equivalent increases each year, due to the compound interest computation relating to the difference between the provisions and the funding. As the interest equivalent increases, other items remaining stable, the maximum provision also increases. The balance of the cumulative difference between funding and the recorded provisions is equal to $92,265 at the end of the 10-year period. This amount is the difference between two annuity streams, i.e., the assumed annuity of $25,000 for accounting purposes and the actual annuity of $18,000 representing the funding. The computation of the balance is shown below:

	Assumed	**Actual**
Amount of the Annuity	$25,000	$18,000
Present Value Factor of An Amount of an Ordinary Annuity of $1 for 10 Periods at Six Percent	13.1808	13.1808
Amount of Annuity	$329,520	$237,255

The difference between the two annuity streams is equal to $92,265 ($329,520 – $237,255). Another way to look at the computation is to take the $7,000 ($25,000 – $18,000) difference between the two annuities and multiply it by the same present value factor shown above, to arrive at the answer of $92,265.

Table IV

Computation of the Maximum Provision

Year	Normal Cost (a)	10% of Past Service Costs (b)	Interest Equivalent (c)=(g)×6%	Maximum Provision (d)=(a+b+c)	Funding (e)	Difference Between Provision and Funding: Current Period (f)	Difference Between Provision and Funding: Cumulative Total (g)=(g+f)
1	$ 10,000	$ 25,000	-0-	$ 35,000	$ 28,000	$ 7,000	$ 7,000
2	10,000	25,000	$ 420	35,420	28,000	7,420	14,420
3	10,000	25,000	865	35,865	28,000	7,865	22,285
4	10,000	25,000	1,337	36,337	28,000	8,337	30,622
5	10,000	25,000	1,837	36,837	28,000	8,837	39,459
6	10,000	25,000	2,368	37,368	28,000	9,368	48,827
7	10,000	25,000	2,930	37,930	28,000	9,930	58,757
8	10,000	25,000	3,525	38,525	28,000	10,525	69,282
9	10,000	25,000	4,157	39,157	28,000	11,157	80,439
10	10,000	25,000	4,826	39,826	28,000	11,826	92,265
	$100,000	$250,000	$ 22,265	$372,265	$280,000		

The closer the actual funding comes to the assumed funding of $25,000, the smaller the interest equivalent, other items remaining the same. If the actual funding included the normal costs and $25,000 of past service costs, there would be no interest equivalent in the determination of the maximum provision.

Table V was developed to illustrate the computation of the defined minimum provision, using the same assumptions. Note that the interest on the unfunded prior service costs decreases over time as the funding takes place. As the interest equivalent decreases, the minimum provision also decreases, other items remaining the same.

The balance of the unfunded prior service cost is equal to $210,457 at the end of the 10-year period. This amount may be calculated by subtracting the $18,000 compound amount of the annuity from the total of the prior service costs of $250,000 plus earnings accumulated on this amount. The computation is shown below:

Total Prior Service Costs	$250,000	
Present Value Factor for the Amount of $1 for 10 periods at 6 percent	1.79084	
Accumulated Amount of Prior Service Costs		$447,710
Amount of Funding Annuity per Year	$ 18,000	
Present Value Factor for the Amount of an Ordinary Annuity of $1 for 10 Periods at 6 Percent	13.1808	
Amount of Annuity		237,255
Difference		$210,455

The difference between the $210,457 amount shown in Table V and the $210,455 is due to rounding.

Table V

Computation of the Minimum Provision

Year	Normal Cost (a)	Interest on Unfunded Prior Service Costs (b)=(e)×6%	Minimum Provisions (c)=(a+b)	Funding Prior Service Cost (d)	Unfunded Prior Service Cost (e)
Initial Value -	-	-	-	-	$250,000
1	$ 10,000	$ 15,000	$ 25,000	$ 18,000	247,000
2	10,000	14,820	24,820	18,000	243,820
3	10,000	14,629	24,629	18,000	240,449
4	10,000	14,427	24,427	18,000	236,876
5	10,000	14,213	24,213	18,000	233,089
6	10,000	13,985	23,985	18,000	229,074
7	10,000	13,744	23,744	18,000	224,818
8	10,000	13,489	23,489	18,000	220,307
9	10,000	13,218	23,218	18,000	215,525
10	10,000	12,932	22,932	18,000	210,457
	$100,000	$140,457	$240,457	$180,000	

The last comprehensive example of pension accounting is designed to illustrate the effects of an amendment to the pension plan subsequent to adoption. The example also assumes that partial funding of the past service costs will take place. The assumptions listed in Exhibit V provide the necessary information about the pension plan.

Exhibit V

Pension Costs with Amendment to the Plan

1. Jar, Inc. adopted a pension plan for its employees on January 1, 197A, several years after the company began operations.
2. At the date of adoption of the plan, the company's actuary calculated the past service costs under the plan to be $250,000.
3. On December 31, 197A, the actuary calculated the normal costs for the year to be $10,000, which was also the actuarially determined normal costs at December 31, 197B.
4. The company funds all normal costs with the trustee of the plan at the end of each year. In addition, the company has decided to fund the past service costs, at the rate of $20,000 per year, at the same time. Funds deposited with the trustee are assumed to earn four percent.
5. The provision for 197A is determined to be $35,000, and the provision for 197B is determined to be $35,200.
6. There are no vested benefits associated with the pension plan.
7. On January 1, 197C, the company amended the plan to increase the benefits payable to employees upon retirement. As a result of the amendment, the actuary determined that *prior* service costs should be increased $50,000. The company increased the funding of past service costs to $24,000 as a result of the amendment. Normal costs for the year ended December 31, 197C, were determined to be $11,000.
8. The provision for 197C is determined to be $41,408.

Many of the computations and journal entries relating to the first two years of the plan (prior to amendment) already have been discussed in detail. To reduce the amount of repetitive computations, Tables VI and VII have been developed to show the maximum and minimum provisions for the plan. Discussion of the Years 4 through 10 will be deferred for a moment.

Table VI

Computation of the Maximum Provision

Year	Normal Cost (a)	10% of Past Service Costs (b)	10% of Prior Service Increments (c)	Interest Equivalent (d)=(h)×4%	Maximum Provision (e)=(a+b+c+d)	Funding (f)	Difference Between Provision and Funding: Current Period (g)	Difference Between Provision and Funding: Cumulative Total (h)=(h+g)
1	$ 10,000	$ 25,000	$ -	$ -0-	$ 35,000	$ 30,000	$ 5,000	$ 5,000
2	10,000	25,000	-	200	35,200	30,000	5,200	10,200
3	11,000	25,000	5,000	408	41,408	34,000	7,408	17,608
4	11,000	25,000	5,000	704	41,704	34,000	7,704	25,312
5	11,000	25,000	5,000	1,012	42,012	34,000	8,012	33,324
6	11,000	25,000	5,000	1,333	42,333	34,000	8,333	41,657
7	11,000	25,000	5,000	1,666	42,666	34,000	8,666	50,323
8	11,000	25,000	5,000	2,013	43,013	34,000	9,013	59,336
9	11,000	25,000	5,000	2,373	43,373	34,000	9,373	68,709
10	11,000	25,000	5,000	2,748	43,748	34,000	9,748	78,457
11	11,000	-	5,000	3,138	19,138	34,000	(14,862)	63,595
12	11,000	-	5,000	2,544	18,544	34,000	(15,456)	48,139
	$130,000	$250,000	$50,000	$18,139	$448,139	$400,000		

Notice that, in Years 1 and 2 (197A and 197B), the company recorded the maximum provisions of $35,000 and $35,200. The reader may wish to take a few minutes to recompute the values shown in the Table. In Year 3 (197C) there was an amendment to the plan that resulted in a $50,000 increase in prior service costs, i.e., a prior service increment. This event is shown in Table VII. As a result of the amendment, the company increased both its normal costs and the funding of its past service costs. The computation of the maximum provision at the end of Year 3 (197C) is shown below:

Normal Costs for 197C	$11,000
10 Percent of Past Service Costs ($250,000 × .10)	25,000
10 Percent of Prior Service Increments ($50,000 × .10)	5,000
Interest Equivalent ($10,200 × .04)	408
Maximum Provision	$41,408

The provision indicated for 197C is $41,408, which is equal to the maximum provision.

For Years 11 and 12, no past service costs are included in the maximum computation. At the end of Year 10 the original past service costs of $250,000 have been fully amortized and drop out of the computation. The $50,000 increment in prior service costs are fully amortized at the end of Year 12, or 10 years from the date of amendment.

Table VII shows the computation of the minimum provision over the 12-year period. The only new item is the $50,000 addition to the prior service costs at the beginning of Year 3 (197C). Once the $50,000 has been included in the prior service costs, the calculation of the minimum proceeds as before.

Table VII

Computation of the Minimum Provision

Year	Normal Cost (a)	Interest on Unfunded Prior Service Costs (b)=(e)×4%	Minimum Provisions (c)=(a+b)	Funding Prior Service Cost (d)	Unfunded Prior Service Cost (e)
Initial Value -	-	-	-	-	$250,000
1	$10,000	$ 10,000	$ 20,000	$ 20,000	240,000
2	10,000	9,600	19,600	20,000	229,600
Amendment to Plan -	-	-	-	-	279,600
3	11,000	11,184	22,184	24,000	266,784
4	11,000	10,671	21,671	24,000	253,455
5	11,000	10,138	21,138	24,000	239,593
6	11,000	9,584	20,584	24,000	225,177
7	11,000	9,007	20,007	24,000	210,184
8	11,000	8,407	19,407	24,000	194,591
9	11,000	7,784	18,784	24,000	178,375
10	11,000	7,135	18,135	24,000	161,510
11	11,000	6,460	17,460	24,000	143,970
12	11,000	5,759	16,759	24,000	125,729
	$130,000	$105,729	$235,729	$280,000	

This final comprehensive example completes the discussion of pension accounting in general. Two special items must be considered before the entire discussion is complete. The first deals with the determination of a required provision for vested benefits, and the second deals with the handling of any actuarial gains or losses resulting from estimates of the pension costs.

Provision for Vested Benefits

Vested benefits are defined in the Opinion (Appendix B) as "benefits that are not contingent on the employee's continuing in the service of the employer." Under many actuarial cost methods, a provision for vested benefits is included in either the normal costs or the past service costs. The Opinion has specified certain procedures to insure that the value of vested benefits is given proper *accounting* recognition.

The accountant must determine a proper accounting provision for vested benefits when:

(1) The actuarially determined value of the vested benefits *exceed* the total of the pension fund and the accounting accruals shown on the balance sheet at the beginning and end of the period, i.e., there is an excess of vested benefits over the fund balance and accounting accrual; and

(2) The excess at the end of the period is not at least five percent less than the excess at the beginning of the period.

These conditions indicate that accounting consideration of vested benefits will occur only when the value of those benefits exceed accounting recognition given to normal and past service costs after funding, and then only if the value of the vested benefits is not decreased by at least five percent.

If the conditions described in (1) and (2) above exist, the additional provision for vested benefits will be the smallest of the following amounts:

(1) Five percent of the beginning excess of the vested benefits over the sum of the accounting balance sheet accrual and the pension fund balance;

(2) An amount required to reduce this beginning excess by five percent; or

(3) An amount that would make the total provision equal to the total of: (a) normal costs; (b) "an amount equivalent to amortization, on a 40-year basis, of the past service costs"; (c) "amounts equivalent to amortization, on a 40-year basis, of the amounts of any increases or decreases in prior service cost arising on amendments of the plan"; and (d) "interest equivalents . . . on the difference between provisions and amounts funded." (APB Opinion No. 8, Paragraph 17(a))

The last item assumes the amortization of the past service cost and the prior service increments on a 40-year basis.

Based upon all of the conditions stated above, it would appear that accounting recognition of vested benefits would occur only in rare cases. If the value of vested benefits were included in the computation of past service costs, and those costs were being amortized over a period of less than 40 years, the accountant would not be concerned with a computation of an additional provision for vested benefits in the determination of the minimum provision. Even if this were not the case, but the excess vested benefits were decreasing by five percent, no separate accounting recognition would be required.

Realizing that an additional provision for vested benefits will enter into the computation of the minimum provision only in very specific situations, the assumptions listed in Exhibit VI will be used to illustrate the computation of the provision.

Exhibit VI
Provision for Vested Benefits

1. Jar, Inc. adopted a pension plan for its employees on January 1, 197A, several years after the company began operations.

2. At the date of adoption of the plan, the actuary calculated the past service costs to be $250,000.
3. The actuarially determined amount of the normal costs for 197A and 197B was $10,000 annually.
4. Jar, Inc. funds all normal costs at the end of each year. The company has elected not to fund the past service costs. Funds deposited with the plan trustee earn interest at the rate of six percent.
5. The actuary has determined that the value of the vested benefits under the plan are as follows:

January 1, 197A	$15,000
December 31, 197A	$35,000
December 31, 197B	$61,330

Since any additional provision for vested benefits only enters into the determination of the minimum provision, the maximum provision will be ignored in this example. The computation of the minimum provision for 197A, before giving consideration to the provision for vested benefits, is shown below:

Normal Costs for 197A	$10,000
Interest Equivalent on the Unfunded Prior Service Costs ($250,000 × .06)	15,000
Minimum Provision Before Considering Vested Benefits	$25,000

Assume that the provision for 197A was determined to be $25,000. The following entry would be made by Jar, Inc. to record the provision in 197A:

Provision for Pension Costs	25,000	
Cash		10,000
Excess of Pension Expense Over Funding		15,000

If this entry were made, the following account balances would result:

	Pension Fund	Balance Sheet Accrual
Balance—January 1, 197A	-0-	-0-
Increase at end of 197A	$10,000	$15,000
Balance—December 31, 197A	$10,000	$15,000

The total of the fund balance and the balance sheet accrual would be zero on January 1, 197A, and $25,000 ($10,000 + $15,000) at the end of 197A. These totals now must be compared with the vested benefits determined by the actuary. The comparison is shown below:

Vested Benefits—January 1, 197A	$15,000	
Accrual and Fund Balance—January 1, 197A	-0-	
Excess Vested Benefits—January 1, 197A		$15,000

Vested Benefits—December 31, 197A	$35,000	
Accrual and Fund Balance—December 31, 197A	(25,000)	
Excess Vested Benefits—December 31, 197A		10,000
Decrease in Excess Vested Benefits		$ 5,000

There will be no additional provision for vested benefits in 197A, because the decrease during the year was more than the five percent required. For purposes of illustration, the tests to be performed to arrive at this answer are shown below:

(1) 5 Percent of the Beginning Excess ($15,000 × .05)	$ 750
(2) Amount Required to Reduce the Beginning Excess by 5 Percent	[a]$-0-
(3) Amortization of Past Service Costs Over a 40-Year Period ($250,000 / 15.0463[b])	$16,615
Interest Equivalent on Unfunded Prior Service Costs	(15,000)
Amount Needed to Make Provision Equal to Amortization Over 40-Year Period	$ 1,615

[a] Since the excess already is reduced by more than $750, the amount required to reduce the beginning excess by five percent is zero.
[b] Present Value Factor for an ordinary annuity for 40 periods at six percent.

Item 3, above, indicates that the minimum provision would have to be increased by $1,615 to equate it with the amortization of the past service costs over a 40-year period. The additional provision for vested benefits will be the smallest of (1), (2) or (3), above; therefore, the additional provision would be equal to zero.

To determine if there is any provision required for vested benefits in 197B, the computation of the minimum provision, before consideration of vested benefits, is shown below:

Normal Costs for 197B		$10,000
Interest Equivalent on the Unfunded Prior Service Costs:		
Prior Service Costs—January 1, 197A	$250,000	
Interest Equivalent in 197A	15,000	
Balance January 1, 197B	$265,000	
Interest Rate	× .06	
Interest Equivalent in 197B		15,900
Minimum Provision Before Considering Vested Benefits		$25,900

If this amount were used to record the provision for the year, the following account balances would result:

	Pension Fund	Balance Sheet Accrual
Balance—January 1, 197B	$10,000	$15,000
Increase at end of 197B	10,000	15,900
Fund Earnings in 197B ($10,000 × .06)	600	
Balance—December 31, 197B	$20,600	$30,900

The total of the fund balance and the balance sheet accrual would be $25,000 on January 1, 197B, and $51,500 ($20,600 + $30,900) on December 31, 197B. These totals are compared with the actuarially determined value of the vested benefits at the beginning and end of 197B to determine if there will be any additional provision for vested benefits. The comparison is shown below:

Vested Benefits—January 1, 197B	$35,000	
Accrual and Fund Balance—January 1, 197B	(25,000)	
Excess Vested Benefits—January 1, 197B		$10,000
Vested Benefits—December 31, 197B	$61,330	
Accrual and Fund Balance—December 31, 197B	(51,500)	
Excess Vested Benefits—December 31, 197B		9,830
Decrease in Excess Vested Benefits		$ 170

While the excess vested benefits did decrease during the year, it must be determined if they decreased by a sufficient amount. To determine this, it will be necessary to conduct the three tests indicated in the Opinion. The results of the tests are shown below:

(1) 5 Percent of Beginning Excess ($10,000 × .05)		$ 500
(2) Amount Required to Reduce the Beginning Excess by 5 Percent:		
Required Reduction	$500	
Reduction Computed Above	(170)	
Additional Reduction		$ 330
(3) Amortization of Past Service Costs Over a 40 Year Period ($250,000/15.0463)		$16,615
Interest Equivalent on Unfunded Prior Service Costs		(15,900)
Amount Needed to Make Provision Equal to Amortization Over 40 Year Period		$ 715

In 197B, an additional provision for vested benefits is required. The amount to be used is $330, the smallest of the three values computed above. The minimum provision recorded in 197B would be equal to the $25,900 previously calculated, plus $330 for vested benefits. The entry to record the provision for 197B would be:

Provision for Pension Costs	26,230	
Cash		10,000
Excess of Pension Expense Over Funding		16,230

After this entry has been made, the balance sheet accrual will have a balance of $31,230 ($15,000 from 197A + $16,230 from 197B), and the balance in the pension fund still will be $20,600. Based upon this information, the following relationship exists between the vested benefits and the total of the accrual and fund balance:

Vested Benefits—December 31, 197B	$61,330
Accrual and Fund Balance—December 31, 197B	(51,830)
Excess Vested Benefits—December 31, 197B	$ 9,500

The beginning excess vested benefits of $10,000 must be reduced by five percent, or $500. As a result of the entry recorded above, the ending excess is equal to $9,500, which is equal to the beginning excess reduced by $500.

The Opinion takes a long-run view of the excess vested benefits at any point in time. The excess vested benefits are amortized over future periods in a systematic manner through adjustments to the minimum provision.

The last major area covered in this discussion deals with the accounting treatment of any actuarial gains or losses resulting from the pension plan.

Actuarial Gains and Losses

Actuarial gains or losses are defined (APB Opinion No. 8, Appendix B) as "the effects on actuarially calculated pension costs of (a) deviations between actual prior experience and the actuarial assumptions used or (b) changes in actuarial assumptions as to future events." For example, the actuarially determined value of the past service costs may have been based upon certain assumptions about employee turnover, among other things; and future events may indicate that the assumed turnover was substantially different than the actual turnover. Another example would be where the funds invested in the plan earned a higher or lower rate of return than anticipated. Both of these events influence the amounts determined by the actuary and result in actuarial gains or losses.

The Opinion states that actuarial gains or losses should be spread or averaged over current and future periods in some reasonable manner. These gains or losses are *not* to be recognized in the current period.

The net gains and losses may be spread or averaged through a separate adjustment to *normal* costs for the period. If this is done, the gains and losses should be spread over a period of 10 to 20 years. The net gains and losses could be spread over this period of time, using a simple straight-line technique or any other systematic method. If the net gains and losses are averaged, an appropriate moving weighted average should be computed.

If an actuarial gain is determined to be $2,000, and it is to be spread over a 10-year period, using the straight-line method, $200 of the gain would serve to reduce normal costs in the current period, and the remaining $1,800 would be deferred for use in future periods.

Net actuarial *gains* also may be spread or averaged through a reduction in the unamortized past service costs. When this method is elected, the reduction should be made prior to the determination of the amount of amortization or the calculation of interest equivalents. A problem is created if there is less than 10 years remaining for the amortization of the past service costs. The Opinion indicates that gains and losses should be spread over 10 to 20 years. If there are less than 10 years remaining in the amortization of the past service costs, this method of spreading should not be used. Regardless of the method used, the actuarial gains and losses should not be spread over a period of time less than 10 years.

Required Disclosures

The disclosures required in connection with the pension plan are identified in Paragraph 46 of the Opinion, and are listed below:

(1) Identification of the plan and the employees covered;

(2) Statement of accounting and funding policies;

(3) Statement of current provision for pension costs;

(4) Identification of any excess vested benefits; and

(5) Identification of any material changes that would prevent interperiod comparability of the information given.

The footnotes to the 1976 Annual Report of General Electric Company have been provided to illustrate the disclosures relating to the various pension plans at the company. As indicated in the notes, funds deposited with the Pension Trust are assumed to earn interest at the rate of six percent. The unfunded liabilities associated with the pension plans are being amortized over a 20-year period. The disclosure is quite interesting, because it provides detailed information about the Pension Trust, as well as the required accounting disclosures.

General Electric Company (Dec)

Summary of Significant Accounting Policies

Pensions—Investments of the General Electric Pension Trust, which funds the obligations of the General Electric Pension Plan, are carried at amortized cost plus programmed appreciation in the common stock portfolio. Recognition of programmed appreciation is carried out on a systematic basis which does not give undue weight to short-term market fluctuations. This recognition of programmed appreciation is limited by a maximum ratio, calculated on a moving basis, of book to market values over a multiyear period.

The funding program for the Pension Trust uses 6% as the estimated rate of future income. This rate includes systematic recognition of appreciation in the common stock portfolio.

Unfunded liabilities of the Trust are being amortized over a 20-year period.

Costs of a separate, supplementary pension plan, primarily affecting long-service professional and managerial employees, are not funded. Current service costs and amortization of past service costs over a period of 20 years are being charged to Company operating costs currently.

Notes to Financial Statements

Note 4: Employee Benefits—General Electric and its affiliates have a number of pension plans, the total Company costs of which was $240.1 million in 1976 and $193.1 million in 1975. The most significant of these plans is the General Electric Pension Plan, in which substantially all employees in the U.S. are participating. Obligations of the Pension Plan are funded through the GE Pension Trust.

The limit described above for recognizing programmed appreciation in the common stock portfolio was not reached at year-end 1976 or 1975.

Earnings of the Trust, including the programmed recognition of appreciation, as a percentage of book value of the portfolio were 6.4% for 1976 and 6.6% for 1975.

Unfunded liabilities of the Trust were estimated to be $707 million at December 31, 1976, compared with $581 million at the end of 1975, the increase resulting primarily from amendments to the Plan which became effective July 1, 1976. Unfunded vested liabilities included in these amounts were $568 million and $447 million at December 31, 1976 and 1975, respectively. Estimated market value of Trust assets at the end of 1976 was $3,636 million and $2,993 million at the end of 1975.

Financial statements of the Pension Trust are below.

Costs of a separate supplementary pension plan, primarily affecting long-service professional and managerial employees, were $9.5 million in 1976 and $4.3 million in 1975. Unamortized liabilities for this supplementary plan were $74 million and $31 million at December 31, 1976 and 1975, respectively. The increase in costs and unamortized liabilities resulted principally from amendments to the plan effective January 1, 1976.

Utah has separate pension plans which are substantially fully funded and the costs of which are included in the total Company costs reported above.

Incentive compensation plans apply to over 3,000 key employees. Amounts included in costs and expenses for incentive compensation, including Utah's Bonus Program, were $40.1 million in 1976 and $35.2 million in 1975.

General Electric Pension Trust

(In millions)	1976	1975
Operating statement		
Total assets at January 1	$3,047.5	$2,762.0
Company contributions	204.5	170.2
Employee contributions	59.4	47.2
	263.9	217.4
Dividends, interest and sundry income	144.9	128.0
Common stock appreciation:		
Realized	11.7	16.7
Accrued	76.6	70.7
Total programmed	88.3	87.4
Pensions paid	(158.5)	(147.3)
Total assets at December 31	$3,386.1	$3,047.5
Financial position—December 31		
U.S. government obligations and guarantees	$ 103.6	$ 97.2
Corporate bonds, notes and mineral interests	318.0	335.5
Real estate and mortgages	672.3	589.2
Common stocks and convertibles	2,177.4	1,831.1
	3,271.3	2,853.0
Cash and short-term investments	57.4	123.1
Other assets—net	57.4	71.4
Total assets	$3,386.1	$3,047.5
Funded liabilities:		
Liability to pensioners	$1,265.9	$1,153.8
Liability for pensions to participants not yet retired	2,120.2	1,893.7
Total funded liabilities	$3,386.1	$3,047.5

Source: *Accounting Trends & Techniques,* Copyright © 1977 by the American Institute of Certified Public Accountants, Inc., p.241.

Topic 10

Foreign Currency

Detail Contents

SFAS No. 8 (October 1975)

Accounting for the Translation of Foreign Currency Transactions and Foreign Currency Financial Statements

and

SFAS No. 20 (December 1977)

Accounting for Forward Exchange Contracts

Note: SFAS No. 20 is basically a modification of certain conditions previously specified for the deferral of gains and losses on forward exchange contracts.

SFAS No. 8 specifies procedures that must be used when accounting for a foreign currency transaction or when translating foreign currency financial statements. A foreign currency transaction is defined in the Statement (Paragraph 3) as a transaction in which an enterprise:

> buys or sells on credit goods or services whose prices are stated in foreign currency, borrows or lends funds and the amounts payable or receivable are denominated in foreign currency, is a party to an unperformed forward exchange contract, or for other reasons, acquires assets or incurs liabilities denominated in foreign currency.

The important detail to remember in connection with foreign currency transactions is that the amount involved is stated in a foreign currency, not in a dollar amount.

For purposes of the Statement, the term "foreign currency financial statements" means those statements whose assets, liabilities, revenues and expenses are measured in a foreign currency and that will be combined, consolidated or subjected to the equity method of accounting for investments. Financial statements that are denominated in a foreign currency, but that will not be combined, consolidated or accounted for by the equity method are not subject to the provisions of the Statement.

The discussion that follows is divided into the two major subjects of the Statement: Foreign Currency Transactions and Foreign Currency Financial Statements.

Foreign Currency Transactions

Because the exchange relationship between the dollar and other foreign currencies is variable, it is possible for a transaction involving foreign currency to result in a gain or loss. The gain or loss is a result of the changing value of the dollar in relation to foreign currencies. Prior to the issuance of SFAS No. 8, some companies recognized these gains or losses currently; others deferred the recognition of the gains or losses through the use of allowance accounts or other means. In an effort to narrow the possible treatment of transaction gains or losses, SFAS No. 8 was issued.

Flowchart I depicts the decision process and accounting procedures to be used in accounting for foreign currency transactions. The following section will discuss the major provisions of the Statement, through the use of the Flowchart, and will provide technical examples to reinforce the general discussion.

Flowchart and General Discussion—Foreign Currency Transactions That Are not the Result of Forward Exchange Contracts

The various types of foreign currency transactions have been identified above. Notice that Flowchart I is divided into two major sections. The left side of the Flowchart deals with foreign currency transactions involving the purchase or sale of goods and the borrowing or lending of funds. The right, and somewhat more complex, side of the Flowchart deals with forward exchange contracts.

FLOWCHART I

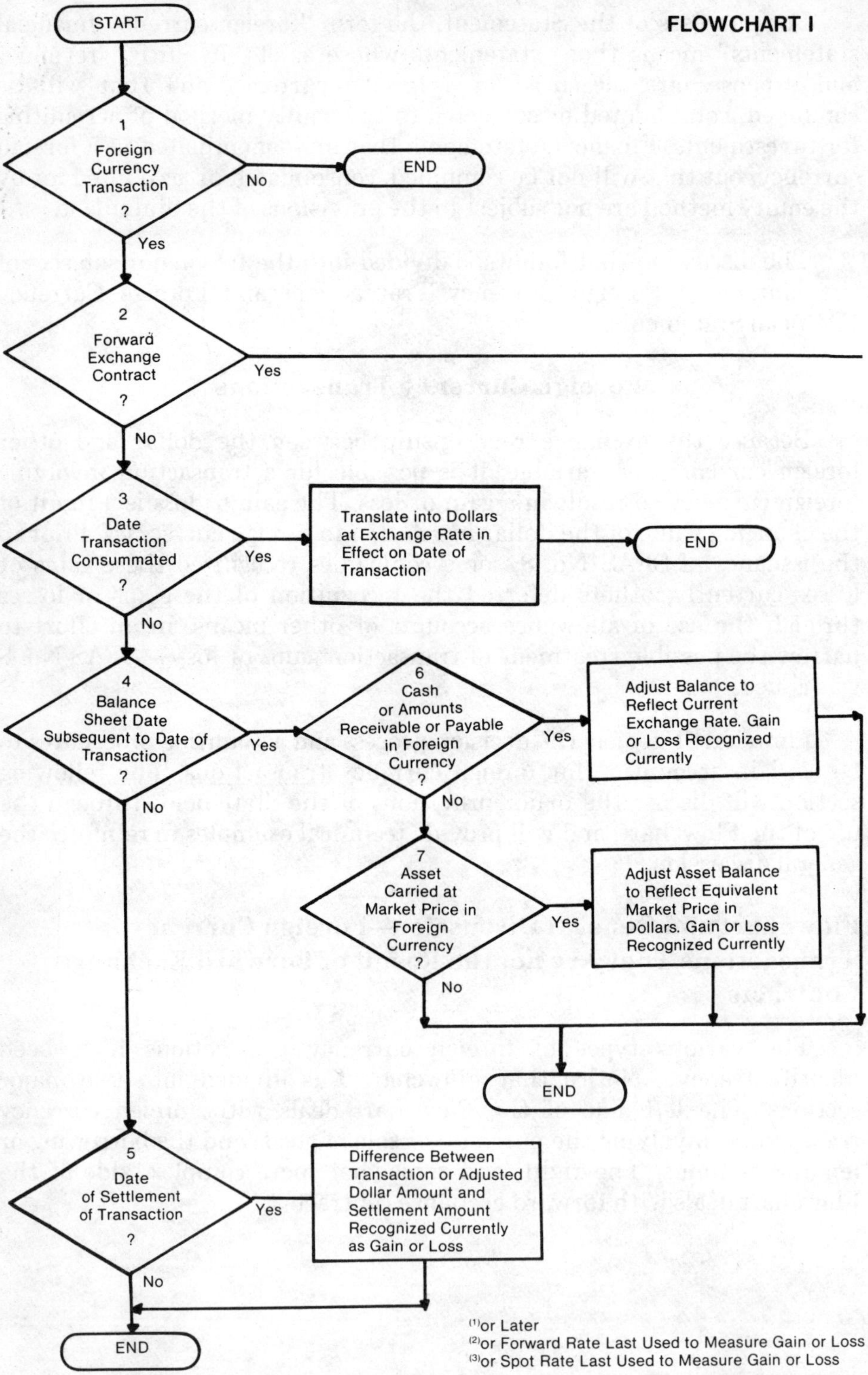
START
1
Foreign
Currency
Transaction
?
No
END
Yes
2
Forward
Exchange
Contract
?
Yes
No
3
Date
Transaction
Consummated
?
Yes
Translate into Dollars
at Exchange Rate in
Effect on Date of
Transaction
END
No
4
Balance
Sheet Date
Subsequent to Date of
Transaction
?
Yes
6
Cash
or Amounts
Receivable or Payable
in Foreign
Currency
?
Yes
Adjust Balance to
Reflect Current
Exchange Rate. Gain
or Loss Recognized
Currently
No
No
7
Asset
Carried at
Market Price in
Foreign
Currency
?
Yes
Adjust Asset Balance
to Reflect Equivalent
Market Price in
Dollars. Gain or Loss
Recognized Currently
No
END
5
Date
of Settlement
of Transaction
?
Yes
Difference Between
Transaction or Adjusted
Dollar Amount and
Settlement Amount
Recognized Currently
as Gain or Loss
No
END
(1)or Later
(2)or Forward Rate Last Used to Measure Gain or Loss
(3)or Spot Rate Last Used to Measure Gain or Loss

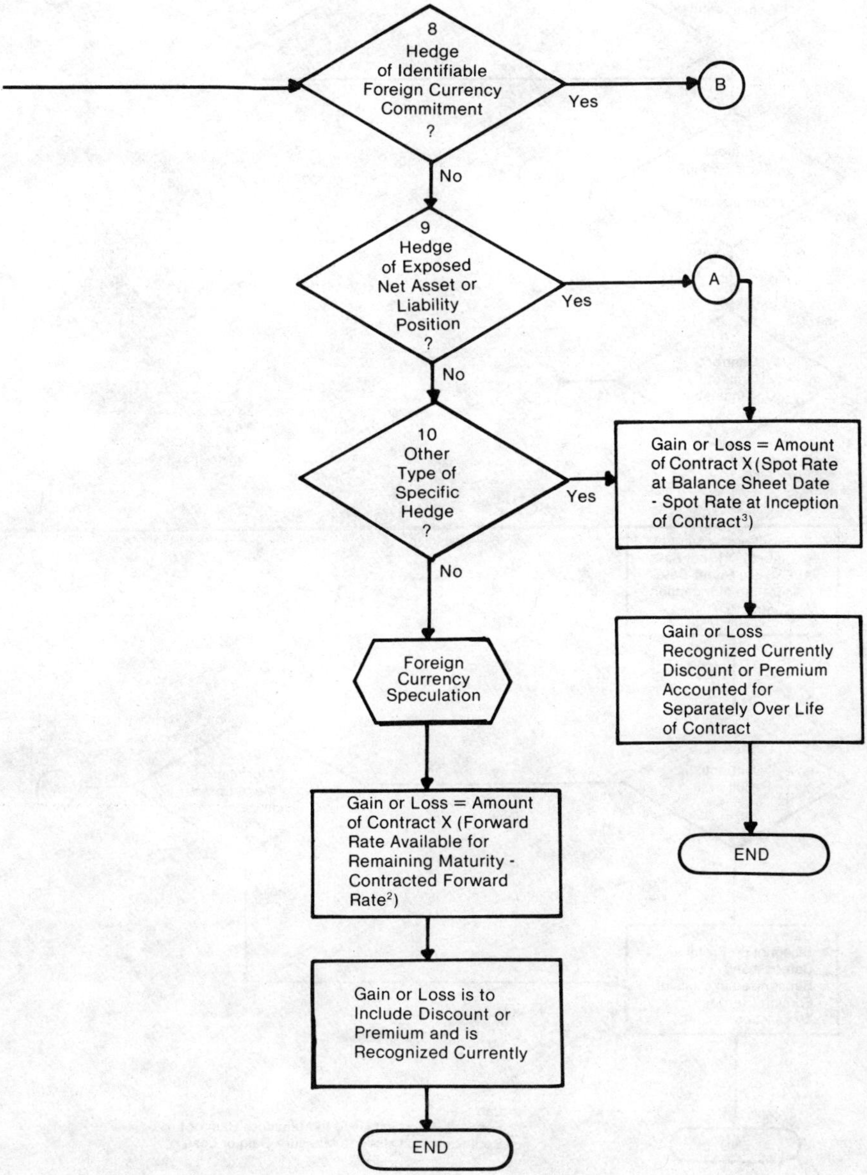
8
Hedge of Identifiable Foreign Currency Commitment ?
Yes
B
No
9
Hedge of Exposed Net Asset or Liability Position ?
Yes
A
No
10
Other Type of Specific Hedge ?
Yes
No
Gain or Loss = Amount of Contract X (Spot Rate at Balance Sheet Date - Spot Rate at Inception of Contract[3])
Gain or Loss Recognized Currently Discount or Premium Accounted for Separately Over Life of Contract
END
Foreign Currency Speculation
Gain or Loss = Amount of Contract X (Forward Rate Available for Remaining Maturity - Contracted Forward Rate[2])
Gain or Loss is to Include Discount or Premium and is Recognized Currently
END

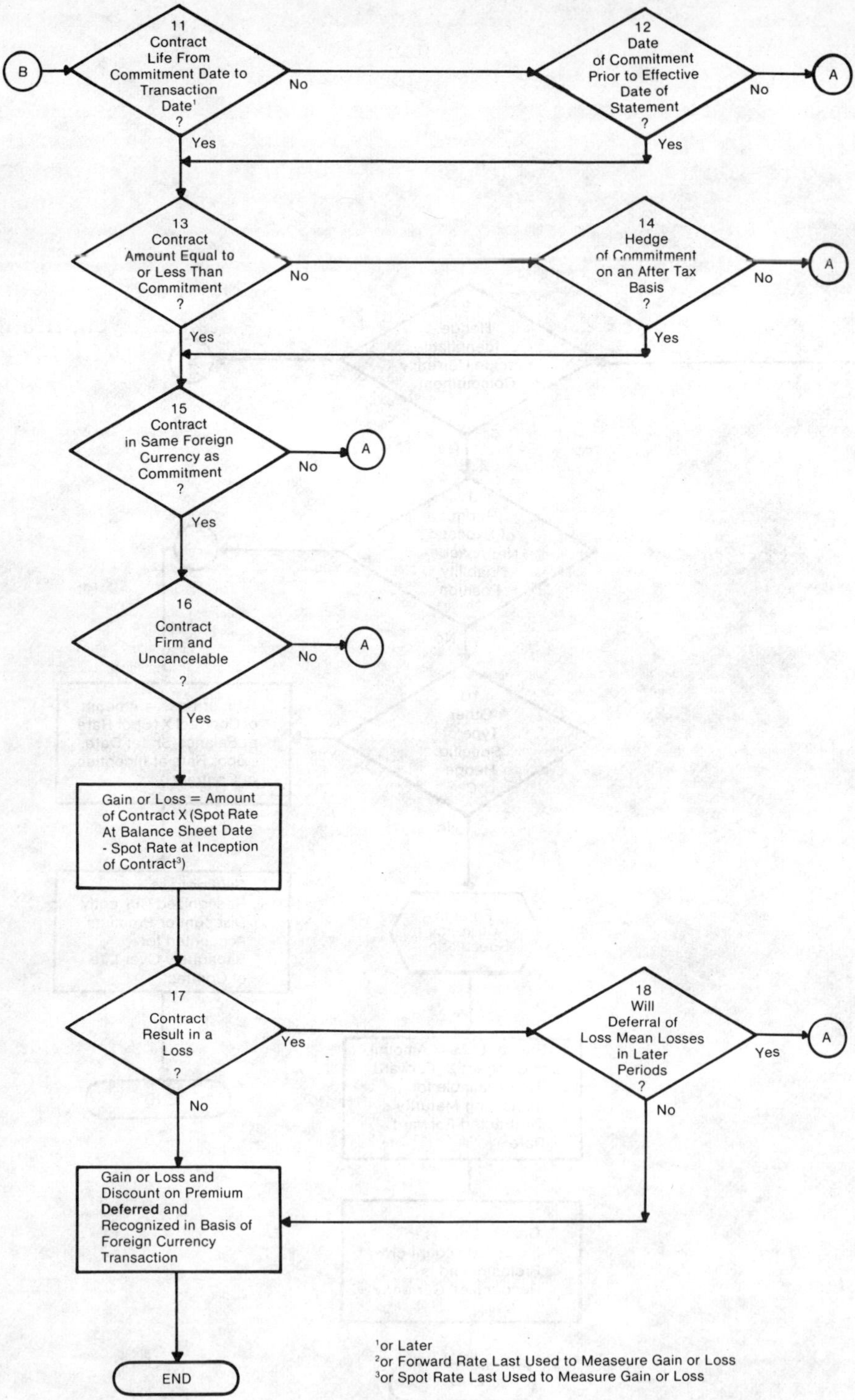

[1]or Later
[2]or Forward Rate Last Used to Measeure Gain or Loss
[3]or Spot Rate Last Used to Measure Gain or Loss

Assume that a company enters into a foreign currency transaction (Block 1) that is not a forward exchange contract (Block 2). There are three dates of importance in determining the proper accounting for such a transaction. The first significant date is the date the transaction is entered into by the company (Block 3). On the date of the transaction, the company should translate the foreign currency amount into dollars at the exchange rate in effect on that date. The exchange rate is nothing more than the cost in dollars of one unit of foreign currency. For example, if it took $1.25 to buy one unit of foreign currency on any particular date, the relationship could be expressed as FC1 = $1.25, where "FC" stands for the name of a specific foreign currency, e.g., pound sterling, yen, lira or peso. Foreign exchange quotations are listed every day in the *Wall Street Journal.* The exchange rate in effect on any given day will be referred to in this discussion as the *current rate,* or the *spot rate,* for that day. The Statement (Paragraph 243) defines the spot rate as "the exchange rate for immediate delivery of currencies exchanged." Once the foreign currency amount has been translated into dollars at the transaction date, the accounts involved will be carried at those dollar balances until the settlement date of the transaction or the next balance sheet date, if it is before the settlement date.

Assume that there is a balance sheet date, either annual or interim, between the date of the transaction and the scheduled settlement date (Block 4). If the account involved in the transaction represents cash or amounts payable or receivable that originally were measured in a foreign currency, the account balance should be adjusted to reflect the current rate in effect on the balance sheet date (Block 6). If the current rate on the balance sheet date is different from the current rate used to translate the amount on the transaction date, a gain or loss will result and should be recognized at the balance sheet date. The gain or loss will be included in the income statement for the current period. Examples of accounts that represent cash or amounts payable or receivable would include cash, accounts and notes receivable and payable, long-term debt, premium or discount on long-term debt, accrued expenses, refundable deposits and cash surrender value of life insurance. Of course, this list is not meant to be all-inclusive, but does indicate the type of accounts under consideration.

If, at a balance sheet date, the account under consideration does not represent cash, or amounts receivable or payable, but does represent an asset account that is carried at market value, that account should be adjusted to reflect the current market price in dollars (Block 7). Examples of these types of accounts would include marketable securities carried at market prices and inventories carried at replacement cost or net realizable value. Any difference between the translated amount at the transaction date and that at the balance sheet date will be a gain or loss that should be recognized currently.

The last date of importance for a foreign currency transaction that is not a forward exchange contract is the date of settlement (Block 5). If there were no intervening balance sheet date between the transaction date and the settlement date, any difference between the translated dollar amount on the transaction date and the dollar amount resulting from the settlement of the foreign currency amount would be recognized as a gain or loss in the current period income statement. On the other hand, if there were an intervening balance sheet date between the transaction date and the settlement date, the gain or loss to be recognized would be measured by the difference between the adjusted dollar balance at the balance sheet date and the dollar amount resulting from the settlement.

Technical Considerations—Foreign Currency Transactions That Are not the Result of Forward Exchange Contracts

To illustrate the accounting for a foreign currency transaction that does not involve a forward exchange contract, assume that a U.S. company purchases merchandise for resale from a foreign supplier for FC500,000 on November 10, 19A. The terms of the sale are "net 30" and the U.S. company is to be billed in foreign currency. The inventories are carried at cost on the books of the U.S. company. On November 10, the current exchange rate is FC1 = $.75.

Based on this information, the dollar equivalent of the FC500,000 at the exchange rate in effect on the transaction date would be $375,000 (FC500,000 × $.75). Therefore, the U.S. company would record the following journal entry on the date of transaction:

11/10/197A	Inventory	375,000	
	Accounts Payable		375,000

Assuming that the U.S. company has a December 31 year end, the next date of importance is the date of settlement, December 10, 197A. For the sake of simplicity, assume that the U.S. company purchases a bank draft payable to the foreign supplier, rather than actually purchasing the foreign currency. On the date of settlement, the current exchange rate is FC1 = $.74. Therefore, the U.S. company would pay $370,000 (FC500,000 × $.74) to the bank to purchase a draft for FC500,000. The journal entry to record the settlement of the amount payable would be as follows:

12/10/19A	Accounts Payable	375,000	
	Exchange Gain		5,000
	Cash		370,000

The transaction results in an exchange gain to the U.S. company, because it takes fewer dollars to purchase the same number of units of foreign currency. The amount of the gain may be computed by multiplying the amount of the obligation by the difference between the exchange rates on the two dates (FC500,000 × \$.01 = \$5,000). The gain will be reported in the current period income statement as a nonoperating item. Had it cost more dollars to purchase the same number of units of foreign currency, e.g., if FC1 = \$.77, the transaction would have resulted in a loss to the U.S. company.

The basic example shown above will be expanded to illustrate the proper accounting when a balance sheet date occurs between the transaction date and the settlement date. For purposes of this second example, again assume that a U.S. company purchases inventory for FC500,000 from the foreign supplier. The merchandise is purchased on December 18, 197A, and the terms of payment are "net 30" in foreign currency. The inventory purchased will be carried at cost on the books of the U.S. company. Once again, the U.S. company will arrange for a bank draft, rather than purchasing the currency. The following exchange rates are in effect on the dates indicated:

December 18, 197A FC1 = \$.75 (date of transaction)
December 31, 197A FC1 = \$.72 (balance sheet date)
January 17, 197B FC1 = \$.74 (settlement date)

On the date of transaction, the dollar equivalent of FC500,000 is \$375,000 (FC500,000 × \$.75), and the following entry would be required:

12/18/197A	Inventory	375,000	
	Accounts Payable		375,000

At the balance sheet date, the account payable must be adjusted, because it represents an amount payable. The inventory account will *not* be adjusted, because it does not represent cash, or amounts receivable or payable, or an asset carried at market price. The determination of the gain or loss to be recognized at the balance sheet date is shown below:

Payable at Transaction Date (FC500,000 × \$.75)	\$375,000
Payable at Balance Sheet Date (FC500,000 × \$.72)	360,000
Exchange Gain for 197A	\$ 15,000

The reason the amount represents a gain is that it took fewer dollars to purchase the same number of units of foreign currency. The journal entry required at December 31, 197A, is as follows:

12/31/197A	Accounts Payable	15,000	
	Exchange Gain		15,000

The carrying amount of the account payable is now \$360,000 (\$375,000 – \$15,000) and has been adjusted to reflect the current exchange rate. The exchange gain will be included in the 197A income statement as a nonoperating item.

At the settlement date, the U.S. company must pay \$370,000 to purchase a bank draft for FC500,000 (FC500,000 × \$.74). Any gain or loss on the settlement date will be determined by comparing the adjusted payable with the cost to liquidate the payable. The gain or loss is calculated below:

Adjusted Amount of the Payable	$360,000
Cost to Settle Payable	370,000
Exchange Loss	$ 10,000

The entry required to record the settlement of the payable is as follows:

1/17/197B Accounts Payable	360,000	
Exchange Loss	10,000	
Cash		370,000

The exchange loss of $10,000 will be included in the 197B income statement. As a result of the above series of entries, an exchange gain of $15,000 was recognized in 197A, and an exchange loss of $10,000 was recognized in 197B.

Both of the examples shown above are quite straightforward and will serve as a good base for the discussion and examples relating to forward exchange contracts.

Flowchart and General Discussion—Forward Exchange Contracts

A forward exchange contract is defined in the Statement (Paragraph 22) as "an agreement to exchange at a specified future date currencies of different countries at a specified rate." A company involved in a foreign currency transaction would enter into a forward exchange contract to protect itself against the risks associated with changing exchange rates. In effect, the forward exchange contract allows the company to negotiate a fixed exchange price for the transaction. A forward exchange contract generally involves a third-party broker in the foreign currency transaction.

To illustrate, a company may negotiate with a foreign currency broker to pay $17,100 for FC9,000, to be delivered in 90 days. In this case the *forward rate* is FC1 = $1.90 ($17,100/FC9,000). If, 90 days hence, on the date the foreign currency is needed, the current rate is FC1 = $1.95, it would cost the company $17,550 to obtain FC9,000. If the company had not entered into the forward contract, a loss of $450 ($17,100 − $17,550) would result. However, because of the forward exchange contract, the company will pay $17,100 and receive FC9,000.

Generally, there is a difference between the current or spot rate and the forward rate on any given day. This difference is treated as a discount or premium on the forward contract. The Statement concludes, in Paragraph 212, that the discount or premium is due to interest rate differentials between the countries whose currencies are involved in the forward exchange contract. Based upon this conclusion, it normally would be appropriate to account for the discount or premium over the life of the forward contract.

If a company is involved in a foreign exchange transaction (Block 1), and enters into a forward exchange contract (Block 2), it is important to determine the reason for the forward contract before the proper accounting can be determined. If the intent of the forward contract is to serve as a hedge on an identifiable foreign currency commitment (Block 8), one accounting treatment is appropriate. However, if the forward contract is intended to hedge an exposed net asset or liability position (Block 9) or serve as some other type of specific hedge (Block 10), a second accounting treatment is required. Finally, if the forward contract is merely an attempt by the company to speculate in the foreign currency market, a third accounting treatment is appropriate.

Hedge of Identifiable Foreign Currency Commitment

The two examples illustrated above for foreign currency transactions involved an identifiable foreign currency commitment, i.e., the obligation to pay a specified amount of foreign currency on a specified future date. In an attempt to offset the effects of foreign currency fluctuations, the U.S. company could have entered into a forward exchange contract.

When a company enters into a forward exchange contract as a hedge of an identifiable foreign currency commitment, any gain or loss, along with any discount or premium, may be *deferred* and included in the basis of the foreign currency transaction. For the gain or loss to be deferred, the forward contract must meet certain conditions. SFAS No. 8 identifies four specific conditions to be met and SFAS No. 20, "Accounting for Forward Exchange Contracts," refines two of the conditions. The first condition states that the life of the forward exchange contract must run from the date of the foreign currency commitment to the date the transaction is consummated, or later (Block 11). SFAS No. 20 modifies this condition by including those forward exchange contracts that were entered into before March 31, 1978, whose life runs to the date of the transaction, or later (Block 12). The second condition specifies that the amount of the forward contract must be equal to, or less than, the amount of the commitment (Block 13). This condition also was modified by SFAS No. 20 to include forward contracts where the contracts exceed the amount of the commitment on a before-tax basis, but the reason for the excess amount is that the hedge was carried out on an "after tax" basis (Block 14). To be able to defer the entire gain or loss on the forward contract, the after-tax amount of the hedge still must be equal to, or less than, the amount of the commitment. If the amount of the forward contract, on an after-tax basis, is greater than the amount of the commitment, only the gain or loss on the amount of the commitment may be deferred. Any gain or loss on the excess amount of the forward contract must be recognized currently. The third condition states that the forward contract must be denominated in the same foreign currency as the commitment (Block 15). The final condition specifies that the forward contract must be firm and uncancelable (Block 16). If *all* these conditions are met, all gains and some losses will be deferred, rather than recognized in the current period. Gains and losses so deferred will enter into the basis of the foreign currency transaction.

The amount of the deferred gain or loss will be equal to the difference between the spot rate at the balance sheet date and the spot rate at the inception of the forward contract, multiplied by the amount of the forward contract. Notice that the *forward rate* does not enter into the calculation of the gain or loss, but is used to determine any discount or premium. The discount or premium is the difference between the forward rate and the spot rate at the inception of the forward contract, multiplied by the amount of the forward contract.

One final test is applicable to any losses in connection with forward exchange contracts that are intended to serve as a hedge of an identifiable foreign currency commitment (Block 17). If the deferral of the loss might lead to recognizing losses in future periods, the loss should not be deferred (Block 18).

To illustrate the proper accounting for a forward exchange contract intended to serve as a hedge of an identifiable foreign currency commitment, assume that, on December 1, 197A, a U.S. company agrees to purchase a piece of equipment from a foreign manufacturer for FC1,500,000. The equipment is to be delivered in 90 days, and payment is due upon receipt of the equipment. On the same day, the company enters into a noncancelable forward exchange contract with an exchange broker for the delivery of FC1,500,000 in 90 days at the cost of $255,000. The forward rate is therefore $.17 ($255,000/FC1,500,000); and, for purposes of this example, the spot rate on December 1 is also FC1 = $.17. There is no discount or premium associated with this particular example.

Because the contract meets the conditions listed below, any gain resulting from it will be deferred and included in the cost basis of the equipment:

(1) The contract life is from the date of the commitment to purchase the equipment to the date of the transaction;

(2) The amount of the forward contract is equal to the amount of the commitment;

(3) The contract is denominated in the same currency as the commitment; and

(4) The contract is noncancelable.

Since the spot rate is equal to the forward rate, the company will establish a receivable and payable relating to the forward currency contract for \$255,000 (FC1,500,000 × \$.17). The journal entry at inception of the contract would be:

Foreign Currency Receivable from Exchange Broker	255,000	
Payable to Exchange Broker		255,000

Assume that the company has a year end of December 31, and that the spot rate on that date is FC1 = \$.18. The gain resulting from the forward exchange contract is equal to \$15,000, and is determined by multiplying the difference between the spot rate at the date of inception of the contract and the spot rate at the balance sheet date by the amount of the forward exchange contract (\$.18 − \$.17 = \$.01 × FC1,500,000 = \$15,000). Even though the gain exists, it will be deferred and included in the cost basis of the equipment. The entry necessary at December 31, 197A, is as follows:

Foreign Currency Receivable from Exchange Broker	15,000	
Deferred Gain on Forward Exchange Contract		15,000

The equipment is delivered on March 1, 197B, and the forward exchange contract expires on the same date. Assume that, on March 1, the spot rate is FC1 = \$.185. The first step is to recognize any deferred gain or loss and take receipt of the foreign currency from the broker. The deferred gain is equal to \$7,500, and is determined by multiplying the difference between the spot rate last used to determine any gain or loss (\$.18 on December 31) and the current spot rate by the amount of the forward exchange contract (\$.185 − \$.18 = \$.005 × FC1,500,000 = \$7,500). The entry to record the deferred gain is shown below:

Foreign Currency Receivable from Exchange Broker	7,500	
Deferred Gain on Forward Exchange Contract		7,500

The balance in the receivable account is now equal to \$277,500 (\$255,000 + \$15,000 + \$7,500). Another way to look at the receivable account is to analyze the number of dollars it would take to purchase FC1,500,000 on March 1, 197B (FC1,500,000 × \$.185 spot rate on March 1 = \$277,500). The entries to record the payment of the obligation to the exchange broker and the receipt of the foreign currency are presented below:

Payable to Exchange Broker	255,000	
Cash		255,000
Foreign Currency	277,500	
Foreign Currency Receivable from Exchange Broker		277,500

The final entry is to record the cost of the equipment received and the payment of the foreign currency to the manufacturer. The deferred gain must be considered now because the company will determine the cost basis of the equipment. The total deferred gain is equal to \$22,500

($15,000 + $7,500). The entry to record the equipment purchased would be:

Equipment	255,000	
Deferred Gain on Forward Exchange Contract	22,500	
Foreign Currency		277,500

Notice that, by entering into the forward exchange contract, the company fixed the cost of the asset acquired at the amount payable for the currency. If the company had not entered into the contract, it would have cost $277,500, rather than $255,000, to pay for the equipment on March 1, 197B.

The preceding example did not have a premium or discount associated with the forward exchange contract. By leaving the basic facts of the transaction the same, and changing the exchange rates, the following example will illustrate the proper accounting when a discount or premium is present.

For purposes of this example, assume the forward rate is still FC1 = $.17, but the spot rate on December 1, 197A, is FC1 = $.165. In this case, there would be a premium on the forward contract of $7,500 ($.17 – $.165 = $.005 × FC1,500,000 = $7,500). The journal entry to record the forward exchange contract must recognize the premium, but further consideration of the amount will be deferred until the cost basis of the equipment is determined. The entry to record the forward contract and related premium would be:

Foreign Currency Receivable from Exchange Broker	247,500	
Premium on Forward Exchange Contract	7,500	
Payable to Exchange Broker		255,000

Assuming the spot rate on December 31, 197A is FC1 = $.175, a deferred gain of $15,000 would be recognized ($.165 – $.175 = $.01 × FC1,500,000). The entry to show the recognition of the deferred gain was illustrated above, and will not be repeated.

On March 1, 197B, the spot rate is FC1 = $.185, so a deferred gain of $15,000 would be recognized ($.175 – $.185 = $.01 × FC1,500,000). The total deferred gain recorded to date is $30,000. The balance in the receivable account would be determined as follows:

Receivable Balance December 1	$247,500
Deferred Gain at December 31	15,000
Deferred Gain at March 1	15,000
Receivable Balance March 1	$277,500

The entries to record the payment to the exchange broker and the receipt are the same as those shown in the last example. The entry shown below is to record the cost of the equipment received. Note that both the deferred gain and the premium on the forward contract enter into the determination of the cost basis.

Deferred Gain on Forward Contract	30,000	
Equipment	255,000	
Foreign Currency		277,500
Premium on Forward Exchange Contract		7,500

Once again, the company has fixed the cost of the equipment at the amount payable to the broker for the FC1,500,000 that will be used to pay for the equipment.

With the issuance of SFAS No. 20, it became permissible to hedge an identifiable foreign currency commitment on an after-tax basis. In this case, the amount of the forward exchange contract may exceed the amount of the commitment, and the portion applicable to the after-tax hedge will be deferred. Losses may be deferred if such deferral will not lead to the recognition of losses in subsequent periods.

In some cases, a company may enter into a forward exchange contract that is intended as a hedge of an identifiable foreign currency commitment, but the amount of the contract may exceed the amount of the commitment. Gains or losses may be deferred on a portion of the forward contract equal to the commitment, and any gain or loss on the excess over the amount of the commitment will be recognized currently.

Gains and losses may be deferred only on forward exchange contracts that are intended to hedge an identifiable foreign currency commitment. All other forward exchange contracts will result in current recognition of any gain or loss.

Hedge of Exposed Net Asset or Liability Position

Another reason identified in the Statement for entering into a forward exchange contract is to hedge an exposed net asset or liability position of a foreign affiliated company (Block 9). Paragraph 243 of the Statement defines an exposed net asset position as "the excess of assets that are measured or denominated in foreign currency and translated at the current rate over liabilities that are measured or denominated in foreign currency and translated at the current rate." An exposed net liability position would exist when the liabilities exceed the assets translated as described above. A company may enter into a forward contract for this reason in an attempt to minimize the adverse consequences of exchange rate fluctuations on the financial statements of the foreign company.

Exchange gains or losses resulting from forward exchange contracts intended to hedge an exposed net asset or liability position will be recognized currently. The gain or loss is determined by multiplying the difference between the spot rate at the inception of the contract and the spot rate at the balance sheet date by the amount of the forward contract. The discount or premium on the forward contract is determined by multiplying the difference between the forward rate and the spot rate at the inception of the contract by the amount of the contract. The premium or discount will be amortized over the life of the contract—generally on a straight-line basis.

To illustrate the use of a forward exchange contract as a hedge of an exposed net asset or liability position, assume that the foreign subsidiary of a U.S. company finds itself in an exposed net liability position. To hedge against this position, the U.S. company enters into a forward exchange contract on December 1, 197A. The contract requires the exchange broker to deliver FC100,000 in 90 days at a cost of $280,000. Because the forward contract is not a hedge of any identifiable foreign currency commitment, gains or losses will be recognized currently. On December 1, 197A, the spot rate is FC1 = $2.77. Since the forward rate is FC1 = $2.80 ($280,000/FC100,000), there is a premium of $3,000 associated with the forward exchange contract ($2.80 – $2.77 = $.03 × FC100,000). The entry to record the forward exchange contract on December 1, 197A, would be:

Foreign Currency Receivable from Exchange Broker	277,000	
Premium on Forward Exchange Contract	3,000	
Payable to Exchange Broker		280,000

The premium is to be amortized over the life of the forward exchange contract, using the straight-line method.

Assuming the U.S. company has a year end of December 31, and that the spot rate on that date is FC1 = $2.79, an exchange gain would be recognized. The exchange gain is computed by multiplying the difference between the spot rate at inception of the forward contract and the spot rate on December 31 by the amount of the forward exchange contract, and is equal to $2,000 ($2.79 – $2.77 = $.02 × FC100,000 = $2,000). Recall that the forward rate is used only to determine the discount or premium. On December 31, the U.S. company would recognize the gain of $2,000, and amortize one-third of the total premium. The entries below reflect these events:

Foreign Currency Receivable from Exchange Broker	2,000	
Gain on Forward Exchange Contract		2,000
Amortization of Premium on Forward Exchange Contract	1,000	
Premium on Forward Exchange Contract		1,000

In the year 197A, the company would recognize a $2,000 gain on the contract and an expense for the amortization of the premium on the contract. The amortization expense is classified as a nonoperating item on the 197A income statement. The recorded value of the receivable is now $279,000 ($277,000 + $2,000), and the unamortized premium is $2,000 ($3,000 − $1,000). The unamortized premium account would be treated as a contra account to the payable, similar to the treatment of discount or premium on other payables.

The forward exchange contract is settled on March 1, 197B, when the broker delivers the foreign currency to the company for the agreed price of $280,000. Assume that, on March 1, the spot rate is FC1 = $2.81. A gain of $2,000 would be recognized in 197B, determined as follows:

Spot Rate at December 31, 197A	$2.79
Spot Rate at March 1, 197B	2.81
Difference	$ .02
Amount of Forward Contract	× FC100,000
Gain to be Recognized	$2,000

In addition to recognizing the gain, the company must amortize the remaining premium on the forward contract. The entries to record the expiration of the forward exchange contract are shown below:

Payable to Exchange Broker	280,000	
Cash		280,000
Foreign Currency (FC100,000 × $2.81)	281,000	
Gain on Forward Exchange Contract		2,000
Foreign Currency Receivable from Exchange Broker		279,000
Amortization of Premium on Forward Exchange Contract	2,000	
Premium on Forward Exchange Contract		2,000

The U.S. company is now in possession of FC100,000, for which it paid $280,000 cash. In the 197B income statement, the company will recognize an exchange gain of $2,000 and an amortization expense in relation to the premium of $2,000.

Hedges of identifiable foreign currency commitments that fail to meet one of the four conditions listed in the above discussion would be accounted for as a hedge of an exposed net asset or liability position would be, i.e., the gain or loss would be recognized currently, rather than being deferred. With the exception of speculation in foreign currency, any other hedge not specifically identified in the Statement would be handled as if it were a hedge of an exposed net asset or liability position.

Foreign Currency Speculation

A company may enter into a forward exchange contract merely as an opportunity to profit from changes in the exchange rates between two currencies. For example, a company may enter into a forward contract to deliver FC250,000 at some specified future date for $87,500 (FC1 = $.35). If, on the date the contract expires, the spot rate is FC1 = $.39, the company would take delivery of the FC250,000 at the agreed price of $87,500, sell the foreign currency for $97,500 (FC250,000 × $.39) and make a profit of $10,000. Of course, the reader is aware that this type of forward contract could just as easily result in a loss.

If the reason for the forward exchange contract is to speculate in foreign currencies, any gain or loss is to be recognized currently. Separate accounting is not given to any discount or premium on the forward contract; rather, the amount is included in the determination of gain or loss. The computation of gain or loss on the forward exchange contract always is based on *forward rates.* Current or spot rates are of no concern in accounting for speculation contracts. The gain or loss is determined by multiplying the difference between the forward rate at inception of the contract and the forward rate applicable to the remaining maturity of the contract by the amount of the forward contract.

To illustrate the accounting for a forward exchange contract intended as a speculation in foreign currency, assume a U.S. company enters into a forward contract on December 1, 197A. The contract requires the broker to deliver FC1,000,000 in 60 days, at a cost of $610,000. So the forward rate on December 1 is FC1 = $.61. Because it is the intent of the company to speculate in currency, it is not necessary to know the spot rate at December 1. The entry to record the forward contract is shown below:

Foreign Currency Receivable from Exchange Broker	610,000	
Payable to Exchange Broker		610,000

Assume the company has a year end of December 31, and, on that date, the forward rate for 30-day delivery of the foreign currency is FC1 = $.62. The 30-day forward rate is used because that is the remaining maturity of the original 60-day contract. On December 31, the company would recognize a $10,000 gain on the contract. The gain is calculated below:

60-Day Forward Rate on December 1	$ .61
30-Day Forward Rate on December 31	.62
Difference	$ .01
Amount of Forward Contract	FC1,000,000
Gain on Forward Contract	$ 10,000

The entry required on December 31 to reflect the gain would be:

Foreign Currency Receivable from Exchange Broker	10,000	
Gain on Forward Exchange Contract		10,000

The gain would be included in the 197A income statement. The recorded amount of the receivable is now $620,000 (FC1,000,000 × $.62).

The contract expires on January 30, 197B. On the date of expiration, the forward rate for the maturity of the contract will be equal to the spot rate on that date. Assume that, on January 30, the spot rate is FC1 = $.625, and that the company takes possession of the foreign currency and immediately sells it to realize the speculation profits. The gain on the contract in 197B is $5,000 ($.625 − $.62 = $.005 × FC1,000,000). The entries to record the settlement with the exchange broker, receipt of the foreign currency and recognition of the gain, and the subsequent sale of the foreign currency are shown below:

Payable to Exchange Broker	610,000	
Cash		610,000
Foreign Currency ($.625 × FC1,000,000)	625,000	
Foreign Currency Receivable from Exchange Broker		620,000
Gain on Forward Exchange Contract		5,000
Cash	625,000	
Foreign Currency		625,000

The total gain on the forward contract was $15,000 ($625,000 − $610,000), with $10,000 being recognized in 197A and $5,000 in 197B. The company could have held the foreign currency in hopes of further profits or entered into another forward contract to sell the foreign currency at some future date.

Other Considerations for Foreign Currency Transactions

To the extent that exchange gains or losses represent timing differences, deferred tax accounting, as specified in APB Opinion No. 11, "Accounting for Income Taxes," should be applied (see Topic 5 for a detailed analysis of income tax allocation).

Disclosure requirements are discussed after the section dealing with foreign currency financial statements.

Foreign Currency Financial Statements

For any one of several reasons, a business enterprise may find it necessary to translate financial statements that are denominated in a foreign currency into dollar amounts. SFAS No. 8 provides specific guidance for the translation process. The particular method emphasized by the Statement is referred to as the "temporal" method. The objective of the temporal method is to translate account balances denominated in a foreign currency in such a manner as to retain the original basis of measurement. The temporal method of translation incorporates some of the attributes of previously used methods. The accounting principles used to determine a particular account balance, if in accordance with U.S. generally accepted accounting principles (GAAP), should be retained; and the only result of the translation should be to convert from the foreign currency to dollars.

Because of the changing relationship between the dollar and other foreign currencies, the translation process may result in a gain or loss at any specific time. Any gain or loss resulting from translation of foreign currency financial statements should be reported in the current period income statement.

Flowchart and General Discussion

Flowchart II shows the decision process and major accounting procedures to be used in translating financial statements denominated in a foreign currency (Block 1). The Flowchart is organized in such a manner that the translation of balance sheet accounts precedes the translation of income statement accounts. While this is a logical arrangement of the provisions of SFAS No. 8, the actual translation of account balances may have to deviate from this pattern.

Before the standards established by the Statement are applicable, the financial statements to be translated must be included by a U.S. parent company or investor company through consolidation, combination or the equity method of accounting for investments (Block 2). If this is the case, the translation process is begun by selecting a specific account to be translated into dollars. A systematic approach to the selection of accounts for translation will be discussed in the section dealing with the technical considerations of the Statement.

The account to be translated must be stated in accordance with U.S. GAAP (Block 3). This is necessary because the foreign currency financial statements are to be consolidated, combined or otherwise associated with parent company or investor company financial statements, which already are prepared on the basis of U.S. GAAP. If the foreign currency account balances were not determined using the same accounting principles, it would be impossible to compare the translated dollar amounts with the dollar balances in the U.S. financial statements. If foreign currency financial statement account balances are prepared on some basis other than U.S. GAAP, they must be adjusted to conform with U.S. GAAP before the translation process can be started.

FLOWCHART II

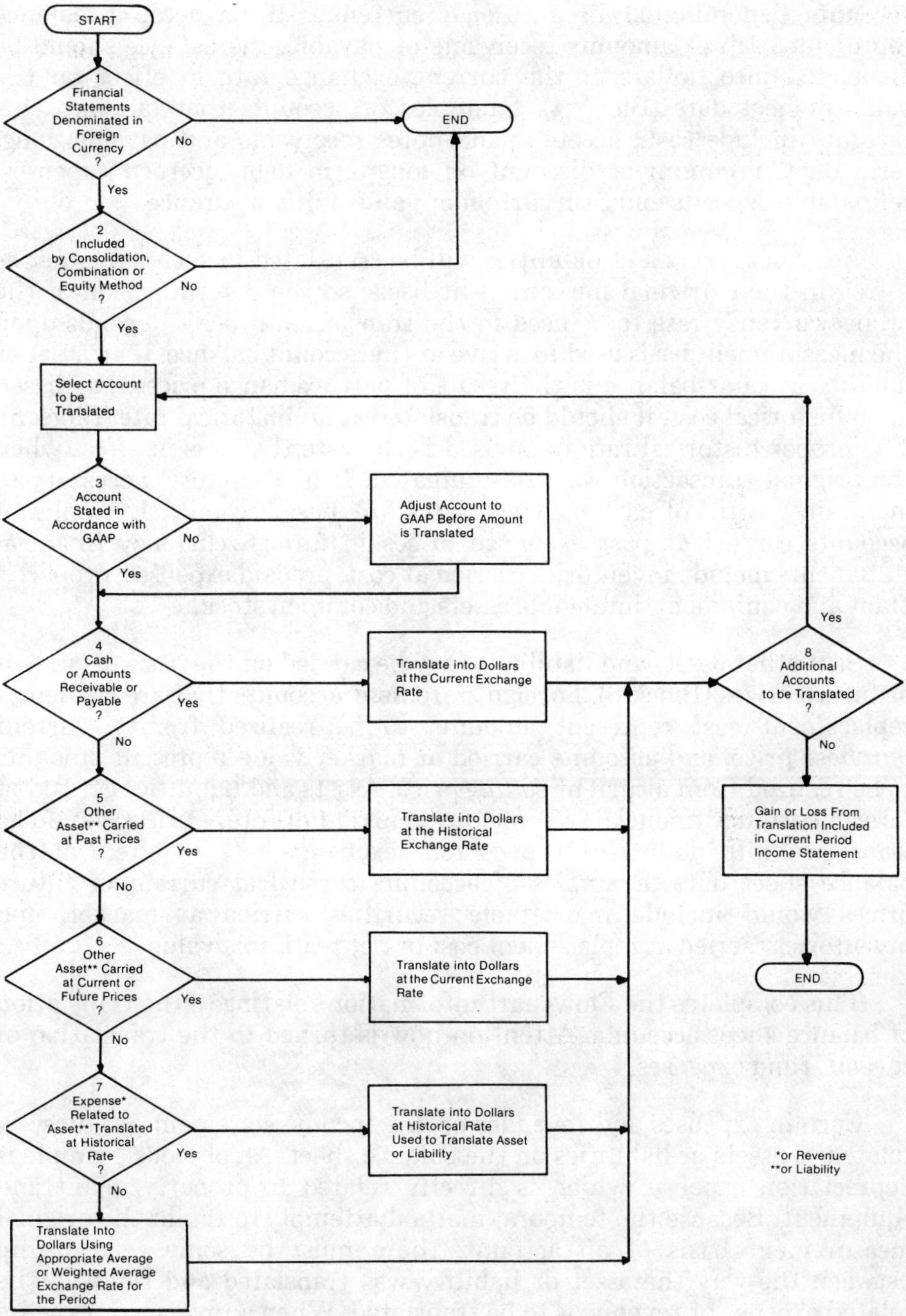

Decision Blocks 4, 5 and 6 relate to the translation of balance sheet accounts denominated in a foreign currency. If an account balance represents cash or amounts receivable or payable, the balance should be translated into dollars at the current exchange rate in effect on the balance sheet date (Block 4). Examples of accounts that fall into this category include cash, accounts and notes receivable and payable, long-term debt, premium or discount on long-term debt, accrued expenses, refundable deposits and cash surrender value of life insurance.

All other assets and liabilities will be translated in such a manner as to retain their original measurement basis, so the determination of the proper currency rate to be used in the translation process depends upon the measurement basis used to arrive at the account balance. If an asset or liability account balance is the result of past exchange prices, i.e., based upon historical cost, it should be translated at an historical rate (Block 5). The proper historical rate to be used is the rate that was in effect when the original transaction was consummated. It is, therefore, necessary to maintain records of past exchange rates for these accounts. Examples of accounts carried at past exchange prices in foreign currency financial statements include inventories carried at cost, prepaid expenses, property, plant and equipment, intangible assets and common stock.

Still other assets and liabilities may be carried on the basis of current or future prices (Block 6). Foreign statement accounts that are carried at replacement cost represent amounts to be realized from a current *purchase* price, and accounts carried at market value represent amounts to be realized from a current *selling* price. Assets and liabilities carried in foreign currency financial statements at current or future prices should be translated into dollars at the current exchange rate in effect at the balance sheet date. Examples of accounts carried at current or future prices would include marketable securities carried at market, and inventories carried at replacement cost or net realizable value.

This completes the Flowchart information relating to the translation of balance sheet accounts. Attention now is turned to the translation of revenues and expenses.

Certain expenses and revenues on the income statement are directly related to assets or liabilities on the balance sheet. An obvious example is depreciation expense, which is directly related to property, plant and equipment. Because the temporal method attempts to retain the original measurement basis of an account, there must be some relationship between the way the asset or liability was translated and the way the related expense or revenue is to be translated. When a revenue or expense is related to an asset or liability account that was translated at an historical rate, the revenue or expense also should be translated at that same historical currency rate (Block 7).

It would be technically correct to translate all other revenues and expenses at the rate in effect on the date the transaction was consummated. However, this would require extensive bookkeeping, and it is doubtful that the benefits derived from such an elaborate accounting system would be greater than the costs incurred. The Statement concludes that these revenues and expenses may be translated at an appropriate average or weighted average exchange rate for the period. In most cases, a monthly average exchange rate is used. If a company's sales are made, and expenses incurred, uniformly throughout the period, the use of an average exchange rate should not yield results significantly different from those that result from using the actual exchange rate in effect when the transaction was consummated.

Once all foreign currency accounts have been translated (Block 8), it is possible to measure the gain or loss resulting from translation. The gain or loss will be included in the current period income statement and thereby will flow through to retained earnings when closing entries are prepared. The computation of the translation gain or loss may be accomplished in several ways. In the technical considerations that follow, much attention will be given to the computation of the gain or loss from translation.

A general overview of the translation process is summarized in Table I below:

Table I

Summary of the Translation Process[1]

TYPE OF ACCOUNT TO BE TRANSLATED	CURRENT RATE	HISTORICAL RATE	AVERAGE RATE
Cash or amounts receivable or payable	X		
Other assets or liabilities carried at past prices		X	
Other assets or liabilities carried at current or future prices	X		
Expenses or revenues directly related to assets or liabilities translated at historical rate		X	
Other revenue or expenses			X

[1] FASB Interpretation No. 15 deals with the translation of certain account balances for stock life insurance companies. The Interpretation concludes that unamortized policy acquisition costs are "deferred charges," and should be translated at the historical rate(s). In addition, reserve deficiency losses that are charged to income in the current period should be shown in dollars after translation of unamortized policy acquisition costs at historical rates and the liability for future policy benefits at the current rate.

Translating Foreign Currency Financial Statements—Technical Considerations

To illustrate the translation of foreign currency financial statements, assume that American Manufacturing Company, Inc., a parent company, wishes to translate the financial statements of its subsidiary, Foreign Enterprise, Ltd. The Foreign Enterprise balance sheet, income statement and statement of retained earnings for the years 197B and 197A are shown in Exhibits I, II and III, respectively. The statement of changes in financial position has been omitted for sake of simplicity; however, the parent company does plan to prepare such a statement after translation has been completed. The financial statements are denominated in the home currency of Foreign Enterprise and were prepared in accordance with U.S. generally accepted accounting principles. Therefore, no adjustment of the account balances as shown will be necessary.

The financial statements presented are from the date of inception of the company. This has been done for illustrative purposes, to demonstrate the accumulation of certain important balance sheet accounts. Exhibit IV contains certain key information about the foreign currency exchange rates necessary to translate the statements. Each quotation represents the dollar equivalent of one unit of foreign currency of the home country of Foreign Enterprise. The translation process will begin by assuming that the 197A financial statements, first year of operations, have not been translated. Once the 197A statements are translated, the 197B statements will be translated. The translation process that follows is quite lengthy, and the reader is encouraged to make frequent reference to Exhibits I through IV.

Table II reflects the details of the translation process and is reproduced from Appendix A of SFAS No. 8. While the general summary found in Table I may be useful in some circumstances, Table II provides the reader with the detailed information required during the translation process.

Table II

Rates Used to Translate Assets and Liabilities

	Translation Rates	
	Current	Historical
ASSETS		
Cash on hand and demand and time deposits	X	
Marketable equity securities:	X	
Carried at cost		X
Carried at current market price	X	
Accounts and notes receivable and related unearned discount	X	
Allowance for doubtful accounts and notes receivable	X	
Inventories:		
Carried at cost		X
Carried at current replacement price or current selling price	X	
Carried at net realizable value	X	
Carried at contract price (produced under fixed price contracts)	X	
Prepaid insurance, advertising, and rent		X
Refundable deposits	X	
Advances to unconsolidated subsidiaries	X	
Property, plant, and equipment		X
Accumulated depreciation of property, plant, and equipment		X
Cash surrender value of life insurance	X	
Patents, trademarks, licenses, and formulas		X
Goodwill		X
Other intangible assets		X
LIABILITIES		
Accounts and notes payable and overdrafts	X	
Accrued expenses payable	X	
Accrued losses on firm purchase commitments	X	
Refundable deposits	X	
Deferred income		X
Bonds payable or other long-term debt	X	
Unamortized premium or discount on bonds or notes payable	X	
Convertible bonds payable	X	
Accrued pension obligations	X	
Obligations under warranties	X	

Exhibit I

Balance Sheet in Foreign Currency—Foreign Enterprise, Ltd.
December 31, 197B and 197A

	197B	197A
Current Assets:		
Cash	1,250,000	956,300
Accounts receivable—trade	3,902,500	2,443,700
Accounts receivable—intercompany	942,500	-0-
Notes receivable	2,970,000	1,000,000
Inventories	9,100,000	7,900,500
Prepaid expenses	425,300	-0-
Accrued interest on notes receivable	35,800	11,400
Total Current Assets	18,626,100	12,311,900
Long-Term Notes Receivable	6,000,000	6,000,000
Property, Plant and Equipment:		
Land	17,000,000	17,000,000
Buildings	156,768,000	149,811,000
Fixtures and equipment	39,932,000	32,626,000
Total Property, Plant and Equipment	213,700,000	199,437,000
Accumulated depreciation	(23,267,200)	(11,265,200)
Net Property, Plant and Equipment	190,432,800	188,171,800
Total Assets	215,058,900	206,483,700
Current Liabilities:		
Accounts payable	2,774,550	3,628,000
Accrued interest on long-term debt	510,000	450,000
Income taxes payable	763,250	766,500
Dividends payable	500,000	250,000
Current maturities on long-term debt	2,500,000	2,500,000
Total Current Liabilities	7,047,800	7,594,500
Long-Term Debt	75,000,000	67,500,000
Deferred Income Taxes	1,858,900	1,096,200
Stockholders' Equity		
Common stock	50,000,000	50,000,000
Contributed capital in excess of par	77,182,400	77,182,400
Retained earnings	3,969,800	3,110,600
Total Stockholders' Equity	131,152,200	130,293,000
Total Liabilities and Stockholders' Equity	215,058,900	206,483,700

Exhibit II

Income Statement in Foreign Currency—Foreign Enterprise, Ltd.
Years Ended December 31, 197B and 197A

		197B		197A
Sales		84,075,500		73,276,000
Costs and Expenses:				
Cost of goods sold:				
Inventory—January 1	7,900,500		-0-	
Production costs	48,462,500		49,965,600	
Goods available for sale	56,363,000		49,965,600	
Inventory—December 31	(9,100,000)		(7,900,500)	
Cost of goods sold		47,263,000		42,065,100
General and administrative		9,731,400		8,245,000
Advertising and selling		7,326,000		4,671,500
Depreciation		12,002,000		11,265,200
Total costs and expenses		76,322,400		66,246,800
Net income from operations		7,753,100		7,029,200
Other income (expenses)		(2,987,500)		(678,200)
Net income before taxes		4,765,600		6,351,000
Income taxes:				
Current		1,143,700		1,144,200
Deferred		762,700		1,096,200
Total taxes		1,906,400		2,240,400
Net income		2,859,200		4,110,600

Exhibit III

Statement of Retained Earnings in Foreign Currency—Foreign Enterprise, Ltd.
Years Ended December 31, 197B and 197A

	197B	197A
Retained earnings - January 1	3,110,600	-0-
Add net income for the year	2,859,200	4,110,600
Deduct dividends for the year	(2,000,000)	(1,000,000)
Retained earnings - December 31	3,969,800	3,110,600

Exhibit IV

Foreign Currency Rates

Explanation of Rates	FC1 197B	FC1 197A
Conversion rate at March 31	$.245	$.25
Conversion rate at June 30	$.25	$.2475
Conversion rate at September 30	$.25	$.245
Conversion rate at December 31	$.245	$.24
Average conversion rate for the year	$.2475	$.2455
Historical conversion rate when stock was issued and land purchased	-	$.255
Historical conversion rate when buildings, fixtures and equipment were purchased	$.245	$.25
Average historical rate applicable to inventories on hand at December 31	$.25	$.2425

The translation of the 197A financial statements will begin by concentrating on as many balance sheet accounts as is possible in the circumstances. At this point, translation of an income statement account will be postponed, unless the translation is needed to complete the translation of a particular balance sheet account.

A logical place to begin is with the translation of current assets. Foreign Enterprise, Ltd. carries its inventories at cost. All current assets except inventories will be translated at the current exchange rate of $.24, because these accounts represent cash or amounts receivable. Foreign Enterprise has determined that the average historical rate applicable to inventories is $.2425. This average rate may have been determined on the basis of inventory turnover or the use of some weighted average rate based upon the age of the inventory. Again, an average rate was used because it would be very expensive and time-consuming to maintain records of all of the actual exchange rates in effect at each inventory transaction date. The translation of the current asset section of the balance sheet for the year 197A is accomplished as follows:

	Foreign Currency Balance	Translation Rate	Dollar Balance
Cash	956,300	$ .24	$ 229,512
Accounts receivable-trade	2,443,700	$ .24	586,488
Notes receivable	1,000,000	$ .24	240,000
Inventories	7,900,500	$ .2425	1,915,871
Accrued interest	11,400	$ .24	2,736
Total current assets	12,311,900		$2,974,607

The next item to be translated on the balance sheet is the long-term note receivable. Since this account represents an amount receivable, it should be translated at the current exchange rate in effect on December 31, 197A, which is the balance sheet date. The FC6,000,000 would translate into $1,440,000 (FC6,000,000 × $.24 = $1,440,000).

The next major section of the balance sheet to be translated consists of property, plant and equipment. Since all accounts in this section are carried at historical cost, the historical rate in effect when the land, building, fixtures and equipment were purchased should be used to translate the accounts. Exhibit IV indicates that the land was purchased when the common stock originally was issued. At that date, the exchange rate was FC1 = \$.255; therefore, the land account should be translated at this rate. The building, fixtures and equipment were purchased when the exchange rate was different, and should be translated at the rate of FC1 = \$.25. Because this is the initial year of operations for the company, the balance in the accumulated depreciation account is equal to the depreciation expense for the year. The accumulated depreciation balance should be translated at the historical rate applicable to the building, fixtures and equipment accounts, because that would be the rate used to translate depreciation expense for the period. The translation of the property, plant and equipment section of the balance sheet for 197A is shown below:

	Foreign Currency Balance	Translation Rate	Dollar Balance
Land	17,000,000	$ .255	$ 4,335,000
Buildings	149,811,000	$ .25	37,452,750
Fixtures and equipment	32,626,000	$ .25	8,156,500
Total property, plant and equipment	199,437,000		$49,944,250
Accumulated depreciation	(11,265,200)	$ .25	(2,816,300)
Net property, plant and equipment	188,171,800		$47,127,950

The translation of the asset side of the balance sheet now is completed. The total assets, expressed in dollars, is shown below:

Current assets	$ 2,974,607
Long-term notes receivable	1,440,000
Property, plant and equipment	47,127,950
Total assets	$51,542,557

The accounts that make up the current liability section of the balance sheet for 197A all represent amounts payable, and should be translated at the current exchange rate at December 31, 197A. The translation of current liabilities is shown below:

	Foreign Currency Balance	Translation Rate	Dollar Balance
Accounts payable	3,628,000	$ .24	$ 870,720
Accrued interest	450,000	$ .24	108,000
Income taxes payable	766,500	$ .24	183,960
Dividends payable	250,000	$ .24	60,000
Current maturities	2,500,000	$ .24	600,000
Total current liabilities	7,594,500		$1,822,680

Long-term debt represent amounts payable, and therefore is translated at the current exchange rate at December 31, 197A. The foreign currency balance in long-term debt would be translated into $16,200,000 (FC67,500,000 × $.24 = $16,200,000).

Because this is the first year of operations for the company, the balance in the deferred income taxes account is equal to the deferred income taxes recorded on the income statement. The proper translation of the balance sheet account for deferred taxes is directly related to the translation of the income tax account on the income statement. If the revenues of a company are earned uniformly throughout the period, and the expenses are incurred in the same manner, then taxes on income would accrue uniformly. This is true because the determination of tax expense is based upon the computation of income. Assume that Foreign Enterprise, Ltd. earns income uniformly during 197A. This being the case, income tax expense would be translated at an appropriate average exchange rate during the year. Therefore, the addition to deferred income taxes would be translated at the same rate. Exhibit IV indicates that the average exchange rate for 197A was FC1 = $.2455. Given this information, the foreign currency balance in the deferred income taxes account would translate into $269,117 (FC1,096,200 × $.2455 = $269,117).

The stockholders' equity section of the balance sheet is the last set of accounts that must be translated. Common stock and contributed capital in excess of par are related and carried at historical cost on the balance sheet. These accounts should be translated at the exchange rate in effect on the date the stock was issued. Exhibit IV indicates that the appropriate rate to use is FC1 = $.255. Using this rate, common stock would translate into $12,750,000 (FC50,000,000 × $.255 = $12,750,000), and the contributed capital would translate into $19,681,512 (FC77,182,400 × $.255 = $19,681,512).

No information has been given concerning the translation of the retained earnings account. In the initial year, the account balance will represent the difference between the income earned and the dividends paid. Direct translation of the retained earnings account is usually not possible. However, it is known that the retained earnings account represents a residual value on the balance sheet. Because all asset, liability and owners' equity accounts have been translated, except for retained earnings, it is possible to determine the balance in the retained earnings account by comparison of all asset, liability and equity accounts translated. To begin the process, first recap the liability and equity accounts that have been translated into dollars. This computation is shown below:

Current liabilities	$ 1,822,680
Long-term debt	16,200,000
Deferred income taxes	269,117
Common stock	12,750,000
Contributed capital in excess of par	19,681,512
Total liabilities and equities translated	$50,723,309

This total amount now may be compared with the total dollar value of the assets translated. The difference between the two balances must represent the balance in the retained earnings account. The computation is made as follows:

Total dollar value of assets translated	$51,542,557
Total dollar value of liabilities and equity accounts (other than retained earnings) translated	50,723,309
Retained earnings balance 12/31/197A	$ 819,248

This residual value assigned to retained earnings is correct because it causes the translated dollar value of the assets to equal the liabilities and stockholders' equity. With this final determination completed, the translation of the income statement accounts can be started. Recall that, during the discussion of translating accumulated depreciation and deferred income taxes, reference has been made to related income statement accounts.

Most items on the income statement will be translated at the average exchange rate during the period. Remember that this is allowed because the cost of keeping track of the historical rate for each income statement item is prohibitive. Income statement accounts that are directly related to balance sheet accounts that were translated at historical rates should be translated at the same historical rates.

The only accounts on the 197A income statement (Exhibit II) that would be translated at historical rates are depreciation expense and the December 31 inventory. All the other accounts would be translated at the average rate during the period. The complete translation of the income statement is shown below:

	Foreign Currency Balance	Translation Rate	Dollar Balance
Sales	73,276,000	$ .2455	$17,989,258
Costs and Expenses:			
Cost of goods sold:			
Inventory—January 1	-0-	-	-0-
Production costs	49,965,600	$ .2455	$12,266,554
Inventory—December 31	(7,900,500)	$ .2425*	(1,915,871)
Cost of goods sold	42,065,100		$10,350,683
General and administrative expenses	8,245,000	$ .2455	2,024,148
Advertising and selling	4,671,500	$ .2455	1,146,853
Depreciation	11,265,200	$ .25*	2,816,300
Total costs and expenses	66,246,800		$16,337,984
Net income from operations	7,029,200		$ 1,651,274
Other income (expense)	(678,200)	$ .2455	(166,498)
Net income before taxes	6,351,000		$ 1,484,776
Income taxes:			
Current	1,144,200	$ .2455	$ 280,901
Deferred	1,096,200	$ .2455*	269,117
Total income taxes	2,240,400		$ 550,018
Net income	4,110,600		$ 934,758

*See balance sheet translation

It is important to note that the income statement translation above ignores the possibility of any translation gains or losses resulting from fluctuations in the exchange rate between the foreign currency and the dollar. Before the translation process is complete, consideration must be given to such gains or losses. To begin this determination, the balance in the retained earnings account must be reviewed (Exhibit III).

The two elements that make up the retained earnings balance are net income for the year and dividends paid. Assume that dividends of FC250,000 were declared at the end of each quarter (FC250,000 × 4 = $1,000,000). The translation of the dividends for 197A would be accomplished by applying the exchange rate in effect at the end of each quarter to the dividends declared. The translation is shown below:

March 31 dividend (FC250,000 × $.25)	$ 62,500
June 30 dividend (FC250,000 × $.2475)	61,875
September 30 dividend (FC250,000 × $.245)	61,250
December 31 dividend (FC250,000 × $.24)	60,000
Translated dividends for 197A	$245,625

After the dividends have been translated, a detailed analysis of the components of retained earnings can be made. With the information developed to this point, a reconstructed retained earnings account would appear as follows:

Retained earnings—January 1, 197A	$ -0-
Add net income for the year (see income statement above)	934,758
Deduct dividends for the year	(245,625)
Retained earnings—December 31, 197A	$689,133

Now refer back to the computation of retained earnings required during the translation of the balance sheet. Notice that the retained earnings balance previously determined is $819,248, and the retained earnings balance computed above is $689,133. Recall that, when the income statement was translated, no recognition was given to possible translation gains or losses. Therefore, the difference between the two calculations of retained earnings must be the translation gain or loss for the period. In 197A, there was a gain from translation in the amount of $130,115 ($819,248 – $689,133). With the gain determined, the income statement for 197A may be recast to reflect the translation gain as follows:

Net income from operations		$1,651,274
Nonoperating items:		
Other income (expense)	$(166,498)	
Translation gain	130,115	(36,383)
Net income before taxes		$1,614,891
Income taxes:		
Current	$ 280,901	
Deferred	269,117	550,018
Net income		$1,064,873

Once the income statement has been recast to reflect the translation gain, the statement of retained earnings would appear as follows:

Retained earnings - January 1, 197A	$ -0-
Add net income for the year	1,064,873
Deduct dividends for the year	(245,625)
Retained earnings - December 31, 197A	$ 819,248

With this final step, the translation of the 197A financial statements is complete. It should be mentioned that there are alternative ways to compute the translation gain or loss. One method commonly used is to determine the net exposed asset or liability position in foreign currency and translate the detail causes of changes in the position from one year to the next. The authors have decided to use the method shown above because it is simple and efficient.

While somewhat lengthy, the translation of the 197A financial statements was relatively straightforward. Some new complexities are added when the translation of the 197B financial statements is undertaken.

The translation of the 197B financial statements will follow the same pattern as was used for the 197A statements. A review of the 197B current assets indicates two new accounts: Intercompany accounts receivable and Prepaid expenses (Exhibit I). The intercompany receivable should be translated at the reciprocal dollar balance on the parent's financial statement. In this case, American Manufacturing Company's payable is carried at $210,000, so this amount will be used to convert from the foreign currency to dollars. Prepaid expenses represent amounts carried at past exchange prices, and should be translated at the historical exchange rate in effect when the prepaid expense was incurred. For purposes of translation, assume that all the prepaid items were incurred on September 30, 197B, when the exchange rate was FC1 = $.25. Inventories will be translated at historical rate, as in the previous translation. All other current assets represent cash or amounts receivable and will be translated at the current exchange rate on December 31, 197B. The translation of the current assets for 197B is shown below:

	Foreign Currency Balance	Translation Rate	Dollar Balance
Cash	1,250,000	$ .245	$ 306,250
Accounts receivable-trade	3,902,500	$ .245	956,113
Accounts receivable-intercompany	942,500	-	210,000
Notes receivable	2,970,000	$ .245	727,650
Inventories	9,100,000	$ .25	2,275,000
Prepaid expenses	425,300	$ .25	106,325
Accrued interest	35,800	$ .245	8,771
Total current assets	18,626,100		$4,590,109

The long-term note receivable represents an amount receivable and will be translated at the current rate of FC1 = $.245. Recall that, in the 197A balance sheet, the long-term note was translated at the then current rate of FC1 = $.24. This is the type of exchange rate change that gives rise to the translation gains and losses. The long-term note will be translated into $1,470,000 (FC6,000,000 × $.245 = $1,470,000).

While property, plant and equipment still will be translated at the historical rate, notice that Foreign Enterprise has purchased some additional buildings, fixtures and equipment during 197B. These additions will be translated at a different historical rate than that used to translate the original acquisitions. The historical rate applicable to the new purchases of property, plant and equipment is FC1 = $.245. The schedule below shows the detail translation of the buildings account:

Buildings Acquired in 197A (FC149,811,000 × $.25)	$37,452,750
Buildings Acquired in 197B (FC6,957,000 × $.245)	1,704,465
Translated Building Account	$39,157,215

The translated value of the fixtures and equipment would be determined in a similar manner, and is shown below:

Fixtures and Equipment Acquired in 197A (FC32,626,000 × $.25)	$8,156,500
Fixtures and Equipment Acquired in 197B (FC7,306,000 × $.245)	1,789,970
Translated Fixtures and Equipment Account	$9,946,470

Land would continue to be translated at the same rate used in 197A.

The calculation of the proper dollar balance in the accumulated depreciation account is somewhat more complex than the procedure used for 197A. For purposes of illustration, assume that Foreign Enterprise is using straight-line depreciation, and that there has been no plant retirement during 197B. Under this set of assumptions, the balance in the accumulated depreciation account must be made up of the following elements:

Straight-line depreciation for 197A	FC11,265,200
Straight-line depreciation for 197B on those assets acquired in 197A	11,265,200
Straight-line depreciation for 197B on those assets acquired in 197B	736,800
Foreign Currency Balance in Accumulated Depreciation	FC23,267,200

The depreciation associated with those assets acquired in 197A will be translated into dollars at the 197A exchange rate of FC1 = $.25, and the depreciation associated with the assets acquired in 197B will be translated at the historical rate of FC1 = $.245 (Exhibit IV). Depreciation would be translated as follows:

Depreciation on Assets Acquired in 197A (FC11,265,200 × 2 years × $.25)	$5,632,600
Depreciation on Assets Acquired in 197B (FC736,800 × 1 year × $.245)	180,516
Accumulated Depreciation	$5,813,116

Based upon the above information, the property, plant and equipment section of the 197B balance sheet would carry the following dollar values:

Land	$ 4,335,000
Buldings	39,157,215
Fixtures and equipment	9,946,470
Total property, plant and equipment	$53,438,685
Accumulated depreciation	(5,813,116)
Net property, plant and equipment	$47,625,569

Total assets, in dollars, can be determined by putting together the individual balance sheet sections.

Current assets	$ 4,590,109
Long-term notes receivable	1,470,000
Property, plant and equipment	47,625,569
Total assets	$53,685,678

It should be obvious to the reader that maintaining records on plant additions and retirements is critical to the successful translation of property, plant and equipment. The process of translation will become more complex as time passes.

All current liability accounts represent amounts payable, and are to be translated at the current exchange rate at December 31, 197B. The conversion is shown below:

	Foreign Currency Balance	Translation Rate	Dollar Balance
Accounts payable	2,774,550	$ .245	$ 679,765
Accrued interest	510,000	$ .245	124,950
Income taxes payable	763,250	$ .245	186,996
Dividends payable	500,000	$ .245	122,500
Current maturities	2,500,000	$ .245	612,500
Total current liabilities	7,047,800		$1,726,711

The long-term debt represents an amount payable, and is translated at the current exchange rate at December 31, 197B. The foreign currency amount translates into $18,375,000 (FC75,000,000 × $.245 = $18,375,000).

The balance in the deferred income taxes account is made up of the carryover from year 197A and the additional deferral recorded in the 197B income statement (FC762,700). Using the assumption of uniform earnings throughout the period, each amount should be translated at the average exchange rate in effect in the year the deferral was created. The computations below show the proper method of translating the deferred income taxes account:

Deferred taxes resulting from 197A operations (FC1,096,200 × $.2455)	$269,117
Deferred increase resulting from 197B operations (FC762,700 × $.2475)(see Exhibit II)	188,768
Deferred income taxes in dollars	$457,885

The final section of the 197B balance sheet to be translated is the stockholders' equity section. Since there have been no additional sales of common stock, the 197B balances will be the same as the 197A balances. Recall that the common stock was translated at $12,750,000, and the contributed capital in excess of par was translated at $19,681,512. It is now time to determine the residual value that will be assigned to the retained earnings account. The recap of liabilities and equities translated appears below:

Current liabilities	$ 1,726,711
Long-term debt	18,375,000
Deferred income taxes	457,885
Common stock	12,750,000
Contributed capital in excess of par	19,681,512
Total liabilities and equities translated	$52,991,108

This total now is compared with the total translated value of the assets to determine the balance in the retained earnings account. The comparison is shown below:

Translated value of assets	$53,685,678
Translated value of liabilities and equity accounts other than retained earnings	52,991,108
Retained earnings balance - 12/31/197B	$ 694,570

Again, this is the residual value that is needed to equate total assets with total liabilities and stockholders' equity. Keep in mind that we will return to this computation when it comes time to consider any translation gains or losses.

The translation of the 197B income statement is shown below. The procedures for translation are similar to those used to translate the 197A income statements. Any difference will be explained.

	Foreign Currency Balance	Translation Rate	Dollar Balance
Sales	84,075,500	$ .2475	$20,808,686
Costs and Expenses:			
Cost of goods sold:			
Inventory—January 1	7,900,500	$ .2425*	$ 1,915,871
Production costs	48,462,500	$ .2475	11,994,468
Cost of goods available	56,363,000		$13,910,339
Inventory—December 31	(9,100,000)	$ .25**	(2,275,000)
Cost of goods sold	47,263,000		$11,635,339
General and Administrative expense	9,731,400	$ .2475	2,408,522
Advertising and selling	7,326,000	$ .2475	1,813,185
Depreciation (see Schedule 1 below)	12,002,000		2,996,816
Total costs and expenses	76,322,400		$18,853,862
Net income from operations	7,753,100		$ 1,954,824
Other income (expense)	(2,987,500)	$ .2475	(739,406)
Net income before taxes	4,765,600		$ 1,215,418
Income taxes:			
Current	1,143,700	$ .2475	$ 283,066
Deferred	762,700	$ .2475	188,768
Total taxes	1,906,400		$ 471,834
Net income	2,859,200		$ 743,584

*See 197A income statement
**See 197B balance sheet translation

Schedule 1
Calculation of Depreciation Expense for 197B

Straight-line depreciation in 197B on assets acquired in 197A (FC11,265,200 × $.25)	$2,816,300
Straight-line depreciation in 197B on assets acquired in 197B (FC736,800 × $.245)	180,516
Depreciation expense - 197B	$2,996,816

As part of the detailed analysis of the statement of retained earnings for 197B, it is necessary to translate the dividend in a manner similar to that used in 197A. Assuming that FC500,000 of dividends are declared quarterly, the following computations are needed to translate the 197B dividends:

March 31 dividend (FC500,000 × $.245)	$122,500
June 30 dividend (FC500,000 × $.25)	125,000
September 30 dividend (FC500,000 × $.25)	125,000
December 31 dividend (FC500,000 × $.245)	122,500
Dividends for 197B	$495,000

Based upon the information generated thus far for 197B, the retained earnings account appears as follows:

Retained earnings—January 1	$ 819,248
Add net income for the year	743,584
Deduct dividends for the year	(495,000)
Retained earnings—December 31	$1,067,832

However, the retained earnings balance determined during the translation of the balance sheet was $694,570. Once again, the difference between the two balances must be the exchange gain or loss for the period. In this particular year, Foreign Enterprise experienced an exchange loss in the amount of $373,262 ($1,067,832 – $694,570). Once the loss has been determined, the income statement for 197B must be recast. The partial income statement is shown below:

Net income from operations		$1,954,824
Nonoperating items:		
Other income (expense)	$(739,406)	
Translation loss	(373,262)	(1,112,668)
Net income before taxes		$ 842,156
Income taxes		
Current	$ 283,066	
Deferred	188,768	471,834
Net income		$ 370,322

The final step is to restate net income in the statement of retained earnings for 197B. This would be accomplished as follows:

Retained earnings—January 1	$819,248
Add net income for the year	370,322
Deduct dividends for the year	(495,000)
Retained earnings—December 31	$694,570

Exhibits V, VI and VII show the translated balance sheets, income statements and statements of retained earnings for Foreign Enterprise, Ltd.

Exhibit V

Balance Sheet—Foreign Enterprise, Ltd.

December 31, 197B and 197A

	197B	197A
Current Assets:		
Cash	$ 306,250	$ 229,512
Accounts receivable—trade	956,113	586,488
Accounts receivable—intercompany	210,000	-0-
Notes receivable	727,650	240,000
Inventories	2,275,000	1,915,871
Prepaid expenses	106,325	-0-
Accrued interest on notes receivable	8,771	2,736
Total Current Assets	$ 4,590,109	$ 2,974,607
Long-Term Notes Receivable	$ 1,470,000	$ 1,440,000
Property, Plant and Equipment:		
Land	$ 4,335,000	$ 4,335,000
Buildings	39,157,215	37,452,750
Fixtures and equipment	9,946,470	8,156,500
Total Property, Plant and Equipment	$53,438,685	$49,944,250
Accumulated depreciation	(5,813,116)	(2,816,300)
Net Property, Plant and Equipment	$47,625,569	$47,127,950
Total Assets	$53,685,678	$51,542,557
Current Liabilities:		
Accounts payable	$ 679,765	$ 870,720
Accrued interest on long-term debt	124,950	108,000
Income taxes payable	186,996	183,960
Dividends payable	122,500	60,000
Current maturities on long-term debt	612,500	600,000
Total Current Liabilities	$ 1,726,711	$ 1,822,680
Long-Term Debt	$18,375,000	$16,200,000
Deferred Income Taxes	$ 457,885	$ 269,117
Stockholders' Equity		
Common stock	$12,750,000	$12,750,000
Contributed capital in excess of par	19,681,512	19,681,512
Retained earnings	694,570	819,248
Total Stockholders' Equity	$33,126,082	$33,250,760
Total Liabilities and Stockholders' Equity	$53,685,678	$51,542,557

Exhibit VI

Income Statement—Foreign Enterprise, Ltd.

Years Ended December 31, 197B and 197A

	197B	197A
Sales	$20,808,686	$17,989,258
Costs and Expenses:		
Cost of goods sold:		
Inventory—January 1	$ 1,915,871	$ -0-
Production costs	11,994,468	12,266,554
Cost of goods available for sale	$13,910,339	$12,266,554
Inventory—December 31	(2,275,000)	(1,915,871)
Cost of goods sold	$11,635,339	$10,350,683
General and administrative	2,408,522	2,024,148
Advertising and selling	1,813,185	1,146,853
Depreciation	2,996,816	2,816,300
Total costs and expenses	$18,853,862	$16,337,984
Net income from operations	$ 1,954,824	$ 1,651,274
Nonoperating items:		
Other income (expense)	$ (739,406)	$ (166,498)
Translation gain (loss)	(373,262)	130,115
Total nonoperating items	$(1,112,668)	$ (36,383)
Net income before income taxes	$ 842,156	$ 1,614,891
Income Taxes:		
Current	$ 283,066	$ 280,901
Deferred	188,768	269,117
Total Taxes	$ 471,834	$ 550,018
Net Income	$ 370,322	$ 1,064,873

Exhibit VII

Statement of Retained Earnings—Foreign Enterprise, Ltd.

Years Ended December 31, 197B and 197A

	197B	197A
Retained earnings—January 1	$ 819,248	$ -0-
Add net income for the year	370,322	1,064,873
Deduct dividends for the year	(495,000)	(245,625)
Retained earnings—December 31	$ 694,570	$ 819,248

With some supplemental information and the translated financial statements, American Manufacturing Company, the parent, could prepare the necessary statement of changes in financial position for Foreign Enterprise, Ltd.

Additional Considerations for the Translation Process

There are several additional problem areas that must be mentioned for a complete understanding of SFAS No. 8.

Recall that deferred income taxes were translated at the average rate during the period. The assumption was made that income was earned uniformly during the period, and that taxes would accrue in a similar manner. However, if the deferral of taxes is the result of assets that were translated at an historical rate, the computation of the deferred amount should be based upon the same historical rate. For example, if the tax deferral in 197A was the result of the use of straight-line depreciation for financial purposes and some accelerated method for tax purposes, the deferral would be the result of differences in depreciation. Since depreciation expense is translated at the appropriate historical rate, the computation of the tax deferral also should be based upon that rate. Before a proper translation of the deferred income tax account can be made, the accountant must first determine the source of the timing difference and then apply the appropriate exchange rate. The use of the average rate in the above example was for illustrative purposes only. In practice, the proper translation of the tax deferral may be quite time-consuming.

Another significant point deals with the valuation of inventory by the foreign company. If inventories are carried at lower of cost or market in the foreign currency balance sheet, the comparison of cost to market should be made in dollars, rather than in the foreign currency. For example, assume that inventories in the foreign company's financial statement had a cost basis of FC100,000 and a market value of FC95,000. Applying the rule of lower of cost or market, the inventories would be valued at market of FC95,000. However, also assume that the current exchange rate at the balance sheet date was FC1 = $.26, and the historical rate applicable to inventories carried at cost was FC1 = $.24. Remember that inventories carried at market would be translated at the current exchange rate, rather than at the historical rate. Given this information, the inventories would be translated into the following dollar amounts:

Inventories at Cost (FC100,000 × $.24)	$24,000
Inventories at Market (FC95,000 × $.26)	$24,700

When the inventories are converted into dollars, market is greater than cost. Therefore, it would be proper to value the inventories at cost of $24,000 on the translated balance sheet. This example points up the importance of making the comparison of cost and market in dollars rather than in the foreign currency.

The translated "market" of $24,700 shown above should be equal to the current foreign currency replacement cost translated at the current exchange rate (see FASB Interpretation No. 17, Paragraph 5). However, translated market value must not exceed the foreign currency net realizable value translated at the current rate, and must not be lower than foreign currency net realizable value reduced by the normal profit margin translated at the current rate. This definition of "market" is consistent with current GAAP. If, in a given case, market was determined to be lower than cost, an inventory write-down would be required. The loss resulting from the write-down should *not* be included in the aggregate exchange gain or loss, but should be disclosed and reported in the income statement.

Disclosures

A U.S. company may find it necessary to include foreign currency financial statements, or summary information from those statements, in statements of the U.S. company for years prior to the effective date of SFAS No. 8 (fiscal years beginning on or after January 1, 1976). If this is the case, the foreign currency statements should be restated to comply with the provisions of the Statement. In addition, the company must disclose the effects of the restatement on income before extraordinary items, net income and earnings per share. In some cases, it may not be possible to restate all prior period financial statements. Where this problem exists, the company should restate as many prior years as is practicable. The cumulative effect of the restatement on retained earnings should be disclosed in a manner consistent with the provisions of APB Opinion No. 20, "Accounting Changes" (see Topic 1 for a complete analysis of APB Opinion No. 20). In addition, the reason for not restating other prior years should be explained.

The basic disclosures required by the Statement include:

(1) The aggregate amount of exchange gains or losses included in income;

(2) If practicable, quantified effects of exchange rate changes on income, other than those disclosed in (1) above; and

(3) If an exchange rate change occurs after the balance sheet date, but before the financial statements are issued, and the change has a material impact on the financial statements, the effects of the rate change.

The example disclosures include a footnote from the 1976 annual reports of Campbell Soup Company and Addressograph-Multigraph Corporation. Notice the disclosure of exchange gains and losses in the Campbell Soup Company note and the fact that prior restatement was not deemed to be necessary. The note of Addressograph-Multigraph deals with the effects of financial statement restatement as a result of SFAS No. 8.

Campbell Soup Company (Jul)

Summary of Significant Accounting Policies

Translation of Foreign Currencies—Foreign currency assets and liabilities are translated at year-end rates of exchange except for inventories, plant assets and related depreciation which are translated at rates in effect at the time of acquisition. Income and expense accounts, except depreciation, are translated at the average exchange rates in effect during the year. All foreign exchange gains and losses are included in income.

In fiscal 1976, the Company changed its method of accounting for foreign currency translation to comply with FASB Statement No. 8, Accounting for the Translation of Foreign Currency Transactions and Foreign Currency Financial Statements. The effect of adopting this statement was not significant and accordingly prior period accounts were not restated:

Notes to Consolidated Financial Statements

(000 omitted from dollar amounts)

Note 1 (in part): Consolidation—Net assets of domestic and foreign companies were:

	1976	1975
Companies in:		
United States	$603,012	$571,917
Foreign countries	101,870	94,483
	$704,882	$666,400

Foreign exchange amounts recorded in earning were the following:

	1976	1975
Exchange gains (losses)	$ (580)	$ 762
Unrealized gains (losses) from currency translation	826	(1,775)
	$ 246	$(1,013)

Income taxes have not been accrued on $77,039 of undistributed earnings of foreign subsidiaries ($69,361 in 1975) which are invested in operating assets and are not expected to be remitted or if remitted will not result in significant tax amounts after considering the effect of available tax credits and adjustments.

Included in Payable to suppliers and others are bank overdrafts of $33,721 in 1976 and $10,984 in 1975.

Addressograph-Multigraph Corporation (Jul)

Consolidated Statement of Retained Earnings

	1976	1975
	($000)	
Retained Earnings at Beginning of Year:		
As previously reported		$115,099
Retroactive restatement of prior years earnings		692
As restated	$122,048	115,791
Net income	6,431	6,257
Retained Earnings at End of Year	$128,479	$122,048

Notes to Financial Statements

Change in Accounting Principle—In 1976, the company changed its method of accounting for the translation of foreign currency transactions and financial statements to comply with a recent statement of the Financial Accounting Standards Board. The 1975 financial statements have been restated for this change. Under this new method foreign subsidiary inventories are translated at historical currency exchange rates rather than current rates and exchange gains and losses are included in current results of operations rather than applied to a reserve.

The effect of this accounting change on net income and net income per share is as follows:

(Dollars in thousands except per share data)	1976	1975
Increase (decrease) in net income	$(612)	$1,349
Increase (decrease) in net income per share of common stock	$(.08)	$ .17

Source: *Accounting Trends & Techniques,* Copyright © 1977 by the American Institute of Certified Public Accountants, Inc., pp. 280 and 306.

Topic 11

Business Combinations

Detail Contents

APB Opinions and SFAS Statements

1. APB Opinion No. 16	–Business Combinations
2. SFAS No. 10	–Extension of "Grandfather" Provision for Business Combinations

FASB Interpretations

1. FASB Interpretation No. 9	–Applying APB Opinion Nos. 16 and 17 When a Savings and Loan Association or a Similar Institution is Acquired in a Business Combination Accounted for by the Purchase Method (Interpretation of APB Opinion Nos. 16 and 17)
2. FASB Interpretation No. 25	–Accounting for an Unused Investment Tax Credit (Interpretation of APB Opinion Nos. 2, 4, 11 and 16)

Future Considerations of the FASB

1. Exposure Draft	–Accounting for Preacquisition Contingencies of Purchased Enterprises (Proposed Amendment to APB Opinion No. 16)

This proposed amendment to APB Opinion No. 16 deals with the proper accounting for contingencies of an acquired company that were in existence at the date of purchase. The Exposure Draft blends SFAS No. 5, Accounting for Contingencies, with APB Opinion No. 16. In effect, the proposal states that a contingency should be recorded as part of the allocation of the cost of the acquired company if (1) events indicate that it is probable that an asset existed, a liability had been incurred or an asset had been impaired at the date of the consummation of the business combination, and (2) the amount of the asset, liability or impairment can be reasonably estimated (See Topic 6 for a detailed explanation of SFAS No. 5).

After the consummation of the combination (which could take as long as one year), any adjustments that are the result of preacquisition contingencies should be included in income in the period in which the adjustment was recognized.

APB Opinion No. 16 (August 1970) Business Combinations

and

SFAS No. 10 (October 1975) Extension of "Grandfather" Provisions for Business Combinations

There are two generally accepted methods of accounting for business combinations. One is referred to as the "purchase" method, and the other is known as the "pooling of interests" method. These two methods are *not* alternative ways to account for the same business combination. Rather, an analysis of the fact situation and the attributes of the combination are studied to determine which of the two methods is applicable. If the purchase method is shown to be applicable in a given situation, the pooling of interests method is of no further concern to the accountant.

As an introduction, some of the general characteristics of a combination that indicate the use of the purchase and pooling of interests methods will be discussed.

In general, the purchase method would be applicable in a situation where one company is "buying out" another. The former company is referred to as the surviving company, and the latter is the acquired company. The combination represents a purchase transaction. The transaction may be viewed as the owners of the acquired company selling their interest to the surviving company. Because the combination is treated as a purchase transaction, the assets acquired and the liabilities assumed must be recorded by the surviving company at their fair values. If there is a difference between the total purchase price and the fair value of the net assets, it is accounted for as either goodwill or negative goodwill. (See APB Opinion No. 17 in Topic 4 for a complete analysis of accounting for goodwill.)[1]

In contrast, the pooling of interests method would be applicable in a situation where two or more companies decide to combine their resources to form a "new" and more effective entity. The owners of the combining companies become the owners of the "new," combined company. It would be inappropriate to refer to any of the combining companies as an acquired company. A classic example of a pooling of interests would be when the shareholders of two companies surrender the stock owned in their respective companies for stock in a newly formed company. This type of transaction is rare. The more common case involves the shareholders of one company surrendering their stock for the stock of another of the combining company. There has been a combining of ownership interests, rather than a purchase transaction; therefore, the *recorded value* of the assets and liabilities combined will be carried forward. Since there was no purchase transaction, goodwill cannot be recognized.

From this short introduction, the reader should be aware that the two methods are intended to apply to totally different fact situations. The two methods have a significantly different impact on the financial statements of the surviving or combined company. Because the impact is so different, many accountants and others viewed the methods as alternatives that could be applied to any business combination. Often the method that effected the most favorable results was used to account for the combination, even in instances where the facts indicated the method selected was inappropriate. Many, including those in the accounting profession, voiced opposition to the practice of choosing either the purchase or pooling of interests methods. As a result, APB Opinion No. 16 was issued. The Opinion set down rigid guidelines for identifying a business combination that qualifies for treatment as a pooling of interests. If a planned combination failed to meet the specified guidelines, it could not be accounted for as a pooling of interests.

---

[1] FASB Interpretation No. 9 deals with the issues involved when an enterprise acquires a savings and loan or similar institution in a business combination accounted for as a purchase. The Board concluded that the "net-spread" method of assigning fair value to assets and liabilities is not appropriate because the method ignores fair values assigned to *individual* assets. Such transactions should be accounted for using the separate-valuation method, since it assigns fair value to *identifiable assets and liabilities either individually or in groups.*

Flowchart and General Discussion of Guidelines

The Flowchart identifies, in shortened form, the guidelines established by APB Opinion No. 16 for the identification of a pooling of interests business combination. The transaction to effect the combination must meet *all* of the conditions included in the Flowchart to be treated as a pooling of interests. Each of the conditions specified in the numbered blocks will need some explanation and elaboration. It is equally important to understand the reason for the conditions specified as to know the conditions themselves. By understanding the intent of the Opinion, one is better able to comply with the spirit of the Pronouncement.

The conditions are listed in the Flowchart under three broad headings. The first set of two conditions relates to an examination of the attributes of the combining companies. The next set of seven conditions relates to the method used to combine the companies, and the last set of three conditions relates to certain events taking place after the combination has been completed.

If, in fact, a pooling of interests is an effort on the part of the owners of two or more companies to combine their resources, those owners must be free to exercise independent judgment as to the desirability of the proposed combination. Therefore, it is essential that each of the combining companies be autonomous and not, in the words of APB Opinion No. 16, Paragraph 46, "a subsidiary or division of another corporation" (Block 1). The combining companies must be autonomous for at least two years prior to the plan to combine. For purposes of this two-year rule, the date of the plan refers to the time when the shareholders are made aware of the terms of the combination, *or* the date the shareholders are given written notice of the terms of the combination, whichever date is earlier.

In addition to being independent of some other corporation, the combining companies must be independent of each other (Block 2). Being independent of each other means that the combining companies own *no more* than 10 percent of the voting common stock of any of the other combining companies. An exception to this general rule is provided for ownership of stock acquired prior to the effective date of the Opinion (November 1, 1970). This exception is referred to as the "grandfather provision," and provides for two ownership exceptions: first, the holding of 50 percent or less of the voting common stock will not prevent the transaction from being accounted for as a pooling of interests; and, second, a company classified as a subsidiary with a significant minority interest in its stock (20 to 50 percent) may be the issuing company in a pooling of interests, provided the pooling does not involve the parent and subsidiary

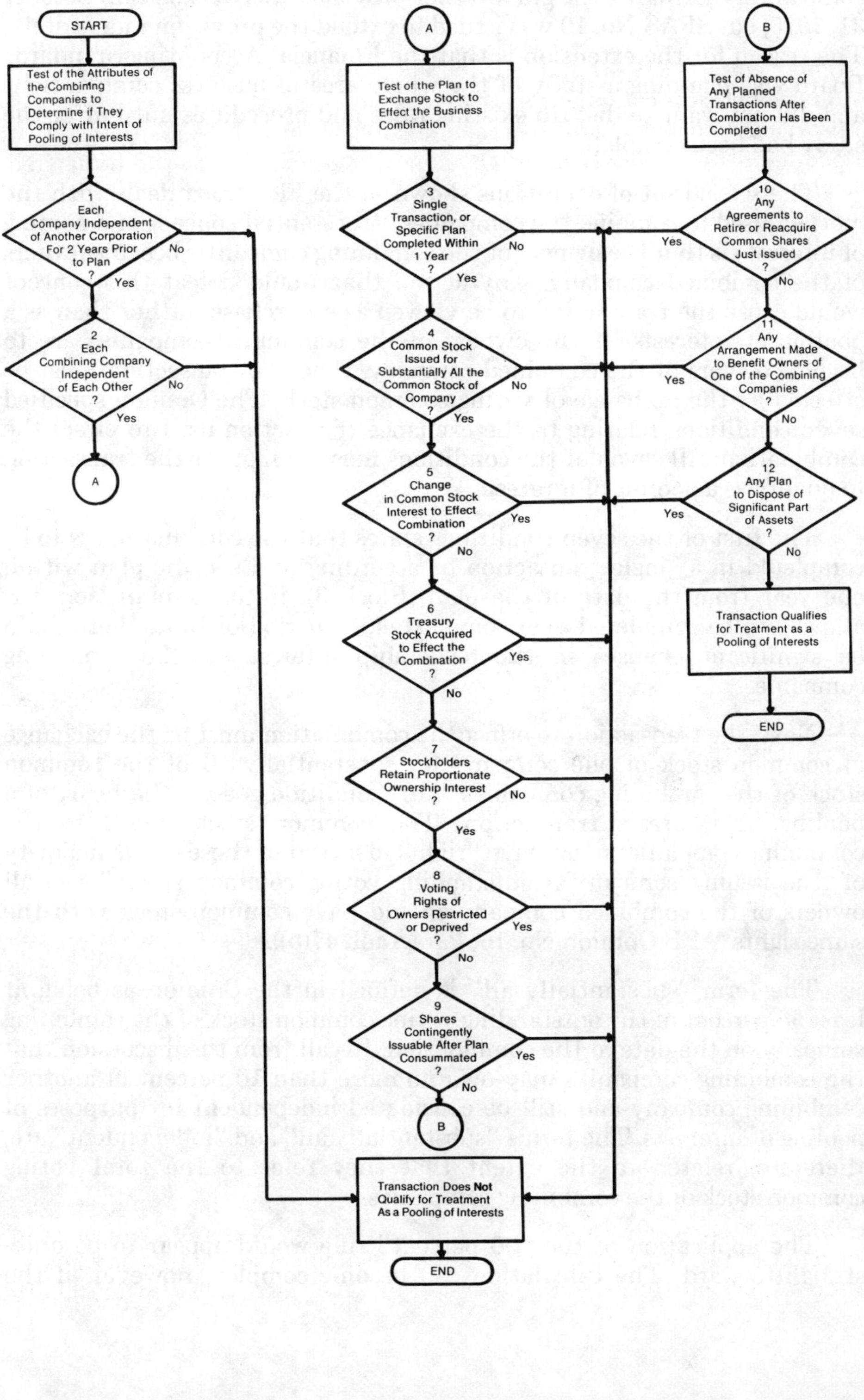
START
Test of the Attributes of the Combining Companies to Determine if They Comply with Intent of Pooling of Interests
1 Each Company Independent of Another Corporation For 2 Years Prior to Plan ?
No
Yes
2 Each Combining Company Independent of Each Other ?
No
Yes
A
A
Test of the Plan to Exchange Stock to Effect the Business Combination
3 Single Transaction, or Specific Plan Completed Within 1 Year ?
No
Yes
4 Common Stock Issued for Substantially All the Common Stock of Company ?
No
Yes
5 Change in Common Stock Interest to Effect Combination ?
Yes
No
6 Treasury Stock Acquired to Effect the Combination ?
Yes
No
7 Stockholders Retain Proportionate Ownership Interest ?
No
Yes
8 Voting Rights of Owners Restricted or Deprived ?
Yes
No
9 Shares Contingently Issuable After Plan Consummated ?
Yes
No
B
Transaction Does Not Qualify for Treatment As a Pooling of Interests
END
B
Test of Absence of Any Planned Transactions After Combination Has Been Completed
10 Any Agreements to Retire or Reacquire Common Shares Just Issued ?
Yes
No
11 Any Arrangement Made to Benefit Owners of One of the Combining Companies ?
Yes
No
12 Any Plan to Dispose of Significant Part of Assets ?
Yes
No
Transaction Qualifies for Treatment as a Pooling of Interests
END

companies. Originally, the grandfather provision was to expire on October 31, 1975, but SFAS No. 10 was issued to extend the provision indefinitely. The reason for the extension is that the Financial Accounting Standards Board was planning a study of the whole area of business combinations and did not want to disturb existing rules and procedures until after the study had been completed.

The second set of conditions shown in the Flowchart deals with the method used to combine the companies. An essential concept of a pooling of interests is that the owners of the combining companies become owners of the combined company. Any action that would defeat this concept would cause the transaction to be viewed as a purchase, rather than as a pooling of interests. If the owners of the combining companies are to become owners of the combined company, then the transaction must be effected by the exchange of voting common stock. The Opinion specified seven conditions relating to the exchange transaction used to effect the combination. All seven of the conditions must be met for the transaction to qualify as a pooling of interests.

The first of the seven conditions states that the combination is to be completed in a single transaction or according to a specific plan within one year from the date of the plan (Block 3). If the combination was allowed to be completed over some extended period of time, there could be significant changes in the ownership interests of the combining companies.

Next, the transaction to effect the combination must be the exchange of common stock of one company for substantially all of the common stock of the combining companies. This condition goes to the heart of a pooling of interests transaction. The common stock issued to the combining companies must have "rights identical to those of the majority of (the issuing company's) outstanding voting common stock," i.e., all owners of the combined company should have common stock with the same rights (APB Opinion No. 16, Paragraph 47(b)).

The term "substantially all" is defined in the Opinion as being at least 90 percent of the outstanding voting common stock of the combining company on the date of the combination. Recall from the discussion that the combining companies may own no more than 10 percent of another combining company and still be considered independent for purposes of pooling of interests. The terms "substantially all" and "independent" are, therefore, related to the extent that they refer to the total voting common stock of the combining companies.

The application of the "90 percent" rule would appear to be quite straightforward. The calculation can become complex, however, if the combining companies have reciprocal holdings of each other's common stock.

The problem is to determine the "equivalent" number of common shares acquired from the combining companies. The existence of intercorporate investments in common stock clouds the issue of the number of shares actually exchanged in the combination. For example, if the company issuing the common stock in a combination (issuing company) owns voting common stock of the company receiving stock in the combination (receiving company), how would the accountant treat the stock already owned by the issuing company? On the other hand, suppose the receiving company owns voting common stock of the issuing company. How would these shares be handled in the combination? In any business combination, the number of shares actually issued can be readily determined. The problem is to determine the number of "equivalent" shares received for the shares issued.

If combining companies have reciprocal holdings of voting common stock, the number of shares of stock of the receiving company outstanding at the date of combination must be adjusted for the intercorporate holdings. The adjusted shares outstanding represent the equivalent number of shares received in the exchange, and serve as the basis of the 90 percent test. To convert from shares outstanding at the date of combination to the equivalent shares received, the following adjustments are required:

(1) Reduce shares outstanding by the number of shares of the receiving company held by the issuing company at the date the plan was initiated;

(2) Reduce shares outstanding by the number of shares of the receiving company purchased by the issuing company between the date of the plan and the date of the combination;

(3) Reduce the shares outstanding by the "equivalent" number of shares of the issuing company held by the receiving company at the date the plan was initiated;

(4) Reduce the shares outstanding by the "equivalent" number of shares of the issuing company acquired by the receiving company between the date of the plan and the date of the combination; and

(5) Reduce the shares outstanding by the number of shares that will remain outstanding after the combination is complete.

Notice that, when the receiving company owns voting common stock of the issuing company, the shares held must be converted to an equivalent number of shares. The conversion is based upon the exchange ratio of the two stocks involved in the combination.

To illustrate the problem involved in determining the number of common shares outstanding for purposes of the 90 percent rule, assume the facts listed in Exhibit I apply to a business combination.

Exhibit I

Computation of Equivalent Number of Shares Outstanding

1. Jar, Inc. and Book-It, Inc. plan to combine resources in a pooling of interests. Jar, Inc. is to issue two of its common shares for each share of Book-It, Inc. common stock outstanding on March 1, 197A.
2. On January 1, 197A, the date of the plan to combine, Jar, Inc. had 50,000,000 common shares outstanding and Book-It, Inc. had 5,000,000 common shares issued and 100,000 shares of common stock held in the treasury.
3. On January 1, 197A, Jar, Inc. held 200,000 common shares of Book-It, Inc. and Book-It, Inc. held 300,000 shares of Jar, Inc.
4. On February 1, 197A, Jar, Inc. acquired an additional 150,000 common shares of Book-It, Inc. for cash.

On March 1, 197A, the date of the exchange of stock, the number of outstanding shares of Book-It, Inc. (for purposes of the exchange) would be determined as follows:

Shares Issued, January 1, 197A	5,000,000
Shares of Treasury Stock Held	(100,000)
Shares Held by Jar, Inc. at Date of Plan	(200,000)
Shares Purchased by Jar, Inc. Subsequent to the Date of the Plan	(150,000)
Common Shares Outstanding, March 1, 197A	4,550,000

On March 1, Jar, Inc. would issue 9,100,000 of its common shares to acquire the common shares of Book-It, Inc. outstanding on that date (4,550,000 × 2 shares). The question is: "Did the combination meet the 90 percent rule?" To answer this question, it is necessary to calculate the number of *equivalent* shares of Book-It, Inc. acquired by Jar, Inc. Intercompany holdings of stock must be used to adjust the number of common shares outstanding. The computation of equivalent shares is shown below:

Shares Issued—January 1	5,000,000
Treasury Shares Held at Date of Combination	(100,000)
Total Shares Outstanding at date of Combination	4,900,000
Shares Held by Jar, Inc. at Date of Plan	200,000
Shares Purchased by Jar, Inc. Subsequent to the Date of the Plan	150,000
Equivalent Number of Jar, Inc. Shares Held by Book-It, Inc. (300,000/2)	150,000
Total Intercompany Shares	500,000
Equivalent Number of Book-It Common Shares Outstanding at Date of Exchange	4,400,000

On the basis of this calculation, Jar, Inc. received an equivalent of 4,400,000 common shares in exchange for 9,100,000 of its common shares. Ninety percent of the common shares outstanding of Book-It, Inc. on the date of combination would be 4,410,000 (4,900,000 × 90%). Jar, Inc. acquired an equivalent of 4,400,000, which is less than 90 percent of the shares outstanding (4,410,000); therefore, the combination *fails* to meet the 90-percent test, and the combination does not qualify as a pooling of interests. For the combination to qualify as a pooling of interests, Jar, Inc. must purchase at least 4,410,000 equivalent shares.

Because the exchange ratio was two shares of Jar, Inc. for each one share of Book-It, Inc. outstanding, the 300,000 shares of Jar, Inc. held by Book-It, Inc. were converted to 150,000 equivalent shares. The 300,000 pre-exchange common shares are equivalent to 150,000 post-exchange shares as a result of the exchange ratio.

As a point of interest, notice that neither company violated the independence rule concerning 10 percent ownership interest. Ten percent of the outstanding common shares of Jar, Inc. would be 5,000,000 (50,000,000 × 10%), and Book-It never owned more than 300,000 shares of Jar, Inc. stock. Ten percent of Book-It common stock outstanding would be 490,000 (4,900,000 × 10%), and Jar, Inc. never owned more than 350,000 common shares of Book-It.

The next condition (APB Opinion No. 16, Paragraph 47(c)) states that none of the combining companies may change the equity interest of its common shareholders "in contemplation of effecting the combination." No such action may take place for two years prior to the plan or between the date of the plan to combine and the actual combination (Block 5). As indicated above, the plan of combination must be executed within one year from the date it is formulated. Changing the interest of common stockholders may be prohibited for as long as three years prior to the consummation of the combination. A change in the equity interest would be indicated by unusual distributions to shareholders in the form of cash or stock dividends, additional issues of common stock or the retirement of outstanding securities.

A related condition prohibits the purchase of treasury stock to effectuate the business combination (Block 6). The time period applicable to this condition is the same as indicated previously, i.e., for two years prior to the plan and between the date of the plan and its execution. Combining companies may purchase treasury stock during this period for some reason other than effecting the combination. However, it is difficult to determine the intended use of the treasury stock. As a result, any treasury shares acquired during this time period are referred to as "tainted" shares. In the absence of substantial evidence to the contrary, the tainted shares are *assumed* to have been purchased to effect the combination. Of course, the combining company that purchased the treasury shares can avoid the problem of tainted shares by selling the stock prior to the combination. Common shares frequently are reacquired and reserved for use in a stock option plan or some other plan to distribute stock to employees. If the company acquiring the treasury shares can demonstrate that the stock is reserved for a specific purpose, the shares generally will not be considered tainted. Treasury shares purchased prior to two years before the plan to combine may be issued in connection with the combination and will not disqualify the transaction from pooling of interests accounting. Tainted treasury shares also may be issued, providing the number of shares is not material in relation to the total number of shares to be issued.

Yet another condition requires that individual common stockholders in a combining company retain their proportionate ownership interest as a result of the exchange (Block 7). This condition does not imply that, if an individual stockholder owns a two percent interest in the combining company, he will own a two percent interest in the combined company. Rather, the owner will retain his proportionate ownership interest relative to other owners of the *combining* company. For example, if after the exchange has been completed, two shareholders in a combining company own one percent and two percent, respectively, of the common stock of the combining company, the relationship between the two shareholders still will be 2 to 1. This is true even though their percentage of ownership in the combined company may be quite small. The relationship among the shareholders of the combining company should remain the same as a result of the combination.

The voting rights of the stockholders of the combined company cannot be restricted or deprived (Block 8). To do so would, in effect, violate the general concept of a pooling of interests, which requires that the owners of the combining companies become the owners of the combined company. If a shareholder receives stock in a business combination, but can't vote the shares, a major right of stock ownership has been taken away. This condition also would be violated if the shares of stock were to be transferred to a voting trust rather than to the shareholders.

The final condition relating to the method of effecting the combination requires that the total consideration involved in the transaction be paid and received at the date of the combination (Block 9). This condition prohibits the existence of contingent consideration in connection with a combination that is to be accounted for as a pooling of interests. Common examples of contingent consideration include issuance of additional shares to the combining company upon obtaining a certain level of profits, or upon the market price of the stock reaching a certain level. Sometimes the contingent consideration is placed in escrow until such time as the conditions of payment are met or expire as a result of the passage of time. These types of arrangements are prohibited if the transaction is to be treated as a pooling of interests.

The final three conditions deal with events that take place after the combination has been completed. An assumption implicit in the notion of a pooling of interests is that there will be some continuity of ownership of the combining companies. This does not mean that a shareholder in a combining company may not sell his shares of the combined company, but rather that the combined company should not enter into any agreement that would disrupt the continuity of ownership interest.

The first condition specified in the Opinion prohibits the combined company from agreeing to retire or reacquire any part of the stock issued to complete the combination (Block 10). If such an agreement were in effect, the owners of one of the combining companies would, in effect, be receiving cash, rather than stock. This type of agreement defeats the purpose of a pooling of interests, which requires the owners of the combining companies to become the owners of the combined company.

The second condition prohibits the combined company from entering into any financial arrangement that would benefit the shareholders of one of the combining companies. All shareholders of the combined company should have the same rights and be treated equally. Preferential treatment of one group of shareholders would violate this concept.

The final condition specifies that the combined company must not plan to sell a significant part of the assets received in the combination for two years after the date of the combination (Block 12). This prohibition does not apply to disposals of assets in the normal course of business or to duplicate facilities, but is meant to apply to major dispositions of assets.

After reading the above discussion, the reader is aware that, for a business combination to qualify for pooling of interests accounting, the events must be carefully planned and executed. The spirit of the concept of pooling of interests as well as the specific rules of the Opinion must be followed for an extended period of time. As a result of the Opinion, the number of combinations qualifying as pooling of interests has dropped drastically. Most business combinations now are treated as purchases. The accountant should play a key role in the planning of a combination that is to be accounted for as a pooling of interests.

To this point, discussion has centered around the identification of a pooling of interests business combination. The discussion and examples that follow will show the different accounting treatments given to a purchase and a pooling transaction.

Purchase Accounting

When a business combination qualifies as a purchase transaction, the assets acquired should be recorded at cost. The cost of the assets to the acquiring company is equal to their fair value on the date of the combination. Any excess of the total purchase price over the fair value of the net assets acquired is accounted for as goodwill.

Exhibit II
Balance Sheet—Book-It, Inc.
June 30, 197B

	Cost	Fair Value	Basis of Fair Value
Current Assets:			
Cash	$ 301,500	$ 301,500	N/A
Marketable securities	125,000	167,200	Realizable Value
Accounts receivable (net)	925,810	898,625	Present Value
Inventories	1,927,350	2,128,170	Schedule 1
Prepaid expenses	102,200	102,200	Appraisal Value
Total Current Assets	$ 3,381,860	$ 3,597,695	
Long-Term Investments	$ 6,000,000	$ 6,500,000	Realizable Value
Property, Plant and Equipment:			
Land	$ 8,950,000	$12,500,000	Appraisal Value
Buildings	15,120,500	21,250,000	Replacement Cost
Equipment	7,881,270	9,675,500	Replacement Cost
Total Property, Plant and Equipment	$31,951,770	$43,425,500	
Accumulated Depreciation	(3,263,100)	(4,332,300)	Replacement Cost
Net Property, Plant and Equipment	$28,688,670	$39,093,200	
Intangible Assets (net):			
Patents	$ 1,762,500	$ 850,000	Appraisal Value
Trademark	123,260	560,000	Appraisal Value
Total Intangible Assets	$ 1,885,760	$ 1,410,000	
Total Assets	$39,956,290	$50,600,895	
Current Liabilities:			
Accounts payable	$ 1,267,370	$ 1,264,500	Present Value
Accrued interest	247,300	247,300	Present Value
Income taxes payable	185,325	181,400	Present Value
Dividends payable	200,000	200,000	Present Value
Current maturities on long-term debt	2,000,000	1,992,575	Present Value
Total Current Liabilities	$ 3,899,995	$ 3,885,775	
Long-Term Debt	$12,375,000	$12,375,000	Present Value
Stockholders' Equity:			
Common stock, $2 par	$ 8,000,000	-	
Contributed capital in excess of par	10,783,960	-	
Retained earnings	4,897,335	-	
Total Stockholders' Equity	$23,681,295	$34,340,120	Residual Value
Total Liabilities and Stockholders' Equity	$39,956,290	$50,600,895	

Schedule 1
Fair Value of Inventories

	Cost	Fair Value	Basis of Fair Value
Raw materials inventory	$ 481,837	$ 503,920	Replacement Cost
Work in process inventory	289,103	296,750	Realizable Value*
Finished goods inventory	1,156,410	1,327,500	Realizable Value*
Total Inventories	$1,927,350	$2,128,170	

* Reduced by a reasonable profit

Exhibit III
Income Statement—Book-It, Inc.
Six Months Ended June 30, 197B

Sales	$20,808,686
Costs and Expenses:	
Cost of goods sold:	
Inventory—January 1, 197B	$ 1,915,871
Production costs	11,994,468
Cost of goods available for sale	$13,910,339
Inventory—June 30, 197B	(1,927,350)
Cost of goods sold	$11,982,989
General and administrative	2,024,148
Advertising and selling	1,813,185
Depreciation	872,937
Total Costs and Expenses	$16,693,259
Net income from operations	$ 4,115,427
Nonoperating income (expense)	(739,406)
Net income before taxes	$ 3,376,021
Income taxes	(1,485,449)
Net Income	$ 1,890,572

For purposes of illustration, assume that Jar, Inc. acquires the net assets of Book-It, Inc. by selling 6,000,000 of its common shares at $6 per share and purchasing all of Book-It's common stock outstanding at a price of $9 per share. To simplify the example, assume there are no direct or indirect costs to Jar, Inc. to effect the combination and that there is no contingent consideration. These two points will be discussed later in this section. Exhibits II and III show the balance sheet and income statement of Book-It, Inc. on June 30, 197B, the date of the combination.

The balance sheet shows both the cost of the assets and liabilities to Book-It and the fair value of the assets and liabilities on the date of acquisition. The far right column indicates the basis used to determine the fair value of each asset and liability. Paragraph 88 of the Opinion provides a guide for the determination of fair values in a purchase transaction. Schedule 1 presents the detailed analysis of the components of inventory and the basis used to determine the fair value of each. Notice that the stockholders' equity section of the fair value balance sheet is just shown as the total residual value. The fair value of the *net* assets acquired by Jar, Inc. is $34,340,120. The costs assigned to the various assets and liabilities will be the fair value at June 30, 197B.

Jar, Inc. sold 6,000,000 of its $1 par value common stock for $6 per share, and used the cash proceeds to purchase the 4,000,000 shares of Book-It, Inc. common stock at $9 per share. The total purchase price of the net assets acquired is $36,000,000 (4,000,000 × $9 per share). The cost basis to Jar, Inc. of the net assets acquired is $34,340,120; the difference between the purchase price ($36,000,000) and the cost of the net assets acquired ($34,340,120) is the amount assigned to goodwill ($1,659,880).[2]

The condensed entries presented are used to illustrate the issuance of the stock by Jar, Inc. and the recording of the assets acquired, and liabilities assumed, in the acquisition:

Cash	36,000,000	
Common Stock (6,000,000 × $1 par)		6,000,000
Contributed capital in excess of par		30,000,000
Current Assets	3,597,695	
Long-term Investments	6,500,000	
Property, Plant and Equipment	39,093,200	
Intangible Assets	1,410,000	
Goodwill	1,659,880	
Current Liabilities		3,885,775
Long-term Debt		12,375,000
Cash (4,000,000 × $9 per share)		36,000,000

Exhibit IV shows the balance sheet of Jar, Inc. immediately after the combination has been completed. The balance sheet of Jar, Inc. prior to the acquisition is shown in Exhibit V, and Exhibit VI shows the income statement for Jar, Inc. for the six months ended June 30, 197B.

---

[2] FASB Interpretation No. 25 addresses the issue of acquired unused investment tax credit in a business combination accounted for as a purchase. The Board concluded that, since APB Opinion No. 2 does not permit the unused credit to be recognized as an asset, special accounting is required for subsequent recognition of the amount. The acquiring company should reduce goodwill recognized in the combination by the amount of tax benefit *realized* from the unused credit in the period in which that credit offsets income taxes payable. Goodwill should not be reduced retroactively.

Exhibit IV
Balance Sheet After Acquisition—Jar, Inc.
June 30, 197B

	Jar, Inc. (Exhibit V)	Book-It, Inc. (Exhibit II)	Combined
Current Assets:			
Cash	$ 6,325,920	$ 301,500	$ 6,627,420
Marketable securities	-	167,200	167,200
Accounts receivable (net)	3,711,050	898,625	4,609,675
Inventories	12,621,307	2,128,170	14,749,477
Prepaid expenses	872,521	102,200	974,721
Total Current Assets	$ 23,530,798	$ 3,597,695	$ 27,128,493
Long-Term Investments	$ 25,006,250	$ 6,500,000	$ 31,506,250
Property, Plant and Equipment:			
Land	$ 18,728,500	$ 12,500,000	$ 31,228,500
Buildings	42,101,290	21,250,000	63,351,290
Equipment	15,271,008	9,675,500	24,946,508
Total Property, Plant and Equipment	$ 76,100,798	$ 43,425,500	$119,526,298
Accumulated Depreciation	(8,265,218)	(4,332,300)	(12,597,518)
Net Property, Plant and Equipment	$ 67,835,580	$ 39,093,200	$106,928,780
Intangible Assets (net):			
Patents	$ 735,600	$ 850,000	$ 1,585,600
Trademark	-	560,000	560,000
Goodwill (see entry to record purchase)	1,659,880	-	1,659,880
Total Intangible Assets	$ 2,395,480	$ 1,410,000	$ 3,805,480
Total Assets	$118,768,108	$ 50,600,895	$169,369,003
Current Liabilities:			
Accounts payable	$ 2,626,721	$ 1,264,500	$ 3,891,221
Accrued interest	625,250	247,300	872,550
Income taxes payable	1,928,700	181,400	2,110,100
Dividends payable	-	200,000	200,000
Current maturities on long-term debt	5,000,000	1,992,575	6,992,575
Total Current Liabilities	$ 10,180,671	$ 3,885,775	$ 14,066,446
Long-Term Debt	$ 40,000,000	$ 12,375,000	$ 52,375,000
Stockholders' Equity:			
Common Stock, $1 par	$ 26,000,000	-	$ 26,000,000
Contributed capital in excess of par	64,854,293	-	64,854,293
Retained earnings	12,073,264	-	12,073,264
Total Stockholders' Equity	$102,927,557		$102,927,557
Total Liabilities and Stockholders' Equity	$153,108,228	$ 16,260,775	$169,369,003

Exhibit V
Balance Sheet—Jar, Inc.
June 30, 197B

Current Assets:	
Cash	$ 6,325,920
Accounts receivable	3,711,050
Inventories	12,621,307
Prepaid expenses	872,521
Total Current Assets	$ 23,530,798
Investments	$ 25,006,250
Property, Plant and Equipment:	
Land	$ 18,728,500
Buildings	42,101,290
Equipment	15,271,008
Total Property, Plant and Equipment	$ 76,100,798
Accumulated Depreciation	(8,265,218)
Net Property, Plant and Equipment	$ 67,835,580
Intangible Assets (net):	
Patents	$ 735,600
Total Assets	$117,108,228
Current Liabilities:	
Accounts payable	$ 2,626,721
Accrued interest	625,250
Income taxes payable	1,928,700
Current maturities on long-term debt	5,000,000
Total Current Liabilities	$ 10,180,671
Long-Term Debt	$ 40,000,000
Stockholders' Equity:	
Common stock, $1 par	$ 20,000,000
Contributed capital in excess of par	34,854,293
Retained earnings	12,073,264
Total Stockholders' Equity	$ 66,927,557
Total Liabilities and Stockholders' Equity	$117,108,228

Exhibit VI
Income Statement—Jar, Inc.
Six Months Ended June 30, 197B

Sales	$35,634,500
Costs and Expenses:	
Cost of goods sold:	
Inventory—January 1, 197B	$13,025,673
Production costs	21,433,520
Cost of goods available for sale	$34,459,193
Inventory—June 30, 197B	(12,621,307)
Cost of goods sold	$21,837,886
General and administrative	3,786,542
Advertising and selling	2,004,655
Depreciation	1,703,500
Total Costs and Expenses	$29,332,583
Net income from operations	$ 6,301,917
Nonoperating income (expense)	(921,583)
Net income before taxes	$ 5,380,334
Income Taxes	(2,421,133)
Net Income	$ 2,959,201

The balance sheet of Jar, Inc. is represented by the combined column in Exhibit IV. It is difficult to review all of the balances in Exhibit IV in detail, but some of the more important balances will be discussed.

As a result of the purchase transaction, $1,659,880 of goodwill was recorded on the books of Jar, Inc. The goodwill is classified as an intangible asset and is subject to the provisions of APB Opinion No. 17. (See APB Opinion No. 17, "Intangible Assets," in Topic 4 for a detailed analysis of accounting for goodwill subsequent to acquisition.) The total proceeds from the sale of the 6,000,000 common shares of Jar, Inc. was $36,000,000. This amount affected Jar. Inc.'s common stock account and contributed capital in excess of par account. The common stock was increased by $6,000,000 (6,000,000 × $1 par value), and the remaining $30,000,000 of proceeds increased the contributed capital account. The balance in the common stock account on the balance sheet of Jar, Inc. is made up of the $20,000,000 from the original issue of stock and the $6,000,000 from the sale of shares to effect the acquisition. The balance in the contributed capital account ($64,854,293) is made up of the $34,854,293 from the original sale of the 20,000,000 shares of common stock and the $30,000,000 excess proceeds from the sale of stock to effect the acquisition.

Notice that there has been no change in the retained earnings account of Jar, Inc. as a result of the purchase transaction. If an income statement were to be prepared immediately after the acquisition, it would be the same as the Jar, Inc. income statement shown in Exhibit VI. There would be no change in net income as a result of the combination. This is an important point to remember, as there will be significant differences in these amounts under the pooling of interests example that follows.

Other Considerations in Purchase Accounting

There usually are costs associated with the arrangement of a business combination. If a company issues common stock in a purchase transaction, the costs of issuing the securities (e.g., preparation of the registration statement, SEC registration fees, etc.) should be used to reduce the contributed capital from the issuance of the stock. Indirect costs not associated with the issuance of securities should be charged to income.

In a purchase transaction, it is permissible to have contingent consideration in connection with the combination. Such consideration may be linked to a certain earnings level, a certain stock price or some other future event. The contingent consideration that is determinable at the date of combination should enter into the determination of the total purchase price of the acquired company. If the contingency is not determinable at the date of combination, it should not enter into the cost determination at that date. Instead, the terms of the contingency should be disclosed in the footnotes to the financial statements.

If the contingency is based upon future earnings, and was not determinable at the acquisition date, the consideration paid when the contingency is resolved should be recorded as an additional cost to the acquiring company. Generally, the additional consideration will be used to adjust the recorded goodwill.

It is possible for a purchase transaction to result in an excess of fair value of assets over cost to acquire those assets, i.e., a bargain purchase. In this case, the acquiring company would be faced with the recognition of "negative" goodwill. This certainly would be a rare occurance. If negative goodwill does result from a business combination recorded as a purchase, it should not be given accounting recognition. Rather, the amount of "negative" goodwill should be used to reduce the amounts assigned to noncurrent assets other than long-term marketable securities. If, after the reduction of noncurrent assets to zero, there is still an amount representing "negative" goodwill, it should be carried on the balance sheet as a deferred credit, and amortized according to the provisions of APB Opinion No. 17.

Disclosures required in a purchase combination will be discussed after the section dealing with pooling of interests.

Pooling of Interests Accounting

Because a pooling of interests represents a combining of resources, rather than a purchase transaction, the assets and liabilities of the combining companies are carried forward at their recorded amounts. No goodwill can result in a pooling of interests. The combining companies will be treated as if they had combined at the beginning of the period in which the combination was completed. This means that not only will assets and liabilities be combined, but so will revenues and expenses. In the purchase method, earnings of the acquired company prior to combination were not included in the income statement of the acquiring company. However, under pooling of interests accounting, income of the combining companies will be combined as if the combination took place at the beginning of the period.

To illustrate the features of pooling of interests accounting, assume that Jar, Inc. and Book-It, Inc. are to combine resources in a transaction that qualifies as a pooling, i.e., meets all 12 conditions listed in the Flowchart. The terms of the combination specify that Jar, Inc. is to issue 1½ shares of its voting common stock for each share of Book-It, Inc. common stock outstanding on June 30, 197B.

Exhibit II contains the balance sheet of Book-It on June 30, 197B. The total number of common shares outstanding is 4,000,000 ($8,000,000 recorded amount/$2 par value). Jar, Inc. will issue 6,000,000 of its common shares to effect the combination (4,000,000 × 1.5 shares). Every shareholder of Book-It, Inc. will receive 1½ shares of Jar, Inc. common for each share of Book-It, Inc. as a result of the combination. The owners of Book-It will become owners of Jar, Inc. Because assets and liabilities are to be carried forward at their recorded amounts, the common stock of Jar, Inc. will be issued at par value of $1 per share. The condensed entry shown below is representative of the type of entry required to record the pooling of interests:

Current Assets	3,381,860	
Long-Term Investments	6,000,000	
Property, Plant and Equipment	28,688,670	
Intangible Assets	1,885,760	
Current Liabilities		3,899,995
Long-Term Debt		12,375,000
Common Stock $1 par		6,000,000
Contributed Capital in Excess of par		12,783,960
Retained Earnings		4,897,335

By referring back to Exhibit II, notice that all assets and liabilities were carried forward at their recorded amounts. The 6,000,000 shares issued take on the value of the total contributed capital of Book-It, Inc.—$18,783,960 ($8,000,000 common stock + $10,783,960 contributed capital in excess of par). Of the $18,783,960, the amount to be assigned to the par value of the common stock issued ($6,000,000), and the remainder ($12,783,960), will be assigned to contributed capital in excess of par.

It is important to note that, if the total par value of the common stock issued is different from the total par value of the stock eliminated, the difference first is used to reduce or increase paid-in capital. If a situation should exist where paid-in capital is reduced to zero, the remaining difference is used to reduce retained earnings.

Exhibit VII shows the balance sheet of the combined company immediately after the pooling of interests.

Exhibit VII
Balance Sheet After Combination—Jar, Inc. and Company
June 30, 197B

	Jar, Inc. (Exhibit V)	Book-It Inc. (Exhibit II)	Combined
Current Assets:			
Cash	$ 6,325,920	$ 301,500	$ 6,627,420
Marketable securities	-	125,000	125,000
Accounts receivable (net)	3,711,050	925,810	4,636,860
Inventories	12,621,307	1,927,350	14,548,657
Prepaid expenses	872,521	102,200	974,721
Total Current Assets	$ 23,530,798	$ 3,381,860	$ 26,912,658
Long-Term Investments	$ 25,006,250	$ 6,000,000	$ 31,006,250
Property, Plant and Equipment:			
Land	$ 18,728,500	$ 8,950,000	$ 27,678,500
Buildings	42,101,290	15,120,500	57,221,790
Equipment	15,271,008	7,881,270	23,152,278
Total Property, Plant and Equipment	$ 76,100,798	$31,951,770	$108,052,568
Accumulated Depreciation	(8,265,218)	(3,263,100)	(11,528,318)
Net Property, Plant and Equipment	$ 67,835,580	$28,688,670	$ 96,524,250
Intangible Assets (net):			
Patents	$ 735,600	$ 1,762,500	$ 2,498,100
Trademark	-	123,260	123,260
Total Intangible Assets	$ 735,600	$ 1,885,760	$ 2,621,360
Total Assets	$117,108,228	$39,956,290	$157,064,518
Current Liabilities:			
Accounts payable	$ 2,626,721	$ 1,267,370	$ 3,894,091
Accrued interest	625,250	247,300	872,550
Income taxes payable	1,928,700	185,325	2,114,025
Dividends payable	-	200,000	200,000
Current maturities on long-term debt	5,000,000	2,000,000	7,000,000
Total Current Liabilities	$ 10,180,671	$ 3,899,995	$ 14,080,666
Long-Term Debt	$ 40,000,000	$12,375,000	$ 52,375,000
Stockholders' Equity:			
Common stock, $1 par	$ 26,000,000	-	$ 26,000,000
Contributed capital in excess of par	47,638,253	-	47,638,253
Retained earnings	16,970,599	-	16,970,599
Total Stockholders' Equity	$ 90,608,852		$ 90,608,852
Total Liabilities and Stockholders' Equity	$140,789,523	$16,274,995	$157,064,518

By looking back through Exhibits II and V, notice that the combined balance sheet just after combination is merely a summation of the amounts in the individual accounts of Jar, Inc. and Book-It, Inc. There were no intercompany transactions to be eliminated. The explanation of the changes in the equity section of the balance sheet has been made previously.

Exhibit VIII presents the combined income statement after acquisition. Jar, Inc. and Company would report income of $4,849,773 after the combination. The assumption is that the combining companies effected the transaction at the beginning of the year. This has an interesting affect on earnings per share reported after the combination. (See APB Opinion No. 15, "Earnings Per Share," in Topic 7 for a detailed analysis of the computation of earnings per share.) Before the combination, Jar, Inc. would have reported earnings per share of $.15 ($2,959,201/20,000,000 shares = $.14796 or $.15), and Book-It, Inc. would have reported earnings per share of $.47 ($1,890,572/4,000,000 shares = $.47264 or $.47).

Exhibit VIII

Income Statement After Combination—Jar, Inc. and Company
Six Months Ended June 30, 197A

	Jar, Inc. (Exhibit VI)	Book-It, Inc. (Exhibit III)	Combined
Sales	$35,634,500	$20,808,686	$56,443,186
Costs and Expenses:			
Cost of goods sold:			
Inventory—January 1, 197B	$13,025,673	$ 1,915,871	$14,941,544
Production costs	21,433,520	11,994,468	33,427,988
Cost of goods available	$34,459,193	$13,910,339	$48,369,532
Inventory—June 30, 197B	(12,621,307)	(1,927,350)	(14,548,657)
Cost of goods sold	$21,837,886	$11,982,989	$33,820,875
General and administrative	3,786,542	2,024,148	5,810,690
Advertising and selling	2,004,655	1,813,185	3,817,840
Depreciation	1,703,500	872,937	2,576,437
Total Costs and Expenses	$29,332,583	$16,693,259	$46,025,842
Net income from operations	$ 6,301,917	$ 4,115,427	$10,417,344
Nonoperating income (expense)	(921,583)	(739,406)	(1,660,989)
Net income before taxes	$ 5,380,334	$ 3,376,021	$ 8,756,355
Income taxes	(2,421,133)	(1,485,449)	(3,906,582)
Net Income	$ 2,959,201	$ 1,890,572	$ 4,849,773

However, after the combination, earnings per share is reported as $.194, determined as follows:

Number of Common Shares of Jar, Inc. Outstanding	20,000,000
Number of Common Shares of Book-It, Inc. Outstanding from January 1 to June 30 (4,000,000 × ½ year)	2,000,000
Number of Common Shares of Book-It, Inc. Outstanding from July 1 to December 31 restated in terms of Jar, Inc.'s shares using exchange ratio (4,000,000 × 1½ = 6,000,000 × ½ year)	3,000,000
Shares Outstanding for Calculation of EPS	25,000,000

$$\frac{\text{Net Income}}{\text{Shares Outstanding}} = \frac{\$\ 4{,}849{,}773}{25{,}000{,}000} = \$.194$$

Had the combination been recorded as a purchase, there would be no change in the earnings per share, assuming no common stock was involved, since earnings of the acquired company prior to acquisition are not combined with the earnings of the acquiring company. However, if stock is exchanged in the purchase transaction, the additional shares issued will be included in the weighted average number of shares outstanding, based on the time from acquisition to the balance sheet date. In effect, the earnings per share would decrease. The difference in reported earnings per share under the two methods often has been referred to as "instant earnings" under the pooling of interests method of accounting.

Another major difference between purchase and pooling of interests accounting has to do with the depreciation and amortization recorded in periods subsequent to the combination. Notice that the cost of the depreciable assets was higher under the purchase method. This would be the typical situation in a period of inflation. The fair market value of the depreciable assets would be higher than the recorded cost of those same assets. In subsequent periods, depreciation expense will be greater under the purchase method; thus, income will be lower. An intangible asset, goodwill, also resulted from the purchase transaction. This asset will have to be amortized in subsequent periods, causing a further reduction in reported income. Pooling of interests accounting has a much more favorable affect upon income than has the purchase method. This is the primary reason why the pooling method led to so many abuses prior to the issuance of APB Opinion No. 16.

Other Considerations in Pooling of Interests Accounting

The cost incurred to carry out the combination should be charged to income. In purchase accounting, certain costs of effecting the combination were treated as a reduction in the contributed capital, and other costs were charged to income. In a pooling of interests, all costs are regarded as expenses, regardless of their nature.

An additional problem is created when one of the combining companies has a different year end than the other combining company(ies) or when one of the combining companies uses different accounting practices than the other combining company(ies) in the same industry. During the process of combination, the companies may wish to utilize the same year end or standardize their accounting practices. If such is the case, disclosure of the adjustments required to accomplish the change should be disclosed by the combined company. Specifics of the disclosures are identified in Exhibit IX.

In some cases a business combination accounted for as a pooling of interests may take place after the balance sheet date of the combining companies and prior to the issuance of the financial statements. In the past, it was permissible to treat such a combination on a retrospective basis and to combine the financial statements of the companies as of the beginning of the period under consideration. However, this practice has been stopped by the issuance of APB Opinion No. 16. Now, a business combination described above should be reported in the footnotes to the financial statements. Specific information about the combination should include, at a minimum, the revenues, income and earnings per share of the combining company, as if the combination had been consummated at the balance sheet date.

Required Disclosures

The disclosures required for a purchase transaction and a pooling of interests transaction are similar. For both, there are disclosures that are required of every combination and other disclosures required only when certain events take place. The latter disclosures are not optional, but may or may not be presented, depending upon the specific facts of the combination. Exhibit IX lists the required disclosures for all purchase transactions and pooling transactions first, then lists the disclosures required in certain given fact situations.

Exhibit IX

Required Disclosures

Combination Accounted for as a Purchase	Combination Accounted for as a Pooling of Interests
I. Required of All Combinations	**I. Required of All Combinations**
1. Name and description of acquired company.	1. Name and description of combined company.
2. Indicate purchase method used.	2. Indicate pooling of interests method used.
3. Time period for which income of acquired company is included in the income statement of the acquiring company.	3. Description of and number of shares issued to effect the combination.
4. Cost of acquired and value assigned to any shares issued to effect the combination.	4. Revenue, extraordinary items, net income and other changes in stockholders' equity of separate companies that are included in the income statement of the combined company for the current period.
5. Pro Forma Information (a)Combined income from the beginning of the period. (b)Combined income for preceding period if comparative financial statements are issued.	5. For the company that issued the stock to effect the combination, reconcile revenue and income reported prior to the combination and to the combined amounts reported after the pooling.
II. Required in Certain Fact Situations	**II. Required in Certain Fact Situations**
1. If goodwill is recorded as a result of the combination state the method used to amortize amount.	1. If a combining company changes its accounting policies to conform with the combined company, indicate the adjustments required.
2. Type and accounting treatment of any contingent consideration in connection with the acquisition.	2. If a combining company changes its fiscal year to correspond with the fiscal year of the combined company, indicate the resulting changes in revenues, expenses, extraordinary items and net income.

The disclosures below show the information for the 1976 Annual Report of General Electric Company, relating to a business combination with Utah International, Inc., accounted for as a pooling of interests, and from the Annual Report of Bird & Son, Inc., relating to a business combination with The Logan-Long Company, accounted for as a purchase. Notice that, in the General Electric Company Note 1, Utah International, Inc. changed its fiscal year from October 31 to December 31, so as to conform with the fiscal year of General Electric. General Electric issued about 41 million shares of its common stock for all of the shares of Utah International to accomplish the pooling.

The combination between Bird & Son, Inc. and The Logan-Long Company involved a cash purchase price of about 17 million dollars. The total purchase price was assigned to the "net tangible assets" of Logan-Long Company, so there was no goodwill associated with the purchase. The pro forma information presents sales, net earnings and earnings per share for the company, as if the purchase took place on January 1, 1975.

General Electric Company (Dec)

Notes to Financial Statements

Note 1: Pooling of Interests—A merger with Utah International Inc. ("Utah" or "Utah International") was effected as of December 20, 1976, whereby Utah became a wholly-owned affiliate of General Electric through the exchange of 41,002,034 shares of General Electric $2.50 par value common stock for all of the outstanding shares of Utah. The principal business of Utah is the extraction and sale of natural resources. The merger was accounted for as a pooling of interests, and accordingly the accompanying financial statements include the accounts of Utah from January 1, 1975.

The sales of products and services to customers and the net earnings applicable to common stock of General Electric and Utah for the years ended December 31, 1976 and December 31, 1975 are shown below.

(In millions)	1976	1975
Sales of products and services to customers:		
General Electric	$14,696.7	$13,399.1
Utah International	1,000.6	706.0
	$15,697.3	$14,105.1
Net earnings applicable to common stock:		
General Electric	$ 749.3	$ 580.8
Utah International	181.3	107.7
	$ 930.6	$ 688.5

Prior to the merger, the fiscal year of Utah ended on October 31. Utah's financial results have been conformed to the calendar-year period used by General Electric.

Bird & Son, Inc. (Dec)

Notes to Consolidated Financial Statements

Note 2: Acquisition—On March 31, 1976, the Company acquired all of the common stock of The Logan-Long Company, a Chicago-based asphalt roofing manufacturer, for a cash purchase price of $16,700,000. The acquisition was accounted for as a purchase and the total purchase price was assigned to the net tangible assets acquired based upon their estimated value and included no goodwill. Operations from the date of acquisition have been included in the Consolidated Statement of Earnings.

Effective June 1, 1976, Logan-Long's Tuscaloosa asphalt roofing plant was sold to comply with an agreement with the Federal Trade Commission to divest this facility.

The following summary, prepared on a pro forma basis, combines the consolidated results of operations of the Company for the years ended December 31, 1976 and 1975, with pre-acquisition earnings of Logan-Long for comparable periods, except that the operating results of Logan-Long's Tuscaloosa facility have been excluded.

	1976	**1975**
Net sales	$240,367,000	$214,130,000
Net earnings	16,041,000	18,692,000
Earnings per share	5.17	6.05

Source: *Accounting Trends & Techniques,* Copyright © 1977 by the American Institute of Certified Public Accountants, Inc., pp. 42-43.

Topic 12

Interim Reporting

Detail Contents

APB Opinion No. 28 (May 1973) Interim Financial Reporting,

SFAS No. 3 (December 1974) Reporting Accounting Changes in Interim Financial Statements

and

SFAS No. 18 (November 1977) Financial Reporting for Segments of a Business Enterprise—Interim Financial Statements

Flowchart and General Discussion

The issuance of APB Opinion No. 28 represents the first attempt by the private rule-making body to develop accounting principles for interim financial reporting. There are two primary objectives of the Opinion: (1) to develop accounting principles and disclosure requirements that are appropriate for interim statements, and (2) to specify minimum guidelines for reporting of interim information by publicly traded companies. Interim financial reporting refers to the issuing of financial information for some time period less than an entire year. An interim period may be a month, a quarter of a year, a half of a year, etc. The issuance of APB Opinion No. 28 created several new problems for the accounting profession, as evidenced by the fact that two additional pronouncements have been issued supplementary to the information in Opinion No. 28.

SFAS No. 3 is an amendment to APB Opinion No. 28 and deals exclusively with the treatment of accounting changes in interim financial statements. The topic will be considered in detail later in the discussion. SFAS No. 18 is actually an amendment to SFAS No. 14, "Financial Reporting for Segments of a Business Enterprise," but deals with segment reporting in the interim period. The basic principle stated in SFAS No. 18 is that segment information is *not* required to be reported in interim financial statements. However, if a company elects to disclose segment information in its interim reports, the information presented must be reported in conformance with the provisions of SFAS No. 14.

The Flowchart of APB Opinion No. 28 depicts, in a general way, the major decisions and related accounting considerations specified by the Opinion. The discussion that follows is organized around the Flowchart presentation, and reference to the Flowchart will be made during the discussion of each major subject area. The Opinion addresses the interim income statement in some detail; therefore, the discussion below begins with the reporting of revenues in the interim period and continues down the income statement until all major items have been covered.

Interim Period Revenues

The basic principle stated in the Opinion (Paragraph 10) is that "the results for each interim period should be based on the accounting principles and practices used by an enterprise in the preparation of its latest annual financial statements unless a change in an accounting practice or policy has been adopted in the current year." This basic principle is applied without exception to the revenues reported in the interim period (Block 1). For example, revenues normally are recognized at the "point of sale" or at the time a service is rendered in the annual statements, and this same procedure would be used for reporting interim revenues.

Interim Period Product Costs and Expenses

The basic principle stated above is applied to product costs or expenses of an interim period, but may require some modification in special circumstances (Block 2). A product cost is one that is directly related to the product sold or the service rendered. In a merchandising enterprise, product costs usually are associated with the account "cost of sales". In a manufacturing enterprise, product costs usually are associated with direct materials, direct labor and the allocation of overhead to the product.

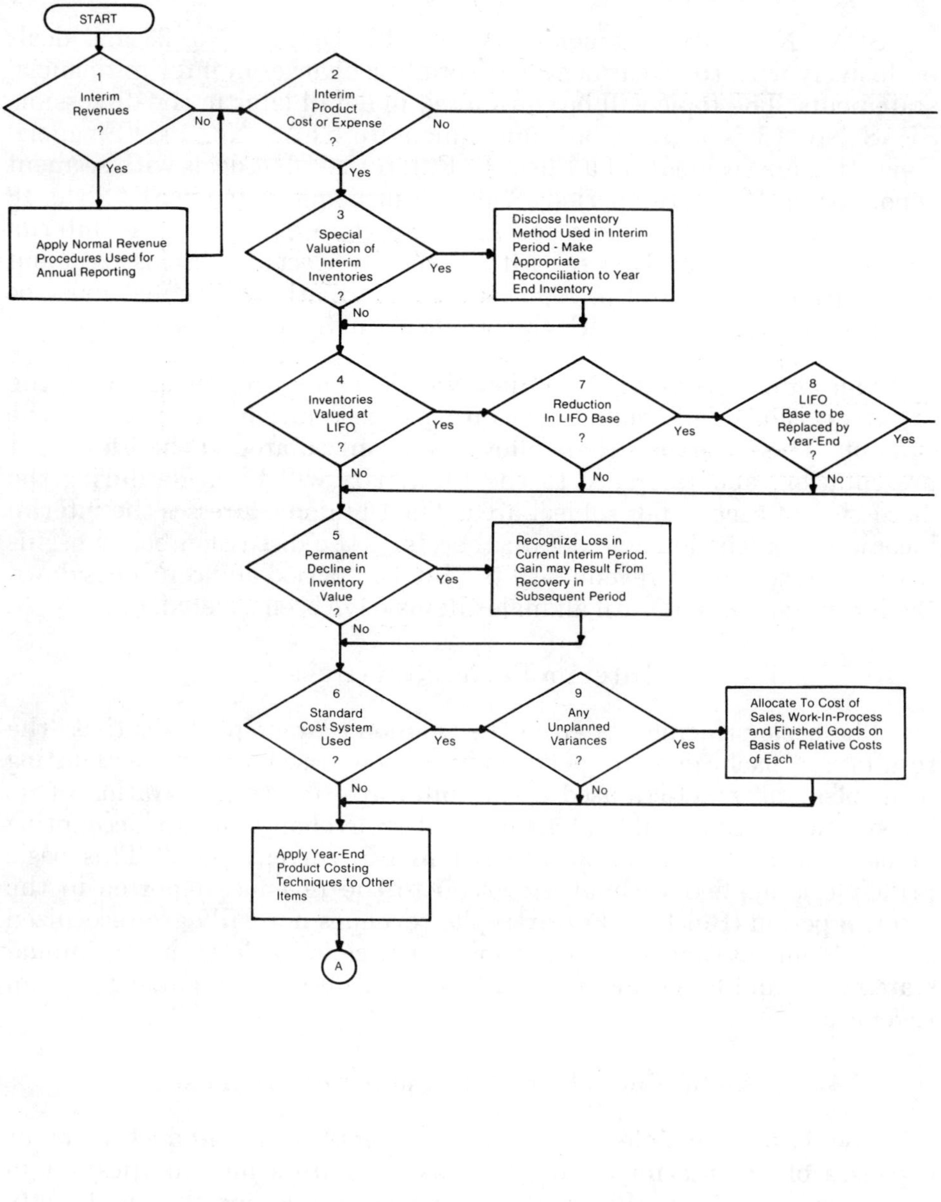
START
1 Interim Revenues ?
No
Yes
Apply Normal Revenue Procedures Used for Annual Reporting
2 Interim Product Cost or Expense ?
No
Yes
3 Special Valuation of Interim Inventories ?
Yes
No
Disclose Inventory Method Used in Interim Period - Make Appropriate Reconciliation to Year End Inventory
4 Inventories Valued at LIFO ?
Yes
No
7 Reduction In LIFO Base ?
Yes
No
8 LIFO Base to be Replaced by Year-End ?
Yes
No
5 Permanent Decline in Inventory Value ?
Yes
No
Recognize Loss in Current Interim Period. Gain may Result From Recovery in Subsequent Period
6 Standard Cost System Used ?
Yes
No
9 Any Unplanned Variances ?
Yes
No
Allocate To Cost of Sales, Work-In-Process and Finished Goods on Basis of Relative Costs of Each
Apply Year-End Product Costing Techniques to Other Items
A

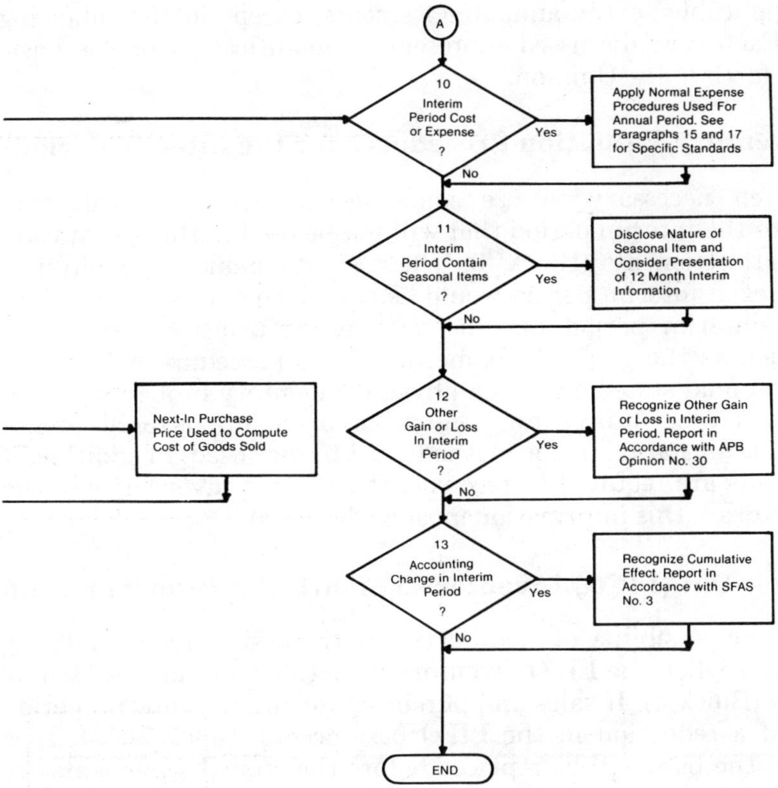
A
10
Interim
Period Cost
or Expense
?
Yes
Apply Normal Expense Procedures Used For Annual Period. See Paragraphs 15 and 17 for Specific Standards
No
11
Interim
Period Contain
Seasonal Items
?
Yes
Disclose Nature of Seasonal Item and Consider Presentation of 12 Month Interim Information
No
Next-In Purchase Price Used to Compute Cost of Goods Sold
12
Other
Gain or Loss
In Interim
Period
?
Yes
Recognize Other Gain or Loss in Interim Period. Report in Accordance with APB Opinion No. 30
No
13
Accounting
Change in Interim
Period
?
Yes
Recognize Cumulative Effect. Report in Accordance with SFAS No. 3
No
END

Product costs are to be accounted for using the same accounting principles applicable to the annual statements, except in the following four cases. Each case discussed represents a modification of the basic principle set forth in the Opinion.

Special Inventory Valuation Procedures for the Interim Period

It is often necessary to use some special inventory valuation procedures for the interim period that will not be used in the preparation of the annual statements (Block 3). The cost of conducting a physical inventory at each interim period would be prohibitive. Inventory values used in the interim period may be determined using an estimating procedure such as the gross profit method. This procedure will not be used for the annual statements, as a physical inventory probably will be taken. When a special inventory valuation procedure is used in the interim period, the nature of the method must be disclosed. In addition, if any adjustments are required to reconcile the interim inventories to the annual inventories, this information must be disclosed.

Last-In-First-Out (LIFO) Inventory Valuation in Interim Period

There is the possibility of modification of the basic principle relating to product costs when the LIFO inventory valuation technique is used by the company (Block 4). If sales and purchases during the interim period are such that a reduction in the LIFO base occurs (Block 7), but it is assumed that the base will be replaced before the annual statements are prepared (Block 8), a modification to the basic principle is required.

In the situation described above, cost of sales should include the price *expected* to be paid for the next inventory items purchased (Next-In Purchase Price), rather than the costs associated with the LIFO base. To illustrate the proper accounting in the interim period for this situation, assume that a company uses the LIFO inventory valuation process and that the LIFO base consists of 10,000 units, at a cost of $10 per unit ($100,000 LIFO base). Prior to the last sale in the second quarter of 197A, the *total* inventory consists of the LIFO base of 10,000 units, plus one layer of 3,000 units, at a cost of $45 per unit ($135,000 Cost of Layer). The last sale of the second quarter of 197A was for 5,000 units. The company has determined that the price of the *next* units purchased will be $50 per unit. Further, the company expects the layer to be replaced prior to the preparation of the annual statements.

Under normal circumstances, the LIFO base would be reduced by 2,000 units. However, the Opinion specifies that, under these conditions, the next purchase price, rather than the costs assigned to the LIFO base, should be used to determine the cost of sales. The following amounts would be used to reflect the cost of the last sale in the second quarter of 197A.

Cost of Goods Sold:	
3,000 units from the layer × $45	$135,000
2,000 units at next purchase price × $50	100,000
Cost of 5,000 Units Sold	$235,000
Reduction in Inventory:	
3,000 units from the layer × $45	$135,000
2,000 units from LIFO base × $10	20,000
Total Inventory Reduction	$155,000

Based upon this information, the following journal entry is required to record the cost of the sale.

Cost of Goods Sold	235,000	
Inventory		155,000
LIFO Base Inventory Liquidation		80,000

The "LIFO Base Inventory Liquidation" account would be classified as a current liability and would be removed when the next purchase is made.

If the purchase price of the next units purchased is $50 per unit, and 10,000 units are purchased at this price, the determination of the amount to assign to inventory would be as follows:

Cost of 10,000 Units Purchased (10,000 × $50)	$500,000
LIFO Base Inventory Liquidation	(80,000)
Cost Assigned to Units Purchased	$420,000

The journal entry required to record the purchase of the additional units would be:

Inventory	420,000	
LIFO Base Inventory Liquidation	80,000	
Accounts Payable		500,000

The units just purchased are made up of 8,000 units at a cost of $50 per unit, and 2,000 units at a cost of $10 per unit. This entry, in effect, replaces the 2,000 units removed in the preceding sale. The LIFO base is restored to 10,000 units at $10 per unit, and the layer is made up of 8,000 units at $50 per unit.

Permanent Decline in Inventory Value During the Interim Period

If there is a permanent decline in the value of inventory during the interim period (Block 5), the resulting loss should be recognized in the interim period and not deferred to the end of the year. No recognition is to be given to temporary declines in the value of inventory. If a permanent inventory decline occurs in an interim period and a loss is recognized, but there is a subsequent recovery in value before the end of the year, a gain should be recognized. The gain recognized may not exceed the amount of the loss previously recognized.

To illustrate the proper accounting for permanent inventory declines in an interim period, assume that a company has inventory of 10,000 units carried at a purchase price of $24 per unit ($240,000). The company expects to sell the units at a price of $30 per unit. The company has estimated that the cost to sell the units amounts to 10 percent of the selling price, and the normal profit margin is 20 percent of the selling price. At the end of the first quarter of 197A, the cost to replace the 10,000 units is determined to be $22 per unit. The decrease in value from $24 to $22 per unit is assumed to represent a permanent decline in value.

Since the decline is assumed to be permanent, a loss must be recognized in the first quarter of 197A. Before the amount of the loss can be determined, the "floor" and "ceiling" values must be computed to find the appropriate market price. This technique is required by Accounting Research Bulletin No. 43, Chapter 4, Statement 6, relating to inventory pricing. This pronouncement specifies that the "ceiling" should not be greater than net realizable value. Net realizable value is equal to the expected selling price, less the cost to complete and sell a unit of inventory. The "floor" is equal to the net realizable value, reduced by the normal profit margin. For this particular case, the ceiling and floor would be computed as follows:

Ceiling:	
Expected Selling Price	$30
Cost to Sell ($30 × 10%)	(3)
Ceiling	$27
Floor:	
Expected Selling Price	$30
Cost to Sell	(3)
Normal Profit ($30 × 20%)	(6)
Floor	$21

The cost to replace the inventory item is $22 per unit, which falls between the ceiling of $27 per unit and the floor of $21 per unit. Therefore, $22 per unit becomes the market value of the inventory item. The market value of $22 per unit is compared with the cost of $24 per unit; and, because market is lower, the inventory item must be written-down by $2 per unit ($22 – $24). A loss of $20,000 (10,000 units × $2 per unit) will be recognized. The entry to record the permanent decline in inventory value would be:

Loss on Decline in Market Value of Inventory	20,000	
Inventory		20,000

This loss would be recognized in the first quarter of 197A.

To extend the example, assume that, at the end of the fourth quarter of 197A, the 10,000 units were not sold, and the cost to replace the units rose from $22 to $23.50 per unit, i.e., there was a recovery in an assumed permanent decline in inventory value. Assuming no change in the expected selling price, cost to sell and normal profit margin, a gain of $15,000 ($23.50 – $22.00 = $1.50 × 10,000 units) would be recognized in the fourth quarter of 197A. The journal entry to record the gain would be:

Inventory	15,000	
Gain on Market Recovery of Inventory Decline		15,000

Regardless of the recovery in value of the inventory item, the gain may never exceed $20,000, the amount of the loss recorded in the second quarter of 197A.

Standard Cost Systems and Interim Reporting

A final situation that may require a modification of the basic principle of recording product costs relates to a company that employs a standard cost accounting system (Block 6). Any variances from standard existing at year end for annual statement presentation will be allocated among finished goods, work-in-process, raw materials inventory and cost of sales, based upon the relative balances in these accounts. Variances from standard can be divided into planned variances and unplanned variances. In the interim period any *planned* variances will be accounted for as assets or liabilities, and any *unplanned* variances will be allocated using the procedures described for year-end handling of variances.

To illustrate the proper handling of *unplanned* variances in the interim period, the information developed in Exhibit I will be used. The information presented in Exhibit I relates to the third quarter of 197A.

Exhibit I
Inventory and Variance Information

	Dollars	Percent
Cost of Sales	$200,000	66.67
Work-In-Process Inventory	35,000	11.67
Finished Goods Inventory	65,000	21.66
Total	$300,000	100.00

	Planned Variance	Unplanned Variance
Material Price	1,000U	2,000U
Material Quantity	4,000F	500F
Labor Rate	3,000F	4,000F
Labor Efficiency	1,000U	3,000U
Budget	500U	5,000U
Volume	6,000U	1,000U

U = Unfavorable variance
F = Favorable variance

The unplanned variances will be allocated to cost of sales, work-in-process inventory and finished goods inventory, based upon the percentages developed in the Exhibit. The allocation process is shown in Table I.

Table I

Allocation of Unplanned Variances

	Total	Cost of Sales (66.67%)	Allocated to: Work-In-Process (11.67%)	Finished Goods (21.66%)
Material Price	$2,000	$1,333	$233	$ 434
Material Quantity	(500)	(333)	(58)	(109)
Labor Rate	(4,000)	(2,667)	(467)	(866)
Labor Efficiency	3,000	2,000	350	650
Budget	5,000	3,333	584	1,083
Volume	1,000	667	117	216
Total	$6,500	$4,333	$759	$1,408

The journal entry required to eliminate the unplanned variances at the end of the third quarter of 197A would be:

Cost of Sales	4,333	
Work-In-Process Inventory	759	
Finished Goods Inventory	1,408	
Material Quantity Variance	500	
Labor Rate Variance	4,000	
Material Price Variance		2,000
Labor Efficiency Variance		3,000
Budget Variance		5,000
Volume Variance		1,000

The planned variances would be carried forward to the year-end.

Other product costs or expenses not described above would be handled in the interim period the same way they would be handled at year end. The next major category of income statement items deals with period costs or expenses.

Period Costs or Expenses in Interim Statements

A period cost or expense is a cost that is not directly related to the product or service (Block 10). These costs generally are expensed when incurred or are assigned to the period on the basis of some allocation process.

Accounting for period costs and expenses presents few accounting difficulties. Paragraphs 15 and 17 of the Opinion establish specific guidelines or standards for the treatment of period costs in the interim statements. The standards identified are:

(1) Period costs are to be charged to interim periods as the expense is incurred, or allocated to interim periods based upon some predetermined allocation method. For example, rent may be allocated based on the passage of time, which implies a straight-line allocation process.

(2) Certain costs incurred in an interim period cannot be determined to benefit any other interim period and should be charged to income in the interim period incurred.

(3) Costs may not be allocated to interim periods on a discretionary basis.

(4) Gains and losses in an interim period should be taken to income in that period and *not* deferred to future interim periods. This standard applies only to gains or losses that would not normally be deferred at year end, when an annual presentation is to be made.

(5) Costs that are normally year-end adjustments or that cannot be determined until the year end, such as bonuses and bad debts, should be estimated and allocated to the interim period.

Additional Considerations of Interim Period Items

Seasonal Influences on Interim Reporting

Many business enterprises experience seasonal fluctuations in operations (Block 11). Interim reports of such an enterprise may be misleading if the user is not aware of the seasonal nature of the company's business. As a result, interim reports of businesses with seasonal fluctuations in operations should disclose the seasonal nature of the business and consideration should be given to the presentation of 12-month statements ending with the current interim period. If the company elects to present 12-month interim information, it should include the current and immediately preceding year.

Other Gains and Losses in Interim Periods

For purposes of these Opinions, "other gains or losses" (Block 12) include the following items:

(1) Gains or losses that are either unusual in nature *or* infrequent in occurance, but *not* both;

(2) Disposal of a segment of a business; and

(3) Extraordinary items.

These gains or losses, if material, should be included in income in the interim period and should not be deferred or allocated to subsequent interim periods. Materiality should be determined on the relationship between the gain or loss and total *estimated* income for the entire year. Materiality should not be determined in relation to the interim period income. Each of the items shown above should be classified separately in the interim period income statement.

In addition to the gains and losses identified above, contingent items may exist at the interim reporting date. Contingent items for interim periods should be accounted for in the same manner as in the annual report (see Topic 6 for an analysis of SFAS No. 5, "Accounting for Contingencies").

Income Taxes in the Interim Period

Income taxes must be accrued in the interim period. The tax rate to be used for the interim period should be the *best estimate* of the effective tax rate for the entire year. The determination of the effective tax rate should give adequate consideration to all available tax credits or tax alternatives. In determining the effective rate, consideration should *not* be given to the tax effects of gains and losses discussed above, i.e., of disposal of a business segment, extraordinary items, etc.

If an operating loss occurs in an interim period, the effect of the loss first should be treated as a net operating loss carryback, if possible. If it is not possible to treat the operating loss as a carryback, the tax effect of the loss should not be recognized in the interim period, unless it is assumed that the effect of the loss will be realized in future interim periods of the current year. Seasonal patterns of losses with subsequent gains should provide assurance that the effect of the carryforward will be realized before the end of the current year.

If realization of the tax effects of a loss deferred in a previous interim period becomes assured in a subsequent interim period, it is appropriate to recognize the tax effect in that subsequent interim period. If the tax effects of losses of preceding interim periods are not recognized, subsequent interim periods in which income is earned should not record income tax expense until the losses of the preceding interim periods have been completely absorbed.

In determining the appropriate amount of taxes for an interim period, the provisions of APB Opinions No. 11, 23 and 24 (see Topic 5 for an analysis of the Opinions) should be applied.

FASB Interpretation No. 18, "Accounting for Income Taxes in Interim Periods" (March, 1977), provides excellent illustrations of the computation of taxes for a wide variety of situations. The reader should refer to this Interpretation for specifics of the computation process. As a result of the Revenue Act of 1978, the FASB issued Technical Bulletin No. 79-9. This Bulletin provides the appropriate accounting for the reduction in the corporate tax rates. The reduction in the tax rate results in a revised annual effective tax rate that should be applied to pretax income on a year-to-date basis.

The last major area for consideration deals with accounting changes in the interim period.

Accounting Changes in Interim Periods

SFAS No. 3, "Reporting Accounting Changes in Interim Financial Statements," is an amendment to APB Opinion No. 28, and specifies the appropriate accounting and disclosures for reporting a change in an accounting principle during an interim period (Block 13). If the reader is not familiar with the provisions of APB Opinion No. 20, "Accounting Changes" (in Topic 1), he should review this material before proceeding with the discussion below. To avoid duplication of material, the authors have assumed that the reader is familiar with the terminology of APB Opinion No. 20, as well with as the calculations necessary to determine the cumulative effect of the change in accounting principle. The primary emphasis of the material presented in this section is to demonstrate the rather complex financial presentation required to report the change.

Change in Accounting Principle Made in First Quarter

The appropriate accounting for a change in an accounting principle (other than a change *to* LIFO or similar changes) made during the first quarter of an annual period is to compute the cumulative effect at the *beginning* of the annual period under consideration and to report the cumulative effect in the income statement of the first quarter.

In addition to reporting the cumulative effect of the change in the income statement of the first quarter, the company also must disclose in the footnotes the nature of the change, the justification of the change, certain "pro forma" information and the effect of the change on specific reporting periods. The pro forma information presented should include income from continuing operations, net income and the related earnings per share amounts. This information should be presented for the quarter or interim period in which the accounting change is made and for any preceding quarters or interim periods presenting financial information with the current interim period. If financial information for preceding interim periods is not presented, actual and pro forma information must be presented for the first quarter of the immediately preceding year.

As indicated above, the effect of the change in accounting principle must be disclosed for certain specified reporting periods. These periods include the quarter or interim periods containing the accounting change, and 12-month-to-date statements containing the first quarter, and subsequent quarters or interim periods of the current annual period in which the new accounting principle is used. The information reported for these periods includes the impact of the change on income from continuing operations, net income and related earnings per share amounts.

It should be obvious to the reader that careful consideration must be given to reporting a change in accounting principle made in an interim period. Very often, it is difficult to understand the reporting presented because of the detailed computations that went into the determination of the amounts shown on the income statement. In an effort to illustrate the accounting and reporting requirements of SFAS No. 3, the authors have compiled all the necessary information in one place: Exhibit II. This Exhibit contains information necessary to calculate the cumulative effect of a change in accounting principles, the reporting requirement relating to a change, the footnote disclosures required and computational information concerning the determination of specific amounts. The Exhibit contains a great deal of information and careful reading is a must.

The basic information that leads to the computations shown in Exhibit II starts with the fact that Reporting Company, Inc. changes from straight-line depreciation to double declining balance depreciation for all assets in February of 197C. Reporting Company, Inc. wishes to prepare interim financial statements for the quarter ending March 31, 197C.

Exhibit II

Computation and Reporting of an Accounting Change in the First Quarter

Information Relating to the Operations of Reporting Company, Inc.

Period	Income From Continuing Operations
1st Quarter, 197B	$ 415,000
2nd Quarter, 197B	435,000
3rd Quarter, 197B	398,000
4th Quarter, 197B	402,000
Total	$1,650,000
1st Quarter, 197C	[a]$ 375,914

Period	Straight-Line Depreciation	Double Declining Balance Depreciation	Difference	After-Tax Difference[b]
Prior to 197B	$100,000	$185,494	$85,494	$42,747
1st Quarter, 197B	$ 25,000	$ 40,725	$15,725	$ 7,863
2nd Quarter, 197B	25,000	38,689	13,689	6,844
3rd Quarter, 197B	25,000	36,755	11,755	5,878
4th Quarter, 197B	25,000	34,917	9,917	4,958
Total	$100,000	$151,086	$51,086	$25,543
1st Quarter, 197C	$ 25,000	$ 33,171	$ 8,171	$ 4,086

Financial Reporting by Reporting Company, Inc.

Partial Income Statement
Reporting Company, Inc.
Three Months Ending March 31, 197C and 197B

	197C	197B
Income From Continuing Operations	$375,914	$415,000
Cumulative Effect of a Change in Accounting Principle (net of taxes of $68,290) Note 1	[c]68,290	
Net Income	$307,624	$415,000
Earnings Per Share:[d]		
Income From Continuing Operations	$ .75	$ .83
Net Income	.62	.83
Pro Forma Information:		
Gross Amounts:		
Income From Continuing Operations	$375,914	[e]$407,137
Net Income	375,914	407,137
Per Share Amounts:[d]		
Income From Continuing Operations	$ .75	$ .81
Net Income	.75	.81

Footnotes to Financial Statements

Note 1: In February, 197C, the Company changed its method of depreciation for all assets owned and for all subsequent assets purchased from the straight-line to the double-declining balance method. The change was made because management believes that double declining balance method is a more appropriate allocation method and more fairly presents income. The cumulative effect of the change of $68,290, for periods prior to the first quarter of 197C is included in income, net of taxes of $68,290, for the first quarter ending March 31, 197C. The change in accounting principle reduced income from continuing operations by $4,086[f] and net income by $72,376[g]. The related earnings per share amounts were decreased by $.01[d] and $.14[d], respectively. Pro forma information is presented to show the retroactive effect of the change in depreciation methods.

Computational Information

[a] First Quarter 197C income is based upon the use of the double declining method adopted in February. The information above shows the difference between the amount that would have been charged for straight-line depreciation in this Quarter.

[b] The effective tax rate of Reporting Company, Inc. is 50 percent. This Column represents the amount in the Difference Column multiplied by the tax rate of 50 percent.

[c] The cumulative effect is determined by using the information given in the After-Tax Difference Column above for all periods prior to 197C. The amount of the cumulative effect is determined as follows:

After-Tax Difference Prior to 197B	$42,747
After-Tax Total for 197B	25,543
Cumulative Effect of the Change	$68,290

Since the tax rate for the Company is 50 percent, the gross cumulative effect is equal to $85,494 plus $51,086, the total difference. The taxes on the cumulative effect are equal to $68,290 because of the 50 percent tax rate.

[d] There were 500,000 shares of common stock outstanding during the entire period. These shares are used in all earnings per share computations.

[e] The pro forma amount is equal to reported income of $415,000 less the after tax difference in depreciation of $7,863 in the first quarter of 197B.

[f] After-tax difference for the first quarter of 197C.

[g] Total after-tax difference through the first quarter of 197C ($42,747 + $25,543 + $4,086 = $72,376)

Exhibit II has summarized the necessary reporting of the cumulative effect and pro forma information of the Quarters ending March 31, 197C and 197B. Notice that, for the interim statements of 197C, the actual income and the pro forma amount are the same. A change in an accounting principle occurring after the beginning of the annual accounting period is treated as if the new accounting principle had been used from the beginning of the accounting period. The cumulative effect is calculated for periods prior to the beginning of the current interim period. The pro forma information presented for 197B shows income restated as if double declining balance depreciation had been used in that period.

Change in Accounting Principle in Other than the First Quarter

A change in an accounting principle may occur in some interim period other than the first quarter of the year. If this should happen, the cumulative effect of the change is presented in the first quarter or in statements that contain the first quarter, e.g., year-to-date or 12-month-to-date financial statements. The cumulative effect is reported in the first quarter, and not in the quarter that the actual change took place. The amount of the cumulative effect is determined for periods prior to the beginning of the first quarter of the current annual period.

In addition to reporting the cumulative effect, the company must disclose the nature of the change, the justification of the change, pro forma information and information relating to certain specified periods. The pro forma information presented must include the quarter or interim period of the current year in which the accounting change actually was adopted and quarters or interim periods of the preceding year for which financial information is presented. If financial information for quarters of the preceding year are not presented, actual and pro forma information for the corresponding quarter of the year prior to the current year must be presented. The pro forma information should present income from continuing operations, net income and the related earnings per share amounts.

The impact of the change in accounting principles on income from continuing operations, net income and related earnings per share amounts must be reported for the following specified periods:

(1) The quarter or interim period in which the change is made;

(2) Each quarter of the current annual period preceding the quarter in which the change is made;

(3) Any 12-month-to-date or year-to-date statements that contain the quarter in which the change in principle is adopted; and

(4) Quarters of the current annual period subsequent to the quarter in which the change in accounting principle is made, if such statements are prepared.

Income amounts for each interim period in the current year should be restated, using the new principle. This restatement is required for all interim periods preceding the quarter in which the new principle is adopted. The income amounts restated should include income from continuing operations, net income and the related earnings per share amounts.

To illustrate a change in accounting principle adopted in other than the first quarter of the year, the same basic facts shown in Exhibit II will be used. The only modification to the information presented is that the change from straight-line to double declining balance depreciation occurred in May 197C. In this case, the change was made in the second quarter of the year. Exhibit III is organized along the same lines as Exhibit II. Notice that information about operations during the second quarter of 197C have been added. The financial reporting and footnote disclosures are for the three months ended June 30, 197C, and the six months ended June 30, 197C. The footnote disclosure becomes somewhat more complex when discussing the two periods covered by the statements. Careful reading of the footnote will prove beneficial. Once again, the computational information is provided so the reader will be able to conclude the manner in which the various amounts were determined.

Exhibit III

Computation and Reporting of an Accounting Change in Other Than the First Quarter

Information Relating to the Operations of Reporting Company, Inc.

Period	Income From Continuing Operations
1st Quarter, 197B	$ 415,000
2nd Quarter, 197B	435,000
3rd Quarter, 197B	398,000
4th Quarter, 197B	402,000
Total	$ 1,650,000
1st Quarter, 197C	$ 380,000
2nd Quarter, 197C	[a]416,744
Total	$ 796,744

Period	Straight-Line Depreciation	Double Declining Balance Depreciation	Difference	After-Tax Difference[b]
Prior to 197B	$100,000	$185,494	$85,494	$42,747
1st Quarter, 197B	$ 25,000	$ 40,725	$15,725	$ 7,863
2nd Quarter, 197B	25,000	38,689	13,689	6,844
3rd Quarter, 197B	25,000	36,755	11,755	5,878
4th Quarter, 197B	25,000	34,917	9,917	4,958
Total	$100,000	$151,086	$51,086	$25,543
1st Quarter, 197C	$ 25,000	$ 33,171	$ 8,171	$ 4,086
2nd Quarter, 197C	25,000	31,512	6,512	3,256
Total	$ 50,000	$ 64,683	$14,683	$ 7,342

Financial Reporting by Reporting Company, Inc.

Partial Income Statement
Reporting Company, Inc.

	For the Three Months Ending June 30		For the Six Months Ending June 30	
	197C	197B	197C	197B
Income from Continuing Operations	$416,744	$435,000	$792,658	$850,000
Cumulative Effect of a Change in Accounting Principle (net of Taxes of $68,290) Note 1			[c]68,290	
Net Income	$416,744	$435,000	$724,368	$850,000
Earnings Per Share:[d]				
Income from Continuing Operations	$ .83	$ .87	$ 1.59	$ 1.70
Net Income	.83	.87	1.45	1.70
Pro Forma Information:				
Gross Amounts:				
Income from Continuing Operations	$416,744	[e]$428,156	$792,658	[f]$835,293
Net Income	416,744	428,156	792,658	835,293
Per Share Amounts:[d]				
Income from Continuing Operations	$ .83	$ .86	$ 1.59	$ 1.67
Net Income	.83	.86	1.59	1.67

Footnotes to Financial Statements

Note 1: In May of 197C, the Company changed its method of depreciation for all assets owned and for all assets subsequently purchased from the straight-line to the double declining balance method. The change was made because management believed that double declining depreciation is a more appropriate allocation method and more fairly presents income. The cumulative effect of the change of $68,290, for periods prior to the first quarter of 197C is included in income, net of taxes of $68,290, of the six month period ending June 30, 197C. The change in accounting principle reduced income from continuing operations and net income by $3,256[g] for the three months ending June 30, 197C, and reduced by $.007[d] the related earnings per share for this period. Income from continuing operations and net income for the six months ending June 30, 197C, were reduced by $7,342[h] ($.015 per share) and $75,632[i] ($.15 per share), respectively as a result of the change in accounting principle. For the first quarter of 197C, income from continuing operations was reduced by $4,086[j] ($.008 per share), and net income was reduced by $72,376[k] ($.145 per share) as a result of the change in accounting principle. The pro forma information is presented to show the retroactive effect of the change in depreciation methods.

Computational Information

[a] Income for the first quarter of 197C is computed using straight-line depreciation and income during the second quarter of 197C is computed using double declining balance depreciation. The income from continuing operations for the six months ending June 30, 197C is computed as follows:

First Quarter Reported Income	$380,000
Adjustment for Depreciation	(4,086)
Restated First Quarter Income	$375,914
Second Quarter Reported Income	416,744
Income for Six Months Ended June 30, 197C	$792,658

[b] The effective tax rate of Reporting Company, Inc. is 50 percent.

[c] The cumulative effect is determined by using the After-Tax Difference information:

After-Tax Difference Prior to 197B	$ 42,747
After-Tax Difference in 197B	25,543
Cumulative effect	$ 68,290

[d] There are 500,000 common shares outstanding during the entire period and these shares are used in all earnings per share computations.

[e] Income Reported	$435,000
Adjustment for After-Tax Effect of Depreciation	(6,844)
Restated income for Second Quarter of 197B	$428,156

[f] Income Reported ($415,000 + $435,000)	$850,000
Adjustment for Depreciation ($7,863 + $6,844)	(14,707)
Restated Income for Six Months Ended June 30, 197B	$835,293

[g] After-tax difference in second quarter of 197C.

[h] After-tax difference for six months ended June 30,197C ($4,086 + $3,256 = $7,342).

[i] Total after-tax difference through June 30, 197C ($42,747 + $25,543 + $7,342 = $75,632).

[j] After-tax difference first quarter of 197C.

[k] After-tax difference through first quarter of 197C ($42,747 + $25,543 + $4,086 = $72,376).

Changes in Accounting Principles Treated Like a Change to LIFO

For some types of changes in accounting principles, it is not possible to calculate the cumulative effect or present pro forma information. The classic example of such a change is when a company changes from some other inventory valuation technique to the LIFO method. Accounting for these types of changes was discussed in detail in APB Opinion No. 20 (see Topic 1). The reader may wish to refer back to this discussion before proceeding with the information below.

If it is not possible to determine the cumulative effect of a change in an accounting principle or to develop the necessary pro forma information, the reason for not computing and disclosing the cumulative effect and pro forma information, as well as the nature and justification of the change, must be disclosed.

If such a change is made in the first quarter of an annual period, the impact of the change on income from continuing operations, net income and related earnings per share amounts must be presented for the following periods:

(1) The quarter or interim period in which the change is made;

(2) Any 12-month-to-date or year-to-date statements containing the quarter in which the change in accounting principle is made; and

(3) Subsequent quarters of the current annual period in which the new accounting principle is used.

If the change in accounting principle is made in a quarter other than the first quarter of an annual period, the impact of the change on income from continuing operations, net income and related earnings per share amounts must be presented for the following specified periods:

(1) The quarter or interim period in which the change is made;

(2) Each quarter or interim period of the current year preceding the interim period in which the change is made;

(3) Any 12-month-to-date or year-to-date statements containing the quarter in which the change in accounting principle is made; and

(4) Subsequent quarters of the current annual period in which the new accounting principle is used.

In addition to these disclosures, information for interim periods preceding the interim period in which the change is made must be restated to give effect to the new accounting principle adopted.

Change in Accounting Principle Made in the Fourth Quarter

Special accounting treatment is required for a publicly held company that makes a change in accounting principles in the fourth quarter of an annual period. If the company provides information concerning the effects of the change in accounting principles in either fourth quarter interim statements or the annual statements, the disclosures shown below are required. If the effects of the change are not disclosed according to the guidelines provided below, they must be disclosed in the footnotes to the annual statements in the manner shown above for a change in accounting principle.

Paragraph 30 of APB Opinion No. 28 specifies the minimum financial reporting and disclosure guidelines for a company that is publicly traded. The minimum reporting and disclosures are as follows:

(1) Sales or gross revenues;

(2) Extraordinary items;

(3) Income tax expense;

(4) Accounting principle changes or estimates;

(5) Disposal of a business segment(s);

(6) Items that are unusual *or* infrequent, but not both;

(7) Earnings per share;

(8) Revenues, costs and expenses that are seasonal in nature;

(9) Significant changes in income tax provisions or estimates;

(10) Contingencies;

(11) Changes in financial position that are significant in nature; and

(12) Net income.

Quarterly financial information for The Signal Company, Inc. for the years 1975 and 1974 is presented below to illustrate some of the required disclosures associated with interim reporting.

Exhibit IV

The Signal Company, Inc. (Dec)

Notes to Financial Statements

Note 19: Comparative Quarterly Financial Information (Unaudited):

(Dollars in thousands, except per share amounts)

1975	First	Second	Third	Fourth	Year
Sales (restated for discontinued operations)	$402,798	$572,911	$601,384	$564,855	$2,141,948
Income from continuing operations	6,256	18,267	14,928	1,966	41,417
Loss from discontinued operations	—	(460)	(444)	(843)	(1,747)
Income before extraordinary income	6,256	17,807	14,484	1,123	39,670
Extraordinary income	366	366	366	367	1,465
Net income	$ 6,622	$ 18,173	$ 14,850	$ 1,490	$ 41,135
Earnings per share:					
Income from continuing operations	$ .28	$ .84	$ .69	$ .09	$ 1.90
Loss from discontinued operations	—	(.02)	(.02)	(.04)	(.08)
Income before extraordinary income	.28	.82	.67	.05	1.82
Extraordinary income	.02	.02	.01	.02	.07
Net income	$ .30	$ .84	$ .68	$ .07	$ 1.89
1974					
Sales	$405,448	$430,561	$396,594	$412,400	$1,645,003
Income from continuing operations	13,219	20,675	16,906	13,619	64,419
Gain from sale of discontinued operations	110,182	—	—	—	110,182
Income before extraordinary income	123,401	20,675	16,906	13,619	174,601
Extraordinary income	367	366	366	366	1,465
Net income	$123,768	$ 21,041	$ 17,272	$ 13,985	$ 176,066
Earnings per share:					
Income from continuing operations	$ .54	$ .86	$ .77	$ .63	$ 2.80
Income from discontinued operations	4.80	—	—	—	4.80
Income before extraordinary income	5.34	.86	.77	.63	7.60
Extraordinary income	.02	.02	.01	.01	.06
Net income	$ 5.36	$ .88	$ .78	$ .64	$ 7.66

Earnings are down in each of the quarters this year compared to last year principally because of Mack Trucks and reduced investment income.

The fourth quarter of 1975 includes year-end adjustments of approximately $2,700,000 as a result of the write-off of receivables, provision for guarantees by UOP and amortization of the excess of purchase price over the book value of net assets acquired.

The fourth quarter of 1974 includes the goodwill write-off of $9,134,000.

Source: *Accounting Trends & Techniques,* Copyright © 1976 by the American Institute of Certified Public Accountants, Inc., p. 25.

Topic 13

Other

Detail Contents

APB Opinions and SFAS Statements

FASB Interpretations

FASB Technical Bulletins

SFAS No. 7 (June 1975)

Accounting and Reporting by Development Stage Enterprises

Flowchart and General Discussion

SFAS No. 7 establishes procedures for identifying a development stage enterprise and specifies the financial reporting and disclosures required of such an entity.

Prior to the issuance of SFAS No. 7, enterprises in the development stage had considerable latitude in the accounting principles used for financial reporting purposes. The form and content of the financial statements issued by development stage enterprises varied widely. Many developing companies initially elected to defer all costs, with little or no consideration given to the expected future benefits of these costs or their recoverability. Another common practice was for an enterprise to not assign monetary amounts to stock issued for assets other than cash. With the promulgation of SFAS No. 7, specific guidelines were presented for financial accounting and reporting of developing enterprises.

The Flowchart depicts the accounting principles and reporting requirements specified in the Statement. The left side of the Flowchart identifies those criteria listed in the Statement for classifying an enterprise as being in the development stage. The right side specifies the proper accounting and disclosure required of a development stage enterprise.

Identification of Development Stage Enterprises

For a business enterprise to be classified as a development stage enterprise, it must meet two basic criteria. First, the enterprise must be devoting substantial effort to establishing a new business (Block 1). The determination of what constitutes "substantial effort" is primarily a management judgment. However, the Statement indicates that the following activities normally are undertaken by a firm in the early stages of development:

(1) Fund raising;

(2) Planning;

(3) Exploration;

(4) Obtaining productive assets; and

(5) Training employees.

This list is not meant to be all-inclusive, but it does provide some guidance as to the types of activities that require considerable management effort during the early stages of development.

If the enterprise is devoting substantial effort to the establishment of a new business, it still must meet an additional condition before it can be classified as a development stage enterprise. If the principal operations of the enterprise have not yet begun, the company meets the conditions necessary for development stage enterprises (Block 2). However, if the company has commenced its principal operations, but has not generated significant revenues from its operations, it also will be classified as a development stage enterprise (Block 3). If principal operations have begun, and significant revenue is being produced, the company will not be classified as being in the development stage. Once operations have begun, the determination of what constitutes "significant revenues" is a matter of management judgment.

Once a business has been classified as a development stage enterprise, it must follow the accounting and reporting requirements specified in the Statement.

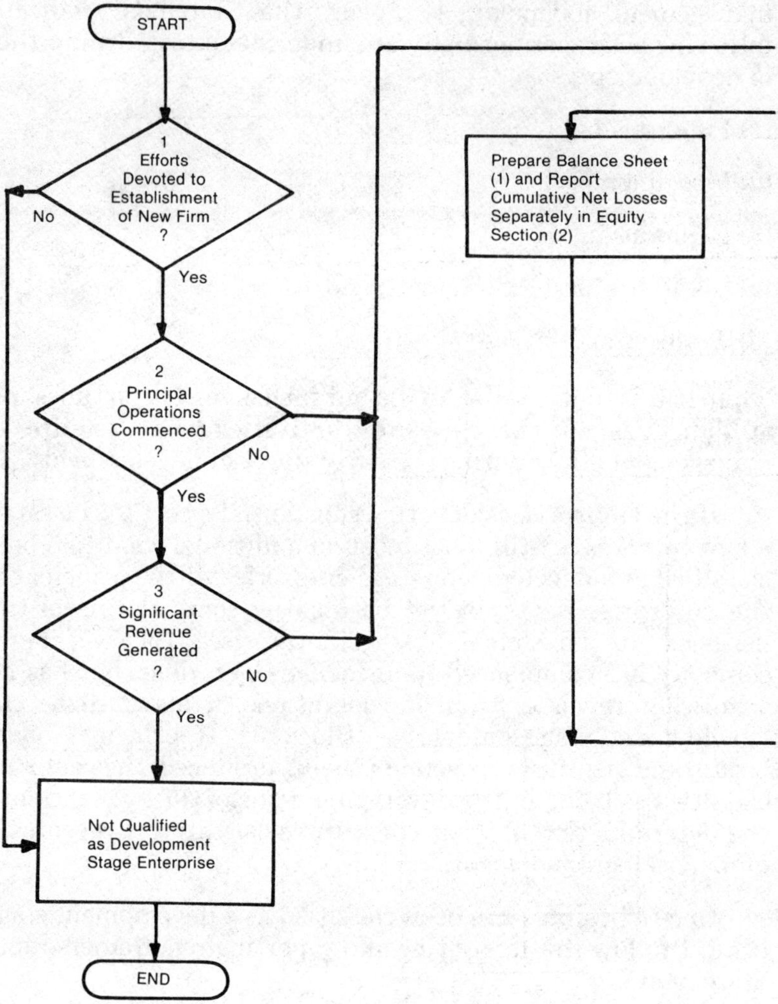

Notes:

(1) Statements should be prepared in conformance with GAAP that apply to established operating enterprises.

(2) Cumulative net losses should be reported under the heading "Deficit Accumulated During The development Stage."

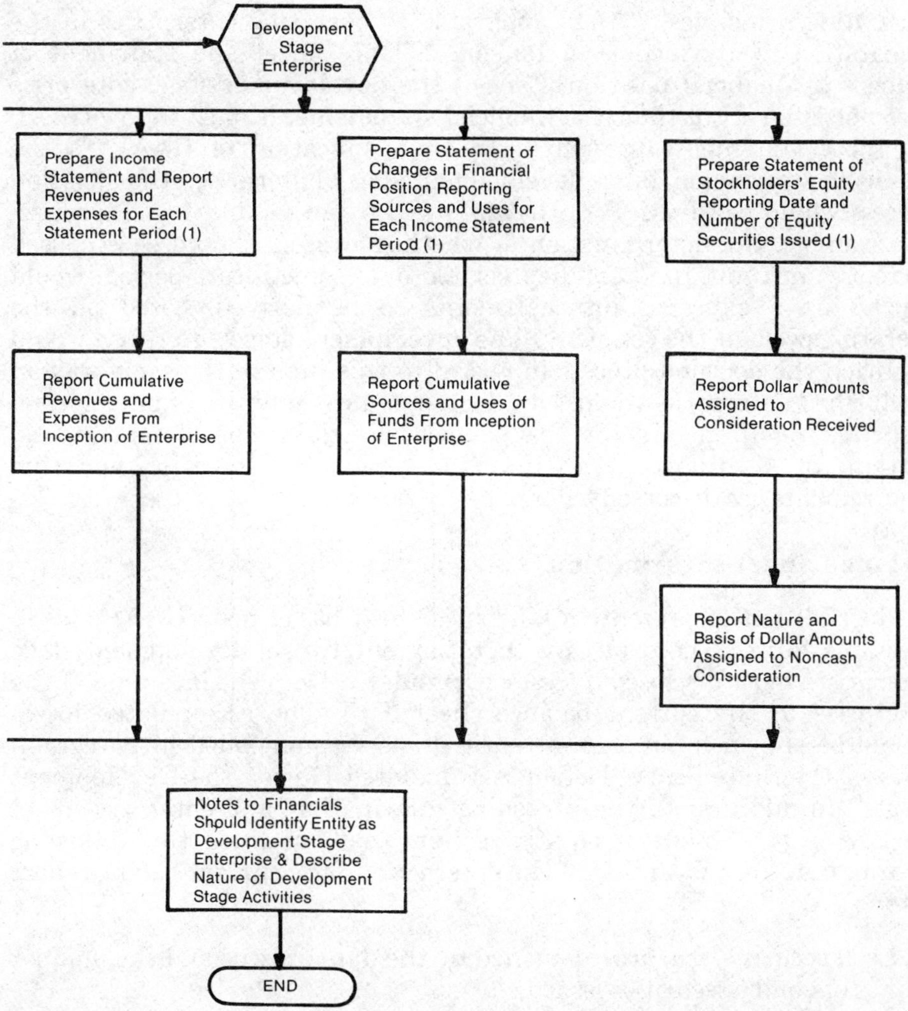
Development Stage Enterprise
Prepare Income Statement and Report Revenues and Expenses for Each Statement Period (1)
Prepare Statement of Changes in Financial Position Reporting Sources and Uses for Each Income Statement Period (1)
Prepare Statement of Stockholders' Equity Reporting Date and Number of Equity Securities Issued (1)
Report Cumulative Revenues and Expenses From Inception of Enterprise
Report Cumulative Sources and Uses of Funds From Inception of Enterprise
Report Dollar Amounts Assigned to Consideration Received
Report Nature and Basis of Dollar Amounts Assigned to Noncash Consideration
Notes to Financials Should Identify Entity as Development Stage Enterprise & Describe Nature of Development Stage Activities
END

Reporting Requirements for Development Stage Enterprises

A development stage enterprise must follow generally accepted accounting principles (GAAP) applicable to operating enterprises in the preparation of its income statement, balance sheet and statement of changes in financial position. Even if the development stage enterprise does not issue all of the basic financial statements, it must follow GAAP for those statements presented. In the application of GAAP to the financial statements of a development stage enterprise, the decision process would be identical to that followed by an established enterprise. For example, the determination of whether an item should be expensed currently, or capitalized and depreciated over some future period, would depend upon expected future benefits to be derived, based on the operating cycle of the company. The development stage enterprise would approach the decision process in regard to this item in the same way an established enterprise would. Development stage enterprises have special reporting requirements for the balance sheet, income statement and statement of changes in financial position. Specific reporting requirements are discussed below.

Balance Sheet Information

In addition to presenting a balance sheet based upon GAAP and in the same form as used by any operating enterprise, development stage enterprises must disclose all losses accumulated from the inception of the enterprise to the current balance sheet date. The accumulated losses should be shown in an account entitled (as recommended in Paragraph 11(a) of the Statement) "Deficit Accumulated During the Development Stage." In addition to the preceding information, the enterprise must prepare a stockholders' equity section that discloses the following information from inception of the enterprise to the current balance sheet date:

(1) Each security issuance, identified by the date of issue and the number of equity securities issued;

(2) Total consideration (monetary or nonmonetary) expressed in dollars for each security issuance and for each equity security;

(3) A description of the nature of the consideration received for each security issuance not involving cash and a description of the method of assigning dollar amounts to that consideration.

Income Statement Information

The development stage enterprise must prepare the income statement for the current period in accordance with GAAP and in a form consistent with that used by an operating enterprise. The enterprise also must disclose cumulative revenues and expenses from the inception of the business to the balance sheet date.

Statement of Changes in Financial Position Information

The statement of changes in financial position also must follow GAAP and be consistent in form with statements prepared by an operating enterprise. The statement of changes in financial position must be presented for each period for which an income statement is prepared. The development stage enterprise also must disclose cumulative sources and uses of working capital (or cash) from the inception of the business to the current balance sheet date.

Other Required Disclosures

In addition to the disclosures discussed above, the development stage enterprise must disclose the fact that it is in the development stage and the reasons why it is so classified. For those companies that previously have been classified as development stage enterprises, but that are not so classified in the current year, appropriate disclosure of the fact that the particular company was in the development stage in the preceding year should be made.

Several accounting problems are created by the transition to SFAS No. 7 and by the transition from a development stage enterprise to an operating enterprise.

Financial statements or summaries of financial information may be presented for the current and prior years by a development stage enterprise. If the financial statements or summary information relate to a time period prior to the effective date of the Statement (January 1, 1976), and the accounting used for those prior periods is different than that required by the Statement, the prior period information should be corrected through the use of a prior period adjustment.[1] Current and prior years' financial statements or summary financial information may be prepared by an established operating entity that would have been classified as a development stage enterprise in the prior period. The company may never have been classified as being in the development stage, because of the effective date of the Statement. If the prior period financial statements or summary information are not prepared in conformance with the provisions of SFAS No. 7, they should be restated to comply with the Statement. For example, the entity may have

---

[1] FASB Interpretation No. 7 requires that, if the development stage enterprise is a subsidiary whose financial statements are included in the consolidated statements of an operating enterprise, the prior period adjustment generally will be reported in the consolidated statements for periods prior to the date the accounting change is made.

capitalized all costs in prior periods (when it would have been classified as a development stage enterprise), without consideration for the recoverability of the costs. Some of these costs may have no future benefit, but are being carried as assets and depreciated. Those costs with no future benefits should be removed through the use of a prior period adjustment. If costs with no future benefits previously were capitalized and are fully depreciated, a prior period adjustment is unnecessary, because the effect of the improper accounting has been completely eliminated.

The effects of any restatement or adjustment, resulting from the application of the procedures described above, on income before extraordinary items, net income and related earnings per share should be disclosed. The disclosure should be made in the period the restatement or adjustment occurs, and for all periods presented. The tax effects, if any, of the restatement or adjustment must be recognized and appropriately disclosed.

SFAS No. 14 (December 1976) Financial Reporting for Segments of a Business Enterprise,

SFAS No. 24 (December 1978) Reporting Segment Information in Financial Statements That Are Presented in Another Enterprise's Financial Report

and

SFAS No. 30 (August 1979) Disclosure of Information About Major Customers

Flowchart and General Discussion

The intent of SFAS No. 14 is to require companies, under appropriate circumstances, to report significant operations in various industries, foreign operations, export sales and sales to major customers. The Statement is meant to apply to cases where companies issue complete financial statements in accordance with generally accepted accounting principles. The basic information to be disclosed is a "disaggregation" of the consolidated financial information of the reporting entity. SFAS No. 14 presents some interesting new reporting and disclosure requirements, but *no new* accounting principles are introduced in the Statement.

Generally speaking, the provisions of SFAS No. 14 apply to all public companies. Nonpublic enterprises are specifically exempted from the provisions of Statement No. 14 by SFAS No. 21 (see Topic 13 for a complete discussion of SFAS No. 21). Paragraph 7 of SFAS No. 14 states that a reporting entity is not required to "disaggregate" financial data relating to *unconsolidated subsidiaries* or other *unconsolidated investees.* While the Statement encourages the application of the disclosure requirements to unconsolidated subsidiaries and other unconsolidated investees, such compliance is purely voluntary.

The last sentence in Paragraph 7 of SFAS No. 14 has been amended by SFAS No. 24, "Reporting Segment Information in Financial Statements That Are Presented In Another Enterprise's Financial Report." In effect, Statement No. 24 identifies other situations where the provisions of SFAS No. 14 need not be applied. For the provisions of SFAS No. 24 to be considered, the consolidated (or combined) financial statements of the reporting entity also must contain separate financial statements of either the parent company or investee company. When this situation occurs, segment information disclosures *may not* be required in connection with the separate financial statements issued. The provisions of SFAS No. 14 would not be applied in the situation described above if the following circumstances exist:

(1) when the separate financial statements are included in the consolidated (or combined) financial statements, and both sets of financials are included in the same financial report;

(2) when the separate financial statements are those of a foreign investee (not a subsidiary) of the primary reporting entity, and the separate financials do not disclose the information required by SFAS No. 14; or

(3) when the separate financial statements are those of an investee company accounted for using the cost or equity method, and the segment information as required by SFAS No. 14 is not significant to the consolidated (or combined) financials.

In the last case mentioned above, the determination of the term "significant" would be made by applying certain tests that will be discussed in detail later in this section.

While this entire amendment process may seem somewhat confusing, remember that SFAS No. 21 and SFAS No. 24 both impact the applicability of the provisions of SFAS No. 14. These two amending Statements limit the situations in which SFAS No. 14 must be applied.

Before determining if various industry operations must be reported separately, the company must group its operations into "industry segments." The determination of an industry segment is perhaps one of the most difficult problems presented in the Statement. An industry segment is defined in Paragraph 10(a) of the Statement as "a component of an enterprise engaged in providing a product or service or a group of related products and services primarily to unaffiliated customers (i.e., customers outside the enterprise) for a profit." This definition of a segment is quite broad, and can be interpreted in a variety of ways. For example, one may have a difficult time determining what constitutes a "group of related products." Appendix D of the Statement provides some guidelines to help the accountant determine the nature of an industry segment. To determine if products or services are, in fact, related, one should consider the following:

(1) Related products or services are those that have similar end uses.

(2) Related products or services may share similar productive techniques. For example, they might be made from similar raw materials or produced using similar equipment and labor techniques.

(3) Related products or services may be sold in similar geographical areas and to similar types of customers.

While these guidelines may prove helpful in many instances, the proper determination of an industry segment is, in the final analysis, primarily a management judgment.

Each industry segment identified by management may or may not be reported separately, depending upon certain conditions established in the Statement. The process of determining which industry segments must be reported separately is outlined in Exhibit I below.

Exhibit I

General Outline of Selection Process

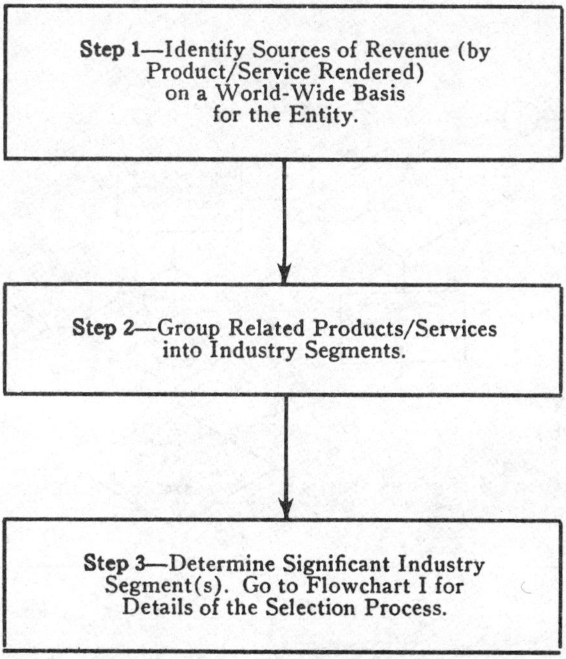

As indicated above, Flowchart I depicts the process of identifying significant industry segments. Flowchart II outlines the decision process and reporting requirements for a company with significant foreign operations, export sales and sales to major customers. Both Flowcharts are designed to help the reader determine when separate reporting is required under the provisions of SFAS No. 14.

The following discussion is organized around the two Flowcharts, i.e., reporting requirements for significant segments will be discussed first, followed by a discussion of foreign operations, export sales and sales to major customers. Each of these major sections will be subdivided into a general discussion of the problem area, followed by the detailed technical considerations.

Determining Reportable Segments—General Discussion

Flowchart I deals exclusively with the problem of determining reportable segments, as defined in SFAS No. 14. Throughout the discussion of Flowchart I and the related example material, it is assumed

FLOWCHART I

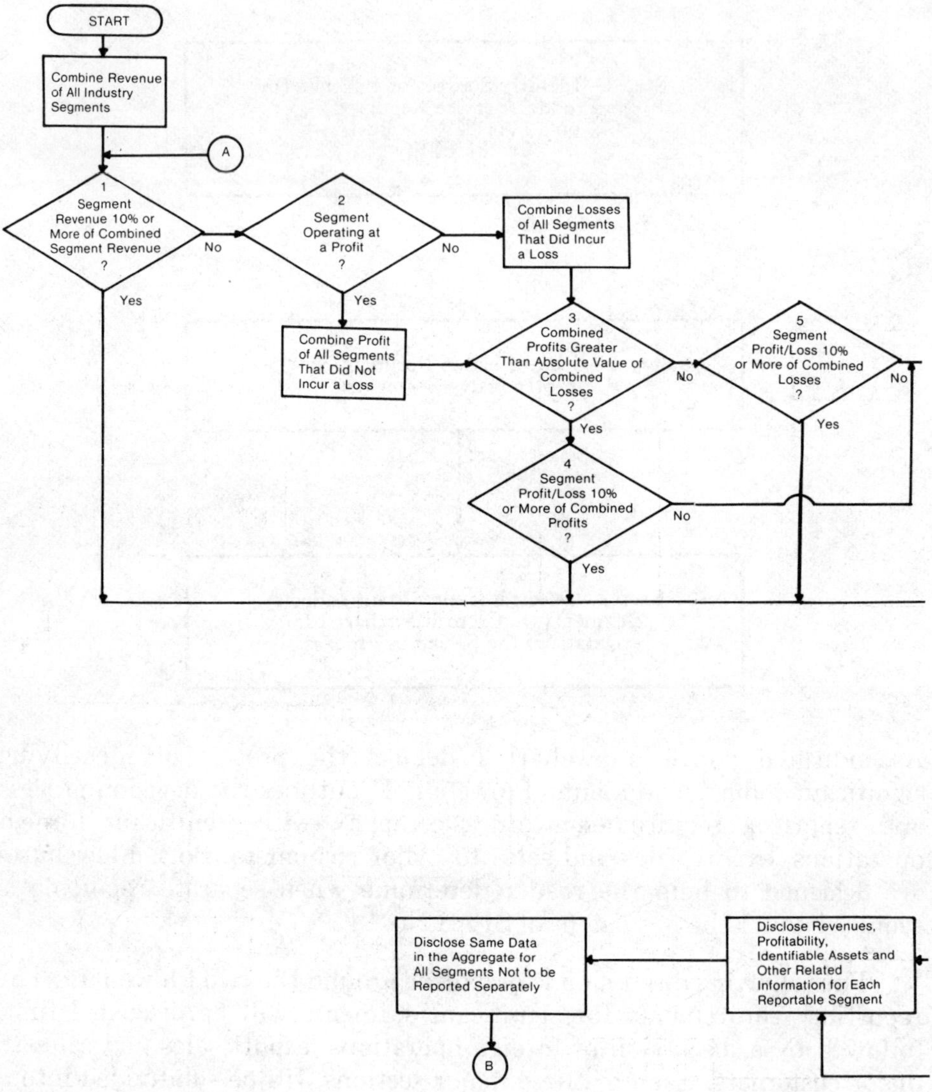
START
Combine Revenue of All Industry Segments
A
1 Segment Revenue 10% or More of Combined Segment Revenue ?
No
Yes
2 Segment Operating at a Profit ?
No
Yes
Combine Losses of All Segments That Did Incur a Loss
Combine Profit of All Segments That Did Not Incur a Loss
3 Combined Profits Greater Than Absolute Value of Combined Losses ?
No
Yes
5 Segment Profit/Loss 10% or More of Combined Losses ?
No
Yes
4 Segment Profit/Loss 10% or More of Combined Profits ?
No
Yes
Disclose Same Data in the Aggregate for All Segments Not to be Reported Separately
Disclose Revenues, Profitability, Identifiable Assets and Other Related Information for Each Reportable Segment
B

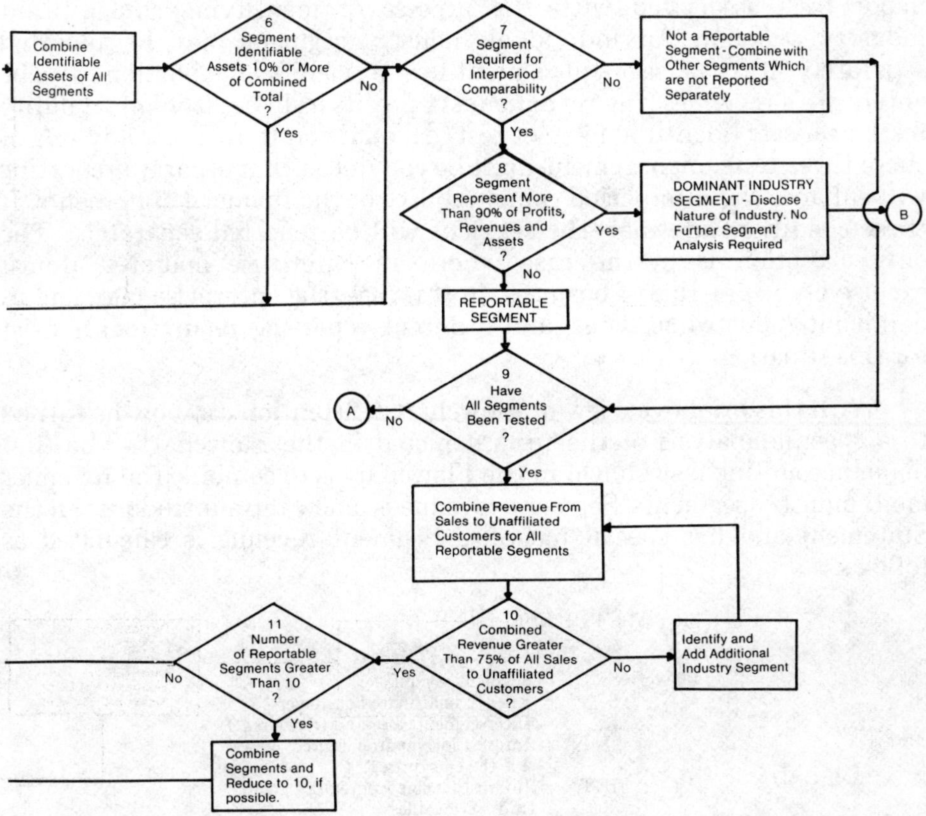
Combine Identifiable Assets of All Segments
6 Segment Identifiable Assets 10% or More of Combined Total ?
No
Yes
7 Segment Required for Interperiod Comparability ?
No
Yes
Not a Reportable Segment - Combine with Other Segments Which are not Reported Separately
8 Segment Represent More Than 90% of Profits, Revenues and Assets ?
Yes
No
DOMINANT INDUSTRY SEGMENT - Disclose Nature of Industry. No Further Segment Analysis Required
B
REPORTABLE SEGMENT
9 Have All Segments Been Tested ?
A
No
Yes
Combine Revenue From Sales to Unaffiliated Customers for All Reportable Segments
10 Combined Revenue Greater Than 75% of All Sales to Unaffiliated Customers ?
No
Yes
Identify and Add Additional Industry Segment
11 Number of Reportable Segments Greater Than 10 ?
No
Yes
Combine Segments and Reduce to 10, if possible.

that management has completed Steps 1 and 2 in Exhibit I. These two steps require judgment on the part of management; and little can be done, through discussion, to structure that decision process. Understanding the specific provisions of the Statement may, in fact, help the reader to reach informed judgments about "related products" and "industry segments." Be that as it may, the following discussion begins with Step 3 of Exhibit I, i.e., with determination of significant industry segments. Generally, each industry that is determined to be significant will be reported separately, and those segments that are not considered significant will be grouped together and reported in the aggregate.

As an overview of Flowchart I, it can be stated that there are three major tests associated with the process of identifying a significant industry segment. An individual industry segment may be reported separately if that segment constitutes a significant portion of the enterprise's revenues (the revenue test), profits or losses (the profitability test), or assets (identifiable asset test). In addition to meeting any *one* of these three tests, management must be convinced that separate reporting will enhance the interperiod comparability of the financial statements. If these conditions are met, the segment will be reported separately. The only exception is in the case where an enterprise operates almost exclusively in one line of business. In this case, the enterprise may have a dominant industry segment, and different reporting requirements exist for this situation.

With this brief overview of Flowchart I, attention can now be turned to a specific analysis of the tests depicted in the Flowchart. The first major accounting task shown in the Flowchart is to combine the revenues of all industry segments. Segment revenue is a new term introduced in the Statement and has special meaning. Segment revenue is calculated as follows:

$$SR = S + IS + INT_o + INT_r$$

Where: SR = Segment revenue.
S = Sales to unaffiliated customers.
IS = Intersegment sales and transfers.
INT_o = Interest income from sources outside the enterprise.
INT_r = Interest income from intersegment trade receivables.[a]

[a] Interest income from intersegment trade receivables will be included in segment revenue only if the related receivable is included in the segment's identifiable assets for purposes of the "asset test."

The summation of all industry segment revenue would be equal to the combined segment revenue. Note that the revenue test is based on combined revenue, and not on consolidated revenue. Intersegment items would be eliminated to get from combined revenues to consolidated revenues.

Once combined segment revenue has been determined, the revenue test can be conducted. If an individual industry segment's revenue is 10 percent or more of the total of all combined segment revenue (Block 1), that segment will be reported separately, if management believes this procedure would enhance interperiod comparability (Block 7), and if the particular segment is not considered to be a *dominant industry segment* (Block 8). Discussion of what constitutes a dominant industry segment will be postponed until after consideration is given to all three major tests.

If an individual industry segment fails to meet the revenue test, the next step is to see if it meets the "profitablity" test. For purposes of this test, it is necessary to separate those segments earning an operating profit from those incurring an operating loss (Block 2). Like segment revenue, operating profit or loss has special meaning for purposes of SFAS No. 14. A general definition of operating profit or loss is segment revenue (as defined above) less all operating expenses. In addition to deducting typical operating expenses, it is appropriate to include as segment operating expenses any reasonable allocation of *enterprise* expenses that are not directly associated with the particular segment. For example, the enterprise may have a central computer facility, and may allocate the costs of the facility to the various companies that receive benefit from the computer services. These allocated costs would be an appropriate operating expense for purposes of calculating operating profit or loss. The Statement indicates that the following items are *not* to be included in the calculation of segment operating profit or loss:

(1) Any revenues earned at the corporate level and not related to any segment;

(2) General corporate expenses;

(3) Interest expense, except if segment operations are primarily of a financial nature;

(4) Domestic and foreign income taxes;

(5) Equity in earnings of unconsolidated subsidiaries or investees;

(6) Extraordinary items;

(7) Gains or losses on discontinued operations;

(8) Minority interest; or

(9) Cumulative effect of changes in accounting principles.

The operating profits of all segments that earned a profit should be combined into one total, and the operating losses for all segments that incurred a loss should be combined into another total. For purposes of the profitability test, the *greater* of the combined profits or the absolute value of the combined losses will be used as the base (Block 3). If the combined profits are greater than combined losses, all segment profits or losses will be compared to the combined profits (Block 4). In this case, it will be necessary to compare the absolute value of the loss with the combined profits for those segments incurring a loss. If the combined losses exceed the combined profits, all segment profits and losses will be compared to combined losses (Block 5).

If a particular industry segment's profit or loss is 10 percent or more of the combined profits or losses, whichever is appropriate in the circumstances, that segment is a candidate for separate reporting. If this test is met, management must believe that separate reporting would enhance interperiod comparability of the statements, and the segment must not be dominant, before a final determination on separate reporting can be made. These two additional conditions are the same as those specified for the revenue test, and they will appear again in the "asset" test.

If an industry segment fails both the revenue and the profitability tests, it still may qualify for separate reporting, depending upon the dollar value of its identifiable assets. Identifiable assets of an industry segment include tangible and intangible assets (net of valuation allowances) used exclusively by the segment and the allocated portion of the cost of assets (net of valuation allowances) used by two or more segments. Assets that are used for general corporate purposes are not considered part of the industry segment's identifiable assets. Loans and advances to, and investments in, other segments generally are not included in identifiable assets. (Loans and advances should be included in the identifiable assets of financial segments, because income from these sources will be included in the operating profit or loss of such a segment.)

If the identifiable assets of a particular industry segment are 10 percent or more of the combined total of all segment identifiable assets, the segment may be reported separately, if the additional conditions mentioned above are met (Blocks 6, 7 and 8).

If an individual industry segment fails to meet any of the three major tests, it still may be reported separately if management feels that separate reporting is needed to achieve interperiod comparability. Obviously, an understanding of what is meant by "interperiod comparability" is important—so important that it can override the three tests specified in the Statement. For example, one industry segment may not have met any of the tests in the past and management may believe it will not meet any of the tests in the future; but, due to unusual circumstances, the segment may meet one or more of the tests in the current period. Management may feel that it would *not* be appropriate to have separate reporting of this segment in the current period because it is not likely to require separate reporting in future periods and did not require separate reporting in the past. In this case, even though the segment meets one or more of the tests, it will not be reported separately. On the other hand, if a particular industry segment fails all three tests, and if management believes that separate reporting of the segment information is required to achieve interperiod comparability of the financial statements, the segment may be treated as a reportable segment (Block 7). This situation may develop when a particular segment has met one or more of the tests in the past and is expected to meet them in the future; but, due to unusual economic conditions, it fails to meet any of the tests in the current period.

If an industry segment has met at least one of the three major tests and the interperiod comparability test, it must be determined whether or not the segment may be classified as dominant. If any one segment represents 90 percent or more of the combined revenues, operating profits or losses *and* identifiable assets, it is considered a dominant industry segment and requires special reporting and disclosure (Block 8).

Each individual industry segment must be tested separately to determine if it will be classified as reportable or non-reportable (Block 9). Once the testing of all industry segments has been completed, and all reportable segments have been isolated, two tests are imposed by the Statement to insure that the information to be disclosed in the financial statements is meaningful.

First, the revenue from sales to unaffiliated customers of all *reportable* segments should be combined. The combined total of the revenue from reportable segments must be 75 percent or more of all revenue from sales to unaffiliated customers (Block 10). If the combined revenues do not meet this test, additional segments must be added, until the test is met. The additional segments to be added will come from the group of segments that failed to meet any of the tests described above. While the Statement does not provide guidance on how to select the additional segments for inclusion, it would seem logical to select those segments that came nearest to meeting the tests. For example, assume that one segment was excluded because it failed all three major tests; that the revenue, profitability and identifiable assets of the segment were about eight percent of the respective totals; and that another segment excluded constituted about five percent of the same totals. Logic would dictate inclusion of the "eight percent" segment before the "five percent" segment for purposes of meeting the 75 percent of sales test.

The final condition identified in the Statement involves the number of separately reportable segments. If the number of reportable segments is greater than 10, every effort should be made to combine segments so as to reduce the total reportable segments to 10 or less (Block 11). The purpose of this test is to keep the reporting and disclosure of segment information from becoming too detailed. When combining reportable segments, those that are most closely related should be combined first.

A detailed discussion of the reporting and disclosure requirements for a segment will be addressed later in this section. Generally, the enterprise must disclose revenues, profitability, identifiable assets and certain related information for each reportable segment.

Determining Reportable Segments—Technical Considerations

To illustrate the provisions of SFAS No. 14, assume that World-Wide Enterprise, Inc. has developed the industry segment information shown in Table I. World-Wide now needs to know which of the various segments must be reported separately.

Table I

Worksheet for Industry Segments

	Corporate	Segment 1	Segment 2	Segment 3	Segment 4	Segment 5	Segment 6	Combined	Eliminations	Consolidated
REVENUES										
Sales to Unaffiliated Customers	-0-	$ 60,000	$ 200,000	$ 25,000	$ 15,000	$ 250,000	$ 50,000	$ 600,000		$ 600,000
Intersegment Sales	-0-	-0-	25,000	-0-	-0-	75,000	-0-	100,000	$ (100,000)	-0-
	$ -0-	$ 60,000	$ 225,000	$ 25,000	$ 15,000	$ 325,000	$ 50,000	$ 700,000	$ (100,000)	$ 600,000
OPERATING PROFITS										
Operating Profit or (Loss)	$ -0-	$ (40,000)	$ 65,000	$ 15,000	$ (3,000)	$ 78,000	$ 10,000	$ 125,000		$ 125,000
Equity in Earnings of Unconsolidated Investee	8,000							8,000		8,000
Corporate Expenses	(10,000)							(10,000)		(10,000)
Interest Expense	(5,000)							(5,000)		(5,000)
Income From Continuing Operations Before Taxes	$ (7,000)	$ (40,000)	$ 65,000	$ 15,000	$ (3,000)	$ 78,000	$ 10,000	$ 118,000	-0-	$ 118,000
IDENTIFIABLE ASSETS										
Identifiable Assets		$ 75,000	$ 275,000	$ 100,000	$ 32,000	$ 350,000	$ 68,000	$ 900,000		$ 900,000
Intersegment Loans	$ 50,000		10,000			20,000		80,000	$ (80,000)	-0-
Investment in Unconsolidated Investee	20,000							20,000		20,000
Corporate Assets	10,000							10,000		10,000
Total Assets	$ 80,000	$ 75,000	$ 285,000	$ 100,000	$ 32,000	$ 370,000	$ 68,000	$1,010,000	$ (80,000)	$ 930,000

Table I indicates that the combined revenue of the enterprise is $700,000. Therefore, any segment with revenue of $70,000 or more ($700,000 × .10) will qualify as a candidate for separate reporting. Segment 2, with revenues of $225,000, and Segment 5, with revenues of $325,000, are the only segments that qualify under the revenue test for separate reporting. Note that the revenue test is based on combined revenues, not on consolidated revenues.

The next test to determine if any additional segments will be reported separately is the profitability test. In the example given, Segments 1 and 4 incurred an operating loss, and all the other segments experienced operating profits. It therefore is necessary to divide the segments into two groups: those with losses and those with profits. The operating profit group is made up of the following segments:

	Operating Profits		Operating Losses
Segment 2	$ 65,000	Segment 1	$(40,000)
Segment 3	15,000	Segment 4	(3,000)
Segment 5	78,000	Total	$(43,000)
Segment 6	10,000		
Total	$168,000		

Next, the $168,000 total profits are compared with the $43,000 absolute value of the combined losses. In this example, the combined profits are greater than the combined losses; therefore, the $168,000 becomes the basis for comparison in the profitability test. For an industry segment to be considered for separate reporting, its operating profit or loss must be at least $16,800 ($168,000 × .10). Based upon this information, Segments 2, 5 and 1 would qualify as reportable segments. While Segment 1 incurred an operating loss, the absolute value of its loss was more than $16,800; and it would qualify under the profitability test.

The last major test for inclusion deals with the identifiable assets of each industry segment. The combined identifiable assets of all industry segments are $900,000. To meet the identifiable asset test, an industry segment must have at least $90,000 ($900,000 × .10) of identifiable assets. Again, Segments 2 and 5 meet this test, but already are included on the basis of the revenue test. Segment 1 does not meet this test, but already is included on the basis of the profitability test. Of the remaining segments, only Segment 3 meets the identifiable asset test ($100,000 in identifiable assets). Note that intersegment loans, corporate assets and investments in unconsolidated investee were excluded from the identifiable assets.

As a result of the three major tests, Segments 1, 2, 3 and 5 are candidates for separate reporting. Segments 4 and 6 may be combined into one group for disclosure purposes if neither is needed to allow interperiod comparability of financial information or to meet the 75-percent-of-revenue test.

Assuming that management has determined that Segments 4 and 6 are not needed to achieve interperiod comparability, they are not specifically excluded until the combined revenues of the reportable segments has been tested. For purposes of this test, only revenue from sales to unaffiliated customers is considered. The combined revenues from this source are shown below:

Reportable Segments
Sales Revenue from Unaffiliated Customers

Segment 1	$ 60,000
Segment 2	200,000
Segment 3	25,000
Segment 5	250,000
Total	$535,000

Revenue from sales to all unaffiliated customers is $600,000. The reportable segments' revenue from this source is 89 percent ($535,000/$600,000) of the total. Therefore, the 75-percent test is met, and no additional segments need be added. Because the 75-percent test has been met, Segments 4 and 6 are excluded as possible reportable segments and will be reported in combined form.

World-Wide has less than 10 reportable segments, so no combination of reportable segments is required. Based on the information presented in this example, World-Wide would report Segments 1, 2, 3 and 5 separately, and would combine Segments 4 and 6 into one reporting group.

Detailed examples of reporting and disclosure requirements will be shown at the end of the discussion of SFAS No. 14. The following section provides a general outline of the disclosures for each reportable segment.

Reportable Segments—Disclosure Requirements

Disclosure requirements under the provisions of SFAS No. 14 can become complex. Flowchart I indicates that, in general, revenues, operating profit or loss, identifiable assets and certain related information must be disclosed for each reportable segment. This same disclosure is required for the combined segments that are not reported separately. In the example material, Segments 4 and 6 are combined, and the disclosures would relate to the aggregate combined amounts.

The Statement identifies three methods that are considered appropriate for presenting the information. Management may choose the method it considers most meaningful. The information may be presented:

(1) In the financial statements, with reference to related footnote disclosures;

(2) In the footnotes to the financial statements; or

(3) In a supplementary schedule, which is not part of the basic financial statements. (If the financial statements are being sent to stockholders, reference must be made in the financial statements to the supplementary schedule, thereby making the schedule an integral part of the entire financial statements.)

It is assumed that, once a method of presentation has been selected, it will be used consistently from period to period.

The required *revenue* disclosures for each reportable segment and for the combined segments not reported separately include the following:

(1) Sales to unaffiliated customers;

(2) Intersegment sales or transfers, along with the basis of accounting for such sales or transfers and, if this accounting basis is changed, the nature of the change and its affect on segment operating profit or loss; and

(3) A reconciliation of the revenue disclosed in 1 and 2 above to the revenue reported on the *consolidated* income statement. (Table I presents a reconciliation for all segments.)

There are both minimum and optional disclosure requirements for reporting the profitability information. The following minimum requirements are identified in the Statement.

(1) Operating profits or losses, as defined above, should be disclosed for each segment;

(2) If the method of allocating operating expenses between segments has been changed, the nature of the change and its effect on segment operating profit or loss should be disclosed; and

(3) Operating profit and loss disclosed in 1 and 2 above should be reconciled to pretax income from continuing operations on the consolidated income statement. (Table I shows such a reconciliation for all segments.)

In addition to the minimum disclosures described above, the enterprise may *elect* to present some other measures of profitability. These measures might include net income or some other value between pretax income from continuing operations and net income. If the company elects this additional disclosure, it must identify each item of revenue or expense that was added or deducted from operating profit or loss. Once the additional disclosure has been elected, it should be used on a consistent basis.

Identifiable assets, as defined earlier in this section, must be reported for each segment. Identifiable assets thus disclosed should be reconciled to consolidated *total* assets. Corporate assets should be identified and reported separately for purposes of the reconciliation.

The other disclosures required by the Statement relate primarily to the assets of the enterprise, and include disclosure of the following:

(1) The total amount of depreciation, depletion and amortization expense for each reportable segment;

(2) Capital expenditures made by each reportable segment;

(3) Whether the enterprise has an investment carried on the equity method, or an unconsolidated investee whose operations are vertically integrated with a reportable segment, and the geographical area of operation of the investee; and

(4) The effect of a change in accounting principle on the operating profit or loss of a reportable segment.

Alternative disclosure is required for a dominant industry segment, i.e., for a reportable segment that represents more than 90 percent of the revenue, operating profits and identifiable assets of the enterprise. The only disclosure requirement for a dominant industry segment is that the industry be identified.

Foreign Operations, Export Sales and Major Customer Information—General Discussion

Flowchart II depicts the decision process and general reporting requirements for identifying significant foreign operations, reportable export sales and major customer information. The discussion that follows will treat each of these three topics separately.

FLOWCHART II

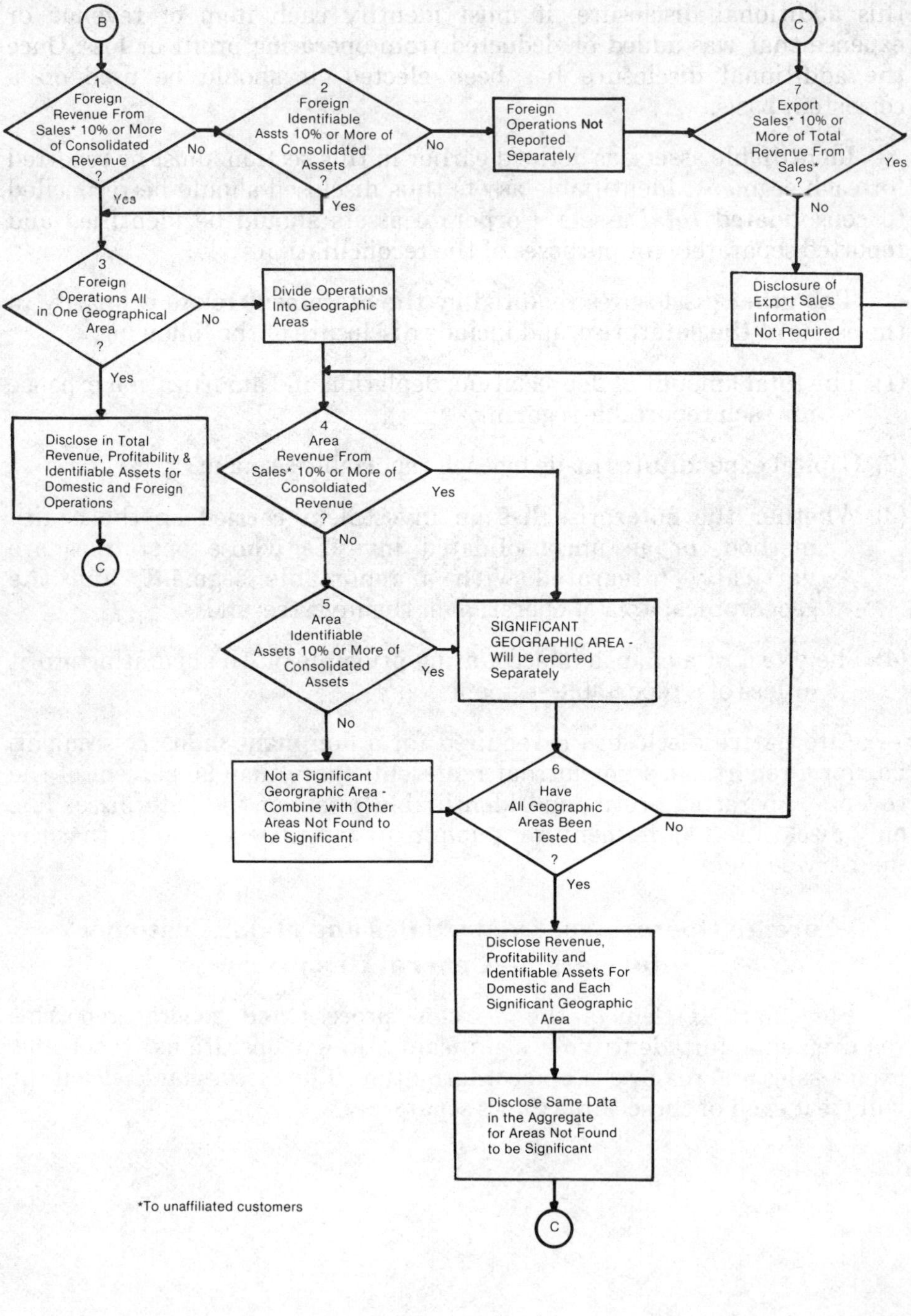

*To unaffiliated customers

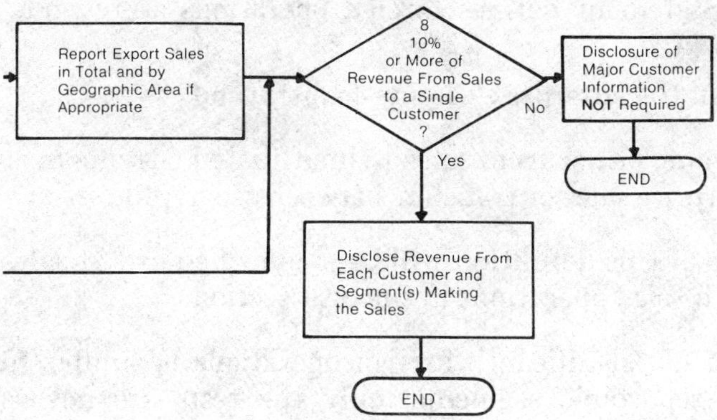
Report Export Sales in Total and by Geographic Area if Appropriate
8
10% or More of Revenue From Sales to a Single Customer ?
No
Yes
Disclosure of Major Customer Information NOT Required
END
Disclose Revenue From Each Customer and Segment(s) Making the Sales
END

Significant Foreign Operations

SFAS No. 14 requires that, where significant foreign operations exist, the enterprise should separately disclose domestic and foreign activities. Paragraph 31 of the Statement defines foreign operations as revenue-producing activities that:[1]

(1) Are located outside of the enterprise's home country; and

(2) Are generating revenue, either from sales to unaffiliated customers or from intra-enterprise sales or transfers between geographic areas.

Additional refinements of this definition will be made when export sales are distinguished from foreign operations in the next section.

The determination of "significant" foreign operations is similar to the determination of reportable segments, only the tests are not as extensive. For foreign operations to be considered significant, revenue from sales to unaffiliated customers must be 10 percent or more of consolidated revenue reported on the enterprise's income statement (Block 1). If the foreign operations fail to meet this test, a second, and final, test is available. If the identifiable assets of the foreign operation are 10 percent or more of the consolidated total assets of the enterprise, the operations are considered to be significant (Block 2). If neither of these two tests are met, foreign operations will not be disclosed separately.

Once it has been determined that foreign operations are significant, the accountant must determine if all foreign operations are carried out in one geographic area (Block 3). Geographic areas are defined (SFAS No. 14, Paragraph 34) as "individual countries or groups of countries as may be determined to be appropriate in an enterprise's circumstances." While the determination of a geographic area is a management judgment, the Statement (Paragraph 34) lists the following factors to consider when grouping foreign operations:

(1) Proximity;

(2) Economic affinity;

(3) Similarities in business environments;

(4) Nature, scale and degree of inter-relationship of the enterprise's operations in the various countries.

---

[1] FASB Technical Bulletin No. 79-4 states that operations in areas under U.S. sovereignty or jurisdiction, such as Puerto Rico, the Virgin Islands and American Samoa, should be considered *domestic* when an enterprise is separating domestic and foreign operations.

A geographic area may be as narrowly defined as Japan, for instance, or as broadly defined as Asia, depending on the circumstances.

If all foreign operations are conducted in one geographic area, disclosure should be made of total domestic and foreign revenues, profitability and identifiable assets. However, if foreign operations are conducted in two or more geographic areas, it is necessary to determine whether each area should be reported separately. The revenue test and the identifiable assets test, as outlined above, will be applied to each geographic area (Blocks 4 and 5). If either of these two tests is met by the operations in a geographic area, that area is considered to be significant for separate reporting purposes. When it is appropriate to report on geographic areas, those areas that are not considered to be significant should be combined and reported in the aggregate.

Table II, which is merely an extension of Table I, shows the operations of World-Wide Enterprise, Inc., divided into foreign and domestic operations. The foreign operations are divided into geographic areas for purposes of testing the provisions of SFAS No. 14.

Table II

Worksheet for Foreign Operations

	Domestic	Geographic Area 1	Geographic Area 2	Geographic Area 3	Geographic Area 4	Combined	Eliminations	Consolidated
REVENUES								
Sales to Unaffiliated Customers	$400,000	$ 40,000	$ 85,000	$ 55,000	$ 20,000	$ 600,000		$600,000
Interarea Sales	100,000					100,000	$(100,000)	-0-
Total Revenues	$500,000	$ 40,000	$ 85,000	$ 55,000	$ 20,000	$ 700,000	$(100,000)	$600,000
IDENTIFIABLE ASSETS								
Identifiable Assets	$575,000	$ 60,000	$100,000	$120,000	$ 45,000	$ 900,000		$900,000
Interarea Loans	70,000	5,000		5,000		80,000	$ (80,000)	-0-
Investment in Unconsolidated Investee	20,000					20,000		20,000
Corporate Assets	10,000					10,000		10,000
Total Assets	$675,000	$ 65,000	$100,000	$125,000	$ 45,000	$1,010,000	$ (80,000)	$930,000

To determine if foreign operations are significant, it is necessary to combine the revenue from sales to unaffiliated customers for all geographic areas. This would result in the following information:

Revenue From Foreign Operations

Geographic Area 1	$ 40,000
Geographic Area 2	85,000
Geographic Area 3	55,000
Geographic Area 4	20,000
Total	$200,000

Foreign operations are significant, because $200,000 in revenue from sales to unaffiliated customers is more than 10 percent of *consolidated* revenues ($600,000 × .10 = $60,000). Therefore, at a minimum, domestic and foreign operations will be reported separately. While it is not necessary for the foreign operations to meet the identifiable asset test, the reader should note that, in this example, the test was met. The $325,000 in identifiable assets of foreign operations ($60,000 + $100,000 + $120,000 + $45,000 = $325,000) is more than 10 percent of consolidated total assets ($930,000 × .10 = $93,000). Note that, in both of these tests, consolidated amounts are used, rather than the *combined* totals used for the determination of reportable segments.

Because foreign operations are in more than one geographic area, it is necessary to determine if any of the geographic areas are significant. Ten percent of consolidated revenues is $60,000 ($600,000 × .10). Any geographic area with revenue from sales to unaffiliated customers of $60,000 or more will be considered to be significant, and therefore to require separate reporting. Of the four geographic areas, only Area 2, with revenues of $85,000, meets the revenue test. In addition, any geographic area with identifiable assets of $93,000 or more will be considered significant. Area 2, which previously was included under the revenue test, also meets the identifiable asset test. Of the remaining three areas, only Area 3, with identifiable assets of $120,000, meets this new test.

As a result of these tests, World-Wide will report its domestic operations, Geographic Areas 2 and 3 separately, and Geographic Areas 1 and 4 in combined form.

The disclosures required for foreign operations are very similar to those required for segments. Revenue from sales to unaffiliated customers and sales or transfers between geographic areas should be disclosed for the enterprise's domestic operations as well as for significant foreign operations. An appropriate reconciliation of revenue thus disclosed to consolidated revenues also must be made. Disclosure of operating profits, net income or some other measure of profitability appearing between these two amounts should be made. Again, appropriate reconciliation is required. The final disclosure is for identifiable assets, which should be reconciled to consolidated total assets.

Export Sales

As a result of the above analysis, enterprise operations are divided into foreign and domestic. A part of the analysis requires the separation of sales to unaffiliated customers into foreign and domestic categories. Export sales represent a further subdivision of domestic sales to unaffiliated customers. Export sales are those sales made by an enterprise's domestic operations to unaffiliated customers in foreign countries.

It sometimes is difficult to distinguish between foreign operations and export sales. The Statement (Footnote 12) offers the following help in distinguishing between the two:

> If revenues are normally identified with the enterprise's foreign operations, revenue generated from abroad would be considered foreign revenue. If they are normally identified with the enterprise's domestic operations, revenue generated abroad would be considered export sales. . . .
>
> Services rendered by the foreign offices of a service enterprise . . . having offices or facilities located both in the home country and in foreign countries would be considered foreign operations. . . . Revenue generated abroad from services provided by domestic offices should be considered export sales.

At times, accountants and others will have difficulty in determining what constitutes foreign operations and what constitutes export sales.

If the domestic operations of an enterprise have sales to unaffiliated foreign customers that amount to 10 percent or more of the total sales to unaffiliated customers, this fact must be disclosed (Block 7). The amount of export sales should be disclosed in the aggregate or by geographic area, whichever is appropriate in the circumstances.

Sufficient examples of testing have been presented above. Because of the simplicity of the test, a specific example will not be presented for export sales.

Sales to Major Customers

As indicated in Flowchart II, if 10 percent or more of the revenue of an enterprise results from sales to a single customer, this information should be disclosed (Block 8).[2] The amount of revenue from each such customer should be identified, along with the segment(s) making the sale

---

[2] FASB Technical Bulletin No. 79-5 indicates that an insurance company, such as Blue Cross, is *not* a customer of a health care facility, even though the insurance company makes payments for the patients to the health care facility.

but the customer's identity is not required to be disclosed. In most cases, the identification of a single customer is very straight-forward. SFAS No. 30, "Disclosure of Information About Major Customers," identifies the following entities as being a single customer for purposes of the 10 percent test; "a group of entities under common control . . ., the federal government, a state government, a local government (for example, a county or municipality), or a foreign government." This refinement of the concept of a single customer was needed because, when selling to the federal government, it is difficult to define the single customer as a particular department, agency or the federal government. With this definition in SFAS No. 30, specific guidance has been given the cases that previously were difficult to handle. SFAS No. 30 encourages the reporting entity to disclose information about concentration of sales to any particular governmental department or agency, however, identification of the specific department or agency is *not required.*

Example Disclosures

The disclosures shown below are from the 1976 annual reports of Celanese Corporation and The Standard Oil Company (Ohio). They illustrate two different approaches to the reporting of segment information. Celanese Corporation has elected to report the segment information in the notes to the financial statements, while Standard Oil Company has elected to show the information in a separate schedule entitled "Business Segments." Both disclosures provide the required reconciliations.

Celanese Corporation (Dec)

Notes to Consolidated Financial Statements (millions)

Note U: Product group information

	Fibers Group U.S. Polyester and Nylon	Fibers Group U.S. Cellulosics	Fibers Group Non-U.S.	Chemicals Group Chemicals	Chemicals Group Plastics	Chemicals Group Polymer Specialities	Inter-product line eliminations and corporate income, expenses and assets	Totals as shown in consolidated financial statements
1976								
Sales: Total	$665	$302	$285	$634	$185	$266	$(214)	$2,123
Inter-product line	20	27	3	157	3	4	(214)	—
Operating income	50	27	(30)	110	4	10	(15)	156
Depreciation	57	27	22	49	21	7	3	186
Assets	484	274	278	521	214	150	(11)	1,910
Capital expenditures	43	17	44	87	20	9	3	223
1975								
Sales: Total	548	285	328	529	128	249	(167)	1,900
Inter-product line	13	16	3	132	1	2	(167)	—
Operating income	20	22	6	93	(18)	(1)	(12)	110
Depreciation	56	27	23	45	15	7	4	177
Assets	490	259	308	457	193	172	29	1,908
Capital expenditures	38	23	41	51	43	9	3	208
1974								
Sales: Total	545	289	328	462	200	257	(153)	1,928
Inter-product line	20	16	3	107	5	2	(153)	—
Operating income	51	(29)	27	101	25	1	(11)	165
Depreciation	47	31	22	43	14	6	3	166
Assets	457	264	297	423	207	178	47	1,873
Capital expenditures	91	20	18	41	37	9	4	220
1973								
Sales: Total	522	260	283	284	170	201	(111)	1,609
Inter-product line	18	11	—	72	9	1	(111)	—
Operating income	99	(7)	34	48	22	9	(8)	198
Depreciation	43	30	22	33	13	5	2	148
Assets	484	271	282	372	166	140	32	1,747
Capital expenditures	68	11	10	40	15	5	10	159
1972								
Sales: Total	425	235	222	250	156	199	(102)	1,385
Inter-product line	12	12	—	65	10	3	(102)	—
Operating income	56	5	7	44	10	8	(8)	122
Depreciation	37	23	20	31	12	4	4	131
Assets	429	315	293	377	178	138	(25)	1,705
Capital expenditures	34	17	16	21	20	11	9	128

Inter-product line and inter-area sales generally are priced with reference to prevailing market prices. In calculating operating income, the $11 million effect of the cost reduction program in 1972 was included in the product lines where the costs were incurred.

During 1974, operating income was affected by the changes in accounting principles. These changes reduced product line operating income as follows: polyester and nylon, $21 million; cellulosics, $14 million; non-U.S. fibers, $7 million; chemicals, $21 million; plastics, $8 million; and polymer specialties, $18 million.

Total and inter-area sales, net income, depreciation, assets and capital expenditures of non-U.S. subsidiaries by geographical area are shown for 1976. Also shown there are the totals for all non-U.S. subsidiaries for these items for 1972 through 1976. The balance of the Corporation's net income, assets, capital expenditures and depreciation relates to U.S. operations, except for equity in net income and investments in affiliates. Total and inter-area sales for U.S. operations for 1976 were $1,790 million and $217 million, respectively. Included in the inter-area sales for the U.S., Canada, and for non-U.S. subsidiaries in total are intercompany sales of $79 million, $13 million, and $6 million, respectively.

Corporate assets included in the next-to-last column in the table for 1972-76 are: $124 million; $212 million; $211 million; $84 million; and $174 million, respectively.

Source: *Accounting Trends & Techniques,* copyright © 1977 by the American Institute of Certified Public Accountants, Inc., p. 15.

The Standard Oil Company (An Ohio Corporation)

Business Segments

	1976	1975	1974	1973	1972
			Thousands of Dollars		
Sales and operating revenue					
Petroleum					
Products	$2,266,328	$1,888,196	$1,657,672	$1,092,290	$ 999,004
Merchandise	93,759	85,091	78,998	76,626	71,875
Crude oil and natural gas	24,047	22,117	17,200	28,759	41,278
Other	59,624	42,076	34,599	6,547	-0-
	2,443,758	2,037,480	1,788,469	1,204,222	1,112,157
Coal	148,952	166,270	114,680	84,608	78,206
Chemicals and plastics					
Industrial chemicals	131,478	96,263	103,032	73,013	56,809
Agricultural and other nitrogen chemicals	132,544	137,072	108,536	71,003	40,236
Plastics	53,902	47,076	51,460	49,148	48,287
	317,924	280,411	263,028	193,164	145,332
Royalties from licenses on patented processes	4,724	22,975	41,012	24,709	21,338
Other	1,062	-0-	-0-	-0-	30,263
	$2,916,420	$2,507,136	$2,207,189	$1,506,703	$1,387,296
Income before interest, income taxes, and extraordinary items					
Petroleum*	$ 155,606	$ 84,216	$ 72,515	$ 60,251	$ 57,623
Coal	32,363	52,083	31,546	12,373	11,577
Chemicals and plastics	46,923	54,162	47,895	23,217	11,807
Royalties	1,879	21,047	39,700	23,692	20,245
Other	(1,615)	(2,713)	2,823	804	2,305
Corporate	213	(1,968)	(1,521)	(421)	(1,039)
	$ 235,369	$ 206,827	$ 192,958	$ 119,916	$ 102,518

Assets					
Petroleum					
Alaska	$4,410,450	$2,495,600	$ 921,071	$ 425,449	$ 319,187
Lower 48 states	1,294,327	1,228,023	1,227,134	1,108,413	1,170,989
Coal	157,209	128,010	100,150	76,402	70,367
Chemicals and plastics	185,916	178,798	145,150	130,395	133,072
Royalties	55,376	67,165	59,276	33,348	21,440
Other	68,696	60,842	47,140	38,784	37,333
Corporate	88,244	62,005	121,563	150,687	50,030
	$6,260,218	$4,220,443	$2,621,484	$1,963,478	$1,802,418
Capital Expenditures					
Petroleum	$1,639,152	$1,571,896	$ 666,625	$ 178,154	$ 101,919
Coal	38,094	29,464	20,351	5,692	16,313
Chemicals and plastics	13,373	19,258	8,465	7,039	4,479
Other	4,898	17,214	3,132	405	14
Corporate	3,282	3,783	1,839	1,307	1,668
	$1,698,799	$1,641,615	$ 700,412	$ 192,597	$ 124,393
Depreciation and depletion expense					
Petroleum	$ 58,012	$ 63,561	$ 51,710	$ 50,465	$ 53,846
Coal	9,513	7,455	5,900	5,930	5,691
Chemicals and plastics	12,097	10,112	9,690	9,251	8,957
Other	278	20	11	7	880
Corporate	1,614	1,344	1,123	1,366	1,502
	$ 81,514	$ 82,492	$ 68,434	$ 67,019	$ 70,876
* Includes a $\frac{5}{12}$ of 1% interest in the Iranian Oil Consortium as follows:					
Income before income taxes	$ 13,274	$ 22,145	$ 38,186	$ 14,484	$ 9,123
Income after Iranian income tax	$ 416	$ 1,931	$ 9,271	$ 1,643	$ 1,996

Products and services of the business segments are described in the Review of Operations. Inter-segment sales are immaterial.

The above information complies with Financial Accounting Standards Board Statement No. 14, "Financial Reporting for Segments of a Business Enterprise."

Source: *Accounting Trends & Techniques,* Copyright © 1977 by the American Institute of Certified Public Accountants, Inc., p. 14.

SFAS No. 15 (June 1977) Accounting By Debtors and Creditors for Troubled Debt Restructurings

Flowchart and General Discussion

SFAS No. 15 establishes accounting and reporting standards for a restructuring of troubled debt. Not all debt restructurings qualify for treatment as a troubled debt restructuring. Debt restructuring, troubled or otherwise, involves the modification or elimination of a debt instrument before, at or after maturity date by means other than those required in the debt instrument. A troubled debt restructuring will exist only if the "creditor for economic or legal reasons related to the debtor's financial difficulties grants a concession to the debtor that it would not otherwise consider" (SFAS No. 15, Paragraph 2). In effect, the creditor is making the concession in hopes that he will receive more from the debtor than he would if the concession were not made.

While there are many types of troubled debt restructurings, the Statement identifies and treats in detail the following:

(1) Transfer of assets from the debtor to the creditor in full settlement of the debt;

(2) Transfer of an equity interest in the debtor to the creditor in full settlement of the debt;

(3) Modification of the terms of the debt through a change in the (1) interest rate, (2) maturity date, (3) face or maturity value of the debt, and (4) accrued interest, or some combination of these items;

(4) Transfer of assets or an equity interest in partial settlement of the debt, *and* modification of the terms as described in 3 above.

It should be noted that this list is not meant to be all-inclusive, and that other types of troubled debt restructurings will have to be evaluated on their merits. Flowcharts I and II are designed to illustrate the major accounting and reporting consequences of these four types of troubled debt restructurings. Flowchart I deals with the restructuring from the viewpoint of the debtor, and Flowchart II is from the view-point of the creditor. Specific provisions of the Statement, as reflected in the Flowcharts, will be discussed under the debtor and creditor captions below.

Troubled Debt Restructuring—Debtor Accounting

As indicated above, the discussion of debtor accounting for a troubled debt restructuring will incorporate the four basic types of restructurings. Each type of restructuring will be treated separately. After the four general types have been discussed, some additional accounting complications will be addressed, followed by the required disclosures specified in SFAS No. 15.

Transfer of Assets in Full Settlement

One possible way to effect a debt restructuring is for the debtor to transfer assets to the creditor (Block 2). When such a restructuring occurs, it still is necessary to determine if the transaction qualifies for *troubled* debt restructuring treatment. The transaction will be considered a troubled debt restructuring only if the fair value of the assets transferred is not equal to or greater than the carrying amount of the payable (Block 3). When the fair value of the asset transferred is less than the carrying amount of the payable, the creditor has made a concession to the debtor. This is a basic requirement of troubled debt restructuring.

The determination of fair value of the asset transferred is basically a matter of judgment on the part of the debtor, but the Statement does provide some guidance in this area. Paragraph 13 defines fair value of the assets as "the amount that the debtor could reasonably expect to receive for them in a current sale between a willing buyer and a willing seller, that is, other than a forced or liquidation sale." The selling price for the same or similar assets also would be an indication of fair value. The Board also suggests that, if a market price is not available, the present value of the assets' future cash flows should be used to estimate fair value. The carrying amount of the payable is equal to the face of the payable plus or minus any adjustments for items such as unamortized discounts or premiums, unamortized debt issue costs, and accrued interest.

Once it has been determined that the fair value of the assets transferred are not equal to or greater than the carrying amount of the payable, the transaction will be accounted for as a troubled debt restructuring. In such a case, the debtor always will recognize a gain on the restructuring itself and, in most cases, also will recognize a gain or loss on the transfer of the assets. The difference between the fair value of the asset transferred and the carrying amount of the payable is to be

FLOWCHART I

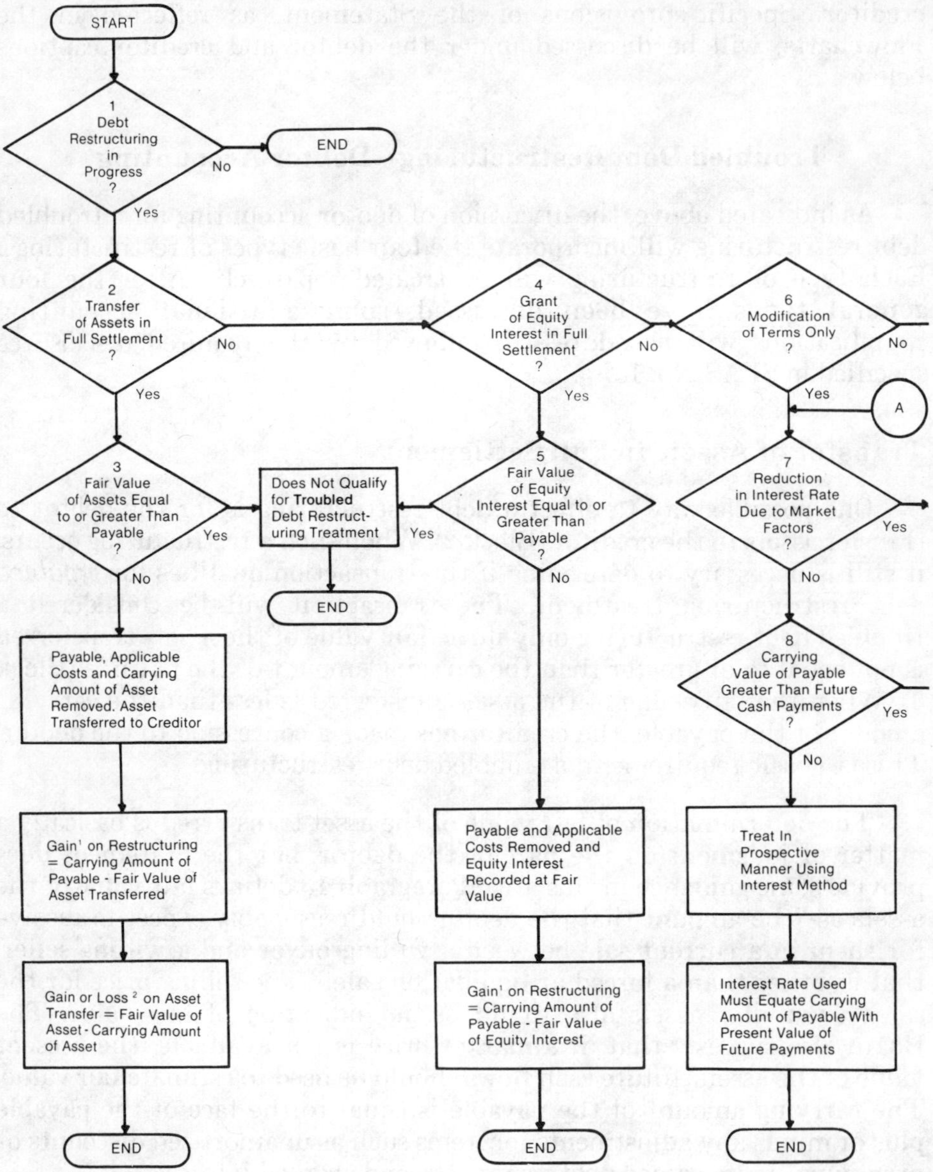

[1]Extraordinary Gain as Specified in SFAS No. 4

[2]Accounted for in Accordance with APB Opinion No. 30

recognized as the gain on restructuring of debt. This gain is classified as an extraordinary gain in accordance with the provisions of SFAS No. 6, "Reporting Gains and Losses from Extinguishment of Debt" (see Topic 6

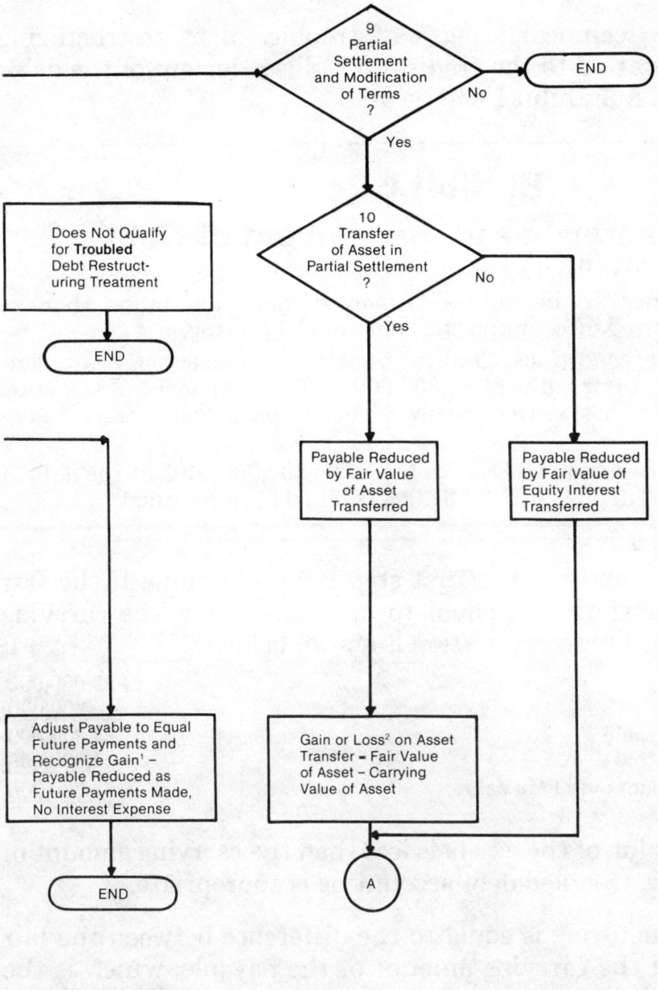

for a detailed analysis of SFAS No. 4). When the asset is removed from the books of the debtor, the difference between the book value of the asset and its fair value represents the gain or loss on the asset transfer.

Any gain or loss on the asset transfer should be classified according to APB Opinion No. 30, "Reporting the Results of Operations" (see Topic 1 for a detailed analysis of APB Opinion No. 30). APB Opinion No. 30 specifies that the gain or loss may be classified in one of the following three ways: (1) as an extraordinary item, (2) as a one-line item in the non-operating section of the income statement or (3) as a part of ordinary operations of the company. The appropriate classification in any particular case will depend upon the circumstances faced by the company in that year.

To illustrate the technical aspects of troubled debt restructuring where assets are transferred to the creditor in full settlement of the debt, the assumptions listed in Exhibit I will be used.

Exhibit I

Asset Transfer in Full Settlement of Debt

1. Debtor, Inc. has a $5,000,000 note payable to Creditor, Inc.
2. The note bears interest at the rate of 10 percent per annum, and there is $200,000 of unamortized discount on the books of Debtor, Inc.
3. Due to severe economic conditions, Creditor, Inc. is willing to accept equipment of Debtor, Inc., with a fair value of $4,000,000, in full settlement of the note. Creditor, Inc. believes that, in the absence of such a concession, it is not likely to collect on the note.
4. The equipment had a cost basis to Debtor, Inc. of $4,500,000; and, at the date of transfer, accumulated depreciation of $1,000,000 had been recorded.

Based on this information, the first step is to determine if the fair value of the asset transferred is equal to or greater than the carrying amount of the payable. This computation is shown below:

Face Amount of Payable	$5,000,000
Unamortized Discount	(200,000)
Carrying Amount of Payable	$4,800,000
Fair Value of Asset Transferred	4,000,000
Excess of Carrying Amount over Fair Value	$ 800,000

In this case, the fair value of the assets is less than the carrying amount of the payable. Therefore, troubled debt accounting is appropriate.

The gain on restructuring is equal to the difference between the fair value of the asset and the carrying amount of the payable, which is the $800,000 determined above.

The next step is to see if there is a gain or loss associated with the transfer of the asset. The gain or loss is the difference between the book value and the fair value of the asset transferred, and is determined as follows:

Cost of Equipment Transferred	$4,500,000
Accumulated Depreciation	(1,000,000)
Book Value of Equipment Transferred	$3,500,000
Fair Value of Equipment Transferred	4,000,000
Gain on Transfer of Asset	$ 500,000

With this information known, the asset and payable must be removed from the books of Debtor, Inc., and the various gains recognized. The entry required to accomplish this is presented below:

Notes Payable	5,000,000	
Accumulated Depreciation	1,000,000	
Discount on Notes Payable		200,000
Equipment		4,500,000
Gain on Restructuring of Debt		800,000
Gain on Transfer of Assets		500,000

The gain on restructuring would be reported as an extraordinary item in the current period income statement. The gain on asset transfer would be classified according to the provisions of APB Opinion No. 30.

Transfer of Equity Interest in Full Settlement

A transfer of equity interest in full settlement of existing debt may be accomplished through the issuance of stock of the debtor company to the creditor. As in the case of asset transfers, the fair value of the equity interest transferred must *not* be equal to or greater than the carrying amount of the debt (Block 5). If the fair value of the equity interest transferred is less than the payable, the transaction qualifies for treatment as a troubled debt restructuring. Unlike the asset transfer situation, there will be no gain or loss resulting from the transfer of the equity interest. There will, however, be a gain from the restructuring. The equities transferred should be recorded on the books of the debtor at fair value. The gain from restructuring will be the difference between the fair value of the stock and the carrying value of the payable. Again, the gain should be classified as extraordinary, in accordance with SFAS No. 4.

The assumptions listed in Exhibit II will be used to illustrate accounting for a transfer of equity interest in full settlement of debt.

Exhibit II
Equity Transfer in Full Settlement of Debt

1. Debtor, Inc. has $8,000,000 in bonds payable that are held by Creditor, Inc.
2. The bonds pay interest at the rate of 12 percent per annum, and there is $300,000 of unamortized premium and $100,000 of unamortized bond issue costs on the books of Debtor, Inc.
3. Due to severe economic conditions, Creditor, Inc. is willing to accept 600,000 common shares of Debtor, Inc. in full settlement of the bonds. Creditor, Inc.

believes that, in the absence of such a concession, it is not likely to collect on the bonds.

4. The common stock has a par value of $2 per share and is currently selling for $10 per share.

To see if the transaction qualifies for troubled debt restructuring accounting, the fair value of the stock transferred must be compared with the carrying amount of the bonds. The computation is shown below:

Face Value of Bonds	$8,000,000
Unamortized Bond Issue Costs	(100,000)
Unamortized Premium	300,000
Carrying Amount of Bonds	$8,200,000
Fair Value of Stock Transferred	
(600,000 shares × $10 per share)	6,000,000
Excess of Carrying Amount over Fair Value	$2,200,000

Because the fair value of the stock is less than the carrying amount of the bonds, the transaction qualifies for troubled debt accounting.

The only gain to be recognized is the gain resulting from the restructuring. The gain is equal to the difference between the fair value of the stock and the carrying amount of the bonds, and is the $2,200,000 computed above. Based upon this information, the following entry is needed to record the transfer:

Bonds Payable	8,000,000	
Premium on Bonds Payable	300,000	
Common Stock		[a]1,200,000
Contributed Capital in Excess of Par		[b]4,800,000
Bond Issue Costs		100,000
Gain on Restructuring of Debt		2,200,000

[a] 600,000 shares × $2 par value per share = $1,200,000.
[b] 600,000 shares × $10 fair value = $6,000,000 − $1,200,000 = $4,800,000.

The reader will have noted by now that it is impossible to have a loss on restructuring, since, if the fair value of the asset or equity interest transferred is greater than the carrying amount of the debt, the transaction does not qualify for troubled debt restructuring accounting.

Modification of Terms

A modification of terms consists of some adjustment to the existing debt, such as a change in interest rate, maturity value, maturity date or some combination of these items (Block 6). However, not all modification of terms will result in troubled debt restructuring accounting. For example, if the modification resulted in a reduction in the stated interest rate, and that reduction were due to market factors (Block 7), this agreement would not qualify for troubled debt restructuring accounting.

If the modification of terms is due to reasons other than this, the transaction will be treated as a troubled debt restructuring.

Before proper accounting can be determined, the debtor must compare the future *gross cash outlays* (principal and interest) under the new terms with the carrying value of the existing payable (Block 8). If the carrying value of the payable is greater than the future cash payments, a gain on restructuring will result. The gain is equal to the difference between the carrying value of the payable and the total future cash payments. In this case, the creditor has made a concession as to the total amount of cash to be received under the new terms. In addition to recognition of the gain from restructuring, the payable is to be written down by an amount that will equate the carrying amount of the payable with the future cash payments. Subsequent payments during the life of the debt will be principal payments only, with no interest being recognized.

If the carrying value of the payable does not exceed the future cash payments, the transaction is to be treated in a prospective manner. The carrying amount of the payable will *not* be adjusted, and no gain will be recognized. It will be necessary to adjust current and future interest expense through the calculation of a new effective interest rate, based upon the new terms. The effective rate will be the rate of interest that equates the present value of the future payments (under the new terms) with the carrying value of the payable. Current and future interest expense will be computed using the interest method at the new effective rate. (The interest method is the application of the discount rate to the unrecovered obligation balance, and is required by SFAS No. 15. The interest method is explained in APB Opinion No. 12, Paragraph 16.)

The following examples are used to illustrate the various possibilities identified above. Exhibit III lists the assumptions that will be used to demonstrate proper accounting in a situation where the carrying value of the payable exceeds the future cash payments.

Exhibit III

Example 1—Modification of Terms

1. Debtor, Inc. has a $3,000,000 note, payable in full to Creditor, Inc. in 10 years.
2. The note bears interest at the rate of 10 percent per annum, and there is $150,000 of unamortized discount on the books of Debtor, Inc.
3. Due to economic conditions, Creditor, Inc. believes that it must grant some type of concession to Debtor, Inc. to collect on the note. Creditor, Inc. is willing to accept the payment of $250,000 a year for the next 10 years in place of the existing note.

The agreement represents a modification as to the terms and amount of repayment of the note. Therefore, the agreement qualifies for troubled debt restructuring accounting. The first step is to compare the carrying value of the note with the gross future cash payments. This computation is shown below:

Face Amount of Note	$3,000,000
Unamortized Discount	(150,000)
Carrying Value of Note	$2,850,000
Future Cash Payments ($250,000 × 10 years)	2,500,000
Excess of Carrying Value over Cash Payments	$ 350,000

In this case, the carrying value of the note is greater than the gross future cash payments, and a gain from restructuring of $350,000 must be recognized. The payable is reduced to $2,500,000, an amount equal to the future cash payments. The entry required to reflect the write-down is as follows:

Notes Payable	500,000	
Discount on Notes Payable		150,000
Gain on Restructuring of Debt		350,000

All subsequent payments will represent repayment of principal, and no interest expense will be recognized. This is the reason for the elimination of the discount on the note in the above entry. Discounts and premiums normally are associated with interest expense; and, in this case, no interest expense will be recognized. The entry necessary to show subsequent annual note payments is shown below:

Notes Payable	250,000	
Cash		250,000

A more complex situation exists when the debtor must calculate a new effective rate of interest as the result of some modification of terms. This would be the case where the total future cash payments are greater than the carrying value of the payable. To illustrate the accounting under these circumstances, the assumptions listed in Exhibit IV will be used.

Exhibit IV

Example 2—Modification of Terms

1. Debtor, Inc. has a $3,000,000 note, payable in full to Creditor, Inc., in four years.
2. The note bears interest at the rate of 10 percent per annum, and there is no unamortized discount or premium associated with the note.
3. Due to economic conditions, Creditor, Inc. has agreed to make certain concessions to Debtor, Inc. in order to insure collectibility of the note. Creditor, Inc. has agreed to accept $2,500,000 at the end of four years *and* to reduce the interest rate from 10 percent to eight percent on the new balance.

This agreement represents a modification as to the amount of repayment and the rate of interest to be paid. Assuming that the reduction in interest was not due to market factors, the agreement qualifies for troubled debt restructuring accounting. As before, the first step is to compare the carrying value of the payable with the total future cash payments. This computation is shown below:

Note Principal Repayment	$2,500,000
Interest Payments ($2,500,000 × 8% × 4 years)	800,000
Total Future Cash Payments	$3,300,000
Carrying Value of Note	3,000,000
Excess of Cash Payments over Carrying Value	$ 300,000

In this case, the total future cash payments exceed the carrying value of the note, and the effects of the modification of terms will be accounted for on a prospective basis. It is now necessary to determine the interest rate that will equate the present value of the $3,300,000 future cash payments with the $3,000,000 carrying value of the note.

The rate may be determined through the trial-and-error method, using the present value of $1 for the principal repayment, and the present value of an ordinary annuity for the interest payments, or through the use of a computer program. The authors used a computer program to calculate the new effective rate of 2.6628 percent. Once the new rate has been determined, an amortization schedule, like Table I, can be prepared.

Table I

Amortization Schedule for Interest Expense and Note

Year	Cash Interest	Interest Expense	Amortization of Note	Note Carrying Value
Initial Value	-	-	-	$3,000,000
1	[a]$200,000	[b]$ 79,884	[c]$120,116	[d]2,879,884
2	200,000	76,686	123,314	2,756,570
3	200,000	73,402	126,598	2,629,972
4	200,000	*70,028	129,972	[e]2,500,000
	$800,000	$300,000	$500,000	

[a] $2,500,000 × 8% = $200,000.
[b] $3,000,000 × 2.6628% = $79,884.
[c] $200,000 − $79,884 = $120,116.
[d] $3,000,000 − $120,116 = $2,879,884.
[e] Represents the modified maturity value at the end of 4 years.
* Rounded.

Table I shows the cash interest paid, the interest expense to be recognized and the amortization of the note over the four-year period. Since the effects of the restructuring are to be accounted for on a prospective basis, no gain or loss is recognized. The entry required for the first year's interest payment is shown below:

Note Payable	120,116	
Interest Expense	79,884	
Cash		200,000

At the date of restructuring, no entry would be required, because no gain is recognized and there is no write-down of the payable.

Partial Settlement and Modification of Terms

A troubled debt settlement may take on a combination of forms or types. For example, a transfer of assets may be combined with a modification of terms. By definition, any time there is a partial settlement of a debt, there has been a modification of terms. If a troubled debt restructuring is to be accomplished through a partial settlement and a modification of terms, the transfer of assets or equity interest is accounted for first, and then the modification of terms is handled. The carrying amount of the payable is reduced by the fair value of the assets or equity interest transferred to the creditor (Block 10). No gain from restructuring is recognized at this point; but, if the settlement involved the transfer of assets, the gain or loss from such transfer should be recognized. After this has been accomplished, the *remaining* carrying value of the payable is compared to the total future cash payments under the new terms. If the remaining carrying value of the payable is greater than the future cash payments, a gain on restructuring will be recognized (Block 8). The gain is equal to the difference in the remaining carrying value of the payable and the future cash payments under the new terms. The payable is to be reduced by an amount that will equate the payable with the future cash payments. No interest expense will be recognized over the remaining life of the payable. Subsequent payments are merely a reduction of the revised carrying value of the payable. If the remaining carrying value of the payable is *not* greater than the future cash payments, a new effective rate of interest must be determined. This rate must equate the present value of the future cash payment under the new terms with the revised carrying value of the payable. No gain is recognized at the time of restructuring. Future interest expense will be recognized, using the interest method based upon the new effective rate.

To illustrate a straightforward example of accounting for a troubled debt restructuring that involves a partial settlement and a modification of terms, the assumptions listed in Exhibit V will be used.

Exhibit V

Example 1—Partial Settlement and Modification of Terms

1. Debtor, Inc. has a $4,000,000 note, payable in full to Creditor, Inc., in four years.

2. The note bears interest at the rate of 10 percent per annum, and there is $100,000 of unamortized discount on the books of Debtor, Inc.
3. Debtor, Inc. is not able to pay the interest on the note, and it is not likely that the company will be able to repay the principal amount when due. Therefore, Creditor, Inc. has agreed to accept a parcel of land owned by Debtor, Inc. and reduce the maturity value of the note to $2,000,000. In addition, the interest rate is reduced from 10 percent to six percent on the new maturity value of the note.
4. The parcel of land had an original cost to Debtor, Inc. of $700,000 and a fair value of $1,000,000 at the date of restructuring.

This transaction represents a troubled debt restructuring with a partial settlement, represented by the payment of land, and a modification of terms, represented by the reduction in interest rate. The first step is to reduce the carrying value of the note by the fair value of the land transferred. This calculation is shown below:

Face Amount of Note	$4,000,000
Unamortized Discount	(100,000)
Carrying Amount of the Note	$3,900,000
Fair Value of Asset Transferred	1,000,000
Revised Carrying Amount of Note	$2,900,000

Because the partial settlement is effected by the transfer of an asset, the gain or loss resulting from the asset transfer must be recognized. The gain or loss is equal to the difference between the fair value and the carrying value of the asset transferred, and is computed below:

Fair Value of Asset Transferred	$1,000,000
Carrying Value of Asset Transferred	700,000
Gain on Asset Transfer	$ 300,000

The journal entry required to reflect the reduction in the carrying value of the note is as follows:

Notes Payable	1,000,000	
Land		700,000
Gain on Transfer of Assets		300,000

Note that no gain on restructuring is recognized at this point, and there has been no reduction in the unamortized discount.

Once the revised carrying value has been determined, it is necessary to evaluate the accounting problems posed by the modification of terms. Assuming that the reduction in interest rate was not due to market factors, the next step is to compare the revised carrying value of the note with the future total cash payments, under the modified terms of the agreement. This comparison is shown below:

Revised Carrying Amount of Note (per above)		$2,900,000
Future Cash Payments:		
Principal	$2,000,000	
Interest (at 6% for 4 years)	480,000	
Total Future Cash Payments		2,480,000
Excess of Carrying Amount over Cash Payments		$ 420,000

Since the revised carrying value of $2,900,000 is greater than the future cash payments of $2,480,000, the carrying value of the note must be written-down, and a gain of $420,000 must be recognized. The carrying value of the note will then be equal to the future cash payments, and no interest will be recognized over the remaining life of the note. Since no interest is to be recognized, the unamortized discount also must be removed at the time of restructuring. The journal entry to accomplish this is:

Notes Payable	520,000	
Discount on Notes Payable		100,000
Gain on Restructuring of Debt		420,000

The two preceding entries could have been combined into one journal entry, but were shown separately for illustrative purposes. This example resulted in a gain on restructuring because the carrying value of the payable, as revised, was greater than the future cash payments under the new terms.

To illustrate a somewhat more complex example of a partial settlement and modification of terms, the assumptions listed in Exhibit VI will be used.

Exhibit VI

Example 2—Partial Settlement and Modification of Terms

1. Debtor, Inc. has a $2,000,000 note, payable in full to Creditor, Inc., in four years.
2. The note bears interest at the rate of 10 percent per annum, and there is no unamortized discount or premium associated with the note.
3. Debtor, Inc. is not able to pay the interest on the note, and it is not likely that the company will be able to repay the principal amount when due. Therefore, Creditor, Inc. has agreed to accept 50,000 common shares of Debtor, Inc. in partial settlement of the note. In addition, Creditor, Inc. has agreed to forgive $200,000 of the note and reduce the interest rate to eight percent on the new maturity value.
4. The common stock of Debtor, Inc. has a par value of $1 per share and a fair value of $10 per share on the date of restructuring.

The acceptance of stock represents a partial settlement of the debt and the forgiveness of $200,000 represents modification of the terms of the note. The first step in the process is to reduce the carrying value of the note by the fair value of the common stock transferred. Remember that no gain or loss results from the transfer of an equity interest, and it is not appropriate to recognize a gain on restructuring at this point. The calculation of the revised carrying value is shown below:

Carrying Amount of the Note	$2,000,000
Fair Value of Common Stock Transferred (50,000 shares × $10 fair value)	500,000
Revised Carrying Amount of the Note	$1,500,000

The journal entry necessary to reflect the reduction in carrying value of the payable and the issuance of the stock is:

Notes Payable	500,000	
Common Stock (50,000 shares × $1 par)		50,000
Contributed Capital in Excess of Par		450,000

Now the revised carrying amount of the note must be compared with the total future cash payments under the modified terms. This comparison is shown below:

Future Cash Payments:	
Principal ($1,500,000 − $200,000 forgiveness)	$1,300,000
Interest ($1,300,000 × 8% × 4 years)	416,000
Total Future Cash Payments	$1,716,000
Revised Carrying Amount of the Note	1,500,000
Excess of Cash Payments over Carrying Amount	$ 216,000

Note that the forgiveness of $200,000 does not affect the revised carrying value of the note, because no asset or equity interest was transferred to obtain the $200,000 concession.

Since the $1,716,000 total future cash payments are greater than the $1,500,000 revised carrying amount of the note, it is necessary to determine a new effective interest rate. The rate must equate the present value of the $1,716,000 with the $1,500,000 carrying amount of the note. The calculation of the rate may be accomplished through the trial-and-error method, using the present value of $1 for the principal amount and the present value of an ordinary annuity for the interest payments. This is a very time-consuming process. The authors used a computer program to calculate the new effective rate of 3.7832 percent. Once the new rate has been determined, an amortization schedule can be prepared. Table II below shows the amortization of the note and resulting interest expense for the note used in this case.

Table II

Amortization Schedule for Interest and Note

Year	Cash Interest	Interest Expense	Note Amortization	Note Carrying Value
Initial Value	-	-	-	$1,500,000
1	[a]$104,000	[b]$ 56,748	[c]$ 47,252	[d]1,452,748
2	104,000	54,960	49,040	1,403,708
3	104,000	53,105	50,895	1,352,813
4	104,000	*51,187	52,813	[e]1,300,000
	$416,000	$216,000	$200,000	

[a] $1,300,000 × 8% = $104,000.
[b] $1,500,000 × 3.7832% = $56,748.
[c] $104,000 − $56,748 = $47,252.
[d] $1,500,000 − $47,252 = $1,452,748.
[e] Represents the maturity value of the note with the modified terms.
* Rounded.

Given the information in Table II, the journal entry to record the first annual interest payment is shown below:

Interest Expense	56,748	
Notes Payable	47,252	
Cash		104,000

Note that the forgiveness of $200,000 is amortized over the four-year period as the interest payments are made. The total of the "Note Amortization" column is equal to the amount of the forgiveness. The new effective rate of interest insured a proper amortization of both interest expense and the note payable. At the end of the four-year period, the carrying value of the note is equal to the maturity value.

While the preceding example was somewhat complex, the solution was highly structured. However, when there is an unamortized discount or premium, or unamortized debt issue costs associated with the note, the solution to the problem becomes quite complicated. Note that, in the above example, once the effective interest rate was determined, it was relatively easy to divide the cash interest payment into interest expense and amortization of the principal amount of the note. When the debtor has unamortized discount, premium or issue costs (hereafter referred to as "unamortized items"), the problem becomes, "How does one divide the cash interest payment into interest expense, amortization of note principal *and* amortization of unamortized items?"

In cases where the future cash payments *exceed* the carrying amount of the debt, the Statement prohibits the write-down of the debt or other unamortized items. In these cases, a new effective rate of interest must be calculated that equates the present value of the future payments with the carrying amount of the note. The carrying amount of the note is equal to the face amount, plus or minus related unamortized items. The new effective rate, when there are unamortized items, is applied against the unrecovered balance, and the resulting principal amortization is actually made up of two elements. One element of the amortization is the part that applies to the forgiveness granted by the creditor and, the other element is the amortization of the original unamortized items. The problem is, "How does one separate these two elements?"

APB Opinion No. 21 (see Topic 6) requires that discounts and premiums on notes be established and reported as a reduction or addition to the related note. Since a separate account will be established for the related unamortized items, it is necessary to determine the amortization applicable to these items. SFAS No. 15 requires the use of the interest method in the determination of amounts to be amortized, unless another method provides results that are not materially different from the interest method. The Statement provides no guidance in making the division between the two elements discussed above.

In an effort to resolve this problem, the authors have devised a logical method of separating the two elements. The first step is to determine the effective rate, *without* consideration being given to the unamortized items; and the note principal then is amortized, using this rate. Next, the effective rate is determined, giving full consideration to the unamortized items; and the note principal again is amortized, using this rate. The difference between the two principal amortization schedules must be the amortization that is applicable to the discount or premium. It should be stressed that other approaches may be just as logical and acceptable.

To illustrate the basic problem and solution, assume the same facts as listed in Exhibit VI, except that there is an unamortized discount of $50,000 associated with the note. Remember that the only *new* element added to the problem is the unamortized discount.

Given this added assumption, the new revised carrying amount of the note would be determined as follows:

Face Amount of the Note	$2,000,000
Unamortized Discount	(50,000)
Carrying Amount of the Note	$1,950,000
Fair Value of Common Stock Transferred	500,000
Revised Carrying Amount of the Note	$1,450,000

The entry to reduce the note by the fair value of the stock transferred is identical to that used in the previous example and need not be repeated. The future cash payments of $1,716,000 exceed the revised carrying amount of $1,450,000; therefore, it is necessary to determine the effective interest rate that will equate the present value of the cash payments with the revised carrying value of the payable. The rate required to equate these two amounts is 4.76385 percent.

Once the effective rate has been determined, an amortization schedule similar to Table III can be developed.

Table III

Amortization Schedule for Interest and Note

Year	Cash Interest	Interest Expense	Note Amortization	Note Carrying Value
Initial Value	-	-	-	$1,450,000
1	[a]$104,000	[b]$ 69,076	[c]$ 34,924	[d]1,415,076
2	104,000	67,412	36,588	1,378,488
3	104,000	65,669	38,331	1,340,157
4	104,000	63,843	40,157	[e]1,300,000
	$416,000	$266,000	$150,000	

[a] $1,300,000 × 8% = $104,000.
[b] $1,450,000 × 4.76385% = $69,076.
[c] $104,000 − $69,076 = $34,924.
[d] $1,450,000 − $34,924 = $1,415,076.
[e] Represents the maturity value of the note under the modified terms.

If one were to use the information in Table III to prepare the entry to record the annual interest payment, it would be as follows:

Interest Expense	69,076	
Notes Payable	34,924	
Cash		104,000

However, this entry is not sufficient, because it fails to record the amortization of the note discount. In effect, the note principal amortization of $34,924 is a *net* amount, which includes the amortization of the principal and the amortization of the discount. If the problem is to be solved correctly, it is necessary to "gross up" the principal amortization shown in Table III. Recall that the principal amortization in Table II amounted to $200,000, and the same amortization in Table III amounted to $150,000. Therefore, the difference between the two numbers ($50,000) must be the amortization of the discount related to the note. Based upon this information, Table IV develops a year-by-year analysis of the difference between the principal amortizations shown on the two Tables.

Table IV

Schedule for Discount Amortization

Year	Table II Note Amortization	Table III Note Amortization	Difference Discount Amortization
1	$ 47,252	$ 34,924	[a]$ 12,328
2	49,040	36,588	12,452
3	50,895	38,331	12,564
4	52,813	40,157	12,656
	$200,000	$150,000	$ 50,000

[a] $47,252 − $34,924 = $12,328.

With the information in Tables III and IV, it now is possible to prepare the correct journal entry to record the first annual interest payment. This entry is shown below:

Interest Expense	69,076	
Notes Payable	47,252	
Discount on Notes Payable		12,328
Cash		104,000

This entry accomplishes all the necessary amortizations. Anything less would result in an error. Note that the difference between the $47,252 note principal amortization and the $12,328 discount amortization is the $34,924 net amortization shown on Table III. The purpose of Tables II and IV is to find the individual amortization amounts of $47,252 and $12,328, rather than the net amount of $34,924.

With the solution to this problem, the discussion of the major types of troubled debt restructurings is completed. Attention now is turned to some special considerations relating to restructuring.

Other Considerations

An agreement in a troubled debt restructuring may be such that the cash payments to be made depend upon some indeterminate or contingent future event. Or it could be that the rate of interest on the debt varies, depending upon some factor such as the bank prime rate.

The Statement concludes that, in cases where the future payments are contingent upon some future event, the provisions of Paragraph 17 of SFAS No. 5, "Accounting for Contingencies" (see Topic 6 for a detailed analysis of SFAS No. 5), should apply. This particular paragraph specifies that a gain should not be recognized until it is *realized.* This being the case, the maximum possible payments or amounts should be included in the future cash payments. This total then will be compared with the carrying amount of the debt to determine if there is a gain on restructuring. In other words, a gain should not be recognized at the time of restructuring if it is possible to offset the gain with contingent future payments.

An interest rate that is allowed to vary after the date of restructuring is not given recognition at the date of restructuring, but is treated as a change in an accounting estimate in subsequent periods when the rate actually changes. The applicable rate to use in determining the future cash payments is the rate that prevails on the date of restructuring.

Any contingent agreement should be reviewed every statement date to determine if a liability and expense should be recorded consistent with the provisions of SFAS No. 5. If it is probable that the contingent amount will now be paid, and that amount can be reasonably estimated, a two-step accounting process is necessary. First, a determination must be made of the amount of the contingent payment included in the future cash payments. Next, the amount that can be reasonably estimated and will probably be paid (hereafter referred to as the liabiliity) must be compared to the contingent payments included in the future cash payments. The excess of the liability over the contingent amounts included in the future cash payments is recorded as interest expense and as a payable. The carrying amount of the restructured payable is reduced by the lesser of the contingent payments included in the future cash payments or the liability.

One final consideration deals with legal fees and direct costs associated with a troubled debt restructuring. Legal fees associated with a transfer of an equity interest should be used to reduce the recorded amount of the equity interest, thereby increasing the gain on restructuring. Direct costs incurred by the debtor should be offset against the gain on restructuring to the extent a gain exists. Direct costs that exceed the gain on restructuring should be charged to expense in the period of restructuring.

To illustrate the accounting for a troubled debt restructuring where a contingent agreement is present, the assumptions set forth in Exhibit VII will be used.

Exhibit VII
Contingent Agreement

1. Debtor, Inc. has a $4,000,000 note, payable to Creditor, Inc., which requires principal repayments of $400,000 at the end of each of the next 10 years.
2. The note bears interest at the rate of 10 percent per annum, and there is no unamortized discount or premium associated with the note.
3. Debtor, Inc. is in financial difficulty and may not be able to make the required interest and principal payments. As a result, Creditor, Inc. is willing to accept 500,000 shares of common stock of Debtor, Inc. and the payment of $250,000 at the end of each of the next 10 years. In addition, Creditor, Inc. specifies that it will receive an additional $25,000 payment for each year in which the earnings of Debtor, Inc. exceed $200,000.
4. The common stock of Debtor, Inc. has a par value of $1 per share and a fair value of $2 per share on the date of restructuring.
5. Debtor, Inc. incurs $10,000 of direct costs in connection with the restructuring. Of that total, $2,500 is directly related to the equity issue.

In this particular case, the first step is to reduce the carrying amount of the note by the fair value of the equity interest transferred. The revised carrying amount is calculated below:

Carrying Amount of the Note	$4,000,000
Fair Value of the Common Stock Transferred (500,000 shares × $2 per share)	1,000,000
Revised Carrying Amount of the Note	$3,000,000

Since $2,500 of the direct costs were associated with the issue of the common stock, the contributed capital will be reduced by this amount. The journal entry necessary to reflect the reduction in the carrying amount of the note and the direct costs related to the stock issue is shown below:

Notes Payable	1,000,000	
Common Stock		[a]500,000
Contributed Capital in Excess of Par		[b]497,500
Cash		2,500

[a] 500,000 shares × $1 par value = $500,000.
[b] $1,000,000 − $500,000 − $2,500 = $497,500.

The next step is to compare the expected future cash payments with the revised carrying amount of the note. In order to make this comparison, the future cash flows must be calculated. Remember that contingent payments are included in the future cash payments, based on an estimate of the maximum amount expected to be paid. The expected future cash payments would be calculated as follows:

Future Cash Payments:	
Required Payments—$250,000 × 10 years	$2,500,000
Contingent Payments—$25,000 × 10 years	250,000
Expected Future Cash Payments	$2,750,000

The revised carrying amount of $3,000,000 is greater than the expected future cash payments of $2,750,000; therefore, a gain on restructuring will be recognized for the difference of $250,000. However, this gain must be reduced by the direct costs not directly associated with the stock issue, which amounts to $7,500. A gain of $242,500 therefore will be recognized. The entry required to record the gain and the direct costs not related to the stock issue is presented below:

Notes Payable	250,000	
Gain on Restructuring of Debt		242,500
Cash		7,500

The $7,500 represents the payment of the direct costs. The note now has been written-down to the amount of the expected future cash payments, and no interest expense will be recognized over the remaining life of the note. The two preceding entries could have been combined, but were shown separately for purposes of illustration.

An example of the accounting required when a troubled debt restructuring contains a provision for variable interest payments will be developed in the section dealing with creditor accounting.

Disclosures

The disclosures required to be presented by the debtor in the preparation of the basic financial statements in the period of restructuring include the following:

(1) Any modification of terms and settlements must be described for each debt restructured;

(2) The gains on debt restructuring must be aggregated and reported along with the related tax effect and related earnings per share information, net of the tax effect; and

(3) The gains and losses on asset transfers must be aggregated and reported in income.

For periods subsequent to the reporting period of the restructuring, the debtor should disclose information concerning contingent payments included in the carrying amount of the payable.

Troubled Debt Restructuring—Creditor Accounting

The discussion of creditor accounting in a troubled debt restructuring is very similar to the previous discussion of debtor accounting. The authors assume that the reader is interested in a particular accounting problem and may not have read the material relating to the debtor accounting. If the previous section has been read, the reader may wish to go directly to the example material, rather than read through the discussion of creditor accounting. If the reader has not completed the section on debtor accounting, the following discussion and related example material will provide the information necessary to gain a full appreciation of the creditor's accounting and reporting requirements.

There are three major types of troubled debt restructurings from the standpoint of the creditor. These include (1) receipt of asset(s) in full settlement of the debt, (2) modification of the terms of the agreement, and (3) a partial settlement of the debt, coupled with a modification of terms. After each of these three topics have been considered in detail, some accounting complexities of the Statement will be taken up, followed by a listing of the required disclosures.

Flowchart II shows the major accounting decisions and related procedures that are identified in the Statement. Specific references to the Flowchart will be made as the various types of restructurings are discussed.

Receipt of Assets in Full Settlement

In a troubled debt restructuring, a creditor may receive assets or stock of the debtor in full settlement of the obligation (Block 2). In this case, the transaction will qualify as a *troubled* debt restructuring only if the fair value of the assets received are not greater than the recorded investment in the receivable (Block 3). The recorded amount of the receivable is defined (SFAS No. 15, Footnote 17) as the face of the receivable, "increased or decreased by applicable accrued interest and unamortized premium, discount, financial charges or acquisition costs." The recorded investment in the receivable does not give consideration to any valuation allowances related to the receivable. The *carrying amount* of the receivable is the recorded investment in the receivable, reduced by any related valuation allowance. Careful attention must be given to the difference between the two terms. For the most part, the following discussion will deal with the recorded investment in the receivable.

If the fair value of the assets received is less than the recorded investment in the receivable, the creditor has made a concession to the debtor. This is one of the essential requirements of the Statement. If no such concession has been made, the transaction will not qualify for troubled debt restructuring accounting. When it has been determined that the fair value of the assets received is less than the recorded investment in the receivable, the creditor will recognize a loss on the restructuring. The loss to be recognized is equal to the difference between the recorded investment in the receivable and the fair value of the assets received. However, if a valuation allowance, such as allowance for uncollectible accounts, has been established in connection with the receivable, the loss may be partially or fully offset against the valuation allowance. Losses on restructuring should be applied first to the valuation allowance, and any loss in excess of the allowance will be reported on the current period income statement. Any losses resulting from restructuring that appear on the income statement must be handled in accordance with the provisions of APB Opinion No. 30 (See Topic 1 for a detailed analysis of APB Opinion No. 30, "Reporting the Results of Operations"). This Opinion provides three different classifications for the loss, depending on the environment of the creditor. The loss may be classified as (1) an extraordinary item, (2) a one-line item in the non-operating section of the income statement or (3) an expense of normal operations, such as general and administrative expenses. For example, a financial institution might treat the loss as a general and administrative expense (charged to a bad debts account), whereas a nonfinancial creditor may treat the loss as a one-line item in the nonoperating section or even as an extraordinary item. The offset of the loss against the valuation allowance is recognition that previous adjusting entries relating to the allowance represented a partial (or complete) recognition of the loss on restructuring. Therefore, the loss should be charged against the valuation allowance, if appropriate

FLOWCHART II

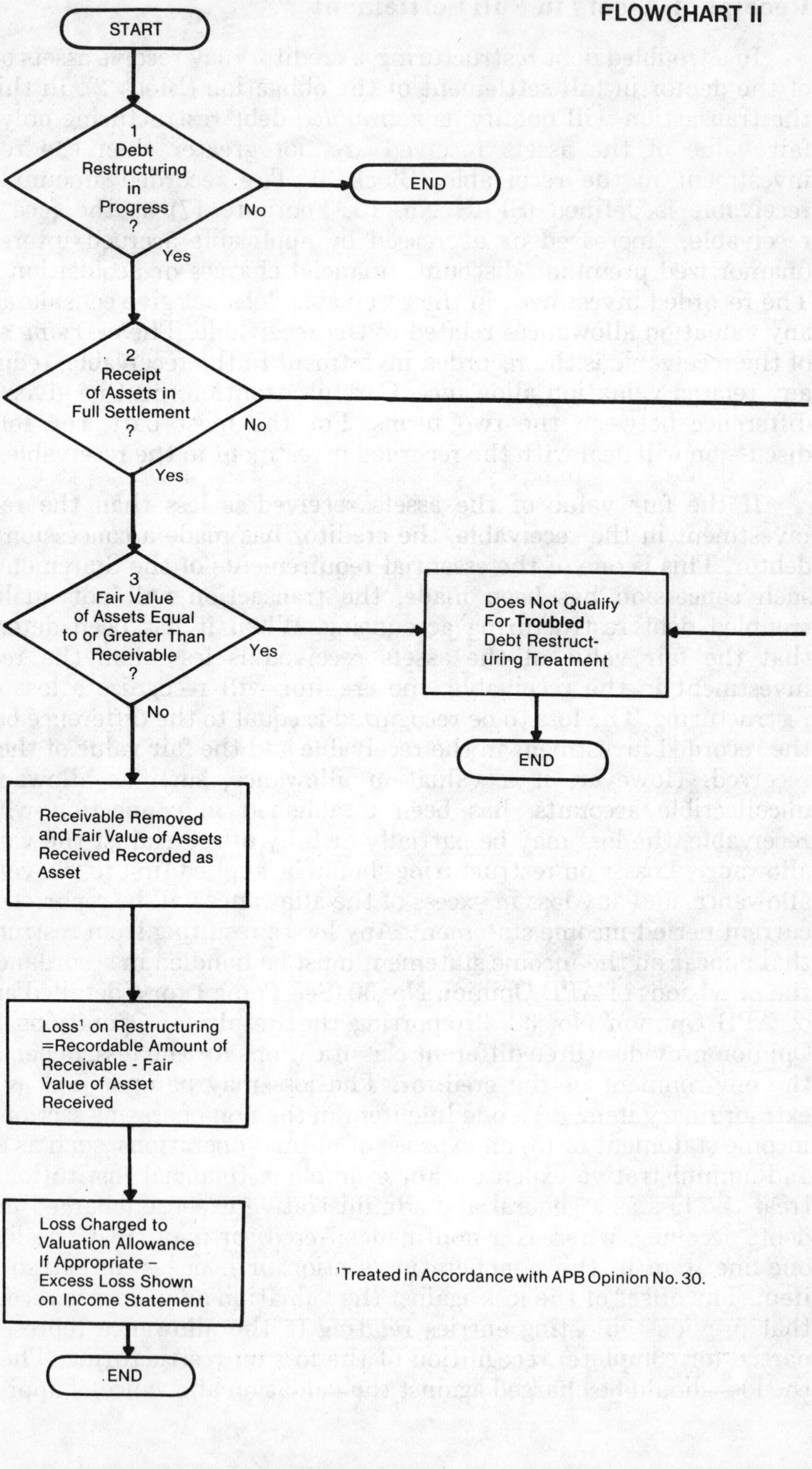
START
1
Debt
Restructuring
in
Progress
?
No
END
Yes
2
Receipt
of Assets in
Full Settlement
?
No
Yes
3
Fair Value
of Assets Equal
to or Greater Than
Receivable
?
Yes
Does Not Qualify
For Troubled
Debt Restruct-
uring Treatment
END
No
Receivable Removed
and Fair Value of Assets
Received Recorded as
Asset
Loss[1] on Restructuring
=Recordable Amount of
Receivable - Fair
Value of Asset
Received
Loss Charged to
Valuation Allowance
If Appropriate –
Excess Loss Shown
on Income Statement
END

[1]Treated in Accordance with APB Opinion No. 30.

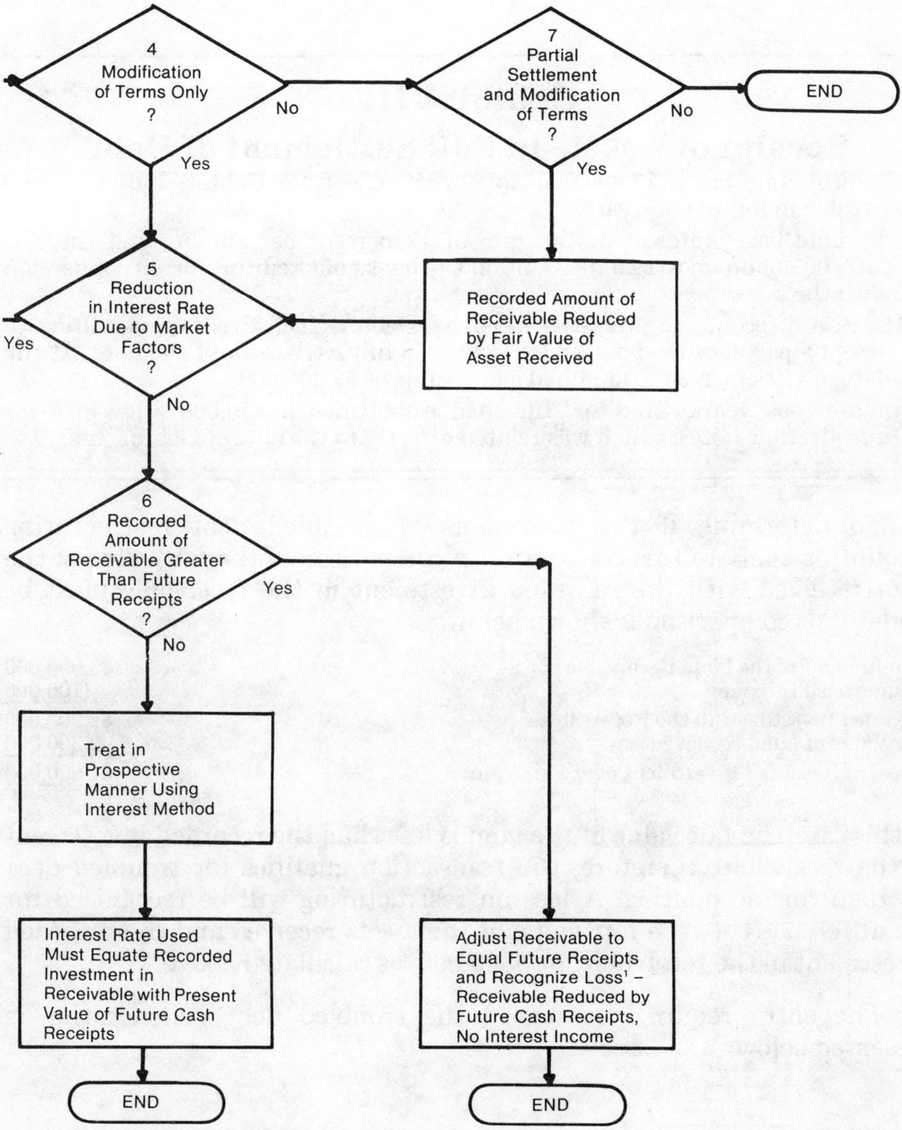
4
Modification
of Terms Only
?
No
Yes
7
Partial
Settlement
and Modification
of Terms
?
No
END
Yes
5
Reduction
in Interest Rate
Due to Market
Factors
?
Yes
No
Recorded Amount of
Receivable Reduced
by Fair Value of
Asset Received
6
Recorded
Amount of
Receivable Greater
Than Future
Receipts
?
Yes
No
Treat in
Prospective
Manner Using
Interest Method
Interest Rate Used
Must Equate Recorded
Investment in
Receivable with Present
Value of Future Cash
Receipts
END
Adjust Receivable to
Equal Future Receipts
and Recognize Loss[1] –
Receivable Reduced by
Future Cash Receipts,
No Interest Income
END

in the circumstances. Of course, if no valuation allowance has been established in connection with the receivable, the entire loss would be reported in the current period income statement.

Any assets received by the creditor in a troubled debt restructuring will be recorded and accounted for in subsequent periods as if the creditor had purchased the assets for cash. The assets received are to be recorded at their fair value on the date of restructuring.

To illustrate the situation where a creditor receives assets in full settlement of a troubled debt, the assumptions listed in Exhibit VIII will be used.

Exhibit VIII

Receipt of Assets in Full Settlement of Debt

1. Creditor, Inc. has a $3,000,000 note receivable from Debtor, Inc., which is payable in full in two years.
2. The note bears interest at the rate of 12 percent per annum, and there is $100,000 of unamortized discount on the books of Creditor, Inc. in connection with the note.
3. Because of economic problems faced by Debtor, Inc., Creditor is willing to accept a parcel of land owned by Debtor in full settlement of the note. At the date of settlement, the land had a fair value of $2,300,000.
4. In previous years, Creditor, Inc. had established a $50,000 allowance for uncollectible notes, which was related directly to the note of Debtor, Inc.

To determine if the provisions of troubled debt restructuring accounting apply to this transaction, a comparison of the fair value of the asset received with the recorded investment in the receivable must be made. This comparison is shown below:

Face Amount of the Note Receivable	$3,000,000
Unamortized Discount	(100,000)
Recorded Investment in the Receivable	$2,900,000
Fair Value of Land Received	2,300,000
Excess of Recorded Investment over Fair Value	$ 600,000

In this case, the fair value of the land is less than the recorded investment in the receivable; therefore, the transaction qualifies for troubled debt restructuring accounting. A loss on restructuring will be recognized for the difference between fair value of the assets received and the recorded investment in the receivable, or $600,000, as calculated above.

The entry required to record the troubled debt restructuring is presented below:

Loss on Restructuring of Receivable	600,000	
Discount on Notes Receivable	100,000	
Land	2,300,000	
Notes Receivable		3,000,000

The loss of $600,000 should be offset against the $50,000 allowance for uncollectibles, since $50,000 of the loss has been recognized in the period when the allowance was established. The entry to accomplish this would be:

Allowance for Uncollectibles	50,000	
Loss on Restructuring of Receivable		50,000

After this entry has been made, Creditor, Inc. would report the excess loss of $550,000 ($600,000 − $50,000) in accordance with APB Opinion No. 30. The two preceding entries could have been combined into one entry, but were shown separately for purposes of illustration.

Modification of Terms

Recall that modification of terms involves some adjustment to the existing debt, such as a change in interest rate, maturity value, maturity date or some combination of these items (Block 4). If a debt restructuring involves a reduction in the interest rate originally specified, the transaction will qualify for *troubled* debt restructuring accounting only if the reduction was not due merely to market factors (Block 5). Once it has been determined that the transaction involves a modification of terms, a comparison must be made between the recorded investment in the receivable and the total gross future cash receipts specified by the new terms (Block 6).

If the recorded investment in the receivable is greater than the future cash receipts, a loss on restructuring must be recognized. The loss will be equal to the difference between the recorded investment and the future cash receipts. The receivable must be reduced by an amount that will equate the receivable with the future cash receipts. No interest income will be recognized in subsequent periods, because the entire payment will be a reduction of the receivable balance.

If the recorded investment in the receivable is less than the future cash receipts specified by the new terms, the transaction will be treated in a prospective manner.[1] The recorded investment will *not* be adjusted, and *no* loss on the restructuring will be recognized. The creditor must determine the effective rate of interest that will equate the present value of the future receipts with the recorded investment in the receivable. This new effective rate will be used to determine current and future interest income.

---

[1] FASB Technical Bulletin No. 79-7 suggests that, if a receivable had been written down prior to the restructuring due to a decline in the value of the receivable, the write-down should *not* be reversed in comparing the future cash receipts with the recorded investment in the receivable.

To begin the illustration of the concepts identified above, the assumptions listed in Exhibit IX will be used.

Exhibit IX
Example 1—Modification of Terms

1. Creditor, Inc. has a $350,000 note receivable from Debtor, Inc., which is payable in full in four years.
2. The note bears interest at the rate of 10 percent per annum, and there is $25,000 of unamortized discount on the books of Creditor, Inc. in connection with the note.
3. Because of economic problems faced by Debtor, Inc., Creditor is willing to accept the payment of $50,000 per year for the next four years, in place of the original note.
4. In previous years, Creditor, Inc. had established a $15,000 allowance for uncollectible notes that was related to the note of Debtor, Inc.

If it is assumed that the elimination of interest was not due to market factors, the modifications of the amount to be paid, the terms of payment and the change in interest rate qualify this transaction for troubled debt restructuring accounting. The first step is to compare the recorded investment in the receivable with the total future cash receipts called for under the new terms. This comparison is shown below:

Face Amount of the Note Receivable	$350,000
Unamortized Discount	(25,000)
Investment in the Receivable	$325,000
Future Cash Receipts ($50,000 × 4 years)	200,000
Excess of Investment over Cash Receipts	$125,000

Note that the investment in the receivable does not consider the allowance account.

Since the investment in the receivable exceeds the future cash receipts by $125,000, the receivable must be written-down to equal the total future cash receipts of $200,000. A loss of $125,000 on the restructuring will be recognized. Because no interest income will be recognized in subsequent periods, it is necessary to remove the discount from the books of Creditor, Inc. The necessary entry is presented below:

Loss on Restructuring of Receivable	125,000	
Discount on Notes Receivable	25,000	
Notes Receivable		150,000

With the elimination of the discount, the face amount of the note is now equal to $200,000 ($350,000 – $150,000), which is the amount of the future cash receipts.

Next the loss must be reduced by the previous amount charged to the valuation allowance of $15,000. The entry to complete the restructuring is:

Allowance for Uncollectibles	15,000	
Loss on Restructuring of Receivable		15,000

This entry leaves a net loss of $110,000 to be included in the income statement in the year of restructuring. No interest income will be recognized over the remaining life of the receivable, and each cash receipt will merely be a reduction of the receivable balance. The following entry would be made each time a cash payment is received:

Cash	50,000	
Notes Receivable		50,000

This first example illustrates the accounting in a case where the recorded investment in the receivable is greater than the total future cash receipts. To demonstrate a second, and more complex, situation, the assumptions listed in Exhibit X will be used.

Exhibit X

Example 2—Modification of Terms

1. Creditor, Inc. has a $1,000,000 note receivable from Debtor, Inc., which is payable in full in five years.
2. The note bears interest at the rate of 12 percent per annum, and there is no unamortized discount or premium associated with the note.
3. Because of economic problems faced by Debtor, Inc., Creditor is willing to: (a) forgive $200,000 on the principal amount of the note; (b) reduce the interest rate to 10 percent on the new note balance; and (c) extend the maturity date to eight years.
4. There has been no allowance for uncollectibles established in relation to the note of Debtor, Inc.

Again assuming that the reduction in interest rate was not due merely to market factors, the transaction qualifies for troubled debt restructuring accounting. The first step is to compare the recorded investment in the receivable with the total future cash receipts under the modified terms. This comparison is shown below:

Face of Note (Recorded Investment in the Note)		$1,000,000
Future Cash Receipts:		
Principal	$800,000	
Interest ($800,000 × 10% × 8 years)	640,000	1,440,000
Excess of Cash Receipts over Investment		$ 440,000

Since the $1,440,000 total future cash receipts are greater than the $1,000,000 recorded investment in the receivable, it is necessary to calculate a new effective interest rate. That rate must equate the present value of the $1,440,000 with the $1,000,000 investment in the receivable. The calculation can be made using the trial-and-error method, with the present value of $1 applied to the principal repayment and the present value of an annuity applied to the interest payments. This is a very time-consuming process and is not suggested. The authors used a computer program to calculate the new rate of 5.9777 percent. Once the new rate has been determined, an amortization schedule similar to Table V can be prepared. This Table shows the cash interest received, the determination of interest income and receivable amortization using the interest method, and the investment in the note.

Table V

Amortization Schedule for Interest and Note

Year	Cash Interest	Interest Income	Receivable Amortization	Investment in Receivable
Initial Value	-	-	-	$1,000,000
1	[a]$ 80,000	[b]$ 59,777	[c]$ 20,223	[d]979,777
2	80,000	58,568	21,432	958,345
3	80,000	57,287	22,713	935,632
4	80,000	55,929	24,071	911,561
5	80,000	54,490	25,510	886,051
6	80,000	52,966	27,034	859,017
7	80,000	51,349	28,651	830,366
8	80,000	*49,634	30,366	[e]800,000
	$640,000	$440,000	$200,000	

[a] $800,000 × 10% = $80,000.
[b] $1,000,000 × 5.9777% = $59,777.
[c] $80,000 − $59,777 = $20,223.
[d] $1,000,000 − $20,223 = $979,777.
[e] Represents the revised maturity value at the end of 8 years.
* Rounded.

Given the information in Table V, the entry required to record the first cash receipt, recognition of interest income and amortization of the receivable is as follows:

Cash	80,000	
Interest Income		59,777
Notes Receivable		20,223

At the end of the eight-year period, the receivable will be reduced to its maturity value of $800,000. The calculation of the new effective interest rate was effected by the forgiveness of principal and the reduction in the stated interest rate. Information for entries for subsequent years is shown in the Table. Notice that, on the date of restructuring, no loss is recognized, and the balance of the receivable is not reduced. This is the primary difference between the first example and this example.

While this second example offers some interesting complexities, the solution is highly structured. The creditor is faced with a very complex solution to the above example if the receivable has any unamortized discount or premium associated with it. Remember, when it is necessary to calculate a new effective rate of interest, the Statement prohibits the reduction in the receivable or the elimination of any related unamortized items. The problem faced by the creditor, where discounts or premiums are present, is the determination of the portion of the total amortization that relates to the other unamortized items. In effect, the new effective rate will give the creditor the "net" amortization; but he needs to know the "gross" amounts, if proper accounting is to be accomplished. The creditor needs some method of dividing the total amortization into the portion applicable to principal and the portion applicable to other unamortized items.

The Statement does not provide any guidance in making this separation. Therefore, the authors have devised a logical method of dividing the two elements of the amortization. First, the effective interest rate is determined without consideration of the unamortized items, and the receivable is amortized using this rate. Next, an effective rate is determined with full consideration given to the unamortized items, and the receivable is amortized using this rate. The difference in the amortization using the first and second rates is the amortization for the unamortized items.

To illustrate this procedure, assume the same facts as shown in Exhibit X, except that the note had an unamortized premium of $50,000 recorded on the books of Creditor, Inc. The only new information added in this example is the premium. Given this additional information, the new revised investment in the receivable is shown below:

Face Amount of Note Receivable	$1,000,000
Unamortized Premium	50,000
Recorded Investment in Receivable	$1,050,000

In the preceding example, the future cash flows were determined to be $1,440,000, which is in excess of the $1,050,000 recorded investment in the receivable. This being the case, it is necessary to calculate a new effective interest rate that will equate the present value of the $1,440,000 with the $1,050,000 investment in the receivable. This rate was determined to be 5.13791 percent.

Once the new effective rate has been determined, a second amortization schedule can be prepared. Table VI was constructed on the basis of the new rate.

Table VI

Amortization Schedule for Interest and Note

Year	Cash Interest	Interest Income	Receivable Amortization	Investment in Receivable
Initial Value		-	-	$1,050,000
1	[a]$ 80,000	[b]$ 53,948	[c]$ 26,052	[d]1,023,948
2	80,000	52,610	27,390	996,558
3	80,000	51,202	28,798	967,760
4	80,000	49,723	30,277	937,483
5	80,000	48,167	31,833	905,650
6	80,000	46,531	33,469	872,181
7	80,000	44,812	35,188	836,993
8	80,000	*43,007	36,993	[e]800,000
	$640,000	$390,000	$250,000	

[a] $800,000 × 10% = $80,000.
[b] $1,050,000 × 5.13791% = $53,948.
[c] $80,000 − $53,948 = $26,052.
[d] $1,050,000 − $26,052 = $1,023,948.
[e] Represents the revised maturity value at the end of 8 years.
* Rounded.

When information from Tables V and VI are combined, sufficient data is provided to allow the creditor to isolate the annual premium amortization. Table VII is constructed from information found on Tables V and VI, and shows the determination of the premium amortization.

Table VII

Schedule for Premium Amortization

Year	Receivable Amortization (Table V)	Receivable Amortization (Table VI)	Premium Amortization (Difference)
1	$ 20,223	$ 26,052	[a]$ 5,829
2	21,432	27,390	5,958
3	22,713	28,798	6,085
4	24,071	30,277	6,206
5	25,510	31,833	6,323
6	27,034	33,469	6,435
7	28,651	35,188	6,537
8	30,366	36,993	6,627
	$200,000	$250,000	$50,000

[a] $26,052 − $20,223 = $5,829.

Given the information in Tables VI and VII, the required journal entry for the first year is presented below:

	Debit	Credit
Cash	80,000	
Notes Receivable		20,223
Premium on Notes Receivable		5,829
Interest Income		53,948

Information for entries in subsequent years is contained in Tables VI and VII.

Partial Settlement and Modification of Terms

Troubled debt restructurings may take on many different forms, two of which have been illustrated in the sections above. In addition to these types of restructurings, it is possible to have a combination of the two. In this case, the creditor would be faced with a partial settlement of the receivable and some modification of the terms of the remaining settlement (Block 7). When faced with this type of restructuring, the creditor first must reduce the recorded investment in the receivable by the fair value of the assets received in the partial settlement. Once this has been accomplished, the balance in the receivable account is referred to as the *remaining* or *revised* investment in the receivable. This remaining investment in the receivable will be used for purposes of all subsequent testing of the transaction. No loss on restructuring is recognized when the receivable is reduced by the fair value of the asset received.

Once this step has been completed, the remaining investment in the receivable is compared to the future cash receipts under the modified terms of the settlement. Remember that a partial settlement alone is, in effect, a modification of terms, because there has been a change in the method of repayment. If the remaining investment in the receivable is greater than the future cash receipts called for under the new terms, a loss on restructuring will be recognized. The loss is equal to the difference between the investment in the receivable and the future cash receipts. The remaining investment in the receivable will be reduced further by an amount necessary to equate the investment with the future cash receipts. No interest income will be recognized over the remaining life of the receivable.

If the remaining investment in the receivable is not greater than the future cash receipts, a new effective interest rate must be determined. This rate must equate the recorded investment in the receivable with the future cash receipts, and will be used to determine interest income over the life of the receivable. In addition, there will be no loss on restructuring.

To illustrate several of the concepts identified above, the assumptions listed in Exhibit XI will be used.

Exhibit XI

Example 1—Partial Settlement and Modification of Terms

1. Creditor, Inc. has a $6,000,000 note receivable from Debtor, Inc., which is payable in full in five years.
2. The note bears interest at the rate of 10 percent per annum, and there is $100,000 of unamortized premium on the books of Creditor, Inc. in connection with the note.
3. Debtor, Inc. is unable to pay the current interest, and it appears that the company will not be able to repay the principal amount when due. As a result, Creditor, Inc. has agreed to: (a) accept, in partial settlement of the note, a parcel of land with a fair value of $3,000,000 at the date of restructuring; (b) forgive $1,000,000 of the principal amount of the note; and (c) reduce the interest rate from 10 percent to 5 percent on the new maturity value of the note.
4. Creditor, Inc. established a $200,000 allowance for uncollectibles in previous years.

Assuming that the reduction in interest rate was not due merely to market factors, the transaction would qualify for troubled debt restructuring accounting. The exchange of land represents a partial settlement of the note; and the forgiveness of principal, reduction in interest rate and acceptance of land in partial settlement represent modifications of the original terms of the note.

The first step in the accounting process is to reduce the recorded investment in the receivable by the fair value of the land received. This computation is shown below:

Face Amount of the Note Receivable	$6,000,000
Unamortized Premium	100,000
Recorded Investment in the Note Receivable	$6,100,000
Fair Value of Land Received	(3,000,000)
Revised Investment in the Note Receivable	$3,100,000

The journal entry to record the reduction in the receivable is as follows:

Land	3,000,000	
Notes Receivable		3,000,000

Once the revised recorded investment in the receivable has been determined, the next step is to compare the revised investment in the receivable with the future cash receipts specified under the new terms. This comparison is shown below:

Revised Investment in the Receivable		$3,100,000
Future Cash Receipts:		
Face Amount of the Note	$3,000,000	
Forgiveness of Principal Amount	(1,000,000)	
Principal Repayment	$2,000,000	
Interest ($2,000,000 × 5% × 5 years)	500,000	
Total Future Cash Receipts		2,500,000
Excess of Investment over Receipts		$ 600,000

Since the $3,100,000 revised investment in the receivable is greater than the $2,500,000 future cash receipts, the investment in the receivable must be reduced; and a loss on restructuring recognized. The loss is equal to the difference between the revised investment in the receivable and the future cash flows, or $600,000, as calculated above. No interest income is to be recognized over the remaining life of the note. Therefore, it is appropriate to eliminate the unamortized premium related to the note. The journal entry necessary to accomplish this would be as follows:

Loss on Restructuring of Receivable	600,000	
Premium on Notes Receivable		100,000
Notes Receivable		500,000

After this entry, the investment in the receivable is equal to the $2,500,000 future cash receipts. This determination is shown below:

Original Face of the Receivable	$6,000,000
Unamortized Premium - per above entry	-0-
Fair Value of Land Received	(3,000,000)
Reduction in Note Balance - per above entry	(500,000)
Remaining Investment in the Receivable	$2,500,000

All subsequent receipts from Debtor, Inc. will represent merely a reduction in the principal amount of $2,500,000. No interest income will be recognized. The cash receipts from Debtor, Inc. will amount to $100,000 ($2,000,000 × 5%), and the entry to record this transaction is as follows:

Cash	100,000	
Notes Receivable		100,000

Since there is an allowance for uncollectibles established, the last step in the process is to offset the loss against the allowance account. The required entry is:

Allowance for Uncollectibles	200,000	
Loss on Restructuring of Receivable		200,000

This leaves a $400,000 net loss on restructuring ($600,000 – $200,000 = $400,000), to be reported on the income statement in accordance with the provisions of APB Opinion No. 30.

The reader should note that the three entries presented above could have been combined into one entry for purposes of recording the restructuring transaction. Individual entries were used for illustrative purposes only. The example just concluded did not require the determination of a new effective interest rate, because the revised recorded investment in the receivable exceeded the total future cash receipts.

The next example illustrates a situation where a new interest rate must be calculated. For purposes of this example, review the assumptions listed in Exhibit XII.

Exhibit XII

Example 2—Partial Settlement and Modification of Terms

1. Creditor, Inc. has a $5,000,000 note receivable from Debtor, Inc., which is payable in 10 years.
2. The note bears interest at the rate of 10 percent per annum, and there is no unamortized discount or premium relating to the note.
3. Debtor, Inc. is unable to pay the current interest, and it appears that the company will not be able to repay the principal amount when due. As a result, Creditor, Inc. has agreed to: (a) accept 100,000 common shares ($20 per share fair value on date of restructure) of Debtor, Inc. in partial settlement of the note; (b) forgive $1,000,000 of the principal amount of the note; and (c) reduce the interest rate from 10 percent to eight percent on the new maturity value of the note.
4. Creditor, Inc. established a $100,000 allowance for uncollectibles in previous years.

Assuming that the reduction in interest rate was not due to market factors, the transaction qualifies for troubled debt restructuring accounting. The exchange of stock represents a partial settlement of the receivable; and the forgiveness of principal, reduction in interest rate and acceptance of stock represent modifications of the original terms of the note.

To begin the accounting process, the investment in the receivable must be reduced by the fair value of the stock received. This computation is shown below:

Recorded Investment in the Receivable	$5,000,000
Fair Value of Stock Received (200,000 Shares × $20 per Share)	(2,000,000)
Revised Investment in the Receivable	$3,000,000

The journal entry necessary to reflect the change in the receivable is shown below:

Investment in Debtor, Inc. Common Stock	2,000,000	
Notes Receivable		2,000,000

Once the revised investment in the receivable has been determined, this amount must be compared to the future cash receipts under the modified terms of the restructuring. This comparison is made as follows:

Revised Investment in the Receivable		$3,000,000
Future Cash Receipts:		
Face Amount of Receivable	$3,000,000	
Forgiveness of Principal	(1,000,000)	
Principal Repayment	$2,000,000	
Interest ($2,000,000 × 8% × 10 years)	1,600,000	
Total Future Cash Receipts		3,600,000
Excess of Receipts over Investment		$ 600,000

Because the $3,600,000 total future cash receipts exceed the $300,000 revised investment in the receivable, it is necessary to calculate a new effective interest rate. That rate must equate the present value of the $3,600,000 with the $3,000,000 investment in the receivable. The new rate was determined to be 2.33551 percent. This rate will be used to determine interest income over the remaining life of the note.

Once the new rate of interest has been determined, an amortization schedule similar to Table VIII can be prepared. Table VIII shows the cash interest to be received, the interest income to be recognized, the amortization of the receivable due to the forgiveness of principal, and the receivable balance.

Table VIII

Amortization Schedule for Interest and Note

Year	Cash Interest	Interest Income	Receivable Amortization	Investment in Receivable
Initial Value	-	-	-	$3,000,000
1	[a]$ 160,000	[b]$ 70,065	[c]$ 89,935	[d]2,910,065
2	160,000	67,965	92,035	2,818,030
3	160,000	65,815	94,185	2,723,845
4	160,000	63,616	96,384	2,627,461
5	160,000	61,365	98,635	2,528,826
6	160,000	59,061	100,939	2,427,887
7	160,000	56,704	103,296	2,324,591
8	160,000	54,291	105,709	2,218,882
9	160,000	51,822	108,178	2,110,704
10	160,000	49,296	110,704	[e]2,000,000
	$1,600,000	$600,000	$1,000,000	

[a] $2,000,000 × 8% = $160,000.
[b] $3,000,000 × 2.33551% = $70,065.
[c] $160,000 − $70,065 = $89,935.
[d] $3,000,000 − $89,935 = $2,910,065.
[e] Represents the revised maturity value at the end of year 10.

Given the information developed in Table VIII, the journal entry to record the first interest payment from Debtor, Inc. would be as follows:

Cash	160,000	
Notes Receivable		89,935
Interest Income		70,065

The balance in the note receivable account is being written-down each year, so that, at the end of the 10 years, the $1,000,000 principal amount that was forgiven will be completely amortized; and the balance in the receivable account will be equal to the maturity value of the note.

One last item that must be considered is the reevaluation of the allowance account that had been previously established. Recall that Creditor, Inc. had established a valuation allowance of $100,000 prior to the restructuring. After the restructuring has been completed, Creditor, Inc. must make a determination as to the collectibility of the restructured receivable. Any change in the valuation resulting from this determination should be recorded currently. Assume that, after the restructuring, Creditor, Inc. expects to collect all of the modified receivable, except for $200,000. Based upon this judgment, the company must increase the valuation account by $100,000 ($200,000 expected loss – $100,000 balance in the valuation allowance). The entry to accomplish this last step would be: [2]

Uncollectibles Expense	100,000	
Allowance for Uncollectibles		100,000

This completes the discussion and related examples for the three major types of troubled debt restructurings. There are some additional accounting problems posed by the Statement that will be considered next.

Other Considerations

A debt restructuring may involve contingent payments or other indeterminate items. For example, a cash receipt may be based on the debtor maintaining a specific profit level in future periods. Another situation may involve the interest rate on the restructured receivable being linked to some variable factor, such as the bank prime rate of interest.

Contingent items involved in a troubled debt restructuring must be evaluated in accordance with the provisions of SFAS No. 5, "Accounting

[2] FASB Technical Bulletin No. 79-6 indicates that SFAS No. 15 does not specify procedures for determining the collectibility of a restructured receivable. However, SFAS No. 5 requires losses to be recognized in the period in which the loss is probable and the amount can be reasonably estimated. The collectibility of the restructured receivable must be evaluated by reference to the provisions of SFAS No. 5 (see Topic 6 for a complete discussion of SFAS No. 5).

for Contingencies," and, in particular, with Paragraph 8 of that Statement (see Topic 6 for a detailed analysis). A determination must be made as to whether or not the items will be included in the calculation of the future cash receipts. If it is probable that the contingent item will be paid, and the amount can be reasonably estimated, the items will be included in the total future cash receipts. Contingent items must meet these criteria before they can be included in the future cash receipts. When the contingent receipts have been earned, they will be used to reduce the receivable balance to the extent that the contingent items were included in the future cash receipts in determining the loss (or avoiding the loss) on restructuring. Any excess of the earned contingent receipts will be treated as interest income.

If the terms of restructuring allow the interest rate to vary, the interest rate at the date of restructuring is used in the computation of the future cash receipts. Subsequent changes in the interest rate require special accounting treatment. When it has been determined that the interest rate has changed, the creditor should recalculate the future cash receipts from that date, based upon the new rate. The future cash receipts so calculated must be compared with the investment in the receivable. If the recorded investment in the receivable is greater than the newly calculated cash receipts, a loss on restructuring will be recognized. The loss will be equal to the difference between the investment in the receivable and the newly calculated cash receipts. The receivable then will be reduced by an amount necessary to equate the receivable with the future cash receipts. No interest income will be recognized in subsequent periods. If the calculation of the new cash receipts indicates that they are greater than the investment in the receivable, the change in interest rate will be treated as a change in an accounting estimate according to APB Opinion No. 20, "Accounting Changes" (see Topic 1).

Any legal fees or direct costs associated with a debt restructuring should be charged to expense in the period incurred.

One final item in the Statement deals with the substitution or addition of debtors in a troubled debt restructuring. A debt restructuring may involve a substitution of the existing debt with debt of another entity, or additional debtor(s) may be added without removing the original debtor. The Statement concludes that, when faced with this situation, the substance of the transaction should dictate the necessary accounting treatment. If the debtors involved in a substitution or addition agreement are related or under common control, e.g., parent and subsidiary, the transaction should be treated as a modification of terms for purposes of applying the provisions of SFAS No. 15. If the debtors are *not* related or under common control, the Statement concludes that the transaction should be handled as a receipt of assets in full settlement and a combination of restructuring types.

The following examples are designed to illustrate the proper accounting for troubled debt restructurings involving contingent payments and variable interest rates. The assumptions listed in Exhibit XIII will be used to demonstrate accounting in a contingent payment situation.

Exhibit XIII
Contingent Receipts

1. Creditor, Inc. has a $2,000,000 note receivable from Debtor, Inc., which is payable in full in 10 years.
2. The note bears interest at the rate of 12 percent per annum, and there is no unamortized discount or premium associated with the note.
3. Debtor, Inc. is unable to pay the current interest, and it appears that the company will not be able to repay the principal amount when due. As a result, Creditor, Inc. has agreed to: (a) accept a parcel of land with a fair value of $1,000,000 in partial settlement of the receivable; and (b) receive an annual payment of $80,000 for each of the next 10 years and an additional $30,000 in each year that the net income of Debtor, Inc. exceeds $200,000.
4. There has been no valuation allowance established in connection with the original note.

After the agreement was concluded, Creditor, Inc. estimated that Debtor's earnings would exceed $200,000 in five out of the next 10 years.

The first step in the accounting process is to reduce the recorded investment in the receivable by the fair value of the land received. The revised investment in the receivable is calculated below:

Recorded Investment in the Receivable	$2,000,000
Fair Value of Land Received	(1,000,000)
Revised Investment in the Receivable	$1,000,000

The journal entry necessary to record the reduction in the receivable is:

Land	1,000,000	
Notes Receivable		1,000,000

Next, the expected future cash receipts must be compared with the revised investment in the receivable. Before the comparison can be made, the future cash receipts must be calculated. Recall from the previous discussion that only the contingent receipts that probably will be collected, and can be reasonably estimated, will be included in the cash receipts. The comparison of the investment to the future cash receipts is shown below:

Revised Investment in the Receivable		$1,000,000
Future Cash Receipts:		
Specified Payments ($80,000 × 10 years)	$800,000	
Contingent Payments ($30,000 × 5 years)	150,000	
Total Expected Future Cash Receipts		950,000
Excess of Investment over Receipts		$ 50,000

Only the probable and reasonably estimated contingent payments of $30,000 for five years were included in the future cash receipts. Since the investment in the receivable is greater than the expected future cash receipts, it is appropriate to recognize a loss on restructuring in the amount of $50,000. The receivable will be reduced by the amount of the loss recognized. The journal entry needed to accomplish this would be:

Loss on Restructuring of Receivable	50,000	
Notes Receivable		50,000

No interest will be recognized over the remaining life of the receivable. Subsequent receipts will represent a reduction in the receivable account.

The assumptions listed in Exhibit XIV will be used to illustrate the proper accounting for a troubled debt restructuring that involves a variable interest rate.

Exhibit XIV
Variable Interest Rate

1. Creditor, Inc. has a $3,500,000 note receivable from Debtor, Inc., which is payable in full in five years.
2. The note bears interest at the rate of 12 percent per annum, and there is no unamortized discount or premium associated with the note.
3. Debtor, Inc. is unable to pay the current interest, and it appears that the company will not be able to repay the principal amount when due. As a result, Creditor, Inc. has agreed to forgive $1,000,000 of principal amount of the note and to charge interest on the new maturity value at the nine percent bank prime rate in effect on the last day of the year.
4. There has been no valuation allowance established in connection with the original note.

The analysis of this situation is begun with the computation of the expected future cash receipts. Recall that the interest rate used in the computation is the nine percent prime rate in effect on the date of restructuring. The computation of the expected future cash receipts is shown below:

Recorded Investment in the Receivable	$3,500,000
Forgiveness of Principal Amount	(1,000,000)
Maturity Value of Revised Receivable	$2,500,000
Interest ($2,500,000 × 9% × 5 years)	1,125,000
Expected Future Cash Receipts	$3,625,000

Since the $3,625,000 in total future cash receipts under the modified terms of the agreement are greater than the $3,500,000 recorded investment in the receivable, it is necessary to determine a new effective interest rate. The rate must equate the present value of $3,625,000 with the investment of $3,500,000. The rate was determined to be .80563 percent. Once the rate has been determined, an amortization schedule like Table IX can be prepared. Table IX shows the cash interest to be received, the interest income to be recognized using the new interest rate, the amortization of the principal forgiveness of $1,000,000, and the balance in the receivable account.

TABLE IX

Amortization Schedule for Interest and Note

Year	Cash Interest	Interest Income	Receivable Amortization	Investment in Receivable
Initial Value		-	-	$3,500,000
1	[a]$ 225,000	[b]$ 28,197	[c]$ 196,803	[d]3,303,197
2	225,000	26,612	198,388	3,104,809
3	225,000	25,013	199,987	2,904,822
4	225,000	23,402	201,598	2,703,224
5	225,000	*21,776	203,224	[e]2,500,000
	$1,125,000	$125,000	$1,000,000	

[a] $2,500,000 × 9% = $225,000.
[b] $3,500,000 × .80563% = $28,197.
[c] $225,000 − $28,197 = $196,803.
[d] $3,500,000 − $196,803 = $3,303,197.
[e] Revised maturity value at the end of the life of the note.
* Rounded.

Based upon the information in Table IX, the following journal entry is required to record the interest income and note amortization on the date of the first interest receipt.

Cash	225,000	
Notes Receivable		196,803
Interest Income		28,197

Now assume that the bank prime rate changed from nine percent to seven percent two years after the restructuring, i.e., at the beginning of Year 3. In this case, the expected cash receipts must be recalculated, based upon the new bank prime rate of seven percent. The computation will be made from the end of Year 2 through Year 5, and would be as follows:

Maturity Value of the Receivable	$2,500,000
Interest ($2,500,000 × 7% × 3 years)	525,000
Expected Future Cash Receipts	$3,025,000

The recorded investment in the receivable at the end of Year 2 is $3,104,809 (see Table IX), which is greater than the expected future cash receipts of $3,025,000. It therefore is appropriate to recognize a loss on restructuring in an amount equal to the difference between the investment and the future cash receipts. The calculation of the loss is shown below:

Recorded Investment in Receivable	$3,104,809
Expected Future Cash Receipts	(3,025,000)
Loss on Restructuring of Receivable	$ 79,809

The entry to record the loss would be as follows:

Loss on Restructuring of Receivable	79,809	
Notes Receivable		79,809

No interest income will be recognized over the remaining life of the receivable. Subsequent payments will be a reduction in the receivable balance.

Disclosures

Paragraph 40 of the Statement presents the disclosures that are required by the creditor in the preparation of the basic financial statements. For troubled debt restructurings involving some modification of terms, the following information should be reported by major types of receivables:

(a) Recorded investment in receivables in the aggregate;

(b) Interest income at gross that would have been reported if there had been no restructuring; and

(c) Interest income, included in current period income, from restructured receivables.

Obligations to lend money to debtors involved in a restructuring of troubled debt also should be disclosed.

SFAS No. 21 (April 1978)

Suspension of the Reporting of Earnings Per Share and Segment Information by Nonpublic Enterprises

General Discussion

SFAS No. 21 amends APB Opinion No. 15, "Earnings Per Share," and SFAS No. 14, "Financial Reporting For Segments of a Business Enterprise." The purpose of Standard No. 21 is to suspend the requirement that earnings per share and segment information be disclosed in the basic financial statements of nonpublic entities. In addition, segment and earnings per share information does not have to be disclosed by nonpublic subsidiaries, investee companies and corporate joint ventures that issue separate financial reports.

A nonpublic entity is defined by SFAS No. 21 (Paragraph 13) in the following manner: [1]

> an enterprise other than one (a) whose debt or equity securities trade in a public market on a foreign or domestic stock exchange or in the over-the-counter market (including securities quoted only locally or regionally) or (b) that is required to file financial statements with the Securities and Exchange Commission.

Standard No. 21 does not prohibit the disclosure of earnings per share and segment information by nonpublic entities. Accordingly, if a nonpublic entity should disclose segment or earnings per share information in financial reports, the disclosures should be presented in accordance with the provisions of APB Opinion No. 15 and SFAS No. 14.

---

[1] FASB Technical Bulletin No. 79-8 states that closely held brokers or dealers in securities are considered to be nonpublic enterprises even though they are required to file financial statements with the SEC.

Appendix A

Table I

Present Value of $1

Periods	8%	9%	10%	11%	12%	13%	14%
1	.92593	.91743	.90909	.90090	.89286	.88496	.87719
2	.85734	.84168	.82645	.81162	.79719	.78315	.76947
3	.79383	.77218	.75131	.73119	.71178	.69305	.67497
4	.73503	.70843	.68301	.65873	.63552	.61332	.59208
5	.68058	.64993	.62092	.59345	.56743	.54276	.51937
6	.63017	.59627	.56447	.53464	.50663	.48032	.45559
7	.58349	.54703	.51316	.48166	.45235	.42506	.39964
8	.54027	.50187	.46651	.43393	.40388	.37616	.35056
9	.50025	.46043	.42410	.39092	.36061	.33289	.30751
10	.46319	.42241	.38554	.35218	.32197	.29459	.26974
11	.42888	.38753	.35049	.31728	.28748	.26070	.23662
12	.39711	.35553	.31863	.28584	.25668	.23071	.20756
13	.36770	.32618	.28966	.25751	.22917	.20417	.18207
14	.34046	.29925	.26333	.23199	.20462	.18068	.15971
15	.31524	.27454	.23939	.20900	.18270	.15989	.14010
16	.29189	.25187	.21763	.18829	.16312	.14150	.12289
17	.27027	.23107	.19784	.16963	.14564	.12522	.10780
18	.25025	.21199	.17986	.15282	.13004	.11081	.09456
19	.23171	.19449	.16351	.13768	.11611	.09806	.08295
20	.21455	.17843	.14864	.12403	.10367	.08678	.07276

Table II

Present Value of an Ordinary Annuity of $1

Periods	8%	9%	10%	11%	12%	13%	14%
1	.92593	.91743	.90909	.90090	.89286	.88496	.87719
2	1.78326	1.75911	1.73554	1.71252	1.69005	1.66810	1.64666
3	2.57710	2.53129	2.48685	2.44371	2.40183	2.36115	2.32163
4	3.31213	3.23972	3.16987	3.10245	3.03735	2.97447	2.91371
5	3.99271	3.88965	3.79079	3.69590	3.60478	3.51723	3.43308
6	4.62288	4.48592	4.35526	4.23054	4.11141	3.99755	3.88869
7	5.20637	5.03295	4.86842	4.71220	4.56376	4.42261	4.28831
8	5.74664	5.53482	5.33493	5.14612	4.96764	4.79877	4.63886
9	6.24689	5.99525	5.75902	5.53705	5.32825	5.13166	4.94637
10	6.71008	6.41766	6.14457	5.88923	5.65022	5.42624	5.21612
11	7.13896	6.80519	6.49506	6.20652	5.93770	5.68694	5.45273
12	7.53608	7.16073	6.81369	6.49236	6.19437	5.91765	5.66029
13	7.90378	7.48690	7.10336	6.74987	6.42355	6.12181	5.84236
14	8.24424	7.78615	7.36669	6.98187	6.62817	6.30249	6.00207
15	8.55948	8.06069	7.60608	7.19087	6.81086	6.46238	6.14317
16	8.85137	8.31256	7.82371	7.37916	6.97399	6.60388	6.26506
17	9.12164	8.54363	8.02155	7.54879	7.11963	6.72909	6.37286
18	9.37189	8.75563	8.20141	7.70162	7.24967	6.83991	6.46742
19	9.60360	8.95011	8.36492	7.83929	7.36578	6.93797	6.55037
20	9.81815	9.12855	8.51356	7.96333	7.46944	7.02475	6.62313

Table III

Present Value of an Annuity Due of $1

Periods	8%	9%	10%	11%	12%	13%	14%
1	1.00000	1.00000	1.00000	1.00000	1.00000	1.00000	1.00000
2	1.92593	1.91743	1.90909	1.90090	1.89286	1.88496	1.87719
3	2.78326	2.75911	2.73554	2.71252	2.69005	2.66810	2.64666
4	3.57710	3.53129	3.48685	3.44371	3.40183	3.36115	3.32163
5	4.31213	4.23972	4.16987	4.10245	4.03735	3.97447	3.91371
6	4.99271	4.88965	4.79079	4.69590	4.60478	4.51723	4.43308
7	5.62288	5.48592	5.35526	5.23054	5.11141	4.99755	4.88869
8	6.20637	6.03295	5.86842	5.71220	5.56376	5.42261	5.28831
9	6.74664	6.53482	6.33493	6.14612	5.96764	5.79877	5.63886
10	7.24689	6.99525	6.75902	6.53705	6.32825	6.13166	5.94637
11	7.71008	7.41766	7.14457	6.88923	6.65022	6.42624	6.21612
12	8.13896	7.80519	7.49506	7.20652	6.93770	6.68694	6.45273
13	8.53608	8.16073	7.81369	7.49236	7.19437	6.91765	6.66029
14	8.90378	8.48690	8.10336	7.74987	7.42355	7.12181	6.84236
15	9.24424	8.78615	8.36669	7.98187	7.62817	7.30249	7.00207
16	9.55948	9.06069	8.60608	8.19087	7.81086	7.46238	7.14317
17	9.85137	9.31256	8.82371	8.37916	7.97399	7.60388	7.26506
18	10.12164	9.54363	9.02155	8.54879	8.11963	7.72909	7.37286
19	10.37189	9.75563	9.20141	8.70162	8.24967	7.83991	7.46742
20	10.60360	9.95011	9.36492	8.83929	8.36578	7.93797	7.55037

Index